DROPPING THE TORCH

Dropping the Torch: Jimmy Carter, the Olympic Boycott, and the Cold War offers a diplomatic history of the 1980 Olympic boycott. Broad in its focus, it looks at events in Washington, D.C., as well as the opposition to the boycott and how this attempted embargo affected the athletic contests in Moscow. Jimmy Carter based his foreign policy on assumptions that had fundamental flaws and reflected a superficial familiarity with the Olympic movement. These basic mistakes led to a campaign that failed to meet its basic mission objectives but did manage to insult the Soviets just enough to destroy détente and restart the Cold War. The book also includes a military history of the Soviet invasion of Afghanistan, which provoked the boycott, and an examination of the boycott's impact four years later at the Los Angeles Olympics, where the Soviet Union retaliated with its own boycott.

Nicholas Evan Sarantakes, a historian specializing in the World War II and Cold War eras, is an associate professor in the Strategy and Policy Department at the U.S. Naval War College. He has published a number of articles that have appeared in academic journals such as the *English Historical Review* and the *Journal of Military History*, military publications like *Joint Forces Quarterly* and the *Royal United Services Institute Journal*, and journalistic publications like *Texas Alcalde* magazine and ESPN.com. Professor Sarantakes is also chair of the Paul Birdsall Prize in European Military and Strategic History book prize committee for the American Historical Association and is a Fellow of the Royal Historical Society.

Dropping the Torch

JIMMY CARTER, THE OLYMPIC BOYCOTT, AND THE COLD WAR

Nicholas Evan Sarantakes

U. S. Naval War College

CAMBRIDGE
UNIVERSITY PRESS

CAMBRIDGE UNIVERSITY PRESS
Cambridge, New York, Melbourne, Madrid, Cape Town, Singapore,
São Paulo, Delhi, Dubai, Tokyo, Mexico City

Cambridge University Press
32 Avenue of the Americas, New York, NY 10013-2473, USA

www.cambridge.org
Information on this title: www.cambridge.org/9780521176668

First published 2011

Printed in the United States of America

A catalog record for this publication is available from the British Library.

Library of Congress Cataloging in Publication data
Sarantakes, Nicholas Evan, 1966–
Dropping the torch : Jimmy Carter, the Olympic boycott, and the
Cold War / Nicholas Evan Sarantakes.
p.   cm.
ISBN 978-0-521-19477-8 (hardback)
1. Sports and state – United States.   2. Olympic Games (22nd : 1980 : Moscow,
Russia)   3. Boycotts – United States.   4. Cold War.   5. United States – Foreign
relations – Soviet Union.   6. Soviet Union – Foreign relations – United States.
7. Carter, Jimmy, 1924–   I. Title.
GV7221980.S27   2010
796.48–dc22   2010030370

ISBN 978-0-521-19477-8 Hardback
ISBN 978-0-521-17666-8 Paperback

This book is dedicated to
Thomas Lang
Commander, USN
Strategy Seminars, 2008–2009,
U.S. Naval War College

Contents

Acknowledgments

When I wrote my first book, one of the things that I learned – and it surprised me – is that a lot more people own the book than just the author. Everyone from the copy editor to the graphic design artist that puts together the dust jacket has some say in the final product. The author's name goes on the book, because ultimately the words that you are reading are the most important element of the publication and the part that takes the longest to produce.

In the case of this book, the writing took roughly five years, and in that half-decade, I encumbered a number of debts. Many people helped me in ways large and small. I tried to express my thanks to them at the time, but this section of the book gives me the opportunity to make a more enduring expression of gratitude.

The research for this book began in 2004 during a trip I took to the Olympic Museum in Lausanne, Switzerland, where I initially did research at the Samaranch Olympic Studies Centre for another project. I was visiting with my brother, then Captain, now Major Andrew T. Sarantakes, who was stationed in Germany, and he helped me with the logistics of that move. Making this trip was rather daunting at first, since I spoke neither French nor German. When I arrived at the museum, the staff was exceptionally polite and professional. I cannot recommend this facility enough, or Lausanne, or Switzerland. I finished that research rather quickly and then turned my attention to 1980. There was a ton of information, and I planned a second trip. The official languages of the Olympic movement are English and French, so all correspondence and records are recorded in both languages. The fact that Lord Killanin was a native English speaker meant that going through his personal papers did not require any additional language skills, which might have been the case were I examining events that transpired when J. Sigfrid Edström of Sweden was International Olympic Committee (IOC) president. While almost all of the material I wanted to examine in Switzerland was in English, the finding aides were available only in French. I was surprised at how much of that language I was able to pick up during my two trips. There were limits, though, and the archivists at the Samaranch Centre helped me when my comprehension of French hit a wall. During a brief conversation at an academic conference, Thomas A. Schwartz of Vanderbilt University encouraged me to pursue this research further and turn it into a book.

Most of the boycott effort took place in public. As a result, newspapers became an exceptionally important resource. While most academics are content to limit their research of public debate to the pages of *The New York Times*, I had no such luxury. A number of media outlets shaped the course of the boycott campaign. Robert G. Kaiser gave the effort an enormous push with his column in *The Washington Post*, and since the boycott was national in scale, it was the subject of commentary not only in general news magazines like *Time* and *Newsweek*, but also in others with a specialized focus like *Business Week* and *Sports Illustrated*. Editorial columnists in newspapers from around the country also weighed in on this topic, and important articles appeared in major newspapers like the *Los Angeles Times* and in smaller ones like the *Colorado Springs Gazette Telegraph*. Since the international Olympic movement is international in fact as well as in name, I had to do a fair amount of research in foreign newspapers. The summer I spent as a Junior Fellow in the newspaper reading room at the Library of Congress paid dividends long after I finished graduate school. Most of the newspaper research I did took place there. It was tough going since even as late as 1980, most major papers outside of a few titles like *The Times* of London and *The New York Times* made no effort to assemble an index. In addition, most electronic databases did not have holdings that reached back to 1980. I made do. I picked key dates and examined the microfilm holdings of particular newspapers at the Library of Congress. This process was slow, but I found a number of gems.

The account in this book is international in focus. There are important elements of the Spanish, Belgian, West German, Australian, and Canadian stories – to name just a few – that did not make it into this account; there are also plenty of studies waiting to be written about these events. The attempt here was to have a broad and international focus. To that end, I was multilingual in my research. French and English might be the official languages of the Olympics, but the movement involves nations that use languages other than those two. Much if not all of this debate was public in nature, and newspapers were an excellent source to examine the politics in countries like Spain and Germany. I used the same method of picking key dates for going through foreign-language newspapers as I did with domestic ones. It was a bit odd to read material I could not really understand, but I was fortunate that "Olympic" translates well into Spanish, French, and German. I found a number of useful items and then made photocopies like crazy. I then had others translate for me.

The boycott was mentioned in several books that journalists wrote shortly after the events, which helped me understand how the issue played in the domestic politics of various nations. Needless to say, books on the Soviet perspective appeared in Russian, while those for West Germany were in German. A number of participants (both political and Olympian) wrote memoirs, and although all members of the International Olympic Committee read and speak either French or English, many chose to write in their native tongues.

As a result, many people helped me with these sources. While I was teaching at the U.S. Army Command & General Staff College (C&GSC), a student, Major Matthew C. Rinke, translated Korean titles. A friend of mine from graduate school, Lise Namakis, helped me acquire an important Russian-language publication, and a colleague of mine at the Staff College, Bruce Menning, did the translations. Since the end of the Cold War, the archives of the former Warsaw Pact have been a new area of exploration for those individuals with reading ability in the relevant languages. The Cold War International History Project has arranged for several scholars to translate and disseminate documents they have found in these archives. Although this work has made only a portion of these archives available, they have provided a useful service. Soviet and Hungarian documents that I used came through this venue. The Federal Republic of Germany was a major player in the boycott, and my friends, Sarandis "Randy" Papadopoulos of the Naval History and Heritage Command, Marc Mulzer, and another C&GSC colleague, Don Myer, translated German-language material for me. I picked up a lot of French while I was in Switzerland – there is no substitute for immersion as a way of acquiring and improving your foreign-language skills – but there was no way I could translate materials with accuracy. I leaned on a number of friends and colleagues for help with the French-language items. They included Michael Creswell of Florida State University, Michael Neiberg of the University of Southern Mississippi, Everett Dague of Benedictine College, and Michael F. Pavković, a colleague of mine at the Naval War College in Newport, Rhode Island.

I was better with Spanish, having studied the language as a teenager, but still was not up to doing translation work on my own. My friend Kyle Longley of Arizona State University and my colleagues at the Command & General Staff College, Mark Montesclaros and Brook Allen, helped with the newspapers articles from Spain and several South American countries.

Robert Eldridge of Osaka University helped me acquire several Japanese-language books about the boycott. I did some of the translations, but Toshi Yoshihara, my colleague at both the Air War College in Montgomery, Alabama, and at Naval War College did most of this work. He also translated some Chinese terms for me.

The boycott was international in nature, and even in countries quite similar to the United States, it played out differently given different political contexts. My friend, Galen Perras of the University of Ottawa, helped explain Canadian politics and gave me some tips on Canadian resources. Randy Papadopoulos grew up in Canada and provided me with even more information about things Canadian. Matthew Hughes of Brunel University in London and Simon Anglim, a graduate student at Aberystwyth University in Wales, helped me acquire material from the archives of the British Olympic Association. Amy Terriere of the BOA helped in this matter as well. I was fortunate to have this assistance. A few weeks later, a flood destroyed the records of the Association. I donated my materials back to the BOA, but future researchers should not expect my citations to these holdings to match those in use at a later date.

The U.S. Olympic Committee (USOC) does not represent a foreign country, but Cindy Slater, the USOC librarian, helped me enormously during a trip to Colorado Springs – far more than I had a right to expect – and she deserves much thanks.

I am particularly grateful to Joe Onek and Anita DeFrantz for allowing me to interview them for this book. Onek and DeFrantz were leading the opposite sides of the boycott in 1980. I interviewed both in the same week – Onek in person and DeFrantz over the phone – and what struck me in both interviews was that both of them saw and respected the other point of view. That perspective was more important than the information they gave in the interview and was often absent – or at least pretty well hidden – from the written records from 1980. After those two sessions, I made an extra effort to not only be fair and balanced in my presentation, but to show that people on both sides of the issue saw and got the other point of view even if it still failed to convince them.

Writing, of course, is one of the production areas that the author dominates, but even then it is not absolute. There are copy editors who catch dangling participles and split infinitives, but even before a book gets to that stage, a good author will need lots of help. I am no different. Three friends read earlier drafts of this manuscript: Mike Creswell, Galen Perras, and Michael Ezra at Sonoma State University saved me from many errors, large and small.

In writing this study, I have tried to maintain – as much as possible – the original flavor of the times. The people writing the documents were busy people and they often made mistakes in grammar. Instead of correcting these with troublesome brackets and [sic]s I have decided to let things stand as much as possible as they were in the original. This will give the reader a feel for the flavor of the day, but will also make for the best read of this period in time.

During my work on this project, I was employed at six different institutions. I expect to be at the sixth, the Naval War College, for a good long while. Commander Thomas Lang, United States Navy, my teaching partner when

I first arrived at the College, helped me make the crucial adjustment to a new institution. This book is dedicated to him as a token of thanks.

Any defects that remain are mine and mine alone and come despite the assistance I have received.

NES

Newport, Rhode Island

Augusta, Georgia

Hattiesburg, Mississippi

Montgomery, Alabama

Shreveport, Louisiana

Midland, Texas

Spring 2009

Abbreviations

Despite valiant efforts to the contrary, a number of acronyms appear in the text. Many of these appeared in the original documents, and in some cases, like the KGB, the letters are better known than the proper name. The following is a list of the abbreviations in the text:

ABC	American Broadcasting Company
AOF	Australian Olympic Federation
BOA	British Olympic Association
BU	Boston University
CAB	Civil Aeronautics Board
C&GSC	U.S. Army Command & General Staff College
CBS	Columbia Broadcasting System
CHL	Central Hockey League
CIA	Central Intelligence Agency
COA	Canadian Olympic Association
EAA	Export Administration Act
EC-9	European Union (before expansion)
FAZ	*Frankfurter Allgemeine Zeitung* (German: Frankfurt General Newspaper)
GANEFO	Games of the New Emerging Forces
GRU	*Glavnoje Razvedyvatel'noje Upravlenije* (Russian: Main Intelligence Directorate)
IEEPA	International Emergency Economic Powers Act
IOC	International Olympic Committee
JOC	Japanese Olympic Committee
KGB	*Komitet Gosudarstvennoy Bezopasnosti* (Russian: Committee for State Security)
LAOOC	Los Angeles Olympic Organizing Committee
MVP	Most Valuable Player
NATO	North Atlantic Treaty Organization
NBC	National Broadcasting Company

NHL	National Hockey League
NOC	National Olympic Committee
NSC	National Security Council
PDPA	People's Democratic Party of Afghanistan
PRC	People's Republic of China
SALT	Strategic Arms Limitation Treaty
UNESCO	United Nations Educational, Scientific and Cultural Organization
USOC	United States Olympic Committee
USS	United States Ship
USSR	Union of Soviet Socialist Republics

INTRODUCTION

Miracle on Ice

MIKE ERUZIONE AS THE TEAM CAPTAIN STOOD ON THE PLATFORM, hand over his heart, with his Olympic gold medal hanging from his neck, as a series of cables attached to the roof of the arena pulled the U.S. flag in the air ahead of those of Finland and the Soviet Union. He was singing words to the "Star Spangled Banner," leading the crowd in the song, as the music played during the medal ceremony. It is difficult to overstate what he and his nineteen teammates on the U.S. Olympic Hockey Team had done to reach this moment. Just in athletic terms, their victory was astonishing. They had defeated a Soviet team that had won the gold medal of the last four Olympiads. During that run, the goal differential between the Soviets and their opponents had been 175–44. After 1980, the Soviets would not lose to another U.S. team for another eleven years. In fact, they would not lose *any* game in international play for another five years.[1]

As impressive as the hockey team's success was in athletic terms – and it was extraordinary – their gold medal was far more significant to the psyche of the nation. "It was what America needed in troubled times," an official of the U.S. Amateur Hockey Association explained a few weeks later. Their win produced "a release of emotion and national pride that swept a country searching for something to bolster its pride."[2]

Their triumph was also of immense importance to the international Olympic movement. The national euphoria that those twenty men produced in the United States helped blunt the efforts of the Carter administration to destroy the modern incarnation of the Olympics.[3]

This significance would come into play in the days, weeks, and months that followed Lake Placid. At the time, though, the television cameras faded back to Eruzione from the three flags, he turned around pumped his fist in the air, and then waved his teammates, who were standing in a row behind him, onto the stand. All twenty managed to crowd onto the platform, hugging each other, thrusting their fingers in the air, declaring that they were number one. Then Eruzione led them in a victory parade around the rink, waving

American flags and proudly showing their medals to the people in the stands. The crowd was cheering and chanting: "U.S.A! U.S.A! U.S.A!"[4]

The person most responsible for this moment was the team's coach, Herb Brooks. A member of the 1960 U.S. National Hockey Team, he was the last player cut before the United States won the gold medal at the Olympics that year. In the two decades that followed, Brooks won three national college championships as the head coach at the University of Minnesota. Convinced that the regular humiliation the United States suffered in international play could be reversed, he developed a new style of play that he dubbed "American hockey." His system combined the aggressive forechecking and improvisation common in North America – mainly Canada – with the open-ice tactics, poise, and heavy physical conditioning typical of the Soviet approach to the game.[5]

To find the right players for this type of hockey, Brooks held a two-week tryout in Colorado Springs, Colorado. He believed it was critical to assemble a team that was on the whole more powerful than the sum of its individual parts. The coach had to find players that would mesh together. He had no interest in putting together a college all-star team. Most of the players he selected, though, were college students; fourteen of them were twenty-two years old or younger. The U.S. team was the youngest that competed at the Olympics. "I think some of 'em are so young they still believe in Santa Claus," Brooks joked.[6]

This team had talent and potential even though it came from only four states: Massachusetts, Michigan, Minnesota, and Wisconsin. Steve Janaszak, one of the goaltenders, helped Brooks win two national titles at the University of Minnesota and had been named Most Valuable Player of the 1979 championship tournament. Every time the Americans had done well at the Olympics, they had the benefit of an exceptional talent in front of the net. Janaszak was good but he was never more than the backup and was the only player never to get on the ice during Olympic play because of the phenomenal work of Jim Craig, the starting goalie. As a goaltender at Boston University, Craig had earned All-American honors and helped his team win the national title. Another fellow Terrier was Jack O'Callahan. He had turned down admission to Harvard to play at Boston University (BU), where he became team captain, team Most Valuable Player (MVP), and an All-American. When the Terriers went to the national championship tournament, Dave Silk ended up on the All-Tournament team. The New York Rangers of the National Hockey League (NHL) drafted him after his sophomore year. Eruzione was another alumnus of BU. The all-time scoring leader in school history, Eruzione's talents were difficult to describe. He had certain intangibles that made him a valuable asset, but since he seemed to be a weak player in the measurable skills of a hockey player, his presence on the team always was a bit at risk.[7]

Unlike Eruzione, there was no question about Mark Johnson's talent. Johnson had been the College Player of the Year in 1978–79, and was the all-time scoring leader in hockey at the University of Wisconsin, where his father was the head coach. He even briefly made the 1976 U.S. National Hockey Team when he was 16, before the final cuts kept him from competing in the Olympics.[8]

Ken Morrow had played for Bowling Green State University, helping turn that Ohio school into a college hockey power by the end of the 1970s. Morrow made All-American, the first player in school history to receive that honor. In difficult financial circumstances following the death of his father, he nearly signed with the Islanders of the NHL. It was only when the Islanders and Morrow agreed to a complex arrangement that provided insurance coverage for his salary in case became injured in the Olympics, that he agreed to join the team.[9]

Each of the twenty that made the final cut had talent: The real task Brooks faced was welding these players into a collective force, a team. This task was easier said than done. In 1976, during the national college championship playoffs, players from BU and Minnesota got into a brawl that emptied both benches and took an hour to bring to an end. Many of the Terriers gathered in Colorado Springs worried that Brooks and his Golden Gophers still harbored grudges from the fight. Despite his talent, Johnson went to the tryouts concerned as well. His father and Brooks were bitter rivals. The elder Johnson believed that Brooks had kept many of his players from trying out for the Olympics in 1976. Would the new coach of the U.S. national team give the son of his rival a fair evaluation?

Johnson and the others need not have worried. What all of them found was a coach focused solely on victory and creating a unified force that represented the entire nation. Nothing else, including history, mattered. "Don't get regional" was a Brooks catch phrases. He had a number of sayings that he repeated as he pushed his players during his long, brutal, and relentless practice sessions:

- Gentlemen, you don't have enough talent to win on talent alone.
- You guys looked like a monkey screwing a football out there.
- Go up to the tiger, spit in his eye, then shoot him.[10]

The team did indeed bond together. "Every team I played on for five years always felt a common bond," Janaszak remarked. "Twenty guys who all hated Herb. You knew the guy sitting next to you had been through all the same crap." When the players saw Brooks, they would remark, "Here comes the Ayatollah." Assistant Coach Craig Patrick was the bridge between the team and the head coach. It was his job to offer the players positive encouragement, while Brooks maintained an emotional distance. "The Ayatollah" was often abusive toward Patrick in front of the team, but this behavior was for show. The two men shared a room on the road.[11]

Brooks had good reasons for this behavior. At the tryouts, he had selected twenty-six players, but he could only take twenty to the Olympics. Six more had to go. Having been cut from the 1960 squad just before the start of the Olympics to make way for another player, he promised that he would not bring in any outsiders at the last minute and would explain his decisions with the individuals being dismissed from the team. When he cut the last two players, he was in tears himself, remembering 1960 all too well.[12]

In addition to finding the right mix of players, Brooks had to teach them the new style he wanted to use in the Olympics. "We had to cram two or three years of experience playing this into five months of exhibition games," he explained to a *Sports Illustrated* reporter. He had one goal: beating the Soviets. "I tried to develop a team that would throw their game right back at them." A key element in this process was a long pre-Olympic exhibition season. Brooks had them play an eclectic mix of other national teams, American and European professionals, American colleges, minor leaguers, and all-stars. The players called the demanding physical training exercises that Brooks inflicted on the team "Herbies." One of the most notorious Herbies came during a tour of Scandinavia. The Americans made a listless effort against the poorly regarded Norwegian National Team. "Hey, if you don't skate tonight, gentlemen, we'll skate after the game," their coach warned them. After playing the Norwegians to a 3–3 tie, Brooks ordered the team back onto the ice and had them skate back and forth the length of the rink. The crowd stayed at first and cheered, thinking it was some kind of skating demonstration. When they realized it was a form of punishment, they booed. The team kept skating back and forth even after the custodial staff turned off the lights in the rink. The next night, the U.S. defeated Norway handily, 9–0.[13]

In 1979, there were two minor leagues that fed players into the NHL, and officials of the U.S. hockey federation and the Central Hockey League had arranged that the Olympians would play every CHL team twice, and that the games would count in the official standings. Brooks and his charges ended up with a final record of 14–3–1, which, combined with their victory over the champions of the American Hockey League, the other semi-pro circuit, made them for all practical purposes but name the best minor league team on the continent. The Americans also won the gold medal at a pre-Olympic international tournament held at Lake Placid, New York, where the Winter Games would be held in a few weeks. Most nations, though, sent their junior teams. Overall, the United States had a pre-Olympic record up to that point of 42–15–3. The team had done well, but the real question remained: Would they be good enough to take on the best team at the Olympics, the Soviets?[14]

The answer came three days before the start of Olympic play – and it was "No." The Soviets humiliated the Americans in an exhibition game played at Madison Square Garden, 10–3. Even that score fails to tell the full story. The Soviets scored four minutes into the game and had four goals in the first fifteen. The Americans had two power play opportunities during the game and at neither time were they even able to take a shot on goal. When the game ended, Viktor Tikhonov, the Soviet head coach, was gracious when he said, "I think the United States team has a very good future."[15]

Far more devastating to the team than the score was an injured knee that O'Callahan suffered. A doctor from the U.S. Olympic Committee was saying that damage would require surgery to fix. His Olympics were over before they began, but a day later, a second doctor said the injury was less severe than originally thought. The physician thought O'Callahan should recover in time to compete in the medal round, if the Americans made it that far. Brooks had a difficult decision to make: go into the Olympics, possibly down one man, or cut a player that was critical to the cohesive chemistry of the team. To make matters worse, he only had a few hours to make his decision. The day before the Olympics began, Brooks walked into the locker room and said, "Jack, we've had a long talk and we don't know if you're going to be able to play, but we're going to stick with you." The team cheered. "Looking back on it," Eurzione reflected a few months afterwards, "that was just about the best thing Herb could have done. The emotion in that locker room was a great way to start off the Olympics."[16]

The team went into the Lake Placid Games believing they had a chance to win a medal. "If I didn't think we could win the gold medal, I wouldn't be here," Rob McClanahan, a Left Wingman on the team, said. The first test of the Winter Olympics came even before the opening ceremonies. The opponent was Sweden, and getting a win would be difficult. No U.S. team had defeated the Swedes in twenty years. The game was a must-win, and the Americans let the pressure get to them; they were tense, tentative, and missing connections. Brooks decided he had to do something. McClanahan had pulled a muscle in the game, and during the break between periods, the coach stormed into the locker room, looked at him, said he was weak, and told him to suit up again. Hurt, insulted, and angry, McClanahan charged Brooks and started yelling at him. Morrow was dismayed at what he was watching. "I remember sitting there thinking, 'Twenty minutes into the Olympics, and we've already imploded,'" he said. The former Bowling Green State star had company. "This is unreal," Silk thought. "Francis Ford Coppola is going to come out in a minute and say, 'Cut. Good,'" he said making a reference to a scene in the film *Apocalypse Now.*[17]

The stunt worked. The Americans were energized during the rest of the game. Still, Brooks had to make another gutsy call. In the last minute, he pulled Craig from the game giving the team another play on offense. With twenty-seven seconds left in the game, Bill Baker scored his only goal of the Olympics to give the United States a tie rather than a loss. Brooks never explained his actions in the locker room to McClanahan. Years passed before he could forgive his coach.[18]

The next game would be even tougher. Czechoslovakia had won the silver medal at the 1976 Innsbruck Olympics and the world championship twice in the 1970s. Olympic officials had arranged a schedule to keep the United States from facing the Soviets until the medal round, but the Americans had never lost to the Czechs and then gone on to win a medal in the Olympics. The Americans basically had to win this game. The visitors scored first and early, but the Americans responded quickly and then took the lead in the second period. They never looked back. The final score was 7–3. "Many people said that, that the Czechs were considered the second best team in the world and the only team that had a chance to beat the Soviets," Eurzione explained. "Well, we pretty much dominated the Czechs." Morrow described how: "The crowd got us going against the Czechs and it just snowballed." O'Callahan agreed. "I think that may have been the best game we played all year, better than the game against Russia," he said. "I can't remember us ever being better than that night." The crowd was chanting "U.S.A., U.S.A., U.S.A." when the game ended. Public and media interest in the hockey team started to grow: the stands were only partially full for the game against Sweden – now they were full. Despite this popularity, Brooks enforced a rule that no players would attend press conferences. Uneven attention from the media could create jealousy on the team.[19]

The next game was against Norway. The Americans won, 5–1, but that score fails to reflect the difficulty the United States faced or the fact that they trailed 1–0 at the end of the first period. Despite the win, no one on the team was happy with the trouble they had against the less-than-stellar Norwegians. "It was kind of a brutal game," Brooks observed. "We just weren't motivated. We didn't move the puck, we didn't do a lot of things. We were drained from the Czech game."[20]

Two days later, the Americans faced the Romanians, another opponent that they took lightly. Romania had never garnered a medal in hockey. The United States won the game, 7–2. Again the score was misleading. The Americans missed a number of scoring opportunities and were starting to worry about the goal differential, which would determine entry into the medal round. If they had the same record as Sweden, goals would decide the awarding of medals. "When we came up here, people thought if we got through the first four games unbeaten it would be unbelievable," Jim Craig observed. "And now, it's not good enough. Beating somebody seven-two in the Olympics is not good enough."[21]

The last game of the first round was against West Germany. If the Americans lost, their Olympics would be over, since it would be impossible for them to advance into the medal round. A simple win was also not good enough for the United States. The Americans wanted to win by at least seven to avoid having to face the Soviets next. They also wanted to avenge a German victory in the 1976 Olympics that cost the United States the bronze. "I wanted to beat them especially bad because of '76," Buzz Schneider, the only member of the U.S. team from the previous Olympic squad, said. "You'd think something like that won't bother you, that you'd forget it. But I hadn't." The West Germans took an early 2–0 lead, before the Americans scored four straight goals. The final score was 4–2, which was good enough to get the team into the second round for the second consecutive Olympiad, but their next opponents would be the defending champions, the Soviets. "No team is invincible," Mike Ramsey, a U.S. defenseman explained, aware of the coming confrontation. "The Russians are close. But any team can be beaten. If we catch them on a bad day, who knows? We got a shot."[22]

The game with the Soviets was daunting enough just in athletic terms. The visitors were clearly the best hockey team, amateur or professional, on the planet, but the American people were investing the game with a good deal of politics and social issues: Vietnam, Watergate, the decade of malaise, the high inflation of the 1970s, the humiliation of the Iranian hostage crisis, the Soviet invasion of Afghanistan, Carter's efforts to boycott the Olympics, the slow, lingering death of détente, and the return of the Cold War. Hundreds of telegrams arrived for the team from around the country. One urged them to "Save us from the cancer of communism." *Newsweek* magazine called the contest "a morality play on ice." The players, for their part, found all these extra issues unsettling.[23]

The Soviets entered this tournament expecting to win their fifth consecutive gold medal. Unlike the Americans, they rarely had much of a challenge. They destroyed the Japanese, 16–0, the Dutch, 17–4, and the Poles, 8–1. Trained to maintain their poise, they remained calm when the Finns took a 2–1 lead into the final five minutes of their game. The Soviets then scored three goals in 79 seconds, to take the victory. The Canadians gave them the toughest challenge at Lake Placid, taking the lead early in the game, then falling behind. The Canadians managed to tie the contest at four before ultimately falling, 6–4.

Brooks watched the game and realized something – the Soviets were bored. In their arrogance, they were sleepwalking through the tournament, which allowed the Finns and the Canadians to stay in the contest much longer than should have otherwise been the case. Soviet goaltender Vladislav Tretiak admitted as much: "We were way stronger, nobody ever doubted that. We were professionals and they were just students. Simply put, we did not respect their team and you can not do that in hockey." Their encounter with the Americans at Madison Square Garden did nothing to alter that attitude. "No matter what we tried we could not get that 10–3 game out of the players' minds," Soviet head coach Viktor Tikhonov said. "The players told me it would be no problem. It turned out to be a very big problem."[24]

Al Michaels of ABC Sports captured the significance of the game at the beginning of the broadcast of the game, "I'm sure there are a lot of people in this building who do not know the difference between a blue line and a clothes line. It's irrelevant. It doesn't matter, because what we have at hand is the rarest of sporting events. An event that needs no build up, no supercilious adjectives."[25]

The U.S. team responded with an energetic and forceful effort that was the product of Brooks' heavy emphasis on physical conditioning. "The Americans were so strong in the first period," Soviet defenseman Zinatula Bilyaletdinov recalled. "It was unexpected for us."[26]

It appeared to matter little, though. The Soviets scored nine minutes into the contest. Buzz Schneider responded charging down the left side of the ice, the one away from the television cameras, and fired a slap shot from a sharp angle that flew into the upper far corner of the net. The Soviets responded quickly with another score of their own. Then, just before the period came to an end, Mark Johnson sensed that the Russian defenders were letting up. "We relaxed a little bit. We felt that the period was over and the horn would sound," Bilyaletdinov explained. "Unfortunately, that was a big mistake." Johnson slid in between two defenders and skated wide to the left of the Soviet net, which created a huge gap between Tretiak and his station. The American blasted a slap shot past him to tie the game at two goals apiece.[27]

Most hockey experts considered Tretiak the best goalie in the world at the time, but he had been playing poorly, and during the break between periods, Tikhonov decided to replace him with Vladimir Myshkin. "The whole team was not happy when Tikhonov made the switch," Sergei Makarov, a Soviet winger, recalled. "It was the worst moment of Vlady's career. Tikhonov was panicking. He couldn't control himself. That's what it was – panic." Defenseman Sergei Starikov agreed, "It felt like a big hole had been put in our team." Even Tikhonov later conceded that he was wrong: "The biggest mistake of my career was replacing Tretiak with Myshkin." Tretiak always played better after giving up a goal, but the coach let his emotion get the better of him.[28]

At first, though, this decision had no impact on the game. The Soviets dominated the second period, scoring the go-ahead goal less than two minutes after it started and outshooting the Americans, 30–10. Learning from his experience in the 10–3 game, Craig stayed back in the net, creating a smaller target and blocking most of these shots.[29]

The Americans were trailing when the third period started, but they were still in the game, and had come from behind before, but these were the Soviets, the best team on the planet. Then the Americans had an opportunity: A Soviet penalty gave the U.S. a power play. The Russians held them off. As the power play ended, however, Dave Silk cut across the ice with the puck, passed it directly to Johnson who was standing in front of the Soviet net, and he slapped it right between the legs of Myshkin. The game was tied again, 3–3. The arena exploded in cheers. "The crowd was an unbelievable big help to us," Brooks said. "The fans displayed excellent sportsmanship, even though we have different ways of life and government. There were no politics on behalf of the Russians and no politics by us. I don't think the fans were an ugly lot. They were positive." Eighty-one seconds later, Eruzione skated around a Soviet defenseman, using him as a screen to block Myshkin's view, and snapped a twenty-five-foot wrist shot off the wrong foot, which went straight into the left side of the net. "And that's when the building went crazy," Al Michaels observed. "I mean that's when sound had feel."[30]

The American players celebrated on the ice for a few seconds, but there were exactly ten minutes left in the game, and they were worried. The Soviets had more than enough time to take the lead back. No one needed to look any further than their three-goal rampage against Finland, which had taken all of seventy-nine seconds. "These are going to be the longest ten minutes of my life," Morrow told himself. Brooks was telling his players not to get rattled, "Play your game." His real message: relax and stay focused. It was a wasted effort. "God couldn't have come down and got us relaxed," Eruzione said.[31]

All the American players on the bench were standing, and the crowd was chanting: "USA! USA! USA!" Their teammates on the ice started to notice something; although none of them spoke Russian, they could tell that the Soviets were beginning to talk in angry and anxious tones, and began taking shots at random, reflecting a good deal of confusion. The American players were also surprised when, in the last sixty seconds, Tikhonov kept Myshkin in the game instead of pulling him and giving the Soviet team an extra skater. The reason: The Russians had never practiced this move. They had little reason to believe that they would ever be behind. Tretiak admitted: "Until the last minute, I thought we would beat them. To lose, that was not possible."[32]

The din of the crowd only grew louder as the seconds ticked off the clock. Al Michaels was screaming into his microphone: "Do you believe in miracles? Yes!" The horn sounded and the game ended. The Americans poured out onto the ice and danced around in ecstasy. "I don't think you can put it into words," Eruzione said. "It was twenty guys pulling for each other, never quitting, sixty minutes of good hockey. I don't think we kicked their butts. We just won."[33]

The Soviets patiently stood on the ice, waiting for the traditional postgame handshake. They were smiling in amusement. The relentless practice sessions had sucked all the joy out of the game for the Soviet players. Tretiak later said he had practiced everyday for twenty-one years, including his wedding day. "It was more than hockey for those guys," Makarov said. "We were happy for them." That evening, several of the Soviet players toasted their American opponents.[34]

The opposing coaches reacted quite differently to the game. Brooks left the floor of the arena, went back to the locker room, locked himself into a toilet stall, and cried. On the other side of the building, in the Soviet locker room, Tikhonov was yelling at his players: "This is your loss." On the plane back to the Soviet Union, the coach continued to rail at his players. Finally, defenseman Valery Vasiliev had enough; he grabbed Tikhonov by the neck and threatened to kill him. Vasiliev's teammates had to pull him off their coach.[35]

After the Soviets left Lake Placid, cleanup workers at the Olympic village found 121 empty vodka bottles in the Soviets' rooms. None of the Russians turned in their silver medals to have their names inscribed on them. Not one. Several of them, in fact, threw their medals away.[36]

Despite the victory, the U.S. team still had one game to play – and it was still a must-win. If they beat Finland, they would win the gold medal; if they lost, the goal differential would determine the medals, and they would finish in fourth place. It was altogether possible that the Soviets could still leave Lake Placid with the gold medal, if they won and the Americans lost. According to Eruzione, "Herb Brooks walked into the locker room, and he looked at us and said, 'If you lose this game you will take it to your fucking grave.' And he stopped, he walked a couple of steps, turned, looked at us again and said, 'Your fucking grave.'"

"He didn't have to say much more than that. We knew he was right," Mark Johnson said.[37]

Throughout the Olympics, the Americans had been outscored in the first two periods. This pattern held again. Finland scored first, and Jorma Valtonen, the Finnish goaltender, was playing well, very well. He blocked fourteen shots in that first period. At the end of the second period, Finland was ahead, 2–1. The Americans had, however, outscored their opponents 27–6 in the third period, which was the product of heavy physical conditioning that Brooks had stressed during practices. That pattern held, as well, in this game. The Americans scored twice in the first six minutes of the third period to take the lead, 3–2. After some sloppy play that gave the Finns power plays, Johnson scored another goal. Now the score was 4–2. Three minutes and thirty five seconds remained in the game. The crowd counted as the last five seconds on the game clock ticked off, and Michaels was yelling into his microphone again: "This impossible dream comes true!"[38]

At the medal ceremony, the Americans followed a superstition that they had developed during the pre-Olympic training. Craig always led the group out of the locker room, followed by John Harrington. Eruzione was always the last in line. They followed this practice one final time, before they watched the raising of the U.S. flag and the playing of the "Star Spangled Banner."[39]

Two presidents watched the U.S. Hockey Team's success and had very different reactions. One was James Earl Carter, Junior, President of the United States. "It was one of the high spots of my year when the young Americans won – a very emotional moment," Carter remarked. He called and congratulated Brooks after the Soviet game, telling him that the team had made the nation proud. Vice-President Walter Mondale was in the stands for the gold medal game and visited the locker room afterwards. He wanted to congratulate the players from his home state of Minnesota. Brooks told him not to get regional.[40]

Carter called again after the victory over the Finns. Technicians from American Broadcasting Company (ABC) had a special room set up for the team to receive the call. Eruzione told them if their conversation was going to be televised, it would be from the locker room. Stunned, the workers from ABC moved the lights and cameras while sportscaster Jim McKay delayed on the air. After the technical set up was finished, Eruzione spoke to the President. Cater told him, "We're all proud of you." Like most other Americans, the hockey team had inspired the President: "I was hoping this victory and the gold medal were an omen of better days ahead."[41]

The other president was The Right Honourable Michael Morris, The Third Baron Killanin of Galway, County Galway, president of the International Olympic Committee Unlike Carter, he was actually in the arena and draped the medals around the necks of the Americans, starting with Harrington and finishing with Eruzione. Observers noted the he seemed amused as he presented medals and shook hands with each player. He was not. He found the nationalism on display that day jingoistic and distasteful.[42]

There was a good deal of irony in these reactions. The "miracle on ice" ended up working against the efforts of the Carter administration that had started a boycott against the Moscow Games, which mutated into an attempt to destroy the Olympic movement. The success of the hockey team ended up helping Lord Killanin in his efforts to fight the White House. Until the hockey team won the gold, there had been strong support among the American people for a boycott of Moscow, but something changed. Eruzione explained that the American people loved his team because it "represented them in an athletic event that was far greater than a hockey game." Their success had suddenly provided the nation with a symbol of glory that made Americans more proud of their country. Their string of victories and the gold medal win showed the power of the Olympic movement, its ability to foster nationalist sentiment, its capacity to direct those energies into nonlethal forums, and in so doing act as a force that encourages mutual understanding.

To see this power – what international relations pundits like to call "soft power" – observers had to look at the situation honestly and assess the Olympics within their proper context. Carter, however, refused – adamantly refused – to do so. As a result, the effort to boycott the Moscow Olympiad became a proxy battle between Carter and Killanin. Given the power available to the U.S. government, it should have been a one-sided contest, with the American winning easily. Carter, however, managed to undermine himself with mismanagement and poor leadership. The President had based his policy on assumptions that had fundamental flaws and reflected a superficial familiarity with the Olympic movement, and these fundamental mistakes led to a campaign that failed to meet its basic mission objectives, but did manage to insult the Soviets just enough to destroy détente and restart the Cold War.

Why is retelling the story of the 1980 Olympic boycott important? There are many answers to this question. As the Olympic movement accepts national contingents, international politics will come into play in some fashion. Despite the amazing amount of "soft power" that the Olympics have in the form of public relations and propaganda, they remain a weak tool for diplomacy. Ask yourself this question: What do people remember about the Berlin Olympiad of 1936? The answer: The success of Jesse Owens, which, to use the words of Eruzione, was "an athletic event that was far greater than a ... game." Owens humiliated Hitler and his master race theories. In fact, in 1936, the Olympic movement forced political concessions from the Nazis. In the 1980 Summer Olympics, the U.S. basketball team could have avenged its highly questionable 1972 loss to the Soviets on their home court, achieving perhaps the same status in America as the hockey team. (People tend to forget that the Soviets won more medals at Lake Placid than any other team, but the story of the hockey team is what people remember from that gathering.) It is also possible that the massive influx of foreign visitors and media contingents could have been too much for the Committee for State Security (KGB) to handle. Media attention cuts both ways, though. Lord Killanin admitted as much: "The boycott of the Moscow Games was the most damaging event since the Games were revived in 1896." As such, he believed it was imperative the committee study and learn lessons from this incident to prevent it from reoccurring in the future. As the outgoing president, however, he had little power to commission such a study. "I regret that the IOC did not make a closer analysis of all the events that occurred between the Soviet Union's occupation of Afghanistan and the opening of the Games in Moscow, which I recommended. The attitude of the IOC that bygones should be bygones and that everything should be swept under the carpet is dangerous."[43] This book can serve such a function, because the Olympics have hardly seen the last of politics.[44]

Another reason this story is important is that it shows that popular perceptions about this administration are on the mark, for the most part. To be direct, Carter was mediocre in his handling of U.S. foreign policy. While he was well informed on the details and innovative in coming up with new ideas, he displayed poor judgment at the strategic level. He was unable to see large, conceptual issues or understand how perceptions in foreign lands might be different from those found in the United States. Opinions of the day that he was weak and indecisive were – to be equally direct – wrong. Carter showed resolution and determination throughout the boycott effort. It was his inability to provide a sustained strategic vision in his foreign policy that produced divisions within his administration and resulted in policies that worked against one another. His staff and national security officials were thoughtful, talented men and women, but they came off as amateurs because of the situation in which the President put them. More damningly, there was a whiff or two of court politics at play in the Carter White House, and these considerations rather than a sound analysis of the facts shaped policies.[45]

This book also tells us something about U.S. foreign policy and the course of the Cold War. It was the Olympic boycott, an American action, rather than the invasion of Afghanistan that killed détente. The boycott never had the potential to damage the political standing of the Communist Party within the Soviet Union, despite what Carter administration officials wanted to believe, but it did humiliate Soviet leaders in a way that they could neither forgive nor forget. Up to this point in time, Carter had mishandled relations with the Soviet Union, but the two countries were still in a position to work together. It was the overreaction of the President to Afghanistan that reinvigorated the Cold War. The Soviets had exposed the ruthless nature of their regime and the limited sovereignty that their dominions enjoyed when they invaded East Germany in 1953, Hungary in 1956, and Czechoslovakia in 1968. There was nothing unusual about their actions in Afghanistan. What was different was the intensity of the American reaction. The rationale that Carter and his subordinates offered for legitimizing their boycott was weak and strained, and one which they United States would be unable to meet years later when it hosted the 2002 Winter Olympics and was fighting in Afghanistan itself.[46]

Perhaps what is most important about the pages that follow is not what it explains about Carter, or Olympic politics, or about the Cold War, but what it shows about the American people and their attitudes about their place in the world. Foreign policy is a national event in that it affects everyone from the leadership of the nation to the average citizens. The Olympic boycott was no different. It was an event that involved large chunks of society, and support for the campaign was strong. The American public was still on the crusade that was the Cold War. The consensus on U.S. foreign policy was holding; Vietnam did nothing to shatter basic views about the outside world. Public attitude was simple: The Americans were the good guys, the Soviets were the bad guys. End of story. The 1970s were not just a time of weak national will and bad hair. The people wanted visionary leadership. Carter understood the desire but was never able to deliver. His successor, Ronald Reagan, could and did.

The Carter-Killanin confrontation invokes more than a little sadness because it pitted two men of high morals and proven ethics against one another. Carter had refused to join the White Citizens Councils in Georgia that opposed the civil rights movement at a time when community leaders were expected to take segregationist stands. Lord Killanin, for his part, had seen the threat of Nazi Germany early on and had voluntarily joined the British Army a year before Hitler started World War II, even though he was a citizen of neutral Ireland and under no legal obligation to serve. These two presidents would meet each other only once, when Killanin came to the White House for a futile, last-minute meeting on the boycott. Their stories, though, start in the refined halls of London and the dusty fields of Georgia, far from Moscow and Afghanistan.

CHAPTER 1

Lord Killanin and the Politics of the Olympics

ANYONE AT ALL FAMILIAR WITH THE MODERN OLYMPICS AND ITS history knows that it has never been free of international politics. Although the political issues that dominate world affairs have had their influence, the movement also has its own set of issues that are often quite different. While it is true that the Olympics fuel nationalism, the Games direct those energies into nonlethal forums and, as a result, encourage mutual understanding. This background was a significant factor in the boycott effort of 1980, and the president of the IOC more than anyone else understood this context. The presence of politics might seem to contradict the Olympic ideal of bringing the people of the world together, but not really.

The very heart of the international Olympic movement is the IOC. Baron Pierre de Frédy de Coubertin of France created the organization in 1894 when he "revived" the Olympics. He picked the founding members, and it has been a self-selecting organization ever since. Lord Killanin described it as basically a "club." The Olympic Charter is the constitution of the movement, which the Committee can interpret as it sees fit. There are many examples of the committee ignoring both the spirit and letter of the document when it so chooses. The IOC essentially answers only to itself, and for a long time having a seat on the committee was a lifetime appointment. There is no rule that the IOC must have a delegate from every country associated with the movement. As a result, several members can be, and often are, from the same nation, while most other lands have no voice at all in this organization. Members of the IOC like to note that they are not envoys of their homelands, but rather representatives of the Olympic movement, ambassadors if you will, in the places where they reside.[1]

In the 1970s, the committee had roughly seventy members and was still littered with generals, admirals, knights, lords, barons, viscounts, counts, marquises, dukes, grand dukes, princes with royal, imperial, and serene titles, sultans, and even a king. Many members without titles often had the noble distinctions of *van, von,* or *de* before their family names. Only a few committeemen – and at this point in time they were all male – had careers in government or much expertise in matters involving foreign policy. Most were wealthy, even those from the less developed nations of Africa, Asia, and South America. Their personal wealth varied significantly, but all of them could afford to travel abroad frequently. These backgrounds were no accident. "As the best means of safeguarding liberty and serving democracy, it is not always best to abandon ourselves to the popular will," de Coubertin explained. "Rather we must maintain, in the midst of the electoral ocean, strong islands that will ensure independence and stability." A number of reforms implemented in the 1990s following corruption scandals lowered the age limit, which was first put in place in the 1970s, increased the size of the committee, and created a number of representative positions for athletes and officials from other sport organizations.[2]

Since the IOC usually meets only once a year, a smaller group of members forms the executive board that handles pressing issues. The most powerful person on the executive board is the president of the IOC. This individual has enormous influence and can initiate any number of policies. Because personality and internal factionalism influences IOC decisions, inconsistency is a major characteristic of its policies. The group structure of the Committee also ensures that slowness is another feature.[3]

The basic administrative units of the movement are the national Olympic committees. These organizations administer the Olympics in the regions they represent. Most of these committees represent sovereign nation-states, but not always. Puerto Rico, the United States Virgin Islands, and Hong Kong all have an Olympic committee. On the other hand, the Olympic Council of Ireland represents all thirty-two counties on the island. Athletes in Northern Ireland do, however, have the choice to compete for a place on the British Olympic team if they want. The main job of all these national committees is to select the teams that will participate in the Summer and Winter Games of each Olympiad.[4]

The international athletic federations are also important administrative components of international sports. These organizations determine the rules and regulations of play, control eligibility (which varies significantly from sport to sport), sanction competitions, and provide judges. There are also national federations that administer the sport within the confines of that country. In most ways, the federations are more important than the national Olympic committees and have enormous influence *within* the Olympic movement. Only the *Federation Internationale de Football Association** that administers the sport known in the United States as soccer has significant standing on its own. The World Cup of football (soccer) is the only international

---

* International Federation of Association Football.

sporting event that rivals – and in many places surpasses – the Olympics in popularity.[5]

Political problems were present in the modern Olympics at the very beginning. Baron de Coubertin, like many other Frenchmen, wanted revenge against the new German Empire for the humiliation it inflicted on France in 1871. He attributed the defeat not to the military incompetence of Emperor Napoleon III, who thought he had the same talent as his uncle, but to the physical weakness of French youth. Turning his back on a military or political career, he decided to become a leader in what Americans would later call "physical education" or "sports management." He traveled extensively early in his life gaining ideas from the British and Americans. During his time in the United States, the Baron met Theodore Roosevelt who advocated something the politician liked to call the "strenuous life." The two became good friends and mutual supporters. By the time de Coubertin established the IOC, his travels had broadened his perspectives. He remained a proud and patriotic Frenchman, but he also believed that international athletic competition could contribute to a more humane world.[6]

To that end, de Coubertin decided to "revive" the Olympics of ancient Greece, which had for twelve centuries embodied much of what he wanted to accomplish. Although a cynic might claim that the baron had just created a world championship system and covered it in the trappings of ancient Greece, this view is a bit misleading. There was an honest effort to model the modern Olympics on those of old. Many of the same sports would be played, the Olympics would take place only once every four years, art festivals and museums would be associated with the athletic competitions, and the Games would be, at least initially, male only. There were some significant changes, though. The original contests were sacred to Zeus, and no one was interested in reviving the pagan religious aspects of the Olympics. He decided instead to replace the religious elements with modern symbols of the nation-state. "If the image of God were replaced for each athlete by the flag of his country, the grandeur of the ceremony could surely not fail to be enhanced and the appropriateness of this modernization is so obvious that there is no need to insist upon it," he explained. Using the garb of the ancient Greeks also bolstered the cause of the modern Olympians, cloaking it with prestige and an intangible mystique. There have been a number of challenges to the authority of the IOC throughout its history. What is important to note is that none of these rival efforts have voiced complaints about the ideals of the movement, but rather about the Committee's stewardship.[7]

Having athletes compete as part of national contingents raised a number of issues. What was a country? In the 1890s, when a number of empires existed, the answer to this question was a complicated one. Would British colonies like Canada and South Africa compete as part of the team from the United Kingdom or would they field their own teams? A number of athletes from the subject regions of Finland, Bohemia, and Ireland objected to the use of the flags that represented their imperial masters. In fact, several wanted to field their own teams.[8]

Other problems developed due to differing cultures and political interests. The British objected to the use of the metric system in measuring race distances. The Germans were initially reluctant to participate in the Games because de Coubertin was French. The Baron realized that the first Olympiad should be played in Greece. (Unlike the ancient Games, which were always played in Olympia, the modern ones move from city to city.) Earlier in the nineteenth century, the Greeks had attempted to revive the Olympics and had little success. Although they were pleased with the resurrection of the Olympics, the Greeks made no mention of de Courbertin in their official bulletins and programs. The royal family and the government of Greece attempted to displace the International Olympic Committee and keep the Games in the land of their birth. This effort failed, but nationalism in the Games only grew stronger with each passing Olympiad. In 1908, British officials objected to American behavior at the London Games. The Americans, for their part, accused British judges of discriminating against them. Such charges are so frequent that judging controversies are an almost regular occurrence at the Olympic Games, but de Coubertin was surprised enough to note with some resignation: "The Olympic Gamers were becoming an affair of state."[9]

The two world wars produced far bigger problems involving nationalism for the Olympics than anything that had come before. At first, it appeared that World War I would be a quick contest, and de Coubertin refused calls to move the Games of the VI Olympiad from Berlin. Although many people believe otherwise, there never was an Olympic truce in ancient Greece, and there was no chance of having one in 1916. When it became clear that war was going to last longer than expected and that there would be no competitions in Germany, de Coubertin moved to Lausanne, Switzerland, to keep the Games neutral. Lausanne has remained the headquarters of the modern Olympics ever since. De Coubertin announced that even though there was no chance to celebrate the Olympiad, the number would remain. The Games of 1920 would bare the designation of Roman numeral seven. When the war ended, the IOC quickly decided that the best symbolism was to have the Games in Antwerp, Belgium, to honor the suffering of that little country. This gesture was hardly neutral, and the IOC decided to expel all of its members from the defeated Central Powers. These actions raised the question about German participation. The ideals of the movement demanded that they be invited, but it was difficult for many IOC members to put aside the passions and hatred of war. In the end, the Committee avoided the issue altogether when they gave responsibility for inviting the contestants to the Antwerp organizers. The Belgians chose not to invite the Germans, nor did the French in 1924.

It was only in 1928 at the Amsterdam Games that the Germ〔 the movement.[10]

The Antwerp Games were small, since organizers only ha〔 nize the event and many countries were still recovering from 〔 is quite nice, but it certainly lacks people," King Albert I of B〔 when he visited.[11]

The King was right, but the important thing about the Games was that they were actually held. The modern Olympics had survived the trial of global war. Despite the brief threat of war in 1924 between Germany and France, the Olympic movement grew stronger during the interwar period. The IOC expanded to sponsor the Winter Olympics. A number of people objected to this move, since the ancient Greeks had never played these sports, but they lost the argument. During this period, the movement expanded the number of events for women, introduced the torch relay from Olympia, and the use of the Olympic flag with the symbol of five interlocked rings. Another important development for the long-term health of the movement came when de Coubertin ended his tenure as IOC president and Count Henri de Baillet-Latour of Belgium succeeded him.[12]

World War II was an even bigger test of the movement's strength than the first one. Nazi Germany hosted both the Winter and Summer Games in 1936. (The IOC had awarded both sets of Olympic Games to Germany before the Nazis came to power.) In Garmisch-Partenkirchen, the Bavarian crowds were rather ill-mannered, and stringent security made for a less than hospitable environment. Anti-Semitic signs were visible, but de Baillet-Latour won a small concession from the Nazis and got these items removed.[13]

The Summer Games of Berlin, though, are far more famous, or infamous, depending on one's perspective. The fact that Hitler would get to use the Games to his advantage began to bother some, and in 1935, Ernest Lee Jahncke, an IOC member from the United States and a former assistant secretary of the navy in the administration of President Herbert Hoover, publicly called on the committee to reverse its decision. A Gallup opinion poll that year found that 43 percent of the American public supported a boycott. Avery Brundage, president of the American Olympic Association, led the fight to keep the United States in the Games. Something of an anti-Semite himself, he dismissed the effort as nothing more than Jewish and Communist propaganda. He never understood that people of good character could and did honestly disagree with him. "I spent a lot of time soul searching, looking for the answer," Sam Balter, a Jew who was a member of the 1936 U.S. basketball team that won a gold medal, remarked years later. "Some told me it was important to compete and show a Jew could win. Others said it was immoral to attend Games in Germany. Even now after 50 years, I'm not sure I made the right decision." Brundage, for his part, was willing to take at face value the statements of German officials that the Nazi regime would honor the Olympic code and

˶llow all Germans, including Jews, to try out for the German national team. He had enough influence and authority in the American sporting world to win the day. Later that year, the IOC expelled Jahncke and replaced him with Brundage.[14]

The Games themselves were a draw on the propaganda front. The Nazis clearly failed to honor their promises to allow unfettered competition for positions on the German national team, and had an international stage upon which to display what they thought was appropriate art, music, and artifacts of ancient Greece. The swastika was visible everywhere, and many visiting dignitaries were wined and dined by leading Nazi officials and came away impressed with their charm. While these achievements were for the good of National Socialism, the Nazis suffered significant public setbacks to their racially charged ideology. South Korean Sohn Kee-chung, competing as part of the Japanese team under the name Kitei Son, won the gold medal in the marathon. The Japanese dominated swimming and diving, while the Egyptians did the same in weightlifting. The most visible success, though, belonged to an American – Jesse Owens. The former Ohio State Buckeye star was black, and his success, particularly in the long jump against German athletes, punched a big hole in the Nazi idea of Aryan superiority. He set two world records and won four gold medals in the four main track-and-field events. Owens was a huge star in Berlin; average Germans stopped him and asked for his autograph; his photograph was published in a favorable context in the German press; film director Leni Riefenstahl featured him more prominently than any other athlete in her documentary *Olympia* despite the objections of Nazi propaganda chief Joseph Goebbels. German sports historian Hans Joachim Teichler notes that Owens forced a "temporary suspension of a core part of National Socialist ideology."[15]

Forty years later, these facts were uncomfortable ones for proponents of a boycott of Moscow. So, a number of Americans just ignored the reverses that Hitler had suffered. "The Nazis were very successful in using the Olympics as propaganda. Jesse Owens was a footnote," a State Department official told *The Washington Post* on the condition of anonymity. Senator David Pryor of Arkansas agreed, dismissing Owens's success in a speech he gave introducing a resolution calling for a U.S. boycott of the 1980 Olympics.[16]

People with memories of this time challenged these views. "I read in the papers that it was a propaganda victory for the Nazis," Robert J. Kane, president of the U.S. Olympic Committee remarked in Congressional testimony, "they are rewriting history. Jesse Owens destroyed their myth of Aryan supremacy." Marty Glickman, a Jewish member of the U.S. track-and-field team in 1980, agreed. "The propaganda argument is nonsense," he remarked. "Who was the hero in 1936, Hitler or Owens? Jesse was a black hero. The best man won." On the floor of the U.S. Senate, Barry Goldwater of Arizona noted that participation could also be important politically: "For those of you who are concerned about making a political statement through the Olympics, please remember that Jesse Owens did more to show Hitler's Aryan theory for the manure that it was than any boycott ever could."[17]

Americans might have little regard for history, but the members of the International Olympic Committee have regularly shown even less for international politics. They voted to award the 1940 Games to Tokyo despite a good deal objections to the Japanese invasion of Manchuria in 1931. The war that broke out between Japan and China in 1937 made no impact on the IOC, but it did bother the United Kingdom. In 1938, British and Commonwealth athletes indicated that they would not attend the 1940 Olympics if Japan was still at war with China by then. The Japanese solved the problem later that year when they informed the IOC that they were no longer able to host the the the gathering. The Committee had a contingency plan to use Helsinki, Finland, as a backup to Tokyo. Plans were going forward with this option when World War II brought about the cancellation of these Games and the ones that would have followed in 1944.[18]

The Olympics barely survived World War II. The IOC found it impossible to hold meetings during the conflict, and de Baillet-Latour was unable to leave Nazi-occupied Belgium. When the Count died in 1942, Nazi sports officials attempted to seize control of the Committee. This effort failed, because IOC headquarters were still in Switzerland. J. Sigfrid Edström of Sweden, the IOC vice-president, became acting president. Only three members attended the first postwar meeting of the executive board, but the IOC decided to hold the Olympic Games of 1948 in London. As was the case after the previous war, the organizing committee extended no invitation to the Germans. A huge controversy then engulfed the IOC about embracing members from the defeated Axis powers. Reflecting the Eurocentric focus of the Committee, the main point of contention was the status of German representatives. Not much got said about the Italians or the Japanese. This issue roiled the waters for five years, with Edström and Brundage determined to put the past behind them and forgive the Germans, even if they were former members of the Nazi party. In a contentious meeting in which the two men refused to allow the Committee to hold a formal vote, they succeeded in getting the Germans back on the IOC.[19]

While the Olympics had survived World War II, the movement faced a more difficult problem of how to adjust to the new era of the Cold War. The IOC had to wrestle with the issue of how, or even if, it would incorporate the Soviet Union and the other Communist nations into the Olympic movement. Imperial Russia had participated in the Olympic Games before World War I, but the Soviet Union had ignored the "bourgeois" pastime.[20] Many of the small nations of Eastern Europe that were now under Soviet political control had been members of the Olympic movement before the war. Edström believed that politics and sport should not mix and was prepared to welcome them back into the movement despite their current political orientation. He, however, had no intention of electing Communists to the IOC. Edström made the first move, writing to Soviet athletic officials and inviting them to join the International Amateur Athletic Federation, which supervised track-and-field contests. The Soviets never responded, but suddenly showed up at the Federation's 1946 European championships unannounced. Edström and Brundage ignored Federation rules that prohibited athletes from competing against those from nations without a recognized federation and allowed the Russians to compete. The Soviets afterward made a formal bid to join the Federation but demanded that the organization make Russian an official language, expel fascist-controlled Spain, and put a Soviet on the executive committee. The Federation rejected all three of these conditions. With their bluff called, the Soviets accepted and joined.[21]

In 1951, when the Soviets had become members of enough federations, the IOC voted to accept the Soviet Union into the Olympic movement. The Soviets made the same three demands of the Committee that they had made of the track-and-field federation, and got the same rejection, which they accepted. The Soviets then announced that Konstantin Andrianov would represent the Soviet Union on the IOC. This move stunned the committeemen. They selected their members, not Josef Stalin, but they were unable to find an alternative. They decided to bend a little, accepting the man that the Kremlin had imposed on them. Of course, the Committee had done the same when they accepted selections that Hitler had forced on them. Andrianov never bothered to learn French or English, the official languages of the Olympics, and the IOC bent again when they allowed him to appear with an interpreter. Far more significant was the IOC and Avery Brundage's willingness to accept Communist explanations about the amateur status of their athletes and that their national Olympic committee was independent of the Soviet government. The presence of the Soviets, while it made the Olympic movement more universal, politicized IOC proceedings along East-West lines.[22]

The Soviet Union competed in the Olympics for the first time in 1952 in Helsinki. The Soviets had thought about competing in London in 1948 but ultimately decided against doing so, believing they lacked the time to put together a competitive team. The Soviet team, though, had minimal contact with other athletes. The Soviets refused to stay in the Olympic village, and political handlers blocked efforts at fraternization. With the Soviets in attendance, the Helsinki Games became another outlet for the Cold War. In this context, what mattered was how many medals the Soviet and American teams won. The results were basically even. The Soviets garnered 71: 22 gold, 30 silver, and 19 bronze. The Americans took 76 medals home: 40–19–17.[23]

Another major problem the Olympic movement faced during the Cold War was which of the two Germanys should participate in the Olympiads. Brundage was determined to get the Germans back into the Olympics and to have them compete as a unified team. In West Germany, the *Nationales Olympisches Komitee für Deutschland** was reformed the day after the founding of the *Bundesrepublik* in 1949. The West Germans insisted that their committee was a continuation of the prewar organization and represented all of Germany, including the "Soviet occupied zone." At the same time, the Federal Republic said it was the only sovereign German government. Neither wanted any recognition of their East German counterparts. When the German Democratic Republic created its own national Olympic committee, the IOC had to make some decisions. The Committee recognized the West Germans in 1951, but Brundage decided he would work out a compromise, creating one organization for the two states similar to the Olympic Council of Ireland. Negotiations in Switzerland did indeed produce a settlement that allowed the East Germans to participate as part of the West German contingent. When the Communist representatives returned to Berlin, their government denounced the agreement. As a result, the Germans that competed in Helsinki in 1952 came only from the western half of the country. The East Germans then requested recognition of their Olympic committee in 1954, which the IOC gave on a provisional basis provided that they compete as one team with the West Germans. This time the Communists accepted. On matters of symbolism, the Germans used as a flag the black-red-gold tricolor that was common to both states with the five Olympic rings superimposed on its stripes. Beethoven rather than either of the national anthems of the two Germanys saluted the victors during their medal ceremonies.[24]

Brundage was quite proud of his accomplishment. "We have obtained in the field of sports what politicians have failed to achieve so far," he bragged. The IOC even got the U.S. government to accept the use of East German passports when the Americans hosted the 1960 Winter Olympics in Squaw Valley, California. This agreement fell apart after the building of the Berlin Wall in 1961. In 1968, the IOC recognized the national Olympic committee of East Germany and starting with the Games of that year, the two Germanys fielded separate teams until reunification in 1990.[25]

German participation in the Olympic movement proved quite easy to solve compared to a similar issue involving China and Taiwan. The IOC had three Chinese members before the Chinese Civil War of 1946–49. All three refused to follow the defeated Chiang Kai-shek to Taiwan. The members of the *Zhonghua Aulinpike Weiyuanhui***, however, were scattered all about mainland China and Taiwan. As a result, two separate organizations developed, and both wanted recognition from the IOC. Edström and Brundage were inclined to ignore the two groups and allow neither team to participate in the Games. Both Chinese delegations, however, refused to make life easy for the

---

*   National Olympic Committee for Germany.
** Chinese Olympic Committee.

IOC. In 1952, representatives of the two organizations showed up in Helsinki, asking for accreditation, and making political and diplomatic arguments that sat poorly with their audience. There was no clear consensus among the Committee, and a French member proposed that they let both Chinese teams compete in the sports in which their national federation had international recognition. The Nationalists from the Republic of China rejected this compromise, while the Communists from the People's Republic of China were unable to get their athletes to Finland in time to compete. In 1956, the IOC invited both teams; the Nationalists accepted, but the Communists rejected this offer. In 1958, Tung Shou-yi, an IOC member who still lived in Beijing, resigned, noting that the "Olympic spirit has been grossly trampled upon."[26]

Tung's departure reflected a policy of self-imposed isolation that the People's Republic was pursuing in world affairs. The Chinese decision resolved the matter before the IOC, but Soviet members objected to Taiwan's claim that it represented all of China. The rest of the Committee agreed and informed the Taiwanese that they would have to adopt a new name. This decision provoked a firestorm of protest in the United States. President Dwight D. Eisenhower publicly criticized the decision, and the U.S. Senate Judiciary Committee's Internal Security Committee subpoenaed Brundage to testify before Congress. "The country seems to have gone off on an emotional binge in unprecedented proportions," he observed. In a note he wrote, his exasperation is quite clear:

AB
Clever fellow
Imperialist
Fascist
Capitalist
Nazi
& now Communist.[27]

Under international pressure, the Chinese Olympic Committee compromised – a little – changing its English-language name to the wordy "Olympic Committee of the Republic of China." (In Chinese, the name of the organization remained the same). The IOC accepted this revision but insisted that when the team marched in the opening ceremonies of the Rome Summer Games, it would do so behind a sign that read "Taiwan." The Nationalist Chinese athletes objected. During the parade of nations, when they passed the presidential box, they flashed a sign that declared, in English: UNDER PROTEST.[28]

The Communists from mainland China, however, still had their own grievances against the IOC. When the committee suspended the *Komite Olahraga Nasional Indonesia** for failing to invite Israel and Taiwan to

---

* Indonesian National Olympic Committee.

the fourth Asian Games as they were required to do, President Sukarno of Indonesia responded by saying that the IOC had failed the ideals that Baron de Coubertin had put forward. He then established the Games of the New Emerging Forces, which was an effort to create athletic contests for athletes in the less developed countries of the world. China supported this effort and was one of the forty-eight nations that sent athletes to the first Games of the New Emerging Forces (GANEFO) games in 1963. The IOC worried about this challenge to its authority and offered to forgive Indonesia and readmit them into the movement if the Indonesians would just ask for readmission, which they were more than willing to do. This crisis, however, was far from over. The federations administering international swimming and athletics (or track-and-field) had not sanctioned these GANEFO contests. China had participated and was a member of neither organization. Ignoring the precedent that Edström and Brundage had set when Brundage had been president of the very same athletics federation, the two organizations insisted on banning certain Indonesian athletes from participating in the Tokyo Olympics of 1964. Indonesia responded with a boycott.[29]

The two Chinas would remain a troubling issue for the international Olympic movement throughout the 1970s. The People's Republic of China (PRC) started making moves to rejoin the world of international sports after they joined the United Nations in 1971. The strategy that sports officials in Beijing followed was simple; they joined only those international sports federations in which Taiwan was not a member. After gaining recognition from the required number of federations, the Chinese applied for accreditation from the IOC in 1975, but insisted that Taiwan be expelled. The Communists saw their participation in the Olympics as a political and diplomatic issue, which was not the way the members of the IOC viewed their organization. Eventually, in 1979, the Committee recognized the Chinese Olympic Committee. The IOC allowed Taiwan to stay in the movement provided they changed their name yet again, which they did, becoming – in English – the "Chinese Taipei Olympic Committee." This solution proved acceptable to officials in Beijing. Despite its repeated name changes, this organization still calls itself in Chinese the "Chinese Olympic Committee."[30]

The man who oversaw the inclusion of China was the sixth president of the International Olympic Committee and the third peer to wear the title of Killanin of Galway. Born in London on July 30, 1914 as Michael Morris, he was a son of Eire but an English gentleman as well. His heritage on both sides of the Irish Sea played a significant role in his rise within the international Olympic movement. He proved to be an acceptable leader to the Irish Olympic movement, which was divided on the same religious and political fault lines that divided the Emerald Isle on all other issues. From the beginning of his involvement with the Olympics, Killanin was fully aware that international politics intruded often into international athletic play.

Killanin's grandfather was the chief justice of Ireland during the reign of Queen Victoria and became a baron in the peerage of the United Kingdom. The third Killanin was often described as an Irish peer, which is accurate but misleading. He was Irish and a peer, but a British peer. The Irish peerage was a separate set of titles that the throne had awarded until 1801 when the United Kingdom of Great Britain formally absorbed the Kingdom of Ireland. After the joining of these two kingdoms, the throne gave individuals titles in the peerage of the United Kingdom. The peers of Ireland kept their older titles, but these honors never included membership in the House of Lords, a body which included the Irish Killanins since they were British nobility. Later in life, the third baron enjoyed the perplexed reactions he got in Ireland when he used his House of Lords identification card.[31]

There was something of a tradition in the Morris family that Irish Catholic males would marry English Protestant females. His father, a career officer in the British Army, followed this pattern marrying an Anglo-Australian, which only added to the international nature of the family. Lieutenant-Colonel The Honourable George Henry Morris should have been the third Killanin, but he died thirty-three days after his son's birth, during the first days of the Great War. As a result, Michael Morris inherited the family title from his childless uncle when he was thirteen.[32]

The young Lord Killanin spent most of his youth in England, attending public schools, then Cambridge. As a result, he spoke with an English accent for the rest of his life. His title proved to be something of a liability. "This is something which is absolutely true in life as one is always considered an 'amateur' if one has a title." He was also fluent in French and did graduate work at the Sorbonne.[33]

He decided to pursue a career in journalism, joining the staff of the *Daily Express*. "I was fairly young because I came down from Cambridge before I was 21, and I was employed in Fleet Street before I was 21. I wasn't very bright. I didn't get a very good degree, but I happened to be a little precocious." He suffered an early career setback after he was fired for failing to check his facts on a story; "a highly unimportant one," he explained later. He quickly found a new job at the *Daily Mail* that doubled his salary. "I found again that having a title made people rather polite for reasons that I disliked. When I worked I virtually never used it." He became a foreign affairs correspondent, covering military, political, and diplomatic issues. He covered the Sino-Japanese War that started in 1937, finding himself in the odd position of being accredited by both China and Japan. In later years, after he had actually served in the military, he remarked, "In some ways I think it is safer being a soldier than being a war correspondent."[34]

After returning to London, he became an editor and began moving up in the world of British journalism with his own column. Then, he decided to join the British Army. This move was a bold act of conscience. It came before the Nazi invasion of Poland that started World War II. "I believe very much in the freedom of the individual and in human rights and I really joined up, although Ireland was neutral, because I felt very strongly about the totalitarian regime and their efforts to dominate the world. Strangely enough, I think I first really learnt about this when reading as a young reporter of Hitler's treatment as a result of the 1936 Games." He joined a Territorial Army regiment – the reserves of the British Army – of the King's Royal Rifles – a unit his father had served in before World War I. He served throughout the war, saw combat during the D-Day invasion of Normandy, and later received membership in the Order of the British Empire – one of several British orders of chivalry – at a rank just below knighthood.[35]

After the war, he returned to Ireland and began rebuilding the family residence in County Galway that had been destroyed during the Irish Civil War. He later described this effort as "a moment of madness." Having an estate was not in his nature. "I realized I was building a kind of yacht that was anchored forever and highly expensive – and I don't like living behind the walls of an estate cut off from people. I haven't the landlord mentality, anyway." He sold the mansion but retained the Episcopal Church that his grandfather had built for his grandmother, converting it into a summer retreat for his family. He settled in Dublin but kept County Galway license plates on his cars for sentimental reasons. He became a book author, writing a biography of Sir Godfrey Kneller, the seventeenth-century painter, and the *Shell Guide to Ireland*. In 1947, he joined the Irish Shell board of directors, which led to his membership on fourteen other corporate panels. In the 1950s, he teamed up with his friend, John Ford, the film director, and produced *The Rising of the Moon*. He worked on this movie and two others using the name Michael Killanin.[36]

It was during this decade that he became involved with the international Olympic movement. Despite partition, there was one Irish team at the Olympics. The Olympic Council of Ireland represented all thirty-two counties, regardless of the political boundaries. The differences that divided the island complicated the process of finding a president that would be acceptable to all of Ireland. Killanin's social status and religion made him acceptable to the Catholic south, while his service in the British Army made him acceptable to the Protestant north. Even though he had never competed in the Olympics as an athlete, he became president of the association in 1950 and would hold that position until 1973. He was attracted to the Olympic movement not because he was a sports fan, but because he thought it did important social work. "Sport for world peace" and "united through sport" were two phrases that characterized his feelings toward the modern Olympics.[37]

Two years later, he became a member of the IOC. After twenty years on the Committee, including stints as a member of the executive board and as a vice-president, he became the sixth president of the IOC in 1972. In the middle of his term, he observed: "I'm five years older and 20 kilos (44 pounds) lighter, but I can say that every moment has been interesting." After leaving office, he was a bit more melancholy, "I can assure you that one of the experiences looking back over the eight years was at times one of complete loneliness."[38]

His administrative style was significantly different from that of his predecessor. "We need a leader," Brundage remarked, "and Michael isn't a leader." As always, Killanin was diplomatic in describing the differences between himself and Brundage: "I have the greatest respect for my predecessor, but he came from a certain generation." The members of the IOC sided with Killanin. After twenty years of Brundage's rule, which had both helped and hurt the Olympic movement, they were ready for a change.[39]

As IOC president, Lord Killanin was, by his own admission, a part-time executive. He spent only about one day a week on the Olympics, devoting the rest of his time to his paid positions as a member of company and bank boards. "The post of President of the International Olympic Committee should not be purchasable but open to anyone who could devote the time," he explained after his tenure in office ended. He operated out of the basement of his Dublin home but found that he was getting so many calls about the Olympics that he had to have his number taken out of the Dublin phone directory.[40]

There were problems with this administrative approach. Monique Berlioux, the executive director of the IOC secretariat, had significantly more power than her formal job description implied. One of her subordinates said she liked to brag that she controlled Killanin. While many people associated with the Olympics in the 1970s probably believed this view to be true, there were other problems with Killanin's administrative style. "The issues he faced proved too complex to be solved with a kitchen-table style of management," Richard W. Pound, a Canadian member of the Committee observed.[41]

Lord Killanin did enjoy good press coverage during his time in office. A reporter from *Sports Illustrated* observed, "He has a genial, commanding presence and an instant likability; he is a man without false dignity." Journalists loved his jovial sense of humor, which made him good copy. When asked how a nude streaker managed to get into the closing ceremonies of the Montreal Games, Killanin admitted he was unsure "because he wasn't wearing the correct badge." On another occasion, he was asked what he thought of the girls performing folk dances at another ceremony. "Much prettier than ladies putting the shot."[42]

It is hardly a surprise then that, with this weak administrative approach and charming personality, assessments of the man differ so much. Olympic historian Allen Guttmann uses the word "ineptitude" to describe the Irishman's performance in office. A long-time member of the IOC, Baron Luke of Pavenham, was equally harsh, "Killanin ... wasn't awfully good." Pound of Canada was a little more generous in his assessment, but only a little, noting he "was well over his head in many of the complicated international problems that arose on his watch." Alain Coupat of the IOC staff, though, was extremely positive in his assessment: "He was the key element in the evolution from this totally closed organization under Brundage to the open regime of Samaranch. He guided the thinking that made the change possible. With his mild manner, it was masterfully done." The political scientist Christopher R. Hill calls him "a shrewd and amiable peer." Peter Ueberroth, the head of the Los Angeles Olympic Organizing Committee, described him as "the epitome of integrity."[43]

The first real test of Killanin's presidency came with the 1976 Montreal Olympiad. The Games were held in the French-speaking province of Quebec, which had separatist political inclinations. Killanin handled these problems easily enough at the opening ceremonies, introducing Queen Elizabeth II in French. Construction problems proved far more difficult and in the end were impossible to solve. Costs quickly exceeded the original estimate of $125 million. The honor of hosting the Olympic Games eventually cost the city of Montreal $2 billion, which took twenty-eight years to pay off. Much of this cost resulted from corruption within the municipal government, the awarding of jobs and contracts to political cronies of the mayor, labor strikes, structural design problems in the architecture of various stadiums, inflated prices, and poor coordination between various branches of government. In his memoirs, James Worrall, a Canadian on the IOC, states, "All that could be done was to hope and pray that the labour unions would continue as promised without further interruptions." Killanin and other IOC members were less passive and began holding discussions about moving the Games to Germany. "We were indignant," Artur Takač, the Technical Director the IOC appointed for the Montreal Games, recalled. "This was a body blow and one which sounded like a vote of no confidence." He and others were both "worried" and "bitter" at this decision. Perhaps, but the concerns the IOC had were well founded. When the Games started, construction work on the main stadium remained unfinished.[44]

As troubling as these problems were, political issues arose that caught the IOC unprepared. The Canadian government promised that it would allow athletes from every national Olympic committee admission into the country so they could compete in Montreal. Just before the Games began, the government of Prime Minister Pierre Trudeau informed Killanin that athletes from Taiwan would be prohibited from entering Canada if they attempted to compete as representatives of the Republic of China. The Canadians, who had just established formal diplomatic relations with the People's Republic of China, had informed Killanin about this issue a year in advance of the Montreal Games. "It was baffling to hear that Lord Killanin was surprised by these reports," Takač notes in his memoirs. He believes the Irishman stalled to limit the political fallout from the United States. The Canadians, though, were prepared to compromise and allow the Taiwanese to compete if they did so as Taiwan and not the Republic of China, and had no problems with whatever flag and anthem they chose to use. The Taiwanese refused this compromise. "How can we stop calling ourselves Chinese," Henry Hsu, the IOC member from Taiwan, asked. Needless to say, the Taiwanese did not participate in the Games of the XXI Olympiad. At a press conference afterwards, Killanin said he was "fed up with politicians interfering with sport." In a spontaneous gesture, the reporters present applauded.[45]

Just as this crisis simmered down, another developed about the participation of New Zealand. The real issue was not New Zealand itself but rather the status of the discriminatory white regimes that controlled several African countries. The International Olympic Committee had prohibited South Africa from competing in the Tokyo and Mexico City Games because its apartheid policy resulted in racial discrimination in sport that violated the letter and spirit of the Olympic charter. In 1970, the IOC expelled South Africa from the Olympic movement. In 1972, the IOC extended its ban to the newly independent Rhodesia. Although investigation found that there were no separate athletic systems in Rhodesia, the Supreme Council for Sport in Africa, an organization of sport federations in black African nations, remained unsatisfied and wanted to isolate the minority white government of Rhodesia. It rejected an IOC compromise and threatened to boycott the gathering in Germany. Despite Brundage's outrage, the Committee voted 36 to 31, with 3 abstentions to ban the Rhodesians. The issue seemed to have been resolved as the Montreal Games approached, but the Supreme Council was upset that the New Zealand Rugby Union was planning to have its national team tour South Africa in violation of the ban on contact with that country. The organization demanded that the IOC ban New Zealand from participating in the Montreal Olympiad. Most IOC members, including Lance Cross of New Zealand, considered this crisis to be contrived. Rugby was not an Olympic sport, and the New Zealand Rugby Union had no relationship with the New Zealand Olympic Committee. There was no inclination to make any concessions on the part of the IOC and the boycott went forward. (The exact number of countries that participated is open to dispute since many had already participated in some events before they withdrew.)[46]

Assessments of the IOC president's performance during these crises vary. "Killanin should have sensed the danger," his successor Juan Antonio Samaranch stated later, "that Africa, more than Trudeau's refusal to admit the Taiwan team to Canada, was the greater threat." The Olympic historian John Lucas is far more positive in his assessment of Lord Killanin, who "kept a typically low profile and allowed the defection to happen without any intervention from the IOC. The Taiwan issue was still hot, the African withdrawal lacked credibility even in the most liberal press, and Killanin sat smoking his pipe, at least in the figurative sense, waiting for the Olympic pageant to begin. Probably it was the wisest move – or lack of action – on his part." The president of the IOC was worried about holding the movement and the athletes together. "Our first responsibilities are to them," he said. In his opinion, retaliatory actions that divided athletic organizations or kept certain groups from competing against another helped no one.[47]

After the Montreal Games ended, Killanin admitted he "enjoyed it in a masochistic sort of way." Shortly thereafter, he suffered a heart attack, which he and his wife blamed on the stress of the Canadian gathering. There is probably some truth to this belief, but he was quite heavy at the time and his weight was probably a bigger factor in his health problems. He quickly decided that one term in office was enough. "There's a lot of pressure on me to run again, but my ulcer says 'No, eight years is enough.' I think there are an adequate number of candidates and I still think eight years is enough, really."[48]

Afterwards, the International Olympic Committee took actions that they thought would prevent future boycotts. The year after Montreal, the IOC adopted a new policy that national committees that withdrew from an Olympiad for political reasons would be suspended for five years, and censured the twenty-three African nations that boycotted the Games in Canada. "I am always just a little frightened at over politicization of sport. I must admit, I am a realist; I am criticized for it. Sport and politics unfortunately are frequently interrelated. Our object is to bring everyone together regardless of race, creed or political beliefs," Killanin remarked in a speech he gave between Montreal and Moscow. "It is our duty to endeavour to understand those of the others, and ensure that we are not marred in our progress by political reservations, or indeed that sport or sportsmen are not used for political purposes, but are protected against abuse for these purposes."[49]

Such words and actions probably seemed appropriate at the time, but the political problems at Montreal were nothing more than a faint indication of what was to come.

CHAPTER 2

Los Angeles versus Moscow

WHAT LORD KILLANIN AND THE MEMBERS OF THE INTERNATIONAL
Olympic Committee did not know was that while they had been fighting
public battles about the politics of participation in the Olympics over China,
Taiwan, and South Africa, the United States government had already politically intervened in the movement. Done quietly, American officials attempted
to influence the process in which the IOC selected the host city in an effort to
bring the Games to the United States. This effort brought about a clash with
the Soviets who were basically trying to do the same thing. The president
responsible – personally responsible – for this confrontation was not Jimmy
Carter, but Richard Nixon. This Cold War contest put the IOC right in the
middle, bribes in the pockets of its members, and the Games of the XXII
Olympiad in Moscow.

When Nixon entered office in 1969, a group of prominent individuals in
the Los Angeles area were trying to bring the Olympics to California. The last
time the United States had hosted the Summer Games was 1932. Ironically,
the host city that year was Los Angeles. The USOC was interested in hosting
the Games again. Since the 1940s, Detroit had been the designated bid city
for the United States. In 1960, the United States hosted the Winter Games,
which were again in California, in the resort of Squaw Valley. Repeated efforts
to bring the Summer Olympics to Michigan were unsuccessful. In 1968, the
USOC replaced Detroit with Los Angeles as the official American nominee
for the 1976 Summer Olympics, and Denver for the Winter Games. The IOC
would vote and make its decision in May of 1970.

Despite the prestige of the Olympics and the fact that the people making
the effort came from his native southern California, Nixon offered exceptionally weak support to this undertaking. The President and his advisors basically ignored the Olympics for their first year in office. There were all of three
sentences in the letter of support that he sent to the Los Angles group for the
portfolio they gave members of the IOC: "Dear John: I want to take this opportunity to congratulate you and the Los Angeles 1976 Olympic Committee

for obtaining the privilege of bidding for the 1976 [Olympic Games]. It was also a pleasant surprise to find so many old friends on the Los Angeles Committee, including Bill Henry, Preston Hotchkis, Marty Samuelson, and Paul Zimmerman. My best wishes to you and to the Committee." In contrast, Governor Ronald Reagan of California composed a much stronger statement of support: "Thanks to its topography and climate, California has long been an international sports center. Los Angels has the facilities and experience necessary for mounting a global athletic event of the scale of the Olympics, and it has the population and resources to insure its success. We Californians are fully cognizant of the honor that would be accorded if Los Angles is selected as the setting for the International Games, and sincerely hope you will extend this honor and responsibility to Los Angeles."[1]

Despite this lack of Presidential interest, members of the Los Angeles committee made several additional efforts to get further support from the administration. These events would have passed without notice in Washington had people representing the Los Angeles effort not injected the Cold War into the bid process. After the Los Angeles 1976 Olympic Committee tried and failed to get an opportunity to make a formal presentation to President Nixon, Bill Nicholas, a committee member, made a direct appeal during an Oval Office visit with a group from the Tournament of Roses Association. John Kilroy, president of the Los Angeles 1976 Olympic Committee, also asked the administration to help finance its operations with a grant of $250,000. Needless to say, these efforts failed. The situation changed dramatically, though, when another committeeman, Rodney Rood, contacted an old acquaintance of his from the public relations and advertising industry – H. R. Haldeman, the White House chief of staff. Rood explained that the Soviet Union had decided to make a bid to host the 1976 Games, and that the selection process had quickly become a contest of prestige with Cold War overtones. "We are now in direct confrontation with the Soviet Union on the level of international politics – a confrontation to determine international public appeal under the guise of non-politics – the award of the Summer Olympic Games of 1976," Rood declared.[2]

What the Los Angeles committee basically wanted was for the government to provide service in support of their private effort. The initial and vague appeal was for the "support and endorsement of our program by the President." Three weeks later, Rood made four specific requests to Haldeman. First, that the President send a personal representative, preferably an astronaut, to the Caribbean Games to be held in Panama. The success of this gathering was extremely important to Virgilio de Leon, a Panamanian on the IOC. The Los Angeles committee hoped to win his vote. Rood also requested that the administration have the National Aeronautics and Space Administration provide a supply of moon rock that could be incorporated into pins that he wanted to give to members of the IOC. The California businessman requested that the U.S. Information Agency provide their organization with a $100,000 grant to finance its operations. Up until that point, county and municipal governments, and private business had funded the committee, putting it at a competitive disadvantage against the Soviets. "We need financial assistance from the Federal Government because of our greatly accelerated visitation program necessitated by the aggressive competition of the Soviet Union." Finally, Rood wanted the administration to provide a waiver from the Civil Aeronautics Board so that Los Angeles committee members could fly the private but regulated U.S. airlines for free, reducing their operating costs. Kilroy later requested that a presidential representative attend the Caribbean Games and that Nixon attend a black tie premiere party in Los Angeles for a documentary film on the 1968 Mexico City Olympics. Many members of the IOC were expected to attend.[3]

The contest between Los Angeles and Moscow and the larger issue of a U.S.-Soviet confrontation got the attention of the Nixon administration, including the interest of the President himself. There was a brief exchange about these requests inside the White House and the Old Executive Office Building. Charles "Bud" Wilkinson, the former head football coach at the University of Oklahoma who had become a member of the President's staff, weighed in on this matter. He noted that in previous years, that the U.S. government had clearly honored the ideals of this international sports movement by not using national resources to support a municipality's bid to host an Olympiad. "I do not believe the President should be personally involved in this campaign, and I am definitely opposed to giving Los Angeles any money." Richard Nixon himself, though, thought differently and committed his administration to supporting the Los Angeles group in its battle with Moscow. Detroit had never enjoyed any support from the U.S. government.[4]

The Denver bid was a complicating factor. The Californians wanted help for Los Angeles but suspected that government officials might feel obliged to provide equal assistance to Denver, which would dilute their efforts. In the history of the modern Olympics, only two nations, the United States in 1932 and Germany in 1936, had hosted both the Winter and Summer Games in the same year. Rood explained that supporting the Los Angeles bid should be a top priority for the U.S. government. "The first objective of the United States should be to obtain the 1976 Summer Games, a far greater victory than the obtaining of the Winter Games in view of the magnitude of the athletic and cultural events associated with the Summer program, and the competition with Moscow and the Soviet Union." He also suggested that the fact that the United States had hosted the 1960 Winter Games would work against Denver, and that Los Angeles had, as a result, a much better chance of winning the Summer Games. "Should Los Angeles fail, after an all-out effort, there may be a possibility for Denver on the Winter Games vote."[5]

Despite the contemporary and historical reputation of the Nixon White House under Haldeman as an efficient machine, the Olympics issue quickly became mired in multiple bureaucratic efforts and attempts to delegate responsibility to others. Individuals from the State Department, the White House staff, and the National Security Council (NSC) – which was the foreign policy branch of the White House staff – worked on this project. White House aide Larry Higby realized having so many different agencies involved in the Olympics issue was counterproductive and thought that one individual should be responsible for the matter. Since the Olympics were an international movement, he thought the NSC was the best organization equipped to coordinate administration efforts. The problem with this idea was that the political scientists and economists working for the NSC knew little about international sports. "I don't mind at all your throwing the ball back at me, because that allows me to engage in the same sport," NSC staff member Helmut Sonnenfeldt told Higby. "Seriously, we share your unfamiliarity with this problem, and as a result I'll offer you all the NSC type guidance I can; but I'm afraid it doesn't cover some of the points." Higby refused to give up his idea of making one person responsible for overseeing Olympic matters. In a memo he sent to Haldeman, he argued, "I feel that this whole operation should be housed in Kissinger's office and would recommend that you sign Tab B, a memorandum to Kissinger asking him to assign a staff man for all Olympic matters." Haldeman response was blunt. He scrawled a large "No" over that entire paragraph.[6]

The chief of staff agreed with advice about making one individual responsible, but he wanted to retain control over the White House effort rather than give it to Kissinger. Haldeman thought about the idea for two days and then appointed Charles Stuart the project manager. "This is a matter that is of the highest priority and you should act to do everything that is reasonably necessary to get the 1976 Olympics here in the U.S.," the chief of staff informed Stuart in the memo assigning him the job. Haldeman was even more blunt in a handwritten notation on another memo: "Do everything necessary to get 1976 Olympics in U.S."[7]

Despite this appointment, conflicting bureaucratic interests continued to shape the actions of the administration. Haldeman had positioned himself and his staff to take credit for the achievement of helping bring the Olympics to the United States, but he also made it clear that others shared responsibility for the effort, if not the day-to-day administration. At the bottom of a routine memo to Kissinger announcing Stuart's appointment, Haldeman had added a sharp, handwritten note: "Henry – we've got to win this one – don't let it get away from us."[8]

The administration initially worked to honor most of the requests that Rood and Kilroy had made on behalf of the Los Angeles committee, but soon began advancing its own ideas. Nixon himself initiated this change. The President sent a letter to all members of the IOC supporting the city's bid. Nixon mentioned the "splendid climate" and "renowned hospitality" of the region. In a subtle dig at the Soviet Union, he also stated that the "freedom of movement and expression" that southern California was known for would make Los Angeles "a particularly suitable and exceptionally attractive site for the Olympic competitions."[9] Thinking the Committee was a miniature version of the United Nations, he wanted to send a personal letter to the U.S. ambassador in each country with a representative on the IOC "putting a personal responsibility on him to deliver that country's vote." He specifically wanted each ambassador to meet with their host foreign ministry and insist that officials in these agencies pressure their Olympic "delegate" to vote for Los Angeles. As Haldeman noted, the ambassadors were to "sell like hell + deliver the vote." The chief of staff told Stuart to provide a list of the undecided delegates and warned, "don't let this delay any longer than you have to because the President will keep pushing on it." Stuart, however, recommended against this action, suggesting instead that the Department of State contact the ambassadors representing these nations in the United States and apply the pressure in Washington. This view prevailed. Major General Alexander Haig of the NSC staff informed the State Department that the administration wanted to target twelve countries: Belgium, Chile, West Germany, Great Britain, Greece, France, Indonesia, Iran, Italy, Pakistan, Switzerland, and Yugoslavia.[10]

Neither of these ideas were particularly effective methods of attempting to influence the international Olympic movement. Nixon and his subordinates were assuming that the International Olympic Committee was similar in structure to the United Nations and were considering policies that would have been good ways of pressuring an international organization comprised of nation-states. The individual members of the committee had no official relationship with the governments of their home countries or even their national Olympic committees. With either of these two proposals, the degree of influence that the United States could have exerted on the IOC would have depended on how much sway foreign governments had or were willing to use on an individual citizen. Given the diffuse organizational structure of the international Olympic movement, U.S. pressure on foreign governments was an extremely ineffective way of influencing Committee members.[11]

Despite its inappropriate and ineffective nature, the transformation that Nixon had initiated from general support to active lobbying accelerated as the White House attempted to obtain a waiver from the Civil Aeronautics Board (CAB). Two airlines, Pan Am and Trans World Airlines, agreed to provide international transportation at no cost for representatives of the Los Angeles bid, but CAB regulations prohibited them from doing so. The board could make exemptions if it were deemed of "paramount national interest." Denver had obtained such an exception in 1969, and the White House began pushing for exemptions for both cities in 1970. Historical precedent worked against this effort, though. In the past, the board had made exemptions only at the request of either the State or Commerce Departments, and only for foreign journalists traveling to the United States. The rationale behind this policy was that free transit would be a subtle way to assure that the nation received favorable coverage in foreign media outlets. In mid-February, Nixon domestic affairs advisor John Ehrlichman, believing the State Department had the power to waive CAB regulations, asked Kissinger to take the matter up with Acting Secretary of State Elliot Richardson. When this memo arrived at the offices of the NSC, Haig recommended that they take no action. He had talked to members of Richardson's staff and was informed that they worried that requesting such a waiver would create expectations of similar treatment from every other equally deserving group. "I am inclined to think that it would be dangerous to push this one too hard and suggest that you talk to Elliot Richardson about it and that we hold with whatever hard-nosed judgment State comes up with." Kissinger accepted this advice. He noted the "paramount national interest" requirement and observed, "This is a most difficult judgment for State to make in this case, and we should not be overly optimistic that the Secretary will be able to arrive at such a judgment."[12]

Since getting a waiver for members of the two committees was proving impossible, Stuart tried to obtain free travel for all national teams that would be traveling to the United States if Los Angeles were hosting the Olympics. This idea was a good one. Such a measure would have made it much easier for some of the poorer national Olympic committees around the world to send their athletes and coaches to Los Angeles. Stuart found the CAB willing to grant this type of waiver, but the International Air Transport Association of America, an aviation industry organization, refused to support this endeavor. Stuart later learned that the two airlines that showed the most resistance were Pan Am and TWA. His proposal was far more expensive than allowing a few members of the Los Angeles committee to fly for free, which is what these corporations had originally volunteered to do.[13]

Under Stuart's direction, the Nixon White House took other actions to win support for Los Angeles, many of which were done without any request from the Californians. Some of these endeavors were nothing more than good lobbying efforts; others were underhanded and suspect. Stuart wrote a series of progress reports for Haldeman that establish a good documentary record of White House initiatives. He sent presidential tie clasps to every member of the IOC. He traveled overseas with Los Angeles committee members as a "White House representative," showing that the city had high-level support. Stuart also arranged to have promotional brochures and other paperwork for both Denver and Los Angeles sent overseas via diplomatic pouch, saving the two committees a considerable amount of money in postage. Officials from the U.S. Embassy presented the publicity material to the individual members of the IOC. These deliveries helped give the Los Angeles and Denver efforts the cast of official sanction. The State Department also provided Stuart with support services that ranged from the mundane – tracking down addresses – to the critical – providing information that Foreign Service officers gained on the Olympics.[14] Considering the power of the U.S. government, though, these actions were fairly minor.

One of the efforts Stuart made, however, shows he had learned a good deal about international sport even if he still had a ways to go. He wanted to influence Brundage on behalf of Los Angeles. "The Los Angeles Olympic Committee people feel that if Brundage were to receive some indication of Presidential recognition prior to his leaving for Amsterdam on May 1st, he would likely be so euphoric as to violate his established principles and really push for Los Angeles," Stuart explained to Haldeman. "I tend to believe this evaluation."[15]

If Stuart were right about Brundage and his principles, it would have been a conversion as dramatic as the one that took place on the road to Damascus, though of far less significance. Brundage had been involved in the international Olympic movement for most of his adult life and was a stalwart believer in the idea that only amateur athletes should compete in the Games, and that politics could and should be kept out of the sporting arena.[16] The President's man was atrociously off the mark in his assessment of Brundage, but the idea of lobbying individual members of the IOC was sound.

Stuart had stumbled, but in fairness it is important to note that he was still learning the structure of international athletics. The cases of Rood, Kilroy, and others on the Los Angeles committee are different stories. Infatuated with the sports world and the high level in which they were engaged, these individuals based many of their decisions on some simplistic assessments about world affairs and the Olympic movement. One prominent Californian believed the United Kingdom and the Commonwealth were not supporting them out of historical embarrassment, suggesting that having the Olympics in Los Angeles during the U.S. bicentennial would be a painful reminder to the British that they had lost the American Revolution. Another member of the committee thought that the Moscow bid was solely designed to undercut their effort, and never considered that the Soviets might want the Olympics for the same reasons the Americans wanted the Games.[17]

With only two years left in his tenure as Committee president, Brundage had no intention of violating or repudiating values he had held dear for decades. He did, however, make himself available to members of the Los Angeles group and gave them advice – but that in no way means he was about to become their agent. He constantly warned the Californians that they could not assume that appreciation for the achievements of U.S. foreign policy would automatically garner them votes in the IOC.[18]

The Californians ignored these warnings and gave Stuart a misleading view of Brundage. Some of the honors Stuart suggested included awarding Brundage the Presidential Medal of Freedom, holding a dinner or luncheon in his honor, staging the premiere of the film on the 1968 Mexico City Olympics at the White House, or just having Nixon meet with him in the Oval Office. "None of the above proposals were acceptable," Stuart noted afterwards. He urged Haldeman to have the President contact Brundage before the IOC vote and inform him that he would be receiving the Medal of Freedom later in the year. There is, however, no indication in White House files that Haldeman ever took the matter up with Nixon. Nor are there any documents in the files Brundage kept on the Los Angeles bid or in his head of state correspondence files that suggest Nixon or anyone else from the White House contacted him.[19]

The effort to influence individual IOC members was the best move the White House staff could have made, and though the effort was wasted on Brundage, there were others who were less principled. Stuart began using subtle bribes to acquire IOC votes. These efforts were tepid compared to the corruption scandals that would rock the Olympic movement in later decades. According to Kilroy, the IOC members from Latin American were the keys to the pending vote. General Jose Clark Flores of Mexico wanted to become president of the IOC and was attempting to deliver votes for Moscow. In return, he expected support from the Communist Eastern Europe members in his personal campaign. "Although General Clark has called for solidarity in the Latin American bloc, we do not believe he controls this vote," Kilroy observed. He suggested that de Leon, Eduardo Dibos of Peru, and Jose Beracasa of Venezuela had as much prestige and influence as Clark. "Mr. De Leon should be given significant support as he appears to be well accepted and friendly with all the Latin American members."[20]

Stuart did as suggested and bought the votes of both men. The U.S. government provided a grant to a Panamanian sports official to take a course at an American school on the topic of athletic stadium management. Another grant went to a Peruvian track coach in order to help him prepare for the Pan American Games. The exact details of these transactions remain unclear. In both cases, however, Stuart reported to Haldeman that de Leon and Dibos initiated the contact and solicited the funds.[21]

White House efforts ended on May 12, when the Committee met in Amsterdam, Holland. Los Angeles was never a strong contender. After the first round of balloting, Moscow led with 28 votes, Montreal had 25, and Los Angeles, 17. According to IOC procedures, the last-place contender dropped from consideration in the next round. After the second ballot, Montreal won over Moscow, 41–28 with one abstention. The Olympians cast their ballots secretly, but one thing is clear from the final result; Moscow failed to gain any support in the second round.[22]

A number of factors contributed to the outcome. The White House became involved in the process at an extremely late date. Stuart noted as much only two weeks after his appointment: "It is unfortunate that we were not asked to aid Los Angeles earlier for the game is now pretty much played out." A number of commentators remarked that the U.S.-Soviet political confrontation that brought the Nixon administration into the effort eventually worked to Montreal's advantage. The IOC wanted to avoid the political issues associated with having to choose between Moscow and Los Angeles. There was also concern about the reception awaiting tourists in the Russian capital that went beyond its hotel housing capacity. Many individuals wondered if a police state would really welcome, or even be prepared for, the massive influx of foreign tourists that come with an Olympiad. Sports columnist Arthur Daley of *The New York Times* noted, "Moscow is dull. The I.O.C. prefers 'fun cities' for its games. Montreal qualifies." In a State Department report, the U.S. Consul General in Amsterdam observed that a desire to avoid making a decision in favor of the United States or the Soviet Union was clearly a factor, but other considerations were far more important. Montreal had an established history with the IOC, having barely lost the bidding process for the 1972 Games to Munich, Germany, and Canada had never hosted any Olympiad.[23]

There is a good deal of truth to these observations, but the records of the IOC and testimony of individuals present show that other dynamics had more influence. The first factor is that the Olympic movement was quite weak in the late 1960s and 1970s. The IOC was operating on money borrowed against revenue it expected from television rights to the 1972 Summer Olympics. The Games had become excessively large and costly as more and more sports joined. The inclusion of additional competitions brought with them numerous officials and athletes and required facilities upon facilities. It is little surprise then that fewer and fewer cities were willing or even able to bear the honor of hosting the Summer Games. In the 1970s, the IOC met three times to decide which municipalities would host the Olympics of 1976, 1980, and 1984. Only three cities during the entire decade made formal bids at these meetings to host the Summer Games: Montreal, Moscow, and Los Angeles. As a result, each one hosted an Olympic festival.[24]

A second dynamic at work stemmed from the exceptional incompetence of the Americans in making their presentation in Amsterdam. Kilroy stumbled and fell down, knocking over a table as he began his talk. The members of the IOC asked the Los Angeles group the most questions. Many of the issues put to the Californians seem fundamental in nature, suggesting that IOC members had serious reservations about the competence of the Americans. The delegation from Moscow was asked a series of substantive questions; Montreal only one. Lord Killanin observed of the American effort: "Los Angeles made a flamboyant bid which did not impress the IOC." The Americans were passing out baseball caps, which members of the IOC noted was not an Olympic sport. The Los Angeles group also had young women in short skimpy clothing operating an orange juice dispenser for IOC members. In 1970, the International

Olympic Committee was an all-male organization, but such crude sexuality struck these refined gentlemen as inappropriate.[25]

Montreal had other advantages over Los Angeles. The Canadians from Quebec made their presentation in both English and French, the two official languages of the Olympic movement. Count Jean de Beaumont, the IOC member who headed the Finance Commission, asked if Montreal would make a financial performance guarantee to the committee to make sure the city did indeed meet its obligations to host the Games. Beaumont had asked the same question of the Americans and they gave a qualified "yes," but Montreal Mayor Jean Drapeau declared that the promise of the city was more valuable than any cash deposit. The members of the committee applauded. That response was a good indication of sentiment on the committee.[26]

Although disappointed, the Americans accepted the decision with grace. Los Angeles Mayor Sam Yorty publicly expressed relief that the Games were staying in the "free world." On another level, with the Games taking place on the same continent, Americans would have little problem traveling to the Games, and U.S. television networks would be spared the difficulties of working across more than one or two time zones.[27]

The Amsterdam meeting of the IOC was not an entirely negative experience for the United States. The committee awarded the Winter Games to Denver on the third ballot. In an ironic way, the defeat of Los Angeles was a victory for Denver. The unexpected success of Montreal undercut the campaign of Vancouver. The IOC was less than enthusiastic about the possibility of awarding both the Summer and Winter Games to the same nation and eliminated the Canadian city in the first round of voting, even though many thought Vancouver had the best technical bid.[28]

Despite the initial euphoria that followed the IOC decision, the Denver Olympics soon became entangled in Colorado state politics, and the city ultimately relinquished the honor of holding the Winter Olympics. The decision of Denver and Colorado voters to bar state money from being used to host the Olympics had ramifications that reached into 1974.

The Coloradoans set in motion forces that almost guaranteed that Moscow would receive the next Summer Olympics. The administration had learned that influencing global sport was difficult, very difficult. In 1974, two American cities – Los Angeles and Lake Placid, New York – were once again competing to bring the Summer and Winter Games to the United States. This time around, the administration made little effort to support either of these initiatives. Lake Placid, however, had done a careful job of preparing and needed little help. A small community of 10,000 people, the town had hosted the 1932 Winter Games and was thorough in securing the support of the public in a referendum, and financial underwriting from the state, before it started lobbying the IOC. The Lake Placid bid committee asked Nixon for an endorsement of their effort, and after the administration checked to make sure that the group had solid support, the President agreed. He sent a short, formal letter to Lord Killanin. Olympic supporters in California had taken no such efforts, and there is no record in White House records of any support for the renewed Los Angeles effort.[29]

As the members of the IOC assembled in Vienna, they were no more eager than they had been in 1970 to award the Summer Games to Moscow. The problem the Committee faced was that Lake Placid was the only municipality that had put in a bid to host the Winter Olympics. The Committee had little choice in awarding the Games to Lake Placid, but this decision was acceptable to most. The little New York community already had most of the facilities it required to host the Olympics.[30]

The lack of municipalities willing to host the Winter Games, however, put the IOC in a difficult position when it came to picking a host for the Summer festival. It faced the disagreeable choice of awarding both editions to the same country and taking a clear side in the Cold War, or giving the Summer Games to Moscow. The minutes make it abundantly clear that the vote was essentially an up or down decision on the Russian city. The delegation from Los Angeles made its presentation, showed a film, and then was asked a few simple questions. The exchange bordered on the perfunctory. The Los Angeles group not only faced the liability of Lake Placid, but also the fact that the Summer Games of 1976 would be held in North America and that the IOC preferred to rotate the Games to different continents. The Soviets then made their presentation on behalf of Moscow. After showing a film, the members of the IOC and the representatives of the international athletic federations that were normally present at these meetings showered the Russians with one query after another. Some questions, like the ability of visitors to convert their currency into rubles and what type of freedom reporters would have in the city, reflected the concerns members had about awarding the Games to a police state known for its inhospitality toward foreigners. Representatives from several of the international athletic federations then spoke about the resources in Moscow. The city had hosted a number of athletic matches and world championships before, and most of the individuals in the room that had participated in these gatherings had positive things to say about their experiences and the resources they had used. Several serious and legitimate reservations did pepper this conversation. Sergei Pavlov, chairman of the Moscow preparatory committee, responded, saying the city had plans to build new stadiums and pools if the IOC gave the Games to the Soviet Union. Remarks of this nature went on and on.[31]

The Committee recessed for the day before making its decision. There was no actual ballot on Lake Placid. With only one candidate city, the IOC was more than content to make the decision through acclamation. Moscow versus Los Angeles was a different matter altogether. Killanin noted that at that moment in 1974, politics and sport administration seemed to converge. "No doubt people thought in casting their vote for Moscow they were supporting the mood of détente. That apart, on the question of sporting infrastructure and organisation, there was only one candidate." Well aware that there was a political context to the contest between Los Angeles and Moscow, the IOC, at its president's suggestion, took the unusual position of deciding that there should be no public announcement of the vote tally. In previous meetings, the IOC had announced the number of votes that had gone to each city in each round, but this time the Committee decided to simply announce the winners as a unanimous decision. Lord Killanin, the Marques of Exeter, and Prince Franz Josef II of Liechtenstein counted the ballots and then informed the rest of the committee of the outcome. "In truth, the vote in favour of Moscow was almost unanimous," the Irish baron observed later.[32]

Lord Killanin was no idiot. He knew that taking the Olympics behind the Iron Curtain was a move fraught with risk. "So much depends upon what the relationships are between the major powers," he remarked after Montreal. The commercial threat is something that can be contained to a certain extent because it is purely about people making money. The political one is much harder because it is like a religion – it becomes so emotional that people won't cede anything one way or another." He was worried about the direction of international affairs in the late 1970s and its impact on the Olympics as well. "There is no doubt at all that Moscow is anxious to run the Games extremely well and there is no doubt afterwards that the United States will want to show that they can do them better. And that is where we have this terrifying competition between Oranising Committees instead of between athletes. We are powerless. We say there must be X number of sports over 17 days and accommodation for athletes, officials and media, but we don't say you must build a 100,000 seat stadium."[33]

There were plenty of warning signs that people were unhappy with the decision to give the Games to the Soviet Union. In a 1976 editorial that appeared in *The New York Times*, Bill Bradley, a member of the 1964 U.S. Olympic Basketball team that won a gold medal, predicted there would be a boycott of Moscow because of Soviet political manipulation: "I believe the United States should discontinue its participation in the Games unless the promotion of mutual understanding among nations becomes a more central focus of the quadrennial festival." In 1976, Bradley was a member of the New York Knicks, but in 1980, he would be a U.S. Senator from New Jersey and one of Carter's strongest supporters. In 1977, two members of the U.S. House of Representatives, Dan Quayle and Jack Kemp, introduced a resolution calling for a boycott of the Moscow Olympics. In 1978, *U.S. News and World Report* magazine interviewed another two U.S. Congressmen about boycotting the Moscow Games because of Soviet treatment of dissidents and anti-Semitic policies in a point-counterpoint format. Robert F. Drinan of Massachusetts argued that the Olympics should return to Montreal. He also dismissed the contention that politics and sport should be separate. "I think that's mythology. The people who raise that don't want any change at all. It's bogus argument – a nonargument – by people who don't want any fuss about moral issues." The Soviets had failed to honor the Helsinki Accords and were unlikely to admit Israel, and should be, as a result, denied the Olympic stage. Leo J. Ryan of California, on the other hand, believed manipulating the Olympics as a political platform was wrong. "Our own youngsters are our own best ambassadors and advertisement."[34]

Similar sentiment was churning in the United Kingdom. A number of anti-Soviet groups were demanding that the British Olympic Association send no team to Moscow in 1980. As a result of this pressure, the organization passed a resolution in September of 1978 that declared:

> Throughout the history of the Olympic Games and in according with the established principles of the Olympic Movement emphasis has always been placed on the participation of the individual competitor in the Games.

> The British Olympic Association therefore is of the opinion that subject to the laws of the each participating nation, and in accordance with the regulation of the International Federation concerned, any competitor, if selected, should not be denied the privilege of participating in the Olympic Games.[35]

Despite this free-floating hostility, Moscow had great financial potential for the IOC. Lord Killanin and the Count de Beaumont used the Winter and Summer Games of 1980 to change the way the Olympic movement negotiated television contracts. Prior to this time, the organizing committees of each host city negotiated the television contracts. When both Montreal and Innsbruck signed contracts that ran counter to the financial interests of the IOC, Killanin become more involved in the negotiation process. The Committee adopted new rules that would make television contracts a joint responsibility. These changes established the foundation that Killanin's successor, Juan Antonio Samaranch, used to produce the massive financial windfalls of the 1980s. Samaranch took the policy a step further and had the IOC take sole responsibility for these negotiations.[36]

There was, though, a serious political edge even to this advantage. Television would bring great profits to the International Olympic Committee, but it would also increase the visibility of this venue, creating a huge propaganda platform that the Soviets could use to their advantage. In the words of the *National Review*, an American magazine of political commentary, the Moscow Olympics were going to be "a sinister and deadly-serious political operation disguised as sport." There actually was nothing particularly odd about this publicity focus. Other host cities and nations before and after had and would do the same. The Soviet Union, though, was a highly ideological entity, and there were many who might also use the forum the Olympics provided to make legitimate criticisms of Soviet society, which television could easily communicate to the rest of the world.[37]

Despite these important developments, the international Olympic movement reached it lowest point a few months later. In 1978, Los Angeles was the only applicant for the Olympiad of 1984. There had been efforts in Tehran to bring the Olympics to Iran. Reflecting the politics inherent in the Olympics, the Shah informed Lord Killanin that if Tehran were awarded the Summer Games, there would be no marathon since it glorified a Persian defeat. That problem disappeared when Tehran dropped out of the bid process in 1977 as revolution engulfed Iran. Canada was still an option. Montreal let the IOC know that it would be willing to host the Games again if the committee was unwilling to award the Olympics to the United States. The Californians had been weak in their previous efforts, but they were not so incompetent as to lose an uncontested election. There was a problem, though. Public opinion polls showed that 70 percent of Los Angeles supported the idea of hosting the Olympics, but those same surveys showed that a clear majority was opposed to using public funds. Organizers in Los Angeles believed the Games could still be successful using private funds. A series of negotiations followed in which the IOC agreed to surrender its claim to all profits from the Games and ended its insistence that the city of Los Angeles assume financial responsibility for any losses. City voters then passed a cost control measure that prohibited the use of public funds. The ironic element in these negotiations is that it would be the success of these Games and the new commercial methodology that the Californians pioneered that would bring vast money to the IOC and strengthen the international Olympic movement, making it less vulnerable to political pressure.[38]

These developments, though, lay in the future. For the time being, Americans were quite happy. Los Angeles had won its contest with the IOC and on October 20, 1978, in a formal ceremony at the White House, Lord Killanin and Mayor Tom Bradley signed the formal contract giving the Games to the city. In a harbinger of what was to come, President Jimmy Carter did not attend the function, even though he was in the building at the time.[39]

CHAPTER 3

Jimmy Carter and U.S.-Soviet Relations

IT IS AN IRONY OF FATE THAT THE OLYMPIC BOYCOTT PITTED TWO principled men against each other. Like Lord Killanin, Jimmy Carter had taken a strong, moral stand against the shortcomings of his society and in the end profited from his convictions. The two men came from backgrounds that, while not diametrically opposite, were still significantly different.

Carter grew up on a farm in Georgia. "My most persistent impression as a farm boy was of the earth," he recalled many years later. "There was a closeness, almost an immersion, in the sand, loam, and red clay that seemed natural, and constant." Neighbors in the countryside were few and far between, and Carter described his life as "isolated but not lonely." Much like Killanin's Ireland, Carter's Georgia still harbored grievances about history and particularly toward the nation's capital. In the case of Georgia, the festering wound was the defeat in the U.S. Civil War. "Although I was born more than half a century after the war was over, it was a living reality in my life," Carter recalled. "I grew up in one of the families whose people could not forget that we had been conquered."[1]

One thing Carter and Killanin had in common was that they both excelled in the classroom. After he finished high school in Plains, Georgia, Carter wanted to attend the U.S. Naval Academy. The problem was getting a Congressional appointment. After his first attempt failed, Carter's Congressman, Steven Pace, suggested that he enroll in a junior college and try again in a year. As a result, Carter started school in September 1941 at Georgia Southwestern College and took courses designed to prepare him for Annapolis. When his second effort to win admission to the Academy failed, Carter and his father had a bit of a confrontational meeting with Pace. In the words of Carter, the Congressman said, "'I'll give Jimmy an appointment next year, and he won't have to take the full entrance examination if he can make good grades in college.' I had my doubts, but Daddy trusted Mr. Steve's firm promise." Instead of staying at Georgia Southwestern, Carter moved to

Atlanta and attended the Georgia Institute of Technology, believing it would better prepare him for the Academy. It apparently did. True to his word, Pace gave Carter a Congressional appointment, and he started at Annapolis in 1943 with the rest of the Class of 1947.[2]

Midshipmen James E. Carter, Jr. did well while at the Academy. He was well liked by his classmates. In one particularly trying incident, Carter got permission to have Albert Rusher become his roommate after Rusher's previous roommate committed suicide. The move actually required a good deal of bureaucratic approval. Although no class leader or academic star, Carter did work that was well above average. He lettered as a cross-country runner and graduated in the top ten percent of his class. He tried and failed to win a Rhodes Scholarship, but what is significant about this episode is not that he was rejected, but that he was competitive for this academic honor.[3]

Carter had a good start to his naval career. After some initially poor assignments on aging surface ships, he joined the submarine force. He enjoyed the close sense of teamwork that service on a "pig boat" produced. "The crew and the officers lived in intimate contact with one another, depending upon the quality of each man and his knowledge of the ship to provide safety and effectiveness for us all," he explained. Service on ships often produced a "work hard, play harder" attitude to compensate for the long and dangerous tours at sea. Although Carter was washed overboard and nearly died while serving on the U.S.S. *Pomfret*, he never apparently indulged in excess when off duty. "As hard as it is to believe about anyone in the navy," the executive officer of one of his ships observed, "there are no sea stories about Jimmy Carter."[4]

After his initial service, the young naval officer met Vice Admiral Hyman Rickover. The son of Austrian Jewish immigrants, Rickover had managed to entrench himself in the submarine nuclear propulsion program to such a degree that Congress and the executive branch allowed him to turn it into his personal kingdom, which he maintained long after he had passed the mandatory retirement age. Getting an assignment to Rickover's command was extremely difficult. It was a competitive process, and the Admiral interviewed finalists himself, usually using demeaning questions and tricks to see how individuals reacted to stress. Rickover insisted that progress required an increase in work quantity and quality, and this approach was what the service required during times of great change. Carter passed the test, and Rickover came to have a profound influence on him equal only to that of his parents. (Sadly, Rickover had no memory of his former protégé and had to consult his files when Carter became a serious presidential candidate.) As an Academy graduate and a member of the submarine nuclear propulsion program, Carter seemed to have a good, solid naval career with a number of promotions in front of him. He likely would have reached the rank of either Commander or Captain and had the command of a ship.[5]

Life had other plans for Jimmy Carter. His father died, and he resigned his commission and returned home to Plains to take over the family business. Given the tight housing market in the town, Carter, his wife Rosalynn, and their children had to move into public housing until they could find a home of their own. Carter had inherited the peanut warehouse that his father had owned. He quickly came to enjoy impressive success, with rapidly growing profits. Within two years, he was making double his navy salary. He moved his family into a rental property and eventually built a large ranch-style house on a lot that was more than two acres in size. As Carter became more and more successful as a businessman, he turned to civic activities. He joined the Lions Club and two professional organizations, the Certified Seed Organization and the Georgia Crop Improvement Association. He later became president of both. He became a member of the school board and, after five years, its chairman. What is most significant about this period, however, was the organization that he would not join. Despite pressure from friends and neighbors, he refused to become a member of the White Citizens Council of Plains. The Ku Klux Klan and the White Citizen Councils basically fought the civil rights movement. The difference was that the Councils had a membership of respectable middle-class social leaders, while Klan members were more likely to be from the working class and were more willing to use violence to get their way. Carter suffered for this decision: "We lost quite a few customers for several months, but eventually most of them came back."[6]

In 1962, Carter decided to enter electoral politics with a run for the state Senate. Few people noticed the start of his political career. "My own announcement was buried even in our local newspaper, the *Americus Times-Recorder*," he reflected wryly. The paper, though, eventually endorsed him. As Carter admits in his memoirs, the main issue in the campaign was not one of policy, but rather the mood and sentiment of the state. The primary election was a close one, but after the final count, Carter had lost to the incumbent, Homer Moore, 3,063 to 2,924. The problem was that Joe Hurst, the political "boss" of Quitman County, had stuffed one of the ballot boxes. Showing a good deal of tenacity, Carter initiated a legal challenge to this outcome. In a decision that came the day before the general election, Judge Tom Marshall, ruled that both candidates should be write-in candidates in the general election. "My main consideration was to let the voters make the decision about who should be their state senator," Marshall explained after he retired from the bench. This solution was fraught with practical difficulties; some ballots had only Moore's name, and the two candidates had little time to alert their supporters. In a suspect final, Carter won, 3,013 to 2,182. Moore, for his part, talked about challenging the result, but his heart apparently was not in the fight. Moore, as Carter admitted, had not been party to any fraud, and he decided that linking his name closer to Hurst's was not in his best interests, so he conceded. "Some of my folks in Stewart County are still asking me not to give up," he told Carter at a conference of agricultural warehouse opera-tors, "but I think I'll be better off staying at home and getting some of your best customers while you're up in Atlanta." Still, he kept changing his mind, and talked about challenging the result in the Senate itself. In his memoirs, Carter states that he remained uncertain about the outcome of his race until the moment he went to the dais of the Senate and took the oath of office.[7]

As a Senator, Carter was an earnest, diligent legislator. He did, though, show early signs of a "technocratic" approach to governance that he would use later in the White House. In fairness, though, it should be pointed out that in state legislature, this approach is far more appropriate than it is as a chief executive. Carter had promised to read every bill and did so, but quickly learned that the mass of legislation made this simple task quite demanding. Some bills were hundreds of pages long. He regularly stayed in Atlanta for the entire work week instead of taking three-day weekends like his colleagues and voted on the "special interest" bills that appeared on the floor only on Fridays. When there was no legislation, he would visit state agencies and talk to their heads about matters involving pending legislation. He was well liked and well respected in the Senate. "It was obvious from his utterances that he did his homework," one of his colleagues remarked.[8]

This attention to detail made him no friend of the journalists covering the legislature. "You just dreaded to see Carter coming down the hallway in the legislative session," one reporter recalled. "You never could talk substantive issues for him wanting to point out little picayune comma faults in stories." Another reporter recalled that "Carter also forced me to start using a tape recorder" since he repeatedly said he was misquoted.[9]

His moral convictions shaped many of his actions in the State. "I try to uti-lize my religious beliefs as a constant guide in making decisions as a private or public citizen," he explained. Although religious, he supported changing the language of the Georgia state constitution to reflect the language of the First Amendment. He also opposed – in extremely mild form – some of the most obvious mechanisms local officials used to disenfranchise black vot-ers. Since this topic was so emotionally charged, given its association with the civil rights movement, he chose to avoid the issue when making public appearences. Noteworthy about his stand on this issue was not that he found practical limits to his morality, but that his values made him take stands that, for the time and place, were less than easy to make.[10]

After two terms in the Senate, ambition got the better of Carter. On March 3, 1966, he announced he was running for an open seat in the U.S. House of Representatives. With the incumbent giving up the position to run for gover-nor, Carter seemed almost certain to win. Then, on June 12, he surprised many political observers when he declared that he would run for governor instead. While Carter seemed certain to win a seat in Congress, he had no chance to get elected Governor. In 1966, there were five candidates running for the

Democratic nomination, and the mood in the state was far more conservative than it had been in 1962. Carter finished third, failing even to make it to
the runoff race. Lester Maddox, an Atlanta restaurateur who gained national
fame when he used a pick axe handle to keep black patrons from integrating
his establishment, ended up winning the nomination, but finished second in
a three-way contest in the general election. According to the state constitution, the Georgia House of Representatives selected the new governor. Since
the House was controlled by the Democrats, they made Maddox the new chief
executive. For Carter, the campaign was a disaster. He had lost, spent most of
his savings, had four friends carrying a significant bank loan, and had split
the liberal bloc in the Democratic Party, guaranteeing a Maddox victory.[11]

Carter was tenacious and decided to run for governor again in 1970. He had
learned from his experiences and was far more organized than he had been
in 1966. He and Rosalynn had been collecting the names of every person with
whom he had any type of association; his staff organized this information in
a master file by zip code, which included their occupation and political philosophy – a time-consuming project in the era before the widespread use of
personal computers. Familiarizing himself with voting patterns in the state,
Carter also studied electoral returns in every race in every Georgia county
since 1952. He also had a public opinion surveying firm conduct polls to help
him determine which issues he should stress on the campaign trail.

One thing the candidate refused to do was describe his political philosophy.
When a reporter asked him if he was a liberal, conservative, or moderate, he
avoided answering the question. "I believe I'm more complicated than that."
His refusal to describe himself or even take consistent stands on a variety of
issues, made it possible for him to draw votes from poor minorities, but also
from racial segregationists that might have supported Alabama Governor
George Wallace. He could see "no trouble in pitching for Wallace votes and
the black votes at the same time."[12]

Without stating his political philosophy, Carter chose to run on character and values instead. This emphasis basically required that he denigrate his
opponent in addition to stressing his own merits. Personal attacks against his
political opponents were a regular feature of every Carter campaign.[13]

Jimmy Carter was no racist, but he was more than willing to use the hate
of others to his advantage. He regularly made campaign appearances before
African American audiences, but at the same time courted the support of
admitted segregationists. He also accused his opponent, former Governor Carl
Sanders, of being a supporter of former Vice-President Hubert H. Humphrey
and of plotting to run for Senator Richard Russell's seat in 1972. The names
Humphrey and Russell were politically loaded terms in the South of that day.
Humphrey had been a vocal supporter of civil rights legislation since the late
1940s and was one of the most liberal members of the U.S. Senate on the issue
of race. Russell, on the other hand, had been the leader of southern resistance

in the Senate to any meaningful civil rights legislation. Carter was attempting to make a point about racial politics when he applied the label of "Humphrey man" to Sanders. In another move that was as clever as it was misleading, Hamilton Jordan, Carter's campaign manager, established two Carter committees in several counties. "One headed by people who supported Maddox or Wallace and one headed by a less conservative element." This move led many to believe Carter was far less liberal than was actually the case.[14]

Whatever moral and ethical judgments one might wish to make about the tactics Carter used, they were effective. He and Sanders were the two top candidates in the Democratic primary, and in the runoff race, Carter won 60 percent of the votes. In the general election, Carter defeated the token candidate the Republicans put up with a similar margin of victory. James Earl Carter, Jr. was the hundredth chief executive of Georgia.[15]

Although a man with a strong sense of moral center, Carter was more than willing to use a certain amount of deception when necessary. In fact, many Georgia politicians thought that he went too far in this area. During his inaugural address, the new Governor announced a new plan to reorganize the government of the state. He had, however, never discussed this issue during the campaign. The old Governor, Lester Maddox, who became Lieutenant Governor in 1970, remarked, "When I put my pennies into a peanut machine, I don't expect to get bubble gum, and neither do the people." Maddox had a point, and Carter's duplicity caused his popularity to drop dramatically. It would have been difficult for him to get reelected or win any other state-wide race in Georgia. Despite his lack of popularity, Carter accomplished a good deal while in office. He supported the passage of "sunshine laws" designed to make state agencies more accountable to the public. He regularly held public forums around the state and moved the governor's office to smaller towns in the state for a day. He used the Judicial Nominating Commission and appointed all of his nominees from the lists the board prepared, even if some of his nominees were political opponents. His support for reforms of the salary structure and the judicial retirement system improved the reputation of the courts in the state.[16]

Many of these actions went over poorly with other politicians. His associates used words like "sincere" and "honest" to describe him. Sometimes these comments were not intended as compliments. "His practice of attempting to do things that he felt were right regardless of the political implications sometimes didn't sit too well," one state official observed. Representative Grace Hamilton remarked that "he thinks he's still commander of a submarine." An editorial in *The Atlanta Constitution* made an important, practical point: "Virtue is on the governor's side, but how many votes has virtue?"[17]

Despite these legitimate questions and reservations about Carter, his campaign for President began in 1972. Hamilton Jordan put together a fifty-page memo on campaign strategy for 1976 that he gave to Carter the day before the presidential election between Richard Nixon and George McGovern. His team of political subordinates – many of whom would follow Carter into the White House – had worked together for a long time and knew each other well. There were no confrontations over job responsibilities or ego. Reflecting Carter's character and technocratic focus, the two themes the campaign would articulate would be morality and competence. This approach worked, but just barely. Public opinion polls showed that a heavy majority of the electorate thought him "a man of high moral character." The problem he faced, though, was that even among most of his supporters in the party, he was not their first choice. Polls of Democratic voters showed that former Vice-President Hubert Humphrey was still their preferred candidate. Carter earned real support among liberals for defeating the presidential aspirations of segregationist Alabama Governor George Wallace in the Florida and North Carolina primaries. These were real triumphs, but many of his victories were close, with small margins over his opponents, and often only those of pluralities. After Humphrey had made it clear that his battle with cancer prohibited any run, Governor Edmund "Jerry" Brown of California declared his candidacy late in the primary season, energizing the party faithful. Brown scored several significant victories over Carter. His candidacy, though, was too little, too late. Bloodied, Carter stumbled into the nomination. It was Carter's good fortune that the Republican nominee, President Gerald R. Ford, had a number of liabilities that made him extremely vulnerable. Ford had never been elected President or Vice-President. Richard Nixon had appointed him to the second position. He had no national following in the Republican Party and barely defeated a primary challenge from former California Governor Ronald Reagan. Ford's pardon of Nixon still bothered many Americans, and it seemed to be part of a corrupt bargain between the Republican presidents. The outcome of the presidential election was close. Carter won, with 49.9 percent of the vote to Ford's 47.9. The remaining ballots went to minor party candidates. In the Electoral College, Carter had 297 votes to Ford's 241. Carter's victory was the closet in a Presidential election since Woodrow Wilson's victory over Charles Evans Hughes in 1916.[18]

Carter attributed the outcome of the election to his performance in the televised debates with Fold. "If it hadn't been for the debates, I would have lost. They established me as competent on foreign and domestic affairs and gave the viewers reason to think that Jimmy Carter had something to offer."[19]

Once in the White House, Carter wanted to pursue two different goals in world affairs. He intended to move the focus of American diplomacy away from the Soviet Union. In his opinion, the relationship the United States had with Soviets had dominated foreign policy for too long. He essentially wanted to continue the policy of détente that he had inherited from the Nixon and Ford administrations. According to Secretary of State Cyrus Vance, "We both believed in the necessity of continuing détente, but we agreed that it must be reciprocal – the Soviets must understand that political, economic, and trade cooperation with us entailed obligations that they act with restraint."[20]

Carter ultimately hoped that this policy would bring about an end to the confrontation between the Soviets and Americans that people called the Cold War. "It is a new world," he told students at the University of Notre Dame shortly after his inauguration, "that calls for a new American foreign policy – a policy based on constant decency in its values and on optimism in our historical values."[21]

Lord Killanin, for one, was unimpressed. He explained, "I am watching Moscow very, very closely. But so much can depend on the relationships of the major powers at the time. The first Carter impact has been of going away from détente. That can create the atmosphere in which the Games have to take place."[22]

Killanin's assessment had merit. Relations between the Soviet Union and the United States started to decline in the late 1970s, despite the wishes of the leadership in both countries. Part of the reason for this turn of events was the other foreign policy objective that Carter pursued. He wanted U.S. foreign policy to emphasize the respect of human rights. He intended to put U.S. allies under more scrutiny on this matter, but also do the same with the Soviet Union. "Sounding like a zealous TV commercial, he seemed to think it was his duty to raise the matter of human rights every time he met a Soviet representative," Soviet Foreign Minister Andrei Gromyko recalled. "I endured it myself." This well-intentioned goal sat poorly with the Russians in the Kremlin and made them less likely to work with the United States in a constructive, nonconfrontational manner. "The successive administrations of Nixon, Ford, and especially Carter did not pursue a consistent course of détente," Soviet Ambassador to the United States Anatoly Dobrynin explained. "Their very concept of detente was contradictory and ambiguous. The policy of linking detente to Soviet internal developments marked a sharp departure from the Nixon and Ford administrations. The Soviet leadership considered it an attempt to weaken if not change its regime."[23]

Soviet leaders were also offended. Human rights, to them at least, seemed to be improving. By Soviet standards, they were right. There were fewer people in prison, and the Politburo was willing to listen to friendly critics, but the Americans wanted to focus on "enemies of the regime." Yuri Andropov, chairman of the Committee for State Security, better known by its Russian acronym, KGB, told his subordinates to resolve individual cases the Americans raised. The Soviets had even given President Ford a list of Jews applying for emigration out of the Soviet Union. Most of these requests had been met. When Vance traveled to Moscow and proposed significantly deeper cuts in land-based missile systems than the Nixon and Ford Administrations had negotiated with the Soviets, Brezhnev was quite angry. He thought he had a deal with the United States, but then that anger turned to "disgust" when Vance began talking about human rights. "Suddenly, right there in Moscow – in Brezhnev's office – to talk about human rights!" the Soviet leader's interpreter commented. "To talk about Soviet violations of somebody's human rights! Unheard of! It was a personal affront. It was taken very, very, very personally by Brezhnev and Gromyko. On the human plane, that's how it was."[24]

This response was predictable. "From my European view of the situation, Carter's first response to Soviet policies in 1977 contained serious flaws," West German Chancellor Helmut Schmidt recalled. "The accusation he publicly leveled over and over, that Soviet citizens were deprived of all human rights, could not, of course, alter their lives in any way, but it would inevitably embitter the Soviet leadership." Schmidt realized that anger would have enormous ramifications elsewhere. "Someone who continually compromised the Soviet leaders by waging a human rights campaign could hardly hope to persuade them to go beyond the old agreements for arms limitation to actual disarmament."[25]

The Soviet Union was equally responsible for the unraveling of détente. This period was basically one of "managed competition." It was a time when the Cold War was "less dangerous" but still ongoing. While Americans considered it a time when they made economic concession in return for good Soviet behavior and negotiated from a position of equality with Moscow, officials in the Kremlin considered it a reward for its military buildup and the proper correlation of political forces. Leonied Brezhnev, General Secretary of the Communist Party of the Soviet Union and Chairman of the Presidium, was personally invested in détente as a way to ensure peace. Many apparatchiks, Communist ideologues, and Russian nationalists resisted détente, though. They believed the Soviet Union was making too many concessions to the United States and other western powers. The internal politics of the Soviet Union were none of the business of any other nation-state. Brezhnev pushed détente personally, but his health was declining. He had developed brain atherosclerosis that would physically exhaust him after prolonged periods of stress or strain. He took opiate-based sedatives to help manage the disease, but often overdosed and ended up comatose or in a groggy, sluggish state. These health issues affected his scheduling and his ability to focus on details. He also became more suspicious. At the same time, Andropov of the KGB, was alert to public opinion. He wanted to leave the position with his reputation intact, which made him reluctant to use his police powers against dissidents and political opponents. The result was that those that opposed détente had little to worry about if they worked against this policy.[26]

Carter, for his part, wanted to find new methods of conducting U.S. foreign policy. As a result, he was receptive toward what is now called "public diplomacy." Although it might easily be dismissed as "propaganda," public diplomacy involves many venues. The Carter administration showed a real interest in international exchanges. The exchanges were to enrich both countries, reflecting an inclination in this administration toward collective action that rejected unilateralism. *The Washington Post* noted that the new administration had "a new and stronger emphasis on the role of information – some may call it propaganda – in the implementation of American foreign policy." Carter also oversaw reforms of bureaucratic reform of the various information agencies in the U.S. government that created the International Communications Agency, which allowed the Voice of America to operate more effectively and to reach a wider audience inside the Soviet Union so as to challenge the claim that Communism represented the wave of the future. When he saw a report on this matter, the President wrote a one-word comment on the document: "good." The new administration was getting results.[27]

Despite this success, a problem that reflected the nebulous foreign policy objectives of the administration – the rivalry between Carter's two main foreign policy advisors, Vance and National Security Advisor Zbigniew Brzezinski – was growing and affecting more and more venues of U.S. foreign policy. The two men came from very different backgrounds. Vance was Yale. Brzezinski was Harvard. Vance was a corporate lawyer and part of the establishment. His cousin had been the Democratic nominee for president in 1924. Vance had held a number of positions in the Department of Defense during the presidencies of John F. Kennedy and Lyndon Johnson. Brzezinski was an academic and a naturalized U.S. citizen. The son of a refugee Polish diplomat, he gained a good deal of influence writing well-read academic pieces from his position at Columbia University. "Ultimately," according to Brzezinski, "the deepest differences between Vance and me were philosophical. Our differing backgrounds had produced substantially different conceptions of how the world works and consequently a different estimate of the proper balance between power and principle in our age."[28]

Both had different assessment of Soviet intentions. Vance believed confrontations might develop over ignorance of local conditions and blundering. He tended to see crises in international affairs as the product of regional factors that had little to do with either superpower. The Secretary of State wanted to pursue principled foreign policies and thought that diplomatic talks and negotiations with the Soviet Union could be productive. Brzezinski disagreed. He believed the Soviets were trying to use détente to spread their Communist ideology. He saw global patterns at work in international crises that often involved the Soviet Union. As a result, the National Security Advisor wanted to pursue a more stringent, hardline policy against the Soviets that put them on the defensive, with an emphasis on human rights. To put these differences in simpler terms, Vance was a "dove," and Brzezinski a "hawk."[29]

Carter was unwilling or unable to decide between the different approaches that these two advocated. To his credit, he wanted debate among his advisors. "He was, if anything, willing to permit debate to go on too long and to try to absorb every detail and nuance before making his decisions," Vance recalled. The problem was quite obvious to outsiders. "From my own experience," Gromyko reflected, "I would say Carter had a certain amount of goodwill, but this quality only showed itself when questions of war and peace were not being discussed. He could raise his glass in ten toasts and do it intelligently. But when the big problems appeared on the agenda he was visibly uncomfortable."[30]

Carter wanted both frank discussion and collegiality. His administration was a team. Vance and Brzezinski managed to keep from making their differences personal – for a while. Brzezinski spends a good deal of his memoirs trying to show that their disputes were nothing more than honest disagreements on matters of policy, noting, "Vance was a gentleman lawyer, patient, cooperative, and clearly a good sport." His account, though, does have a slightly condescending tone. Vance, according to Brzezinski, "preferred to litigate issues endlessly, to shy away from the unavoidable ingredient of force in dealing with contemporary international realities, and to have an excessive faith that all issues can be resolved by compromise." Vance basically ignored discussing Brzezinski at any length in his memoirs, and that silence speaks volumes.[31]

Carter's management style in the White House created an environment that fostered a combative atmosphere in his administration. In the slang of Washington, he was a "technocrat," or "policy wonk." Reflecting his scientific and technical education, he wanted to familiarize himself with – and even master the details of – various policy options. There is a certain intellectual arrogance behind trying to master the details of the wide-ranging issues that any president must face, but the real problem with this approach is that he had a difficult time considering strategy, defining priorities, and making choices between various options. One staff member on the National Security Council admitted that Carter had an impressive ability to absorb data, but also observed, "He had great difficulty, however, connecting, relating, and interpreting these facts. He could not see patterns and trends, and had little sense of history." It was also difficult for Carter to master all the details and nuances of various different matters in front of him, regardless of how hard he tried. In a comment that tells one as much about Gromyko as it does about Carter, the Soviet Foreign Minister recalled, "Being a diligent man, Carter did his best, but when he tried to pronounce the names of towns and regions in the Soviet Union all that came out was a sequence of incomprehensible noises. More worryingly, we quickly discovered that he had difficulty in grasping even the most elementary basic features of the Soviet-US relationship."[32]

American allies noticed these traits as well. Helmut Schmidt, chancellor of the Federal Republic of Germany, had reservations about Carter's foreign policy and leadership skills. "Because he served as an officer on a nuclear submarine he thinks he knows atomic energy," he bitterly confided to French

President Valéry Giscard d'Estaing. "But he has no notion of strategy and that is what counts."[33]

The result was a vacuum at the highest level of U.S. foreign policy. The administration attempted to pursue many contradictory objectives with little rhyme or reason. Brzezinski admitted later that "we attempted to do too much all at once."[34] Another result was that his two main advisors tried to fill this vacuum. The disagreements between Vance and Brzezinski were disputes not over specific issues – though technically they were – but for the very soul of Jimmy Carter's approach to world affairs. It was clear to the Russians which of the two advisors was winning. "During his term of office, Carter himself slid steadily towards confrontation," Gromyko observed.[35]

The most visible example of the conflict within the administration came when the President retuned to his alma matter, the Naval Academy, and delivered a speech on U.S.-Soviet relations. Many observers believed that Carter had simply grafted two different drafts that Vance and Brzezinski had prepared into one speech. Vance actually claims as much in his memoirs. A reporter for *The Washington Post* captured this sentiment with the first sentence in the news story on the address: "President Carter, in effect, made two speeches at Annapolis yesterday." Brzezinski later explained that the President himself was the primary author of the speech and immediately afterward seemed very upbeat. He had little reason for such optimism. "The end result was a stitched-together speech," Vance explained. "Instead of combating the growing perception of an administration rent with internal discussions, the image of an inconsistent and uncertain government was underlined."[36]

The biggest issue in U.S.-Soviet relations in the late 1970s was arms control. Carter wanted to introduce neutron bombs into the North Atlantic Treaty Organization (NATO) arsenal and deploy them in West Germany. Schmidt opposed this effort. He feared that this move would energize the pacifists in his party, creating an enormous amount of political controversy that would weaken him while delivering nothing but modest strategic improvements in return. Carter eventually retreated on this issue, but not before doing enormous damage to his relationship with Schmidt.[37]

Despite this setback, the President remained determined to go further and turn arms limitation talks into arms reduction. He also wanted to discuss a number of other related issues, including a comprehensive nuclear test ban treaty, nuclear nonproliferation, demilitarizing the Indian Ocean, banning the development of antisatellite, chemical, and radiological weapons, and limiting the proliferation of conventional weapons to the minor nations of the Third World.[38]

Although the Soviets arguably needed arms control and détente more than the United States, there was a good deal of ambiguity in their defense policies. The Soviet Union worked to improve the quality of their weapons even while honoring the numbers of the Strategic Arms Limitation Treaty (SALT) that it had signed with the United States. Soviet military doctrine continued to stress offensive ground operations and deployed intermediate-range missiles in their European territory. American critics of détente used these moves to point out the shortcomings of any foreign policy that involved trusting the Soviets to any significant degree. Although Carter continued to authorize arms control talks with the Soviets, he also approved the development of new weapons systems like the "stealth" bomber and the MX missile. He also ordered the deployment of cruise missiles and Pershing II intermediate missiles in nations of the North Atlantic Treaty Organization to counter Soviet moves.[39]

Despite these actions, efforts to include human rights (which the Soviets resented), and the U.S. diplomatic recognition of the Peoples' Republic of China, the two countries managed to sign another arms control treaty, commonly called SALT II. Carter and Brezhnev met in Vienna, Austria, in June 1979 to sign the appropriate documents. The agreement reduced the number of strategic delivery systems each country could deploy, and these systems included those on land, submarines, and in the air. The treaty also limited the number of warheads on these missiles. Brezhnev even liked Carter personally. "Quite a nice guy, after all," he remarked about Carter. The President and his team had gotten results.[40]

The euphoria over this success quickly vanished. The summer after the Vienna summit, a "crisis" over a Soviet infantry brigade raised serious questions about the administration's basic competence in foreign policy matters. Administration officials made public intelligence reports that the Soviets had a brigade stationed in Cuba. Vance declared, "I will not be satisfied with the maintenance of the status quo," and the President said the continued presence of the Soviet soldiers in the Western Hemisphere was "not acceptable." Brzezinski wanted to use the incident as an excuse to build up U.S. resources. It was only then that presidential advisors discovered that the unit had been stationed in Cuba since 1962, and that the United States had consented to its presence in the agreement that ended the Cuban Missile Crisis. "It was a very costly lapse in memory," Vance admitted in an understatement. The Secretary of State brought White House Counsel Lloyd Cutler into the discussions and, over Brzezinski's objections, convinced President Carter to hold a gathering of "wise men" – a group of former officials from previous Republican and Democratic administrations – similar to the ones Lyndon Johnson had used during the Vietnam War. The group put much of the blame for the pseudocrisis on Brzezinski and recommended that Carter take only minor actions. Vance and Cutler basically suggested that the administration order certain unilateral actions mainly designed to get past this episode. Carter agreed. This crisis had a number of important consequences. Cutler became a rising star within the administration for his role in resolving the matter. Reports from the intelligence agencies were taken with a little more skepticism. The damage was more significant. Brzezinski conceded that "the Cuban crisis shook public confidence in the Administration." The Carter White House needed to be more certain and resolute in dealing with the Soviets.[41]

The reaction in Moscow was entirely understandable. According to Dobrynin, the Soviets saw Carter as an unpredictable man determined to revive the Cold War. The Politburo never really considered that Carter was inept. He was, instead, the most dangerous American president since Harry S. Truman. He questioned the legitimacy of, and was determined to destroy, the Soviet Union.[42]

It was against this backdrop in U.S-Soviet relations that the leaders in the Kremlin decided to make their move in Afghanistan. These actions would soon pit two men of character, Carter and Lord Killanin, against each other in a battle for the future of the international Olympic movement and eventually the course of the Cold War itself.

CHAPTER 4

The Soviet Invasion of Afghanistan

ON THE NIGHT OF DECEMBER 24–25, 1979, THE SOVIET ARMY DID something it had not done since 1945. The invasion of Afghanistan was the first military operation that the Soviet Union had conducted since the end of World War II designed to seize territory the Soviets had not controlled at the end of that conflict. While this move seemed in Washington to indicate a new period in Communist aggression, the perspective was significantly different in Moscow. Soviet leaders wanted to bolster a flailing regime in a country that bordered the Soviet Union and looked at this move as nothing more than a short-term, regional action in their backyard of no real importance to any other nation. They had no expectation that it would affect U.S.-Soviet relations or damage their Olympic party.

One of the bigger mysteries in history is who made the decision to invade Afghanistan. In 1989, Georgi Arbatov was the chairman of the Subcommittee on Political Issues and Negotiations of the Supreme Soviet Committee on International Affairs and had the job of preparing a report on the decision to intervene in Afghanistan. Even after conducting an official report, which condemned the invasion, Arbatov admitted that he had learned only "some" of the facts about the decision and remained uncertain about who was involved in committing the Soviet Union to the invasion.[1]

The fact that such a basic issue remains blanketed in doubt even to officials at the time reflects the political structure of the Soviet Union in 1979. Brezhnev was head of both the party and the Soviet state. In 1974, though, he became quite ill following a summit meeting with President Ford. He never really recovered. As a result, his job performance began to flag. He found it difficult to concentrate during meetings and had trouble remembering information. Documents had to be prepared for him using extra-large print. The Politburo was full of a number of weak individuals who had risen to the top because they were careful and cautious, and made sure to assess the prevailing trends before expressing their views on policy matters. A situation such as this allowed Brezhnev to dominate the Politburo when he was healthy and vigorous, but after 1974, the result was drift and indecision. The Soviets formally made the decision to invade on December 12, but according to a number of participants, this action was just a formality. "There can be no doubt about Brezhnev's responsibility," Arbatov observed, "although I am not sure that he was physically capable of clearly understanding the situation in Afghanistan or the consequences of the decision."[2]

In a reflection of the limited number of people involved in authorizing the invasion, no Politburo member informed Dobrynin. The ambassador was back in Moscow for an annual physical and heard the news over the radio. "No one in our embassy in Washington was asked about possible repercussions, and I was not consulted by Gromyko even though I was in Moscow at the time," he remarked. Worried about American reactions, Dobrynin met with Brezhnev just before he left to return to the United States. "It'll be over in three to four weeks," Brezhnev told him, dismissing the concerns of the ambassador about the American reaction.[3]

While the "who" is still controversial, the "why" of the invasion has never been that confusing. "Our concerns about the danger of a region with which we shared a border were genuine," Arbatov explained. In 1978, a group of Communists overthrew the government in Afghanistan. Their hold on power, however, was weak, and most Afghans had no interest in being part of a Marxist social revolution. In September 1979, Hafizullah Amin seized control of the faction-ridden party and government apparatus. Many of his opponents sought refuge in the Soviet Union, and an insurgency against his government started. Even the KGB found Amin's administration particularly brutal. The Soviets tried to get him to reduce his use of terror against his political opponents. Amin responded by asking the Soviet Union to recall Ambassador Alexsandr Puzanov. The Soviets realized the situation in Afghanistan was on the verge of disaster. Andropov warned Brezhnev in early December, "All of this has created, on the one hand, the danger of losing the gains made by the April [1978] revolution (the scale of insurgent attacks will increase by spring) within the country, while on the other hand – the threat to our positions in Afghanistan (right now there is no guarantee that Amin, in order to protect his power, will not shift to the West)."[4]

The Soviets began thinking along the same lines they had used when they had intervened in Czechoslovakia and Hungary. The problem with this type of thinking is that no two situations are ever the same. The social structure of the country, the terrain, and the size of Afghanistan were significantly different from the Soviet-dominated states of eastern and central Europe. Despite these facts, the rationale the Soviets used was almost the same. Amin, who had earned a master's degree from Columbia University, was always suspect in Russian eyes. Many thought he was an agent of the Central Intelligence Agency. In Soviet terms, they feared he was "doing a Sadat on us." His efforts to eliminate his rivals within the People's Democratic Party of Afghanistan (PDPA) looked dangerous to the Soviets. "The scale of political repression was taking on increasingly mass proportions," a high-level Politburo report declared. "Just during the period following the events of September, more than 600 members of the PDPA, military personnel and other persons suspected of anti-Amin sentiments were executed without trial or investigation. In effect, the objective was to liquidate the party."[5]

The decision was one made out of desperation rather than out of an effort to exploit or gain advantage, and Soviet documents make it clear that it was not reached easily. In a series of discussions, the Politburo had on March 17 and 18, 1979, the old men that ran the country knew what was at risk. Brezhnev was absent for the first day of the discussion, and the group quickly reached a consensus to invade Afghanistan. The second day, when Brezhnev was present for the discussion, the group reversed itself. Brezhnev was still committed to détente and, given the weak personalities on the Politburo, it was easy enough for them to reverse their positions. Gromyko declared, "We would be throwing everything we achieved with such difficulty, particularly détente, the SALT II negotiations would fly by the wayside, there would be no signing of an agreement (and however you look at it that is for us the greatest political priority), there would be no meeting of Leonid Ilych with Carter." Andropov was also thinking along these lines, "We will look like aggressors, and we cannot permit that to occur." Such sensible attitudes carried the day then, but after the Vienna summit and Amin's coup, attitudes began to change. Minister of Defense Dmitri Ustinov and Andropov began pushing for intervention. Amin's behavior and his coup bothered them to no end. He had killed his political opponents, people who had trusted and worked with the Soviets. Such challenges to Soviet leadership could not be tolerated. Ustinov and Andropov isolated members of the Politburo, making sure they never saw dissenting opinions on intervention.[6]

The Soviet leaders could not have picked a worse place to invade. The phrase "military genius" is tossed about too frequently, but it is a good description of Alexander III of Macedonia, commonly known as Alexander the Great. Despite his skill, Afghanistan brought him to near ruin. In the nineteenth and early twentieth centuries, the British Empire fought a series of wars in this country and was largely thwarted. The mountainous terrain of Afghanistan and the xenophobic populace worked against any outside force. Scholars at the Institute of Oriental Studies of the Soviet Academy of Science quickly realized that the Politburo had made a crucial error, but they had no influence on the course of events.[7]

When the Soviets intervened in Czechoslovakia in 1968, they announced the Brezhnev Doctrine, which declared that it was their duty to prevent counterrevolutionary forces from overthrowing another Socialist regime. According to a classified Politburo report: "In this extremely difficult situation, which has threatened the gains of the April revolution and the interests of maintaining our national security, it has become necessary to render additional military assistance to Afghanistan, especially since such requests had been made by the previous administration in the PDPA. In accordance with the provisions of the Soviet-Afghan treaty of 1978, a decision has been made to send the necessary contingent of the Soviet Army to Afghanistan." Amin had asked for Soviet troops earlier in the year and was quite pleased when he learned the evening of December 22–23 that Soviet Politburo had agreed to his request.[8]

Another factor in the Soviet decision was that they had a relatively free hand in South and Southwest Asia. There was no other power in the immediate vicinity that could thwart their ambitions in the region. The United Kingdom had left India in 1947 and was no longer able to counter Russia. The United States had played a significant role in Iran, but the Islamic revolution that overthrew the Shah had also ended U.S. influence. As a result, the Soviets understandably believed there would be few international repercussions to their actions in this area.[9]

The invasion force that the Soviet military cobbled together reflected the poor decision-making process that sent these soldiers to Afghanistan in the first place. The day after the Politburo gave its formal approval, Colonel-General Yuri Maksimov, the commander of the Turkestan Military district, approved plans for the Limited Contingent of Soviet Forces to move into Afghanistan. He gave the job to Lieutenant-General Yuri Tukharinov, commanding general of the newly formed Fortieth Army. In its order of battle, this new formation had two motorized rifle divisions, one airborne division, one air assault brigade, and two motorized rifle regiments.[10]

The Fortieth Army had 52,000 men under arms as it entered Afghanistan, but many were poorly prepared for what awaited them. A good number were reservists suddenly called up for active duty. Yuri Tinkov, a paratrooper, recalled that when his regiment received orders to muster out, they thought it was a training exercise. "We didn't have any idea where we were going," he later explained. "Even the officers didn't know our final destination."[11]

The Soviets had a strategy that focused on achieving two operational objectives. The first was to stage a coup d'etat against the Amin government. The KGB began filtering opponents of the Amin regime back into Afghanistan, so they could argue that they had not overthrown the regime. These efforts often threatened to expose the invasion before it took place. In one incident, a KGB officer left a briefcase in a mud hut at Bagram airfield. The case contained a cassette tape recording of the new President of Afghanistan, Babrak Karmal, giving a speech explaining the reasons for the coup. The Soviets had selected Karmal, and if the tape became public before intended, the invasion could easily have been ruined before it started.[12]

Despite such disregard for basic operational security, the 103rd Guards Airborne quickly seized control of all the major political and military installations in the Afghan capital of Kabul on Christmas Day, sealing it off from the rest of the country. "Fear was gnawing at the pit of everyone's stomach," Tinkov recalled as his plane landed. It took 343 sorties and a total of 47 hours for the Soviets to get the division into Kabul. Mechanized infantry formations seized control of the roads leading into the city. Key targets in the city included Taj-Bek Palace – the official residence of the Afghani president – various military headquarters in the city, key ministry buildings, and communication facilities like radio stations and post offices.[13]

The battle to take Taj-Bek Palace was particularly brutal. The building sat on a high, terraced hill, with heavy tree and shrub growth on its sides. Its thick walls were capable of withstanding an artillery strike, and the road leading to the palace spiraled around the entire knoll that, when viewed from above, resembled a tadpole. These features were important because they channeled the attack and gave the advantage to the defenders. Winter weather conditions had ruled out a helicopter assault. Amin also had 2,500 personnel assigned to his personal defense, which included an anti-aircraft regiment and a number of tanks. A battalion from the Soviet Army's Main Intelligence Directorate, or GRU, also contributed to Amin's personal protection. The night of the battle, the Afghan dictator was in a good mood. At dinner that evening at the palace, he told his guests he was building a close relationship with Brezhnev. Then, everyone at the table became ill. Amin's guard sent for Soviet military doctors. After undergoing a stringent examination of their identity documents, Colonels Viktor Kuznechenkov and Anatoliy Alekseyev found Amin with almost no pulse. After pumping his stomach, giving him several injections, and an intravenous drip, they managed to stabilize his condition.[14]

While the two doctors were working to save Amin's life, other Soviets initiated the attack on the palace. Over 500 Spetsnaz commandos from the GRU and the KGB conducted the operation. The attack was under the command of Colonel Grigoriy Boyarinov, an army officer who had arrived in Afghanistan two days earlier. Many of these soldiers were supposedly part of Amin's personal security detail. "Immediately before the operation some drank vodka, others valerian, but all the same it didn't help," Lieutenant Colonel Pavel Klimov recalled. "The excitement and stress was great. For many this was the end of the biographies; everyone understood the danger."[15]

The Soviets were wearing Afghan uniforms in an effort to support the official party line that a domestic coup had removed Amin. The Soviets opened fire with two ZSU 23–4 self-propelled anti-aircraft guns and charged the traffic barriers on the road to the palace in their armored personnel carriers, running over Afghan defenders that stayed at their posts. The soldiers assigned to Amin's personal bodyguard refused to surrender and directed an intense amount of light weapons fire toward these vehicles. Captain Viktor Karpukhin led one of the assault waves. His driver hesitated as they came under fire. "I told him not to spare the ammunition just shoot as fast as you can. And he tried; it was impossible to breath in the vehicle from the smoke. All the shells and rounds for the machine gun coupled with the gun were expended very quickly." He then had his driver stop at the very walls of the building. "I jumped out first and Sasha Plyusnin ended up next to me. We began to shoot at everyone who was exposed and was shooting from the windows, allowing the rest of the soldiers of our subgroup to get out."[16]

Other elements of the assault were less fortunate. The bullets of the ZSU 23–4s did not have enough velocity to penetrate the granite walls of the palace and were ricocheting back on to the Soviet armored personnel carriers and doing considerable damage. As a result, the crews of these other vehicles stopped a considerable distance from the palace and found themselves getting hit as they exited. Colonel Ehval'd Kozlov, who had developed the plan for the assault, was shot in the foot before he even got out. The Soviets found themselves pinned down. The mission was in danger of failing. The Afghan defenders were using 9mm West German Keckler & Koch MP5 submachine guns, which lacked the velocity to penetrate the flak jackets the Soviets were wearing. Still, limbs and groins were vulnerable, and heavy machine gun fire could and did cut through body armor.[17]

The commandos would have been in even worse shape if not for the actions of the Soviet advisors attached to the anti-aircraft regiment guarding Amin. The unit's heavy guns were positioned in the mountains surrounding the palace to protect against an air assault, but they could be easily aimed at ground targets and had enough firepower to take out the armored personnel carriers the Soviets were using. The advisors attached to this unit simply removed the gun sights from the guns, which effectively neutralized these weapons.[18]

A number of officers, including Kozlov, Boyarinov, and Karpukhin, found the courage to move forward. "Initially the situation was on the edge of panic," one KGB officer recalled. "I saw that we could not get a large number of people to the Palace. The shooting was horrible. The firing locations, which should have been neutralized by the army guys, were shooting at everything. If we had flinched just a bit everything would have turned out differently."[19]

The survivors rallied and managed to break into the palace through a window. Colonel Boyarinov was shouting above the din, "Upstairs men! We need to go upstairs! And defend the corridors here on the first floor!" In the room-to-room fighting that followed, he was fatally wounded. "Each step there had to be fought for, just like in the Reichstag," Karpukhin recalled. The Soviets managed to reach the communications center and cut off contact with the outside world. None of the other formations tasked with protecting Amin would be coming to his aid.[20]

Upstairs, Amin thought he was under attack from other Afghans. Dazed from his attempted poisoning, he instructed one of his aides to contact the Soviets. The fact that the attackers were cursing in Russian quickly exposed the political façade for what it was. His assistant informed him that the Soviets were the ones actually conducting the attack. "You're lying, it can't be!" After failing to reach his Army chief of staff on the telephone, he accepted his fate. "I suspected this; it's all true." He wandered about the room aimlessly, with his five-year old son hugging his leg.[21]

Colonel Kozlov, despite the wound to his foot, rushed up the staircase that lead to the second floor of the palace with a group of seven other Soviet commandos. They were throwing grenades and firing automatic weapons as fast as they could. At the time, the staircase seemed huge to Kozlov, and reminded him of a famous scene in director Sergei Eisenstein's silent film *The Battleship Potemkin* where the Czar's Cossack troops massacre civilians on the Odessa steps. Returning to the palace years later, he was stunned to find that the staircase was that of an ordinary house. "How we eight traveled up it together I don't know; the main thing is we stayed alive. It happened that I was fighting without a bulletproof vest, which even now is horrific to imagine but on that day I didn't remember it. It seemed I had become empty inside and everything was forced out by the desire to carry out the mission. Even the noise of battle and the shouts of the people were perceived differently from the usual way. Everything in me operated only for battle and I was to be victorious in battle."[22]

The firefight only intensified when the eight reached the second floor. Sergey Golov was one of the soldiers charging up the stairs with Kozlov: "I don't know why he had ended up without a bulletproof vest but Ehval'd bravely forged ahead with a pistol in his hands. I didn't notice when I myself was wounded. Possibly it was when, having thrown a grenade into a window and got into trouble and it rolled back. I quickly managed to throw a second grenade and lie on the floor. The grenades detonated and we stayed alive. The main goal was to reach Amin's location at any cost."[23]

The smoke and noise inside the building had a surreal effect, cutting off soldiers from one another. According to Karpukhin, "It was quite hard for us to converse during the battle; we had other concerns. You were to reload faster and in any case look in order to orient yourself and not get a bullet from somewhere."[24]

After breaching the second floor, the Soviets then began methodically moving from room to room. "I ended up paired with Lenya Gumenny and we 'cleaned' all the rooms in sequence," one Soviet remembered. "First we opened the door, threw in a grenade and shot everything. Then we stopped throwing grenades and just shone a flashlight since there was no more resistance. We ran through the entire floor and then returned."[25]

During an initial sweep, Soviet soldiers found Amin lying dazed and incapacitated on the floor. Not knowing who the man was, they moved on.[26]

The battle lasted forty-three minutes. "Suddenly the shooting stopped," Major Yakov Semenov explained. During a survey of the building, the Soviets found Amin dead, wrapped in a carpet. His five-year-old and eight-year-old sons were also dead. Colonel Kuznechenkov, one of the two doctors who had been tending to him, had also been killed in a friendly-fire incident during the room-to-room "cleaning." Boyarinov, the overall attack commander, was posthumously made a Hero of the Soviet Union. Kozlov also received this decoration. Karpukhin received this medal for other actions and was a major general when his KGB career ended. Although the fatalities were light, almost everyone in the attack force had been wounded.[27]

There was also a difficult fight at the new headquarters of the General Staff of the Afghan Army. A detachment of fourteen Spetsnaz commandos accompanied KGB Major Valeriy Rozin, General A. A. Vlasov, and General I. F. Ryabchenko to the General Staff building. The cover story for the attack was a get-acquainted meeting between Ryabchenko, the commander of the 103rd Airborne Division, and General M. Yakub, chief of the Afghan General Staff. The signal for the attack on the General Staff was an explosion in the city center that would also destroy communication equipment. Yakub realized what was going on and attempted to grab a gun that was lying on a table. Rozin lunged at him and the two were quickly grappling with one another. Several Soviets entered the room and started firing. General Ryabchenko, unaware of the planned action, sat in his chair, stunned.[28]

At the same time, Soviet soldiers had managed to move to the second floor before the explosion and were chatting with their Afghan comrades, exchanging cigarettes. The commandos then took control of the ground floor and the entrance to the building. Room-to-room fighting followed. The Spetsnaz destroyed the communications equipment that connected the General Staff with the rest of the Afghan Army, effectively paralyzing that force. The Afghans in the building retreated to the third floor, but the Soviets did not follow. The defenders were contained. The fight in the building took more than an hour. The Soviets had taken over a hundred prisoners, and it was difficult for the small detachment of commandos to guard this large group. A company of paratroopers from 103rd Airborne Division arrived shortly thereafter and started shooting into the building. After a bit of delay, Ryabchenko got his men to stop shooting. There were no friendly-fire incidents, and with these reinforcements, the Soviets managed to take control of the building. Yakub had been wounded in the fray and was under guard. An Afghan collaborator went to where he was being held, talked with him for a good bit in Pashtu, and then shot him. Taking the rest of Kabul was relatively easy. No other group of Afghans put up as much resistance as the detachments at Taj-Bek Palace and the General Staff building.[29]

The second Soviet operational goal was to seize control of the major centers of population in Afghanistan. The Fortieth Army made a three-pronged advance into Afghanistan. The first was the air bridge that had dropped Soviet troops into Kabul. At the same time, ground troops crossed the Soviet-Afghan border at Kushka in the west and Termez in the east. These two prongs advanced around the edge of the country and met in Kandahar, a city in southern Afghanistan that Alexander the Great founded in the fourth century BC. This effort took roughly seven weeks due mainly to the distances that Soviet troops had to cover. "Many residents greeted Soviet Soldiers with flowers," Major General Aleksandr Lyakhovskiy recalled in a history he wrote of the operation. "They chanted slogans of Soviet-Afghan friendship."[30]

A major assumption that many Soviet officers had was that the sheer size and weaponry of the Fortieth Army should be enough to "sober up" the Mujahideen rebels. The Soviet Army made no effort to study the history, culture, or even geography of Afghanistan before invading. "The Soviet High Command made a serious initial error," the officers of the Soviet General Staff observed in a postwar staff study. The Soviets sent soldiers from the Central Asian regions of the Union of Soviet Socialist Republics (USSR), thinking that they would receive a better welcome in Afghanistan than troops from the various European regions of the Soviet Union. This decision, however, ignored the ancient rivalries that had existed between the Uzbek, Tadjik, and Turkmen peoples of the Soviet Union and the Pushtun tribes of Afghanistan. These soldiers also often lacked an adequate command of basic Russian and were liabilities to their units.[31]

There were two initial results of the invasion. First, the Soviets did indeed establish stability in Afghanistan. For two months, the Afghans put up little resistance as the Soviets seized control of the country.[32] Then in March, everything changed. The Soviets had badly misjudged the strength and determination of the Afghan rebels and had managed to unify the populace. "Never before in Afghan history had so many people been as united as they now were in opposition to an invader," M. Hassan Kakar, an Afghan academic, notes in a book about the response to the Soviets. "The opposition to the invasion was thus national, crossing regional, ethnic, and linguistic lines." About 40 percent of the Limited Contingent of Soviet Forces was involved in stability operations and guard duty. According to the Soviet General Staff, failure to destroy the Mujahideen was political rather than military. To use the understated language of a Soviet staff study, the new government of Babrak Karmal that the Soviets had installed after Amin's execution "did not live up to expectations." The rebels moved into the hills and started conducting raids against the foreign occupier.[33]

The Soviet response was quite predictable. "Because the forces of the opposition began raiding our units and naturally we had to defend ourselves in such a situation," General Valentin Varennikov, deputy chief of the Soviet General Staff at the time of the invasion, later explained. "And after that, all this began growing like a snowball, and events began developing in an undesirable direction."[34]

Even in Kabul, the Soviets never fully eradicated the rebel threat. The city was a fortress, with a complex security belt ringing the municipality. The three-layered system was ten to twenty miles in depth. The network included bunkers, gun emplacements, and mines. The Soviets had outposts along the major roads leading into the city. Despite these efforts, the Karmal regime had problems in protecting the security of its own officials. The rebels managed to carry out bombings, shootings, and assassinations in Kabul. Things were so bad that even the Soviet media reported on conditions in the city. "Circumstances change with the approach of night," a Soviet journalist admitted. "Streets and alleys become empty. The footsteps of guards echo hollowly in the quiet that sets in, and patrol vehicles move around slowly." In one famous example, an Afghan wrestler who went to Moscow to participate in the Olympics despite warnings from the Mujahideen returned to Kabul and had to go into hiding. Eventually, the resistance found and murdered him in 1982.[35]

The problem the Soviets had was that in training, equipment, and doctrine, they were prepared to fight in Central Europe against the militaries of NATO, not irregular fighters in the mountains of Afghanistan. Soviet officers had designed their army to punch holes in the enemy lines with artillery and air strikes, and rush deep into the enemy's rear area with armor columns. Tanks, armored personnel carriers, and self-propelled artillery were ineffective in the steep terrain of Afghanistan and were unable to mass fire or maneuver quickly.[36]

The war that the Mujahideen were fighting was one in which light infantry tactics would dominate. The Soviet Army, though, had deliberately chosen tactical predictability for a war against NATO in which they believed operational flexibility would be key. In Afghanistan, this predictability became a huge liability. The Soviets compounded this problem with the use of timid tactics. One of the most common weapons the Afghan rebels had was the World War I–era British Enfield rifle. These firearms had enough power to penetrate Soviet body armor. As a result, troops of the Fortieth Army tended to stay about 300 meters away from their enemy. At this range, their own rifles and light machine guns were at the maximum range of accuracy and were less capable of thwarting the ambush-and-pursuit tactics the Mujahideen used. "We did not expect such a powerful enemy would abandon an almost certain victory and retire empty-handed," one rebel remarked.[37]

The Soviets did have certain technological advantages in the helicopter and antipersonnel mines. Helicopters increased Soviet infantry mobility and were deadly when used as gun platforms. "Traveling with the guerrillas in Nangrahar province in mid-1980, I found tribesmen panic-stricken by the appearance of gunships on the horizon," journalist Edward Girardet observed. Unaware that they were invisible to the crews of these machines, the rebels would scatter and seek shelter. The helicopters were impervious to the light weapons the Afghans had, at least in the early stages of the conflict. Most of the helicopters that the Mujahideen claimed to have shot down landed due to mechanical problems.[38]

Land mines were another important technological advantage the Soviets used against the Mujahideen. The mines made it difficult for the rebels to maneuver and created a number of supply problems. In both instances, the Soviets placed antipersonnel mines along the trails and footpaths that the Mujahideen used. These weapons also stripped the resistance of their cover among the people. The rest of Afghan society used these routes, and as traveling on them became dangerous, seven million Afghans decided they were safer living as refugees in Pakistan and Iran.[39]

In a way, though, the mass of refugees rebounded back on the Soviets. Many of these Afghans had nothing to do other than fight. Their homes had been destroyed, their livelihood ruined, and their families killed or scattered. There was nothing holding them back from joining the fray.[40]

While certain technologies mitigated against tactical timidity, logistics limited the number of these weapons. Supply efforts were poor when the invasion started and never got better. During the first year of the war, Soviet battalions simply lacked the weapons and ammunition necessary to engage with their enemy. Other items were also less than abundant. One soldier told Russian journalist Gennady Bocharov in February, "We live like animals. We haven't been able to wash even once. There's no firewood, so we freeze. And the food's hardly fit for pigs. Some of us already have body lice." This complaint reflected a tendency in the Soviet Army to ignore sanitary conditions. It is hardly surprising then that during the first half of the war in Afghanistan, noncombat fatalities (disease, illness, etc.) accounted for 17.7 percent of total Soviet fatalities.[41]

Even if the Soviets had been supplied adequately, it might not have mattered. The army was not designed to fight an insurgency nor did it make any effort to study the history of irregular war. The Soviets had defeated this type of warfare in the past, as had other armies. The average Soviet soldier was poorly trained, and there was an expectation among training personnel that the troops would learn on the job. It is hardly surprising then that the Soviets tended to stick to strong points. "They're outside the city," an Afghan student told Girardet. "They don't come into town."[42]

The army failed to perform basic tasks with either imagination or vigor. It was quite common for sweeping operations to move through valleys and towns without posting any blocking forces, which gave their enemy an escape route. Commanders also often refused to adapt to the terrain. One of the biggest mistakes Soviet officers made on a regular basis during the early months of the war was making no effort to secure the high ground. After studying one engagement in a small Afghan village, observers from the Frunze Military Academy noted that "the company had insufficient experience in conducting combat in mountainous regions and neither the officers, sergeants, nor soldiers knew the enemy's tactics." During this period, the Soviets made little use of air power to protect convoys or seize dominant terrain features and deny them to the Mujahideen. Instead, the Soviets used tanks to spearhead their convoy formations, which was a bad idea. The restricted terrain in the mountainous regions of Afghanistan gave these vehicles little room to maneuver. The Soviets quickly learned some painful lessons, and before the end of 1980, the Soviets began using helicopters to protect their convoys. According to Western analysts, the number of Soviet helicopters in Afghanistan jumped from an estimated low of 15 in January to a high of 300 in September.[43]

There were other manifestations of Soviet tactical timidity. Soldiers preferred to stay in their vehicles rather than dismount and avoided maneuvering at night. They also failed to take defensive precautions and slept in unprotected tents. Only when the Mujahideen fired into these shelters at night, did Soviet soldiers begin digging trenches.[44]

Even the terrain worked against the Soviets. Tactical communication was uncertain in the mountains. The atmospheric conditions in high elevations, in addition to the uneven, hilly ground, made radios unreliable. Batteries ran out of power faster in the thin air, and motors were less efficient in their work than they were at lower altitudes.[45]

The only exception to this generally poor performance on the part of the Soviets came in the performance of their elite units: the paratroopers, Spetsnaz commandos, and reconnaissance forces. These formations generally had better training and a stronger esprit de corps than the average Soviet soldier. Many of the individuals serving in these formations were professionals who that had volunteered for their assignments. "They had the courage to face us and the ability to climb mountains quickly," Ali Ahmad Jalali, a Mujahideen commander, noted.[46]

Poor morale was a natural byproduct of poor performance in the field. The Soviets brutalized the Afghan population on a regular basis. Soldiers would commit random acts of vandalism, and patrols in cities and towns would regularly take money and other valuables from Afghans that they stopped and searched. Such behavior only alienated the people and undermined Soviet efforts to stabilize the country. "An all-encompassing moral corruption prevailed in our officer corps. Everyone had an incomprehensible urge to grab for himself as much as possible," Yurchenko recalled. "What surprised me most was how all-encompassing that degeneration was. It seemed that the only thing that people thought about was grabbing things for themselves, from the lowest rank of the hierarchy all the way to the top."[47]

A major problem the Soviets faced in this war was that they had no ally of any significance in the fight with them. Soviet propaganda claimed that the intervention was at the request of the Afghan government, but events on the ground quickly exposed this lie for what it was. Following the invasion, the 8th Infantry Division stationed near Kabul actually fought the Soviets in a battle that lasted until January 5. Another division, the 15th, also revolted against the foreign occupation a few weeks later, and there was fighting in a number of Afghan cities like Kandahar and Jalalabad. Even after establishing control in Afghanistan, the Soviets still had problems. In July, the 14th Mechanized Division revolted. These clashes, however, had more to do with confrontations between Amin and Karmal supporters rather than with direct hostility toward the Soviet Union.[48]

The bigger problem the Red Army faced with its Afghan allies was not active opposition from the Army, but rather its collapse. There was a massive amount of desertion in the immediate aftermath of the Soviet invasion. Kakar estimates that by the middle of March, 80 percent of the soldiers in the Army had deserted and that by May, this number was 90 percent.[49]

The Karmal regime, as a result, quickly became totally dependent on the Limited Contingent of Soviet Forces. Conscription, despite its unpopularity, became the mechanism the Kabul government attempted to use to rebuild the Afghan Army. Actually, kidnapping is a better term to describe Afghan military manpower policies. Yurchenko recalled, "Our battalion surrounded a village from one side, and from the other side the Afghan police drove the draft-age men toward us."[50]

It is easy to understand then why the Afghan Army was such a week reed. Mujahideen leaders would later explain that they had many followers within the Army. These individuals were both officers and enlisted men. These sympathizers acted as spies and provided information to the rebels. In other situations, these men would switch sides and join the Mujahideen. It was not unusual for officers to negotiate the surrender of their units and hand over all their weapons to the rebels.[51]

The Soviets had more dependable allies from a number of foreign countries that sent combat forces to Afghanistan. These nations included Bulgaria, East Germany, Czechoslovakia, Vietnam, and Cuba. What is odd about the contribution of these contingents is that the Soviet Union made no effort to draw attention to their presence and show the solidarity of the international Communist movement.[52] If they had, these allies could have had an impact disproportionate to their size and actually military mission.

It is also clear that the Soviets failed to understand who they were fighting. The Soviet General Staff described the Mujahideen as well-trained, disciplined, and organized. These Afghan rebels were anything but, particularly in the early months of the war. According to the Soviet General Staff, the Mujahideen were regularly receiving formal military training in Pakistan at schools and centers that the United States, China, and NATO nations had established. The rebels also had a formal logistical system and regular military identification cards and established defensive positions, like trenches, upon which to fall back on.[53]

As good Marxists, Soviets officers had a difficult time in understanding that there were people who defined their identities by factors other than class. This ideological focus made it difficult for them to understand the religious views of their opponents and fathom that this resistance might have a popular basis in the country. According to a report that four Politburo members made for their colleagues, "The situation in Afghanistan remains complicated and tense. The class struggle, represented in armed counterrevolutionary insurrections, encouraged and actively supported from abroad is occurring in the circumstances where a genuine unity of the PDPA is still absent, where the state and party apparatus is weak in terms of organization and ideology, which is reflected in the practical non-existence of local government organs, where financial and economic difficulties are mounting, and where the combat readiness of the Afghan armed forces and the people's militia is still insufficient."[54]

This confusion was the product of factors other than ideological blinders. Part of it was that the Soviets had no good intelligence of the enemy. Afghanistan was also an extremely undeveloped country that was radically different from Soviet society. Gennady Bocharov, a Russian journalist, thought visiting Afghanistan was like going back in time nearly seven centuries, to the year 1358. Soviet soldiers shared this view. Yuri Yurchenko drove an armored personnel carrier during the first days of the war. After leaving Kabul, he observed, "It seemed as though we had traveled back in time to medieval Asia."[55]

Despite thinking in the Red Army to the contrary, there was no central resistance. The Soviet intervention united the Afghans, but it is important to note that this unity went only so far. The Afghans were united against a common foe, the Soviets. Divisions within Afghan society remained. The decentralized nature of the insurgency was both its strength and its weakness. It was extremely difficult for the Soviets to decapitate or coopt the guerrilla movement. On the other hand, the commitment of the various resistance bands varied significantly as did their motivation. Some fighters had little interest in destroying the enemy. They intended to use their membership in the movement to improve their own social standing in their villages and tribes, and their commitment to fight the Soviets ended once these foreign troops left the immediate region. Other Mujahideen organizations operated as governments in areas that they controlled, assessing taxes and enforcing Islamic law. There were problems, though. The rebels only pursued local objectives. Many Mujahideen fighters were from different parts of the country and these individuals needed more support from the people since they were not fighting out of their own homes. The feuds between the various resistance bands often had little to do with fighting the Soviets, and their inability to work together against the foreign occupation disillusioned many people. Others also objected to the harsh justice and execution of party members and associates. Many of these individuals had extensive family ties in the area, which was not the case for the Mujahideen.[56]

Neccessity dictated much of what the rebels did militarily. According to a Soviet General Staff Study, "The armed opposition forces abandoned positional warfare and widely employed maneuver. The Mujahideen could only be forced to accept battle under compelling circumstances. These circumstances included defense of a base or base region or when the Mujahideen were encircled and had no other options." Even then the rebels found ways to limit the danger the Soviets posed to them. "In this case, the blocked Mujahideen detachments moved into close combat, where it was practically impossible for the Soviets to use their aviation and which sharply restricted their possibility of using artillery, especially from indirect firing positions."[57]

The rebels were using the same tactics that their grandfathers and great-grandfathers had used against the British Army in the nineteenth century. The Afghans used these tried and true methods, because they had little or no military training. Most guerrilla bands lacked discipline and never did any serious training. Although the Mujahideen fighters improved with experience as the war continued into the 1980s, they never developed anything other than a basic approach toward fighting. As a result, most were unable to use weapons more advanced than heavy machine guns. "It was impossible to force the Afghan soldiers to fight seriously," Tinkov said.[58]

The resistances also had a highly uncertain supply situation. Although the CIA would eventually get military equipment to the rebels, that was not the case in the early days of the Soviet intervention. The Mujahideen got most of their weapons from the Soviets, directly or indirectly. Many Afghan soldiers defected and brought with them their Soviet-supplied weapons. Before the end of 1980, the Soviets gave heavy anti-tank and anti-aircraft guns to only the most reliable Afghan units because of these large-scale defections. The rebels also took weapons and bullets from Soviet prisoners and the dead, showing a marked preference for the AK-74 Kalashnikov assault rifle.[59]

It is little surprise then that the rebels made a number of tactical mistakes in the first days of the war. The Mujahideen made easy targets for Soviet fliers as they assembled in large bands of hundreds and thousands. Nor were they able to block Soviet advances.[60]

The war that the Soviet Union ended up fighting in Afghanistan was not the war that the leadership in the Politburo had intended to fight. Such is often the case in war. The war did reflect the crude and simplistic politics of Soviet society and actually worked against Soviet interests. Arbatov stated, "We became participants in the dismantling of the détente we had launched a few years earlier. We helped the enemies of détente in the United States and other NATO countries to start another cold war."[61]

That hostile response was one Soviet leaders never considered. That surprise was perhaps understandable. Afghanistan was a neighboring country of the Soviet Union and within its regional sphere of influence. Why should the United States care about what happened in this primitive nation? How the United States responded also stunned Soviet leaders. It is to that response, and the decision of Jimmy Carter to bend the Olympic movement to his needs, that this story now turns.

CHAPTER 5

The American Response

THE QUESTION THAT FACED THE CARTER ADMINISTRATION WAS HOW to react to the Soviet invasion. It was clear that the Americans would object and that U.S.-Soviet relations would suffer to some degree, but the Carter Administration had two important options. It could either see this intervention as a regional issue of limited importance outside Central Asia, or it could define this move as a major initiative in international affairs. Domestic political factors were always in play during this time and were the primary influences, rather than international considerations that shaped Carter's decision. As things turned out, the boycott had significant impact on the international Olympic movement but very little on the situation in Afghanistan.

Most Americans saw the Soviet intervention in Afghanistan in dire terms – none more so than Brzezinski. He was the person most responsible for defining the administration's view of the invasion. Soviet actions in Afghanistan only confirmed his hostile view of the Soviets. In assessing the strategic ramifications of this move, he looked not at the history of rivalry in Central Asia, but rather to the international confrontation that was the Cold War. For an American official, this view was predictable and probably understandable. Brzezinski decided, though, that this Soviet action was different than the ones that had come in East Germany, Hungary, and Czechoslovakia. "The Soviet occupation of Afghanistan is the first time since 1945 that the Soviet Union used its military forces directly to expand its power." The intervention, direct though it may be, was in keeping with the increased aggression in Soviet foreign policy that the 1970s had witnessed. Brzezinski reminded Carter that "Afghanistan is the seventh state since 1975 in which communist parties have come to power with Soviet guns and tanks, with Soviet military power and assistance."[1]

Brzezinski's stringent view was predictable, but what he remained uncertain of was which Jimmy Carter would show up during this crisis. The National Security Advisor cleverly appealed to both the best and worst in Carter. He bluntly warned the President that "four of these takeovers occurred since

January 1977." The message was clear: One Soviet advance was unfortunate, but four represented weak American leadership in world affairs. At the same time, he told the President the crisis was an opportunity: The moment at hand now "required major decisions by you, but I believe that a major historical turning point has been reached. You have the opportunity to do what President Truman did on Greece and Turkey, and I believe that this is desirable both for domestic and international reasons."[2]

The National Security Advisor was prodding Carter. He needed to be strong on foreign policy. His poll numbers were declining. After Iranian students had seized control of the U.S. embassy in Tehran, the American people had rallied around his leadership. As the crisis continued, his numbers began to fade. He was facing political challenges to his leadership within the Democratic Party under the leadership of Senator Edward M. Kennedy of Massachusetts and Governor Edmund "Jerry" Brown of California. Of these two, Kennedy appeared to be a far more serious threat. In September 1978, a poll showed that he was the choice of Democrats and independents to be the next president by 40 percent to Carter's 21. Just before the beginning of the Iranian hostage crisis, Carter had an approval rating of 29 percent in another poll. Kennedy had a two-to-one lead over Carter among Democrats. Polls in early January showed that most Americans had come to agree with Kennedy's complaints that the Shah of Iran was nothing more than a thug, and that it had been a mistake to support him. While respondents in these surveys gave Carter good marks for his handling of the crisis, they also showed that their patience was wearing thin. Americans wanted the hostage crisis resolved in days and weeks, not months. Whatever boost Carter had gotten from the crisis was over.[3]

Brzezinski believed that the United States had to intervene directly in Southwestern and Central Asia. "We have to move deliberately to fashion a wider security arrangement for the region, lest Soviet influence spread rapidly from Afghanistan to Pakistan and Iran. I cannot emphasize strongly enough the strategic consequences of such a development. It would place in direct jeopardy our most vital interests in the Middle East."[4]

This analysis was deeply flawed. While the Soviet invasion might have looked dangerous on a map, the terrain of Afghanistan worked against easy movement toward either Iran or Pakistan. Brzezinski had company in this mistaken assessment. Admiral Stansfield Turner, Director of Central Intelligence, warned that while the invasion appeared to be unplanned, it could be an indicator of further aggressive activity in the Third World. "How assertative the Soviets will be in the future will very likely depend upon how 'successful' the Soviet leadership views their intervention in Afghanistan to have been," he warned. Years later, after the end of the Cold War, Dobrynin explained that this analysis was extremely inaccurate. "There was no grand strategic plan designed by Moscow to seize a new footing on the way to the oil riches of the Middle East and thus gain global superiority over the United States." The decision had little to do with international issues. "It was a Soviet reaction to a local situation in which the security of our southern boarders was threatened by the growing instability inside Afghanistan and the obvious ineptitude of the Amin government (as well as by troubles in neighboring Iran)." At the time, people in Moscow thought regional security issues and U.S.-Soviet relations were two different matters, with no direct connection to one another. "In any case, it can be unambiguously stated that the appearance of Soviet troops in Afghanistan was not the result of a conscious choice between expansionism and detente made by the Kremlin leadership. To my knowledge the Kremlin was not even considering this kind of choice," the ambassador explained. Research in Soviet archives basically supports the ambassador's argument.[5]

Carter and his subordinates saw things differently at the time and believed that Afghanistan had destabilized U.S.-Soviet relations. This initiative demanded a response from the White House. The question was: What did the United States hope to accomplish? A U.S. State Department paper prepared for Carter attempted to address this issue directly:

> The first is punitive: we want them to pay a price for infringing fundamental principles of international behavior. The second is coercive: we want them to withdraw their troops and allow Afghanistan to return to a semblance of sovereignty and neutrality. The third is deterrent: we want to prevent the Soviets from crossing further thresholds, such as hot pursuit of rebels across international frontiers or escalation of the fighting with the rebels to a massive scale.[6]

Carter was one to write comments on papers and documents that came across his desk. In this fashion, he often made his views known to his administration. He disagreed with the analysis the State Department had offered. When he read this paper, he wrote on the side in his fine, tight handwriting: "1 + 3 inter-related[;] 2 unlikely." In other words, he knew coercion simply was not possible and that there was nothing the United States could do to force the Soviets out of Afghanistan.[7]

What then could the United States hope to do about the Soviet intervention? Carter quickly wrote a letter to Brezhnev. In strong language, he warned the Soviet leader that he did not believe their cover story, and that Afghanistan was putting their relations with the United States at risk. Brezhnev wrote back, bluntly telling Carter to mind his own business. "The attempt made in your letter to cast doubt on the very fact of the request of the government of Afghanistan to send our troops to this country seems strange," he observed. "The immoderate tone of some of the wording of your message is striking. And to what purpose? Wouldn't it be better to assess the situation more quietly, keeping in mind the higher interests of peace and not putting the relations between our two countries in last priority?" Brezhnev and the other members of the Politburo saw Afghanistan as being a regional issue having little to do with their relations with the United States. What had the Soviet Union done in response to U.S. intervention in the Dominican Republic in 1965? He still wanted and believed détente could continue. "I don't think that the work to create more stable and productive relations between the USSR and US could become useless if, of course, the American side does not want this. We don't want this. I think that this would also not be to the advantage of the United States of America itself. It is our conviction that it is a mutual matter how relations between the USSR and US develop. We think that they ought not to be subject to fluctuations under the influence of any outside factors or events."[8]

Carter's comments on a memo that Vance prepared documenting a meeting he had with Chancellor Helmut Schmidt of the Federal Republic of Germany show that the President was unable to make the distinctions Brezhnev was making. The conversation between Vance and Schmidt, according to Vance's account, was one of frankness between two professional diplomats attempting to honestly discuss the differences between allies. Carter, on the other hand, emerges from his "exchange" with Vance and Schmidt as petty and overly sensitive to criticism:

Vance/Schmidt: We believe that we should seek to achieve a return to the status quo ante in Afghanistan, along the general lines suggested by the recent statement of the EC-9 in their Rome meeting.

Carter: "Status quo ante"? ante when? Not 12/23/79.

* * *

Vance/Schmidt: The Chancellor then raised the possibility that the Soviets, despite all of the sanctions taken against them by the West, may simply refuse to pull out of Afghanistan.

Carter: Most likely response.

* * *

Vance/Schmidt: What should the West do if the Soviets refuse to leave Afghanistan? In Schmidt's view – and he emphasized he was "thinking out loud" – he thought it would make sense in such a situation to try to push the Soviets out of some other area where they have established a foothold – i.e., Angola, Libya, Ethiopia, or North Yemen.

Carter: How about trade restraints, boycotting Olympics, stronger NATO Allied unity – world condemnation.

* * *

Vance/Schmidt: We must do something in order not to appear impotent.

Carter: Just what we are trying to do with doubtful support.[9]

The Carter that emerges from this "exchange" is a man torn by his wish to force change and his realization that there is really very little he can do to alter the situation. At the same time, he also knew he had to do something – anything – to avoid looking weak. Although Schmidt never saw the President's commentary on his meeting with Vance, he understood the basic situation that the man was in at the time. "Carter quite obviously thought of nothing but showing himself firm in his relations with the Soviets because of his reelection campaign. But this firmness was merely a pretense – with which he fooled himself as well. Because in fact he was not prepared actually to put pressure on the Soviet Union when it came to Afghanistan." The German chancellor also believed that Carter made his decisions in a hasty manner. "Television theatrics frequently take the place of statecraft. Out of such situations grew Carter's rashness in proclaiming the grain embargo and the boycott of the Olympic Games after the Soviet invasion of Afghanistan."[10]

The President certainly would have disputed this last statement. He believed that his staff was responding in good fashion, giving him the options he needed and seeking outside opinion when appropriate as they began to consider an Olympic boycott. In his memoirs, he states, "I held many meetings with my advisors and consulted closely with other heads of state and with sport leaders in our country."[11]

The only problem with this statement is – it is not true. Peter Ueberroth, the head of the Los Angeles Olympic Organizing Committee (LAOOC) that was planning the summer games of 1984, observed that he had had no contact with Carter and "no one from his administration ever contacted me or anyone else at the LAOOC either to enlist our aid or to give us a courtesy briefing." He had company. When reporters asked Lord Killanin if he would be meeting with Carter, the Irishman answered, "He has not requested to see me, and I have not requested to see him, and I don't have a vote in the United States."[12]

Robert Kane and F. Don Miller, the president and executive director of the U.S. Olympic Committee, were watching and listening to the loose talk about a boycott. They took the initiative to write Carter about it: "This proposal is diametrically opposed to the principles of the worldwide Olympic movement which has been, for more than 80 years, a significant force in creating international amity and engendering goodwill among the youth of the world."[13]

The NSC met on the second day of the new year to consider what responses the United States would take. The State Department prepared a special paper for this meeting, listing the available options that could be used to retaliate against the Soviet Union. The president littered the margins of this paper with many comments. Some of them were nothing more than a check mark, approving a policy option. At other times, he wrote a simple "Yes" or "No." He showed a preference for using propaganda and economic tools against the Soviets, refusing to take strong actions like increasing the military presence in the Persian Gulf. His notations show that the headwaters of the naïve arrogance that ran through his administration came from the Oval Office itself. In response to a recommendation that the U.S. work to limit the nations that extended diplomatic recognition to the new regime, he thought he could dictate what actions U.S. allies should take: "Leave minimum; no more than 10. UK, Canada – no recognition. Italy, Federal Republic of Germany, Ambassador out. France – no political contact." When it came to the Olympics, the discussions of the options exaggerated the importance of the United States or any other nation to the status of the games: "US withdrawal from Summer Olympics in Moscow would be serious blow to Soviet international prestige." The paper also noted that the Olympics option had limited utility and cut both ways. "Refusal to participate in the summer games would be too delayed a response, and would hurt American athletes far more than it would affect Soviet policies or actions." What is most interesting about this section is that Carter passed over it without making any comment.[14]

The administration did discuss the boycott idea. The NSC discussed a number of different responses before turning to the Olympics. Based on the reaction of Rolf Pauls, the West German ambassador to NATO, Undersecretary of State Warren Christopher, the number-two man in the State Department, told the President and the others that there was widespread support for a boycott in Europe. (Pauls had suggested the boycott during an emergency meeting of the organization to discuss responses to Afghanistan. He remarked that a boycott of the Berlin Games in 1936 might have altered history.) White House Press Secretary Jody Powell said the time to strike was now; if the United States waited to try and organize a wider boycott, it would fail. He wanted to target just a few countries and then others would jump on the bandwagon. White House Counsel Lloyd Cutler was also present at the meeting. He warned that the United States should boycott the Olympics only if it was combined with other strong action. He had no problem with seizing passports as a way of keeping athletes from traveling overseas. He also suggested that the United States could organize an alternate set of games to compensate the athletes. Cutler and Vance then began arguing about the need to combine an Olympic boycott with other action. Cutler warned that a boycott of just the Games would trivialize U.S. policy. During this exchange, Christopher entered into the conversation, warning against cutting off contact in this nonpolitical venue. He also observed that it was a harsh way of treating U.S. athletes who might only have one chance to compete in the Olympics. This view carried little weight in the discussion that followed. Brzezinski said going to Moscow would send a message that would "be interpreted as business as usual." Mondale jumped in and claimed that a boycott "could capture the imagination of the American people."[15]

This discussion was hardly the type of foreign policy Carter wanted to be implementing. In the third-person language of the minutes of this meeting, the president said this talk was sending "cold chills down his spine." The discussion then shifted immediately. White House Chief of Staff Hamilton Jordon tried to bolster his boss's confidence. He said the United States could organize alternative games. Brzesinski began backtracking. He said if thirty nations refused to go to Moscow, they would have accomplished something, but if it was only three it was hardly worthwhile. Cutler and Secretary of Defense Harold Brown said the Olympic boycott had to be one of several responses, but Brown added that the Olympics was the one most meaningful to the Soviets.[16]

The discussion was hardly extensive or meaningful. Many of the participants chose to remember differently, though. "The thing that stood out there," Mondale recalled, "that we really debated about because we knew it could have such serious consequences to our best young athletes, was whether we should try to spoil the Moscow Olympics." Carter's diary, though, shows that he had seen in that paper and heard in the discussion what he wanted to see about an Olympic boycott, but that he was alert to the very clear limits of this option: "We had a long discussion about the 1980 Olympics. We will make a statement saying that this issue is in doubt, but not make a decision yet about whether to participate. This one would cause me the most trouble, and also would be the most severe blow to the Soviet Union. Only if many nations act in concert would I consider it to be a good idea." Carter and his administration would in a few weeks ignore the important qualification about international cooperation.[17]

After the NSC meeting, Brzezinski announced the official administration position on the summer games as Carter had stipulated. "On the Olympics, we will take the following position which may be used publicly: 'Our European Allies have questioned whether we should proceed to participate in the Olympic games in Moscow. We will assess this question and review the position taken by other countries in reaching our decision.'"[18]

There was truth to these directions, but only a little. There was not much effort to work with other countries beyond listening to the simple suggestion of Pauls. Schmidt later stated that "Carter had not discussed the joint Western reaction he was outlining with his allies ahead of time." Ignoring sports administrators – even the IOC President – was one thing, but making no effort to consult with the leaders of allied nations was another thing altogether.[19]

When Carter spoke to the country from the Oval Office about Afghanistan on the night of January 4, the administration's policy toward the Olympics still remained unresolved. Toward the end of his broadcasted remarks, he declared, "Although the United States would prefer not to withdraw from the Olympic games scheduled in Moscow this summer, the Soviet Union must realize that this continued aggressive actions will endanger both the participation of athletes and the travel to Moscow by spectators who would normally wish to attend the Olympic games." These comments were the type that Olympic and Soviet officials would have listened to with care but could easily have dismissed as nothing more than some well-qualified positioning.[20]

These individuals might have been more concerned had they been privy to Carter's thoughts. Behind the scenes, he was moving toward a stronger and harder line with each passing day. "We discussed how far we wanted to go with economic measures against the Soviet Union," the President recorded in his diary. "I want to go the maximum degree – interrupting grain sales, high technology, canceling fishing rights, reexamining our commerce guidelines, establishing a difference in COCOM [an international committee which set rules for trade with communist nations] between the Soviet Union and China, canceling visits to the Soviet Union, restricting any sort of negotiations on culture, trade and forth."[21]

Commentators in the media warned that an Olympic boycott would restart the worst elements of the U.S.-Soviet confrontation. In a *Newsweek* cover story, entitled "The Chill of a New Cold War," reporters from the magazine quoted Carter: "This is most serious threat to world peace during my Administration." The President also added, "It's even more serious than Hungary or Czechoslovakia." With that type of rhetoric, the team of reporters writing the story noted that "rising tensions were snuffing out what was left of detente."[22]

Carter was quite pleased with the way his administration had been working. In a short, handwritten note, he gave his lieutenants clear instructions on how he wished to proceed:

1–9–80
To Key advisors on Afghanistan

1) Make no public statements on policy unless I have approved it.
2) Maintain strict confidentiality on discussions in progress.

So far we've done well. We must not confuse the American people or other nations.

Jimmy Carter[23]

One of the contributing factors to this crisis was a breakdown in diplomatic communication between the two superpowers. Both nations bore responsibility for this problem. As Brezhnev's health collapsed, there was no central authority in the Soviet Politburo. Personal rivalries and petty bickering drove the decision-making process just as much as the merits of different policy options. No Soviet consulted with Dobrynin about the invasion beforehand,

and his American counterpart, Ambassador Thomas J. Watson, was having problems of his own. Officials in the NSC were unhappy about the quality of his administrative work in the embassy and believed he was failing to explain with appropriate force and clarity American feelings about Afghanistan. A former chief executive officer of the International Business Machines Corporation – better known as IBM – Watson was a political appointee and, according to Canadian Ambassador Robert A. D. Ford, admitted that he was intimidated and lost in this new setting of international diplomacy.[24]

Such an admission seems probable, but complaints about his job performance are a bit of a dodge. Watson had only just started in Moscow. "I hadn't even been on the job a month when we began getting reports of Red Army units building up along the border with Afghanistan. Probably the U.S. should have paid more attention, but the White House and State Department were preoccupied with the hostage crisis in Iran." Even after Dobrynin returned to the United States, the communication problems remained. The Soviet Ambassador and Vance held a series of meetings in February. Vance's failure to take notes during these meetings frustrated others in the national security bureaucracy.[25] It is important to keep these communication problems in perspective. They certainly enflamed differences in foreign policy objectives and interests, but communication was neither the cause nor the cure to the crisis.

Carter wanted more than just a boycott; he wanted to hurt the Soviets. The State Department had called Watson back to Washington for consultations. "Carter was determined to make the Soviets pay for their aggression, but in fact there was very little we could do," the ambassador observed. Carter had a series of meetings on January 4 and decided to initiate a grain embargo against the Soviet Union. Mondale argued against this move; it would be unpopular in the farm states, but Carter had made his decision. Watson was stunned at what he saw in these meetings. "I didn't know the president very well, and I was a little surprised at how vehemently he reacted." Even Brzezinski, the ultimate hawk, thought the President was overreacting. Carter clearly felt burned. His waffling, indecisive image had cost him domestically, and now it had been for naught. He needed to react strongly: "I was determined to make them pay for their unwarranted aggression without yielding to political pressures here at home."[26]

Ambassador Watson knew better than others what was coming as a result of the anti-Soviet moves Carter was making. "This meant taking apart practically all the cooperative arrangments we had with the Russians under détente."[27]

Most of the actions Carter had approved amounted to nothing more than pinpricks, but the Soviets were vulnerable to economic measures. Mikahail Gorbachev was a new Candidate Member of the Politburo, having just joined that body in 1979. The first serious topic he had to address was the "alarming grain shortage" after Carter embargoed further shipments. "What I said disturbed everyone present."[28]

The Carter administration was keeping its options open on the Olympic question, but the news media intervened and became the decisive factor in tipping the scales in favor of a boycott. On January 10, Robert G. Kaiser, the former Moscow correspondent for *The Washington Post*, wrote in an editorial column for his paper, "There should be no underestimating the significance the Soviets themselves put on their selection. They have been treating this Olympiad as one of the great events of their modern history." He believed that the summer games gave Western nations some leverage over the Soviet Union that they normally never enjoyed. "The idea that an Olympiad could collapse because of international disapproval of actions by the Soviet government would certainly sink in." As a result, "an effective boycott of the Games this summer would be a tremendous blow to Soviet prestige; but perhaps more significant, the collapse of this Olympiad would send a genuine shock through Soviet society." Kaiser even argued that "these Olympics could cause the first serious challenge to the legitimacy of Soviet power in many years.[29]

This column had an enormous impact on the Carter administration because they saw in it something they wanted to see. "Oddly enough," Cutler recalled, "the first recommendations that we should not go to Moscow came from the Americans reporters who had spent time in the Soviet Union." Brzezinski liked Kaiser's arguments and made sure that Carter saw the column.[30]

A number of important sports columnists addressed the boycott issue as well. Shirley Povich of *The Washington Post* and Red Smith of *The New York Times* were journalists at work in this field in 1980, and instead of making calls for keeping the Olympics out of politics, which would have serviced their professional interests in having something significant to write about, they supported the boycott idea. "To have the United States team there and competing would be a dishonor to America," Povich declared. "The games aren't as important as self-perpetuating Olympic officials think," he added. "The Games have bred more ill will than good will. Their image of friendly strife is a hoax and the amateurism of the athletes, particularly in the Soviet bloc, a complete sham." Smith wrote seven columns that focused either entirely or in part on the boycott, taking a strong and consistent position in favor. "It is unthinkable that in existing circumstances we could go play games with Ivan in Ivan's yard and participate in a great lawn party showing off Russian splendors to the world." He acknowledged that many American athletes would have their dreams shattered and see years of practice go for naught, which would be particularly painful for those in sports that had limited outlets, but he explained that those losses would be minimal compared to the anguish of the Afghanis. Smith, however, often refused to deal with the substance of people's positions who disagreed with him. His language was that of a rabid

Cold War warrior. Although the *Times* would run twenty-nine editorials and columns on the boycott with only three in opposition in its opinion section, editors at the paper found his language to be extreme and his facts suspect and refused to print his submission. The column did, however, go out over *The New York Times* news service and quickly led to exaggerated stories that Smith's own paper had censored him. His writings had influence. Cutler later told Smith's son, "Your father's column gave the Olympic boycott legitimacy and momentum."[31]

Admiral Stansfield Turner, the Director of Central Intelligence Agency (CIA), disagreed with the direction of this thinking. He forwarded to the White House a CIA study that found that an action against the Olympics would have limited impact on the Soviet Union. He also argued that such an effort could backfire on the United States. "The Soviets would also be able to play the role of an aggrieved party before a partially sympathetic international audience and to utilize international disagreements over the boycott to exacerbate tensions between the U.S. and non-boycotting (or reluctantly boycotting) states, probably including some close U.S. allies." He foresaw little economic damage to the Soviet Union from such an action.[32]

Brzezinski told Carter that the Admiral was wrong, because the *Post* said so. "As Robert Kaiser point out in Thursday's Washington Post (see attached article), taking away the Olympics would unquestionably be an action which would hurt the Soviet leaders." He also added another argument. "Moreover, as Kaiser points out, the Soviets would almost certainly regard the holding of a successful Olympiad as convincing evidence that the decision to invade Afghanistan had not cost them a real price in their relations with the West."[33]

The issue came to a head in mid-January. There were three key meetings in which the administration decided to initiate an effort to destroy the international Olympic movement rather than a boycott of the Moscow games. On January 11, at the regular Tuesday breakfast meetings Carter had on foreign policy, Vice President Walter Mondale pushed the idea. A boycott was popular with the public and it would hurt the Soviets. Mondale had suggested the idea in public the day before, but Vance was skeptical and their conversation became, in Brzezinski's words, "heated."[34]

Despite this exchange, the job of raising a test balloon fell to the Secretary of State. A day later, he suggested to *The New York Times* that it might be best if the games were held someplace other than Moscow. In Ireland, Lord Killanin quickly poked holes in this balloon. "It is virtually physically impossible to move them at this stage." The logistics of hosting the Olympics required years of planning. In Canada, Jim Worrall, a Canadian member of the IOC, remarked, "I don't think Montreal or any other city is in a position to hold the Games on such short notice." In London, Ian Woolridge, a sports columnist for the *Daily Mail*, predicted the boycott would fail. "The reason is that

Mr Carter's and Mrs Thatcher's advisers are unaware of the quaint idealism on which the Olympics were revived at the turn of the century."[35]

Being a democracy, public opinion in the U.S. was an important consideration in the boycott effort. Sport was a major recreational activity in American society. The United States was a founding nation in the revival of the international Olympic movement. Would American sports fans support the boycott, or would they turn their ire against a President who was trying to destroy the premier international sporting event? There are several ways of measuring public sentiment, and most indicated that in January 1980, there was broad support among the American people for a boycott. The House of Representatives of the State of Washington passed a resolution requesting that the IOC "relocate the XXII Summer Olympiad to a country whose concept of civilized conduct more closely reflects the philosophy of the Olympics than does the Soviet Union."[36]

Several newspapers conducted regional polls of their readers and found large majorities in favor of the boycott. *The Washington Star* conducted an unscientific survey of its readership. The results were lopsided. In response to the question, "Should the U.S. boycott the Moscow Olympics?" – 85.8 of the respondents said yes and 14.2 said no. Roughly half of the readers wanted to prohibit the Soviets from participating in the Lake Placid Winter Olympics, with 51.6 percent saying yes, while the other 48.4 percent said no. In New Hampshire, the Manchester *Union Leader* conducted a similar survey and found 91.1 percent in favor of keeping the U.S. team out of Moscow. The *Boston Herald American* found 85.5 percent of its readers in favor of a boycott. The *San Francisco Chronicle* conducted a scientific poll that produced similar results. A total of 75 percent favored a boycott. The *Chicago Tribune* found 63 percent Chicagoland residents in favor of a boycott.[37]

Three major national polls were conducted in mid-January and each found significant majorities in favor of the boycott, if not as overwhelming as the unscientific regional newspaper surveys. An ABC-Louis Harris reported that 55 percent of the American people supported a boycott, with another 39 percent in opposition, and the remaining 6 percent being uncertain. A Gallup Poll conducted a few days later produced similar results: 56 percent in support, 34 opposed, and 10 undecided. An National Broadcasting Company (NBC) poll that started its survey the day the Gallup poll ended suggested that the division was tighter, with proponents of the boycott at 49 percent, those opposing at 41 percent, and the undecided at 10 percent.[38]

Support in the media for a boycott was overwhelming from both national outlets and regional publications. Both *Time* and *The New York Times* voiced their approval, doing a total reversal from their editorial policies in 1976 about mixing of sports and politics from 1976, when the Trudeau Cabinet blocked the participation of Taiwan in Montreal. Many believed that the symbolism of the boycott was important. An editorial in the *Akron Beacon*

Journal declared: "Such a boycott would impose considerable moral and economic pressure on the Soviet Union." In New York, the *Daily News* believed something more important was at stake: "It is our belief that other nations will boycott the Olympics, too, if the U.S. takes the lead. But we should not hesitate to act whatever others do. A man or a nation should stand up for a great principle, even if it means standing alone."[39]

Others believed that this action would truly hurt the Soviet Union. The editorial board of *The Washington Star* argued: "A U.S. boycott of the Moscow Olympics would constitute both a symbolic retort and substantial punishment to Soviet imperialism." Mary McGrory, the Pulitzer Prize winner who wrote a column for the paper, declared: "It's hard to think of much, short of a nuclear strike, that would inflict more pain." In Denver, the editors of the *Rocky Mountain News* offered a more sound rationale for their position: "A boycott of the games by the decent countries of the world won't get the Soviet army out of Afghanistan," they observed, but it would have an impact economically and psychologically. "We must not reward aggression nor follow the rape of another of Russia's neighbors with fun and games as usual."[40]

If it did not hurt them, at least it would send a message. An editorial in *The Philadelphia Inquirer* declared: "As long as we continue to do business as usual, it gives the impression the United States does not care. In fact, the United States cares a great deal. Boycotting the Olympics would send that message to Moscow in no uncertain terms."[41]

In other papers, the idea that the Olympics were a fraud was a popular theme. The editors of the *Arkansas Democrat* argued that "all this talk about keeping politics out is a farce." Others believed that it was time to bring the games to an end. Frederick Klein, the sports columnist for *The Wall Street Journal*, argued the Olympics "have been turned into an orgy of nationalism by cheating by both contestants and officials and by a universal flouting of their rules of eligibility. It's a spectacle we well can do without."[42]

A good deal of this analysis made some questionable assumptions about the importance of world public opinion and that the Soviet peoples saw the American people in much the same way that Americans saw themselves. One of the most realistic assessments in favor of the boycott came from conservative columnist George Will. He knew it would do little to reverse the invasion of Afghanistan, but it would kill the foolish idea of détente. "Boycotting the Olympics would help put an end to the dangerous delusion that, regarding the Soviet Union, the period of maximum danger has passed," he argued. "A boycott would be a fireball in the night, arousing Americans from the slumbers of détente."[43]

The Olympians were the only major group that opposed to this idea. "Any boycott isn't going to change the Soviets' mind and isn't going to get troops out of Afghanistan," Julian Roosevelt, an American member of the IOC remarked. "I'm as patriotic as the next guy, but the patriotic thing to do is for us to send a team over there and whip their ass." Al Oerter, the four-time gold medalist in the discus, who was trying to make a comeback at age 42, agreed: "The only way to compete against Moscow is to stuff it down their throats in their own backyard." Roy Kissin, a marathoner, was even more outspoken: "Frankly, I'm sick and tired of being someone's political pawn," he snapped. "The people suggesting a U.S. boycott are taking a pretty self-righteous position. Most of them have absolutely noting to lose. What do they care if we go to Moscow or not?" Reporters were literally ringing the phone off the hook at the home of Tracy Caulkins, a leading contender for a number of gold medals in swimming events. Her mother released a statement on behalf of her 17-year-old daughter: "I do not feel it will have a serious impact on the Russians if the United States is the only country to boycott the Games, and the athletes would suffer." The younger Caulkins added: "I cannot believe this is happening. But I will continue my training and hope the problem can be resolved, so the Games can be held."[44]

Former Olympians rallied to the cause. In Cleveland, Harrison Dillard, an Olympic gold medalist at the 1948 and 1952 Olympics, argued in an editorial in the *Cleveland Press*: "I cannot see how a boycott of the games by the American team can contribute in any possible way toward a withdrawal of Russian troops from Afghanistan." All that would happen is that a number of American athletes would have their dreams shattered. It would do nothing to stop the invasion. "If a boycott would help to get the Soviets out of Afghanistan, I would agree with that action."[45]

Robert Kane, President of the U.S. Olympic Committee, was a major figure that the media turned to as a source. Appearing on NBC's *Today* show, he took an equivocal position. He said if "there's a problem with the site, it ought to be focused on that. A boycott is just not the right way to do it. It's disloyal to the organization we belong to – the International Olympic Committee." This argument was weak, had no chance of winning any public support, and almost guaranteed that administration would win on this issue.[46]

Two major themes emerged in opposition to a boycott in various media outlets. The first was that this effort would be ineffective and would have no impact on the Soviet Union. The editors of *The Boston Globe* declared: "There are better ways to protest Soviet aggression than by staying away from an international sports competition." Their colleagues at the *Dallas Times-Herald* agreed, observing that this action "would hardly be effective as an act of national reprisal." The position of the *Milwaukee Sentinel* was a little more nationalistic, but got at the fact that a boycott cuts both ways: "Let's not skip a chance to go to Moscow and whip their athletes." *The Atlanta Journal*, which had a fairly conservative editorial staff, declared: "We would recommend against the use of the Olympics as an expression of political anger over the Soviets' moves in Afghanistan. Any such mass protest would have little impact on Soviet foreign policy, but it would almost certainly push the games over the brink and ruin them forever."[47]

The other theme was the nature of the sacrifices that individual athletes had made to prepare for the games, and that these efforts would be for nothing. "I've only given up seven years of my life and my whole future," noted Flora Hyman, a member of the U.S. Women's Volleyball Team, which was a leading contender for a gold medal. "If there are no Olympics, what have I done with my life?" She and her teammates trained and lived in Colorado Springs, Colorado, under austere conditions, receiving room and board and $120 a week for incidental expenses. "I gave up getting married," Rita Crockett, another member of the team explained. "My boyfriend and I were discussing getting married. Now, we just discuss getting to be friends again. My phone bill to him is $150 a week, but I only get to see him four times a year."[48]

The National Broadcasting Company – or NBC as it is more commonly known – which had the rights to televise the Moscow Games, started airing stories that focused on the life of the average athlete in January. These stories were a strong theme throughout the network's coverage of the boycott debate. These stories were antiboycott in their very nature and often had no counterbalancing position from the administration. Their peers in the industry noticed. "I'm not accusing them of anything at all," Roone Arledge, President of both ABC Sports and News, said. "But if we had ever done that I would never live it down. Being as involved as they are in the Olympics, I should think they would be very, very careful."[49]

The idea of a boycott also had a lot of support overseas. In the United Kingdom, Prime Minister Margaret Thatcher was out in front of Carter on the issue. She had already discussed the issue with Schmidt on January 15. On January 17, during Prime Minister Question Time, she declared, "We favour trying to move the venue from Moscow to elsewhere, if it is possible to do so. That cannot be done alone, and we believe that we should try to do it by taking concerted action with our allies in making an approach to the International Olympic Committee, in whose lap the decision lies." After leaving office, she explained, "Like President Carter, I was sure that the most effective thing we could do would be to prevent their using the forthcoming Moscow Olympics for propaganda purposes."[50]

There was strong support for this proposal among the British. An editorial in The Economist stated, "The removal of the Olympics from Moscow would be a startling sign to the average man hanging on to an Omsk omnibus that the rest of the world detests the invasion of Afghanistan by the insecure autocrats who are his rulers. It would black out the expensive worldwide television spectacular now being designed (more nationalistically than the 1936 Nazi Olympics) to show him that those autocrats enjoy international legitimacy and acclaim."[51]

Like Carter, Thatcher wanted to avoid the onus of destroying the Olympics. As she explained to Sir Denis Follows, Chairman of the British Olympic

Association, "In an ideal world, I would share entirely the philosophy of the Olympic movement that sport should be divorced from politics. Sadly, however, this is no longer a realistic view." She then got to the heart of the matter, "For the Soviet Union the Olympic Games are a major political event which will be used to boost Soviet prestige in the world. It would be wrong for those people and countries which deplore aggression to co-operate in giving the Soviet Union the success it is seeking." Unlike the American president, she had no interest in issuing an ultimatum or deadline. She instead wanted to take action right then and there. "We therefore ask that the British Olympic Association should approach the International Olympic Committee urgently and propose that the Summer Games be moved from the Soviet Union." She said that Her Majesty's Government would be willing to help pay for the coast of relocating the Olympics. This offer was one that the Carter administration never made.[52]

The boycott idea also played well in Australia. On January 9, the Cabinet had taken a stand against the Olympics. Ten days later, Prime Minister Malcolm Fraser announced that he would be visiting the United States and would push Carter to take some type of action against the Moscow Olympics.[53]

Syd Grange, president of the Australian Olympic Federation (AOF), was called from a meeting of the municipal council meeting of Manly, on which he sat as an alderman, to take a phone call. Fraser was on the other line and told Grange he wanted the AOF to boycott Moscow. Grange recalled that the Prime Minister was friendly and "the way he spoke he just felt I could do this without much trouble." Grange said the whole Australian Olympic Federation would have to make that decision, but that he would bring the issue before the organization.[54]

The situation in West Germany was far more complex. The editors of the *Rheinische Post* observed after the IOC selected the Soviets to host: "Olympic Games in Moscow – a big opportunity, but also a big risk." Their colleagues at the *Frankfurter Allgemeine Zeitung* were also skeptical. The Soviets, they observed, have promised to fulfill all requirements for freedom of information for the guests, to organize the Games strictly following the Olympic rules, and to prevent any political discrimination. These are big words. The entire world will watch to see if actions will follow." As the Soviets prepared for the Olympics, they found that they lacked technical expertise and turned to foreign firms for help. The West Germans led the way, signing contracts worth 250 million Deutschmarks. In the late 1970s, after human rights and conservative political activists urged that some action be taken against the Moscow Olympics, Willi Weyer, president of the *Deutscher Sportsbund**, said, "The fight for human rights is fought on a different battlefield. Sports does not fit into the role of Attack Unit for political goals."[55]

---

* German Sports Federation.

The main West German concern at the time was maintaining good relations with the Soviet Union. Many people worried, not about the invasion of Afghanistan or boycotting the Summer Games, but that the Soviets might require that athletes from Berlin be distinguished from the other members of the West German team. After Afghanistan, there was a great fear that this action might be a precursor to another world war. (The Germans were not alone in thinking that their decisions and theirs alone would determine the fate of world peace. This view was expressed in France, Britain, the United States, and Australia.) The result was even less desire to use the Olympics politically. "Cooperation, not confrontation. Collaboration not boycott. Understanding not separation," Weyer stated.[56]

Politicians in the Bundestag agreed. Marie Schlei of the *Sozialdemokratische Partei Deutschlands*[†] said, "It would not be good for the Western side to jeopardize our conflict resolution politics, arms control negotiations, and bilateral relationships in reaction to Soviet actions. The suggestion to boycott the Olympic Games will not help resolve this issue. Those are two separate areas. International conflicts will not be solved by this." The Christian Democrat opposition took the same position. Hans-Joachim Jentsch of the *Christlich Demokratische Union Deutschlands*[‡] remarked: "NATO officials are taking the wrong approach when they play with the thought to boycott the Olympic Summer Games in Moscow in reaction to USSR's invasion of Afghanistan. Realistic politics that characterize the Soviets correctly, are the commandments of the hour. Let's not demand Sports Organizations to straighten out what politicians messed up by applying the wrong politics. Sports cannot do that." A leading member of the *Freie Demokratische Partei*[**], Juergen Moellemann added that "during times of tension, Sports must build bridges, not destroy them."[57]

With this near-universal support for the Olympics, the position of Chancellor Helmut Schmidt, a Social Democrat, on the boycott should have been easy. Things started to change in January, though, as U.S. officials talked about the Olympics. Heinrich Lummer, head of the Christian Democrats, decided to support the boycott: "The defenders of human rights must ask themselves the question what powers they possess to help justice prevail. They don't have a lot of choices. A big one is the plea to the world's conscience, the mobilization of the world's public. The aggressor and violator of the human rights must be isolated intellectually and politically. Under this aspect, a boycott of the Olympic Games cannot simply be denied by pointing at the neutrality of sports. A unified boycott would seriously impact the Soviet Union, both internally as well as in foreign affairs. It could not suggest

---

[†] Social Democratic Party of Germany.
[‡] Christian Democratic Union of Germany.
[**] Free Democratic Party.

to its own people that the invasion of Afghanistan was legitimate. A boycott as the world's response could not be concealed on the inside. It would demonstrate the political isolation of the aggressor." Two hundred and fifty former prisoners of East Germany sent Schmidt a telegram supporting some action against the Olympics. Political dissident Niko Huebner and writer Siegmar Faust argued that it was a "perversion of the Olympic idea to host the Games in a country that wages war."[58] Attitudes were moving in Carter's direction.

Against this backdrop of international support, Carter met with a number of his domestic political advisors on the morning of January 16. This meeting touched on number of topics including the Olympics. This was the second key meeting in which the administration moved toward boycott. Since it was a gathering to discuss domestic affairs, neither Vance nor Brzezinski was present. According to both the notes that White House Staff Director Alonzo McDonald took and the formal memo he wrote documenting the decision, Carter tasked Lloyd Cutler with the job of "pulling together the Government's position on the Olympics." Cutler had two days to produce a memo recommending the policies and strategies the United States should follow. Cutler was to see what restrictions the Olympic charter had that were relevant. The only other stipulation that Carter gave Cutler was that the United States would not participate if the Soviets were in Afghanistan, and that a decision needed to be made by mid-February.[59]

This meeting signaled the beginning of Cutler's inept and amateurish effort to impose Carter's will on the international Olympic movement, and even at this early date reflected some of the shortcomings of the approach that would distinguish this undertaking. Cutler was a rising star within the Carter administration and was one of the few "Washington insiders" with direct access to the President. A 62-year-old lawyer, he had been an influential figure in Democratic circles and had ended up on the infamous enemies list that the Nixon Administration compiled. He joined the Carter administration in 1979 as White House Counsel and helped Carter find a way out of the Soviet brigade fiasco. What made Cutler influential was not his courtly style or measured speech, but his willingness to do exactly as the President wished. When he spoke, people knew he was speaking for Carter. The President made this point bluntly in a handwritten note he sent to Powell the next day:

1–17–80

Jody

Tell State & others (& you) to get out of the Olympics business. Let Lloyd & me handle it.

JC

Throughout the Olympic boycott, Cutler doggedly did as the President instructed and often invoked these desires as reasons enough to pursue various options even when these actions blurred the focus of U.S. strategy and policy. At the same time, he also showed a marked unwillingness to disagree with Carter, give him contrary advice, or report bad news. In giving Cutler his instructions, Carter had essentially decided to take actions against the summer Olympics and had even established a rough timeframe for action. As far as Cutler was concerned, his job was policy implementation rather than formulation.[60] Cutler's deputy, Joe Onek, did much of the day-to-day work on the boycott.[61]

A day after his appointment, Cutler provided the President with a four-page memo on the Olympics, providing information on the two options Carter wanted to consider: relocating the games and/or a boycott. This document was as close as he came to giving Carter advice the President did not want to hear. "You do not have any legal authority to prevent American athletes or spectators from attending the Olympic Games in Moscow, unless you invoke the International Economic Emergency Controls Act." To invoke that legislation, the President had to declare a national emergency. Cutler carefully explained the organizational structure of the international Olympic movement and the relevant powers the IOC had under its charter, the procedural rules for a vote of the committee, and requirements about when and where the winter and summer games were to be held. He made reference to Red Smith's columns but noted they were in error when it came to providing the IOC with a reason for moving the summer games. The Soviet Union was actually in full accord with the letter of the Olympic charter. "There is no evidence yet that the Soviets intend to violate these rules." He then said the President had three options: take no action on a boycott; announce that he would ask the U.S. Olympic Committee to boycott unless the games were moved but take no additional effort; or pursue the second option and make an additional effort like organizing a counter-Olympics, expanding the boycott to include other nations, and trying to get the IOC to relocate the athletic festival. Knowing his audience, Cutler never bothered to discuss the pluses and minuses of taking no boycott action. "An immediate announcement that you request the USOC not to send the U.S. team to Moscow unless the Soviets promptly withdraw their forces from Afghanistan would make a major impression on Soviet leaders and would, on balance, be popular at home. Without such an announcement, there is no chance that the USOC will itself take such an initiative or ask the IOC to change the site." Cutler warned, though, that moving the games from Moscow or a boycott would have negative repercussions and could "even lead to the end of the modern-day Olympics." He believed that any effort to relocate the summer games would fail. "Nevertheless, the effort should probably be made in order to give the IOC every chance to preserve the Olympics."[62]

The next day, at the weekly foreign policy breakfast, Carter finally made the decision to initiate action against the Olympics. The conversation focused on Afghanistan until Vance raised the issue of the Moscow games. The President was perplexed and told his lieutenants: "It's the toughest question of all for me." He was fully aware that he was about to set in motion events that would destroy the Olympic movement. "I don't want the onus for the failure of the Olympics to fall exclusively on the United States." He had a good reason for wanting to avoid such responsibility. He told the group, "It must be seen as a legitimate worldwide political reaction to what the Russians are doing in Afghanistan." Then, with what Jordon called a sly grin, he said, "After the grain embargo, the farmers raised hell, but after I announce our Olympics boycott, we'll face the wrath of an even more power force – Howard Cosell, telling the sports fans that Jimmy Carter killed the Olympics." The announcement of the boycott itself would take place on January 20 when the President appeared on the news program *Meet the Press*.[63]

Carter had referred to sportscaster Howard Cossell, but he had little reason to worry about him or sports fans. There was strong sentiment in the United States to bring the Olympics to an end. *Business Week* and the *San Francisco Chronicle* ran editorials calling for such action. On the pages of *Newsweek*, columnist Pete Axthelm argued, "The Olympics have simply grown too big, too political, too artificial. Avery Brundage was wrong. The Games need not go on." In addition, Cosell himself spoke on the air in support of the boycott. "I harbored no illusions about the sanctity of Olympics," he wrote years later. "It seemed absolutely wrong to me to let them use our athletes and our technological capabilities to broadcast their perverse propaganda to every corner of the globe – and I'll always admire President Carter for having the guts to spoil their party."[64]

What Cosell was saying was that the boycott played well domestically. As far as the American people were concerned, the Soviets were evil and they were good. There could be no compromise with evil doing and that certainly was a good description of the Soviet move into Afghanistan. Cosell was right, domestic factors rather than an assessment of international affairs led to the boycott. Implementing this policy, though, turned out to be much more difficult for the Carter administration than anyone in the White House expected, and for that they had only themselves to blame.

CHAPTER 6

Easy Victories

WITH THE DECISION MADE, THE CARTER ADMINISTRATION INITIATED their efforts to impose its political will on the international Olympic movement. Early endeavors were largely successful. These victories came on the domestic front and made it clear that regardless of the tool used to measure public sentiment, Carter was on solid ground. The American people supported a boycott against Moscow.

The President started the process himself. He took the boycott message to the American people on January 20, appearing on the Sunday morning television talk show *Meet the Press*. After the appropriate introductions, moderator Bill Monroe of NBC News had the first question and asked if the United States would boycott the Olympics. "Neither I nor the American people would support the sending of an American team to Moscow with Soviet invasion troops in Afghanistan," Carter replied. "I have sent a message today to the United States Olympic Committee spelling out my own position, that unless the Soviets withdraw their troops within a month from Afghanistan that the Olympic games be moved from Moscow to an alternative site, or multiple sites, or postponed or cancelled."[1]

That deadline of one month was controversial at the time and ever since. Many domestic critics saw it is as an example of Carter's generally inept handling of foreign policy; that in setting a date he robbed himself of flexibility, committing himself to action against the Soviet Union sooner than circumstances demanded. An editorial in *Sports Illustrated* argued that waiting longer "would have been ideal for making the Soviets squirm." Delay also would have made it possible for Carter to line up support from other nations and, more importantly, their national Olympic committees. Otherwise there was the real danger that the boycott could end making the U.S. look ineffectual. William Loeb, editor of the Manchester *Union Leader*, called the deadline "ridiculous," saying the time to act was now. The deadline, though, served a purpose. It was an effort to show the moral stand of the administration and take the onus off the United States and Carter for ruining or even destroying the Olympic games to which many people, foreign and domestic, had considerable attachment and considered a positive force for peace, and put it on the Soviet Union. Of course, once he had announced the deadline personally, Carter's own credibility was at stake. There then is some truth to Gromyko's claim that "the Carter administration set out to undermine the process of détente in Europe."[2]

The forum of the Sunday morning talk shows often allows guests to elaborate on issues and Carter, took full advantage of this platform. He continued, saying that he thought the Olympics should have a regular location. "In my opinion, the most appropriate permanent site for the summer games would be Greece." He also thought the Winter Games deserved a fixed home, although he offered no suggestions. He also expressed an expectation that the boycott would be a success since 104 nations had condemned the invasion in a United Nations vote. These statements also made it easier for his administration to challenge the International Olympic Committee's stewardship over the international Olympic movement should it fail to heed the wisdom of his plan.[3]

This question initiated a follow-up from Monroe. What if no one joined in the boycott? Carter's response was forthright: "Regardless of what other nations might do, I would not favor the sending of an American Olympic team to Moscow while the Soviet invasion troops are in Afghanistan."[4]

Monroe then turned over the questioning to Carl T. Rowan of the *Chicago Sun-Times*. He asked the President if the United States was on the verge of war. "As I said earlier, Mr. Rowan, this in my opinion is the most serious threat to world peace since the Second World War. It is an unprecedented act on the part of the Soviet Union." More questions followed, concentrating primarily on foreign policy and economic issues. Carter responded in direct and powerful fashion to those on world affairs. On the economic issues, he was evasive, dodging the central thrust of various inquiries.[5]

Immediately after *Meet the Press* ended, Cutler and Powell held a press briefing at the White House. Their intention was to shape and influence the coverage of the President's appearance. Cutler and Powell were both speaking under normal rules of no direct quotation or attribution. Already showing a profound ignorance of the complex logistical, transportation, and housing issues involved in hosting an Olympic festival, Culter said either Montreal or Los Angeles could host an alternative set of games. If it was held in Canada, he added, athletes could be housed in colleges in southern Canada and in northern New England. In another comment indicating that he saw the boycott as a simple exercise in political diplomacy rather than a confrontation with a nonstate entity, he said he expected wide support in NATO.[6]

Being inquisitive is a good professional trait for reporters, and Cutler's audience took advantage of his presence to ask him a number of substantial questions about the boycott. These inquiries were understandable; Powell had introduced him as the key administration official on the boycott. Cutler was a powerful Washington, D.C. lawyer – a "mover and shaker" or a "rainmaker," to use popular terms to describe his legal activity – but he had not been in the courtroom for years and was less than savvy when it came to interacting with the media. The result was that he answered a number of questions poorly. When asked if the administration thought the boycott would force the Soviets out of Afghanistan, he replied: "We don't." Realizing his mistake, he quickly added, "We will see just how much importance they attach to the games." Another reporter immediately asked another question about what powers the U.S. government had to keep American athletes from going to Moscow. Cutler answered, mentioning passports and currency exchanges. "There are various ways in which, I feel sure the U.S. Government, if necessary, and if it decided to do so, could prevent U.S. athletes from participating in the games."[7]

"Wait a minute, wait a minute," Powell said, jumping in. He realized that Cutler was sending out the wrong message, and was weakening the argument that Carter and the United States were taking a moral position. "Let's underline what was said before, since several people apparently didn't listen to the earlier answer either. We do not anticipate that that would be necessary. That is a bridge that we have not crossed, and we do not think it will be necessary to cross."[8]

Cutler realized he had blundered. When asked again what the administration would do if the U.S. Olympic Committee decided to send a team to Moscow anyway, he replied. "We expect the force of public opinion and reasoning that is set forth in this is sufficient." Cutler, ironically enough, had ignored talking points he had prepared for Carter on the very topic of the legal power that White House could employ to enforce a boycott. Still, the damage was done, and his comments ended up in the lead story on the *NBC Nightly News.*[9]

Powell also provided the rationale for the boycott. At another gathering of White House reporters. he read from the English translation of a Soviet document entitled *Handbook for Party Activists.* The document asserts that the USSR received the honor of hosting the Olympic games as a recognition of its peaceful foreign policy. The importance of this minor document was exaggerated over the course of the next few months. Carter read the document three weeks later and instructed Powell to "read & promulgate."[10]

Despite this mistake, the reaction to the President's announcement was strong and positive. In Minnesota, the editors of *St. Paul Pioneer Press* hoped that others would join the boycott: "President Carter deserves international support in his efforts to move the Olympic Games to a place other than Moscow." The editorial board of the *Akron Beacon Journal* believed, "Moving the Olympic games or boycotting them in Moscow is one of the most powerful, peaceful weapons we have to humiliate Russian leaders and to hurt them economically." In Virginia, the editorial board of the *Richmond Times-Dispatch* called for an even tougher response: "Encouraging our athletes and our Olympic fans to shun Moscow is only a small part, a very small part, of the kind of foreign policy reorientation that will be needed to halt the Soviet march."[11]

There were, though, several newspaper editorial boards that opposed the boycott. The general theme running through the positions of these newspapers was that a boycott would be ineffective. "Obviously such a threat lacks the leverage to pry a single Soviet soldier out of Kabul, and both Carter and the Soviet leaders know that," the editors of *Newsday* argued. Those at the *Dallas Times Herald* worried that the United States would be standing alone. "The current circumstances do not suggest that anything would be gained by a U.S. boycott of the Olympics. Without the support of every other nation in the Olympic movement, American withdrawal doesn't even make for good symbolism." In California, the editorial board of the *Oakland Tribune* worried that something far more valuable was in danger, "The Olympics should not be boycotted even if they are held in Moscow. The games are perhaps the only example of international cooperation whose origins can be traced back to antiquity. They surely should not be allowed to collapse because of a single nation's wrongdoings."[12]

Such a concern was on the mind of Lord Killanin and other Olympians. The same day Carter was announcing his boycott policy, an interview Killanin did appeared in the German newspaper *Bild am Sonntag*. "I am very concerned about the situation," he told Joerg Wigand, the reporter interviewing him. "At the moment we are definitely experiencing the most difficult and hazardous phase of the entire Olympic movement." When Wigand asked if it might be possible to move the games, Killanin replied, "There is no alternative besides Moscow any more. Montreal or Munich are absolutely out of the question as alternatives. It's Moscow or nothing."[13]

Despite this strong stand, there were many in the Olympic movement that questioned Killanin's leadership. Richard W. Pound, President of the Canadian Olympic Committee and a member of the IOC, was one of them. In his memoirs, Pound called the Irishman "bland" and "softer" than other IOC presidents and damned him with faint praise: "Although he had not been a powerful president and was well over his head in many of the complicated problems that arose on his watch, Killanin was a thoroughly nice man and excellent company."[14]

Just before Carter's announcement, Pound warned the Irish baron that he needed to do something to save the Americans from themselves. In his opinion, Killanin had to deflect the idea of a boycott: "It seems to me that without some firm advice from you, the situation may get out of hand even before the IOC session at Lake Placid." He foresaw a number of scenarios that might develop and none of them were particularly good. Some of them came close to developing as he predicted. Because of the presidential election in the United States, he believed the United States was about to initiate policies that could destroy the Olympic movement. If that were the case it would cause enormous resentment across the globe that would be directed towards the Americans. Another real possibility was that a boycott would produce a situation where the United States would have to use an enormous amount of political muscle to convince others to take part in the boycott. If that happened, the Soviet Union would achieve a significant propaganda victory for either thwarting the U.S. effort to destroy the Olympics or by showing that the United States had refused to honor the peaceful intentions of the movement.[15]

American Olympians were less than enthusiastic about the boycott. Although the Los Angeles County Board of Supervisors adopted a resolution on January 22 calling on Lord Killanin to hold an emergency session of the IOC to designate an alternative site for the summer games, this represented a minority view among those Americans closely involved with the Olympic movement. "My first impression was that our country must be very weak if this was our best retaliatory shot," Peter Ueberroth, Chairman of the Los Angeles Olympic Organizing Committee, reflected on hearing the news. Most of those preparing for the Moscow Olympics could do nothing more than hope. "All I can do is keep on training, keep my fingers crossed, and pray for the best," Bob Lewis, a steeplechaser, told the *Detroit Free Press* when asked for his reaction to Carter's announcement.[16]

While all indications were that Carter believed the argument he was making, others in his administration were more realistic. Cutler asked Attorney General Benjamin Civiletti to examine the legal options open to the government. The day after Carter appeared on *Meet the Press*, Civiletti delivered his assessment. "The presidential announcement of an American boycott of the Olympics will depend upon the United States Olympic Committee's compliance for its success unless additional steps are taken," he declared in his first sentence. "Of course, voluntary compliance may well be sufficient, but if you determine that you want your plan to have a compulsory effect, some legal mechanism beyond a simple Executive Order will be necessary." In that case, it would be necessary to turn to Congress to pass some legislation. "My recommendation is that you keep this congressional option in reserve, for use if you decide that a voluntary program will not work." Legislative possibilities included asking Congress to amend the amateur sports act to prohibit participation in the Moscow Olympics, a statute that prohibited any American sports organization from participating in the Moscow games, or a bill allowing the President to revoke passports of athletes. The attorneys that prepared the study were of the opinion, though, that the best option was the voluntary route. Cutler forwarded the memo to Carter. "I agree with Ben's suggestion that the best method would be to amend the Amateur Sports Act of 1978," he stated. "There seems to be little doubt that Congress would pass such an amendment if the need arises and you decide to request it." He requested permission to mention this option when he met with the USOC in Colorado later in the week. Carter agreed. Suddenly the velvet of moral force was wrapped around the hard steel of political power.[17]

Cutler's estimate of Congress was on the mark. The boycott was popular with the American people and, in a reflection of that sentiment, both chambers held hearings. Members in the House and the Senate introduced several resolutions supporting the boycott. Representative Carroll Hubbard, Jr. of Kentucky said a boycott would be a good way of showing the Soviet Union "that we no longer believe in the illusion of détente." Robert Dornan, a Republican from California, declared, "The United States must, if we are to retain any honor at all, withdraw from the Olympic games if the site is not moved from the shadow of the Kremlin." Despite a reputation for being a buffoon, Dornan was one of the few people in the legislative branch seriously thinking about the implementation of this policy. He said the United States government should provide financial assistance to the IOC in order to move the games.[18]

The House Committee on Foreign Relations, under the leadership of Clement Zablocki, held hearings on January 23. The focus of the hearings was House Concurrent Resolution 249. Zablocki had introduced this nonbinding resolution that called on the IOC to move the games and then called on the USOC and other national Olympic committees to boycott Moscow. Kane of the USOC was the first witness to testify. Two themes emerged from his prepared remarks and the questions-and-answers session that followed. The first was his belief in the Olympics. "I have never been the least bit cynical about the great good that the Olympic does in the world." He was proud that the United States had competed in Berlin in 1936. Jesse Owens had exposed Nazism as a fraud, inflicting a huge propaganda defeat on Hitler's regime.[19]

Kane also worried that Carter's proposed boycott would destroy the Olympics. "The United States is absolutely the only country I think that could undercut the Olympic games to extermination, by not participating." He believed any action against Moscow would result in some action against the next set of Summer games. "The Olympic games will never be the same, because Eastern Bloc countries, if that happened, would not enter the 1984 games at Los Angeles." He remained skeptical about the feasibility of moving the games. He figured that it would probably cost half a billion dollars.[20]

Kane was testifying to a hostile audience. Congressman Dante Fascell of Florida made this point clear just before Kane began his testimony: "We asked the President if the time has not come to question the so-called modern Olympics and to establish alternative games at a different, perhaps permanent, site, which will be conducted under the auspices of a new set of rules which will truly eliminate both professionalism and politicization of sport."

The harshest and at the same time the silliest exchange came when Daniel Mica of Florida asked Kane what it would take to get the IOC to move the games:

Mr.Mica: Would it be fair to say, then, if the Russians invaded the United States they would not violate any IOC tenets?

Mr.Kane: I will ask Lord Killanin when I see him.

Kane maintained his composure throughout. "I am trying to answer the questions in the most truthful way I can," he explained to his audience. In the end, he managed to impress most of the representatives with his honesty even if he failed to change any of their minds. After he finished his remarks, the committee recessed for lunch.[21]

In the afternoon, the committee reconvened and heard from their next witness, Christopher. He advanced two distinct themes in his remarks. The first was that the administration wanted to punish the Soviet Union for its invasion of Afghanistan. The Olympics were a good means to that end: "To pursue sports as usual, at the same time we have said there is to be no business as usual, would send precisely the wrong message." Such symbolism was important for both domestic and diplomatic reasons. "In short, Mr. Chairman, I do not believe the American people want to see our athletes participating in games in Moscow at the same time that Soviet soldiers are crushing the independence of a free nation." Christopher was one of the people that Kane saw rewriting history. The comparison between Moscow and Berlin was easy for him to make, and it was not something that made the United States look good. "We and other nations who participated in the 1936 Olympics who understand those tragic circumstances must remember it was not among our proudest moments."[22]

In the questioning that followed, Christopher tried to explain why the administration had issued a one-month deadline. Being forthright in public about wanting to avoid responsibility for damaging the Olympics would have required the administration to face the full implications of the boycott – something the President was unwilling to do in private much less in public. Christopher's answer was that they wanted to give the Soviets a reasonable warning before they initiated the boycott "and a month seemed like a reasonable period of time." He showed little understand of military operational requirements, particularly the demands associated with a withdrawal when he explained, "I think if they got them in within a month, they could get them out within a month."[23]

The Undersecretary argued that the boycott would expose illegitimate Soviet actions to the Soviet peoples. "If the Olympics are not held in Moscow, it will not be something that they can hide from their people." As a result, he explained, "I think the removal of the Olympics from Moscow is probably the strongest single step we could take to persuade them to withdraw their troops from Afghanistan." Paul Findley, an Illinois Republican who had previously served as a member of the NATO Parliamentary Assembly, challenged Christopher. He had no problem with the boycott: "It seems to me that that step is desirable and that, in fact, it would be indecent for us to go to Moscow under these circumstances." His problem was with Carter's defense policies: "It also seems to me that what is greatly needed is to get military might in the right places in right hands in that part of the world." Christopher quickly dodged this partisan thrust, telling Findley that the administration was discussing other options. He was there to discuss the Olympics and only the Olympics.[24]

In addition to wanting to punish the Soviet Union, Christopher believed it would be best if the Olympians moved the Games to another city and nation. He later remarked, "I believe that if the International Olympic Committee were to decide that it would like to go elsewhere, that is legally and technically possible. With 5 or 6 months leadtime, and with the possibility of delaying the games somewhat, but still holding them this year, I think it is possible to find an alternate site if the will were there to do it." He focused on Montreal and said it was the best option open to the IOC. The only shortcoming the Canadian city faced was having enough adequate housing, and Christopher said that problem could be solved. He never mentioned who would pay for this solution – the IOC, the Canadian government, the City of Montreal, or the U.S. government – and no one asked him about the comments that Jean Drapeau, the mayor of Montreal, had already made saying his city was unable to host a relocated version of the games. In addition, Christopher thought the National Collegiate Athletic Association or the Amateur Athletic Association could take over administration of the Olympics from the IOC.[25]

Christopher communicated the policy that President Carter wanted to pursue with clarity and precision, and for that effort he deserves high marks. In his testimony, however, he never addressed the serious issues associated with this policy and, in fact, was uncertain as to what option he wanted the IOC to pursue. This confusion and uncertainty was a by-product of the President's determination to avoid the onus of being the person responsible for destroying the Olympic movement. It also reflected Carter's tendency to immerse himself in the details and an unwillingness to choose between various options, which was at the heart of strategic-level thinking. Judging from the reaction of the Committee, few of the Congressmen in attendance of either party cared about these shortcomings. "I think if we had stayed out of the 1936 Olympics by ourselves we would be proud of that action today," Democrat Jonathan Bingham of New York remarked. Robert Lagomarsino, a Republican from California, was like Christopher in his disregard for the logistical issues involved in hosting the Olympics and thought the IOC could easily move the games if they had the will: "I think they could, frankly, if they really tried." Republican Representative Dan Quayle of Indiana remarked, "Your optimism is encouraging from this member's point of view, because I think that would be the best thing that could happen." It is no surprise then that the Committee reported Resolution 249 on a voice vote.[26]

Such support boded well for Carter. The boycott policy enjoyed significant support among the American people. Despite Cutler's candid admission that the boycott would probably fail, the President and his lieutenants were committed to the effort. Later that evening, after the Committee had voted, Carter gave his State of the Union Address and received, as was customary, a standing ovation from the joint session of Congress as he walked into the House of Representatives. Carter delivered the speech in what one observer called "firm but subdued tones." His speech focused almost entirely on foreign affairs and was interrupted with applause twenty times. About a fourth of the way into his remarks, he turned his attention toward the Olympics. "I have notified the Olympic Committee that with Soviet invading forces in Afghanistan, neither the American people nor I will support sending an Olympic team to Moscow." Kane sadly noted that this line received the loudest applause that evening. Carter made it clear that this response was not about the Olympic movement, but rather about Soviet intervention in a region that the United States considered extremely important to its own well-being: "Let our position be absolutely clear: An attempt by any outside force to gain control of the Persian Gulf region will be regarded as an assault on the vital interests of the United States of America, and such an assault will be repelled by any means necessary, including military force." A *New York Times* reporter covering the event noted, "the language of détente was largely replaced by the language of containment."[27]

There was considerable support for this approach toward the Soviet Union. "Carter's message was made of stern stuff," the editors of *The Atlanta Constitution* noted approvingly. In Massachusetts, *The Boston Globe* declared, "The statement by the President, in the spirit of Harry Truman, will be popular with many Americans." In Truman's home state, the editorial board of the *St. Louis Post-Dispatch* thought Carter had the right mix: "The tone of President Carter's State of the Union Message last night was tough and confident, but the actions he recommended were measured and restrained. The combination was impressive, we thought."[28]

The House of Representatives also approved. The next day, Zablocki managed a floor debate on House Concurrent Resolution 249. The fact that the resolution now had 100 members acting as cosponsors was a good indication that the House would act on it in a positive fashion. In fact, there was almost no counterargument. Barry Goldwater, Jr. of California was one of the few representatives that spoke out against the resolution. "This administration has failed miserably in the conduct of foreign affairs," he declared with evident contempt. "The politicians have botched it, and now that they are faced with the consequences of their past mistakes, we are going to sink to the level of the very countries we are criticizing and politicize the Olympic games." These comments were those of a hawk when it came to the Soviet Union. "I have always thought détente was a rather one-sided figment of our imagination, and while I was angered, I was not surprised by the Soviet intervention in Afghanistan." His opposition to the boycott also had an idealistic bent. "I know that it has been used for political purposes in the past, but I have always been rather proud that the U.S. Olympic Committee and team as a whole have abided by the ideal." In his closing remarks, he also suggested that the United States was giving up on a powerful propaganda tool. "For those of you who are concerned about making a political statement through the Olympics, please remember that in 1936, Jesse Owens did more to show Hitler's Aryan theory for the manure it was than any boycott ever could." Such arguments carried little weight with the rest of the House, and the final vote on the resolution was an impressive 386–12.[29]

Far more significant than these domestic reactions were those of Soviet leaders. Put simply, the Soviets were unprepared for the boycott. Gromyko's assertion that Carter was trying to destroy détente "without any excuse" reflected the fact that most members of the Politburo failed to understand what Carter was trying to do. Sitting in Washington, Dobrynin had a better understanding of the American reaction: "Carter's entourage in the White House was handed a rare opportunity to convince the president of their thesis that the Soviet Union posed a global threat to the United States." What hurt the ambassador was that there was no question his country was in the wrong. "The deeply erroneous Soviet action provided the American right with a solid political pretext for another spiral of the arms race and renewed attacks on detente."[30]

Such candid views were largely absent in Politburo discussions. Gromyko told his colleagues that the United States was responding weakly to Afghanistan and dismissed the threat of an Olympic boycott before Carter's announcement as unofficial talk that could be ignored. Only after his appearance on *Meet the Press* and the State of the Union Address did the Politburo realize Carter was serious. Some members thought the man was emotionally unstable. Such a view, absurd as it may sound in later years, was understandable given how important personalities and cliques were in the political culture of the Soviet Union. Brezhnev's fading health hindered the operation of the Politburo – why should not the same be true in the U.S. government? Many thought mental health problems explained the zig-zag nature of U.S. foreign policy under Carter. Others, taking a more rational view, believed Brzesinski had finally won his battles with Vance for control of U.S. foreign policy.[31]

In the discussions that followed, the Politburo had the good sense to order Dobrynin back to Moscow. When he arrived, he explained that the American people had turned against détente because the Carter Administration had convinced them the Soviets were the aggressor and cooperation with an aggressor was impossible. He personally doubted that Carter had come to some sudden dramatic change in his view about the Soviet Union, nor did he think that the Americans had any realistic expectation that the Soviets would reverse themselves on Afghanistan: "He assumed a tough, anti-communist attitude in public, apparently out of electoral considerations, which I thought, suited him perfectly."[32]

The Politburo wanted to preserve détente but was also determined to stay the course in Afghanistan. "In general I found in the Kremlin a stubborn determination to continue its course in Afghanistan and stand fast against Carter," Dobrynin stated. The decision the group reached was to avoid challenging the United States directly. Their official policy read: "In this complicated situation, the leadership of the CPSU does not intend to adopt a policy of 'fighting fire with fire.' We shall do everything possible to prevent the Carter administration from drawing us into confrontation and undermining detente." Preserving the Olympics would service this goal. "We shall not engage, as the American administration is doing, in impulsive acts which can only intensify the situation and play into the hands of the proponents of the 'Cold War.' The American side, forgetting the elementary principals of restraint and prudence, is conducting a policy leading to the destruction of all inter-governmental ties which were constructed with such difficulty during the past years."[33]

A major difference between American and Soviet leaders was that the latter believed their own rhetoric. While Carter and his administration were looking for some type of rationalization for the boycott, be it an argument that the USSR had already politicized the Olympics or historical precedent from ancient Greece, officials in Moscow argued that the boycott was a threat to détente. Vladimir Kotelnikov, vice-president of the Soviet Academy of Sciences, argued that "objectively, the U.S. line, aimed at wrecking the 1980 Olympics in Moscow, contradicts the idea of peace, international cooperation and détente." This position became one that officials from the USSR tasked with publicly arguing against the boycott would repeat regularly. One Soviet propagandist claimed on the pages of *Sovetskiy Sport*: "Such tactics, as we all know, have always characterized the authors of the cold war. Now they have been borrowed by the present opponents of friendship and détente." The nations of Eastern Europe followed this line regularly.[34]

Since the Politburo believed – correctly – that Carter was primarily responsible for the boycott, much of their propaganda focused on him. Soviet radio services argued that the American president was "undermining the policy of détente and reviving the cold war." The *Televizionnoye Agenstvo Sovetskogo Soyuza** better known in English by its acronym as TASS aired an editorial

---

* Television Agency of the Soviet Union.

the day after Carter appeared on *Meet the Press*. Political analyst Vladimir Goncharov argued, "The president's demand is clearly political and its aim is to disrupt détente and undermine peaceful cooperation of the peoples." Vadim Zagladin, first deputy of the International Department of the Soviet Communist Party's Central Committee, said Afghanistan was a "pretext to do what he wanted to do before." A major theme that appeared in a number of Russian-language media outlets was that Carter had initiated the boycott in service of his own political interests as the United States entered its presidential election.[35]

Another theme was the threat of the boycott to the future of the Olympic movement. Warnings against "a split in the Olympic movement" were quite common. There was a good deal of irony to this argument given the threat that Soviet Union had posed to the Olympics before it joined the movement[36]

Despite his calm analysis, Dobrynin was stunned at what he found back in Washington. "For all my experience of anti-Soviet campaigns in the United States, I had never encountered anything like the intensity and scale of this one. What particularly caught my attention was the president's personal obsession with Afghanistan." He thought the rhetoric coming out of the White House was the most excessive during his time in Washington. "Not even the Reagan administration with its active policy of confrontation repeated Carter's most extreme claims." The Ambassador knew what was at stake. "All this threatened to destroy the success of detente irreparably."[37]

These Soviet views would come into play later as the United States tried to rally other nations to the cause of the boycott, but for now the Carter Administration was scoring success after success. The next battle came in convincing American Olympians to support the boycott. This effort was one that was going to be difficult. The Olympians, unlike other Americans, were well invested in attending the summer games. "Just what right does Carter have to keep us from going anyway?" Edwin Moses, the defending Olympic champion in 400-meter hurdles, demanded to know after the President's announcement. "Those are *our* Games. The athletes' games."[38]

This view was fairly common. One hundred and twenty-five athletes at the Olympic Training Center released a statement two days after the State of the Union Address. They reminded the public that they could claim the moral high ground just as much as the President. "The very foundations of the Olympic Games began as an instrument of fostering peace," they declared. The athletes also argued that the boycott was doomed to fail. "We must use actions which achieve results, not symbolic gestures which only vent emotions. The Olympic Games should be used as a vehicle for peace, thus it is vitally important in these troubled times." The U.S. Women's Handball Team issued a statement of their own, saying they wanted to compete in Moscow because they were patriotic Americans. "Out team feels that amateur athletes are a powerful form of patriotism for the United States, not only in the Olympics, but at all times and in all forms of competition. We are proud to wear 'U.S.A.' on our backs." Debbie Green of the U.S Women's Volleyball Team reflected in a soft voice, "We have worked for six years to represent our country in international competition, and when we say we want to go, to do what we've trained to do, they call us unpatriotic."[39]

This sentiment probably would have been stronger had the athletes known that Carter made the boycott decision without any consultation with U.S. Olympic leaders. No one in the administration made any effort to contact the USOC officials until after the President had determined his policy. Joe Onek, Cutler's deputy, agreed to a meeting with Miller and Kane: "I tentatively said yes, since I believe it would be a mistake to make any public decision without having heard their views." Although Miller and Kane indicated that they would support any decision the President made, they wanted to make sure he got both sides of the issue.

They never got the chance. Kane and Miller met with Culter, Onek, and Vance the day before Carter went on *Meet the Press*. Kane and Miller quickly opposed this idea but used arguments that had little potential to influence the administration. A boycott, they said, might provoke a Soviet boycott against the Lake Placid Winter Olympics or could easily splinter the Olympic movement. If the USOC took an early stand against the Moscow games, the Americans would lose any influence they had with the IOC, which had agreed to discuss relocation at its next meeting. Miller and Kane made one other argument that Vance, Cutler, and the others should have heeded. They two Olympians warned that action on the part of the United States against the Olympics without support from other nations would result in a major propaganda win for the Soviet Union. According to the clipped language of the notes Kane made, "Vance, Cutler can't believe we USOC would ever defy Pres. of US on such a sensitive issue." They were so convinced that the Soviets needed validation from the American participation in the games that they failed to understand that it was the contests themselves that had the legitimacy.[40]

Miller and Kane never had an opportunity to meet with Carter during their visit to the White House, and the administration made no effort to consult with them. They had been informed, nothing more. Kane was well aware of this fact. His notes for a speech he gave on the boycott read: "No notice to other nations, no consultations. Microcosm."[41]

Kane was right, but Cutler and Onek suggested that Carter meet with Killanin and Berlioux only after the President had committed himself to the boycott. Carter approved "but only if there is some real possibility of their agreeing to move the Olympics out of Moscow. I don't favor giving them a forum just to disagree with me."[42]

The next day, Carter made his appearance on *Meet the Press* and sent a letter to Kane, which the White House released to the press. "This invasion also endangers neighboring independent countries and access to a major part of the world's oil supplies. It therefore threatens our national security." He further explained that the Soviets had to be punished for what they had done. "We must make clear to the Soviet Union that it cannot trample upon an independent nation and at the same time do business as usual with the rest of the world." Carter claimed that he knew what was best for the Olympics. "If Soviet troops do not fully withdraw from Afghanistan within the next month, Moscow will become an unsuitable site for a festival meant to celebrate peace and good will."[43]

Cutler went to Colorado for a regularly scheduled meeting of the USOC to make the administration's case. "The nation faces a very grave situation. It is the most serious threat to world peace since World War II," he said in his presentation. "What is at stake is simply this, Should the Games be held in Moscow at a time after the USSR has completed the subjugation of a friendly nation, in a vital area?" Cutler appears to have expected that the Committee members would quickly bend to what a *Sports Illustrated* reporter called his "hard-sell." Instead he got a two-and-a-half-hour discussion of U.S. foreign policy in which Cutler became, according to observers, "huffy" when the Olympians dared question Carter's decision.[44]

Cutler wanted immediate compliance, but what he got instead was a resolution calling on the IOC to move the games from Moscow. Joe Onek, Cutler's deputy, quickly argued that this was a victory for the administration: "It is the first step in signaling to the Russians that their aggression in Afghanistan will not go unanswered. This is precisely what the President requested." There was more truth than fiction in this statement. The resolution reflected the unwillingness of the USOC to challenge the President's direction of foreign policy, and was in keeping with Carter's stated preference that the IOC move the games to another location.[45]

As a practical matter, the idea of moving the Olympics at this late date was impossible. Lord Killanin had already made that point clear. There is a reason that municipalities need six to eight years to plan for the games. The logistical challenges were immense. Just finding a city with the vacant hotel capacity to house all the athletes, officials, and fans that go along with the athletic festival would have required several years of advance notice. Foreign Service Officer Nelson Ledsky, the head of the State Department's boycott task force, disagreed. "It seems almost beyond belief that, given the entrepreneurship of the Western world, a major sports event cannot be organized in six months."[46]

Kane had no illusions about the IOC moving the games. He was playing for time. His private explanation of his approach to other members of the Committee was blunt: "We have, all along, relied on time perhaps changing the tensions of the world, so that it would make it more propitious to have the Games in Moscow, and then we'd stand up hard and firm, against the President, if he still insisted."[47]

Kane was also worried about sanctions from the International Olympic Committee. Killanin had publicly warned the Americans about the boycott. If the USOC complied with the administration, it would "be in complete conflict with rule 24C, regarding its autonomy, which could have very dangerous repercussions." Killanin added that "it would appear that President Carter and members of your government are not aware of the Olympic rules." The issue was discussed at the meeting, and Cutler was rather skeptical about this concern. "If this is the rule that requires each national Olympic committee to be autonomous and free of political influence, then the problem goes back to the incompatibility of the rule with the membership of the Soviet Union's national committee," he told the media afterwards. "It's just inconceivable ... that the Olympic committee of the Soviet Union could be autonomous and free of political influence." Cutler had a good argument, but reporters noticed that he seemed tense and uneasy.[48]

An additional reason the Olympians refused to go along fully with the administration was that they felt the movement itself was at stake. Bob Mathias, a gold medalist at the 1948 and 1952 games, who had gone on to become a four-term Congressman from California, believed such a development was a real possibility. In 1980, he was the director of the Olympic Training Center. "We're going to fight to the end," he said. "We're fighting for the life of the Olympic Games. It's almost too late. I'm afraid it might be."[49]

Despite the refusal of the USOC to become pawns of the administration, the President decided to declare victory. "The decision was difficult, and it was a courageous action which deserves our praise and our support." Their action was saving the "noble ideals" of the Olympics from "desecration" and was actually in the best interests of the movement. "It reaffirmed the principles that the Olympics should not become some meaningless or even hypocritical spectacle, but athletic competition as a genuine expression of international friendship and peace."[50]

The U.S. Senate got involved in the issue as well. The upper chamber has a reputation for being more deliberate, thoughtful, and even-handed in its handling of issues than the House of Representatives. Such was the case in the Olympics boycott. The Senate Foreign Relations Committee did a far better job of exploring both sides of the issue than its counterpart in the House. In the end, though, it might not have mattered. "There is no point in pretending that this drama is likely to have a happy ending," Senator Frank Church, chairman of the Committee, pointed out in his opening remarks. "It will not – not for the athletes, not for the Olympics, nor for a U.S. policy that ends by leaving us isolated; that is not the role we seek and it is not the one we should write in haste or carelessly for ourselves."[51]

One way in which the Committee distinguished itself from its counterpart in the House was taking testimony from both sides of the issue. The first witness the Committee heard from was Senator Ted Stevens of Alaska.

While having Senators testify as a witness to other Senators might seem a little inbred – like journalists interviewing other journalists – Stevens had some unique credentials. He had served on the President's Commission on Olympic Sports that Gerald Ford had authorized, and had been the primary author of the legislation that it recommended, the one that became known as the Ted Stevens Olympic and Amateur Sports Act. "I believe that the decision as to whether or not American athletes should participate, should be made by the athletes themselves and not by Congress and not be the President," the Alaska Republican told his colleagues. "The United States has far more to lose from staying home from Moscow than we will ever gain from a boycott." The Olympics was a unique opportunity that would not develop again for decades. Reporters in the thousands from all over the planet would be in the Soviet Union, and that massive number would probably overwhelm restrictive Soviet security measures. Many of these journalists would also be attending the 1980 Winter Olympics and 1984 Summer Olympics. These three sets of games were an excellent opportunity to compare and contrast the Soviet and American ways of life. "The President overreacted," Stevens declared. "Now what we are trying to do is put up the façade of protest at the expense of some athletes."[52]

The Committee then heard from yet another member of the Senate. Bill Bradley, a Democrat from New Jersey, had won an Olympic gold medal in 1964, but was in favor of a boycott. "After my visit to Moscow last summer along with Senator Biden and a number of other Senators it was clear to me that the Soviets will spare nothing to make the Olympics the biggest peacetime propaganda event since Sputnik." He believed that the IOC had to find a permanent home for the Olympics. His preference was Greece. Such an action would prevent host governments from exploiting or trampling on the Olympic ideals. Church quickly noticed a fairly big hole in this proposal: If a number of previous host nations had manipulated the games, would not Greece do the same? Bradley had no ready answer and it was only when he brought his comments to a close that he finally provided an answer to Church's question. "One could make the argument that the Olympic games in a revised format with a permanent home would indeed transcend nationalism. Further, I don't think any Greek Government, whatever its political complexion, would throw the Olympic games out of Greece; it is part of the heritage of the country that can be celebrated by all factions of political opinion."[53]

The committee then heard from Warren Christopher. The arguments he put forward in his testimony were largely the same as those that he made when he testified in front of the House Committee. His comments, though, showed that the Carter Administration really never considered the national Olympic committees independent actors. "Other governments around the world have adopted positions roughly paralleling that of President Carter and my own expectation is that many more will join us in the days ahead in that effort." The administration was assuming that if they convinced the government of a nation to support the boycott that their Olympic committee would comply. No one on the Committee challenged this view. In fact, a memo the Committee's staff prepared told them the same thing.[54]

Although supportive of the boycott, these Senators were hardly a rubber stamp. Muskie asked about contingency planning if the national Olympic committees refused to comply and said, "We are sort of flying by the seat of our pants." Christopher had to agree, but he said the USOC vote would influence other Olympic committees to join the boycott. Others were disturbed at reports that the administration was thinking of revoking passports. Joseph Biden, a Democrat from Delaware, called such an effort "outrageous." He added, "For us to suggest that we have to coerce American citizens not to participate in foreign policy decisions by threatening to lift visas is counterproductive." The reasons for his criticism were quite substantial: "We cannot have a foreign policy that does not have overwhelming American public support and expect that foreign policy to succeed."[55]

The Senate Committee then heard from a number of Olympians: Miller and three medalists – Anita De Frantz, Al Oerter, and John Thompson. De Frantz had won bronze at Montreal in rowing, Oerter was a four-time gold medalist in the discus competition, and Thompson coached the U.S. Men's Basketball Team to gold in Montreal. Miller's testimony was almost identical to that of Kane's. He made no apologies for his work with the Olympics. "The Olympic movement must survive. It represents what is good and wholesome in life." He was particularly worried about the ramifications of Carter's efforts. "I don't think anyone in this Nation would rest easily with the thought that the United States was responsible for the demise of the Olympic games, or that it knowingly contributed to the end of a movement that has stood as an instrument of international brotherhood, amity, and goodwill for more than 80 years." De Frantz was adamant in her opposition to the boycott and made a clumsy effort to inject race into the discussion. The issue had no impact on any of the Senators. In brief comments, both Thompson and Oerter expressed their support for the Olympic movement but supported the boycott, which reflected a change in Oerter's thinking.[56]

After hearing from the witnesses, the committee then debated the resolution, tinkering with the language a bit. The committee then approved the document, 14–0, and arranged to have it sent to the floor of the Senate that afternoon. In both speed and margin, the actions of the Committee were victories for the administration, but there was an important theme running underneath the surface. The Senators had found a number of shortcomings in administration policy, and their inquiry had been neither rigorous nor hostile. In addition, a number of them were rather skeptical about the boycott.

"It is an easy way out," Richard Lugar, a Republican from Indiana, remarked. He was going to vote for the resolution but had no illusions about the power of the boycott to affect a change. "In fact, it won't get very far at all."[57]

That afternoon, the whole Senate debated and voted on the resolution. The discussion on the floor was one-sided. Stevens was the only Senator to speak out strongly against the boycott. His remarks were extensive: "I think that history will show that the action that is being taken by the Senate, the action that was taken by the House of Representatives, and the position that was taken by the President were wrong." For the most part, though, most of the "debate" was between Senators expressing their support. The final vote was almost unanimous.[58]

On this issue, the American public was with Carter, and so was the Prime Minister of Australia, Malcolm Fraser. When Carter went public with his decision on *Meet the Press*, Fraser followed up a day later. He informed the AOF that "an effective boycott of the Games will bring home to the Russian Government and people, perhaps in a way no other step could, the great seriousness in the eyes of independent nations of the steps the USSR has taken." He also put some muscle behind the request. The Australian government was scheduled to make a payment to the AOF of $500,000, and Fraser informed the organization they could have the money only if it was not used to support sending a team to Moscow.[59]

The executive board of the AOF held a meeting at the Lakeside Hotel in Canberra to discuss the prime minister's letter. Kevan Gosper, a member of this organization as well as the International Olympic Committee, was not present at the meeting since he was living in London doing some preparatory work required of him before he became chief executive officer of Shell Australia. He had an international long distance phone call with Bob Ellicott, Minister for Home Affairs. "I told him," Gosper later explained, "I thought the Australian team should go to Moscow but I could sense the issue was going to be a very serious one." In the end, the board decided to pass Fraser's letter on to the IOC without comment. As a result, the president of the organization took a legalistic position that ignored political realities. "Neither the Prime Minister nor the Australian Government has asked us to boycott the Games." The organization, though, complied with Fraser financial requirements and used the $500,000 to purchase a building and planned to draw on other funds to finance the travel of its team to the Soviet Union.[60]

The Prime Minister hardly was one to let this issue go. He traveled to Washington and met with Carter at the White House on January 31. After first discussing the problem of Vietnamese refugees, Fraser's host turned the conversation to Afghanistan. The President was worried about Western unity on this issue and asked that Fraser discuss the issue as he toured Europe. The Australian liked what he heard. Fraser had been deeply suspicious of Carter and had for some time questioned both his leadership and policies. "But then of course, events moved on and President Carter got some good, hard lessons, about the way in which he could trust the Russians, or the Soviets," Fraser told an interviewer years later. "And at one point he said to me, 'But Malcolm, the President of the Soviet Union – the Chairman – lied to me, he lied to me!'"[61]

After their meeting ended, Fraser told reporters he supported the boycott and wished the AOF would do as the USOC had done. Russell Schneider, an Australian newspaper columnist following the prime minister, noted that Fraser was on a personal crusade: "The reason for Fraser's anti-Soviet crusade is a simple one: he believes in it."[62] Carter had company in the boycott.

Fraser's trip continued on to the heart of the old empire, London. He met with Margaret Thatcher, and much of their discussion revolved around the Olympic boycott. Thatcher said she supported Carter, but Fraser was less than keen on the American. He wanted a stronger push. He was afraid Carter was allowing the situation to drift with his one-month deadline. He wanted someone to agree to host an alternative Olympics. His preference was Montreal, and that required that they, Fraser and Thatcher, put pressure on the Canadian government. All Thatcher would do in this regard was agree to a meeting between Australian, British, and American diplomats.[63] Carter was in the lead on the boycott, for better or worse.

Fraser was pushing for domestic political reasons. The public in Australia was evenly split on the issue at the time. Gallup polls in February showed 48 percent of Australians in favor of a boycott and 46 percent opposed.[64] The Prime Minister wanted the weight of international affairs to push Australians further in his direction.

The administration had won a number of easy victories, but these successes obscured a number of problems with the policy. The Senate Foreign Relations Committee had pointed out a number of these shortcomings in a helpful fashion – or what passed for helpful in Washington. Under Cutler's direction, though, the Administration made no effort to use this constructive commentary to their advantage. There seemed no reason to do so. The first few days of the boycott had gone well for the Carter White House. February would be less kind.

CHAPTER 7

Painful Losses

AS JANUARY TURNED INTO FEBRUARY, THE CARTER WHITE HOUSE made a number of efforts to implement the boycott on an international scale. It was at this time that the policy started to encounter a number of serious problems. The idealism and operational structure of the Olympic movement proved to be far more difficult to overcome than Carter expected.

The first major reversal came on February 2 in the library of Lord Killanin's Dublin home. Lloyd Cutler had traveled to Ireland to meet personally with the IOC President. Killanin's account of the meeting brings credit to neither man. "The first positive sign of trouble reached me on January 28," the Baron noted in his memoirs. While the public record clearly indicates otherwise, his dismissal of Carter's public remarks as "rumblings" shows that he failed to realize how serious the Americans were about the boycott, giving ammunition to his critics in the Olympic movement. Cutler started with what Killanin considered a long speech on the Soviet intervention in Afghanistan and how control of that country would put them in a good position to seize oil fields in Iran or move toward the Persian Gulf. "I was, as it turned out, to get a great shock," he recalled. "I discovered that Cutler had not flown in from Washington to discuss, but rather instruct." Killanin noted that Cutler tended to drop his head as he talked while maintaining his gaze, which gave the Baron the feeling that "he was looking at you out of the top of his eyes with the stabbing penetration of a lawyer." Cutler told his host that the United States wanted the IOC to postpone or cancel the games. According to Killanin, Cutler put this statement in the form of a demand. He found it all rather patronizing. "Here again was the American attitude of bringing out the bulldozer to save someone from an awful fate, or what America thought was an awful fate. It was this sense of arrogance, not personally shown by Cutler but evident in the high-handed approach of the White House, that raised my hackles."[1]

As the meeting continued, it became obvious to Killanin that the American did not know what he was talking about. "Cutler told me to my surprise that under Olympic rules the Games could only be held with an international truce in effect and this rule should be invoked." The problem Killanin had with this statement was that it was incorrect. The truce was not part of the modern Olympics. Another problem was that Carter and Cutler were advocating a standard that the United States had failed to meet in 1952, 1968, 1972, and would fail to meet again in 2002. Cutler also told his host that Carter had instructed the USOC to present the issue to Killanin's committee when they met in Lake Placid in a week. Killanin grew exasperated as he listened. There was no federal nature to the structure of the international Olympic movement, and he and only he controlled the agenda of IOC meetings. Cutler had no excuse for making this mistake. He had a copy of an intelligence memorandum the CIA's National Foreign Assessment Center had prepared on the Olympic movement that accurately explained the "diffused" structure of the Olympics. Killanin's complaint, while legitimate, reflected his tendency and that of many other Olympic officials to focus on issues of protocol instead of responding directly to matters of substance. Killanin also questioned Carter's integrity. "Whatever the rights and wrongs of the Afghanistan affair, the judgment of one man, already scrambling for his political life in the American presidential election campaign, which occurs in the Olympic year, had turned the Olympic arena into what was to be its own battleground."[2]

Cutler's mission had failed, but Killanin had a moment of doubt. As he said goodbye to Cutler and saw him to his car, he wondered to himself, "Oh, God, after Montreal do I deserve this?" He regained his determination before he reached his front door, inspired in part from the roar of the crowd watching a nearby rugby match.[3]

While Killanin was pondering his fate, the Carter administration was in the process of suffering another setback and this one was extremely public. The U.S. State Department had commissioned Muhammad Ali, a professional boxer and former Olympic gold medalist, to represent the United States in Africa in an effort to build public support for the boycott. The idea came from three Foreign Service officers who were black and had served in Africa. The idea quickly made its way to the White House where Carter approved the proposal. Years later in retirement, he explained his reasons to an Ali biographer. "There was a specific interest on my part in having Muhammad Ali explain our country's position on the Olympic boycott, and also in his pointing out what our nation is, what its basic policies are, our commitment to freedom and human rights, and the fact that we have black Americans who have been successful with a diversity of religious commitments."[4]

While creative, this approach soon ran afoul of logistics. When he agreed to undertake this mission, Ali was in India doing charity work. A group of Foreign Service officers went to India to meet with the boxer and accompany him on the trip. They had no time to brief the boxing legend about the reasons behind the boycott. The night before he left for Tanzania, the first stop on his diplomatic tour, Ali had a late-night meeting with Yuli Vorontsov, the Soviet

Ambassador to India. Vorontsov tried to convince Ali against making the trip. The ambassador failed, but the exhausted boxer spent his flight sleeping because of his meeting and arrived in Dar es Salaam poorly informed on U.S. foreign policy.[5]

At first, it seemed it might not matter. Crowds waiting on the airport tarmac were chanting: "ALI, ALI, ALI." A White House official accompanying the boxer was stunned: "The welcome was phenomenal." President Julius Nyerere, though, was insulted that Carter had sent a mere athlete to discuss the boycott and refused to meet with the special envoy. After Ali arrived, he participated in a press conference that became combative. When asked why the United States was not assisting with the liberation movements in southern Africa while the Soviet Union was, Ali replied: "They didn't tell me in America that Russia supports these countries. Maybe I'm being used to do something that ain't right. You have given me some questions which are good and which are making me look at things different." The lack of U.S. support for the 1976 Olympic boycott was another issue thrown at him. "I am not representing America," he replied. "If you believe in freedom you are naturally offended when a country like Russia invades a country." The boxer was stunned when he was asked if he was a puppet of the White House. "Nobody made me come here and I'm nobody's Uncle Tom."[6]

A number of observers, both Tanzanian and American, thought Ali had handled the press conference well, but the boxer thought differently. "Ali began to talk about jumping ship," one member of the delegation reported back to Carter. Ali soon found new resolve in indignation. In a meeting with Tanzanian Minister of Youth and Culture, Chediel Mgonja, someone slipped him a note calling him a stooge of Jimmy Carter. Ali responded with an emotional speech. He was not in Tanzania to talk about what the U.S. had done or failed to do in the past – he was there to talk about Afghanistan. He asked Mgonja if he thought he was Carter's puppet. The Sports Minister responded that he thought Ali was an excellent representative of the United States on this issue since he had won an Olympic medal. He added that the attacks on Ali were probably the product of Soviet publicists.[7]

Ali's public statements had done significant damage to the credibility of his diplomatic mission. The editorial commentary back in the United States was savage and aimed at Carter and his subordinates, not at Ali. The criticisms came from every corner of the country. The editors of the *Des Moines Register* called the Ali mission an "idiotic move." In South Carolina, an editorial in the *Charleston News & Courier* declared: "Any adverse reaction to what Muhammad Ali said in Tanzania can be blamed less on him than on the Carter administration. He's a boxer, not a diplomat or student of foreign affairs. His candid remarks were typical of the predictable consequences of the Carter penchant for picking emissaries by who they are rather than what they know and can do." In New Orleans, *The Times-Picayune* made an exceptionally good point: "There is no reason to expect a fighter to excel as a diplomat, and it was simply inept for the President to allow the United States to be represented by the uninhibited ex-champion even in a sports-related matter. It makes as much sense as putting Cyrus Vance in the ring with Larry Holmes."[8]

The mission continued despite this commentary. An official in the Dar es Salaam cabled his counterparts in Nairobi, Kenya, the next stop on Ali's trip: "Good luck and Godspeed to our colleagues down the line. This visit should keep AF [the State Department's African Affairs office] staff meetings in stories for at least six months. Believe me, they're all true." The reception in Nairobi was strong and positive. Crowds were chanting: "ALI, ALI, ALI!" He had to get on top of a truck and direct traffic to unsnarl a traffic jam. The day before, President Daniel arap Moi announced that he would support the boycott and agreed to meet with the American boxer.[9]

In Nigeria, Ali received another massive outpouring of public enthusiasm when he arrived. By this time, he was properly briefed and prepared for the less welcoming response of the Nigerian government when President Alhaji Shehu Shagari refused to meet with him. From there, Ali went to Liberia, and just before he arrived, President William Tolbert announced he would support the boycott. Tolbert agreed to meet with the boxer and told him his country needed more assistance from the United States. In Senegal, Ali received a warm welcome from President Leopold Sedar Senghor. The two men met at Senghor's beachside villa, discussing the boycott over champagne and reading poetry to one another. Such hospitality, though, did not translate into support for the boycott. Senghor was no friend of the Soviet Union but believed that sport and politics should be kept separate. Senegal had been one of the few African nations to defy the boycott of New Zealand at the Montreal Olympics, and its team would be present in Moscow as well.[10]

The Ali mission never recovered from the bad press it received in the beginning. Sports Columnist Shirley Povich of *The Washington Post* declared, "The whole fiasco was not all Ali's fault. Much of the blunder can be traded to the White House, where the president unforgivably overrated Ali as a diplomat. Carter was mistaken in thinking Ali's charm and popularity as an international black personality could be persuasive factors in Africa." Povich's colleague at the *Post*, Dave Kindred, declared, "To make Muhammad Ali an instant diplomat is unfair to him and condescending to those African nations we seek to sway." An editorial in *The Economist* summarized it best: "It seemed, no doubt, like a good idea at the time."[11]

Carter saw the initiative through to the end. On February 11, he met with the boxer for what was officially described as a report on the trip. There were a number of State Department and NSC officials in the Cabinet Room for the meeting, but it basically amounted to a twenty-minute photo opportunity. Ali had prepared a formal written report for the President, but he also managed to discuss some matters of substance with Carter during their meeting. Most of his comments focused on foreign policy issues involving Africa that had little to do with the boycott. Many African leaders were critical that the United States had not taken a strong stand against South Africa and insisted the United States needed to take some "drastic moves" against that nation. Africa had real problems with hunger and disease that the United States could and should help resolve. Many officials were skeptical that the United States would really boycott Moscow, and Ali said the United States had to develop the alternate games to show the Africans that it was serious. He also suggested that the United States develop a sports exchange program that would foster relationships between the U.S. and the developing world. Ali was quite proud of his efforts. "As I look back over the past week of the Mission, I can't help but feel a sense of accomplishment," he declared in his written report.[12]

Ali had no reason to feel proud. He changed no policies on his trip. Instead, he managed to generate a good deal of ridicule. Some of it was aimed at him but much more was focused on Carter, and deservedly so. The diplomatic tour was the product of patronizing attitudes at work in the Carter White House that Killanin had first noticed.[13]

Far more typical of the boycott was the effort to work through traditional venues, but Carter and others in his administration never took the Olympic movement and its ideology seriously, which was the major reason the boycott campaign failed. The administration approached this issue thinking it would be a cheap and easy way to lash back at the Soviets. Carter admits as much in his memoirs: "I know the decision was controversial, but I had no idea at the time how difficult it would be for me to implement it or to convince other nations to join us."[14]

This confession would have seemed typical of Carter to Helmut Schmidt, Chancellor of West Germany. "The world image of most Americans – and of most American politicians – does not go far beyond the borders of their own country. This is the reason for the American naïveté in assessing and dealing with other nations and their interests that we have often enough observed."[15]

Carter initially responded with correspondence to the other leaders of foreign nations. The day after his State of the Union Address, he told Schmidt that a boycott was "the most significant and effective action we can take to convince the Soviet leaders of the seriousness of their invasion." The initial response in Europe was supportive. Preferring to act through the European Economic Community rather than NATO to show some political independence from the United States, the foreign ministers of the member nations endorsed the boycott. Attilio Ruffini, foreign minister of Italy and chair of the meeting, remarked that the Soviets had "destroyed the conditions that ought to exist for holding such games." The French were a notable exception. Jean François-Poncet was courteous, but believed the boycott was the product of emotion rather than sound analysis. It was also wrong, and France would offer no support for such a policy.[16]

This consensus fell apart under the weight of a good deal of skepticism. Schmidt made two telling criticisms that were both on the mark. First, "Carter had not discussed the joint Western reaction he was outlining with his allies ahead of time." Second, "there was no logical and self-contained overall strategy for managing the crisis." The Chancellor began to wonder. "Washington's attempt to force Brezhnev to retreat with a dozen pinpricks was hardly persuasive; after studying this long letter, I had to ask myself whether Carter was sincere in his efforts to achieve a Soviet retreat from Afghanistan."[17]

Back in North America, the boycott began foundering. Canadian Prime Minister Joe Clark had a reputation for flip-flopping similar to Carter's. On January 4, he responded to a question at a press conference and said the Canadian government had no plans under consideration to support a boycott. He explained that the boycott would have "no practical effects" on the Soviet Union and would be a gesture of little significance. Then on January 24, Clark said he was reconsidering his position. Two days later, he met with James Worrall and Richard Pound, the two Canadians on the International Olympic Committee, and told him that he wanted the IOC to move the games or Canada would boycott the Olympics. Unlike Carter, he had met directly with Olympic officials and was honest in explaining a position he had already decided to take. While making a campaign appearance in front of a group of Ukrainian Canadians, he announced his new policy. "In an ideal world, international sport should be separate from international politics but the Soviet Union does not separate sport from politics," he stated. "They expected the West to be weak. We shall not be weak." He issued the same February 20 deadline as Carter.[18]

The Prime Minister had reasons for changing his position. Clark was in a precarious political position. He had lead the Progressive Conservative Party to an upset victory over Pierre Trudeau's Liberals in the 1979 general election and, at thirty-nine, became the youngest man ever to serve as Prime Minister of Canada. His government, though, was a minority one and before the end of the year, the House of Commons voted no confidence. There would be a new election, and Trudeau was doing well against him in the polls. A boycott was the best option Clark had because it solidified support for him among the right-wing voters of his party who were as anti-Soviet as their cousins to the south. "I predicted the move a week ago when President Carter started getting huge public support for his boycott idea," Greg Joy, who won a silver medal for Canada at the Montreal games, remarked. "Isn't it obvious Clark decided this was a good political idea for him?"[19]

Clark was making himself an easy target for Trudeau in the election. "Every time Joe Clark talks to his Toronto candidates, Canadian foreign policy is set back 20 years," the former Prime Minister joked.[20]

Two days before the February 20 deadline, Trudeau had his revenge. He defeated Clark and became Prime Minister of Canada again and found himself in an odd situation in regards to the boycott. His government had manipulated the Olympics and prevented Taiwan from competing in Montreal. Now the question was would he do so again, even if it meant supporting the policy of a man he had just defeated. According to his memoirs, written in the third-person, "Trudeau did not believe the boycott would work. He believed that sporting events could be held hostage in future years and knew that a boycott would destroy the dreams of many Canadian athletes. He refused to endorse the boycott until the Canadian Olympic committee made its decision." As a result, Canada remained an open question mark for anyone at the White House trying to count the nations supporting the boycott.[21]

The situation in Germany was far more complicated. Schmidt and Carter held each other in mutual contempt. Schmidt believed that Carter was being inconsistent in his moral foreign policy. He also believed that the President had an exaggerated view of his own power. "Carter and Brzesinksi both over-estimated the ability of the White House to shape the world merely by taking stands."[22] Although neither man liked the other, they were the leaders of two countries that had important ties to one another, and both had an interest in working together. The bad relationship complicated matters between the two men, but it was no barrier to common action.

Another factor creating even more difficulties was that 1980 was an election year for Schmidt, and he was facing a serious challenge from the political right over the *Ostpolitik* policies that had normalized relations between the two Germanys. On the other hand, he was facing challenges within his own party from the left among those that thought a boycott would jeopardize *Ostpolitik* and détente. In addition, Willi Daume, a German on the IOC, had taken a strong stand against the boycott and wanted to replace Killanin as president. A West German boycott would do significant damage to Daume's ambitions. Like other Olympians, his arguments focused on sports issues. He warned against the danger of "emotionalization" and the "long-term effect of boycott." Unlike other Olympians, he also used political arguments, seeing a negative "impact on the inner-German relationship." He was referring to contact between East and West Germany.[23]

If this situation were not tricky enough, both Brzezinski and Deputy Secretary of State Warren added to Schmidt's problems when they gave him misleading information about American intentions. In January, Christopher traveled to Germany, and the Chancellor met with him and asked if the U.S. planned to boycott the Olympics. He said, no. Berndt von Staden, West Germany's ambassador to the United States, had a similar meeting with Brzezinski in Washington and got a similar response. As a result, Schmidt felt comfortable in omitting any mention of the issue to the Bundestag. Then, three days later, Carter appeared on *Meet the Press*, suddenly putting Schmidt into an exposed position. If he changed his position, he would face questions about both his policies and his political independence. When Vance toured Europe in February, the Chancellor complained with "some vigor," to use Vance's subdued language. Schmidt made it clear that the American attitude that the allies should simply do as they were told was unacceptable. Vance replied that this was the work of others in the administration who he thought knew or should have known better. The Secretary of State chose not to include this last comment in the memorandum that he prepared after this meeting.[24]

The situation was fairly obvious to most observers. Australian Prime Minister Malcolm Fraser observed, "The United States can often be pretty cavalier with its friends."[25]

The President let his personal feelings bleed into his alliance management duties. When Carter read the report Vance produced documenting his meeting with Schmidt, his handwritten comment was simple: "Don't apologize." Schmidt said West Germany would support the United States in the Olympic boycott, but he would need time. "I have a queasy feeling still," Carter noted. Schmidt said he was a dependable ally but told Vance he was worried about the policies the United States was advancing, the future of détente – which had direct ties to *Ostpolitik* – and the quality of U.S. leadership. Carter clearly found these views insulting, and when he finished reading the memo, he made a marginal comment for Vance and Brzezinski: "Overall, I see nothing encouraging here. FRG opposes any sanctions against Iran or Soviets, are continuing business as usual with SU, refuse to commit publicly to Olympic boycott, & privately & in press are very critical of us."[26]

Lord Killanin was watching these efforts from his home in Dublin. He called the idea of moving the games "glib." It was also apparent to him that the Carter White House was unfamiliar with the structure of international sport. In these observations, he was absolutely correct. Members of the Carter administration, including the President himself, never took seriously the idea that national Olympic committees were independent of their national governments. Marshall Brement, a Foreign Service Officer and an expert on the Soviet Union assigned to the National Security Council, called this idea a "fiction in most countries." Lloyd Cutler and Joe Onek shared this view: "In many third world countries, the governments have full control over their NOC's." While these assessments were correct for the Warsaw Pact nations and probably fairly accurate for many of the poorer nations, they were wrong in their entirety for Western Europe, which was the heart of the Olympic movement. The administration never made this distinction, which explains why the administration focused on foreign governments for so long in the boycott effort.[27]

All the events that had transpired so far in the boycott effort were minor compared to those that came in the middle of February in the small town of Lake Placid, New York. The United States was the host for the Winter

Olympics, and the IOC usually met just before the start of each set of games. This time was no different. What was unique about this gathering, though, was its significance. Everyone at the time realized that the actions that the committee took or did not take were going to be important in determining the course of the boycott. The first round of the battle came on the morning of Friday, February 8, when the IOC Executive Board met at the Lake Placid Club. Robert J. Kane was present to explain the position of the USOC. The lean, former track star made it clear that both committees had been put into a political situation against their wills. He also made it clear that his organization wanted to avoid becoming a tool of U.S. foreign policy. The problem was that the Soviet Union had violated the Olympic charter. He then read from a prepared statement: "I appear before you to urge that the Olympic Summer Games of 1980 be held at a site other than Moscow on the grounds that the contract between the International Olympic and the Moscow Olympic Organising Committee has been broken." Many thought he was advancing an argument only at the behest of the White House, but Kane's notes make it clear that he truly believed that the Soviets were in the wrong. "The military invasion of Afghanistan by the Soviet Union has, in our opinion, violated the basic concepts not only of world order and peaceful accommodation between countries, but it is also an act of war by the Soviet Union against its neighbour that violated the fundamental principles of the International Olympic committee and of the Olympic movement." He then quoted the Olympic Charter to show where the Soviets were in violation of rules 1, 3, 4, 6, 11, and 24, which he liked to call a "contemptuous, insolent affront" to the Olympic movement. He, however, avoided using these terms before the IOC. After Kane finished, Killanin – the good Anglo-Celtic gentleman that he was – thanked him, and said he thought, based on his meetings with Cutler, that the Carter administration had made a quick and ill-considered decision. The Irish baron and several other members of the Board asked him a series of questions about U.S. foreign policy that Kane was in no real position to answer. "I must say, they were very friendly," he later told his colleagues on the USOC. "It was a fair, and I think, helpful conversation that we had." He had no illusions about his chances of success. "It became clear that we were not going to get very far." Killanin, though, asked him to be present the next day when the whole committee met.[28]

After a break for lunch, the board reconvened in the afternoon and heard from the Australians. David McKenzie, Vice-President of the AOF, presented Fraser's letter announcing the boycott as official Australian foreign policy to the Executive Board and also included his organization's response. He made it clear that he was only presenting Fraser's letter and had no wish to make a presentation to the whole committee. Killanin thanked him. McKenzie and the other Australians then left the room. Their business before the Executive Board had taken all of fifteen minutes.[29] Despite this rather perfunctory presentation, the debate on the boycott would roil Australia like no other issue in 1980.

The next day, the entire membership of the IOC assembled for the meeting that regularly preceded the start of the each set of games. Despite the largely conservative political views of the majority of the committee, a number worried that Carter would use the ceremonial setting to make some type of political statement. The administration decided late that Cyrus Vance would open the meeting. Killanin was also concerned. He warned Cutler that the meeting was largely ceremonial and that political statements were inappropriate at the time. Vance, however, had not provided the IOC with an advanced copy of the speech, which the Committee's secretariat needed in order to translate it into French. Some members suggested that the Secretary of State not be allowed to speak unless they had copies of the speech. Then the State Department released the speech to the media. "Vance was virtually ordering the IOC to cancel or postpone the Moscow Games," Killanin complained in his memoirs. The baron was exaggerating. The speech was political, but it was hardly abrupt or uncivil in tone. The IOC president figured that the representatives of the Moscow Olympic Organizing Committee would be offended at the speech and, wishing to avoid a counterdemonstration, warned them in advance of what Vance was going to say. The Russians were discreet in their absence. The Secretary of State, however, did nothing to improve matters when he just walked into Killanin's hotel room as if it were his own, which the Irishman understandably found off-putting.[30]

As he started the meeting, Lord Killanin was fully aware of what was at stake. "The opening of this Session of the International Olympic Committee is the opening of one of the most important Sessions ever held by this body, since its inception in 1894," he remarked. There was no exaggeration in that statement. He, however, tried to make a moral equivalency argument, questioning the integrity of the U.S. government to take a stand on principle. "Are there any countries which can claim to fully respect human rights, and not to practise discrimination of some kind?" Intellectually, he had a legitimate argument, but it had no chance of convincing any Americans. He was on stronger ground when he told his audience, which included Vance, "Do not use the Olympic Games to divide the world, but to unite it – do not use athletes for the solution of political problems!" He repeated this position as he brought his remarks to an end, "We call upon all competitors and participants, besides of course the spectators and the media, to respect each other within the principles of the Olympic Movement."[31]

Vance stood before the Committee and welcomed them to Lake Placid. He then quickly turned his attention toward contemporary world affairs. He reminded them that the ancient Greeks had practiced "a 'truce of the Gods'" that prohibited warfare during the Olympics. This statement was factually incorrect, but that mattered little to Vance. The Secretary of State then explained, "To hold the Olympics in any nation that is warring on another is to lend the Olympic mantle to that nation's actions." The Carter Administration respected the work of the Committee, but the IOC had to comply with U.S. policy. "We do not want to see the Olympic movement damaged. But if the basic principles of the Olympics are ignored, the future of the Games themselves will be placed in jeopardy." As the speech came to an end, Vance informed his audience of that policy: "Let me make my government's position clear: we will oppose the participation of an American team in any Olympic Games in the capital of an invading nation." He finished, arguing that the Carter administration was acting in the best interest of the Olympic movement: "By upholding the principles of the Olympics when they are under challenge, we will preserve the meaning of the Olympics for years to come."[32]

The Secretary of State could not have delivered a more counterproductive speech if he had tried. The IOC responded, to use the words of Richard Pound, in "stony silence." There is no exaggeration in that statement. Several accounts of that meeting mention the lack of the applause when Vance finished his remarks. Even the Americans in the audience thought the speech was a disaster. "That night was the only time in my life I've been embarrassed to be an American," Phil Wolff, the chief of staff of the Lake Placid games, said. "I spent three years fighting in World War II. Nobody has a deeper love of this country than I do, but that was not right to be so derogatory and political when we're supposed to be welcoming all our guests from around the world."[33]

Vance had actually helped the Soviet cause. Ignati T. Novikov, president of the Moscow Organizing Committee, in his final report described the speech as a Soviet public relations victory: "The IOC, the International Sports Federations and the majority of National Olympic Committees demonstrated cohesion and solidarity in the struggle for the very future of Olympism. It was with a feeling of satisfaction that the international public received the decisions of the IOC Session in Lake Placid, the participants of which rebuffed the political interference in sport, and unanimously reaffirmed Moscow's right to hold the Games of the XXIInd Olympiad." He added: "The attempts to disrupt the Games in Moscow suffered a resounding defeat."[34]

Novikov's assessment was accurate. "I was mad as hell and even more determined that the IOC must never yield to political pressure," Worrall of Canada stated. Lord Killanin observed, "Vance's speech had drawn the IOC membership together as though someone had lassoed them with an enormous rope. On every side, in the corridors of the country club, in the restaurant, and among callers to my suite, there were words of disgust at what the United States government was doing and the way it was going about it."[35]

Killanin was not the only one who saw the widespread anger that Vance had generated. Vitaly Smirnov, a member of the Committee from the Soviet

Union, recalled, "Many people came to me to express support for Moscow from who I would not have expected it: General [Niels] Holst-Sorenson from Denmark, serving with the NATO air force, made a firm statement in support of Moscow, and subsequently had difficulties at home on account of this. The same with [Syed] Wajid Ali [of Pakistan]: people for whom it was not easy to make such views public, but who wanted them to be recorded. From that moment, I really understood that whether we are from the east or from the west, what we care about is the Olympic Games. It was a big lesson for me."[36]

The next day, Lord Killanin officially declared the eighty-second session of the IOC open since Vance had failed to perform this ceremonial task in what, according to the minutes, he called "the most embarrassing ceremony ever held." The Committee decided to hold off discussion of the boycott for another day until the Lords Exeter and Luke could arrive. On the morning of February 10, the full membership of the Committee took up the issue of the Moscow Olympics. Killanin had circulated Kane's statement to the Executive Board, and the American was present to explain his position. "There, again, I thought we were received in good grace," the American observed. Several members questioned both the actions of the USOC and of the U.S. government. Killanin pointed out that the United States had been engaged in combat during previous Olympic festivals and no effort had been made to exclude the Americans. Kane replied that this situation was different because it was the host nation that was at war.[37]

After some more discussion, Killanin pointed out that the U.S. government had made very little effort to use other elements of national power, like economic embargos and trade sanctions, against the Soviet Union. Alexandru Siperco of Romania asked if the USOC would be involved in establishing alternate games. According to the minutes, "Mr. Kane's answer was an emphatic 'no.'" Killanin wondered how the USOC executive committee could have unanimously recommended this proposal. Doug Roby, who was a member of both the IOC and the USOC, explained that he had only supported the resolution requesting that the IOC consider relocation. Alejandro Rivera Bascur of Chile said he believed that the games should stay in Moscow, even though his country would be absent from the festival. This decision was a voluntary one on the part of the Comité Olímpico de Chile*. The Soviet Union had boycotted Chile in past international sports competitions, and the Chileans had no intention of traveling to Moscow pretending that bygones were bygones.[38]

After this discussion ended, the Committee heard a report from the Moscow organizers and then, once this business concluded, discussed the Afghanistan issue in earnest without the American or Soviet delegations present. Lord Exeter, Philipp von Schoeller of Austria, and Marc Holder of

* Olympic Committee of Chile.

Switzerland praised Kane for his dignified manner and presentation of a position he did not hold. Lord Exeter, Prince Alexandre de Mérode of Belgium, and Wlodimierz Reczek of Poland all expressed the view that the future of the Olympics was at stake.[39]

Killnanin then asked a three-man committee of Worrall, Daume, and Reginald Alexander of Kenya to come up with a statement on the boycott. The Committee examined the statement in its English and French versions and approved it unanimously. "The overriding decision I think was a reaction against, basically against Secretary of State Vance's speech at the Opening of the Session, where he came and attacked us," Killanin told the BBC later in the year. He released the statement publicly in his name: "The very existence of the Olympic Games, the Olympic Movement and the organization of sports through the International Federations is at stake. All 73 members present at the 82nd session of the International Olympic Committee are unanimous that the Games must be held in Moscow as planned." The New York Times coverage of this meeting drew explicit attention to the fact that the two Americans on the committee, Roby and Julian Roosevelt, had voted in support of this statement.[40]

Kane had failed, but the nature of his presentation had been extremely important. According to the Olympic Charter, the USOC was in violation. The Charter required that all national committees be independent of their governments. Kane had clearly been pursuing the foreign policy objects of the Carter White House. The International Olympic Committee, however, had no intention of taking any action against the Americans. "I must congratulate you and Don Miller on the way you handled the very delicate situation in which your President placed you," Killanin wrote Kane. Richard Pound of Canada agreed, "Now that the some of the smoke has cleared, I wanted to drop you a short note to express my personal admiration (and in this respect, I think every member of the International Olympic Committee feels the same way) for the manner in which you conducted yourself at the IOC Session in Lake Placid. I think everyone knew the extremely difficult position in which you found yourself and sympathized very deeply with you." Such understanding was in the interests of the Committee. The United States was one of the leading powers in international sport and was scheduled to host the games of the XXIII Olympiad. The idea of banning the United States from participating in the next set of summer games, which they were to host, was absurd. "I resolved at Lake Placid to avoid that sort of maneuvering," Lord Killanin stated.[41]

Proponents of the boycott were quite disappointed with this outcome. Clark said the decision was "clearly wrong." The White House Staff released a public statement of its own: "We regret the decision of the International Olympic Committee to conduct the Olympic games in Moscow." Thatcher declared in Parliament that it was now the policy of her government that Britain should boycott the Olympic games.[42]

There was little surprise to this outcome for those that understood the organization of international sport. The *Association des Comités Nationaux Olympiques** met in Mexico City a few days before the IOC gathered in Lake Placid. This group passed a resolution urging the IOC to resist pressure to postpone, move, or cancel the Moscow games. Since there was a good deal of overlap in membership between the two organizations, this vote was a good indicator of what transpired in New York. There is no indication, though, that the Carter administration had any idea that this meeting was taking place, much less its significance.[43]

Kane and the USOC were still in a difficult bind. The IOC had rejected their position, but Kane still wanted to play for time. He released a heavily qualified statement that seemed to support the policy of the White House: "We must remain open to the President's views of what is best in the international interest and to the will of the American people."[44]

Carter decided to ignore these qualifications, releasing a public statement and a letter thanking Kane for his support. Jimmy Carter never signed anything without reading it first and often made small changes in his correspondence. In a small sign indicative of the sloppy administrative work that was typical of this White House staff, Kane received two versions of this letter, both signed by the President, but one with a typographical error that Carter had hand-corrected.[45]

Cutler and his lieutenants realized that they were no longer scoring victories as easily as they had in January and were growing frustrated. "We need a prompt USOC decision to build momentum for the boycott and beg[i]n planning for alternative games, objectives USOC does not share," Onek stated. "We may be forced to say soon that American athletes will not go to Moscow regardless of what the USOC decides." In a meeting with U.S. Olympic officials at Lake Placid, Onek said that the White House would destroy both the USOC and international Olympic movement if they refused to comply with the administration. Kane used the term "phony arrogance of power" afterwards to describe Onek. The White House lawyer quickly apologized, but there was nothing idle in this threat. He also noted many years later that Cutler never repudiated his statement.[46]

Cutler made an even bigger mistake. With the February 20 deadline approaching and it being clear that Soviet troops would be in Afghanistan after that date, reporters in Lake Placid asked Cutler if there would still be a boycott of the Moscow games if the Soviets withdrew some time afterwards but before the start of the Summer Olympics. "If there were a bona fide withdrawal, or a plan for a withdrawal, it would have to be considered," he replied. "After all, the objective of this is not to inflict a punishment but to achieve a result." Cutler had blundered with the media again. His comments were clearly

* Association of National Olympic Committees.

haphazard and informal, but reporters quickly exaggerated their importance, suggesting that they represented a shift in administration policy.[47]

Two days later, Carter tried to set the record straight at the end of a press conference. "We have no desire to use the Olympics to punish," he said. This statement, though, clearly contradicted what other government officials had said about the purpose of the boycott. Carter himself had been consistent in not wanting to use the Olympics in such a fashion, but this statement would come back to haunt him later. When asked the same question that had been put to Cutler about troop withdrawals before the Olympics, he answered, "I don't see any possibility of that." Reporters had generated this controversy, but despite its artificiality, it had hurt the Carter White House, perpetuating the "waffling" public image of the administration. The controversy was also misleading. There was no uncertainty of purpose in the White House on the issue of the boycott.[48]

It was at this time that Cutler decided that the U.S. government should destroy the international Olympic movement. "In my judgment there is probable cause to believe that the IOC and international federations have for some time been violating the antitrust laws of the United States, and that the illegal arrangements among them will obstruct our present efforts and those of the U.S. Olympic Committee to arrange for alternate games." The IOC was the legislature, judge, jury, and executioner when it came to regulating the Olympic movement. "The rules and the lack of reasonable hearing procedures would appear to be unreasonable restraints of trade under *Silver v. New York Stock Exchange.*" Although contracts with U.S. television networks provided the IOC with their single largest source of revenue, the White House had little leverage over the Committee. As a way of gaining leverage over the Olympic movement, Onek had proposed to Cutler in January that the United States get the United Nations Educational, Scientific and Cultural Organization (UNESCO) to take the place of the International Olympic Committee, since it had a charge to advance physical education. "The IOC would undoubtedly fear that once [UNESCO] gets its nose in the tent it would try to take over the international competitions."[49]

As the White Counsel, the in-house legal advisor to the President, Cutler had no power to initiate legal action himself. He hoped the Attorney General would do it for the administration. He told Civiletti that the IOC was both judge and jury in all matters involving the Olympic movement, even those within the United States. "Under these circumstances, you may want to consider initiating an appropriate investigation and the service of civil investigative demands on the IOC while its top officials are in Lake Placid."[50]

Cutler also drafted legislation that would give the President legal authority to prevent the USOC from participating in the Olympics and all U.S. media organizations from sending any reporters to Moscow. Lawyers in the Department of Justice warned Civiletti that there were serious problems with the draft. "Our very preliminary analysis of the constitutional issues raised by that proposal suggests that much further thought and study, which we are undertaking, will have to be done before we can draw any firm conclusions as to subsection (b)'s constitutionality." Congress had consistently refused to grant the President the power to control the communications industry – even as a war power. The courts had also been consistent in ruling against legislation that specifically targeted this industry. "If subsection (b) has a theoretical capacity to reduce coverage of the 1980 games, we think the courts will have little difficulty finding a burden on the First Amendment interests." Civiletti sent the paper to Cutler. "I agree with their preliminary assessment that subsection (b) raises substantial constitutional questions."[51]

The Attorney General also told Cutler to drop the idea of destroying the International Olympic Committee. "I do not think that we will serve that objective by beginning to seriously examine either the IOC or the international sports federations on antitrust grounds." He had two reasons for taking this position. "All foreign nations and particularly western countries are violently opposed to the extra territorial application of our anitrust laws." He also believed that such an effort would be one designed to attack "the entire concept, principles, and organization of the Olympics in perpetuity. That battle is one we are unlikely to win, either in the United States or elsewhere in the world." Such a move would be bad. The President had repeatedly said he believed in the Olympics and was opposed only to Soviet efforts to manipulate the games. "I think that any action in this regard on a policy ground would be totally unproductive to achieve our objective and seriously undermine the President's position."[52]

A week later, Department of Justice lawyers produced a preliminary and pessimistic examination of the relevant case law. Assistant Attorney General Stanford Litvack of the Antitrust Division, declared, "It seems very difficult to construct a serious antirust challenge to the IOC's basic control over the Olympic games or to link its decision on the question of where to hold the 1980 summer games to competition." Civiletti considered the issue closed. "This preliminary view confirms my dim view of the utility of antitrust law application to this subject."[53]

Cutler, however, refused to give up on this subject. "While I agree with many of the conclusions, the memo does not deal with the central question of whether it could violate the antitrust laws for the IOC and the international sports federations (the IF's) to conspire to refuse to sanction 'alternate games' about two weeks after the Olympics, to be held at several sites including an American site, open to athletes from all nations, including those who go to Moscow."[54]

With Cutler advancing these ideas, some people were beginning to wonder if he should continue to oversee boycott efforts. Al McDonald in particular had some profound reservations about the White House Counsel wandering from his assigned tasks. "The issue should be kept narrow and specific," he told Cutler. On February 14, during Carter's regular Thursday morning meetings with his senior White House staff, he asked if attacking the antitrust status of the IOC was wise. Efforts that might result in a direct attack on the international Olympic movement or change the status of amateur sport in the United States required careful study and consideration of all possible ramifications. Without directly blaming Cutler, he suggested in a memo that he prepared the next day that the White House Counsel was using heavy-handed methods that were turning counterproductive. "The Onek flap in Lake Placid was unfortunate. On balance, Secretary Vance's speech probably had a negative impact also." He suggested it might be time to hand off the boycott to the State Department and pursue the policy through traditional diplomatic channels: "For the moment, we are riding the crest of a gigantic and successful wave on the Olympic issue. Perhaps I am dead wrong, but I am concerned that we are pressing our luck too hard. If not handled with great care, the situation could turn from a solid, positive movement with great punitive damage to the USSR into a broad international squabble that has nothing to do with our national security response to the Soviet invasion of Afghanistan which is our only reason to be involved."[55]

Cutler had no interest in giving up his duties on the Olympic boycott. He had real influence with Carter and was becoming an even more important figure in Washington. In his response to McDonald, he backed away a bit from the idea of challenging the IOC's legal status. He believed establishing counter-Olympics was necessary, because "the President's prestige is fully engaged," and a rival set of competitions would convince other nations to join the boycott. No one at the State Department or the NSC had the time to offer the strong leadership that the boycott required. "To pick up your metaphor of riding the gigantic wave, the surfboard is only half way to shore, and we still run a great risk of wiping out. Is this the time to change riders?"[56]

Perhaps it was. The boycott had started coughing and sputtering. Many of the mistakes the administration had made were self-inflicted, ranging from Warren Christopher's comments to Helmut Schmidt to Vance's speech at Lake Placid. None of this damage was irreversible. In the second half of February and in March, these mistakes become permanent. Much was again self-inflicted, but some of the damage came from unlikely sources, including Herb Brooks and his hockey team.

CHAPTER 8

The White House Games

IN MID-FEBRUARY, CUTLER'S ASSESSMENT LOOKED TO BE ACCURATE. The Carter White House had suffered several defeats, but none of them were irreversible. Over the course of the next six weeks, the boycott effort would stall as the public mood started to shift. During this time, Cutler led the administration into a strategic cul-de-sac, exposing some of the worst elements of Carter's leadership methods.

Much of the fading public support, though, had to do with the Winter Olympics taking place in Lake Placid. As figure skater Scott Hamilton carried the U.S. flag and led his teammates clad in their official team uniforms of brown sheepskin coats and cowboy hats into the brisk air of the opening ceremonies, a shift was taking place in public opinion. Sports columnist Ken Denlinger of *The Washington Post* argued that this change had already taken place. The boycott had been "a miscalculation of American passion for Olympic sport." Denlinger explained, "Americans are wildly apathetic about the Olympic sports, until a month or so before they take place."[1]

Carter, however, refused to reconsider his position. At the annual meeting of the American Legion, he said the Soviet invasion of Afghanistan had "altered the careful balance of forces in a vital and a volatile area of the world." He characterized the response of his administration as equitable but strong, and that included the boycott of the Moscow Olympics. "That deadline is tomorrow, and it will not be changed." The *Washington Post* reporter covering the story noted this statement drew "strong applause" from an otherwise silent crowd. To add strength to this message, Carter, relying on Cutler's advice, ordered the U.S. Army to cut all ties to the U.S. Olympic Committee that was in support of the trip to Moscow.[2]

As if there was any doubt to the President's meaning, the White House staff reinforced his message. Lloyd Cutler appeared on the NBC television network's *Today* show the morning of February 20. Only a week removed from his blunder at Lake Placid, Cutler was careful to stay on message. There was no chance now, he said, that U.S. athletes would compete in Moscow. He also predicted that thirty–forty nations would take part in the boycott. The White House press office also released a statement, noting that "Soviet forces have not even begun to withdraw from Afghanistan." As a result, the President's "decision remains unchanged."[3]

Editorial coverage in response was still strong at this point. "The U.S. Olympic Committee can't have it both ways. Either it stands with the President or with the Kremlin," declared the editors of the *Philadelphia Inquirer*. One of Carter's hometown papers, *The Atlanta Constitution*, praised his actions. "Setting a deadline on Afghanistan was the right decision and following through was the proper course to take. Let the world know Uncle Sam's word is his bond." *The Commercial Appeal* of Memphis declared: "The boycott will work, regardless of how many countries join in." This editorial also added, "The boycott can be a symbol of U.S. determination."[4]

There was, though, a clear trend among a number of commentators who began thinking that this policy was ill-conceived. In New Jersey, the editors of *The Bergen County Record* observed, "With no assurance that the rest of the world will follow America's lead, we find ourselves locked into an intractable position a full five months before the Olympics. A lot can happen in those five months to make us regret the President's hasty decision." The editors of *The Des Moines Register* wondered if the Olympics was an area into which the government should be intruding: "U.S. athletes are free as individuals to stay away from Moscow if that is what their consciences tell them. They should be equally free to participate in a world event that this year happens to be held in Russia." Others questioned Carter's resolve. After the boycott deadline passed, the editors of *The Salt Lake Tribune* were pleasantly surprised: "For once, Jimmy Carter seems determined to stand his ground. Too bad that this belated show of resolve is reserved for a cause that may already have been lost."[5]

At this point, the Soviets pushed back a little. For the most part, the boycott was a battle between the U.S. government and the international Olympic movement. The Soviets, though, attempted to put some pressure on the West Germans. Deputy Soviet Foreign Minister Vladimir Semenov told Schmidt that the Olympics were "indispensable" to the future of détente. The Federal Republic should not take part in the boycott if they wanted to continue to improve relations with the Soviets and the East Germans.[6]

Events quickly began turning against the boycott. The start of the winter Olympics showed the American people that there was a moral and ethical stand to be had for participating in the games of summer. The magic of the winter Olympics was one thing. The stunning success of the U.S. hockey team was another thing altogether. Marshall Brement of the NSC realized the "miracle on ice" had changed public sentiment. "The Olympic situation seems to be disintegrating," he warned Brzezinski. "If we are not careful, our magnificent hockey win may fuel domestic sentiment against the boycott." He was right, and others saw this change in sentiment as well. A week later, a headline for an article in *The New York Times* declared: "THE OLYMPIC BOYCOTT, NOW LAGGING, STILL FACES HURDLES: THE CARTER ADMINISTRATION MAY AT LEAST GET A GOLD MEDAL FOR TRYING."[7]

Brzezinski claims he saw that public sentiment had turned against the boycott and recommended to the President that the administration give up on the effort. In his memoirs, the National Security Advisor writes: "By late February it became clear to me that [Cutler's] efforts were getting nowhere and that at best we would obtain only a partial boycott by other states of the Moscow Olympics. I briefed the President on February 22, and soon thereafter we dropped our effort to organize an alternative event, concentrating on making certain that in addition to the United States some other key countries refrained from participating." While this account sounds reasonable, Brzenzinski is quite wrong; the administration and Carter were still committed to the idea of alternate games.[8]

A public opinion poll that the U.S. Olympic Committee commissioned showed that while the boycott still had public support, it was much weaker than at the beginning of the year. The Roper organization conducted this survey during the first week of March. In response to this question – "Now that the Winter Olympic Games are over, would you say they made you feel more proud of our country, or less proud, or didn't affect your feelings one way or the other?" – 75 percent replied "more proud." When asked if the U.S. should still boycott Moscow in the wake of what happened at Lake Placid, 58 percent still favored the boycott. This figure still represented a majority, but it was down from the astronomical figures that some polls found in January. A survey from the Gallup organization conducted at roughly the same time reported similar sentiment; 63 percent of the public supported a boycott. What is important to note about this survey is that it showed that the support for the boycott was hollow. When asked if it was "proper" to use the Olympics for political purposes regardless of what might have been done in the past, 67 percent said it was wrong. When asked if the U.S. should send a team to Moscow if the Soviets withdrew even though it would be after Carter's February 20 deadline, 63 percent of the public said the Americans should be present. Foreign Service Officer William J. Dyess studied these figures in a report that ended up on Carter's desk and noted, "It seems there is sizable and strong support, at the present, for reconsidering the U.S. position, 'if the Russians should pull out of Afghanistan before the games take place.'"[9]

The Soviets were coming to similar views about Carter's boycott. Boris Ponomarev, Central Committee Secretary for International Relations of the Communist Party of the Soviet Union, met with his Bulgarian, Czechoslovakian, East German, Hungarian, and Polish counterparts on February 26. He told them that Carter's efforts to use the boycott against international socialism had failed. The boycott crisis was far from over, but the Games would go on as scheduled regardless. It was also in the political interests of the Soviet Union to have as many athletes from as many countries as possible take part in the Olympics.[10]

At a press conference held just after the Winter Olympics ended, a reporter asked Carter if he was worried about fading support for his policy. "I do believe that the overwhelming support that I've so far seen in America will not wane for our refusal to go to the Olympics in Moscow," he replied.[11]

Carter, along with almost every American sports fan, had rooted for the U.S. hockey team, and he decided to do something that was out of character for him: He hosted a reception for the Winter Olympians at the White House. Although it has become commonplace in the years since for championship teams to have a reception at the White House, it was still a fairly new exercise in 1980. Carter was initially only interested in bringing the hockey team to the White House. The rest of the Olympic team was an afterthought. Carter made this point inadvertently in his public comments at the reception, explaining that his initial invitation had been a narrow one.[12]

With that point made, Carter was personally excited about the event. In a speech he gave earlier in the day to a youth organization, he declared with obvious pride that the "American hockey team whipped the Soviets and went on to bring the gold medal to our people." He was also looking forward to meeting Eric Heiden, who had won five gold medals in speed skating. He then managed to tie the Olympics to the idealism he saw in the audience before him.[13]

The 1980 U.S. Winter Olympic Team, clad in various different combinations of their team uniforms and warmup suits, arrived at the South Lawn of the White House just before noon. They assembled on both sets of steps leading up to the portico and on both sides of that balcony. A crowd of several hundred watched from the grounds below. A sign near the White House declared: "USA Hockey Team – Best thing on Ice Since Scotch!"[14]

With Olympic athletes flanking him on either side, Carter declared, "For me, as President of the United States of America, this is one of the proudest moments that I've ever experienced." Although his initial comments were about Herb Brooks, he took time to praise other medalists: "Eric Heiden's performance at these winter games will be remembered for years to come." Heiden and the hockey team had accounted for all the gold medals the Americans won at Lake Placid, but Carter had words of praise for the other medalists, some of whom were seen as losers for failing to live up to expectations. He introduced Leah Poulos Mueller, who had won two silver medals in speedskating, and Linda Fratianne, the defending world champion in figure skating who had finished second behind Anett Pötzsch of East Germany. Many people had expected Beth Heiden to win as many gold medals as her brother. In fact, both Heidens had appeared on the cover of *Time* magazine just before the Olympics started. This attention seemed reasonable. She was the defending world champion in three different distances, but instead she managed to win one bronze medal. "And I would like to say that my heart went out especially to Beth Heiden, who did a tremendous job. And I think she deserves an awful lot of credit." He also praised skier Phil Mahre who had won a silver medal in the slalom after coming back from a broken leg that he suffered a year before on the same mountain.[15]

Afterwards each individual member of the team walked up the south-western steps of the portico and shook the President's hand. Carter gave Eric Heiden a bear hug after they shook hands. Beth Heiden, who had been driven to tears at Lake Placid, hugged him. He kissed her on the forehead. The mood was electric. Haynes Johnson in an article of commentary for *The Washington Post* noted, "After a long run of lousy luck, Americans finally had something to cheer." Lesley Stahl in her story for the *CBS Evening News* compared the White House event to the reception soldiers get after coming home from a war.[16]

A reception inside the White House followed. The Olympians milled around the executive mansion, ate, and posed for pictures with the President, administration officials, and one another. There was a good deal of autograph signing as well. Many were in awe. "One of the things that always strikes you is how impressed people are – and you tend to forget – just to have an opportunity to meet the President and to be in the White House, and sometimes they're really taken aback by it all and they're sort of bashful and inarticulate and so forth," White House Press Secretary Jody Powell reflected later on this event. "And almost afraid to speak or move for fear they might do something wrong."[17]

Perhaps – perhaps not. Looking out over the South Lawn, Mike Eruzione said, "I'd love to hit a few golf balls on that."[18]

Jerry Rafshoon, former White House director of communication who was then working for the reelection campaign, and White House Chief of Staff Hamilton Jordan were gloating – as professional political operatives often do – over the publicity they would get on the evening news telecasts. Jordan's secretary told them that using the Winter Olympics to support a boycott against the Summer Olympics was one of "the most shameless things I have ever seen." Rafshoon, laughing in mock anger, disagreed. The most shameless thing he had ever done was arrange Carter's appearance on *What's My Line* when he was governor of Georgia.[19]

The Carter lieutenants were probably disappointed when they saw the news. Eric Heiden had taken the point in soliciting a petition in which the winter athletes denounced the boycott, and all three networks insisted on mentioning this effort. "The winter athletes in general just don't feel that a boycott is the right thing," Heiden said when he appeared in Sam Donaldson's story for ABC's *World News Tonight*. The stories that appeared on both ABC and Columbia Broadcasting System (CBS) gave the impression that the athletes were united in their opposition.[20]

The truth was a little more complex. Sports reporters Tony Kornheiser and John Feinstein in their story for *The Washington Post* found that the winter athletes were divided on the subject. "I didn't sign anything," Mike Eruzione said, "and I don't think any of my hockey players would have." Kornheiser and Feinstein found similar sentiment elsewhere among the Winter Olympians. "I feel sorry for the people training for the Summer Games," David Santee, a figure skater, told the two reporters. "But I'm probably better off if I don't comment on the boycott." Among the television networks, only NBC quoted an athlete supporting Carter. Hockey goaltender Jim Craig basically said the U.S. Olympic Committee should do whatever the President instructed.[21] The damage was done, though. More people watched the television networks then read *The Washington Post*.

Carter had little grounds for complaint. The athletes themselves were extremely deferential in their behavior at the White House. No one made an effort to make a political statement or discuss policy during the ceremony. In the petition, the athletes thanked him for inviting them to the White House and said they were "extremely proud" for having had the chance to represent their country at the Olympics. They stressed the opportunities they had to meet with others from a number of different countries and exchange ideas. "Mr. President, we urge you to use your most prestigious office to assure that our fellow athletes who have trained diligently for the Olympic Summer Games are provided the same opportunity which we have just experienced." The letter had the signatures of many that had or would go on to acquire fame in the 1980s: Fratianne, Mueller, both Heidens, Scott Hamilton, Tai Babilonia, and Randy Gardner, to name just a few.[22]

The document had no impact on the President or on the White House staff. There were, however, members of the White House staff that worried about what influence it might have on public opinion. Two days after the reception, a memo that ended up Cutler's desk advised him that the administration should hold a briefing for the summer Olympians "to counter the post-Lake Placid erosion of support which has begun."[23]

The main focus of the administration at this time was on organizing the alternative Olympics. "The primary purpose for holding alternative international games is to increase the number of major nations which decide not to send teams to Moscow this summer," Lloyd Cutler and Joe Onek informed the Special Coordination Committee, a subcommittee of the National Security Council that Brzezinski chaired. "A secondary purpose is to alleviate the disappointment of athletes who might otherwise be deprived of a major world class competition this summer."[24]

This second sentiment was significant. Carter and his lieutenants understood that the athletes were going to suffer. Onek observed years later:

> Obviously for many of the athletes it was an extraordinary – all were disappointed. For some it is a bigger thing than others, obviously. Although

I must say I began to feel less sorry for the athletes the more I met them only because they had their whole lives had such charmed lives. I met with the volleyball team. Very nice women, and they said something like, 'Oh, we are so disappointed because we wanted to play' – I can't even remember – 'we wanted to play the Chinese again. And we played them in Japan and we played them in China and we really wanted to meet them in Moscow' or whatever. Okay, I haven't been to Japan. In other words, these were people who were leading very full and happy lives as athletes and they weren't exactly the underprivileged of the world.[25]

There was popular support for the counter-Olympics among the public. "There can – and should – be summer alternatives," an editorial in *The Washington Post* declared. "That calls for serious planning now." Carter understood this fact. At a press conference that predated the editorial, he stated, "I am going to pursue aggressively – already am – the holding of international, quality, alternate games." He added, "I believe the Americans will support this alternative effort. I do not believe, under any circumstances, that Americans would support our going to the Moscow Olympics this summer."[26]

Work on establishing an alternate Olympics began early in the boycott campaign. In January, the British government had their embassies begin sounding out the municipal governments of the last four summer Olympics about the possibility of hosting some type of replacement sports festival. The results were mixed, and in a letter Thatcher sent to Carter two days after his appearance on *Meet the Press*, she said the United Kingdom would help, but holding major events in Britain was not possible. Lloyd Cutler and the U.S. government quickly took over this effort despite concerns from the British over the political ramifications of perceived U.S. unilateralism. The State Department issued invitations to eleven different governments to begin planning a replacement for the Olympics. The meeting was held quietly at the State Department on February 12, the same day the IOC debated the status of the Moscow Games. Only five governments (Australia, Canada, the Netherlands, Great Britain, and the United States) sent representatives. Officials from Saudi Arabia and the Philippines were present, but only as observers. The meeting took most of the day. Cy Taylor, an Assistant Under Secretary in the Canadian Department of External Affairs, chaired the meeting as the senior diplomat in the room.[27]

Using the experiences of 1976, the Canadian delegation presented a sobering assessment about the feasability of staging an alternative set of games. Looking at the numbers that had participated in Montreal, over half had come from nations that were already on record as opposing a boycott. Cutler and Onek ignored these facts and led a long discussion on the political need to have an alternate set of game in order to support the boycott. Although everyone in the room agreed with the diplomatic objectives, many kept noting the practical obstacles to the boycott. Taylor noted that most Western governments had no direct control over their Olympic movements. A long discussion followed about mechanisms that could be used to influence Olympic officials. Cutler even made reference to the ancient games as offering political precedent. The discussion turned to the issue of receiving sanction from the international athletic federations. Everyone acknowledged the problems these organizations faced, but none were willing to admit the effort stood little chance of success. The Canadians then returned the conversation to the practical: In 1976, Montreal required housing for 6,000 athletes and 4,000 support personnel (coaches, trainers, judges, etc.), the military provided 15,000 personnel for logistical support, nineteen separate law enforcement agencies had been involved in providing security, and it would require a year and a half to set up the new television equipment. No mention was made of who would pay for all this effort. For all these reasons, the Canadians argued it was impossible to have an alternate set of games.[28]

The Americans, however, did not want to hear this information. An incident that occurred late in the day encapsulated much of the Carter administration's approach to the boycott. Warren Christopher entered the room and said the boycott was a moral issue and that the United States appreciated the support of the other six countries. He wanted Europe to join in this effort. A British cable documenting the meeting made it clear that the Americans warned the assembled diplomats that the boycott was a litmus test of the U.S. alliance with Europe. If the allies failed to respond in sufficient fashion, the Americans would have to rethink their commitment to Europe. When given a short summary of the discussion that had dominated the meeting, Christopher said "ingenuity" and "hard work" could overcome whatever difficulties they faced.[29]

The main reason such cold hard facts failed to alter the American determination to set up some sort of replacement for the Olympics was that Jimmy Carter was committed personally to this objective. In a memo he sent to the President, Cutler stated, "Other governments believe their NOC's and athletes would prefer a set of international world class competitions to replace the Olympics." Next to this sentence, Carter wrote: "So would I."[30]

Thatcher also still believed in the importance of holding alternative games. She, however, was far more realistic than Carter. When Vance visited London at the end of the month, she told him that alternative games were a critical element in making the boycott effective. She was willing to pay for these games. He replied that the U.S. government did not want to get into the business of sports administration and expected that the international athletic federations would pay the bill.[31] The fact that the U.S. government was unwilling to commit real resources to this effort did little to ensure success of the effort.

The discussion in the room that day, though, did convince Graham Dempster of the Australian Department of Tourism and Recreation. In later years, he presented himself as working against the idea of alternate games.

"My task was to convince the US State Department that they were crazy," he explained. "It wasn't a very clever idea at all. There really could be no alternative to the Olympics as there was no body to organise such a thing, the scope was just too great and it was doubtful any international body would fall for it and lose face with the IOC."[32] Records of the meeting hardly support this contention, though.[33]

The same day as his press conference, Carter expressed his interest in having Greece serve as the permanent home of the Olympics. In an example of the patronizing approach toward ethnic politics at work in the Carter White House, the President told the Order of the American Hellenic Educational Progressive Association: "wouldn't it be wonderful if we have a permanent Summer Olympic site in Greece." Appearing at the organization's annual dinner, Carter told the formally attired Greek Americans that returning the games to the land of their ancestors would solve all future political problems: "I think all of you realize that the Olympic games this summer should not be held in Moscow, because Russia is an invading nation. To do so would violate those very principles of peace and of brotherhood and of nonpolitical alignment of those who participate in the games – exactly the kind of defects that would be corrected with a permanent site." This speech might have been patronizing, but it worked. The Greek Americans cheered.[34]

The President had personally committed his administration to three different Olympic-related policy initiatives: a boycott of the Moscow games; the establishment of an alternative set of games; and the establishment of a permanent home for the summer Olympics in Greece. Since Carter was personally involved, Lloyd Cutler knew he had to deliver. He invoked the President's name and authority to win arguments and overcome opposition. The document recording one of these meetings reads: "Mr. Cutler said it is necessary to take some action. Time is running out, and unless we are prepared to show determination, there is a high risk that this issue, where the President's prestige is so heavily committed, will fall apart."[35]

The result of this presidential push was a rigidity in policy that ran almost 180 degrees counter to the public image of the administration. This inflexibility worried Al McDonald. He believed that organizing alternate games is going to be a difficult deal to pull off at best and feared that "it could prove to be an embarrassment to the President." He suggested, "the more general his statements on specifics the better while reaffirming his commitment to do his best for the athletes."[36]

This advice was wasted. Carter had no interest in backing away from the boycott. On March 5, he welcomed Helmut Schmidt to the White House. Their talks covered a number of topics, including the Olympics. Carter, by his own admission, was "sharply critical" of Schmidt's leadership. He spent a good deal of the meeting pushing Schmidt, asking him what West Germany had done to put pressure on the Soviet Union or provide assistance to the

Afghans. "The answer to both those questions apparently is 'Nothing,'" Carter noted in his diary.[37]

Schmidt, though, did promise that West Germany would support the boycott. The Americans thought this pledge was important. Culter believed and told Carter that West Germany was a key battleground for the boycott. If they joined, so would most of Western Europe. Although the animosity between the chancellor and the president was well-known, Cutler believed that Schmidt was living up to his pledge and said so in meetings. Schmidt, he said, was trying to be a good ally. The West German, though, came into the meeting with several grievances toward Carter and his lieutenants. He was still angry about his meeting with Christopher and von Staden's with Brzezinski.[38]

Schmidt clearly had grounds for his complaints. Carter had not offered strong leadership, and in addition, it was becoming obvious to many people associated with Olympic administration that the White House staff was ill-informed. "I told Cutler the alternate games would fail because they require the sanction of the international federations," Ueberroth wrote in his memoirs. "It was clear he and his associates didn't know a thing about international amateur sports." He got even angrier after he attended a White House meeting on setting up alternate games in March. At the meeting, a list of nations that the U.S. was asking for support was distributed. "South Africa stood out like a beacon. Damn it, I thought, Carter, Cutler, and the rest of them didn't have a clue." The IOC still banned South Africa from participating in the Olympics. Bob Berenson, a physician serving on the domestic policy staff of the White House, was candid about this shortcoming: "Look, we don't have anyone in the White House who works on sports. When all this started, I was the only one there who even knew anyone on the U.S. Olympic Committee. We were listing countries who would boycott that didn't even have Olympic teams. We've learned an awful lot lately."[39]

Even if the Carter White House could have overcome the administrative issues involving the federations, logistics was another huge problem. Cities need six to eight years to prepare for the Olympics for a reason. Few cities have an existing mass transit system or police force capable of handling the influx of people normally associated with the Olympics. Nor could any city produce fifty or sixty thousand empty hotels rooms needed to house the competitors, officials, media, and fans in the time available. "It's more complicated than organizing a burlap-bag foot race for a Sunday picnic," one coach told *The Christian Science Monitor*.[40]

These difficulties started becoming apparent to some within the administration even before the Lake Placid games ended. Few countries responded to a White House invitation to attend a meeting to begin planning for a new set of competitions. The Canadians in their response stated that Montreal was not a possibility. Marshall Brement told Cutler he was "uneasy and considerably less optimistic about our prospects." There was no chance of putting together any competition at the same time of the Moscow Olympics. The chances of organizing some event that would take place after Moscow were better. "However, the odds of achieving this are nevertheless still quite slim." His advice to Cutler was blunt. "If we are not willing to go all out on this, the chances of failure are large, and we would probably be better off dropping the idea of alternate games altogether and concentrating only on an Olympic embargo." This recommendation was sound, but with the President personally committed to the idea, Cutler had to move forward in this area.[41]

Others were worried as well. Nelson Ledsky, head of the State Department task force on the boycott, warned Vance in early March: "The starch seems to be slowly going out of our boycott effort." A number of foreign governments were having difficulty getting their national Olympic committees to honor the boycott. "The fact that many states and national Olympic committees (including the USOC) are waiting as long as possible before accepting or declining their invitation to Moscow in the hope of a change in the situation in Afghanistan has prevented us from developing a bandwagon of support especially in Africa and Latin America."[42]

Cutler, though, had already begun work on establishing the alternate games. A problem he faced – and one he did not know he faced – was the role of the international athletic federations. In early February, Michael Scott, an attorney with the legal firm Squire, Sanders & Dempsy, met with Onek, an old acquaintance, and they discussed the role of the federations. Scott was counsel to the National Collegiate Athletic Association and knew something about sports administration. At Onek's request, he investigated the role of the federations. A week later, he wrote to Onek, and his news was not particularly good: "An effort to hold an event 'competitive' with the summer Olympic Games will encounter substantial difficulties, particularly with reference to the asserted 'jurisdiction' of the various IFs. That jurisdiction, however, rests exclusively upon an international network of de facto consensual arrangements among private parties, and can be effectively exercised only by means of threats of disqualification to athletes who participate in events not approved within the framework of this private network." There was hope, but only if the administration wanted and was prepared to challenge the various federations. "The essential issue posed for proponents of 'competitive' games is whether they are prepared directly to confront this IOC-based international cartel, and to encourage participating athletes to do so as well." After getting this letter, Onek and Berenson made some phone calls to several U.S. athletic federations and discovered Scott was right.[43]

Cutler quickly adapted to this information and arranged a meeting with Thomas Keller, the president of the *Fédération Internationale des Sociétés* *d'Aviron**, which took place the day after the White House reception. The decision to talk with the Swiss chemical engineer was a smart one. In addition to his work with the Rowing Federation, he was also president of the *Association Générale des Fédérations Internationales de Sports†*, an organization of all international sports federations, even those not associated with the Olympics, and had a good deal of influence among the people that regulated international sport. The problem was that Cutler and Onek knew little of Keller's personal history. He had been a rower in the 1950s but never got to compete in the Olympics because the Swiss Olympic Association decided to boycott the 1956 Olympics in Melbourne, Australia, in protest over the Soviet Union's invasion of Hungary.[44]

In the discussion that followed, Keller appeared more knowledgeable about domestic American politics and U.S. foreign policy than his hosts were about international sports. Cutler and Onek told Keller that they had assurances from the governments of most Western European nations that they would boycott the Moscow Olympics and as a result, the IOC would end up canceling the games. The U.S. government wanted the international federations to authorize a two-week event in August and wanted them open to all athletes regardless of nationality, including the Soviets. Cutler then told him that the Soviet Union was unacceptable to serve as an Olympic host since it had invaded another country and said that the U.S. position had historical precedent since during the Games of antiquity, the city-state of Elis could not wage war during the Games. There is no record of how Keller reacted to this weak historical precedent, but according to the sanitized language of the memorandum documenting this meeting, Keller told the Americans that their proposal "would be a knife in the back of the IOC." He said it was one thing for an individual federation to sponsor events following the conclusion of the Olympiad, but it was another thing entirely for them to band together and stage what amounted to a set of counter-Games. When Onek argued that the U.S. government wanted to provide a venue for athletes to compete at the highest level, Keller dismissed the idea. An athlete that competed at Moscow was unlikely to appear at another event a few weeks later. There was only so long they could stay in peak physical condition, and medalists were unlikely to risk the stature of their Olympic achievement at some ad hoc contest. He also added that sport was a poor diplomatic tool. Onek and Nelson Ledsky quickly disagreed, telling him that the games were extremely important to the Soviets. According to the minutes, "Mr. Keller again regretted the American decision, but said he understood that the train had left the station and that it was now too late to change the American position." And on that note, this highly unproductive meeting came to an end.[45]

---

* International Rowing Foundation.
† General Association of International Sports Federations.

The White House Counsel and his staff were soon privately admitting what they had denied in public a few weeks before – organizing another set of competitions would be difficult. "Alternative games are impractical unless the planning begins now and firm commitments are made within a month," Cutler and Onek informed the Special Coordination Committee. "There is no single site other than the Soviet Union which can host all the Olympic events in 1980."[46]

The problem was Carter. When Cutler informed him that it was "impracticable" to hold a series of contests in one site, but that it would be possible to hold the contests at different locations around the world, the President noted on the margin: "good." According to the record of the March 6 meeting of the Special Coordination Committee, Cutler told the group that the administration "should know by the end of March whether the alternative games are a realistic prospect." There was no question for Carter, though. When he saw that line, he underlined it and wrote in the margin: "They must [be] held."[47]

Cutler was not one to deny the obvious. Organizing an alternative to Moscow faced a number of problems. "Foremost is the persisting opposition of the international federations." Cutler, though, was one to put his own spin on events. According to him, there were a number of factors why these organizations refused to cooperate. "The federations are entrenched, ably led, Soviet-infiltrated and totally unsympathetic to the boycott." His solution in late March was the same as it had been in late February – use U.S. antitrust laws against the collusion of the federations and the IOC.[48]

Sitting back in Dublin, Lord Killanin watched the White House effort without much concern. The Carter administration was "doomed to failure," to use his words: "What they did not understand was that without the cooperation of the international federations no such competition would be possible. The IFs agree, for their own benefit as much as for that of the Olympic Movement, not to hold major competitions just before or during the period of the Games."[49]

The White House had no intention of consulting Killanin on their efforts, but there were a number of commentators in American media outlets large and small who knew this endeavor would fail. Harrison Dillard, who won four gold medals at the 1948 and 1952 Olympics in various sprinting and hurdling events, denounced the idea early on. "Staging the various events in different cities is not only impractical but totally foreign to the Olympic concept," he declared in a *Cleveland Press* editorial. The idea of putting on alternate games subsidized by the United States is simply ridiculous on the face of it."[50]

Others agreed. "Excuse me, Mr. President, but your latest plan for an alternative Olympics – or whatever you choose to call it – is a bad one," Ken Denlinger declared in *The Washington Post*. The "semi-Olympics" would undermine the boycott. Even though they were open to all, it was unlikely that the Soviets and Eastern Europeans would participate, and these nations were major powers in most of the twenty-one Olympic sports. He also wondered who would pay for them. "The bottom line here, it seems, is that there is no happy alternative for an Olympic experience, no reality that will replace shattered dreams." In a *Los Angeles Times* guest editorial, sociologist Harry Edwards of the University of California at Berkeley noted that the logistical, economic, and political requirements of hosting an Olympics-like event made such an event almost impossible to organize. The alternative games proposal "portends some problems of a size matched only by the naivete exhibited by the Carter Administration in its approach to the issue." This idea, according to Edwards, was both incompetent and weak: "Is the White House serious in asking the American public to accept the notion that this nation's foreign policy has been reduced to employing a boycott of a sports event as the principal non-military response to what Carter has called the 'greatest threat to world peace and security since World War II'? If so, we should be debating questions of considerably greater gravity than whether this country should participate in the 1980 Summer Games." The boycott was bad policy, he declared, but knew that Carter had put his personal credibility on the line: "The President appears to have painted himself into a corner and then set the wall behind him on fire."[51]

Serious efforts at implementing the alternate games started only in the middle of March. Australian Minister of Home Affairs Robert Ellicott met with Under Secretary of State for Political Affairs David Newsom and informed the U.S. government that if the alternate games were ever going to happen, they needed to have some agreed-upon plans in place by the end of March. "I agree," Carter noted on the margin of the memo informing him of this meeting.[52]

Carter and his subordinates had missed the message the Australians were trying to send. Malcolm Fraser had serious reservations about the quality of Carter's leadership. Fraser believed the alternative games were vital in bringing about an Australian boycott. He called Margaret Thatcher on March 4, without any prior notice. According to one British official listening to the conversation, he "showed considerable impatience." Most of it was aimed at the Americans in general and Carter in particular. "Nothing much is happening," he told Thatcher. "I am worried that if we don't start to get some decisions and action of a hard nature that it is just going to run out from us." Thatcher agreed. Fraser figured the best chance to get an Australian boycott was if Canada agreed to host an alternate set of games, and the only way to do that was to get Carter to put political pressure on the government in Ottawa. Since that was not happening, he wanted Thatcher to join him in trying to pressure the Canadians. The British prime minister told him to wait, they needed to find out what Carter had already done in this regard. Fraser also wanted a pending meeting on setting up alternative games to be a meeting at the cabinet level to add some political weight to the effort and get some concrete results. He was going to do that one way or another.[53]

The problem the administration faced was finding someone to administer this effort with the appropriate expertise. "Promotion of alternative games is not a job for amateurs, even high-ranking public officials," Culter and Onek declared. They had four people in mind: Ueberroth; Petr Spurney, executive director of the Lake Placid Organizing Committee; Steven Ross, chief executive officer of Warner Communications and principle shareholder of the New York Cosmos soccer team; and television producer David Wolper, who was head of the television committee for the Los Angeles Olympics. Spurney met with Onek and was willing to help but still had work to do wrapping things up with Lake Placid and would not be available until mid-April. Ueberroth and Wolper agreed to attend a White House meeting on the alternate games. "I offered my assistance in making the best of a bad situation," Ueberroth noted. Wolper agreed to help because of his concerns about the welfare of athletes.[54]

Information about Wolper's involvement got back to Killanin, and he decided to take action. He wrote Kane and told him that the USOC and the LAOC needed to steer clear of any involvement with the effort. "It has been rumoured that certain persons connected with the Games in Los Angeles are assisting the White House Staff in regard to 'their' games. This of course could jeopardise the Olympic Games in Los Angeles." He was worried that Carter administration in its ignorance would get the USOC suspended. Kane got the message. "The so called Alternative Games are the mechanism of the White House," he told Killanin. "We have not associated with them at all. In fact, the very name is abhorrent to us and we've said so." He closed, telling Killanin that he still held out hope that the U.S. might attend the Moscow games.[55]

Ueberroth was also worried. Uncertainty about Moscow was making its way to Los Angeles and slowing down progress on 1984. He told the *Los Angeles Times*: "We have no involvement in such proposed games and believe they are counterproductive for our mutual objectives." Still, another month would pass before he got Killanin to issue a press release that reassured the Californians that the IOC would take no action to strip them of the games.[56]

Efforts to organize a set of countergames basically died with a whimper in Geneva, Switzerland. In mid-March, Cutler, Wolper, and other U.S. officials traveled to Europe for a planning meeting for the alternate games. Lord Killanin called the gathering "a Gilbert and Sullivan style meeting." Only twelve nations of the twenty-five invited sent representatives to the meetings held at the British Consulate General. According to British records of the meeting, Cutler admitted that time was against them. Cy Taylor of Canada warned that trying to impose an alternative set of games on the Olympic movement would backfire on the boycott effort. As a result, very little was decided on. The group selected no name for this competition, no site, and no organizer. Douglas Hurd, Secretary of State at the British Foreign Office, made it clear that none of the governments involved were going to get into the business of organizing sporting events. At a press conference that followed, Hurd and Cutler stressed the positive and argued that they had made significant progress. "What we have to do now, as a result of these meetings, is to get in touch with the various sporting organisations some national, some international," Hurd explained. British reporters tended to ask questions of Hurd, while Americans focused on Cutler. The White House lawyer went out of his way to explain that the games they were planning were benign in intent: "They would pose no threat to the future of the unitary Olympic movement." Hurd made this same point. Of course, what none of the reporters or Hurd knew was that Cutler was still arguing that the U.S. government should use antitrust laws against the IOC and the athletic federations. A *New York Times* reporter asked what would happen if the Soviets changed their policy in Afghanistan. "Then that would be a completely new suggestion," Hurd replied. Cutler, burned at Lake Placid on this question, was stringent in his response. The United States would "not send a team under any circumstances."[57]

The Soviets made it clear that they had no interest in participating in any alternative contests. Interviewed on French radio, Vladimir Popov, first deputy chairman of the Moscow Olympic Organizing Committee, said, "You see, quite naturally we reject this meeting because it contradicts the regulations and rules of international athletic federations. This is nothing but an additional act in the show some are attempting to set up around the Olympic games in Moscow, a show rooted in speculative political theories."[58]

While Cutler was in Europe, an intense debate was taking place in the United Kingdom. The boycott had become a partisan issue in British politics. Although Margret Thatcher's government was strongly in favor of this effort, the Labour Party and the British Olympic Association (BOA) were of different minds. Sir Denis Follows, chairman of the BOA, surveyed the members of the association and then reported to Thatcher, "There is little or no support for the suggestion that the Summer Games be moved from Moscow." Denis Howell, a Member of Parliament who had served as the United Kingdom's first minister of sport in the cabinet of Harold Wilson, circulated a memo that indicated that the position of the government "is not shared by HM opposition." Thatcher had been in office for just under a year, and the Labour Party, smarting over its defeat, was looking for a fight. This development was significantly different from the generally bipartisan support that the boycott had in the United States. What took place in Britain was no small battle. "We decided that every statement of Government had to be contested in Parliament and in the media," Howell explained.[59]

Even before the end of January, opposition had developed in Britain. "The campaign to protect the integrity of the Olympic movement in the Moscow Olympic Games of 1980 was the most epic political battle in which I have ever been engaged," Howell stated many years later.[60]

Politics sometimes make for strange alliances. Even though he was Irish, Lord Kilanin could speak in the House of Lords. He felt that using his peerage to speak out against the boycott was inappropriate. As a result, the Marquess of Exeter became the primary defender of the Moscow Olympics among the Lords. Given the history of Exeter's family, the defense of anything associated with the Soviets seemed a bit incompatible. David George Brownlow Cecil, the Sixth Marquess of Exeter was a member of a rich and powerful clan that had been active in English politics for centuries. The founder of this political dynasty was Sir William Cecil, who had been the primary political advisor to Queen Elizabeth I. During the reign of Queen Victoria, another Cecil, the third Marquess of Salisbury, served as Conservative Party prime minister three times. The Sixth Marquess had been active in politics in his own right, having held a seat in the House of Commons for twelve years before inheriting the title that made him a member of the House of Lords. Lord Exeter, though, was not defending the Soviet Union. He was attempting to protect the international Olympic movement. A member of the IOC, he had competed in three Olympics, winning gold in the hurdles at the 1928 Amsterdam games and silver four years later in Los Angeles. He was the first and, at the time, the only person to have ever completed the race around the Great Court at Trinity College, Cambridge, before the tower clock struck twelve. As a result, he was the inspiration for the Lord Andrew Lindsay character in the 1981 film *Chariots of Fire*. After his athletic career came to an end, Exeter was chair of the organizing committee for the 1948 London Olympics and served as president of the International Amateur Athletics Federation for several decades. "Transferring the Games elsewhere at such short notice is quite impractical," he told the other peers.[61]

Lord Exeter opposed the boycott on principle. He quickly made his feelings known at the highest levels of the British government. He called Thatcher in January, and although he never talked to her, she saw the memo of the conversation the former Olympic champion had with one of her subordinates. She was getting bad advice. The IOC and only the IOC controlled the Olympic movement. There was no possibility of moving the games or arranging an alternative set of athletic contests. He was more than willing to meet with her personally to discuss matters further and had no intention of leaking to the media that he had contacted 10 Downing Street.[62]

Exeter also provoked a debate within the House of Lords on the Olympics. "International sport is the one great worldwide, generally accepted movement bringing the young together in friendship and understanding and it would be a tragedy to do something which would damage it," he said. An under-secretary in Thatcher's cabinet, Baron Bellwin of the City of Leeds, responded, saying "To carry on as if nothing had happened would be to acquiesce and contribute to a massive propaganda success for Russia. He added that it might be difficult to move the games from Moscow but "impossible it is not."[63]

Bernard Levin, a columnist for *The Times*, dismissed Exeter's arguments as "foolish and empty." In a two-part essay that appeared in his paper on back-to-back days, he noted that under the Olympic charter, the Soviet Union never should have been awarded the games in the first place. "The *whole* of the Soviet Union's participation in the Games and more particular her holding of them in Moscow is designed with a view to political profit." Aiming his wrath directly at Follows and Lords Exeter and Killanin, he argued that the Olympic movement gave the three a deluded sense of their own self-importance, which allowed them to make the absurd argument that politics was not a factor in Moscow's role as host. "How can such men live in a moral miasma of this kind and still swear – nay, believe – that the air is sweet? There is only one way, and it is by no means original, nor are they the only men who follow it. They accept in their honest, gullible good will, any lie the Soviet authorities tell them, however transparent, preposterous or disgusting, instead of ruthlessly seeing the turn in their own hearts."[64]

Howell challenged these views. "It is absurd to suggest that participation in this summer's Olympics is an endorsement of Russian policy as it is to suggest that our presence at Lake Placid automatically endorses American policy," he argued on the pages of *The Daily Telegraph*.[65]

These arguments carried little weight with the British Olympic Association. On March 4, the organization approved a simple statement:

> The National Olympic Committee confirms that it is its present intention to send a British team to the Olympic Games. However it will defer its reply to the invitation to participate until its next meeting on 25th March.

The reason for delaying was an effort to coordinate their response with other European committees and out of respect for actions that Thatcher said were underway to convince the Soviets to leave Afghanistan.[66]

The next day, Follows appeared before the Foreign Affairs Committee of the House of Commons. Like Kane, Follows faced a hostile audience. The major difference was that the Members of Parliament were far better informed than the U.S. Senators and Representatives that had questioned Kane. Follows was also far better prepared for the grilling that he faced than Kane had been. In 1978, the BOA had passed a resolution, declaring that it would not boycott the 1980 Olympics. This decision was a response from dissident groups that wanted to make a statement long before Afghanistan. The British Olympians decided to make their position clear in order to avoid additional campaigns attempting to persuade them to boycott: "We have seen no reason to change our opinion because of the invasion of Afghanistan."[67]

One Member of Parliament asked him what the BOA would do if the legislature took a strong stand on the Olympics. "If the House of Commons took a particular point, I am sure the British Olympic Association would give great consideration to it," Sir Denis replied. Sir Anthony Royle, whose father competed at the 1920 Olympics, noted the ambiguity in this response and asked if he or the BOA claimed better judgment in assessing the interests of the British people. Follows said no, it would be "impertinent" to claim otherwise, but the BOA did have a good understanding of world affairs. The last half of the response enflamed Royle, and he repeated the question. Follows maintained his course, "I am saying, on the basis of our experience of international affairs it is likely we have as much experience as most Members of Parliament."[68]

Peter Mills of West Devon asked him what he and other British Olympians could add to the effort to contain the Soviet Union. Follows refused to answer this question, giving his own preferred response: "Sport – and I know this from many years of experience – is the most unifying influence there is in the world today." He also made it clear that he resented the intrusion of Parliament into sports administration since it had ignored the subject up until then. He said he and others in the British Olympic movement believed they were being used as a "pawn."[69]

Parliament was in the process of debating a boycott, and that discussion continued in one form or another until the start of the summer games in Moscow, but the critical moment came two weeks later during the period Cutler was in Switzerland. The House of Commons spent seven hours on March 17 debating British participation in the Olympics. The Lord Privy Seal, Sir Ian Gilmour, introduced the following resolution:

> That this House condemns the Soviet invasion of Afghanistan and believes that Great Britain should not take part in the Olympic Games in Moscow.

It was the first time this body had debated sports. [70]

The BOA was hardly passive on this matter. It prepared a three-page memo that it sent to individual Members of Parliament. The Association was a member of the international Olympic movement and would support the Games, not the Soviet Union. It also repeated the advice that Lord Exeter had given to Thatcher – there was no substitute for the Olympics, and only the IOC could make decisions controlling the movement. It also added that Parliament had few resources to influence the association. The British government only provided £15,000, which was a small amount for an organization that would spend over £1 million to send a team to Moscow.[71]

As the debate began, the Speaker of the House indicated at the start of the debate that he had indications that fifty members wanted to address the issue.

Allowing that many to speak was "quite impossible," but just barely. Forty-nine individuals addressed the Commons that evening.[72]

Gilmour gave a long speech that was interrupted several times. His reasoning was quite similar to the one prevailing in the Carter White House at the time: "There is no question but that for the Soviet Union, holding the Olympic Games i[n] Moscow is of supreme importance. It sees the Games as a propaganda exercise from which it hopes to derive very great advantage. Conversely, a decision by several Western countries to absent themselves from the Games will have a powerful impact upon the Soviet population at large." Numerous speakers favoring the same position followed. Geoffrey Rippon of Hexham asked rhetorically, "Do British athletes really want to go and pay tribute of that kind at this time to the Soviet Union?" Sometimes the positions people took were unexpected. Nicholas Winterton, a Conservative from Macclesfield, was disappointed with Thatcher: "The limited action the Government have taken to register disapproval of Soviet tyranny in Afghanistan is totally inadequate."[73]

Much more of the debate followed predictable courses. Winston Churchill, grandson and namesake of the former prime minister, directed attention to a Misha the Bear lapel pin he was wearing, which had been made with slave labor. Raymond Fletcher, a Labour MP representing Ikleston, who was secretly spying for the KGB, invoked the historical example of Jesse Owens at the Berlin Olympics as a reason for going to Moscow. He also warned, "A boycott would strengthen the hand of the hardliners." Tam Dalyell, a Labour MP from West Lothian in Scotland, noted that many British and U.S. banks were still doing business in the Soviet Union: "In these circumstances, how can anyone, like Hon. Members opposite talk about 'equality of sacrifice'?"[74]

As the debate rolled past 7 PM, Labour came to dominate the comments as the Conservatives had at the beginning. Ron Brown of Edinburgh, Leith, declared, "It is quite clear that the Prime Minister is using Afghanistan to divert attention from the record unemployment and rampant inflation in this country." Toward the end, Howell spoke. "If country after country decides that the only way to confront evil is to destroy the good contained in the Olympic Games and international sport, that is a prescription for the end of international sport as we know it." He also asked a question of Conservative MP Michael Heseltine: "After August, when the Olympics are over, how do we protest at the next Russian act of aggression? If the right Hon. Gentleman has no sportsmen upon whom to urge a boycott, what will he do?"[75]

The debate came to an end at 10:14 PM. The House divided, 315–147, in approving the resolution.[76]

Although the House of Commons had endorsed the boycott, it was a less than impressive victory. With public opinion polls in Great Britain showing the public opposed to the boycott, many MPs skipped the vote. "It is impossible to pretend that the Commons vote on British participation in the Olympics was the decisive, clear-cut, moral pronouncement which ideally it should have been," the editors of *The Daily Telegraph* declared in an editorial.[77]

Cutler stopped off in England just after this vote. He was trying to line up foreign support for the alternate games. The situation he encountered was much more fluid than he expected. The boycott was in serious trouble in the United Kingdom. Although Margret Thatcher's government was strongly in favor of this effort, she was unwilling to use any authoritarian or legal mechanisms, like the seizure of passports, against the Olympians. Cutler arranged to meet with Follows at the Bath Club in London in order to lobby for boycott support rather than the alternate games as he had expected. Sir Denis made it clear to Cutler that his organization would have nothing to do with the boycott. He also met with Howell at the U.S. embassy. Cutler began by reviewing the situation, predicting that more than 100 countries would boycott, and that President Carter wanted to give the athletes a chance to compete since they had invested so much in their training. "Within minutes it was obvious that Cutler knew little about sport and less about international sport," Howell noted. He replied that nothing would compensate the athletes for the loss of the Olympics. Cutler did not understand or chose not to understand what his guest was attempting to explain. Howell later commented, "It was as though he believed the Olympic Games was a commodity to be bought and sold on the money markets of the world." He then tried to explain that the Olympics were an international movement and had to transcend foreign policy of any one nation, even that of the Soviet Union.[78]

Cutler had been outargued, so he tried another approach. He asked what would trouble Howell enough to call off the games. A Soviet invasion of Austria? Yugoslavia? "I want to discover your breaking point," Cutler asked, pointedly. Howell had been elected to the Birmingham City Council when he was seventeen and had been an MP for over twenty years; he knew how to argue and refused to respond to Cutler's question. He told the American lawyer that the questions were hypothetical as far as the 1980 Olympics went. When the conversation ended, Cutler admitted he had never encountered the arguments that Howell had made. This admission might be true given the weak counterarguments that Cutler had heard up to this point. As he was leaving, Cutler clumsily tried to impress Howell with his authority. He would be meeting with the President of the United States, he said, and asked if the British politician had any message for him. Howell replied, "This country is governed by Magna Carta not Jimmy Carter."[79]

Cutler had mishandled his meetings in London and they had gone poorly as a result. He knew the situation in the United Kingdom was dire and he reported as much when he returned to Washington: "we are in serious danger of losing the British." The ramifications were immense. If the United Kingdom attended, so might many of the nations on the continent: "Other West European Governments and NOCs may say that this makes an effective boycott impossible, and make this an excuse for going to Moscow themselves." Cutler, however, excelled at covering his own mistakes. In his memo, he made no mention of his meeting with Howell and dismissed Follows. "Sir Dennis is a living Colonel Blimp," he stated. "He is a pure Olympian who puts aside all responsibilities as a citizen of the West in favor of sports as the last hope of world peace." In small signs of his own cultural ignorance, Cutler misspelled Follow's name, gave incorrect information about his professional background, and called the British Olympic Association the "British Olympic Committee."[80]

Although Cutler could hide or minimize his mistakes within the administration, it was obvious to outside observers that the meeting in Switzerland had been a disaster. In the *Los Angeles Times*, Kenneth Reich, a political reporter, wrote that the Olympians were "fighting back effectively against the boycott drive." Reich referred to a number of unnamed sources from the White House and the State Department who had been trying to build support abroad, and they admitted things were going poorly. "Some believe the White House is being outmaneuvered."[81]

Work would continue on the semi-, counter-, or alternate-Olympics well into May, but after March, the effort was pro forma. "The federations do not now share our concept of international sports festival," Berenson informed Cutler and Ledsky. "Almost all raise very practical concerns." One of the biggest problems was scheduling issues. A number of sports already had planned events during the time the White House staff wanted to hold the event, nor did most want to take part in competitions that would involve the federations of other sports.[82]

The Olympics were the Olympics. "For the athletes, there simply is no alternative to the Olympics," Robert Helmick, president of the Amateur Athletic Union, noted.[83]

This type of thinking frustrated Berenson: "In short, the federations have not gotten into the spirit of the thing and are not thinking big." Many thought sports officials like Miller feared these contests would create a "schism" that would "be the demise of the modern Olympic movement."[84]

The main reason, though, that work came to an end on establishing another set of games was that the boycott itself was in trouble. Cutler, following Carter's rigid directions, had led the administration into a strategic cul-de-sac. The expected moral outrage that the President thought would fuel action against the Moscow Olympics had never materialized. The President only had himself to blame. His "hands on" leadership style had squandered valuable energy, and more importantly time, in a futile effort that was doomed even before it began. Now, Cutler had to return to basics and try to salvage a policy that Carter had committed himself to publicly. The time he had available could be measured in days rather than weeks or months.

1. Killanin of Galway. Michael Morris, the third Baron Killanin, became president of the International Olympic Committee in 1972. His time in office was one of the most difficult for the international Olympic movement. Facilities in Montreal were unfinished when the 1976 Olympics started, the Games themselves were a financial disaster, and only one city was interested in hosting the summer Games in 1984. These problems were minor compared to the boycott of 1980, which had the potential to destroy the movement and which officials in the Carter administration briefly considered. (Photo: TIR_03_000029_01)

2. Boom. President Jimmy Carter appeared on the television program *Meet the Press* on January 20, 1980. He announced that the United States would boycott the 1980 Summer Olympics. The President had not met with any official of either the U.S. Olympic Committee or the International Olympic Committee prior to this announcement. Photograph courtesy of The Jimmy Carter Presidential Library and Museum. (Photo NLC 15199.5)

3. The Lawyer. Carter assigned the task of overseeing the boycott campaign to White House Counsel Lloyd Cutler. While quite good at using the power of the U.S. government to intimidate domestic opponents of the boycott, Cutler was in over his head in the international dimension. Photograph courtesy of The Jimmy Carter Presidential Library and Museum. (Photo NLC 15795.5)

4. Breakfast at Jimmy's. Carter met with his foreign policy advisors regularly for breakfast. In a sign of how much the boycott mattered to the President, Cutler began attending these meetings. From right to left are Secretary of Defense Harold Brown, Secretary of State Cyrus Vance, President Jimmy Carter, National Security Advisor Zbigniew Brzezinski, and Cutler. Photograph courtesy of The Jimmy Carter Presidential Library and Museum. (Photo NLC 16202.8)

5. State of the Union. During his annual address to Congress, Carter repeated his declaration that the United States would boycott the Moscow Olympics. This statement drew strong applause. The boycott was extremely popular with the American public early in 1980. Photograph courtesy of The Jimmy Carter Presidential Library and Museum. (Photo NLC 15378.10a)

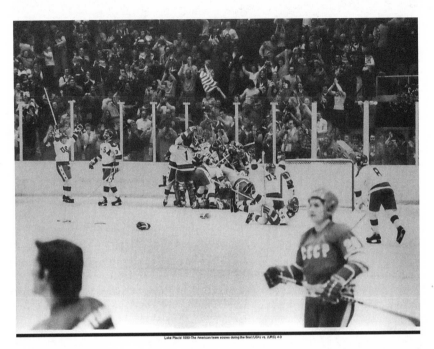

Lake Placid 1980-The American team scores during the final (USA) vs. (URS) 4-3

6. Heroes on Ice. The U.S. Olympic Hockey Team was ecstatic with its victory over the Soviet Union. The U.S. team was a collection of amateur players, while the Soviets were basically a professional team in everything but name and were generally considered to be the best team in the world at any level of play. The win and the team's gold medal victory over Finland two days later began eroding support among the American public for a boycott of Moscow. (Photo: VAAAB019)

7. Special Ambassador. In order to convince the nations of Africa to support the boycott, Carter asked Muhammad Ali to travel across the continent and lobby them on his
behalf. While a distinguished athlete – he had won a gold medal at the 1960 Olympics –
Ali was no diplomat. Many of the political leaders in Africa found Ali's selection condescending. The mission was a diplomatic disaster to everyone but Ali and the Carter
administration. After making a report to the President on the trip, White House staff-
ers asked the boxer for his autograph, and Ali gave Carter an enthusiastic handshake
before the two embraced. Photographs courtesy of The Jimmy Carter Presidential
Library and Museum. (Photo NLC 15530.5/Photo NLC 15530.6)

8. Good Day Mate, I Guess. Australian Prime Minister Malcolm Fraser met with Carter in February. The boycott was a major political issue in Australia. The reason: 1980 was an election year in the dominion. The debate about Moscow among Australians was perhaps stronger and more intense than in any other country. A strong and vocal proponent of the boycott, Fraser had serious reservations about the President's leadership ability and worried that the American might compromise on the issue. His trip to Washington was to offer his support and to make sure that Carter maintained a hard line toward the Soviet Union. Photograph courtesy of The Jimmy Carter Presidential Library and Museum. (Photo NLC15372.9)

9. American Heroes. Public opinion on the boycott in the United States began to change in February with the success of the U.S. Olympic Hockey Team at the Winter Olympics in Lake Placid, New York. The Carter administration responded by hosting a reception at the White House for the U.S. Olympic team. Although it became quite common in later years to have sports teams visit the White House, this function was the first such event of the Carter presidency. Photograph courtesy of The Jimmy Carter Presidential Library and Museum. (Photo NLC 15733.2a)

10. Redemption. During his public remarks, Carter praised the efforts of Beth Heiden, who had been on the cover of *Time* magazine with her brother, Eric, and was widely expected to win numerous gold medals. Many people saw her single bronze medal as a failure. The President thought otherwise. Carter greeted each individual athlete and shook their hand as they walked up to the balcony of the portico. He and Beth Heiden, however, hugged. Photograph courtesy of The Jimmy Carter Presidential Library and Museum. (Photo NLC 15732.32)

11. Power and Glory. During the reception, President Jimmy Carter and First Lady Roselyn Carter chatted with Mike Eruzione, captain of the hockey team. The White House staff was initially interested in only having Eruzione and his teammates, but decided to invite all the winter Olympians. Carter's lieutenants expected the event to play well in the media and bolster their Olympic embargo efforts, but were disappointed when most news coverage gave prominent attention to a statement many of the winter athletes signed, opposing the initiative. Photograph courtesy of The Jimmy Carter Presidential Library and Museum. (Photo NLC 15739.19)

12. Nein, Mein Herr. Helmut Schmidt, Chancellor of Federal German Republic, visited Washington in March. Schmidt had twice asked Carter administration officials if they planned to take action against the Moscow Games and both times they told him no. Only after the chancellor had come out against the boycott did Carter announce that the United States would pursue such a policy. Schmidt eventually reversed himself and took a political beating for it in Germany. He believed the President had a superficial grasp of strategy, and that his behavior toward his German allies reflected a naïve, American provincialism. Schmidt told his host as much to his face. Although there was much truth to these views, Carter did not like being criticized, and this meeting went poorly. At another, the two got into a yelling match. Photograph courtesy of The Jimmy Carter Presidential Library and Museum. (Photo NLC 15852.31)

13. The Ides of March Plus Six. In an effort to end resistance to the boycott, the Carter administration invited a number of Olympic athletes to the White House to explain the reasons for the boycott on March 21, 1980. Despite the humidity in the East Room on that day, the President delivered an impressive presentation, speaking in a solemn, somber tone with an icy look in his eyes. News stories reporting on this speech, however, repeatedly mentioned that none of the athletes – not one – stood or applauded when Carter arrived. Photograph courtesy of The Jimmy Carter Presidential Library and Museum. (Photo NLC 16083.16)

14. Carter versus Killanin. In May, Lord Killanin met with Jimmy Carter in the Oval Office. The meeting was a waste of time. Both were supporting diametrically opposite positions on the Moscow Olympics and were too committed to their stances at that point to change. In his memoirs, Killanin made much of Brzezinski's empty chair and the fact that the conversation had to wait until the National Security Advisor arrived. The Baron thought it was sign of how little power Carter had within his own administration. Brzezinski's tardiness was probably actually a reflection of how little the meeting mattered to him. Photograph courtesy of The Jimmy Carter Presidential Library and Museum. (Photo NLC 17097.19)

15. Dancing Fools. Despite fears that the Games would be a propaganda windfall for the Soviet Union, the opening ceremonies were basically the standard fare of Olympic symbols and references to the host country's culture. Flashcards had been a major feature of the opening games and displayed many images of these images. Dancers dressed in traditional Russian folk clothing and children wearing Misha the bear costumes entertained the crowd in Lenin Stadium. (Photo AAASZoo6 and AAASZoo7)

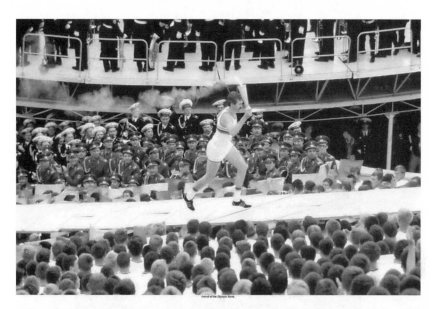

16. Running Man. The honor of lighting the Olympic flame went to Sergei Belov of the Soviet Men's Basketball Team. The flame jutted out from the rim of the stadium, and in a move that impressed many in the crowd, Soviet troops held flashcards above their heads forming a staircase that allowed Belov to climb to the top of the arena. (Photo AAASZ009)

Moscow 1980-Athletics-800m-KIROV Nikolai (URS) 3rd OVETT Steve (GBR) 1st COE Sebastian (GBR) 2nd.

17. Olympic Heroes. With the United States absent from the Games of the XXII Olympiad, Soviet athletes won 195 medals, including 80 gold. Host nations generally enjoy better than average success, but the extent of Soviet results was unusually excessive. The athletes of the British track-and-field team, though, scored some important victories in marquee events. Steve Ovett of the United Kingdom won gold in the 800 meters. In the final run, he upset Sebastian Coe, the world record holder in the event. Here Ovett, in the middle, stands on the victory stand. Behind him, to the left, is Coe, the silver medalist, and in front of him is Nikolai Kirov of the Soviet Union, the bronze medalist. (Photo AAAEU010)

18. Battle of the Ages. The confrontation between Ovett and Coe was one of the most famous in Olympic competition. Having upset Coe's in his specialty, the 800 meters, Ovett's was the favorite to win the gold in the 1,500 meters, a race he had not lost in three years and a distance in which he held the world record. Coe, however, upset Ovett. Jürgen Straub of East Germany, with his arms extended above his head, won the silver, and Ovett, on the far left, won the bronze. (Photo AAABO001)

19. The World's Greatest Athlete, Again. Daley Thompson of the United Kingdom won gold in the decathlon in Moscow. His main rival, Guido Kratschmer of West Germany, had just broken Thompson's world record, but was absent because of the boycott. Four years later in Los Angeles, the West Germans made a good showing, placing second, third, and fourth, but Thompson defended his Olympic title coming one point short of setting a new world record. (Photo AAACY004)

CHAPTER 9

Coca-Cola, NBC, and the Defeat
of the Iron Lady

THE BOYCOTT WAS IN TROUBLE. LLOYD CUTLER KNEW THIS. HE ALSO knew it was his job to get results. Despite this realization, the boycott campaign continued to bleed out, taking one of its worst defeats before the month ended. The problem was that the administration continued to have trouble staying focused. The nature of the global economy caught Carter, Cutler, and the rest of the administration short. Economic and commercial issues absorbed an enormous amount of attention from the administration and also showed to what lengths Jimmy Carter was prepared to go to implement his policy.

There were a number of U.S. firms with ties to the Olympics. Some were major corporations, while others were medium-sized firms or privately owned businesses. Both types of business had different relationships with the Olympics, and many remained skeptical about the Carter administration's prospects of success. In mid-January, *The Wall Street Journal* took a survey of fifty executive and found only four in support of the policy. Most preferred to take no position and see how things developed. Ambassador Dobrynin had no illusions about the power of these capitalists, even if such a view contradicted Communist theory. In his memoirs, he wrote, "Carter publicly called for a boycott of the summer Olympic Games in Moscow, an appeal that a number of companies who had committed themselves to supporting the athletes told us privately they could not challenge."[1]

Most of these businessmen worried about lost opportunities rather than sunk costs. The Olympics were special, coming once every four years. The promotional opportunities were unique and quite valuable. Stanford Blum, a Los Angeles businessman who owned the rights to merchandise the Moscow Olympics, remained fairly upbeat, even though he was willing to face facts: "The sales being blown away are between $50 million and $100 million. Premium promotions are hurting because companies don't want to be identified with things that have 'Moscow' written on them," he explained.

"As of now, Misha the Bear is dead. Nobody wants to have the stigma of Russia attached to them." Blum's Image Factory Sports Incorporated was a small business for which $100 million was a lot of money, but he had other marketing agreements. "Everything is on hold, but I'll survive – I've got Bo Derek." Apparently not. Selling posters of the actress that starred in the movie 10 failed to keep Blum solvent. He went out of business. He, however, was the exception rather than the rule.[2]

Another way in which the boycott affected corporations was the impact it had on agreements to provide supplies to both the U.S. team and the Soviets. These ties with Moscow mattered much more to the administration than the support they gave to the USOC. These firms included Miller Brewing Company, Gillette, Levi Strauss, and Coca-Cola. The administration ended up spending considerable time on those last two corporations. Coca-Cola was particularly important because of its visibility, the status of its main beverage as an American icon, and its home in Georgia, Carter's own state. After delaying for a good while, the company announced in late March that it would support Carter's boycott. "Cheers for Coca-Cola!" *The Atlanta Constitution* declared in an editorial. "The decision is a major one for Coca-Cola because the company had been trying for years to break into the potentially very lucrative Russian market – and the Olympics sales were considered a major step forward in that goal." America was getting serious about the boycott: "Now no Coke. That'll teach 'em."[3]

Still some major problems remained. J. Paul Allen, the chairman of the company, wrote Carter on March 18 to alert him to these issues. "The Coca-Cola Company, of course, supports totally the foreign polices of the United States. With regard to the Olympics, there is a complication which I wish to bring to your personal attention." The company had contracts with the Soviets, and under the terms of this agreement, retail establishments in Moscow were already selling the company's Fanta Orange beverage. Coca-Cola had also supplied the 1979 Spartakiada Sports Festival with the concentrate of both Fanta Orange and their flagship beverage. The company sold little of what they had shipped to the Soviet Union. At the time, its officers decided to leave the surplus in their Moscow plant in anticipation of the Olympics. Allen said he was trying to comply with the boycott. "Realistically, however, if the Soviets choose to distribute the drinks themselves, there is nothing we can physically do to stop this."[4]

Levi Strauss & Company had an even bigger problem in complying with the boycott. The company was inclined to support the administration efforts, but it had signed a contract with West Nally, a subsidiary of Adidas, to supply 35,000 uniforms for the Soviets. The clothing was physically located in Hong Kong. The company was exposed to civil action in French courts for nonperformance. "I do not need to point out to you the possible political effects of action by a French court in ordering Levi Strauss & Co. to deliver the uniforms to the Soviet Union or in awarding substantial damages," John C. Jaqua, an attorney with Sullivan & Cromwell who represented the corporation, informed Cutler.[5]

The corporation with the most visible problem, though, was the NBC. The television network had purchased the rights to broadcast the Moscow games in the United States and hoped to use their coverage of the games as a base on which to promote their new programs and make a bid to move out of the third spot they presently occupied. Early on, though, network executives decided that if the United States sent no team, they would not bother telecasting the games. Over the years, American television networks have been extremely nationalistic in their coverage of the Olympics, and this decision was a strong reflection of that sentiment. The problem the network faced was that for two and half months, the question about U.S. attendance remained in doubt. If Americans ended up in Moscow, the network needed to begin the logistical efforts required to support coverage of the two-week-long sports festival. If not, then they needed to begin planning for a way to fill vacant air time. "The terrible part is the waiting," one executive remarked. "What happens next is totally out of our control. I don't remember when we've had such a complicated problem."[6]

The uncertainty was difficult for the corporation to deal with, but it was even worse for the morale of its employees. Many had no idea if they were going to Moscow. "My bags to be sure, were not packed," Frank Shorter, a runner the network had hired to be part of its on-air team, noted. NBC sportscaster Dick Enberg explained, "It's a little like having a 3½-year gestation period and then having someone come along and take away the baby." His boss, Don Ohlmeyer, executive producer of NBC Sports, agreed: "The Olympics would have been a real opportunity to show what we can do, and I had no doubt about ability to pull it off."[7]

Like the athletes, the boycott resulted in lost opportunities for the broadcasters. "The cameraman and technicians who were assigned to Moscow were assigned because they were the best," Ohlmeyer said. "The Olympics can be a great catalyst for people's careers. They certainly were a catalyst for mine. I wouldn't be where I am today if it were not for the attention I got from working on the Olympics." The lost opportunity "is going to be a very difficult thing to recover from emotionally at NBC sports. For three years, the Moscow Olympics gave everybody at NBC sports a concrete goal to work for."[8]

As demoralizing as the boycott was to the broadcast personnel, NBC's economic relationship with the Soviet Union and the IOC was one that troubled the Carter White House much more. "We believed," Cutler explained later, "that if the April 1 payment went forward it would undermine the entire boycott effort by leading many nations to believe that in the end the United States would go to Moscow." The network had agreed to pay the Soviets $85 million in installments for the broadcast rights to the games. Only $35 million was actually for the broadcast rights, and the IOC got a third of this amount. The other $50 million was for logistical support and technical assistance that went exclusively to the Moscow Olympic Organizing Committee. The network still had three payments of $17.6 million to make, and the next was scheduled for April 1. An insurance policy with Lloyd's of London would cover most of the payments, but this policy required that NBC not be in default. Even though there was a good chance that they would not be televising the games, NBC officials believed that they were still legally required to make their contracted payments.[9]

Cutler and Onek wanted to stop NBC from making any further payments because of the message it would send to foreigners and the Olympic community. "If NBC is allowed to make its remaining payments, this will reinforce their belief that the U.S. is hedging and may ultimately go to Moscow. Particularly in the Third World, few will believe that the National Broadcasting Company is an independent private firm, acting free of government direction. On the other hand, if NBC were required by the government not to make the payments, this would be a strong confirmation of the American position." They also thought their might be some advantage in using these contracts as leverage to get the IOC and the federations to cooperate with the counter-Olympics. Their proposal was that Carter use the powers of the International Emergency Economic Powers Act to block the NBC payments.[10]

Earlier in the year, Carter had rejected similar recommendations. His preference was that the companies voluntarily end their commercial ties with the Soviet Union. He was prepared, though, to issue regulations prohibiting this commerce should it be necessary.[11]

The Special Coordination Committee of the NSC thrashed the issue about in the White House Situation Room on March 20. The meeting started with discussion on grain exports to Hungary, and there was a worry that this might be a way of funneling American wheat to the Soviet Union. Then the group turned to the issue of the Olympics. Cutler gave a general report on the Olympics. The boycott was going well, he said. Despite this effort at staying positive, he admitted they were about to lose the British. Everyone in the room believed that the Thatcher government had done everything possible to convince the BOA. Signs indicated, Cutler said, that Germany and France were about to take firm stands against sending a team to Moscow. Cutler then made an almost total about face and argued that the boycott was about to fall apart. To stop this from happening, he believed the administration needed to use some of the legal powers it had available. Too many people in Europe considered the boycott nothing more than an election ploy to help get Carter reelected. Work on the alternate games was going well, despite what *The*

Washington Post was reporting. In order to make it clear that the U.S. was serious about the boycott, it needed to block payment to both the Soviets and the IOC. Cutting off payment to the Committee would show that the U.S. government had the power to attack their basic source of revenue and would get the committee and federations to end their opposition to the alternate games. Getting Congress to pass legislation before April 1, when NBC was to make its next payment, was impossible. Legislation would also require hearings, and given collapsing public support for the boycott, it might not be wise to give the athletes and other opponents a public forum to voice their views. As a result, the best option available to the administration was using the powers of the Act.[12]

An official from the Treasury Department, C. Fred Bergsten, quickly argued against this idea. Using International Emergency Economic Powers Act (IEEPA) just to stop NBC from paying the Soviets was overkill and would make the administration look "foolish" and "trigger happy." More importantly, such a move would weaken the international position of the dollar and, as a result, increase inflation.[13]

Cutler responded in a classic bureaucratic move, invoking the boss's name. He said dollars were flowing into the United States at the moment, so the risk was small. The U.S. could sell the action as part of a response to the Soviet invasion of Afghanistan and not an action against NBC, the IOC, and the Soviets. Time was short, though, and the President's personal prestige was committed to the boycott. The administration needed to get results.[14]

Attorney General Civiletti then joined in the debate. Once again, he said, the administration – and by this he meant Cutler – was losing focus. The issue at the moment was the resistance of the IOC and the federations. Stopping the NBC payment would have no impact on those organizations. Using IEEPA simply to stop the network would make the administration look "foolish," he said, using the same word as Bergsten.[15]

Deputy National Security Advisor David Aaron ended the conversation, saying the exchange of ideas had been good. He said he wanted Treasury to produce a memo on alternatives to IEEPA before the end of the day. Most of the participants in the meeting got up and left – they were present only to discuss the Olympics – and the committee turned its attention toward Iran.[16]

In the battle of memos that followed this meeting, Cutler was ready with some strong arguments. He warned the President that the boycott faced a "high risk of failure." As a result, he recommended "on an urgent basis" that the President use the IEEPA to block NBC from making its payments. Legislation that would serve this need "would be virtually impossible." He also reminded Carter of his own stakes in this issue. Thatcher was about to suffer a humiliating defeat, because she was unwilling to use the full legal powers of Her Majesty's Government: "We have an even greater investment in the success of the Olympic boycott. The risks of failure are significant, particularly if the British Olympic Committee defects. Our main weapons must continue to be persuasion and moral authority, but in my judgment we must not shirk from showing the IOC, the international federations, and the governments and peoples of Europe' – not to mention the Soviets – that we also have legal authority and are willing to use it judiciously when necessary."[17]

Secretary of the Treasury G. William Miller warned against Cutler's proposal. "Such action could only intensify the nervousness of foreign dollar holders that their claims or assets might be subjected to similar action if they found themselves in disagreement with the United States over important foreign policy issues." Using the legislation would also be an abuse, since its purpose was to protect the U.S. financial system from attack. The administration needed a stable dollar if it was going to fight inflation and provide international monetary leadership. Using commercial coercion against the Olympics would put all that at risk: "I believe that it would be a mistake to risk undermining our objectives in these areas by invoking IEEPA for any very narrow purpose in the present circumstances."[18]

Miller's arguments were strong, but Admiral Stansfield Turner suggested in a memo of his own that the risk was less dire than the Treasury Secretary indicated. "There would be no perceptible effect on the value of the dollar over the long run and probably little impact on exchange markets in the short run."[19]

Civiletti still worried about the use of IEEPA and produced a memo of his own. He agreed with Miller's concern about abuse. "It is my view that the action of blocking a payment by NBC to the Soviets is an inadequate reason for calling upon the broad emergency powers that accompany a declaration of a national emergency." Unlike Miller, he offered an alternative. The administration should get legislation from Congress to stop further payments. He admitted, though, that there was no way that they would get the bill passed before NBC needed to make another payment to the Soviets.[20]

Since the immediate issue for the administration was stopping the NBC payments, this advice was meaningless. Jaqua of Sullivan & Cromwell soon came up with a proposal to limit the legal liability of Levi Strauss that might have solved Carter's NBC problem. He suggested to Cutler that the best solution was for the U.S. government to use the powers it had under the Export Administration Act of 1979 to prevent his client from delivering the clothing. Lawyers with the Commerce Department, though, had already considered this possibility and warned that there was no way that legislation provided the legal foundation for such a move. "Reliance on the Export Administration Act would involve a novel interpretation of that statute that greatly stretches its plain meaning, and a literal reading suggests that such controls are simply not authorized by the Act." There was some thinking within the administration that nothing more than a letter from the President was required to block the NBC payments. Cutler and Onek believed that *Eastern Airlines v.*

McDonnell-Douglas provided the legal foundations for this position. This Vietnam-era case stemmed from a lawsuit the airline filed when the airplane manufacturer failed to provide jets as contractually required. McDonnell-Douglas failed to deliver the jets, because Department of Defense demands for more planes during the Vietnam War took priority over civilian production. Both contracts had provisions giving Defense Department requests preference over those of others. As a result, lawyers representing the network informed Onek that a mere letter would be insufficient for their legal needs. "To some extent this may be a bluff, since it would be difficult for NBC to turn down the President," Onek informed Cutler.[21]

While Carter's lieutenants debated this issue, the administration began conducting a series of briefings for the members of the Olympic movement in the United States. There were many reasons for having these briefings. In part, it was an effort to get around the leadership of the USOC, which many White House officials considered an obstacle, and discuss the issue directly with committee members. The State Department wanted the group to commit to the boycott soon in order to keep the momentum they had in convincing other governments – rather than national Olympic committees – to support the effort. The administration also wanted to get the athletes on board with the alternate games concept. Many high-ranking members of the administration conducted these briefings, including Vance, Warren Christopher, Secretary of Defense Harold Brown, and General David C. Jones, Chairman of the Joint Chiefs of Staff. These meetings always stressed national security and were never a forum to exchange ideas about alternatives to a boycott. These administration briefing teams ultimately managed to meet with about 40 percent of the individuals with votes on the committee.

The President also needed to express some sympathy to the summer athletes. There was a good deal of resentment in this community that Carter had treated the winter Olympic athletes to a reception at the White House but was attempting to block those that competed in the Summer Games from going to Moscow. "They feel they are being used for political purposes, perhaps even narrow domestic political purposes," Berenson warned. Two members of the NSC staff made an additional warning. There was a racial edge to this resentment. "Some Blacks, for instance, tend to argue that the boycott is aimed at discriminating against them, since more Blacks participate in the summer Olympics than the winter Olympics, which we did not boycott. Ridiculous as this is, the view is strongly held among the Blacks."[22]

The most important of these briefings is one that Carter conducted on March 21, the day after the Special Coordination Committee had debated export bans. Olympic athletes gathered in the East Room of the White

House. The meeting began with a briefing from Brzezinski on the situation in Afghanistan. The room was warm and humid as he spoke. He explained that the Soviets had established a "strategic wedge" and now could reach the Strait of Hormuz with bombers. Evidence suggested the Soviets were using chemical weapons, sealing the boarders, and building permanent bases in the country. "They are creating no impression that the invasion will be reversed. We might as well face that fact." Brzezinski was ignorant of Afghanistan's terrain in making some of these statements, but he was honestly explaining the views of the administration. The invasion was part of a larger pattern of reckless Soviet actions in foreign policy. "To the U.S.S.R., sport is an extension of politics," he said. As a result, a boycott against the summer Games was an appropriate response: "We do not oppose the Olympics. It is the site we oppose. We have determined that we cannot permit business as usual in social, cultural, scientific or commercial activities. We can't say of sport that 'this is somehow immune.' It's not logical, not possible. Worse, it is symbolically wrong, *morally* wrong to hold this festival of peace in the capital of an aggressor nation posing a threat of such strategic significance."[23]

His presentation was made of daunting stuff. Sitting in the audience, Jane Frederick, a pentathlete, was thinking to herself, "Yesterday I was on a sunny track in Santa Barbara. Today I'm being exposed to the iron realities of the world." When Fred Newhouse, a gold and silver medalist in Montreal, asked if there was anything that might allow them to compete in Moscow, Brzezinski deviated from the official White House line, but only just a little: "We certainly will reconsider if they depart, but that seems very, very unlikely."[24]

Onek followed with a presentation on efforts to organize a set of alternatives to the Olympics. Despite the disastrous meeting in Geneva, he offered optimistic words but was vague on details. He had just started taking questions from the audience when the White House press corps suddenly barged in.[25]

They were there to report on the President. Carter walked into the room, and for the first time since he had come into office, no one stood or applauded. This incident was mentioned prominently in news accounts of the meeting. Sam Donaldson of ABC News called it "a grim moment for President Carter." The insult was not intentional but was once again the product of the bad staff work that characterized the Carter White House. No one had bothered to advise the athletes on protocol – few had ever been to the executive mansion before – and he had appeared abruptly without warning.[26]

Speaking in a solemn and sober tone with an icy look in his eyes, Carter rarely referred to his notes. He admitted at the beginning that he was speaking to the athletes "with some degree of trepidation." He said history was clear; had there been a boycott of the 1936 Berlin Olympics, there never would have been a Second World War. The situation today was far more dangerous.

Then he made his position bluntly clear: "I can't say at this moment what other nations will not go to the Summer Olympics in Moscow. Ours will not go. I say that not with any equivocation; the decision has been made." He said he had not made this choice easily. "It's not a pleasant time for me. You occupy a special place in American life." He explained, "You represent the personification of the highest ideals of our country." As symbols of the United States, though, the athletes had to think about what was best for their nation. "That's why it's particularly important that you join in with us, not in condemnation, even of the Soviet Union, not in a negative sense at all, but in a positive sense of what's best for our country and best for world peace." Reflecting the power of the Olympic ideal, Carter – like those that had attempted to manipulate or destroy the movement before him – declared that he was actually true to the faith. "In my judgment what we are doing is preserving the principles and the quality of the Olympics, not destroying it." The audience applauded at the end, and the press corps left the room.[27]

Carter then took questions from the athletes. During this session, he said he had the power to prevent athletes from using their passports and that he would use that power. "He closed the door," Willie Davenport, a gold medalist at the 1968 Mexico City Olympics remarked. "Not only did he close the door, he locked it and threw away the key." Terry Anderson, a coach with the U.S. shooting team, said, "The president was very impressive. He changed some minds."[28]

Not that many. "I thought I had been had," Anita DeFrantz declared. She had expected that there would be a dialogue between the athletes and the president in exploring alternatives to a boycott. "When we arrived, I realized that I was – how naïve I was," she said with a chuckle. "Lets put it that way. How naïve I was." Afterwards, a number of the Olympians gathered at the nearby Hay-Adams Hotel and took an informal poll. The results: 44 opposed to a boycott; 29 in favor; and 24 abstentions. "It seems a choice between logic and emotion," Dick Tillman, a member of the sailing team remarked. "Today we got the facts, and they leave little room for hope. But emotionally, Lord, it's hard to give up."[29]

Carter's presentation led to an increase in news media coverage and commentary on the boycott. The fact that other nations, American allies, were going to be in Moscow mattered little to *The Kansas City Times*: "If it should turn out the U.S. is the only major nation to boycott the Games – then so be it." In Norfolk, *The Virginian-Pilot* argued, "The Olympic boycott is the only response to the Afghanistan invasion that seems to be hurting the Russians." An editorial in *The Houston Post* explained why: "By giving up their dream of going to Moscow, several hundred American athletes might help save their generation of from an ordeal that could only be costly to the whole world. It would not be easy for the Kremlin to explain to the people of Soviet Union why so many people of the free world refused to come to the heralded Olympics of 1980 in Moscow." The *Chicago Tribune* also warned American Olympic athletes about the ramifications of competing in the Soviet Union. "They might even manage to defeat a few of Eastern Europe's hormone-laden 'amateurs' and come back with gold around their necks. But they'll have blood on their hands."[30]

Despite such sentiment, things only got worse for Carter. On March 25, the BOA ignored the vote in Parliament and the position of Margaret Thatcher's government and accepted the Soviet invitation to participate in the Moscow games. Thatcher had fought this decision. "We have the highest admiration for the Olympic ideals," she informed Follows after the vote in the House of Commons. "It is not we who are perverting that idea; rather, it is the Soviet Union which is making cynical use of the idealism of sportsmen to try to convince the world that its invasion of Afghanistan is a little local matter of no importance." The Soviet Union was a threat and it was the duty of all British subjects to oppose their evil: "Free countries must bring home as dramatically as possible that this sort of action cannot be taken with impunity." The athletes would suffer, and she supported the efforts to organize a set of counter-Olympics to make up for their loss: "Decisions must be for the individuals and their sporting organizations. I am well aware how hard those decisions must be. The Government's part is to give a lead and to bring into focus the conclusions which would be drawn from participation in the Moscow Olympics."[31]

Follows was less than encouraging in his response. He said he would make sure all BOA members saw her letter. The Association, though, had no interest in any alternative to Moscow: "We exist solely for the purpose of organising and co-ordinating the United Kingdom's participation in the Olympic Games."[32]

Follows did as he promised. At the beginning of the meeting, he circulated the Prime Minister's correspondence. The Lord Exeter made a speech about the Olympics. Then the organization voted to go to Moscow. The rather perfunctory nature of the matter rankled some supporters of the boycott and would give Thatcher's government an excuse to keep pressuring British Olympians well into the early summer.[33]

When the BOA made its decision public, its reasoning was straightforward. "The British Olympic Association, which exists to organise and co-ordinate British participation in the Olympic Games, has agreed to accept forthwith to send a team to Moscow this summer," declared a statement the organization released. Fifteen of the nineteen national sports federations supported this decision. In making this decision, the association had rejected the request of the Thatcher government that it wait until May: "The BOA has not come to this decision lightly. It has given careful and we hope proper attention to the views expressed in Parliament as it has taken note of the responses of the public and aspirations of the competitors."[34]

The Baron Noel-Baker of the City of Derby, a silver medalist at the 1920 Antwerp Olympics and recipient of the Nobel Peace Prize in 1959, explained why the Olympians had decided to go to Moscow. The games, he argued, "have given the whole world a vision of all-embracing international friendship and co-operation, which was in sharp contrast to the folly and wastes of the arms race of war ... The Games in Moscow will serve the short-time and long-time cause of peace."[35]

The British Olympians were also operating in a political climate that made it easy to take that stand. A poll that *The Washington Post* commissioned found an overwhelming majority of Britons in favor of participating in the sports festival. The question put to the public was: "Do you agree or disagree with this statement: Great Britain should boycott the Moscow Olympics because of the Russian invasion of Afghanistan?" Sixty-two percent of the Britons survey disagreed and only 28 percent agreed.[36]

The decision of the BOA did not sit well with the Conservative Party. A few weeks later during Prime Minister's Question Time, Cranley Onslow, a Conservative representing Working, urged Thatcher to "get it into the thick skull of Sir Denis Follows that there is a war going on in Afghanistan." The Prime Minister responded in the positive: "I understand Sir Denis said only a war would change the decision of the British Olympic Committee to go to Moscow. There is just such a war going on in Afghanistan."[37]

Thatcher's response to the BOA vote was abrupt: She resigned as patron of the British Olympic Appeal, the main fundraising organization for the BOA. It was an understandable response: Why should she lend her name to an organization that was raising money for another that had challenged her leadership in foreign policy? As it was, it was a largely futile gesture. Sir Anthony Tuke, chairman of the Appeal, wrote back, informing her that they had raised no money since the invasion of Afghanistan.[38]

Follows remained unphased: "We took this decision even though we know that American might decide not to send a team. The [BOA members] were subject to considerable pressures – and their decision was not really a surprise."[39]

The Carter administration knew the British vote was yet another defeat. What worried Cutler, though, was the ripple effect: "The other West European Governments and NOCs may say that this makes an effective boycott impossible, and make this an excuse for going to Moscow themselves."[40]

Americans, even those supporting the boycott, respected British integrity. The editors of the *Chicago Tribune* criticized the decision, but at least the Europeans had come out and voted against the boycott in a forthright manner. The continued "simpering" of the USOC, on the other hand, was "stupid and cowardly."[41]

Cutler was right to worry. In Germany, Schmidt was facing opposition to the boycott even within his own cabinet. Minister of Economics Otto Graf

Lambsdorff declared, "The Olympic boycott is nonsense." He also thought it was dangerous. A boycott would change the focus of the public: "Then everyone talks only about the busted Games and nobody mentions the Invasion of Afghanistan anymore." Businessmen were also concerned about its huge economic impact. They feared that there would be ramifications to a boycott in German-Soviet relations that had little do to with sports. Over 1,800 businesses had some sort of commercial relationship with the Soviet Union. German exports to the Soviets were worth 20 billion Deutschmarks, and some 300,000 jobs were connected to the export of goods to the East.[42]

The vote in London was worse than Cutler could have imagined. Despite its international nature, the Olympic movement was primarily a European phenomenon. The games, modern and ancient, had started in Europe. At that point in time, only one Asian nation, Japan, had ever hosted the Olympics. The Games had never been held in South America or Africa. The United States was the only Olympic power located outside of Europe. Five of the six IOC presidents had been Europeans. It had become clear to many observers – but not the Carter administration – that Europe would determine the fate of the boycott. As a result, a coordinated move on the part of the national Olympic committees of France, Spain, and Italy was exceptionally important. These three organizations voted to go to Moscow the same day the British made their decision. The actions in these countries failed to garner as much attention in the United States and in the White House as the decision in London, but the Carter White House had suffered another major defeat.[43]

The British vote only added to the collapse of the boycott in the United States. Kane said he could tell that the national mood was changing. "My mail, which was two-thirds for not going is now 50–50. So there is a shifting, although it is not extensive."[44]

Reflecting the shift in public sentiment that had started after the Winter Olympics, ABC and CBS began joining with NBC in focusing more and more on the impact the boycott would have on American athletes. In March and April, the three networks ran forty-six stories of this nature. The editors of the *Seattle Post-Intelligencer* recommended that the President accept defeat gracefully. "It's time for Carter to admit to himself the boycott's a bust and pass a quiet signal to the U.S. Olympics Committee that if it votes to go to Moscow, the president won't help but he won't hinder, either." Their colleagues at the *Chicago Tribune* disagreed in an editorial that conceded the fact that the athletic embargo was failing: "Even if the United States alone boycotts the games, the Soviets will be hurt."[45]

With this sentiment swirling about among the public, Carter studied the memos and the memorandum of conversation that documented the discussions of his lieutenants. He understood the risks that Miller had identified, but Civiletti's recommendation for legislation was a nonstarter. There was no other way, so he decided to use the export controls that existing legislation gave him. In reading Cutler's recommendations that the use of the IEEPA be explained as part of a response to Afghanistan and not the Olympic boycott, he added on the margins of the document: "We must emphasize this. Deemphasize Olympics – except to key people and a little later." He made these initial comments quickly but he still wanted time to consider his position.[46]

When he made his final decision, his instructions were simple. "Lloyd – ok – proceed – you & AG decide between 'extending' [or establishing] 'new' nat emergency. Work out PR w Jody, State, Treasury, Com & Justice to assure consistency." He also liked Cutler's idea on how to sell this proposal. "In PR maximize non-Olympic items."[47]

Cutler and Civiletti worked out an agreement for using the law and submitted the paperwork to Carter on March 27. Miller and his subordinates at the Commerce Department, the agency implementing and enforcing this decision, still worried about the fiscal ramifications of using the IEEPA and developed a formula using the Export Administration Act (EAA). Under this proposal, Carter could avoid declaring a national emergency and risking the status of the dollar, but individuals, be they spectators or journalists, could still travel to Moscow.[48]

Although less stringent, this proposal posed less risk. Carter liked this compromise. He sent the Secretary of Commerce a memorandum the following day that prohibited international transactions related to the Moscow Olympics under the EAA. That same day, the White House Press Office provided copies to the press. "I hereby direct the Secretary of Commerce, by appropriate regulations and to the extent he deems appropriate to carry out the purposes of this direction to prohibit the export to the U.S.S.R. directly on indirectly of any goods or technology by any person subject to the jurisdiction of the United States which are in connection with such games." Jody Powell, White House Press Secretary, also read a public statement to the reporters assembled in the Briefing Room, calling the invasion of Afghanistan "an unusual and extraordinary threat to the national security, foreign policy, and economy of the United States."[49]

Despite this action, the boycott seemed to have suffered fatal wounds. Carter's efforts to inject himself and the power of the Presidency into the campaign had ended in a series of painful, self-inflicted defeats. It had, however, done little to reverse general trends. The decision of the BOA was a huge defeat, but it was an action that had more to do with the institutional interests of that organization than with the actions or failures of the Carter administration or the Thatcher Cabinet. What made it all the more costly a defeat was the ripple effect it had in Europe, the heart of the Olympic movement. Even though Cutler and Carter had nothing to do with this disaster, it hurt their cause nonetheless. Efforts to stop the NBC payments had been a victory of sorts, and it showed to what lengths the President was willing to go to salvage a position that he had unwisely committed himself to with little advanced planning. Under Cutler's supervision the administration had once again lost its focus and done a better job of beating up on Americans rather than Soviets. The USOC would soon feel the full force of a desperate Carter administration.

CHAPTER 10

The Vote in Colorado

THE STALLING-FOR-TIME APPROACH THAT LORD KILLANIN AND members of the USOC had been using appeared to be working. Public support was beginning to fade. Something had to be done to salvage this initiative and avoid embarrassing Jimmy Carter. Lloyd Cutler knew what was at stake and began to focus administration efforts on convincing the USOC to vote against participating in the Moscow Olympics. It was a battle the administration had to win, and Carter and Cutler were willing to use whatever tactics got results.

The administration was painfully aware that the boycott was falling apart, and Carter admitted as much in late April after the USOC had made its decision: "We are inducing dozens and dozens of other nations to join with us in a boycott of the Moscow Olympics this summer, an issue that was severely in doubt a few months ago." To combat this trend, Jimmy Carter decided in early April to get more involved in the boycott. He instructed his staff to inject more boycott comments into his speeches.[1]

Stalling for time seemed to be working. The Olympians were receiving information from their American friends that there might, in the end, be no damage to the gathering in Moscow when it was all said and done. Peter Ueberroth advised Monique Berlioux, "I firmly believe that there is still a good chance to salvage the Games of the XXIInd Olympiad if the Soviet Union would make a major gesture that would give President Carter the opportunity to change his position."[2]

The American Olympians were even beginning to feel bold enough to challenge Carter on the boycott. "From my viewpoint," Miller told the *Los Angeles Times*, "the British Olympic Association showed a lot of courage in doing what they did, and also insured their compliance with International Olympic Committee rules." As a result, the Administrative Committee of the USOC, which basically performed the functions of an executive board, developed a proposal that the House of Delegates wait until the week of May 24 – the deadline for acceptance – to make their decision and decline an invitation only if the President explicitly stated that national security was at risk. "I think that's the key to it," Miller said. "In our judgment the president never has actually said that sending a team to Moscow compromises national security." Robert Helmick, president of the Amateur Athletic Union and a member of the USOC, went further in his public comments, "After two and a half months, it's very clear the boycott is not going to work and we shouldn't victimize our athletes for something that's meaningless." He also added, "I am not going to cast my vote to hang my athletes as the only athletes to be hung." The Athletes Advisory Council, a subcommittee of the USOC, began advocating a compromise that would allow the athletes to boycott the medal presentations, the opening and closing ceremonies, or participate without using the U.S. flag, and stay in facilities other than the Olympic Village. "These measures would seem to be a more appropriate way of protesting Soviet aggression without boycotting the Games which belong to the IOC and not to Moscow," Kane remarked.[3]

Those ideas sounded nice, but as Jack Murphy, sports editor of *The San Diego Union*, noted when they first popped up, "That's wishful thinking. Having rallied the Congress and the nation behind a boycott, the President will be vulnerable to more charges of wishy washy leadership if he retreats."[4]

Murphy was on the mark. When Cutler learned of these proposals, he said, "It's not acceptable. It is no substitute for a decision not to send a team." An editorial in *The Washington Star* declared that Helmick's comments were typical of the "self-absorption" of American Olympians in their inability to see the bigger issues involved.[5]

Despite the negative trend in public opinion polls, Carter's many political opponents in the presidential campaign were uncertain of how to approach the issue. Public support might be fading, but a majority still supported the boycott. More importantly, it was a foreign policy issue on which Carter looked strong, which ran counter to a general perception among many that he was weak and indecisive. Kennedy's challenge was dashing against the rocks of Carter's newfound support in wake of the Iranian hostage crisis. He tried to question Carter's handling of foreign policy matters, but largely failed. While this political challenge failed, the American people were hardly indifferent to the shortcomings of Carter's leadership. The issue gripped the public. The majority of news coverage focused on the plight of the individual hostages and their families. Individual Americans expressed their support by displaying yellow ribbons in remembrance of the hostages. There was also a good deal of resentment and frustration about the impotence of the United States toward Iran. The hard line against the Soviet Union for invading Afghanistan was appreciated. On March 26, while campaigning in Wisconsin, Ronald Reagan, the former governor of California who was a candidate for the Republican nomination, said he was conflicted over the issue. He realized that a number of athletes had invested a lot of time and energy into their training for the

Olympics and was quite sympathetic about their plight, but then again the Soviets were brutal, and it would be "hypocritical" to allow them to host the games. "It's a tough one … You'll just have to let me stew about that one for awhile."[6]

This indecision drew fire. The editors of *The Atlanta Constitution* declared, "Looks like Ronald Reagan is losing his nerve over the proposed U.S. boycott of the Summer Olympics in Moscow. We haven't been among his biggest supporters but this move by the former California governor surprises even us." The next day, Reagan addressed the issue directly at a press conference in the Kansas City area, "I would leave that decision to the athletes themselves. I don't believe our government should be in the position of saying you can't have a visa, you can't leave the country or go." In short, he was against the boycott. "There's something about our government telling our people they can't leave our shores that I can't buy."[7]

Seeking to establish bipartisan support for the boycott, Cutler contacted William Casey, Reagan's campaign manager, and discussed the issue. Casey admitted the issue was catching him off guard. Ed Meese, one of Reagan's closest advisors, called back shortly and told Cutler they were releasing a statement to the press clarifying Reagan's position. To make sure the news got out, the White House lawyer contacted Kenneth Reich, a sports reporter with the *Los Angeles Times* to whom he had given information earlier and told him to call Reagan's headquarters. Reich found it odd that a Carter administration official was helping get the word out for the Reagan campaign and mentioned this strange development in the story he eventually wrote. "We should boycott the Moscow Olympics," the Reagan statement declared. "It is hypocritical to permit the games to be held in a nation which actively engaged in aggression. Still I think we must use persuasion, not coercion, to obtain the cooperation of our own athletes to boycott the 1980 Olympics." He also favored taking the games out of international politics by giving them a permanent home in Greece and was prepared to show American good faith by surrendering the 1984 Olympics.[8]

Reagan only drew more criticism with this statement. Mayor Tom Bradley of Los Angeles, a Democrat, used the opportunity to score some political hits on Reagan. "I am disappointed that Ronald Reagan is not displaying a greater sense of pride and patriotism in this country's plans to host the Olympic Games in 1984." Even Ueberroth, who would later run for office as a Republican, criticized this idea: "I am disappointed in what appears to me to be a very uniformed opinion." Returning the Olympics to Greece sounded nice until one looked at it in a practical light: "I am disappointed that Mr. Reagan did not consider the political instability of Greece, which historically does not seem to be the best site." *New York Times* columnist James Reston noted the Olympics miscue reflected a larger problem: "Ronald Reagan has a backside-foremost way of saying things first and thinking about them later." Reston noted that his flip-flop on the boycott was not really a reversal since he had added the qualification about coercion.[9]

Reagan continued to take hits, not from Carter and the Democrats, but from other Republicans. In a press release, Congressman George Bush, Reagan's main rival, declared, "I'm appalled that my principal opponent for the Republican presidential nomination, Gov. Ronald Reagan, has taken a wishy-washy position on this issue." Bush then turned his sights on Carter. In a patronizing manner, he urged the President to stand strong and suspend the passports of the Olympic athletes. On the campaign trail of the Pennsylvania Primary, Bush told reporters, "I'm not sure its necessary." His press release explained that he expected that most of the athletes would do the right thing and not go to Moscow. He also said the Carter White House needed to try other actions before going after passports. "I think they [the Carter administration] ought to lean on the U.S. Olympic Committee. That's the first thing they need to do."[10]

Reagan took a beating on this issue from the media. The *New York Daily News* blasted Reagan: "The only consistent thing about Ronald Reagan's position on the Olympic boycott has been his inconsistency. By turns, his attitude has been yes, no, and maybe." The editorial board of the *Chicago Tribune*, a right-leaning newspaper, agreed: "It is difficult to say whether Gov. Reagan will gain or lose votes by waffling on the boycott. There is one group, however, that must be giving him a hearty vote of thanks: the Soviet Politburo."[11]

Reagan, though, could give as good as he got. In a statement he released, he repeated his support for the boycott but not if it required coercion. He then managed to turn this seemingly indecisive statement on Carter. "If the president cannot persuade the athletes to stay away from Moscow, he has only himself to blame."[12] This little episode of political theatrics shows why so many people underestimated Reagan and why they were so wrong in doing so.

An important thing about this political intramural is that it made it clear to the American Olympians that the boycott had bipartisan support. Congress made the same point. Thomas "Tip" O'Neill, Jr., Speaker of the U.S. House of Representatives, sent a mass mailing to all the members of the USOC. He reminded them of the vote in the House and Senate. "We must not let the Olympic be prostituted by the Soviets. We are therefore totally opposed to the participation of U.S. athletes in the Moscow games in any shape, form, or fashion." The letter was cosigned by the Republican and Democratic leadership in the House. Senators, from both parties, sent a similar letter to Kane a day later.[13]

The willingness of the American Olympians to "defy" Carter led the administration to pursue a "carrot-and-stick" approach in securing the support of the USOC. Problem was, there was not much carrot. Cutler and others began contacting major corporate donors to the USOC, advising them that they should hold off on making payment on tax-deductible donations to the committee until it voted on the boycott. Presidential advisor Anne Wexler contacted Edward R. Teiling, chairman of Sears, Roebuck and Company, and asked him to withhold a $25,000 contribution his corporation was scheduled to make. When Walter Wriston, chairman of Citibank, visited the White House, Cutler did the same. The administration also approached Bob Sheppard of Allstate Insurance. All told, fifteen corporations ended up withholding $175,000 in previously pledged donations. The administration also told Congress they could revoke the organization's tax-exempt status, strip the USOC of federal land it was using for its training center, and amend its federal charter. Cutler, as an anonymous source in a newspaper story, took a legalistic view, saying, "If you look at the whole universe of things we could do then this is one of those things, but were not proposing it, were not suggesting it."[14]

Cutler and his staff were applying the stick because they distrusted Kane and Miller. Onek and Berenson observed, "Some of the USOC officers, who have at various times publicly indicated support for the President's position, have been working behind the scenes to generate opposition."[15] This comment was a little exaggerated, but not much.

The use of the stick was also a sign of desperation. "We just couldn't afford to lose it, when you have the prestige of the President involved," Cutler explained. "Just think how ridiculous the United States would have looked, if not withstanding an appeal from the President, if the team then decided to go anyway." Recently declassified British documents also attest to the desperation of the administration. Ledsky of the State Department admitted to British diplomats that they were not sure they would get a vote in their favor, and he personally saw an alternative set of games as an objective that would have to change. He was quick to note, though, that the administration planned to get some type of results in this area.[16]

These rough tactic, however, were politically embarrassing. "This is not something Carter and I would've done," Mondale observed years later. "We didn't deal that way."[17]

The dynamic of the boycott effort changed when Jesse Owens, the Olympic legend, lost his battle with cancer on March 31. Owens had been conflicted over the boycott. He was a patriotic citizen, but he also knew his achievements at the 1936 Berlin Olympics had a far greater significance than is usually attached to athletic achievements. "A way must be found, I feel to have our 'boycott' and our Olympics, too," he wrote just before he died. On April 4, Olympic officials gathered from far and wide at his funeral services in the Gothic, milk-colored Rockefeller Memorial Chapel at the University of Chicago to honor him and his legacy.[18]

Cutler was there as well. He came to Chicago not so much to pay tribute to the memory of Owens as to discuss the boycott. His timing, though, was in poor taste, and when his efforts to get corporate contributors to cut off donations leaked to the news media, it made a bad situation even worse. Miller learned of these efforts as he was leaving the church service, when a reporter asked him for a comment. He snapped and said, "It's blatant black-mail." The funeral only underscored the fact that there was a legitimate moral argument for going to Moscow. Miller made this point when he told reporters with emotion, "We never would have been here to honor Jesse if there was a boycott of the 1936 Olympics." Even after he heard Cutler's legal distinction, it carried little weight with him. "They weren't threatening to do it, but the implication was there." He later recalled, "Our fund raising all but stopped and there was very little money coming in."[19]

Cutler, Kane, and Miller had a four-hour meeting after the funeral. (Cutler said it was three). The first hour was a fairly intense confrontation. Miller told Cutler bluntly that the administration had mishandled the boycott. He had asked both Cutler and Wexler directly if they were targeting their fundrais-ing efforts, and they had both lied to him. The USOC had never been willing to be the administration's pawn, but they had not opposed the White House either. An honest approach, they told Cutler, would have been much more constructive. It was also difficult to take the administration seriously when it was saying nations without Olympic teams were part of the boycott. After an hour, the conversation turned constructive, and Cutler stressed, according to Kane, larger issues: "The emphasis seems to be, now, that, in light of the perilous conditions in the world and the confrontation with the Soviet Union, that the United States Olympic Committee must support the President, or not only he but the United States will look bad in the eyes of the world; that we can't let him down; that we must support him."[20]

At this point, Carter became even more involved in the campaign. He called Miller the next day to seek his support. Miller was a retired U.S. Army colonel, and his daughter worked in Vice-President Mondale's office. His politics were similar to the President's, and their conversation should have been congenial. It should have been, but it was not. There are two different accounts of this phone conversation and both focus on the actions of the man on the other end of the connection. According to Miller, he told Carter he was disappointed that the White House staff was putting pressure on corpo-rations to deny donations to the USOC. "There was a long pause on the other end of the phone. Then Carter said, 'I don't know anything about that ...'" On the other hand, according to the notes the President made of the phone call, Miller was "equivocal, but promised to help. Concerned re alternative games which would be 'competitive' [with] Olympics. Needs help [with] fundraising. (I'll help if USOC backs my position.)" Both accounts are fairly accurate rep-resentations – as far as they go – of what transpired that day.[21]

The day after this conversation, Carter sent Kane a telegram. The President reminded him that the Soviet invasion was brutal. "IT JEOPARDIZES THE SECURITY OF THE PERSIAN GULF AREA AND THREATENS

WORLD PEACE AND STABILITY." If the USOC sent a team to Moscow, the Soviets would portray it as a vindication of their approach to world affairs. Participation in the games would inject more politics into the Olympics. "IT WOULD WEAKEN THE INTERNATIONAL OLYMPIC MOVEMENT." Without admitting it, Carter said the problems the boycott had encountered so far were of little consequence. "IF WE CLEARLY AND RESOLUTELY SHOW THE WAY, OTHER NATIONS WILL FOLLOW."[22]

Carter was also not above applying the stick personally. Speaking at the annual convention of the American Society of Newspaper Editors, Attorney General Benjamin Civiletti said the U.S. government had the legal power to keep American athletes from traveling to Moscow. The next day, Carter appeared before the same group and gave a speech on U.S. foreign policy that concentrated on U.S.-Soviet relations. He explained what made the Soviet invasion of Afghanistan so important. "The subjugation of Afghanistan represents the first direct intrusion of Soviet armed forces beyond the borders of the Warsaw Pact nation since the Second World War." The location of this intervention was also quite important. "There can be no doubt that the Soviet invasion poses an increased threat to the independence of nations in the region and to the world's access to vital resources and to vital sealanes." Since Afghanistan is a landlocked nation, the second half of this argument seems a bit dubious. He argued that his administration had taken peaceful steps in response to this assault to avoid escalating the crisis. "America and Americans are not motivated by relentless hostility, by a desire for indiscriminate confrontation or a return to the cold war." He then turned to the boycott and directly compared Moscow in 1980 to Berlin in 1936. He read sections from the political pamphlet for party activists. He then made it clear that there was no way the United States would be in Moscow come July, repeating Civiletti's statement: "If legal actions are necessary to enforce the decision not to send a team to Moscow, then I will take those legal actions."[23]

Carter and his administration took a beating in the news media for wielding these sticks. "Now it's Carter – a leading apostle of human rights – who is putting the strong arm on those who dissent from his policies," the editors of *The Des Moines Register* declared. Former Secretary of the Treasury William E. Simon, the treasurer of the USOC, said the Carter administration was using "ham-handed, thoughtless ... police state tactics." Even one of Carter's hometown papers criticized these methods. The editorial board of *The Atlanta Journal* observed, "It is alarming that anybody in the administration for one moment could have considered revoking the tax exempt status of the [USOC] if it did not support the boycott." Kane even took a political shot at Carter, "I'm sorry the administration had to resort to this kind of contentiousness. I think it has created a backlash." He added: "If only they'd played this as if we were friends and colleagues and part of the United States, it would have been different," he told Frank Dolson, sports editor of *The Philadelphia Inquirer*. "It makes you wonder if they handle all diplomatic matters this way. It's scary. I've learned things in the last three months that I'm sorry I know."[24]

When Eleanor Randolph, a reporter for the *Los Angeles Times*, asked Cutler about Simon's quote, he responded: "That's a bit strong." According to Randolph, Cutler's body language indicated irritation at the question. The lawyer added, "I don't think it's police state tactics to exercise the power of government to say 'you can't go, you can't send a team that purports to represent the United States … when I think by now it is clear that this nation does not want to be represented. To propose, or make a list in response to a professional request of possible legislative matters, I wouldn't call that police tactics."[25]

The presidential intervention and the threats of legal action produced two distinctly different reactions among USOC members. The first was a backlash. "A lot of delegates I've talked to are determined we should go," Helmick, said. He was not alone in seeing this shift. In a phone conversation that took place some time before the vote, Miller warned Cutler, according to the lawyer's notes: "Very very close on go – no go." Cutler wanted to know why Miller had been making public remarks critical of the administration. According to the notes: "Statements to maintain cred. With constituency." Miller warned Cutler again, "No way of assuming outcome – do think they will end up OK – close vote." He also reassured Cutler that he could count on him. "If he feels going badly, DM will take hard pos. before in favor of [Administrative Committee] res."[26]

There was more to this assessment than wishful thinking on Miller's part. On April 3, the *CBS Evening News* reported the results of a telephone poll it conducted among members of the USOC and found 27 in favor of sending a team, 16 opposed, and 36 undecided.[27]

The second reaction worked against the backlash. The leadership of the USOC decided it was better to bend rather than break and committed to support the boycott, even if it was without much enthusiasm. "I am sorry to say that I have reached the conclusion that we have no 'out,' that we are licked," Kane told a meeting of the Administrative Committee. "So, that means that, if we decide to go, he is going to give it to us; we are going to lose our charter, lose our everything." In essence, the Carter administration would destroy the committee and the Olympic movement within the United States. "If you will accept that conclusion, then we ought to try to milk them for everything we can get, and this is the time to do it." In fact, Kane and Miller had already decided to do just that. Most of the meeting they had with Cutler after Owens' funeral focused on carrots that the administration could use to secure a ballot in favor of the boycott. Kane and Miller then worked to convince the rest of the committee to support the boycott. One of the few exceptions was Anita DeFrantz, who was still active as an athlete despite her prominent position on the Administrative Committee. She was getting a lot of hate mail and prank phone calls for her vocal opposition. "With all that was going on and all the attention, I'm sure my phone was tapped, I know it was," she said many years later." She also told the Administrative Committee just prior to the vote on the boycott that there would be a legal challenge from the athletes. Since she had just graduated from the University of Pennsylvania Law School, there could be little doubt about who would be doing the litigation. The Administrative Committee recommended that the USOC boycott on a 9–1 vote. DeFrantz was the lone dissenter. "I did not give up, ever," she said years afterwards.[28]

It would seem that the bulk of USOC had surrendered. Six days after the CBS poll, *The Atlanta Journal* published a survey that it had taken of almost all of the delegates and found that they would vote to boycott in overwhelming numbers. Several delegates said Carter's decision took the onus off them for their vote. Bill Wall, executive director of the Amateur Basketball Association, declared, "A decision has to be made at this time. Carter has done many things that have ticked off [delegates], and they'll let him know it here. But until now he has only intimated what he'd do, and I applaud him for finally putting it in writing."[29]

Cutler was using some of the biggest carrots he had to get Miller and Kane's support. In two phone conversations that Miller and Cutler had on April 6 and 7, they negotiated the type of federal assistance the USOC would receive. The retired colonel made it clear that the U.S. government was going to have to do something to help the committee deal with the fundraising problems it was facing as a result of the boycott. Cutler's notes read: "Bottom line – some Cong. Support."[30]

Miller also wanted something in writing, and since the agreement had not been formalized at the time the USOC met, he was recommending they delay the vote until May. This stand was unnecessary. Cutler had the standing with Carter to deliver. He informed the President, "I am persuaded we can win the House of Delegates vote this weekend if we develop and announce a program (1) to honor the 1980 Olympic athletes who will be giving up their chance to compete in the Moscow Games, and (2) to help the USOC stave of the financial disaster it faces." In the end, Carter agreed to be the honorary chair of a special fundraising committee, with Reagan serving as co-chair. He was also willing to record television commercials to encourage donations to the committee. Miller originally pushed for the figure of $35–50 million, but the administration refused to go that far. Cutler told Carter $15 million. Carter rejected this figure. "I would not be responsible for a specific amount," he told Cutler. Despite this position, he was still willing to help. "I'd make TV spot, etc." He, however, wanted Cutler to be frugal. "Lloyd – This may be too much of a personal commitment. I dont want to be taking Kane's job. Define my commitment narrowly – J." The Committee ended up getting a matching funds agreement. A few weeks later, an editorial in the *Rocky Mountain News* noted that neither the USOC nor the White House was calling this payment a bribe. "So there," the editorialists noted with some healthy skepticism.[31]

Before the USOC could hold its vote, the Carter administration suffered another defeat. The *Comité Olímpico de Puerto Rico** voted to send a team to Moscow. Although Puerto Rico was U.S. territory, it had its own national Olympic committee. Reflecting the ignorance the Carter administration had of international sport, Puerto Rico had never figured in any of their boycott efforts. On April 9, the Puerto Rican committee in the "best tradition of the Olympic spirit," – to use the words of their president – voted 21–3 in favor of going to Moscow. In doing so, they had rejected calls from the government of Puerto Rico to support the boycott. The Resident Commissioner wanted Carter to use his powers to prevent the team from attending. Cutler recommended against this action "because of the political sensitivity of the Independence issue in Puerto Rico and because the presence of a Puerto Rican team is not that significant to the success or failure of the boycott." The Virgin Island Olympic Committee, on the other hand, said it would send no team. This victory was a minor one since this territory had never won a medal in the Olympics, but it was a gesture that Carter believed was worthy of "special credit."[32]

Editorial commentary in newspapers around the country picked up as the vote of the USOC approached, and much of it was exaggerated in tone. In a column for *The Washington Post*, Robert G. Kaiser suggested that the future of America's status as a superpower was at stake. In New York, the editorial board of *The Wall Street Journal* argued that if an indecisive president was finally taking a strong position, it was because the policy was so clearly needed: "It is hard to imagine how a great nation can survive if the President is unable to obtain public support and loyalty for his efforts to resist aggression." Much of the commentary was aimed directly at the USOC. The editors of *The Christian Science Monitor* observed, "Just as President Carter should not have delayed in calling for an international boycott of Moscow as host of the Summer Olympics, so the United States Olympic Committee should not now delay in supporting this gesture against the brutal Soviet invasion of Afghanistan." These sports officials had only themselves to blame. An editorial in the *Los Angeles Times* declared, "The pressures being put on the USOC could and should have been avoidable, if only that body had acted promptly to do what respect for national honor and an enlightened regard for its own self-interest required it to do." Others with more partisan agendas took shots at Carter and détente. Columnist Patrick Buchanan observed that the boycott was turning into a "diplomatic fiasco." The reason for this failure was that Carter "had been preaching the soothing heresies of detente since the day he took office" and could hardly expect others to join in him in a sudden 180-degree pivot in policy.[33]

This type of pressure caught many members of the USOC off guard. They were important people in the world of sports, but most had little experience

---

* Puerto Rican Olympic Committee.

with the national politics and found the attention unexpectedly intense. Doris Brown Heritage, a five-time world cross-country champion, told a *Sports Illustrated* reporter, "I didn't realize this whole thing could get so vicious."[34]

Kane, for his part, was convinced that other national Olympic committees would follow their lead. When Miller recommended at the meeting of the USOC Administrative Committee the night before the decision on Moscow that they hold off on a vote for a number of reasons, including the fact that the administration had not yet made a firm financial commitment and that delay would take pressure off these other committees, Patrick H. Sullivan, the counsel for the committee, rejected this position: "They are big boys, Don; they can do what they want. They are big boys, and don't have to follow us."[35]

Reflecting the enormous pressure he was under, Kane said larger issues of war and peace rested on their vote: "It appears that we have no choice but to boycott. But, once we do, and the other free nations come along – and some of the other nations, too, perhaps – the breach between the East and West becomes much greater, because we have instituted, engineered a boycott, which brings worldwide embarrassment to the Soviet Union. I think that's inevitable."[36]

William E. Simon, the former Secretary of the Treasury who was serving as the organization's treasurer, disputed this idea and tried to put the events into context. His remarks at the meeting show that even this experienced political figure was overreacting. "I don't happen to believe that the fact that we are pulling out of the Olympic Games, that that's going to bring us any closer to war than we are, already. I think we are close to 'World War Three,' now, as we were at the time of Pearl Harbor – but that is a separate consideration, and the Olympics is just another grain of sand in the hourglass, that's all."[37]

Still worried about the outcome of the vote, Carter sent Vice-President Walter Mondale to address the committee. Citing Carter's position as honorary president of the USOC, the White House staff informed Kane that Mondale was coming. Problem was that none of the Administrative Committee wanted the Vice-President in the room. Kane believed it was unwise and politically impossible to keep Mondale from speaking: "It was only when the President of the United States asked that Don felt he should agree to let the vice-president speak," he told the local media. "But there will be no others."[38]

The most significant meeting in the history of the USOC started at 9:02 the next morning when Kane gaveled the House of Delegates to order in the ballroom of the Antlers Hotel. One of the committee's vice-presidents, E. Newbold Black, in an effort to avoid the silence that had greeted Carter at the White House, asked the audience to stand and welcome their guest. Mondale delivered his speech from behind a podium that prominently displayed the name of the hotel. One observer called his speech "powerful"; another called it "ludicrous." [39]

One way or another, his rhetoric was extreme: "As we meet today, the lesson of the Soviet invasion of Afghanistan still waits to be drawn. History holds its breath; for what is at stake is no less than the future security of the civilized world. If one nation can be subjugated by Soviet aggression, is any sovereign nation truly safe from that fate?" With the Olympics, though, these murdering Russians were going to present themselves as a progressive force in world affairs, who were advancing the cause of peace: "I am convinced that the American people do not want their athletes cast as pawns in that tawdry propaganda charade." A boycott would serve the best interest of the United States: "It is an unambiguous statement of our national resolve." The time for decision was now: "Your vote is a test of our will, our confidence, our values, and our power to keep the peace through peaceful means." This obligation was a weighty one, but it was also appropriate: "It is fitting that the same ancient nation that gave us the Olympics also gave us democracy; for your decision here is truly a referendum on freedom."[40]

Mondale then spent a good deal of time comparing Moscow to Berlin in 1936. If there had been a boycott then, there might never have been a World War II. This argument was a powerful one that resonated with the American people, but not with the delegates in the room. Since Jesse Owens had died only two weeks earlier, and many people in the room believed that his victories had exposed Nazi racial ideology as a fraud, this section required some finesse on Mondale's part. He delivered, paying tribute to Owens, "but neither Jesse's achievements in Berlin nor any words spoken at the games prevented the Reich from exploiting the Olympics toward their own brutal ends."[41]

As the Vice-President brought his comments to a close, he told the delegates he respected their work. "Like you, I am in awe of the Olympic tradition – stretching over centuries, reaching out across cultures." Many people had sacrificed to train for the games, "but I also know, as you know, that some goals surpass even personal achievement." In short, preventing the Olympics from being manipulated would be, in the long run, the best thing: "I believe that the Olympic movement will be forever strengthened by your courage."[42]

After Mondale finished, the committee began conducting a number of routine business matters like calling the roll. Kane then reviewed the chronology of events that had led them to the decision they were going to make that day. The resolution that the Administrative Committee had adopted was formally introduced before lunch. Christopher Knepp, a delegate from the U.S. Baseball Federation, also introduced a resolution calling on the USOC to accept the invitation to Moscow. After lunch, Kane agreed to limit debate to three people on either side of the issue. Gene Edwards of the U.S. Soccer Federation and Brice Durbin of the National Federation of State High School Associations spoke in favor of the boycott. The third speaker was William Simon.[43]

If there was any chance of the committee voting against the boycott, it ended when Simon spoke. The former Secretary of the Treasury was conflicted, though. He worried about the future of the Olympic movement. He also was concerned about U.S. foreign policy if Carter were unable to react forcefully against Soviet aggression. Simon had stayed up the night before, writing and rewriting what he planned to say. He, however, was torn and actually wrote two different speeches. In his memoirs, he claims he did not decide which address he was going to give until he reached the podium. There is probably a little truth in that memory, but only a little. He had committed to speaking in favor of the boycott when Kane limited the debate to six people. He began by saying the committee faced a moral issue. "I am somewhat incredulous that a group of mature and what I consider to be among the most patriotic of Americans – our Olympians – can seriously discuss defying the President of the United States on a national-security issue. We aren't defying a man; we are defying the office, the highest elected Office in our land." He also questioned the expertise of the delegates to even consider voting against the boycott. "I ask you, are we, all of a sudden, foreign-policy and national-security experts?"[44]

This imperial presidency argument is one that almost every administration uses. Simon, though, blended it with both patriotism and concern about the future of the Olympics. "What we ought to decide here, today, in my judgment, is not the legalese of various amendments, but an unequivocal vote of support for our country." Applause interrupted him at this point. "And I suggest to you that, if the route you wish to take is to vote to defy the President, you will be voting to destroy the United States Olympic Committee, the Olympic movement, and denying future generations of Americans the privilege and the honor of representing our country in future Olympic games."[45]

He repeated these themes several times in a speech that was twenty minutes in length. At several points, he observed that the USOC was being put into a difficult position and that there was no easy answer. "As I said at the outset, it's a moral decision – and, they are the toughest kind."[46]

As he finished, he told the delegates the issue of 1980 had already been decided. They needed to keep other considerations in mind. "Really, the reality of it all is that, regardless of what side you come down on in this issue, the President has said that we aren't going to Moscow. He has made that national-security determination, and it's overwhelmingly supported by the American people. And, indeed, if there's any who have a death wish and vote to defy the President, God help us."[47]

When he finished, the room exploded in applause and then a standing ovation. "Bill gave one of the great speeches of all time," Michael Lenard, an athlete representative observed. "As soon as Bill gave his speech, I said 'uh-oh.' I was going to vote 'no' and nothing was going to change my mind, but if anyone was on the fence, Bill's speech changed their mind. Bill's speech was very, very, very effective."[48]

It was then the turn of the boycott opponents to speak. It is a reflection of the mixed sentiment among even individual delegates that their audience applauded after each finished. Knepp said, "I just disagree, and I am not convinced with the reasons that the Administration has put forth." Colonel Don Hull of the national Boxing federation warned that a boycott might lead the IOC to suspend the USOC. The last was DeFrantz. Her argument was more legalistic than Simon's. She said the USOC had a legal obligation to send a team. Without mentioning the Carter administration by name, she said threats to prevent the U.S. Olympic team from traveling overseas struck at the very core of self-determination and self-expression that were at the heart of what it was to be an American. "I also offer to you a few words from a gentleman older than I – Ben Franklin – who said, in 1758, 'They that can give up essential liberty to obtain a little temporary safety deserve neither liberty nor safety.'" In closing she said, "Let's not boycott freedom."[49]

Colonel Miller then collected the ballots in an empty water pitcher. In the complex USOC voting process, the tally of the 275 delegates, most of whom had more than one vote, was 1,604–797 in favor of the boycott. Kane then announced the results of the vote publicly to a mob of 200 reporters assembled in the lobby of the hotel. "I am completely satisfied that it was the right decision," he said. "At the same time, I am desperately sorry for American athletes who have been hurt by it." He was in tears.[50]

Peter Schnugg, a member of the water polo team and a delegate, was angry at the outcome. "The administration twisted arms," he said. "I'm not learned in politics, and maybe I'm full of naivete but a lot of things the president did shocked me. Those are the things that scared the Olympic committee." He also explained why he had voted to go to Moscow. "William Simon said we were closer to World War III than ever. No doubt that affected a lot of people but what it came down to was, 'Who do you believe?' I had a difficult time accepting everything the president said. I just couldn't say I honestly believed him."[51]

The vote was an unqualified victory for the White House. It was the first major contest in the boycott that had gone in favor of Carter's policy. White House Press Secretary Jody Powell quickly released a statement: "The President welcomes the strong vote of the United States Olympic Committee House of Delegates not to send a United States team to the Moscow Olympics in light of his advice that to send a team would be contrary to our national interest." He also added that there was no chance that the administration would change its policy.[52]

In private, the administration officials knew that it was a win they needed and that it had been close. Al McDonald wrote Cutler a quick note: "Congratulations on the Olympic vote Saturday, we all breathed a sigh of relief."[53]

After the USOC vote, Cutler no longer had any reluctance in admitting what he had done. The *Los Angeles Times* ran a lengthy profile of him a week after the vote that presented him as a well-dressed street fighter and even gave him credit for coming up with the idea of the boycott in the first place. Cutler gave an interview for the article: "Ultimately, we had to exert every effort and leave nothing to chance. I can't tell you which things we did that worked and which things didn't, but I'm glad we did them all. Because, if we hadn't done them, we might not have won."[54]

Assessments about the vote varied significantly, but the Carter administration had no monopoly on the political praise. In the Senate, Harry Byrd, the West Virginia Democrat, congratulated the Olympians: "In my view, this unselfish act by the U.S. Olympic Committee is the single strongest statement of disapproval of the Soviet invasion of Afghanistan." He also added: "The committee's decision also has very significant consequences abroad."[55]

The U.S. Olympic community was divided on how to assess the vote. "We are athletes," said Andy Toro, a former kayaker who would have been the coach for the U.S. team in Moscow. "We know how to handle defeat. On the field, we are defeated many times. Obviously, we got defeated here today because we all wanted to go." Another USOC official observed, "We thought we were pretty independent, but we found out how much pressure the president can bring to bear." Julian Roosevelt, an American member of the IOC, said, "I think the USOC has knuckled under to political pressure unnecessarily." Privately, Kane agreed. In notes he used for a speech afterwards, he wrote: "USOC – chastity defiled."[56]

The politics of the day translated poorly overseas. "It was almost embarrassing to watch the emotional nationalism that charged the meeting," Neil Macfarland, a Conservative Member of Parliament, who would later join Thatcher's cabinet as minister of sport, commented.[57]

Lord Killanin agreed. "I watched the Colorado Springs meeting on television in Dublin and found the national emotionalism embarrassing." More importantly, he thought the debate was inappropriate: "The USOC met at Colorado Springs, Colorado, its headquarters, to discuss national security, which to my way of thinking is not a matter for an NOC." He also tried to find what little positive there was in the situation. "In view of what was happening in the United States that figure of 797 surprised and delighted me. At least if we were to lose the United States in Moscow there would still be people who could maintain the Olympic cause from a position of loyalty."[58]

Lord Killanin was focusing just on the numbers. Many of the USOC members voted with little enthusiasm. One of the reporters present observed that the delegates had "wooden and preoccupied" expressions on their faces as they conducted their business. "I feel I have no choice but to support the

President or be perceived as supporting the Russians," T.E. Dillon, a delegate representing the National Rifle Association, remarked. "I *resent* that."[59]

The main theme that emerged in the U.S. media was the importance of the boycott even as an act of symbolism. "The list of boycotting nations may be a small one, but it could grow by summer. Whether it does or not, it amounts to a high-volume – and valid – protest," an editorial in *The Arizona Republic* declared. The official position of the *Dayton Daily News* was similar: "Whether other nations go along or not, this country has taken the stand it should take, expressed in a way that Soviet officials, even with all their propaganda machinery, cannot hide totally." Many, many similar editorials praising the vote appeared in newspapers around the country.[60]

As far as the domestic ramifications of the vote go, columnist Mary McGrory zeroed in on its significance: "It may have looked a bit crass but the president couldn't be fussy. The arm-wrestling contest with the recalcitrant Olympians was one he had to win."[61]

There was another vote that the USOC took that the White House staff ignored. The delegates voted against participating in any type of counter-Olympics. There "is no substitute for the Olympic Games," Miller remarked. Cutler put a perfect spin on this vote, explaining that the White House had been exploring this option only for the benefit of the athletes: "If this is something that the athletes and national governing boards don't want, that would resolve the issue." The President, though, was personally committed to the issue, and the White House staff spent another month attempting to establish games that USOC had publicly said no Americans would participate in.[62]

The vote in Colorado had, for better or worse, gone in favor of the Carter Administration. It was an important victory, but only two weeks later Carter would suffer the greatest humiliation while in office when the U.S. military failed in its efforts to rescue the hostages being held captive in the U.S. Embassy in Tehran, Iran. Carter made this decision against the advice of Vance, which led the Secretary of State to resign. Carter replaced him with Senator Edmund Muskie of Maine.[63]

Since the President had committed himself to a boycott, a number of events had gone against them. The vote of the USOC was the first key battle that had gone in favor of the White House. Had the vote been in favor of attending the Olympics, the Americans might not have been able to make it to Moscow anyway, but the U.S. Olympians had bent under the relentless pressure the White House had directed at them. Carter's subordinates had beaten Killanin's proxies. In the United Kingdom, Killanin's associates had successfully resisted Carter's ally at 10 Downing Street. The repercussions of both these decisions would travel far and wide.

CHAPTER 11

Civil Wars

IT WAS ONLY WITH THE VOTE OF THE USOC THAT CARTER'S CAMPAIGN gained momentum. The vote in Colorado also set in motion a series of civil wars between the followers of Jimmy Carter and Lord Killanin for control of the international Olympic movement. It was these battles that would determine the success or failure of the boycott.

The Carter administration quickly scored another victory north of the border. An intense struggle for control of the Olympic movement in Canada broke out despite the uncertainty of the new Trudeau Government. According to Eric S. Morse, head of international sports relations in the Canadian Department of External Affairs, "The boycott question dominated the Canadian public foreign policy debate to the virtual exclusion of all other topics." Richard Pound, who in addition to his membership on the IOC was president of the Canadian Olympic Association (COA), agreed. The media, he believed, "jumped on the issue with all the self-restraint of a sailor on shore leave." Trudeau for his part believed that boycott would fail. That view was a fairly common one in Ottawa. "At almost all levels with government, then, the feeling was that the boycott was inevitable, if perhaps ill-advised," Morse recalled. In his memoirs, written in the third person, the Prime Minister explained, "He believed that sporting events could be held hostage in future years and knew that a boycott would destroy the dreams of many Canadian athletes."[1]

The COA acted quickly on this issue. Richard Pound, who was the president of the organization in addition to his membership on the IOC, believed that the boycott was nothing but an election year gambit on the part of Carter. The executive board of the COA voted on March 20 to go to Moscow. The vote was not particularly close: 25–5–1.[2]

The Olympic Trust of Canada, though, had different ideas. This organization existed to raise money to finance the Canadian Olympic movement and make it financially independent of the government. Trudeau had still not taken a position on the issue, and the new Parliament had not even convened when Wally Halder, executive director of the Trust, informed Pound that they would be providing no funding if Canada went to Moscow. "Our corporate community was more American in opposition to going to Moscow than even the U.S. business community," Pound observed.[3]

Trudeau realized the boycott was going to happen one way or another and instructed External Affairs Minister Mark MacGuigan get some type of quid pro quo from the Carter administration. MacGuigan did not take this recommendation seriously and spent most of his energy trying to find a way to present this decision as one taken independently of the White House. As MacGuigan looked for the right moment and setting, Australian Prime Minister Malcolm Fraser complicated his life. The two men met in Zimbabwe to help that country celebrate its independence, and after MacGuigan told him of the Trudeau Cabinet's plans, Fraser shared that news with the press, violating diplomatic protocol. It was only on April 22 that the new Cabinet took a formal position on the boycott when the External Affairs Minister announced in the House of Commons that Canada officially supported this effort in retaliation for the Soviet invasion of Afghanistan. Trudeau had finally come out in support of the boycott when it was clear that a good deal of the Canadian public and the Canadian Olympic movement itself was in support of this idea. In Commons, MacGuigan made it clear that he would take no legal actions to block travel to the Soviet Union if the COA decided to participate in the Olympic Games.[4]

Four days later the COA had its annual meeting. The main issue on the agenda was deciding if it would send a team to Moscow. Pound at the time and afterwards believed that the position of the Trudeau Cabinet determined the vote. James Worrall recalled, "My s 'pirits sank as I could tell from the debate that the full COA membership was moving towards a pro-boycott position." The vote was 137–35.[5] Pound, as a good member of the IOC, had opposed the boycott. Afterwards Denis Whitaker, a member of the COA, told him sarcastically, "That was a great speech, Dick." Thinking Whitaker was serious, Pound thanked him.

Whitaker sputtered in rage, "You are a disgrace. You should resign."

Pound was in no mood to hear such sermonizing: "It had been the end of a long struggle, in which I had managed to hold off the inevitable until the last minute, but had failed. 'Denis,' I said, 'fuck off.'"[6]

Trudeau had attempted to pursue a course independent of the United States and failed. "I'm disappointed in Prime Minister Trudeau," Dave Johnson, the coach of the Canadian swim team, remarked. "I though he could be a leader, instead of following big brother. We shouldn't sell ourselves short on our value to the United States. We have to take a stand on our value as Canadians, but I can't see the boycott as being a complete success."[7]

Pound made a more telling observation. "The boycott attracted a good deal of media attention and allowed politicians to sound firm and resolute, while doing nothing more than preventing their athletes from going to the Games." He believed there was a reason for this deception. "The slight of hand had the desired effect of drawing attention away from the real issue of powerlessness in the face of the Soviets."[8]

Despite this rancor, the confrontation in Europe was far more important than what was taking place in Canada. Margaret Thatcher refused to accept defeat. The BOA had said that it would reconsider its decision if the international climate changed, and this qualification provided an opening for Thatcher. After the USOC vote, journalist Gordon Burns interviewed the Prime Minister for *Reports Politics*, a British television program. "I think matters have changed. I was very pleased with the decision of the American Olympic Committee," she declared. "They felt that the defence of freedom was the over-riding need at the moment. They have decided. That is a lead which other nations cannot ignore and I hope that our own will reconsider their decision and, perhaps, change it." Thatcher believed that few nations would end up in Moscow and that the gathering would be unworthy of the Olympic name. Burns pushed, asking if her government would use legal mechanisms to prevent British athletes from traveling to Russia. The Prime Minister was succinct in her response: "A free country does not do that."[9]

Legal action was one thing, but political pressure was altogether different. George Gardiner, a Conservative Member of Parliament, argued, "It is the crimes against humanity being committed by the occupying army that today cry out for our most vehement censure." He continued, believing it was up to the young men and women planning to go to Moscow to do the right thing. "Each individual athlete has to consult his conscience, and ask himself whether those corpses strewn in the streets or children gassed can really be traded off against the prospect of winning a gold medal."[10]

There was no political posturing to Thatcher's stand. She believed in the cause and thought the tide of victory was with her, particularly after the U.S. vote. "The Association said 'should circumstances, change the BOA would re-examine the situation,'" she reminded one sports official sympathetic to her stand. "I believe that the circumstances, as the Association meant them, are changing and that as the news spreads they will continue to change. I feel with you that the tide of public opinion is indeed starting to flow strongly in our favour."[11]

After Malcolm Fraser's unexpected telephone call of March 5, she had written her Australian counterpart. "We need to move the public debate to more positive ground." She was trying to take that stand. A memo her government prepared made clear the moral terms, it wanted a boycott. These issues also reflected the stark terms of world politics: "If we are to preserve peace it is essential that the free countries of the West and the Third World should make known their anger. Otherwise we risk a repetition." The Olympics was a worthy target because it would "bring home to the Russians the enormity of their action."[12]

The BOA refused to reconsider its decision, so the Cabinet began targeting individual British athletes, trying to convince them not to go. Douglas Hurd had a meeting with Peter Coe, father and manager of middle distance runner Sebastian Coe. "I remember very clearly when my dad was asked to go and see Douglas Hurd. In the nicest way they were essentially saying to my father, 'Can you not keep your troublesome son quiet?'" Lord Coe told *The Guardian* years later when this effort came to light, "My gut instinct was that there was an intellectual dishonesty about what we were trying to achieve."[13]

The French situation was similar to the British one. Only Greece had more of its heritage wrapped up in the Olympic movement than France. Baron de Coubertin had been French, and Paris had hosted the Games twice. No city had hosted the athletic festival three times. French, along with English, was the official language of the movement. It was no surprise then that the *Comité National Olympique et Sportif Français** announced three days after Carter's appearance on *Meet the Press* that they would be sending a team to Moscow for simple reasons of sport.[14]

Unlike Thatcher's Cabinet, the government of Valéry Giscard d'Estaing made no effort to put political pressure on the French Olympic Committee. This position made sense. The French public opposed the idea of a boycott. There were, of course, those who believed that striking at the Olympics made sense. Writing on the pages of the conservative newspaper *Le Figaro*, columnist Alain Besançon argued that a boycott would strike at Soviet legitimacy and show that the invasion of Afghanistan was unacceptable. "I don't know the 'purely sporting reasons' that have led the French Olympic Committee to take the decision to go to Moscow. It could be the spirit to play to the crowd of a concentration camp. However going to Moscow or not is ever foremost a political decision that interests the government."[15]

Under such pressure, Giscard d'Estaing slowly and tepidly changed his position. He was responding less to critics like Besançon than out of a desire to help Helmut Schmidt who was facing an intense electoral challenge that had become entwined in the boycott issue. The problem was that the French President wanted to avoid looking like a puppet of Jimmy Carter. Needless to say, this weak and uncertain position played poorly in the United States. "The French could find themselves more isolated in Moscow this summer than they care to be," the editors of the *Rocky Mountain News* declared in predicting that most of Europe would follow the expected German boycott vote.[16]

Carter shared this frustration. When asked about support that U.S. allies were giving, the President said – in public no less, "We do have times when we get aggravated and displeased, for instance, with the French." There was nothing accidental about this comment. He made no effort to hide his hostility toward Giscard d'Estaing from other foreign leaders.[17]

* National Olympic and French Sports Committee.

Although the French Olympic Committee had already accepted an invitation to Moscow, boycott supporters had enough strength to have the decision reconsidered. Two days before the committee met, French Foreign Minister Jean François–Poncet announced that the government would make no effort to influence this vote. Despite this hands-off approach, the issue looked in doubt. Only twenty-three of the eighty members attended the meeting. A number of members opposed having any vote, feeling that the issue had already been decided, and that such a small number of representatives had no right to speak for the entire organization. These individuals clearly expected a boycott vote would carry the day. Six hours of debate followed, before the committee made its vote. Whatever fear boycott opponents had were misplaced. Despite charges that athletes would only win worthless "medals of chocolate," the French voted 17–2 to once again accept the invitation to the Moscow Games. Claude Collard, president of the committee, announced their decision, explaining that the vote had been made without regard to politics. "We have taken a purely sporting decision, I repeat to you," he told reporters. "We have recognized the position of our athletes and certain of them are of high-level and deserve to go to the games."[18]

This decision drew a good deal of public praise in France. Using the French acronym for the Olympic committee, Jacques Chaban-Delmas, president of the National Assembly, praised the vote. "The decision of the CNSOF conforms to the position that I have always held." The Communist Group of the National Assembly denounced "the unacceptable pressure of President Carter and the German Federal Republic for largely electoral reasons to recreate a 'Cold War' climate." Foreign affairs columnist Daniel Vernet of *Le Monde* believed that the vote had saved détente, which the Germans and Americans were attempting to "torpedo." Other French journalist predicted the vote would have a ripple affect across Europe and throughout the French-speaking countries of Africa.[19]

Despite French views, most observers and participants in the boycott believed that West Germany was the central battleground for the entire boycott. This belief is understandable. The two Germanys were Olympic superpowers, regularly earning more medals than any other nation except the United States and the Soviet Union. Carter's fears about Helmut Schmidt were genuine. Schmidt had been temporizing, but from his perspective it was mandatory. His cabinet was divided on the issue, and Carter had left him exposed to charges of being an American puppet. More significantly, Carter's reputation for indecision, legitimate question about what the USOC would do, and the Chancellor's fears that a boycott would kill détente and *Ostpolitik* gave him good reasons to wait. Given his makeup, it would have been difficult for Carter to accept Schmidt's position since it would require him to acknowledge his own mistakes, but Cutler during his trips overseas saw that Schmidt was moving in the direction of a boycott. The German was being helpful and told the Special Coordination Committee as much.[20]

On March 20, Schmidt took a major step toward a boycott. Right-wing political pressure was developing in favor of the boycott even within the German Olympic movement. Dieter Graf von Landsberg-Valen, president of the *Deutsche Olympiade-Komitee für Reiterei**, released a press release that criticized the "shortage of objectivity" and "naivety" the IOC had in dealing with the Soviet Union. Schmidt announced that German participation was "impossible" as long as the Soviets were in Afghanistan. This statement, though, was no firm announcement that a boycott would be official policy. That final step had to wait until April 26, two weeks after the vote in Colorado. Unlike Carter, Schmidt had a private meeting with leaders of the German Olympic movement, before he announced in the *Bundestag* that the *Bundesrepublik* would boycott the Moscow Olympics. Politically, at least, he had made the right move. The *Bundestag* voted 445 to 8, with 3 abstentions, to support this policy.[21]

The question remained what position would the National Olympic Committee for Germany take. Schmidt's announcement initiated a three-week-long battle for control of the German Olympic movement. The two main antagonists were Willi Daume, president of the Committee, and Willy Weyer, president of the German Sports Federation. Weyer believed a boycott was necessary because of the "crass failure of the IOC" to deal with the Soviet violations of the Olympic charter. Daume, like Samaranch, wanted to be the next president of the IOC and to have any chance of gaining that office needed to make sure that his Olympic committee sent a team to Moscow. Boycott opponents managed to delay the vote for a week to limit the political ramifications of the vote on other European national committees should they lose. The climax to the German debate came in a four-hour-long meeting in Düsseldorf that saw twenty-on members of the committee speak. Afterwards Daume complained that the meeting had not been civil in tone. Alexander Pusch, a fencer who had won gold in Montreal, watched the vote as "my pulse rose higher than it would in a championship." Arguing that Germany had to maintain solidarity with the United States, Weyer carried the day. The vote was fifty-nine in favor of boycott, forty opposed. In a front-page editorial, the editors of the *Frankfurter Allgemeine Zeitung* (FAZ) called the vote "clearer than expected." They also added, "The athletes and the Presidents of the organization have given us an example of democratic decision making which one should not be so rash as to forget." This sentiment was hardly universal, even among the staff of the newspaper. An editorial appearing in the sports section declared that athletic administrators had "made a political decision." The FAZ sports editors worried that the ramifications of this vote might very well likely end up destroying international sport.[22]

Such fears were common among the defeated German opponents of the boycott. "I must accept this decision," Berthold Beitz, a member of the IOC

* German Olympic Equestrian Committee.

remarked, "but I see coming in Moscow that the DDR [East Germany] will stand for the German voice in sport." Hans Hansen, vice-president of the DSB, feared that other efforts to manipulate international sports would follow. For Jürgen Bruhn, a swimmer expected to medal at Moscow, the vote "killed my last hopes." He explained, "I am depressed. I have sacrificed a year of study for the Olympics. There is no substitute." Like Hansen, he expected that one international crisis after another would undermine Olympiad after Olympiad.[23]

The German vote, though, failed to have the impact that the Carter Administration and most observers expected it to have. The Americans had been hoping that events in Düsseldorf would initiate a bandwagon effect in Europe, but the vote in the United Kingdom had blunted whatever advantage the German decision might have given to the boycott effort. Muskie, the new Secretary of State, made this point clear to Carter: "We may yet win one or two Europeans – perhaps the Spanish or Turks or Luxembourgers – but it is now certain that the German coattails are not as strong as we had hoped."[24]

Events in other parts of Europe bore out this assessment. In Italy, the government of Prime Minister Francesco Cossiga offered the United States unqualified support in condemning the Soviet invasion. In many ways, Italy was one of the front lines of the Cold War, despite being a NATO member. The nation was political unstable, faced serious security threats from left-wing terrorists, and had a strong Communist Party with exceptional electoral strength. Most cabinets stayed in office less than a year. The support Cossiga offered was significant, but he had little power over the *Comitato Olimpico Nazionale Italiano*.* Richard N. Gardner, the U.S. ambassador in Rome, was exceptionally well qualified for this post. He was married to an Italian, spoke the language as did his two children, and had taught for a year as a visiting professor at the University of Rome. Despite this expertise, Gardner made the same mistake that the Carter White House did and believed the government had authority over the committee. Gardner, unlike many U.S. diplomats, met with Italian Olympic officials, but most of his efforts focused on Cossiga's Cabinet.[25]

The best the prime minister could do was to recommend that Italy not go to Moscow. On May 19, the government issued a press release that it would prohibit the use of the national anthem or national flag in the opening and closing ceremonies or in the presentation of any medals. "I knew immediately that we had lost our struggle to keep the Italians from participating in the Olympic games," Gardner declared. He was wrong. His defeat had come weeks earlier. The day after Cossiga's press release, the Committee voted again to attend the Summer Olympics. "I felt this outcome was probably inevitable given the Italian enthusiasm for sports and for the Olympics and because of

---

* Italian National Olympic Committee.

the fact that the French and other important European countries had already decided to go," the ambassador explained.[26]

A small crisis developed in the principality of Lichtenstein. The national legislature voted to boycott the Olympics. The problem was that their sovereign, Prince Franz Josef II, was a member of the IOC. The Prince had real executive authority – and had the political power to ignore the vote, but he decided that it would be best for his nation if he heeded public sentiment. As a result, he resigned from the Committee. He was the only IOC casualty associated with the 1980 boycott.[27]

In trying to get Norway to join the boycott, Vice-President Mondale – his family had come to the United States from Norway – took the lead in another example of the patronizing approach to ethnic politics at work in the White House. This approach had little success. The Royal Norwegian Government was one of the few in Europe that never put any pressure on its national Olympic committee. "My Government's position on Norwegian participation has been in principle that this question must be decided upon by the athletic associations themselves," Prime Minister Odvar Nordli wrote to Mondale in English. "On this basis it is my firm conviction that only a decision taken by the athletic associations themselves, without any Government pressure, would receive understanding and support in Norway as well as internationally." Even without pressure from Nordli, the *Norges Idrettsforbund og Olympiske Komité** was deeply conflicted. The committee was the first in Europe to vote to boycott. After the British vote, the Norwegians reversed themselves. Then, after the West German vote, the committee changed its position yet again. The final decision: boycott.[28]

The Olympics became an issue of debate in the Republic of Ireland. Discussion on the topic broke out in the *Dáil Éireann*,[†] the lower chamber of the legislature. Foreign Minister Brian Lenihan said the government was already on record in objecting to the Soviet invasion, but they had no position on a boycott. He also said he had had no contact on the matter with Lord Killanin. "It makes the utmost commonsense for civilised countries such as Ireland and our European colleagues to hasten slowly in this matter."[29]

This attitude might have been perfectly fine, since the Irish Republic had no direct authority over the Olympic Council of Ireland, but U.S. Ambassador William Shannon decided to enter the fray. In a speech he gave to the Sligo Chamber of Commerce, he warned his audience that Ireland's very independence was at stake. "Insofar as the invasion of Afghanistan poses a threat to Western Europe than it is to the United States," the Ambassador said. "And by Western Europe, I would specifically include Ireland which, unlike my own country, has no oil, only a small natural gas field and almost no coal."

* Norwegian Olympic Committee and Confederation of Sports.
† Assembly of Ireland.

He then gave another speech attacking neutrality. It was time to pick sides. That did not sit well in an Ireland that had sat out World War II, refused to join the NATO, and was neutral in the Cold War. An editorial in *The Irish Times* told Shannon to mind his own business: "Just because not everyone in Ireland appears to be toeing President Carter's attitude to the Soviet invasion of Afghanistan (is Killanin a Red agent?) does not mean that we are in need of any special instruction or have lost our political marbles." Lord Killanin enjoyed watching one of Carter's agents take his comeuppance. "It had been considered in many quarters to have been most undiplomatic, but, of course, Ambassador Shannon is a newspaper man and not a professional diplomat."[30]

Despite the clumsiness of Shannon's efforts, the *Seanad Éireann** had an extensive debate on the boycott. On March 26, Senator Gemma Hussey introduced a resolution calling on the government "to make a clear statement of Ireland's foreign policy in the light of recent events in Iran and Afghanistan." One of the things she wanted was for the cabinet to take a strong position against Irish participation in the Moscow Olympics. "To go to the Olympic Games is a political gesture in itself." There was another reason to boycott. It was what Jimmy Carter wanted. "Ireland," she said, "has an enormous amount to gain from having maximum friendly relations with the United States." Hussey was a member of the Fine Gael political party, which was in the minority at the time and was attempting to score some points against the government of Taoiseach – the Irish term for Prime Minister – Jack Lynch. In an exchange with Hussey, Lenihan defended the government's policy of inaction: "As a free country, with free association, free bodies, our national Olympic Committee are quite free to utilize their Irish passports and bring Irish athletes to Moscow and there can be no way in which an Irish Government in a free society can deter them from doing that. That is precisely the situation and we are presenting it in that way." There were important reasons for delay. Lenihan believed that détente itself was at risk. Another senator, Patrick Cooney, took up Hussey's argument: "We should align ourselves firmly in the American western camp. For that reason I am disappointed that the Minister in his speech has been extremely vague and possibly deliberately vague, as to where this Government stand in regard to what position we want to take in the world today as between the opposing blocs." Lynch took a beating. Mary Robinson, a future president of Ireland, said his position was a joke. The Olympic boycott was about getting Jimmy Carter reelected. Michael Lanigan argued against the boycott: "I cannot see what the difference is between keeping the sporting nations of the world out of Russia for one reason and allowing the whole lot of them into America at the same time. It is rubbish. The Minister should advise the Government to let our athletes

---

* Senate of Ireland.

compete in the Olympics in Russia or wherever they are held." This discussion continued until the *Seanad Éireann* adjourned that evening.[31]

On May 16, the Lynch Cabinet issued a statement in which it outlined its belief in open dialogue between nation-states: "As matters now stand, however, the Government after careful consideration of all the issues involved strongly advise the Irish Olympic Committee not to send a team to Moscow." In the *Dáil Éireann*, Lenihan explained the Soviet presence in Afghanistan had ruined the charter of this international festival: "This has resulted in a situation where it is not possible to ensure that the established character of the Olympic Games will be upheld." Carter had won a victory over Killanin in the Baron's home country, but it was a meaningless victory, since the Olympic Council of Ireland represented all thirty-two counties of Emerald Isle, and the Republic had no legal authority over some of the athletes that competed for Ireland in the Olympics.[32]

The battle in Spain, however, was far more significant. Juan Antonio Samaranch, Spanish ambassador to the Soviet Union, wanted to succeed Killanin as IOC president. If Spain boycotted Moscow, that dream would come to an end. He traveled back to Spain to use his influence. The final vote of the *Comité Olímpico Español** was close: 18–11, with 7 abstentions. Spain would be in Moscow. Spanish journalist Jordi Garcia Candau argued on the pages of *El Pais* that the Spanish were trying to help Samaranch get elected and that "they forgot the reason for the boycott." On the other hand, the editorial board of the newspaper *ABC* argued that Jimmy Carter had made a knee-jerk reaction based on the immediate circumstances, and that a boycott was hardly meaningful as a response to Afghanistan. Given these extreme views, it is hardly surprising that the Spanish Olympic Committee made a bit of a compromise and decided that they would not use their national colors in the Soviet Union. "I'm not worried about this issue," Juan Manuel de Hoz, a member of the committee told reporters, "besides they enter the games for the competition between athletes, not between nations." This compromise reflected public sentiment in Spain, with most Spaniards wanting to participate with some type of qualification to avoid giving the Soviets a propaganda festival.[33]

The boycott fared better in other parts of the globe, but only marginally so. The Olympic movement had never developed deep roots in Central and South America. Soccer and the World Cup were far more popular. Despite this shallow association, boycott proponents had limited success in the region. Meeting in Guatemala, the congress of the *Organización Deportiva Panamericana*** issued a resolution in which it declared that the Organization "reaffirms the faith and loyalty of the Olympic movement."[34]

Carter appealed to Rodrigo Carazo, President of the Republic of Costa Rica, as a "friend of the United States" for his support. This request was a

* Spanish Olympic Committee.
** Pan-American Sports Organization.

futile gesture. Costa Rica had just qualified for the Olympic soccer tournament for the first time ever and there was no chance that it would join the boycott. Carazo told Carter that the popularity of soccer in his country made it impossible for him to consider supporting action against the Soviet Union. Others disagreed. The assistant editor of *La Nacion* of San Jose argued, "Costa Rica, a tiny nation without an army and a lover of all human liberties and peace, should never even have considered participation in the Moscow Games." In essence, Carter had been right. "Costa Rica should have placed itself beside the United States and demonstrated its solidarity with the nation which we owe so much."[35]

Journalists in other countries in the region made similar observations. When Guatemala decided to go to the Olympics, an *El Imparcial* editorial declared: "We cannot be indifferent to the invasion of Afghanistan and the aggression of the Soviet Army, nor can we forget that we are being attacked by Communist subversion." In Caracas, *El Universal* ran a front-page editorial denouncing the decision of the *Comité Olímpico Venezolano** to send a team to the summer Games: "To say that we are going to Moscow because sports has nothing to do with politics is folly and sheer hypocrisy. It is to play the game by the rules of a country considered a threat to the peace and well being of humanity."[36]

The Carter administration had better success in the cone of South America. Chile was already on record in its support of the boycott. The *Comité Olímpico Argentino*† decided not to send a team. "National interests need to prevail over sport," Antonio Rodríguez, president of the committee, explained. In neighboring Bolivia, the Carter administration got lucky. The *Comité Olímpico Boliviano*‡ voted not to go to Moscow mainly because it could not afford to send a team. Even after the IOC offered to pay Bolivian expenses, the committee declined to field a team, believing it would not be competitive. In Uruguay, the United States pursued counterproductive policies. President Aparicio Méndez had no problem in informing Carter about these shortcomings. "The decision to participate in the Moscow Olympics does not lie with the Government," he wrote. "Such a decision lies exclusively with the Uruguayan Olympic Committee." Carter was rather skeptical about this claim: "They control everything else in Uruguay." Despite placing no effective pressure on the country, Carter got lucky again when Uruguay decided against going to Moscow.[37]

The administration enjoyed a good deal of success in Asia, but these achievements mattered little. There were few Olympic powers in this region. In 1980, Japan was the only Asian nation to have ever hosted the Olympic

---

* Venezuelan Olympic Committee.
† Argentinean Olympic Committee.
‡ Bolivian Olympic Committee.

games. A number of nations on this continent agreed to support the boycott. China quickly came out in support. On February 1, Hua Guofeng, Premier of the State Council of the PRC, informed Carter that China would support a move to relocate the games, and if that failed, would not attend. Turkey took a strong stand in opposition to the Russian invasion of Afghanistan, but it was not until May 23 that Prime Minister Soyeman Demirel could inform Carter that his country would indeed boycott.[38]

Japan was similar. The *Nihon Orimpikku Iinkai** was opposed to the boycott, but Prime Minister Ohira Masayoshi had mixed feelings on the issue. "Problems involving either sports or religion must be handled with special care," he remarked. "If not, the results can be pretty bad." Representatives of the Physical Education Bureau of the Ministry of Education met with the leadership of the Japanese Olympic Committee. Nothing came of the meeting, except an agreement that the decision would be made later, and initially that Japanese government was content to leave the decision to the JOC.[39]

There was good reason for delay. The public was divided. The *Yomiuri shimbun* conducted a public opinion poll and found 52 percent of the public thought that a nation at war should not serve as host of the games. The *Asahi shimbun*, however, found 55 percent opposed to the boycott and an authoritative 75 percent favoring a strict separation between sports and politics.[40]

Japan was under enormous diplomatic pressure. Kiyokawa Masaji sat on the IOC and was a classmate of the Prime Minister. At a class reunion, Ohira told him that Carter was pressuring him to support the boycott and made it clear that if the nation had to choose between sports and its main ally, then there was no choice. The vote of the USOC tipped the balance in favor of those favoring the boycott. Shibata Katsuji, president of Japan's Olympic committee, called it a "serious new development." On April 25, Ohira's government issued a press release calling on the national Olympic committee to show "self-restraint." The Committee ignored this petition and voted to send a team to Moscow. Under political pressure, though, the organization reversed itself. The final vote was 29–13 for a boycott. Kiyokawa was distraught: "For the last 80 years, the Japanese had a wonderful sport history and in this one decision threw away the trust of the international sports world with this one move and left a major stain."[41]

The situation the Indian Olympic Association faced and the decision it made was much different. India would be at the Olympics. The actions of the Carter administration played poorly in India. An editorial in *The Statesman* declared that the President had "been inept in the follow-up action, both at home and abroad." A reporter for the paper also predicted a Soviet boycott of Los Angeles in four years as a form of payback.[42]

---

* Japanese Olympic Committee.

In the Oceania nations of Australia and New Zealand, the debate was more intense and ugly than any other place on the planet. The debate became a huge issue in Australia because 1980 was – as was the case in Canada, Germany, and the United States – an election year. The boycott became a serious issue that dominated both sport and political reporting in the Dominion, and came to divide the nation the way Vietnam and the conscription battle of 1917 had done in previous decades. Olympic officials and athletes began receiving hate mail and death threats. The issue destroyed many friendships. Others lost their jobs, and the government won the support of many Olympic officials with what were basically bribes.[43]

When Fraser returned to Australia following his meeting with Carter, he addressed the nation on television and then met with executives of the AOF. A major theme of his presentations was that the Soviets were attaching a good deal of political importance to this international gathering and he cited the party activists' pamphlet. Another theme was an exaggerated sense of national peril. At one point he claimed World War III was only three days off. The editors of *The Australian* bought this argument: "If all the nations of the free world refused to go to the Games, it would be a crushing propaganda blow." The editorial board of *The Age*, the leading newspaper in Australia, disagreed. These journalists argued that to describe Afghanistan as the beginning of a Soviet move into the Middle East was an exaggeration, plain and simple. So was using the pamphlet to legitimize the boycott. Those fine points hardly mattered, though. "On principle, and without any delusion about its likely effectiveness, a boycott of the Moscow Olympics is justified," the paper declared in an editorial.[44]

Fraser was willing to use other tools against the Soviets, but one thing that was off limits was embargoing wool imports to the Soviet Union. The prime minister had his staff study the issue and document the exact nature of the dominion's commercial ties with the Soviet Union. The study that his staff produced showed that Soviet demand and resources were highly elastic and they could make good any shortfall in wool. Fraser's explanation was simple: "There's no point in taking measures that will only hurt Australians." In refusing to consider using this economic tool, Fraser took a political beating because of his background in the sheep industry, and charges that wool from his own ranch was shipped to the Soviet Union.[45]

On April 19, the AOF met to vote on its participation in the Moscow Games. Doug Anthony, the deputy prime minister, insisted on speaking to the group afterwards. He warned them that the Soviet Union was destabilizing Southwest Asia and asked them to reverse their decision. He warned them that a division over the boycott between the United States and its allies would only benefit the Soviets. The speech was powerful and, in the opinion of most people in the room, had carried the day. The opponents of the boycott had enough pull to delay the final decision. As a result, the Federation decided to give final authority on this matter to its executive board. The eleven people on this board were not eager to undercut the efforts of their athletes. They continued to delay until the last minute.[46]

It is difficult to measure public support for the boycott. Some public opinion polls show that there was little support at first for the idea, but this support grew as fall turned to winter in the Southern Hemisphere. Another set of polls shows the exact opposite. What we do know is that Australia was the one and only country where a member of the IOC turned on the movement. Kevan Gosper, who had been a member of the committee since 1977, began rethinking his support after the USOC vote. "After much soul-searching, I decided I had no option but to support the request the democratically elected government of Australia was making of its national Olympic committee," he explained. Gosper later recanted and blamed his vote on the IOC president: "I think Lord Killanin was too easy going and we were lucky to survive his presidency. I went off on the wrong line, and argued for the postponement of Moscow, that it should be delayed, and I soon realized there was a lack of reality in that approach. A strong president might have pulled me up on that view. Killanin was insufficiently active with Carter and Brezhnev, and took three months before he met them, following the emergence of the crisis at the end of 1979, during which damage limitation was the requirement."[47]

The delay brought out the conflict in public opinion in many other ways. As in the United States, many corporations that had promised financial support to the AOF began backing out of their commitments. Many found the Olympics too controversial to be associated with. Most remained but almost all lost money. At the same time, labor unions began raising funds among their members. Their fundraising eventually became crucial. The athletes were caught in the middle of this division. Many were not sure if they should bother training anymore.[48]

While the Australian public was conflicted over the boycott, the media was not. Studies show that newspaper coverage was one-sided in favor of the boycott. This bias manifested itself in every way, shape, and form imaginable: number of editorials, the type of language used in news articles, tone and message of editorial cartoons, headlines, and limited coverage of opposing views. When John Hoggett, the sports editor of the Sydney *Daily Telegraph*, wrote a column opposing the boycott, which ran counter to the editorial position of his paper, he lost his job, getting demoted to becoming a general assignments editor in the news department. In the five weeks before the AOF held its vote, 70 percent of the material appearing on the front page of *The Age* was in favor of a boycott and 30 percent was neutral. There was nothing on the front page in support of going to Moscow. The editors of *The Age* explained why: "It is because the Olympics are glamorous, that they are an ideal means of conveying the message that the free world wishes to impart to the government and the people of the Soviet Union. No other acceptable and practicable method offers such impact."[49]

The only major media outlet that took a less than strong position in favor of the boycott was the Seven Network that had the contract to televise the Olympic Games in Australia. There was a strong internal debate among the media groups that owned the network whether they should cover these athletic contests, regardless of the AOF's decision. Despite intense lobbying from the Fraser government, which television executives saw as threats, the network decided to provide television coverage if Australian athletes attended. They would lose money either way, but this decision minimized the losses.[50]

After one of the many delayed Executive Board votes, Gosper held a press conference announcing his support for the boycott. He and David McKenzie, another IOC member from Australia, got into a public shouting match in the hotel where the organization had just met. At the same time, Fraser's rhetoric grew more strident. "My assessment," McKenzie informed Killanin, "is that Prime Minister Fraser's attack on the movement will become more bitter as his likelihood of success diminishes. I believe we should accept the situation and take no steps which might allow the prime minister to take advantage of any statements we might make." The Cabinet, though, decided not to attack the Federation financially; the organization would continue to receive federal funds.[51]

The final decision came on May 23 at the Sheraton Hotel in Melbourne, where the eleven members of the Executive Board met to make their final decision. The stress of the past few months had worn on their health. "It was one of those things, where you couldn't shake hands and say, gee you look good, because everyone looked horrible," one of them recalled. Some went into the meeting having had no sleep the night before. Grange had each individual in the room explain their reasons behind their vote. The group was evenly divided, and the tally stood at 5 to 5. The final decision came down to Lewis Luxton, a fundraiser for Fraser's Liberal Party, but also a former member of the IOC like his father before him. Luxton had before the meeting decided to vote for a boycott, and many people in the room thought that was what the final decision would be when it came down to him, but he had spent an hour on the phone with Malcolm Fraser listening to a lecture on why Australia should boycott. "The hide of him," Luxton said. "I knew his mother!" The final vote was 6–5. Australia would be in Moscow. In making this decision, the organization refused to hear from two cabinet ministers who wanted to speak before them.[52]

"It wasn't an easy task," Grange, explained in a public statement he released after the vote.[53]

At a press conference in Canberra, a reporter asked Fraser if the Olympians had put their interest before that of the nations. The prime minister's response was direct: "Quite plainly."[54]

Australian athletes were jubilant about their victory. Chris Wardlaw, a marathoner, declared: "It's a victory for the LITTLE people." Another runner, Bill Scott, wanted the five dissenters to resign, "The ones who voted that way have gone against the ideal demanded of them in the position that they hold."[55]

Fraser, though, refused to give up. In a public statement he released, he made it clear that there might be terrible ramifications: "I pray the Olympians who do go to Moscow will not pay the price that many of those who went to the Berlin Olympics paid once the World War started in 1939." He also added: "I pray that the Soviet Union will not interpret this and other decisions of Olympic Federations as a weakening of Western will, as Nazi Germany did in 1936." Calls were made almost immediately for the organization to reverse itself. "Whoever and whatever goes to Moscow for the Summer Olympics, it will not be the pride of Australian sport," an editorial in *The Herald* of Melbourne declared.[56]

The AOF had made its decision, but the individual federations could choose on their own not to send a team. "I and my Ministers shall do all that we can to persuade the Executive to reconsider its decision," Fraser told Thatcher. He also added that they would lobby the national federations and attempt to persuade the individual athletes. "The most frantic and appalling week in Australian sport was about to begin," Lisa Forrest, captain of the 1980 Australian swim team, noted in her memoir/history of the boycott. The government offered many of these cash-strapped organizations subsidies if they stayed away from Moscow. Years later, when Forrest conducted an interview with Fraser, she asked if these payments were bribes. He winced, and then said, "Somebody else might say it was a reasonable compensation under the circumstances."[57]

Individual federations, though, were not near as important as the AOF itself. Fraser wrote to Grange on June 13, asking the organization to reconsider. "In deciding to attend the Moscow Games, Australia is virtually alone in the region, in company with only Communist Laos, Communist Vietnam and Communist North Korea. I have to say that I find that a shameful position to be in." The AOF met with Fraser a week later, where the Prime Minister spoke for two hours and fifteen minutes. He failed to convince them. In fact, several of the Olympians called him on his exaggerated rhetoric to his face. In the end, the prime minister had no choice but to reluctantly accept defeat. He refused to seize passports or use some other type of legal mechanism to keep the Olympic team from traveling. "That is not a proper power for a democratic government to use in these circumstances," he explained. Individual athletes, citing the stress of the national controversy, backed out on their own, and five national federations withdrew their teams.[58]

Over in New Zealand, the decision was even closer. Going back to January, there were immediate calls in New Zealand for a boycott. The Cabinet of

Prime Minister Robert Muldoon officially declared itself in favor of moving the Games from Moscow. The editorial board of *The Evening Post* declared: "Strong action is necessary to show the Soviet Union that naked aggression carries a price and that, until Russian troops are back on their own territory, there will be little participation in a civilised discourse with other nations in the world." Their colleagues at *The New Zealand Herald* made similar demands. Support for this position, even among the staffs of these papers, was hardly universal, however. The sports editor of the *Herald* warned that a boycott could kill the modern Olympics: "The absence of the Americans could be the final disaster to the Olympics," he warned.[59]

The New Zealand Olympic and Commonwealth Games Association was torn on this issue. "It's a principle in Olympic administration to be independent of political pressure – that's one of the things that has kept the movement alive," Harold Austad, president of the organization told reporters. In keeping with Lord Killanin's approach of stalling for time, the Association delayed until early May before voting 12–5, with one abstention, to go to Moscow. [60]

Some members of the Association, reflecting their small-nation view of international affairs, worried that New Zealand might be in Moscow without any of its allies. "We must consider our country's position and the fierce public opinion the association would face," Lance Cross, a member of the both the IOC and the New Zealand Olympic Association, told reporters. Cross never turned on the IOC the way Gosper of Australia did, but he was suspect in Killanin's eyes.[61]

Newspaper editorials blasted this decision. "New Zealand should not attend the Olympic Games in Moscow," *The Evening Post* declared. The editors of *The Press* argued that the vote "is disappointing and may well be regretted by the association and athletes."[62]

That regret was not long in coming. "We just crumbled," one Kiwi Olympian observed. *The Evening Post* conducted a random and unscientific poll on the streets of Wellington, the national capital, and found that 60 percent of the people they surveyed were opposed to New Zealand going to Moscow. The Association quickly declared that it would reconsider its decision on May 29. At the same time, individual athletes began backing out of the Olympics on their own. In addition, many of the national athletic federations announced, often against the expressed interests of the athletes they represented, that they would make no effort to organize a team to send to Moscow. "It is faintly irritating to find there's still some pussyfooting on the question of whether New Zealand should send a team to the Moscow Olympics," columnist Tony Garnier declared in *The Evening Post*. He favored a boycott, because "the Olympics give joy, drama and the spectacle. To survive, it must stay outside of politics, not by ignoring but remaining scrupulously detached from them. And that is the real problem with the Moscow Olympics." In the end, both sides could claim victory. New Zealand was at the Olympics, but with a team of only four athletes.[63]

After the disaster of trying to use Muhammad Ali as a roving ambassador, the Carter administration ignored the nations of Africa. The decision of most of these countries had little to do with the United States. The Secretary General of the Supreme Council for Sport in Africa, Lamine Ba, declared that he and the council had no reservations in expressing their "wholehearted support for the Olympic Games in Moscow." In Nigeria, the semi-official *Sunday Sketch* declared, "It is absolutely clear now how badly the United States has hurt itself by choosing the Olympic Games as an arena for U.S.-Soviet confrontation in the cold war style." While a number of African nations decided to boycott Moscow, their absence looked good only on a map. They were weak athletic powers and most people would not have noticed their presence had they been at the Olympics.[64]

On May 24, the battles for control of the Olympic movement seemed to have ended. The result was basically a stalemate, and that worked to the advantage of the IOC. Appearances soon proved to be misleading. Although the deadline had passed, the boycott effort was far from over.

CHAPTER 12

Carter versus Killanin

THE BOYCOTT SEEMED TO BE OVER. THE POSITIONS OF MOST national Olympic committees were made clear several days before the formal deadline, and while these battles took place largely in public, Carter and Killanin worked behind the scenes to gain an advantage before the public climax. These efforts brought about the only face-to-face meeting of these two presidents and also, more importantly, showed the limitations of both men's leadership.

While various factions battled across the planet, the IOC Executive Board met in Switzerland. The big issue it faced during three days of talks was should it penalize the American Olympians. According to Killanin, Carter's boycott was "a clear case of political interference and, unless the USOC rebuffed it, we could move towards taking action against the committee, and that in turn would affect the Los Angeles Games in 1984." Killanin, though, realized such an action would be counterproductive. Having the Olympics in Los Angeles without the United States being allowed to compete was a recipe for disaster. "I am doing all I can to protect the USOC," he warned Kane.[1]

Before the meeting, Killanin had a private talk with Ueberroth over dinner at the Intercontinental Hotel in Geneva. The Californian was worried about the future of his Games. During their meal, Killanin agreed to issue a press release stating that the IOC would take no action to strip Los Angeles of the games.[2] The participation of the USOC in 1984 was still technically an open question, but this move on Killanin's part went a long way to resolve this question long before the Executive Board formally addressed the matter.

During that first day of the meeting, the Baron dominated the entire eight hours of the discussion. After dealing with some procedural issues, the Board took up the status of the USOC. Miller had sent the IOC a telegram officially explaining that "since the President of the United States has advised the USOC that in light of international events that the national security of the country is threatened, the USOC has decided not to send a team to the 1980 summer Games in Moscow." The committee would still select an Olympic team on the off-chance that Carter changed his mind before May 20, so they still might send a team. All the members of the Board were provided with a copy of this message. Lord Killanin also reported that Julian Roosevelt had contacted him and told him that he believed the USOC was in violation of the Olympic charter and should be disciplined. Even though he was an American, Roosevelt would support sanctions against the USOC. Killanin chose not to share this message with the others and said things were a bit confusing about the stand of the USOC, and that the Board should not come to conclusions about the United States until they knew more.[3]

The discussion then turned to the boycott itself. The IOC had only received seven firm refusals: Albania, Honduras, Kenya, Malawi, Paraguay, Saudi Arabia, and the United States. Since Saudi Arabia, Malawi, and Albania declared in 1979 before the Soviets invaded Afghanistan that they would not be going, they were not doing so for political reasons. A number of other countries – Australia, Canada, Japan, New Zealand, Norway, and West Germany – wanted to attend but were under enormous pressure from their governments to decline their invitations. In most of these cases, the boycott had become entangled in political elections, and there was enormous public support for the boycott.[4]

The Board then heard a report on the status of the preparations for the Moscow games from Vitaly Smirnov. He promised that at the next meeting of the full membership of the IOC, all the speeches from their hosts would be nonpolitical and that they would provide English- and French-language translations weeks in advance. Remembering that Vance had failed to provide a French translation of his speech, Lord Killanin called the Secretary of State's remarks "a disgrace." The Committee, he said, had learned much from Lake Placid. Smirnov also informed the Board that Coca-Cola had canceled its contract with the Moscow Olympic Organizing Committee, but it would not matter. Just as Coke officials had feared, the Soviets had enough concentrate on hand to serve the expected Olympic crowds.[5]

After Smirnov finished, the Board then met with a delegation from the various European national Olympic committees. Colonel Raoul Mollet, president of the *Comité Olympique et Interfédéral Belge**, told the Executive Board that many national Olympic committees were facing economic coercion. Donations from their public sponsors were smaller than expected and a number of governments were cutting off their own financial support. Sir Denis Follows of the British Olympic Association made some remarks after Mollet. He said a number of national committees wanted to participate in Moscow but needed to show publicly that being in Moscow was not an endorsement of Soviet foreign policy. These committees needed the help of the IOC on that matter, as well as of the Moscow Olympic Organizing Committee. In the

---

* Belgian Olympic and Interfederal Committee.

extensive discussion that followed these presentations, Mollet praised Fallow and his national committee. Their stand against the Thatcher Cabinet had had an enormous impact in Europe. Killanin said the IOC would be providing some funds to help NOCs operate. Smirnov said the Soviets could also provide funding, if they were asked. They wanted to avoid the suggestion that they were buying people's support, so the committees would have to make a request for financial support.[6]

During the discussion that followed, the Board examined the possibility of allowing individual participants. Killanin said the Board believed such a move might undermine the authority of the national committees. The Executive Board minutes read: "He felt very strongly indeed about this point." Perhaps, but it was also a move that had people in the Carter White House genuinely scared. Marshall Brement warned Brzezinski that the IOC was considering such a move: "Such a decision could break the back of an Olympic boycott."[7]

The first day of talks ended at 6:30 in the evening and the second day started just after nine the next morning. Worried about the meeting, Carter had sent Killanin a telegram in between the two sessions. In it, he reiterated his personal support for the Olympic movement. The boycott was just in opposition to the Soviet invasion of Afghanistan. He did not want to see any governmental involvement in international sports. "We shall continue to oppose the efforts of other governments to establish UNESCO Games, and we shall welcome the IOC and athletes from all eligible Olympic nations at Los Angeles, as we did at Lake Placid." The telegram is odd in that UNESCO had not played any significant role in the boycott up to this point in time. In fact, only the Carter White House had attempted to inject this organization into the debate, and even then it had been nothing more than one of the semi-informed ideas that the White House staff had generated. The Administration was learning from its mistakes a bit and was trying to let the IOC know that it was not a threat to them in the hope they would take no action against the USOC and the Los Angeles Olympics.[8]

After some discussion on the telegram, Killanin threw out an idea to the Executive Board. He suggested that he visit both Carter and Brezhnev in the hope that it would do something to alter the pressure that the national Olympic committees of Western Europe were facing. He wanted the Board to consider the idea for a day and give him their recommendations on May 23. Smirnov told him he was sure that Brezhnev would see him.[9]

The Board then considered extending the May 24 deadline in order to give national committees more time to overcome the political pressure they faced. Back in January when the boycott was just picking up steam, the Soviets had been talking about a March 1 deadline. "This is very unwise and I feel you should leave it to the last possible date May 19th," Monique Berlioux had informed Novikov. "I cannot stress to you the ever increasing opposition to Moscow and only time may assist you." The Board agreed that sticking with the original deadline for simple planning needs was best. Smirnov added that if one or two committees were able to come after the deadline, the Soviets could deal with the situation on an ad hoc basis.[10]

Discussion then turned to the real issue the Board had to resolve: the fate of the USOC. The consensus in the room was that the weighted voting of the USOC's constitution was inappropriate and in conflict with the IOC charter. Monique Berlioux, the director of the IOC's staff, took this occasion to speak. She rarely participated in discussions of the Executive Committee or the full Committee. Her influence came from running Olympic operations on a day-to-day basis – for most of its members, including the president – the IOC was a part-time job. She said the USOC had with its vote violated both its constitution and the Olympic charter. Killanin admitted this might be true, but during the discussion he made a number of comments designed to keep pressure from developing for taking an action against the Americans, reminding his colleagues that USOC officials would meet with them tomorrow to explain the actions of their committee.[11]

Much of that second day was spent meeting with representatives of the various international athletic foundations. One of those present was His Royal Highness The Prince Philip, Duke of Edinburgh, in his role as president of the International Equestrian Federation. Since the Thatcher government was opposed to the Moscow Olympics, there was a good deal of speculation that he, as the spouse of a good constitutional monarch, would announce that the federation would skip the Olympics. If it did so, the horsemen would be the first federation to boycott and would deliver a devastating blow to the integrity of the Moscow Games. "We lunched at the same table," Killanin stated. "In his conversation with other people at the table some of them formed the impression that he was opposed to the boycott, and that view got through to some reporters." Later that day, Thomas Keller of the rowing federation gave a press conference and said that all the athletic organizations represented in Lausanne would support the IOC and released a statement to that end. Keller added, "A lot of people collaborated in this text and the finishing touches were even made by Prince Philip." Killanin watched this scene with bemusement as both the IOC President and as a former journalist: "At that moment I could feel a movement among the reporters and realised that it was the British moving swiftly to the telephones. Here indeed was a story."[12]

Back in London, representatives of Buckingham Palace tried to deny what the Prince had done: "This is nothing to do with the Duke of Edinburgh. He was present at the discussion but he has no part in any such resolution." There was only so far Prince Philip could go, and before leaving Switzerland, he made it clear that he could not travel to Moscow for the Olympics.[13]

On Wednesday, April 23, the third and final day of the Executive Board meeting started at 9:20 AM. The group went through a good deal of business before addressing what to do about the Americans. Kane, Miller, and Patrick

H. Sullivan, the USOC's lawyer, entered the room, and Killanin reminded his colleagues they needed to get a full explanation from the three about the actions of their committee. Kane made a long presentation. He stressed that the Carter administration had developed its policy without any input from, or consultation with the USOC. The Committee had refused to cooperate with the establishment of a set of alternate games. He also explained that there was a good deal of opposition in American society to the Moscow Olympics and that this sentiment had been manifested in a number of ways. With the President of the United States of America saying that American athletes going to Moscow would endanger national security, there was little the committee could do, unless they were prepared to challenge Carter and claim that they knew better about world affairs. In the minutes, Kane describes taking such a stand as a "ridiculous" possibility. Given the overstated and exaggerated claims the administration had made about Afghanistan and the Olympics since January, claiming that the Carter knew more about the situation was actually a bit of a dodge. Sullivan added that the USOC had made no effort to help the administration and influence other national Olympic committees to boycott. His statement was correct, factually, but it was equally misleading given his own comments just before the vote in Colorado. This view, of course, ignored the politics and diplomacy of the boycott debate.[14]

Miller then followed with a detailed explanation of the vote and who had participated, since USOC voting standards were unclear. After he finished, a whole series of hostile questions followed, which even the generally sanitized and bland IOC minutes documenting the meeting cannot hide. Even Killanin was angry, although his feelings were directed more toward Carter than any of the Americans in the room. When he learned about the financial support that the U.S. government was giving to the USOC, he came to believe the Carter White House had bought the Committee's vote. At the time, though, he was offering support to the USOC representatives. His help did little to mollify the anger the three Americans faced, which the IOC members were aiming at the United States for Carter's boycott and at them personally. Samaranch asked Miller if the IOC Charter requirements about the national Olympic committee composition applied to the USOC, to which Miller said it did. Kiyokawa Masaji of Japan questioned the independence of the USOC from the administration, asking what kind of contact they had with the White House staff. Kane argued that the USOC was one of the most independent of the national committees. Members of the Executive Board can be forgiven for questioning that statement, but Miller explained that opinion polls showed that a vast majority of the American people were in support of a boycott and believed that sending a team to Moscow would be an acceptance of the invasion of Afghanistan. With memories of Pierre Trudeau blocking the Taiwanese athletes from participating in the Montreal games, Kiyokawa asked Kane if the United States would use the Los Angeles Olympics to make a political statement. Kane admitted that was a possibility. Alexandru Siperco of Romania wondered about the views of American athletes. Miller said most wanted to compete and offered compromises, but that there was no possibility of compromise with the Carter White House.[15]

Smirnov had been quiet up until then, but he spoke up at this point. The invasion of Afghanistan was nothing more than a pretense. Various officials of the U.S. government had been calling for a boycott for quite some time. Americans did not want to go to Moscow simply because the USSR was a socialist country. Kane responded, refuting this statement. He explained that these remarks had been few in number and had little support at the time. Smirnov said the USOC should have resisted the White House more. The Committee was basically entering into politics, and such a move could destroy the IOC. There was also a certain amount of hypocrisy to U.S. attitudes. No one had tried to use the Olympics to oppose U.S. actions during the Vietnam War. Miller responded, saying the two situations were different. The United States had been fighting a war, yes, but they had not been serving as the host country. Lord Killanin jumped in at this point and reminded the Americans that while that was true, the IOC had awarded hosting duties to the United States for the winter Olympics of 1960 and 1980 when it had been fighting in Korea and Vietnam. Carter was inventing new criteria to legitimize the boycott. (His Lordship was wrong in use of historical examples; the IOC selected Lake Placid a year after U.S. involvement in Vietnam had ended). Siperco took a political shot at the United States and said it should live up to its claims about free speech and allow the athletes' voices to be heard. Killanin interjected that dealing with the Carter Administration was "almost a blank wall." Carter had made up his mind and had no wish to listen to contrary information. The USOC had been in an impossible set of circumstances. Miller supported this position, making the factually incorrect statement that the situation was no longer under their control. The three Americans left the room after two hours and twenty minutes of discussion.[16]

Without the USOC representatives present, the Executive Board began considering sanctions. Lord Killanin took a legalistic view and said until May 24, the USOC had done nothing deserving of any penalty. As a result, there was nothing the Executive Board could do at the moment. Maitre Carrard, the counsel for the IOC, ignored this legalistic argument and said there had been political pressure from the White House and the USOC had failed to resist that pressure. Smirnov projected some of his own culture on the United States when he offered a description of what he had seen when he had visited. The people there were afraid to discuss the boycott. The popularity of this policy was tied into the fact that 1980 was a presidential election year. He agreed with Killanin's view about May 24, and while the IOC could not expel a national committee for not sending a team, the USOC needed to be warned that they were harming the international Olympic movement. Berlioux, taking her cue from Killanin, argued that the USOC should not be singled out. After a bit more discussion, the Executive Board agreed to wait until after May 24 and allow the full membership of the IOC to decide what action, if any, they would take against the USOC. Killanin had carried the day.[17]

After discussing a number of issues, the group returned to Lord Killanin's idea about meeting with both Carter and Brezhnev. The Board approved and then authorized a resolution that it released to the press. It basically restated basic Olympic ideology: "It must be stressed that the Olympic Games are a series of contests among individuals and not countries, and that participation of an athlete in the Games in no way infers support for the political ideology or for the actions of the country in which a city is staging them." The IOC and only the IOC was the guardian of the Olympic movement. The games "are awarded to a city purely on consideration of organisational capabilities and never on political grounds." The Executive Board also said Lord Killanin wished to meet with Carter and Brezhnev to make these points in person.[18]

The only reason the IOC president agreed to have these meeting was because of the Executive Board's input. He had realized since Lake Placid that meeting with Jimmy Carter would be a waste of time. "I felt that Carter, having set his position without consultation, had been rebuffed by the IOC statement and would not have been very receptive. I also cancelled a long-planned trip to Moscow in March for a meeting of the IOC Press Commission because I believe the Soviets might make public relations capital out of it."

Brezhnev did indeed agree to meet with Killanin. In conducting this Olympic version of "shuttle diplomacy," he decided to take Berlioux with him. She was not happy. "Do you want to make me more unpopular with some of your members than I already am?" she asked.[19]

When the baron and Berlioux arrived in Moscow, Novikov and Smirnov greeted them on the tarmac. The Soviets were not particularly worried about the boycott. Novikov could not believe that Carter was seriously trying to use the Olympics to influence the foreign policy of the Soviet Union: "The hopes for the 'crucial' effect of these actions are little more than absurd and incompatible in relation to the mighty economic and technical resources of our great country." This attitude reflected the general sentiment of the Soviet government. "People remarked to me with a mixture of incredulity and irony that Carter seemed to be channeling all his official energies into the boycott to the Moscow Olympic Games," Dobrynin observed after returning to Moscow to consult with Soviet officials. "In general I found in the Kremlin a stubborn determination to continue its course in Afghanistan and stand fast against Carter."[20]

Although the Soviets had a long and less than noble history of manipulating the Olympics and other elements of international sports to their own end, Carter's boycott left them occupying the moral high ground. Constantin

Andrianov, a member of the IOC, doubted that Carter could do any significant damage to the Olympic movement over the long run: "The history of the Games has not been without clouds and there have been difficulties of various sorts, including those of a political nature. But with each Olympiad grew the popularity and influence of the Olympic movement, and it became more and more universal, playing an ever greater role in the life of mankind." He expected little would come of Carter's boycott: "I have no doubt that the present artificial difficulties will also be overcome and that the Games of the XXIInd Olympiad will be staged in the terms established by the IOC as a bright impressive festival of youth."[21]

Killanin was less optimistic than his hosts. After spending a night at an estate with spacious rooms and luxury that made him think of the czar's era, he met with Brezhnev. Novikov and Smirnov were present for the meeting as well. Killanin thought Novikov was "worried" and "ill at ease." The Irishman did not have good news; he expected only about fifty countries would participate in these games. Brezhnev was friendly and covered in decorations because he was leaving soon for the funeral of Marshal Josip Tito, president of Yugoslavia. Killanin thought that Novikov and Smirnov were intimidated at meeting Brezhnev. The Soviet leader said that the rest of Europe would probably follow West Germany. Killanin agreed. He added that he would do whatever he could to help the Olympics but would not let the Soviets use himself or the Olympics for political purposes. One of the things that the United States was using to legitimize the boycott was the *Handbook for Party Activists*. As Lord Killanin read the passage and it was translated back into Russian, Brezhnev interrupted him. "What's wrong with that?" The Irish baron thought the issue a minor one that Carter had exaggerated – and discovered that Brezhnev had never seen the document before. In his memoirs, Novikov though Killanin was confused and embarrassed at the fact that he had to raise the issue at all. Killanin's memoirs certainly offer nothing to contradict this view. The conversation then returned to more serious topics. After the meeting ended, Killanin refused to meet with the organizing committee or take any tours of the facilities out of fear that the Soviets might use this for some type of propaganda. This caution was prudent, but Killanin also tended to exaggerate his own importance.[22]

Immediately after Lord Killanin returned from Moscow, Cutler traveled to Dublin to meet with him. "I think he was agitated at the possibility that I was going to play Brezhnev versus Carter and vice versa," the Baron recalled. "We went through the tiresome discussion yet again about postponing or cancelling the Games and he informed me, with a brave attempt to put authority into his voice, that West Germany was about to withdraw (which turned out to be correct) and the rest of Europe would collapse too (which was not)." Even before this meeting ended, Killanin was wondering if the meeting with Carter would be a waste of time.[23]

Killanin was on the mark in his assessment of Cutler. The American was indeed worried about Killanin's meeting with Brezhnev and how it might look if Carter refused to meet with the baron. The President had made it clear that he did not want to meet with Killanin unless there was a real possibility that he could influence him to support some type of action against the Soviet Union. Cutler knew that Carter had to meet with Killanin. "I recommend the meeting as helpful to our boycott effort and to maintaining Western influence in the IOC movement," he explained to the President. Carter was not interested in having a meeting where they would disagree over U.S. foreign policy, and while such a qualification sounded reasonable, Cutler knew that Carter had to meet with the IOC president if for no other reason than for appearances' sake. In writing this memo, Cutler had decided to protect Carter from himself. In order to convince the President to meet with Killanin, the lawyer gave Carter information that was false and that Cutler knew to be false. In his memo to Carter, Cutler stated of Killanin: "He now estimates that not more than 50 will attend the Moscow games. He proposed a one-year postponement to Brezhnev but did not receive any encouragement." He hoped this information would encourage Carter to agree to talk with Killanin, and the gambit worked. The President checked the line approving the meeting.[24]

This type of misleading behavior was actually a frequent occurrence in the Carter White House. Brzezinski sent daily reports to the President on foreign policy developments. Throughout the spring these documents regularly mentioned the boycott and were often quite misleading. They gave Carter the impression that the campaign against the Olympics was working. In one, a Polish diplomat was directly quoted as saying, "there is nothing you possibly could have done to upset the Soviets more."[25]

Suspecting that this meeting would draw a lot of attention from the media, Killanin traveled under his original name of Michael Morris and Berlioux traveled under her married name, Mme. Serge Broussard. Having just been at the Kremlin, "Morris" could not help notice the similarities between it and the White House. There were long lines of average citizens wanting to take tours of the building, and both came from the outer provinces, be it the Ukraine or Kansas.[26]

Cutler met with Killanin just before the meeting in the Oval Office. He introduced his guest to his staff and then told him that people did not take notes during meetings with the president. Cutler was misleading everyone. Note taking is a regular practice in meeting with any U.S. president, but Cutler did not want more than one record of the meeting. Killanin warned Berlioux not to take any notes, but she still put together a memo documenting the meeting, which is significantly different from the one Onek wrote. Although there is a good deal of overlap between the two, the White House document attributes positions to Killanin that were significantly different from remarks he had made in public over the years. These two documents and Killanin's memoirs reflect the cultural values and understanding of the boycott. Despite the fact that everyone in the room was fluent in English, they often failed to understand what the other was saying and why.[27]

One example came even before the meeting started. Cutler said that they should include Brzezinski and Warren Christopher in the meeting. "It was not until this occasion that I realised Cutler was a powerful man behind a powerful man behind a weak president," Killanin observed. "It appeared it was Cutler who had decided who should be present when I saw the president, and not the president himself." The fact that Brzezinski was late and the meeting waited on him convinced the Irishman that Carter was weak, and that it was his subordinates who were in control, particularly Cutler. In actuality, Brzezinski's late arrival probably reflected the lack of importance he gave meeting with Killanin rather than Cutler's control over Carter's schedule.[28]

By all accounts, the meeting started off with Carter being gracious and expressing what was genuine support for the Olympic movement. "He could not have been more courteous, smiling or friendly," Killanin observed. Carter said he wanted to make sure that boycott did no damage to the games in Sarajevo and Los Angeles. He also discussed the possibility of postponing the Moscow Olympics for a year. If so, the U.S. would be willing to participate if the Soviets withdrew from Afghanistan. Killanin said such a move was impossible. He said he wanted to discuss the future of the Olympic movement. He wanted to make sure that officials and judges from boycotting countries were able to be in Moscow. If not, there was real danger that the United States would be allowing the Communist nations of Eastern Europe to take control of the international athletic federations. According to Killanin's memoirs and Berlioux's record, Carter agreed. For whatever reason, probably unfamiliarity with its significance, Onek made no mention of this issue.[29]

An issue discussed only in the American record was the possibility that the USOC would be punished for boycotting the Olympics. According to the letter of the Olympic charter, sanctions were possible. Three of the five administration officials in the room (Cutler, Onek, and Christopher) were lawyers and worried about the letter of the charter. The IOC, however, ignored its charter when it suited its interests to do so. As a result, Killanin and Berlioux failed to understand the concern of the Americans.[30]

Killanin also raised the issue of press coverage. There is a certain irony to the boycott that it was the United States, even with its First Amendment, that was seen as the major obstacle to fair, full, and balanced coverage of the Olympics in Moscow. Carter said the U.S. would take no action to block press coverage. Cutler jumped in at this point, though, and said NBC would not be providing sports coverage of the games. The television network had, of course, reached this decision on their own given the absence of American athletes. Both Killanin and Berlioux, however, thought the decision had been reached at the White House, and that NBC was being "prevented" from telecasting the games.[31]

The issue of giving the Olympics a permanent home was the next topic of discussion. According to Killanin, it was Carter who raised the issue. According to Onek's version, it was Killanin. The IOC president thought very little of this idea. He told Carter that the biggest proponents of it were the boycotting nations. He considered it nothing more than "a diversion" and an issue his host was pursuing to win Greek-American votes. There was a good deal of truth in these views. Killanin quickly dismissed the idea, but according to Onek, he said it was an issue that the IOC was actively considering.[32]

Killanin then described his meeting with Brezhnev. Carter, in an effort to show that he was not opposed to the Olympic movement, asked what he could do to help make it stronger. Killanin thought the question rather naïve but quickly responded. He said Carter should allow U.S. athletes to compete in Moscow. "At this moment the president's smile vanished for a second, and he replied that of course this was not possible."[33]

As the meeting was breaking up, Killanin asked a naïve question of his own. He wondered if it would be possible to have Los Angeles declared an "Olympic zone" during the games. The IOC would be the legal authority over the region. He essentially wanted the United States government, the State of California, and the City of Los Angeles to cede their sovereignty to his organization. Accounts vary on which of the Americans rejected this rather silly proposal, but the reason was the same: security. Killanin then told Carter he thought the boycott was nothing more than a stunt to get himself reelected in November. There is no record of Carter's response. Afterwards Killanin and Berlioux had lunch with Cutler and Onek and then took questions from reporters as he was leaving the White House. "I was asked a large number of ignorant questions again about cancelling the Games and alternate Games, as well as being asked what I would do if this were 1940 and the Games were being held in Germany," Killanin observed with clear disdain for his former press colleagues.[34]

With the advantage of historical analysis, several observations about this meeting are in order. First, it was a conference that should have taken place in late December or early January, before Carter committed himself and his administration to a boycott. He should have consulted Olympic leaders like he claimed, but never did. In late May, three days before the deadline for accepting invitations to Moscow, Killanin was also right to wonder what good the meeting could do. It is a tragedy that Carter and Killanin found themselves in a battle with one another. Both were men of character who had taken strong moral stands before in their lives. Both, on occasion, ended up advancing simplistic or naïve ideas because of their noble ideals. Lord Killanin can be forgiven a bit for this habit. His responsibilities paled in significance to Carter's. The Irishman noted this trend in Carter: "The more I look back the more it is extraordinary that a vast country like the United States could not produce a greater leader or statesman than Carter."[35]

Killanin informed the IOC Executive Board two and a half weeks later about his two meetings. His report was an honest rendition of the facts as he had seen them. He did not believe Carter was taking any other actions against the Soviets and was using the Olympics as a medium for protest politics because it would cost him nothing. During the second day of the meeting, the Board met with representatives of the international federations, and Thomas Keller tore into Killanin. The IOC – by which he meant its president – had been passive in opposing the boycott. He was also angry that members of the Committee had turned on Moscow. The news media was by and large hostile to the Olympic movement. Keller was afraid that the Olympics might be coming to an end and it was all Killanin's fault. The Irish baron replied that the next eight years, in other words the next two Olympiads, would make or break the movement. Gosper strangely agreed with all of Keller's points. Lord Killanin, in his opinion, "should have moved faster to talk with Carter and Brezhnev. Given the heavy pressure that many Olympic committees around the world were under, one would have thought they could have expected a bit more public support from their leader than they got."[36]

While many in the movement blamed Killanin, the Soviets had a difficult time taking the boycott seriously, considering it a publicity stunt on Carter's part. Gromyko made this point bluntly in his first meeting with Muskie. The new Secretary of State told Gromyko that the United States wanted to resurrect détente. "We are ready to normalize relations," the Soviet responded. "You must stop boycott politics. Maybe you can find a way so the American athletes can participate in the Olympic Games. Maybe they will find a solution that smoothes the way."

Muskie told him that was impossible. Carter had settled on his policy months ago.

Yes, but so what, Gromyko replied. He should just change his mind, again. "The President decides sometimes this way and sometimes that way."[37]

Such sentiment suggests that the boycott was less than the weapon that the Carter administration claimed. The real test, though, would come in Moscow. How would the boycott affect the quality of the competitions at the Olympic Games? The United States would have little influence on this outcome. Instead the public and the athletes of the world would decide this issue.

CHAPTER 13

Moscow: The Olympics Are the Olympics

THE OLYMPICS TURNED OUT TO BE FAR MORE RESILIENT THAN Carter ever imagined. There is no question that the boycott did damage, but the athletic competitions in Moscow themselves were worthy of their Olympic name. No one in Moscow questioned the merit of their achievements or really missed the boycotters. The same could not be said of their rivals in the United States. Despite efforts on the part of the administration to make up for the boycott, the playing careers and sometimes the lives of American athletes became nothing more than dust thrown to the wind.

One of the ways that many observers attempted to measure the success of the boycott was by counting the number of countries going to Moscow and those that were staying away. As simple as this task might sound, there was a good deal of squabbling between the IOC and the White House over the exact numbers. The U.S. government basically asserted that all absent countries were boycotting. The IOC argued that many of these nations were undecided, and that several teams were not going to Moscow because of limited resources rather than an effort to make a political statement. In the end, eighty nations participated in the Moscow Olympics. According to a State Department press release, the boycott had worked: "Those national teams and sports federations not participating in Moscow won 73% (58 out of 80) of all the gold medals won at Montreal by athletes from nations outside the Soviet bloc." If all medals were included, the number was a little lower, 71 percent. "Perhaps," a reporter for *Time* magazine noted, "but the fact is that nations the U.S. says are not boycotting Moscow accounted for 72% of the gold medals and 70% of the total medals in 1976."[1]

Counting medals seemed like a fairly straightforward way to assess the boycott, but geography was a better indicator. The administration tried to claim victory using this standard as well. "The boycott was extremely successful in the third world," Onek informed Cutler. Such triumph, though, was meaningless. The core of the Olympic movement was in Europe, which Lord Killanin realized. "The more I look back on the year of 1980, the more

I realise that but for the support of the West European countries, such as Belgium, Britain, Denmark, France, Ireland, Italy, Holland, Spain, Sweden, and Switzerland, together with Australia and New Zealand, among others, the Olympic Games would now be something of the past."[2]

In that sense, the efforts of Carter's State Department in May 1980 to spin or shape views of the boycott made sense. Behind closed doors, such misleading analysis unfortunately passed for informed judgment. "Although many seem to accept the Soviet and the IOC propaganda position that the outcome on attendance at the Olympics was a defeat for the United Sates, the fact of the matter is that we achieved most of our aims," Brzezinski informed the President. He was particularly pleased that China, West Germany, and Japan were boycotting. They, along with the United States, were the four most important countries in the world. "Even if all other nations had decided to participate, the fact that these four nations were not attending would have been enough to get the political message across to Moscow." He also added that though the boycott had not fared well in Europe, it had been highly successful in East Asia. China, Japan, Indonesia, Thailand, and the Philippines were staying away from Moscow.[3]

Brzezinski's analysis was riddled with errors. These nations might be important players in regional diplomacy, but they were far less significant in international sport. In 1980, no Indonesian athlete had ever won an Olympic medal of any type. Thailand had won exactly one medal since it joined the movement in 1946. The Philippines, during the same time, had won a silver medal. The National Security Advisor probably knew none of this sports trivia, but it did not matter. Brzezinski was telling Carter what he wanted to hear.[4]

Margaret Thatcher was far more realistic. She kept fighting the good fight for the boycott, writing Sir Denis Follows in late May still wanting the BOA to reconsider its decision. The Games would be nothing more than a "charade." She struck from the final version of the letter a line: "There is now an effective boycott." That claim was clearly untenable.[5]

Given the differences in power between the IOC and the United States government, there never should have been much of a contest between these two entities. The ignorance and arrogance that the administration had shown on the boycott had actually made its task more difficult. "We had to struggle all the way; the outcome was always in doubt," Carter admitted in his memoirs.[6] Onek agreed. "I am not sure we could have done very much better," he observed years later. Unfortunately, the President rarely commanded such candor from his subordinates when he was in office. The fact that national Olympic committees were independent of their governments in many Western democracies and were government-controlled in other parts of the globe was an issue that the Carter administration simply could not overcome.[7]

Most media outlets in the United States viewed the effort against the Moscow Games as something less than a success. A news analysis in *The*

Christian Science Monitor declared: "At its current size the boycott has to be considered something of a failure in terms of what the United States originally had hoped to achieve." The magazine *Sports Illustrated* conducted a careful study of medal results in Montreal and reported in its "Scorecard" section: "It is a startling fact that of the 198 gold medals and 612 total medals awarded in the 1976 Games, the countries planning, at latest word, to compete in Moscow won 152 and 456 respectively." As a result, the staff of the magazine concluded, "This suggest that, from an athletic point of view, boycott proponents may have overestimated the extent to which the Games, assuming they take place as scheduled, will be diminished by the absence of the U.S. and its friends."[8]

Foreign assessments varied significantly depending on people's positions on the boycott itself. In West Germany, a *Berliner Morgenpost* editorial called Killanin "the Baron Muenchhausen of international sport" for suggesting that the Olympics would be a success with a third of the national teams absent. In France, the editors of *Le Monde* stated, "The boycott...could not be a true means of pressure on the USSR given the fact that it will be totally without effect at the end of the Games."[9]

On the other hand, Olympians of every nationality were unified in their belief that the boycott had failed. In the United Kingdom, the Princess Royal, who had competed in the Montreal Olympics and would later serve as the President of the International Equestrian Federation and a member of the IOC, questioned the merit of the entire effort. "Do you think the boycott devalued *those* Games, were they any less of an occasion? It is more of a loss for those who don't turn up, especially those who have got not choice and had a genuine chance of a medal. I think boycotts are self defeating."[10]

American Olympians shared these views. Peter Ueberroth visited Moscow to watch the organization and implementation of these games in order to prepare for 1984. He could not help making a political observation: "The failure of the Carter boycott was evident: Most of our staunchest allies were present in Moscow." Kane of the USOC had a slightly different view: "If anything it was a propaganda victory for the Soviet Union because the foremost allies and friends of the United States were there."[11]

Of the Olympians, Killanin was the most vocal. After being at the forefront of the battle against Carter, he could not keep from gloating at his rival's expense. "I don't want to be offensive in any way, but I think it's unfortunate that the president of the United States on sporting matters, was not fully informed on facts. I think this led to the trouble," he told reporters at a Moscow press conference just before the Games started. He also worried about larger diplomatic issues, because there were troubling implications about the competence of the Carter White House. "I only hope that some of the heads of state I've met, and the governments I've met, are better advised on important matters than they are on sport, because if they are not, God help us all." It had been obvious that the administration was clueless about the structure of international athletic competition, and Killanin said so. "I think, first of all, they did not understand how sport is organized in the world. They did not understand the working of the International Olympic Committee. They did not understand the workings of the international federations and national federations. To my mind, they had virtually no knowledge other than about American football and baseball, which if they had been in the Olympic Games, perhaps we wouldn't have had the boycott."[12]

Killanin had made some highly perceptive observations, but they were not particularly well received in the United States. An editorial in *The Wall Street Journal* called these comments "the whining, petulant outbursts of Lord Killanin." Red Smith wrote a column full of invective aimed directly at Killanin, titled: "His Lordship's Tantrum." Smith observed, "He goes out on a note of petty spite, having a tantrum because the United States chose not to attend his farewell party." Smith avoided addressing the main thrust of Killanin's comments about the Carter administration, choosing instead to dispute the Irishman's assessment of sports in America. The United States had won more medals than any other nation in Olympic sports like rowing, swimming, basketball, boxing, weight lifting, and track-and-field, and had hosted successful summer and winter games. "The arrogance of the I.O.C. and the people who head the organization surpasses understanding."[13]

The Soviets also understandably argued the boycott was a failure. "In the opinion of the sports public and many statesmen, the idea of boycotting the Games has failed," Novikov said publicly. Harrison Salisbury, a former Moscow correspondent for *The New York Times*, basically agreed with this assessment in his syndicated column. According to Sailsbury, the average Soviet citizen understood that Afghanistan was the issue between their country and the United States but had no idea what it had to do with the Olympics. Whatever message the Carter administration thought it was sending got lost in translation.[14]

In private, Soviet leaders also failed to understand Carter and, much like Lord Killanin, worried about larger political issues. Brezhnev told a meeting of the Central Committee Plenum of the Soviet Communist Party a month before the Olympics started: "Not a day goes by when Washington has not tried to revive the spirit of the 'Cold War,' to heat up militarist passions. Any grounds are used for this, real or imagined. One example of this is Afghanistan."[15]

Gromyko spoke to the same group after Brezhnev and made it clear that the Soviets still wanted détente. "We have proposed and propose that Washington be led in our mutual relations by the principles of equality, equal security, mutual advantage, non-interference in each other's domestic affairs. In a single word, we have built and are ready in the future to build our relations with the USA on the principles of peaceful coexistence. Declaring our readiness to maintain normal relations with the USA, we proceed from the fact that hostility between the two powers is not only unwise, but also dangerous." The problem was the unpredictability of the United States, particularly the Carter administration. "Many of you, evidently, have in your memory how during the terms of office of various Presidents throughout the post-war period, American policy rocked from side to side. It cost the Soviet Union considerable effort to lead the USA to an acknowledgement of the single reliable basis of our relations – a policy of peaceful coexistence. Now the American administration has once again begun to veer wildly." The Soviets would have to be resolute if they wanted to save détente.[16]

Despite this approach, it was soon impossible to hide the fact that détente was dead. On the eve of the Olympics, the Plenum of the Central Committee of the Communist Party of the Soviet Union approved the following resolution: "Attempting to bend other states to their will, ruling circles in the USA took the road of economic 'sanctions' and curtailment of scientific-technical, cultural and sports exchanges, refusing obligations that had been accepted, and violating treaties and agreements signed by them. Anti-Sovietism and anti-Communism have been transformed into instruments for pressing forward the arms race, and into weapons of struggle not only against the USSR and other lands of socialist solidarity, not only against Communists, but against all adversaries of war, peace-loving forces, and into a means of undermining détente."[17] It was official. Détente was dead. The boycott had been the final blow.

Unlike in the Soviet Union, foreign policy in the United States is the province of many people. As a result, it is a subject of interest across the nation and often has enormous direct and indirect impact on the lives of average citizens. The American athletes of 1980 are proof of that fact. The boycott was a disaster for them. The only question was the degree of the damage done. "Just what right does Carter have to keep us from going, anyway?" Edwin Moses, the world record holder in the 400-meter hurdles, demanded to know. "Those are *our* Games. The athletes' games."[18]

What people in the administration never understood was that American amateur athletes who competed in Olympic sports needed some type of hope to keep up with their training. Runner Evelyn Ashford best explained the situation. "All the talk of the boycott has really taken a lot out of me," she said after winning a race at the USA Indoor Track and Field Championships. "I've been pretty depressed. It's been difficult. Realistically, I know we probably won't go to Moscow. I'm still hoping – I have to hold on to that hope. But it has affected me. I don't have a goal anymore. I don't know what to do now. I've tried to set new goals, but the Olympic Games were going to be everything."[19]

Tracy Caulkins suffered from a similar lack of motivation as the boycott became a reality. She, however, found new purpose when Petra Schneider of East Germany began breaking all her records as the East German prepared to go to Moscow. "The thing that's happened to her was when Schneider came along and broke all those records," Caulkins' coach, Don Talbot, observed. "I've seen a change in her workouts already. She has a new goal, and that's to get those back. And she'll do it." Talbot added: "this boycott business, it doesn't matter to the kids. They can set new goals. But what is truly sad is that the Olympics is the only way to really bring out the greatness in an athlete. The bloody politicians will never know what they put their sportsmen through."[20]

Several federations still held their Olympic trials that spring and summer. The track-and-field meet took nine days in Eugene, Oregon, and being one of the premier Olympic sports, still managed to attract a good deal of public attention. The atmosphere, though, differed from previous years. "These aren't the Olympic Trials," Al Oerter declared. "I'm sure they're not the Trials because I've been sleeping at night. It's a wonderful track meet, but a meet for its own sake, nothing more." Another thrower in the discus event disagreed. "Being an Olympian, even in name only, is *rare*," said John Powell. "It doesn't do much on resumes, I can attest, but you have to go for what you can get. It *is* important."[21]

Some interesting stories emerged from this contest. Al Oerter finished fourth and did not qualify for the team, but he was throwing further than he had in 1968 when he set an Olympic record. Had he been competing for a real chance to go to the Olympics, he might have done better. The key phrase: *might have.* Jodi Anderson won the pentathlon, and in the process set an American record in the long jump, becoming only the second woman to jump seven meters. Moses won his thirty-eighth consecutive race in the 400-meter hurdles. "I'm disappointed, every athlete in America is disappointed," he said still nursing his grudge against the President.[22]

Many of these athletes realized time was not on their side. Competing in the Olympics is an event for the young. In many sports, the athletes reach they physical peak in their teens and early twenties. It is also a time-consuming activity, and for many there were other things they wanted to do with their lives. Caulkins was 17 but figured her future had limits. She wanted to compete in Los Angeles but thought that was unlikely. "I suppose I could be over the hill in 1984," she observed. "I don't worry about it, but I'm aware it could happen."[23]

The Olympics are the Olympics, and on July 19, they went on without these American athletes. An editorial in the *Detroit Free Press* summarized the feelings of most supporters of the boycott: "The response of Europe's Olympic committees to the call for a boycott of the 1980 summer Olympics is disappointing, but the fact remains that the Moscow Games have already been reduced to a mockery of Olympic tradition. The boycott represents an effective protest of the Soviet Union's invasion of Afghanistan."[24]

Events in Russia suggest otherwise. The Moscow games began in impressive fashion honoring the Olympic ideal. The opening ceremonies lasted three hours. Paying tribute to the ancient origins of the Olympics, men wearing

Greek tunics marched into Lenin Stadium carrying a giant metal display of the five Olympic rings on their shoulders. Women wearing togas sprinkled rose petals along the stadium track. During this procession, the stadium flashcard section depicted displays of Mount Olympus and the Acropolis. Gymnasts then filled the field of the stadium and danced. Some wore the ethnic dress of the various countries of the Soviet Union, while others were wearing Misha the Bear costumes. More performers formed huge displays of flowers and the Olympic rings on the floor of the stadium. Another group, using a metal frame on which they draped themselves, formed a giant Olympic torch using nine-layers of people stacked on top of each other. "It was an astonishing display of mass physical cohesion which with the music, the continuous cheering (even from the journalists), the exploding, swaying, expanding and contracting patters of colour laid out below us, was quite mesmerizing," one British reporter observed.[25]

The parade of nations came next. Sixteen of the eighty teams participating in this festival refused to carry their national flags. Ten boycotted the parade altogether and another six had their administrators participate carrying the Olympic banner. These mild forms of protest were wasted efforts. Soviet television cameras carefully focused only on the name cards of these nations, cutting away as quickly as possible to the next contingent. The team from Afghanistan marched in full and received a huge roar from the crowd. In Red Square, Ron Fimrite of *Sports Illustrated* found an English-speaking school teacher from the Ukraine and asked if he knew why the United States was absent. "Yes," he replied in English. "There is a discrepancy between the policies of President Carter and our government." When asked what that dispute was about, the Ukrainian said, "Afghanistan."[26] The Soviet people understood the moral position of the U.S. government, but it was less important to them then individuals in the White House thought.

Other rituals followed. Novikov, Lord Killanin, and Brezhnev made brief remarks welcoming the athletes and opening the games. Killanin praised "those who have shown their complete independence to travel to compete despite many pressures placed on them." Twenty-two doves representing the twenty-second Olympiad were released into the air. Montreal handed over the Olympic flag. The giant screens at each end of the stadium then showed a distant runner approaching, carrying the Olympic torch. Viktor Saneyev, a three-time gold medalist in the triple jump, handed the flame to basketball player Sergei Belov, who ran toward the giant Olympic torch that jutted out from the rim of the stadium directly above the flashcard section. There was no apparent way for Belov to get from the track to the top of the stadium to light the torch, but then a white line started appearing at the bottom of the flashcard section. People were holding shields above their heads that were creating a path that lead straight up to the bottom of the giant torch. As Belov jogged up this improvised bridge, the rest of the flashcard section fluttered to a blue background as he passed by. At the top of the stadium, he paused, holding the flame aloft and looked out over the assembled masses. The Soviet television cameras panned across the field of the stadium where the flags of the assembled nations were fluttering. They caught some of the Olympic banners that contingents were using, but in the kaleidoscope of colors they were easy to miss. Belov then lit the giant cauldron. "That opening ceremony was one of the most spectacular things I have ever seen," a Philadelphia resident, who had made the trip, explained.[27]

Despite the boycott, there was an American presence at this edition of the Olympics. There were some tourists in Moscow, not many, but a few. There was also a small group of U.S. nationals competing on other teams. Long jumper Bill Rea was a twenty-eight-year old dentist born in Austria to an American father and an Austrian mother. He had narrowly missed qualifying for the U.S. team in 1972 and 1976. Starting in 1979, he had put his dental career on hold and lived off his savings in a determined bid to compete for Austria. Rea had no intention of following the boycott: "The athletes have been doing it for themselves all these years, handing out towels and jockstraps to finance their training, and all of sudden Carter wants them to help him out of his own political bind. If he had just quietly tried to get the support of the athletes instead of ordering them: 'Look, you're not going,' he would've gotten better results."[28]

Mike Sylvester had a different perspective. A native of Cincinnati, Ohio, Sylvester was a guard for the basketball team of Italy where he played professional basketball and had dual citizenship. "When I first heard of President Carter's idea for a boycott, I thought it was great. Then our so-called allies didn't stand behind us. As an Italian citizen, I had no choice in the matter. If I didn't respond to the invitation, I would have been disqualified for life from playing in Italy. So it was a question of putting bread on the table for my family, or going along with the boycott." He had fought for the boycott, though: "Our basketball team voted 14-1 to go, he explained. "I was the one no vote. I decided to go along with my team, to keep it together."[29]

There were also a number of athletes in Moscow who had gone to college in the United States. These schools included, among others, the University of Texas at El Paso, Brigham Young University, and North Carolina State University. These athletes had faced a lot controversy in both the United States and their home countries. "The pressure just kept mounting," Rosemary Brown, an Australian swimmer and a sophomore at the University of Florida, remarked. "It was unbelievable. We kept saying, 'What will we do?' Three papers ran a total of 45 editorials about how wrong we were. One of them said the blood of the Afghans will be on our hands." Holding out her hands to a reporter, she asked, "Do you see any blood on them?"[30]

Olympic host nations generally do better than usual in their medal wins, and with the United States, the only major rival to the power of the Soviet sports machine, missing, the number of Soviet victories was just that much larger. Alexander Melentiev, a Soviet, was the first gold medalist of these games. His medal came in pistol shooting. And with that win, the rampage started. Soviet athletes won 80 gold medals and 195 overall. While the Soviets and the East Germans dominated the medal results, any effort to call these Olympics a hollow shell would be misleading. There were also several upsets, and a total of thirty-six nations won medals at these games. In Montreal, the number had been forty-one.[31]

The boycott made little difference in gymnastics. Since 1968, the nations of Eastern Europe had dominated the sport. This trend grew greater and greater with each passing Olympiad, and Moscow was nothing more than a continuation of this development. Soviet gymnast Nikolai Andrianov won seven medals in Canada. Four years later competing on his home turf, he earned another six (two in each type of metal). His teammate Alexander Dityatin did even better. He won eight medals (three gold, four silver, and one bronze), which set a record for most medals won in one Olympic gathering. On the horse vault, Dityatin scored a ten, which was the first time in Olympic history that a male gymnast had earned a perfect score.

Dityatin, however, was not the biggest star of these competitions.[32] That distinction still belonged to the star of Montreal, Nadia Comaneci of Romania. The defending champion in the women's all-around competition, Comaneci seemed to be in good position to win again until she fell to the floor during the uneven bars competition. As a result, Maxi Gnauck of East Germany had the lead and the gold medal until she faltered on the vault. Comaneci did poorly in the vault herself, giving the lead to Yeleana Davydova of the Soviet Union. Comaneci, however, was in fourth place and if she scored 9.95 or better on the balance beam, she could make up the distance and take the gold. Her performance in this event was impressive. She did a handstand, a hand-aided flip, and then a forward flip with a half twist so that when she landed she was looking back at the spot she jumped from. When she landed she wobbled a bit and took a small step backwards, both of which were flaws. The Soviet crowd, though, was cheering and applauding her performance. Then one of the judging controversies that seem to be mandatory at any Olympics occurred. A panel of four judges evaluates each contestant, the high and low scores are normally thrown out, and the middle two scores averaged together. The result was a 9.85, which head judge Maria Simionescu of Romania thought was too low. She protested, and a panel of gymnastic officials took more than twenty minutes before they overruled her complaint. Siminescu then refused to punch the score into the computer. A representative of the Moscow Organizing Committee had to do the job while she looked at him with rage. The 9.85 gave Davydova the gold and Comaneci a tie for silver with Gnauck. These Olympics were not a total loss for Comaneci. In the individual competitions she managed to win gold twice and silver once.[33]

As strong as the Soviets were in gymnastics, they were even more dominating in the swimming events. The Soviet men won more gold and silver medals than the next five nations combined. The boycott played a role in this outcome, but head coach Sergi Vaitsekhovsky had been pursuing a strategic plan over the past five years to turn the Soviet Union into a swimming power. Part of this design included training in Florida with U.S. swimmers. "The Americans surprised us by not keeping any of their training secrets from us, which means there must still be some decent people left in the world. We're sorry they aren't here," Vaitsekhovsky observed. Sergei Fesenko was the first Soviet swimmer to earn gold. The absence of the Americans bothered him not in the least. "But even with everyone here, I think I would have a chance to win," he explained. The biggest star of the swimming events, though, was Vladimir Salnikov. He had been in Florida with Vaitsekhovsky and had trained with his American rivals. Salnikov won three gold medals, but what was most impressive was his time. He broke the fifteen-minute barrier in the 1,500 meters. This achievement was the aquatic equivalent of Roger Banister breaking the four-minute mile. When asked if the absence of the United States, which was the main power in swimming, had tarnished his achievements, he replied in a quiet voice that he would have gone that much faster. "I have swum 1,500 meters under 15 minutes," he added. "Nobody has done that before." During this meet, swimmers set four Olympic records in addition to this world record. In the women's contests, there were six world and eleven Olympic records.[34] The Americans were missed, but their absence mattered less than people in the White House expected.

There was also a touch of irony in these competitions. When the Australian men's 4x100 medley relay team won gold, it put Prime Minister Malcolm Fraser, one of the earliest advocates of the boycott, in a difficult position. Should he make some type of public comments congratulating them? Eventually he decided to send them a note: "You know I did not and do not approve of Australia being represented at these Olympic Games. I do want to say however that your performance in the relay was a truly great sporting achievement. My personal congratulations."[35]

As in most Olympics, some of the most important contests of the festival came in the track-and-field events, which, unlike many other sports, traced their lineage straight back to the games of ancient Greece. The British had a particularly strong showing. The 100 meters dash is one of the prime contests, and the winner gets the title of the "fastest man alive." Allan Wells of the United Kingdom, a former long jumper who had his wife train him for the event, won the quarterfinals. In this same race, defending champion Hasely Crawford of Trinidad failed to qualify for the finals. As a result, the favorite seemed to be Silvio Leonard of Cuba. Wells was optimistic about his chances until he ended up in lane eight. "The British always seem to draw the worst lanes," he grumbled. After a long delay in starting the race, Wells took off in a powerful way when the gun sounded. He and Leonard were even at fifty meters. Both reached the finish line at the same time. Wells leaned forward and instant replay showed that this effort put his shoulders across the line before Leonard's chest. Wells had won, making him the first Briton to win the event since Harold Abrahams in 1924. "There is a Scottish tradition of banging heads in the pubs on Saturday night when looped," his wife Margot said as he took his victory lap. "It's called nutting. You try to get your forehead down and break the other man's nose. That must be the training that won it for him."[36]

The British also dominated another premier event, the decathlon. Daley Thompson, a Scotsman like Wells, had set the world record at the beginning of the summer. That record did not last long. His main rival in the sport, Guido Kratschmer of West Germany, broke it a few weeks later. Since Kratschmer would not be in Moscow because of the boycott, Thompson was confident of his victory. "Well, I've been training for this for five years, I ought to be good," he quipped. He dominated the first day of the event. In the decathlon, medals are determined by an overall point total, and it is not necessary for an athlete to win all – or any – of the ten events outright provided they score high enough in each contest. Thompson, though, was on a tear. He won the long jump, recording the third-longest distance in British history. He then won the 100 meter dash with a time that would have allowed him to earn a bronze if he had been competing in the medal event rather than the decathlon. He was on a pace to set a new world record, but the second day started off wet and windy. "I knew the record wasn't on, so I concentrated on what I came here for, winning." He coasted to an easy victory. When asked about his future, he replied, "Why films, blue movies, you give me the details and I'll do it." Turning serious, he declared he would be back in 1984 and then asked, "What happened in the 800?"[37]

Thompson was asking about the 800 meters final in which two of his countrymen were competing. Most informed observes considered Sebastian Coe, the world record holder in the event, and Steve Ovett to be the best middle distance runners of their generation. Prior to that day, they had only raced against each other once before. At the halfway point, though, Nikolai Kirov of the Soviet Union was leading, and the packed crowd at Lenin Stadium was cheering for him. Kirov, knowing the two Britons were well positioned to challenge him, kicked early. Too early, as it turned out. Going into the last turn, Ovett made his move for the lead and at the end of the turn was in front. Coe, who had at one point been in seventh place, had closed and was in fourth. He had ten meters to make up if he wanted the lead. He managed to pass Kirov but was a half second behind at the finish. "Some days you race well and some days you don't," he said afterwards. "Another battle is coming along." At that moment, the British fans in the stadium did not care. Ovett, a British athlete, had won. They waved Union Jacks and sang "God Save the Queen" in celebration. Soviet television cameras recorded their national ecstasy in full.[38]

There were limits to British glory, though. Wells went into the 200 meters final, hoping to win gold a second time. Pietro Mennaea of Italy, a major power in this event, was deeply conflicted about participating in these Olympics. He worried about the moral issues associated with doing anything that would serve Soviet interests in the wake of Afghanistan. He also wondered if these contests deserved the title of Olympics. "The Games should be total, not with a whole slice of them absent," he explained. "That's what makes me sick." He finally decided to participate. "I had a lot of doubts, but I wanted to see the games continue, I thought my presence would help." Running from the outside lane, he won gold, forcing Wells to settle for silver.[39]

Another Coe-Ovett confrontation in the 1,500 meters dominated public attention. Both men shared the world record, Ovett had not lost a match in this event since 1977. The two men approached this race in very different manners. "Losing the 800 was a terrible disappointment," Coe explained. "If I hadn't had the 1,500 coming up, I'd have been tortured with recriminations. But the 1,500 was there. There was no choice. I *had* to make myself ready for it." Ovett had a more difficult time preparing: "I was so high after the 800 that I couldn't get up again." But when the race started, neither man was in the lead. Instead, it was Jürgen Straub of East Germany. Coe and Ovett followed. The German maintained his position at the halfway mark and through the next lap. With 200 meters to go, he was still in first place. Going into the last turn, Straub faltered and Coe, running wide, passed him. Ovett tried to follow but was unable to pass the German. Coe crossed the finish line first and fell to his knees in exhilaration. He bowed, touching his forehead to the track. "I was surprised by the strength of my reaction," he said the next day. "When I watched that display on the replay it was a bit embarrassing. But it was such a bloody marvelous relief."[40]

Another impressive display of athletics came in the long jump. Lutz Dombrowski of East Germany won the gold. One of his jumps was – at that time – the second longest in history. It was only the second time someone had gone over twenty-eight feet, but he was still more than a foot away from Bob Beamon's world record. "Beamon's record isn't eternal, but I don't think I'll ever break it," Dombrowski said. Rhea, the American on the Austrian team, got injured and missed qualifying for the finals by two inches. "I thought I could still compete with pain," he said. "I guess when you look at it, jumping 7.74 [meters] with a torn ligament in the ankle that requires an operation isn't all that bad." When asked if he should have respected the boycott, he gave a mixed answer. "I didn't want to give up my job and train for a year and not get anything out of it. Right now, I've gotten a trip out of it which isn't the greatest in the world but at least I've competed in the Games."[41]

In the men's high jump, another East German, Gerd Wessig, won, setting a world record in the process at 7 feet and 8¾ inches. He was ecstatic. "It is absolutely crazy to jump such a height," he exclaimed. After setting the new record, he jumped in celebration and did a back flip. He landed on his back and fell off the landing pad, taking the force of the hit on his neck and shoulders. He crumpled on the ground. Track officials rushed over to him, afraid he had broken his neck. Turned out he was fine.[42]

Poland's Wladysla Kozakiewicz set another world record in the pole vault. His mark was the first time in sixty years that the record was set in this event at the Olympics. He did so by beating out Konstantin Volkov of the Soviet Union. The crowd in Lenin Stadium was playing favorites and cheering for Volkov while jeering Kozakiewicz, his fellow countryman Tadeusz Slusarski, and Philippe Houvion of France. After Kozakiewicz had secured the gold, he turned to the crowd and made an obscene gesture in defiance. He seemed quite happy. He then made another jump and set a new world record.[43]

The boorish behavior of the crowd was typical of the Soviet peoples during this Olympic gathering. When the winners of the 4,000 meter individual pursuit cycling competition stood on the victory stand to receive their medals, it was the first time in Olympic history that no national flags were displayed. The medalists were from Switzerland, France, and Denmark and all three countries had decided to compete under the Olympic flag instead of their national banner as a way of protesting the Soviet presence in Afghanistan. The crowd reacted with catcalls. Western political protests, even tepid ones, were unwelcome. Of course, politics can only go so far in explaining these actions. Soviet crowds jeered their own athletes when they performed to less than what was expected of them.[44]

That sort of reaction begs the question of how the Soviet people received this politically charged and boycott-tinged gathering. Kevin Klose of *The Washington Post* spent time in Moscow trying to answer that question. "There is no evidence, after two days of random interviews with Soviets in the sporting crowds, individual citizens on their daily shopping rounds or with Moscow's shrunken group of political dissenters that President Carter's boycott has in any way achieved its intended purpose – bringing home to ordinary Soviets the aggressive nature and international dangers posed by Moscow's intervention in Afghanistan," Klose concluded. A young scientist, who was a member of the Communist Party, explained why: "The Soviets didn't suffer from the boycott. It hasn't done anything bad to us. Our press is convinced that if Carter had not found the Afghan invasion as a pretense, he would have found some other reason to keep the American[s] home." Christopher Booker of *The Daily Mail* in London came to similar conclusions. "Anyone who thought that the boycott could have such an effect has no conception of what a cut-off, insulated society this is, how totally differently the world looks when one is sitting in the middle of the Soviet Union, informed and guided as to what is going on solely by the endless reassuring tones of Radio Moscow."[45]

Because of the boycott, the Soviets managed to medal in every team sport, but even then, there were upsets. In 1980, the Soviets were the only other nation to have won gold in men's basketball, taking an extremely controversial game from the United States in 1972. They appeared to be the frontrunners to win gold on their home court, but there is no substitute for actual play. The Soviets lost to Italy, 87–85, and then 101–91 to Yugoslavia. As a result, these two countries, not the home team, played for the gold medal, and Yugoslavia won, 86–77. Mike Sylvester and his Italian teammates took the silver. The Soviets had to settle for the bronze. In field hockey, which many believed had suffered the most from the boycott, the women from Zimbabwe (the former Rhodesia) won the nation's first-ever gold medal. In the men's tournament, India, which had medaled in the sport every time since 1928, won gold, defeating Spain.[46]

The closing ceremonies on August 3 brought the XXII Olympiad to an end. The stadium was once again at capacity. The screens at both ends replayed some of the highlights of the games. The athletes then paraded into the stadium in one large group without regard to nationality, as is Olympic custom. One of the regular features of the closing ceremony is that the flag of the next host nation gets run up a flagpole, but the administration had objected to this practice even though it really had no power to stop the IOC from doing whatever it wanted, as White House officials admitted privately. Nonetheless, the committee heeded these objections and used the flag of the City of Los Angeles. "The Carter administration's vendetta toward the Olympic Games never subsided; it just got pettier," Ueberroth noted.[47]

Lord Killanin started the events, making a few closing remarks and took the opportunity to attack Carter in an ever so subtle fashion: "I have shortly to close the Games in accordance with tradition, but before doing so, I would ask as I did at the close of the Winter Games at Lake Placid to implore the sportsmen of the world to unite in peace before a holocaust descends." Without mentioning Carter by name, he accused the American president of incompetence: "Alas, sport is intertwined with politics but, and I do not mind being accused of being naive, sport and the Olympic Games must not be used for political purposes, especially when other political, diplomatic and economic means have not been tried." The Olympic colors were then struck and the flame in the giant torch above the stadium went out. Gymnasts, dancers, and acrobats performed in folk costumes on the field. The festivities culminated with the appearance of a twenty-five-foot-high balloon of Misha the Bear, holding a bunch of smaller balloons. The giant Misha waved his paw in farewell and then gently rose above the stadium before disappearing. A huge fireworks display followed. The Moscow Olympics were over.[48]

So what is posterity to make of the Moscow Olympics? Two members of the IOC, Lord Killanin and Richard Pound of Canada, described these games as "joyless." No doubt after the battles these two fought in the spring, the damage the boycott did was the reason for the lack of joy, but these comments tell us more about Killanin and Pound than the general sentiment at the games. Just like beauty, bliss and happiness are often in the eye of the beholder. Another member of the IOC, Kiyokawa Masaji of Japan, using four criteria (number of countries and athletes participating, the quality of the facilities, the caliber of the management of the Games, and the quality of the athletic competitions themselves), called Moscow a "very traditional Olympics."[49]

This view was hardly that of a biased IOC member. Susan Bickelhaupt, a copy editor for *The Boston Globe*, went to Moscow to improve her Russian-language ability. "The Olympics were by all means impressive," she told the readers of the *Globe*. "Nor did I think the Olympics were as 'joyless' as some reporters here described."[50]

It would be absurd to argue that the boycott had no impact on the athletic contests themselves, but overall the Olympics resisted political pressure far better than Carter and his lieutenants expected. A total of 5,179 athletes competed at these games, compared to the 7,134 at Munich, and 6,084 at Montreal. Thirty-six world records were set in Moscow, the same number as those set in Montreal, which kept these games from becoming a socialist invitational despite the absence of the Americans and West Germans.[51]

Many boycott supporters liked to think that their campaign cost the Soviet Union financially. This might be true, but only to the extent of reducing profit margins. The boycott in no way turned the honor of hosting the games into a financial liability as they had been in Canada four years before. According to Novikov, hosting the games cost 431.3 million rubles. The Olympics generated 744.8 million, turning a profit for the USSR.[52]

What many in Moscow objected to most was not the absence of certain nations, but the heavy and excessive security apparatus the Soviets had put in place. In one absurd example, after winning his gold medal, Coe had to spend an hour and a half filling out forms just to enter the media center to be the subject of a press conference. A French newspaper observed, "The most significant thing is the attitude of the Soviet authorities vis-à-vis the foreign press which alternates between the stick and the carrot." Even Bickelhaupt of *The Boston Globe*, who was quite positive in her assessment, noticed this response. "With cultures and languages so drastically different, we couldn't help but feel paranoid about their paranoia."[53]

The athletes living in the Olympic Village noticed and complained. Herbert McKenley, coach of the Jamaican track team and a gold medalist from 1952, remarked, "I don't feel the Olympic spirit as I have in other years. The Village is a little dead." It is no surprise then that after dealing with this repression, several athletes snapped and started a food fight in the Village restaurant, yelling "Free Afghanistan."[54]

According to Booker, it was Communism itself that was at fault for this atmosphere. The Olympic Games celebrate the human spirit, but the Soviets were inherently unable to host such a gathering because the Communist system was unable to touch that intangible element: "Part of the clue as to what that is lies in what even the most hardened men of the world among the sportswriters have had to admit has been the regimented joylessness of these Games, the instant repressive response to anything spontaneous or 'unplanned.'" The only acceptable impromptu celebrations were those that were approved in advance. Testimony to this view came on a British flight full of reporters as well as Sir Denis Follows, Lord Exeter, and Lord Killanin. When the plane pulled off the runway, the cabin burst into applause. A round of cheers then followed after the captain announced they had left Soviet air space.[55]

Despite this sentiment, the Soviets actually profited politically from the boycott. They dominated the Olympics in a fashion unlike any other host nation had done before. They also appeared reasonable and supportive of the sports movements in other countries. The United States, on the other hand, looked difficult and manipulative. In his final report, Novikov stated: "It is the general consensus that the Games of the XXIInd Olympiad not only saved the international Olympic movement from degradation and collapse, but also served as stimulus for the broad dissemination of the noble ideals of Olympism to all the contents of the world."[56] There is some exaggeration in this claim, but not that much.

Back in the United States, sports administrators and the U.S. government attempted to honor the American athletes that never went to Moscow. Administration efforts to organize a counter-Olympics had failed badly. The Liberty Bell Track and Field Classic gave 300 athletes from 26 nations a chance to compete. This meet was the largest international track event held in the United States since the 1932 Olympics and drew 20,000 spectators. The Athletic Congress, which organized the competition, got some of its funding from the U.S. Congress, but the caliber of the competition was hardly equal to that of the Olympics. "An alternative?" Steve Scott a U.S. runner said, repeating a reporter's question. "This wasn't even a good international meet." He was right. Seventeen of the thirty-four winners of the Olympic trials decided not to participate in this event. The throwing contests were particularly weak. Only three men participated in the shot put, which took place on an intramural field at the University of Pennsylvania. Only five participated in the decathlon.[57]

A week and a half later, the U.S. Olympic team gathered in Washington, D.C. The USOC had arranged a series of functions over the course of four days to honor the team that never went to Moscow. These events included a special demonstration of the Marine Corps Silent Drill Team at the Marine Corps Barracks, special tours of the National Mall and the other monuments in Washington, D.C., and a gala dinner at the Museum of History and Technology (which later became the National Museum of American History). The highlight of this visit to the nation's capital was the presentation of a special gold medal that Congress had approved. The legislature had authorized over 650 medals – one for each member of the 1980 team. It was the most medals Congress had ever awarded. For a moment, Carter had second thoughts on giving one to all the athletes, but the bill ordering their minting was extremely popular, having attracted over 228 cosponsors. The athletes assembled at the bottom of the west steps of the U.S. Capitol building that overlooked the National Mall.[58]

Carter attended the event, praised the Olympics – even though his administration had discussed destroying the movement – encouraged donations to the USOC as he said he would, and then defended the boycott: "The overwhelming call by the Congress for a strong response and the decision of the United States Olympic Committee and by fifty other nations not to participate in the Moscow Olympics was a vital and indispensable reaction to the Soviet invasion of Afghanistan. It was the only correct course of action for our Nation. If our Olympic team had been in Moscow these past days, with all the pageantry and spectacle, it would have been impossible for us credibly to maintain our leadership on the world scale in our continuing effort to seek freedom in Afghanistan."[59]

The resentment in the audience was intense. No one applauded the President. "I was feeling just a little bitter," Linda Dragan, a kayaker explained, "when all of a sudden the president appears in his blue suit. You see him and hear him. Then I felt more bitterness. Even though I'd like to show some respect for him." Holly Hatton, a rower, agreed: "All the remarks he made today were directed to voters. If he had any compassion for us, he wouldn't have made political statements."[60]

Carter then left, and Senator Gary Hart of Colorado made some brief remarks. Then Robert Kane and other officers of the USOC presented the medals to the athletes as Donna de Vorna, a gold medalist from 1964, served as master of ceremonies.[61]

There was a reception and buffet dinner for the team at the White House later that day, but a number of the athletes skipped this function. "Nobody wanted to make a scene," Carol Brown, a rower, explained. "But I didn't want to be recognized by the president so I did not join his reception line. I resent being so-called 'honored' by the person who prevented us from going to Moscow." Others showed their anger in other ways. "Not shaking his hand was my personal way to disagree with his boycott," Andy Toro, the kayak coach, explained. "This administration is the biggest enemy of amateur athletics in the world."[62]

Just as this function finished, the U.S. Long Course Swimming Championships and Olympic Trials opened in Irvine, California. The first three finishers in each event made the Olympic team. During this meet, the scoreboard showed the results of the individual matches, but also the times of the same events in Moscow. Mary T. Meagher, a fifteen-year-old high school sophomore from Louisville, Kentucky, set a world record in the women's 200-meter butterfly. Craig Beardsley, a junior at the University of Florida, set the world record in the male version of that event. A reporter with *Sports Illustrated* calculated that the U.S. would have won ten gold, twelve silver, and five bronze medals in Moscow. "Beating the Olympic time doesn't really prove anything," Rowdy Gaines, a swimmer from Auburn University, remarked. Others agreed. "I could guarantee you that if this were the real Olympics, 90% of the swimmers here would go faster," explained Mike Bruner, the previous holder of the world record in the 200-meter butterfly. Cynthia "Sippy" Woodhead, who won the women's 100- and 200-meter freestyles, agreed: "Head-to-head competition is all that counts."[63]

Many of the athletes that were honored in Washington never received any more accolades for their sacrifices. Americans preferred Olympic heroes that had actually competed in the Games. At the time, some knew their fate. "I am 21," Gains told *The New York Times*. "Most swimmers peak at 21 or 22. In 1984, I'll be too old."[64]

What Gaines and many other athletes knew was that the Olympic Games have a magic and authority that makes them something more than just another international sporting event. When asked about the legacy of the boycott, Anita DeFrantz observed, "The important effect was to show that the games could continue without the U.S. athletes being present, and they were great games."[65]

The resilience of the Moscow Olympics was a fact that was hard to hide and was readily reported on. Despite the success of the modern international Olympic movement in resisting the biggest political challenge to its authority in its history, there would be repercussions to this boycott that would travel into 1984.

CHAPTER 14

Los Angeles: The Olympics Are the Olympics

THE REPERCUSSIONS OF THE 1980 BOYCOTT WOULD ECHO FOUR years later in Los Angeles. In an ironic twist, the crisis that surrounded these games would actually make the Olympic movement stronger than it had ever been. Jimmy Carter, though, would not be around to deal with these problems.

What is remarkable, in retrospect, about Carter's electoral defeat is not the outcome. That result had been foreordained – or as close to that as is possible in American politics – for over a year. Rather what is amazing is that for a time he managed to make the contest close. Carter was vulnerable on two important issues: the economy and foreign policy. Public discontent was strong enough on either one of these topics that they could have cost him the election in and of themselves.

Back in 1976, Carter and his lieutenants had pursued a campaign strategy that had stressed his status as an outsider – but four years later, he and his staff made a near-perfect about-face. Carter would stand for reelection but he would do little electioneering. The phrase at the time for this approach was a "Rose Garden strategy." Carter would campaign instead by focusing on his job, avoiding too many overtly partisan efforts, and invoking the power and prestige of his office to rally the American public to his leadership.[1]

This approach worked – for a while. Carter effectively turned back the challenge that Senator Edward M. Kennedy of Massachusetts and Governor Edmund "Jerry" Brown, Jr. of California posed. The two insurgencies were doomed. No incumbent president in the twentieth century had ever been denied the nomination of his party. This strategic plan stopped working for Carter after the primaries ended. At first, the Carter campaign staff believed the general election would be easier for them than the primaries. As the President explained in his memoirs, "I was pleased that Governor Reagan was the nominee. With him as my opponent, the issues would be clearly drawn. At the time, all my political team believed that he was the weakest candidate the Republicans could have chosen. My campaign analysts had been carefully studying what he had been saying during the Republican primary elections, and it seemed inconceivable that he would be acceptable as President when his positions were exposed clearly to the public."[2]

Ronald Reagan was no Ted Kennedy. He had a record of strong executive leadership, which he could use to highlight Carter's weak record, and his challenge involved no question of internal disloyalty. The President's take on the comparison was a little different: "As the Democratic Convention approached, I continued to suffer an erosion of popular support. Too many of my current efforts, though necessary, were politically damaging." One of those initiatives was "the boycott of the Olympics."[3]

This assessment is an after-the-fact rationalization. The policy had been immensely popular at first. In fact, during the campaign Carter attempted to use the boycott as a way of winning votes. He praised the nations that had stayed away from Moscow, claiming that it had denied the Soviets a propaganda victory and delivered a stark message to the Soviet people about the behavior of their government. He hammered Reagan for flip-flopping on the Olympics, saying that he had "yielded to the temptation of weakness" in playing to the crowd for popularity and in doing so had underestimated the staunch patriotism of American athletes. "He doesn't seem to know what to do with the Russians," Carter told the Democratic National Convention during his acceptance speech. "He's not sure if he wants to feed them or play with them or fight with them." A month later in a town hall meeting in Corpus Christi, Texas, he was even more direct: "He's been on both sides of the Olympic boycott – first he was strongly for it, then later he was against it."[4]

There was a realization among Carter's people that the President could not simply stress his experience. "I was troubled by the insinuation of my own analysis that we couldn't just run on our record," he later observed. Attacking Reagan, his record, and his ideas seemed a good alternative. At first, this approach seemed to work, but it had two significant drawbacks. First, Carter delivered the attacks personally, and his comments had a mean, strident tone that many thought demeaning of his office. These attacks on Reagan undercut the perception that Carter was a nice, decent man, which had been one of his major strengths. "We have a major problem on our hands, and we are going to have to eat a little crow to put this 'meanness' thing behind us," Jordon warned the President. Despite these concerns, the polls showed that the attacks were working.[5]

A second problem in attacking Reagan's record was that Carter opened himself up for an examination of his own, and the former California governor was more than capable of using this topic effectively. With Carter closing the distance, the Reagan campaign agreed to a televised one-on-one debate with the President. On October 28 in Cleveland, Ohio, with just a week remaining in the campaign, the two met for their debate. Carter was solid on policy matters, but he trivialized the serious issue of nuclear arms control when he said he took his lead after consulting his thirteen-year-old daughter. Reagan refused to make any blunders during the event and then as the debate came to an end, he delivered a series of withering rhetorical blows: "Are you better off than you were four years ago? Is it easier for you to go and buy things than it was four years ago? Is there more or less employment in the country?" he asked. He then turned the public's attention to foreign policy: "Is America as respected throughout the world at it was? Do you feel that our security is safe, that we're as strong as we were four years ago?" With those simple questions he had focused the debate and campaign on Carter's leadership, making it a referendum on the President's ability and competency. If the answer to these questions was "no," Reagan concluded, "Why then I think your choice is very obvious as to whom you'll vote for."[6] For all practical purposes, the election was over.

The new president confronted a new phase in U.S. relations with the Soviet Union. "When Ronald Reagan was inaugurated as president on January 20, 1981, he inherited a legacy of ruined detente in Soviet-American relations and new era of the cold war," Dobrynin noted in his memoirs. The ambassador believed each nation was equally responsible for this state of affairs. "Each actually followed its own vision of detente. Each applied a double standard that favored its own motives when judging the behavior of the other. At the same time the leaders of both sides failed to explain to the public the limits of détente as well as its promises."[7]

Dobrynin was right, détente was dead, and the climate that followed the return to the Cold War made the boycott of the 1984 Olympics inevitable. The Olympians, though, worked hard to keep the games on track. Under the presidency of Juan-Antonio Samaranch, the IOC attempted to repair the damage it had suffered. "The Olympic Movement learned that if it remained united, it was much stronger than most had imagined, including those within the movement itself," Dick Pound noted. The first item of business toward repairing the Olympics came in 1981, at the Olympic Congress that convened in Baden-Baden, West Germany. (An Olympic Congress is a gathering of all organizations – including federations – involved in the Olympic movement, not just the IOC itself). "Everyone knew just how lucky they had been to dodge the missile launched at the Olympic Movement the year before," Pound recalled. "There was a definite undercurrent of resentment against the Soviet Union for having created the crisis. The socialist countries were similarly resentful for the insult of the refusal to attend 'their' Games. And there was, for perhaps the first time, a realization that the Olympic Games could be destroyed, if political forces were to be aligned with that objective in mind."[8]

Peter Ueberroth saw that the Los Angeles Olympics would be both the mechanism and test of the rebuilding process. The events of 1980 had damaged American interest and influence in the movement. There was no retaliation against individual U.S. nationals, but American individuals could no longer expect to move forward. Federations meeting during the Moscow Olympics made decisions that often worked against the interest of strong athletic powers, like the United States, like reducing the number of athletes any nation could send to compete in an event. Ueberroth developed initiatives to rebuild interest in the Olympics. A national torch relay was one way. Various groups would pay to allow volunteers to carry the flame. All profits went to local charities in the area. Many IOC members and Greek officials back at Olympus complained about the commercialization of the games. "We know we needed to change public opinion. You can't have an Olympic Games in a country that doesn't want to have them," he argued, defending his decision. "I considered that if we could get thought of kids involved, they would sway local public opinion. The idea of the torch was that if it went through cities and towns, those people carrying the flame and donating the money would build up a huge caring attitude, would make the public more friendly, and make competitors more caring."[9]

The threat of a Soviet counterboycott in 1984 had loomed over the Olympic movement since 1980. The Soviets were difficult on many things long before the start of the Los Angeles games. In 1982, Sergei Pavlov, president of the USSR Olympic Committee, raised questions about a number of matters surrounding the Los Angeles Olympics, including entry procedures, custom regulations, regulations for importing horses for the equine events, entry procedures for tourists, and landing authorization for charter flights and Soviet vessels at the Port of Los Angeles. Soviet officials kept raising these issues for the next two years. They also worried about the Coalition to Ban the Soviets. A small political fringe organization that had a membership of only a few dozen, the Coalition was making public statements that they were going to get fifty Communists to defect during the Olympics. Since no Soviet athlete had ever defected before during any previous Olympic gathering, this claim was extremely suspect. The group, nevertheless, was garnering publicity, which either infuriated the Soviets or was exactly what they wanted. Olympic officials from the Soviet Union informed the IOC and the LAOOC that they would need to house their team outside of the village in Soviet ships that would dock at the Port of Los Angeles.[10]

The U.S. government agreed to grant the required authorization. Secretary of State George Schultz explained, "We had in fact, bent over backward to meet all Soviet concerns and had developed a plan for 17,000 people to be involved in Olympic security. We were prepared to spend up to $50 million to assure security, $1 million of which was for the Soviet delegation, including $500,000 to be certain that the Soviet ship that was to house their officials and supporters would have the utmost security. The Soviets knew all this." There is a bit of righteous indignation in these comments. The fact of the matter is that the U.S. government dawdled in its response – which is the way of bureaucracy.[11]

The problem was that this slowness allowed the issue to fester. On April 11, Marat Gramov, president of the Soviet national Olympic committee, sent Samaranch a telegram requesting that the IOC Executive Board hold a meeting to discuss the actions of the U.S. government. In a public statement, the committee declared: "The U.S. administration is trying to use the Olympic Games on the eve of the elections for its selfish purposes." They were also worried about groups like "Ban the Soviets" that were threatening violence against Soviet athletes, and "the uncontrollable commercialisation of the Los Angeles Games."[12]

The executive board did indeed hold a meeting on April 24 at the Château de Vidy, their headquarters in Lausanne, Switzerland. Ueberroth was apprehensive. He attributed the change in Soviet policy to the transition that followed the death of Yuri Andropov, General Secretary of the Communist Party of the Soviet Union, and the power of his successor, Konstantin Chernenko. The new General Secretary had been a political rival of Andropov's and wanted to chart a course different from that of his predecessor. Chernenko had also been close to Brezhnev, remembered the 1980 boycott, and wanted to embarrass the Reagan administration for taking hardline, anti-Soviet policies. "I was beginning to smell a rat," Ueberroth noted. "As with Carter in 1980, the Olympics could become an easy target for Chernenko to make himself look strong."[13]

Samaranch, who had more experience in dealing with the Soviet Union having served as Spain's ambassador to Moscow, agreed: "You could feel their new uncertainty."[14]

The IOC president and vice presidents met privately with delegations from the Soviet Union and then the United States. There were some light moments surrounding these meetings. The U.S. delegation at this meeting included William Simon, now president of the USOC. It was his first trip to Switzerland and he wanted to have a genuine Swiss hot chocolate at breakfast. "His smile drooped when the waiter produced with great fanfare a cup of hot water and an envelope of premixed instant cocoa," Ueberroth recalled.[15]

The crucial meetings came that afternoon with the Executive Board. Meeting separately from the Americans, the Soviets raised a number of issues about inspection of their vessels at the Port of Los Angeles and their desire to have Soviet athletes stay on a cruise ship rather than at the Olympic Village. Samaranch responded in carefully guarded language. The inspections would follow international norms, and the Soviets could keep their athletes on the luxury liners if they wanted. Samaranch and Ueberroth, of course, had no authority over customs officials and port security and could really promise nothing more than what they said. These answers seemed to satisfy Gramov.[16]

After the meeting but before a press conference that Samaranch had scheduled, Ueberroth approached Gramov and offered to travel to the Soviet

Union. The Soviet Olympian took a few moments to respond and then said, "Mr. Ueberroth, we in the Soviet Union regard you with the highest esteem. I will let you know if it is a good idea for you to come to Moscow. Soviet participation will be decided at the highest levels of my government. Please understand, whatever decision is reached will not be a reflection on your efforts."[17]

That response troubled Ueberroth as he participated in Samaranch's press conference. "Gramov's message could only be interpreted one way." He tried to stay positive in his comments, but "feared the worst."[18]

Those concerns were well placed. "By 1984, we were at liberty to express an opinion, to a degree," Smirnov explained after the end of the Cold War. "My opinion was that we should go to Los Angeles, and I had been campaigning for that. Then Andrianov and I were invited to meet the Central Committee. What was our view regarding the Games? I said I considered we ought to go. The Committee said that politically it would be wrong to do that. I said: 'If we don't go, we'll win nothing. If we want to achieve the political effect of sporting success, we should send our athletes. If we send six hundred young men and women, some of them will be heroes. They will be happy we went, and the country will celebrate. Why sacrifice the athletes?' That's interesting, the Committee said, but it's already been decided."[19]

Samaranch was making every effort to ensure that the games went on. He met with Ronald Reagan on May 8 at the White House, taking Ueberroth along with him. The morning of these meeting, press reports were stating that the Soviets were going to boycott. This news only made Samaranch more determined to go ahead with the meeting and get a firm commitment from Reagan that his administration would not manipulate the games. The two sports administrators found the president and his subordinates supportive but not terribly engaged with matters of international sport. Reagan agreed to write a letter declaring, "The United States is totally committed to upholding the Olympic Charter and fulfilling its responsibilities as the host nation of the games. The Olympic games should not be used for political purposes." He had denounced Jimmy Carter without ever mentioning his name.[20]

Ueberroth then put an idea of his own forward. "I suggested that the president perhaps ought to invite Chernenko to attend the Games as his personal guest. It would be a marvelous gesture of statesmanship, I said, whether he accepted or not, and might allay Soviet fears and criticisms."[21]

This idea was a bold one. It would have represented a clear moment when the international Olympic movement had intentionally pushed its own agenda. Reagan seemed interested. Schultz arrived at this meeting late and immediately rejected Ueberroth's proposal, saying it could complicate other issues, which was probably true. "The idea of inviting Chernenko was revolutionary for the time, four years before the first summit meeting with Gorbachev, and I suppose it was too much at the time for the White House to contemplate," Samaranch said reflecting on this lost opportunity. Actually,

Reagan had already been considering the idea. He finally dropped the idea three days later when his ambassador in Moscow told him that he would have no success in extending an invitation.[22]

Gramov confirmed Ueberroth and Samaranch's fears on May 9. He sent a telegram to Samaranch and included a statement that had already been released to the public. It was a highly misleading account of the recent past. "At its meeting on 24th April 1984 the IOC found the stand of the USSR NOC to be just and substantiated." The Reagan administration, the Soviets claimed, had refused to respect these agreements and others that the U.S. government had made previously. "Washington has recently made assurances of the readiness to observe the rules of the 'Olympic Charter'. The practical deeds by the American side, however, show that it does not intend to ensure the security of all athletes, respect their rights and human dignity, and create normal conditions for the Games." These types of actions were unacceptable: "In these conditions the USSR National Olympic Committee is compelled to declare that participation of Soviet athletes in the Games of the XXIIIrd Olympiad in Los Angeles is impossible."[23]

Dobrynin confirmed the views of Ueberroth and Samaranch when he published his memoirs. "In May Moscow refused to attend the Olympics in Los Angeles; they were looking for some way to express their dislike of Reagan and remembered the Carter boycott of the 1980 Moscow Olympics," the retired ambassador wrote.[24]

Under Samaranch, the Olympians responded quickly to the Soviet boycott. "The difference between Samaranch and Killanin, is that the moment the Soviet withdrawal happened, Samaranch was on his way around the world, not just to see Chernkenko and Reagan, but many other leaders, in the attempt to hold the Games together," Dick Pound explained.[25]

The IOC Executive Board held a special meeting a week and a half later in Lausanne and invited Lord Killanin to get his perspective. The Soviet and U.S. national Olympic committees were invited to attend. Samaranch started the meeting recounting all the actions that had led up to the boycott announcement. He believed that the decision was final and the main focus had to be on limiting the damage to the Los Angeles games. Lord Killanin said whatever explanation was being offered in public, the real reason for the boycott was political, and the Soviets were doing nothing other than following the precedent that Carter set four years before.[26]

After an hour of discussion, the Board invited the Soviet delegation into the room. Samaranch said he was quite disappointed in the Soviet decision, but since he had met with Reagan, he should also meet with Chernenko. Lord Killanin reminded the Soviets that the IOC had defended them four years before and that their publicly offered reasons for the boycott were weak. He told them he was convinced that it was just a function of politics, and that athletes would be the only ones to suffer. Gramov responded with a long explanation of Soviet security concerns. He went out of his way to explain that these issues had nothing to do with Ueberroth or the LAOOC. Relations with these Americans had always been good. The problem was that the U.S. government was supporting groups that were hostile toward the Soviet Union and were threatening its athletes. The decision had been made, and Samaranch going to Moscow would make little difference. After listening to Gramov's explanations, Lord Killanin reiterated that the decision was political and only political in nature. Pound said he found Gramov's explanations confusing because they had no foundation in truth. Mario Vázquez-Raña, president of both the *Comité Olympico Mexicano** and the Association of National Olympic Committees, asked if the sporting officials of Socialist nations were going to meet in Prague, Czechoslovakia, on May 24. This question led Samaranch to ask if the Soviet Olympic committee was going to try and organize other countries in a boycott against Los Angeles. Gramov said the Soviets were meeting with other officials in Prague but had no intention of organizing a boycott, which was a misleading statement, if not totally false.[27]

This meeting ended, and the executive board then met with an American delegation that included Ueberroth, Simon, and F. Don Miller at noon. Ueberroth quickly explained what steps had been taken on security matters and informed the group that the LAOOC was coordinating these efforts with the federal government. He did not take Soviet objections on these grounds seriously.[28]

Simon then made a formal speech. "I view this crisis as an opportunity," he told the board. "Well, let us have this crisis act as a catalyst to bring about the changes that are so critical to the survival of the entity (notwithstanding all its warts) that has done so much for peace, understanding and goodwill in this troubled world." He apologized – sort of – for the boycott in 1980. "While the United States Olympic Committee has always resisted the intrusion of politics, we are by no means blameless after our decision not to attend the Moscow Games in 1980, but I am sure everyone can see the difference between the U.S. government calling for the free world's withdrawal for the 1980 Games in the wake of the senseless invasion of Afghanistan, as opposed to the actions by the USSR now in retaliation." Simon was still as conflicted about the boycott of Moscow in 1984 as he had been in 1980. A few minutes later, he added, "We would be naïve to believe that an NOC can withstand forever the withering opposition of a scheming government. We experienced that just four years ago." He then proposed that American and Soviet sports officials negotiate a bilateral agreement in which they promised not to use international sports for political purposes. Other nations could sign this document as well and thereby ensure that athletes could plan on participating in

* Mexican Olympic Committee.

scheduled events: "I have with me a copy of the proposal and I am prepared to sign for the USA."[29]

This idea sounded nice but it was meaningless. Such a promise would have done nothing to prevent the Carter administration from pursuing a boycott in 1980 or the Soviets in 1984.[30]

Simon then proposed that the IOC establish an all-sport facility on each of the continents that could host the Olympics on a rotating basis. He wanted the Committee to address how it would raise money to pay for the games. "'Commercialization' is as much a part of the Olympic Games today as the release of the doves of peace during the opening ceremony, or the raising of the flag of the winner, or the extinguishing of the flame during the closing ceremony."[31]

These ideas went over poorly with the executive board. Samaranch replied, saying that Los Angeles was the immediate issue. Ueberroth then responded, repeating what he had said earlier: There was no serious threat to Soviet athletes, and this boycott was the result of 1980. Lord Killanin agreed and said the USOC had nothing to improve the situation. Simon responded defensively, saying the two situations were extremely different. Ueberroth then made some extended comments about the LAOOC, saying it could handle any security or programming concerns. Simon tried to revive interest in his ideas, insisting that the IOC had to address problems threatening the future of the international Olympic movement. This comment provoked Lord Killanin like no other. He said in a harsh manner that Simon's proposals were irrelevant to the matter at hand. The problem they faced was political, and Reagan's hardline anti-Soviet policies had only enflamed the situation.[32]

"Explaining something sensible to Lord Killanin is akin to explaining something to a cauliflower," Simon observed in a column he wrote for *The New York Times*. "The advantage of the cauliflower is that if all else fails, you can always cover it with melted cheese and eat it."[33]

Samaranch was convinced that the main reasons for the boycott were political. When he went to Moscow, he had these views confirmed when the Soviets allowed him to meet with only minor foreign ministry officials. "I sensed that Russia's decision was absolute, and that the official excuse remained the question of security. We failed to meet either Chernenko or Gromyko, and it was emphasized that the decision had been taken not by the NOC but by the government."[34]

Under Ueberroth, the Los Angeles organizers were ready for the boycott. The fear that the Soviets would boycott in retaliation for 1980 had existed since 1980. The contract the LAOOC had negotiated with the American Broadcasting Company required full payment, even if the Soviets and other Europeans failed to show, but the agreement did have provisions for a rebate if rating figures were low. Ueberroth also had his organization sell tickets and receive full payment in advance. This revenue was placed in interest-bearing accounts, and many sponsors received no contingency clauses. Frugal spending habits kept the Committee from living beyond its means and helped maintain cash reserves. Members of the committee, including Anita DeFrantz, who had earned a good deal of respect for her stringent opposition to the boycott four years before, were calling all their contacts in the sporting world, attempting to limit the damage.[35]

American athletes and officials, though, were almost as disappointed about this boycott as they had been of the one four years prior. "We have to admit we were *wrong* last time," explained Doris Brown Heritage, now an assistant coach for the women's track team. Jim Dunaway, a track writer, agreed, "Their politicians have shown that they know even less about the meaning of sport than ours do and that is really saying something."[36]

Simon had apologized to the IOC in private, but he was unwilling to make that statement in public or take responsibility for providing the Soviets with a pretext for this boycott. "We'll always have problems with the Games because they're too big a spectacle for politicians not to monkey with," he told *Sports Illustrated*.[37]

There was also a fear that the damage this boycott would do, combined with the injuries that Carter had inflicted on the movement four years earlier, would make the continuation of Olympic gatherings impossible. Worrall of Canada worried along similar lines. "This certainly brings us pretty damn close to the end," he said.[38]

Samaranch was less concerned. "The Olympic Movement is one of the greatest social forces of our era," he said in his opening remarks to the IOC meeting in Los Angeles. The movement had grown since 1896 and did more than organize one set of games. Nine decades after its founding, the IOC sponsored or gave its patronage to the winter Olympics, regional athletic meets, contests for disabled athletes, art exhibits that accompanied the games, and the establishment of permanent sports museums. Boycotts limited the good that the committee could do out in the world: "One thing is certain: such decisions can only cause harm to the whole Olympic Movement." Samaranch explained why: "In the first place, because, as always those who suffer most are the athletes, and the athletes alone." It was also a weak, political policy "because it allows the intrusion of political elements into sport while at the same time failing to offer any valid solution for the tense situation in international affairs."[39]

In the end, Samaranch, the IOC, Ueberroth, and the LAOOC were extremely successful. The deadline for accepting an invitation to the games was June 4, and 142 nations accepted, setting a new record. The only absences – and they were noticeable – were the Soviets and their eastern European satellites. As Kenny Moore of *Sports Illustrated* put it, "Only the athletes save the Olympic Games. Each Olympiad, winter and summer, the months before the competition are rancid with boycott, eligibility squabbles, drug accusations and plain, adrenaline-fired suspicion. Then suddenly the flame is kindled, and it becomes the athletes' obligation to somehow redeem the whole Olympic movement by virtue of their performances, to leave flawed Games shining in memory because they produced a Shorter or Spitz, a Korbut or Comaneci." In other words: The Soviets were hardly missed in Los Angeles.[40]

Several American athletes were missing. Many of those that had been honored on the west steps of the U.S. Capitol building in 1980 never competed in Los Angeles or any other Olympic festival. Craig Beardsley was a typical example. Beardsley, who set the world record at the U.S. trials in 1980 with a time that would have won him gold in Moscow, failed to qualify for the 1984 team. In fact, for nearly half of the 1980 team, it was the only time they qualified for the Olympics. "I couldn't even watch the 1984 Olympic Games on TV because I was so disappointed to not be there," Luci Collins, a member of the 1980 Gymnastics Team, explained. "It was heartbreaking for me. There were people on that team that I had placed ahead of just four years prior, even a year prior because I was still competing. To see them on that team and not me was just … just … I couldn't even watch."[41]

As a result, the opening ceremonies were extra special for the veterans. The Los Angeles Coliseum was filled with 90,000 people. There was an hour and a half of music and on-field performers. Big copper-colored and white balloons were released into the air. Skywriters painted the five rings of the Olympics in the sky above the stadium. Eighty-four baby grand pianos and pianists appeared between the columns of the stadium and pounded out *Rhapsody in Blue*. Each pianist was wearing blue. The ceremony was interactive. The audience held up flashcards that decorated the bowl of the arena with each flag of the 140 nations participating in this Olympic festival.[42]

The march of the athletes followed. Greece as the originators of the ancient games went first, an honor accorded them at every Olympics. Romania and Yugoslavia got ovations from the crowd for being the only two Communist nations to defy the Soviet boycott. This applause was nothing compared to what welcomed the U.S. team into the stadium. Ed Burke, a hammer thrower, led the team on to the track, carrying the American flag in his right hand with his right arm extended out in a proud, symbolic show of national power. "As we came out of that tunnel into the cheers and flags, those cheers were for *me*," Anne Donovan of the women's basketball team reflected with astonishment.[43]

Ronald Reagan was there to open the games, an honor that Theodore Roosevelt, Herbert Hoover, Dwight Eisenhower, and Jimmy Carter had all passed on when the United States had hosted previous editions of the Olympics. Samaranch in his opening remarks said, "Our thoughts also go to those athletes who have not been able to join us." Seven former Olympic medalists – Bruce Jenner, Wyomia Tyus, Parry O'Brien, Al Oerter, Billy Mills, John Naber, and Mack Robinson – and Jim Thorpe's grandson, Bill Thorpe,

Jr. – carried the Olympic flag into stadium. The peaceful symbolism continued with a 1,000-person choir singing the Olympic Hymn and the release of pigeons into the skies of Los Angeles.[44]

The culmination started with the lighting of the Olympic torch. One of Jesse Owens' granddaughters carried the torch into the stadium and handed it off to Rafer Johnson, Olympic gold medalist in the 1960 decathlon. Johnson ran up the steps of the Coliseum at the end of the stadium and lit a fuse that ignited the flame that stood above the entire gathering. "There has never *been* anything like this," U.S. high jumper Dwight Stones, a veteran of Munich and Montreal, marveled. "I stayed as long as I could, just to soak up the energy."[45]

Host nations always win an extra large number of medals at the Olympics. With the Soviet Union and East Germany sitting out these games, the haul of medals for the United States was going to be just that much larger. This development was the other side of the coin of a boycott; it was the case in 1980 and so it was again in 1984. In the swimming and diving events, the United States won medal after medal. Greg Louganis dominated both diving competitions, making him the first male to win the events at the same Olympic games. Had Louganis received a perfect score from every judge, he would have scored only 79 more points. "I doubt this performance will ever be equaled," Sammy Lee, a gold medalist at the 1948 and 1952 Olympics, stated. "It won't happen in my lifetime – or yours," the sixty-four-year-old physician told a *Sports Illustrated* reporter in his late twenties. All told, the Americans won eight of the twelve diving medals.[46]

The men's swim team won nine of the fifteen gold medals and the women won eleven of fourteen. Sixteen of the male swimmers were veterans of the 1980 team and eleven of them won some type of medal. When asked if he had taken off his gold medal since the United States won the 4x200 meter relay, team captain Jeff Float, one of the 1980 alumni replied, "No way. It attracts women like a magnet." Other American swimmers that would have been in Moscow relished the games of this Olympiad. Mary T. Meagher, the teenage phenomenon of 1980, was still a teenager at Los Angeles and won three gold medals. Nancy Hogshead won four medals – three gold, one silver. "Every one of these has been a highlight of my life," she declared.[47]

Despite holding forty-eight national records, Tracy Caulkins was competing in her first Olympics in 1984. She won three gold medals and savored the moments. "You look up and wave to someone special and *everybody* waves back," she reflected in astonishment. Australian swimmer Mark Stockwell gave her more reason to treasure her Olympic experiences. He jumped in the warm-up pool and introduced himself. Seven years later, they married. The two only met because Caulkins was competing in Los Angeles as a result of never getting the chance to go to Moscow.[48]

Her teammate Cynthia "Sippy" Woodhead had a more difficult time in the XXIII Olympiad. During the early 1980s, she broke her leg and had two serious illnesses that sapped her strength. "It was awful. Those four years felt like ten," Woodhead said. "It seemed like everything went wrong. But I felt I owed it to myself to compete in 1984, make the team, and actually go to an Olympics, so I pressed on." She barely made the U.S. team, qualifying for just one event, the 200-meter freestyle. She won silver in Los Angeles. "I enjoyed it, but I didn't," Woodhead said. "It felt like I was watching a movie and wishing I could have been there in my top form, at my peak. It certainly wasn't a highlight of my life."[49]

In gymnastics, the Romanians won the team title, defeating the defending world champion Chinese team. The United States placed second. In the individual all-around competition, Mary Lou Retton of the United States won the title. "Well, nobody thought it could be done. But you know what? I went and *did* it," she exclaimed.[50]

The track-and-field events are always the core of any summer Olympics. These contests produced some of the best and worst moments in Los Angeles. Edwin Moses took a streak of eighty-nine consecutive victories into the 400-meter hurdles finals that extended back to 1977. He won and was gracious in victory. "Yes, I've done the training. I concentrate on every single race. But I've been very lucky, too," he said, ignoring his own experiences four years earlier.[51]

Carl Lewis of the United States won four gold medals, equaling the feat of Jesse Owens at the 1936 Berlin Olympics in the very same events. For months prior to the Olympics, Lewis had been flirting with breaking Bob Beamon's world record in the long jump of 29 feet 2½ inches. The general expectation was that he was waiting until the summer games to set a new record. Lewis effectively won the gold with his first jump, going 28 feet ¼ inch. His second jump was a foul, and with none of the other competitors coming within a foot of his mark, he decided to pass on his last four attempts to conserve his strength for his other events. The crowd in the Coliseum started to boo him. "I was shocked at first," he said. "But after I thought about it, I realized that they were booing because they wanted to see more of Carl Lewis. I guess that was flattering."[52]

Middle-distance runner Mary Decker's Olympic experience was the exact opposite of Lewis's. Due to injury and boycott, she was competing in her first Olympics at age thirty-six. Named *Sports Illustrated*'s "Sportswoman of the Year" the year before, Decker was the crowd favorite. Her two biggest rivals in the 3,000 meters race were Zola Budd of Great Britain and Maricica Puică of Romania. Budd had grown up in South Africa but had recently acquired British citizenship as a way around the ban on South African competitors in the Olympics. Puică held the world record in the mile and was the current cross-country champion. Decker led the race for the first half of the contest, but the barefoot Budd passed her on her right in the curve at 1,600 meters. Puică was in fourth place, waiting to make her move. Budd then attempted to move toward the rail. She was too close, but Decker, an experienced runner, made no move to warn her. Suddenly the American's stride hit Budd's leg. This contact nearly knocked Budd over, but Decker lost her balance and fell headlong and then to her side over the rail into the infield: "My first thought was, 'I have to get up." Trying, she discovered that she had pulled a muscle in her leg. "It felt like I was tied to the ground." Decker twisted in the grass in pain and disappointment as officials came to her aid. The race continued, but Budd, stunned at what happened to her role model, was in tears as boos showered down on her. Puică and Wendy Sly of Great Britain passed Budd with one lap to go. Puică finally took the lead with 250 meters to go and won the gold. Budd faded, placing seventh in the race.[53]

Decker blamed Budd for the incident. "She tried to cut in without being, basically ahead." A track referee agreed and disqualified Budd, but on appeal judges disagreed with this ruling and reinstated Budd. "When you're behind, you're the one to have to watch out. It was Mary's fault," fifth-place finisher Cornelia Bürki of Switzerland explained.[54]

There were the usual Olympic judging controversies. The U.S. boxing team won nine of the twelve gold medals awarded at Los Angeles. A good deal of controversy surrounded the actions of a Yugoslavian referee in the fight between Evander Holyfield of the United States and Kevin Barry of New Zealand. Barry was outmatched in talent and delivered a number of illegal blows. The referee issued a number of cautions to the Kiwi boxer, which escalated to warnings, and then went back down to cautions. He issued over six of these reprimands to Barry, which should have resulted in his disqualification. "I couldn't believe what I was seeing," John Holaus, an American boxing official working the match, remarked. These actions were nothing compared to what happened next. Holyfield delivered a blow that knocked Barry to the mat, but the referee ruled the shot illegal and disqualified the American. Barry, despite having been knocked down, won the match and the silver medal. This decision also made Anton Josipovic of Yugoslavia, the winner of the previous bout, the gold medalist.[55]

The South Koreans agreed that the judging and referring was suspect – in favor of the United States. When Jerry Page won a decision over Kim Dong-Kil, the Koreans protested and threatened to withdraw their remaining boxers and go home. "There's too much influence for the United States," Kim Seung-Youn, president of the *Dae Han Amateur Boxing Yunmaeng**, complained. "We are over here not only to win but to learn for 1988. They way things are going, there's nothing to learn. They say they pick the judges by computer, but no one seems to know how to run the computer. As you can see, when the Americans get in the ring they always win, and personally I believe some of them lose. They should be fair. But I have a very small voice, and nobody

---

* Korean Amateur Boxing Federation.

listens to me, and that's why I went public. I'm personally upset. If they run it like this here, then should we run it the same way in Seoul in 1988? Should I just give twelve gold medals to the Korean fighters?"[56]

There were other Olympic stories that ended on better notes. Carlos Lopes of Portugal had a victory going into the last lap of the 10,000-meter race in Montreal before he lost the gold. Eight years later, he was running the marathon and had readied himself for the possibility that he would finish his career without one major victory. "I was prepared to win," he explained. "I was prepared also to lose." He won the race, setting an Olympic record along the way.[57]

After two years of poor health, Sebastian Coe of Great Britain returned to the Olympics to defend his title in the 1,500 meters. In second place for most of the run, he exploded with extra energy in the last stretch, becoming the first man in Olympic history to win this race twice. Like Lopes, he set an Olympic record in the process.[58]

Some of the more memorable moments came on the victory stands. After defending his Olympic title in the decathlon that he first won in Moscow, Daley Thompson of Great Britain showed some jauntiness, whistling "God Save the Queen" as the national anthem of the United Kingdom played during the medal ceremony. Chen Wei-Qiang of the People's Republic of China won gold in the 132-pound weightlifting class and during the medal ceremony held aloft the hand of bronze medalist Tsai Wen-Yee of Chinese Taipei as Taiwan was now called in international sports arenas. Glynis Nunn of Australia won gold in the heptathlon and held a stuffed koala bear on the victory stand, which she used to wave to the crowd.[59]

Both of the U.S. volleyball teams medaled at these Olympics. The women's team lost to the Chinese in the finals and took home the silver. Most of the veterans of 1980 had remained on the team. It was the first medal the United States had ever earned in the sport. Four days later, the men's team won the second when they defeated Brazil to win the gold.[60]

In basketball, the United States dominated both the women's and men's tournaments. Under Pat Summit, the head coach at the University of Tennessee, the women's team won its first gold medal in Olympic play, going undefeated. Summit was the first person to win a medal in women's basketball as both player and coach. (She had been on the U.S. team in Montreal that won silver.) Cheryl Miller of the University of Southern California emerged as the main celebrity of either American basketball team. The 85–55 victory over South Korea in the gold medal game was, statistically speaking, one of the closer contests they faced. [61]

The men's team had an equally easy time, also going undefeated. "We knew we were going to lose. We just didn't want to get beat by 50 or 60," Christian Welp, a player on the West German team, remarked. Head coach Bobby Knight of Indiana University pushed his team relentlessly. "When I get back to Oklahoma," Wayman Tisdale, a player for the University of Oklahoma, remarked, "I'm going to hug every mean person I used to think was mean."[62]

The final victory was an emotional moment for both teams. The women carried Summit off the court on their shoulders. She was lying on her back, holding up both arms and indicating that the U.S. women were number one with her pointer fingers. The men also carried Knight off the court on their shoulders. The net from one of the baskets was hanging around his neck. He was in tears.[63]

The United States won 174 medals (83 gold, 61 silver, and 30 bronze). The American public followed the success of their athletes with uninhibited enthusiasm, which was particularly manifest with ABC's broadcast. At one point, the network refused to carry events in which foreigners were winning medals. This myopic nationalism led Samaranch to complain about the coverage. Frank Deford of *Sports Illustrated* joked that ABC really was short for "Always Be Cheerleaders." Daley Thompson made a point about the television coverage after he won the gold in the decathlon. He put on a t-shirt that read on the front: "THANKS AMERICA FOR A GOOD GAMES AND A GREAT TIME" and on the back: "BUT WHAT ABOUT THE TV COVERAGE?" In the second week of the games, there was more coverage of foreign competitors. It needs to be noted that the network was catering to what the public wanted. Like four years before in Moscow, the fans in the stands were boorish toward their guests. "They are like children," Monique Berlioiux observed. "We have in French a word for this – *chauvinistes*."[64]

This type of chauvinism, which was hardly unique to the American experience, helped the Olympics a great deal. The commercial mode that Ueberroth had pioneered helped the Los Angeles games turn a huge profit. The number of cities interested in hosting the Olympics began to grow. In 1981, there were only two candidates for the 1988 games – Seoul, South Korea, and Nagoya, Japan – but in 1986, the IOC had six applications from municipalities that wanted to host the 1992 summer games and seven for the winter games. To put that number in context, more cities bid on these games than the combined totals during the entire decade of the 1970s. That number held when it came to competing for the 1996 games, and then dropped by one for 2000. The number then exploded to eleven for the 2004 games. The winter Olympics also grew in popularity. In 1994, nine cities – an Olympic record – competed for the right to host the 2002 winter Olympics. The quality of the proposals improved, and Samaranch decided to make the selection process a televised event.[65]

The jingoism of ABC and the southern California fans helped bolster television ratings and sales of Olympics-related items. Smirnov later admitted that both boycotts had been "bad decisions" and that "neither of these political actions served any purpose except to spoil the lives of hundreds of athletes who had given up everything to take part in the Olympic Games."

The irony is that had the Soviets been in Los Angeles, they would have won many events and limited the number of medals the American athletes took home and would have produced less revenue for the Olympians.[66]

After two massive boycotts, it became clear that these types of sanctions, even those from the major athletic powers of international sports, would never alter either the foreign policies of their hosts or the celebration and distinction of the Olympics. As a result, these types of actions became weaker and weaker in the years that followed. At the same time, more and more people wanted to host the games. That was the true legacy of Los Angeles.

CHAPTER 15

Conclusion

HISTORY IS A NEVER ENDING STORY. AS SUCH, IT CAN NEVER REALLY have any conclusion. A good storyteller, though, can make the audience think, and the political crisis of the XXII Olympiad offers many questions to ponder. Historians know that there are as many lessons in the study of the past as there are grains of sand on a beach. The events surrounding the boycott of the 1980 Moscow Olympics are no different. Grains of sand, though, do tend to lump together to form dunes, and four questions – one of process and three others of environment – loom larger than others.

What of Jimmy Carter and his presidency?

The boycott was a failure of Olympic proportions, and Carter should be grateful. Destroying the Olympics, which despite all its various shortcomings has been a positive force in world affairs, is not exactly the kind of achievement that Carter could have used to establish an enduring historical legacy. The United States government certainly had the resources to destroy the international Olympic movement, and a more competent effort could have effectively done so. The President's technocratic approach to governance was counterproductive. He had difficulty setting priorities and often projected himself deep into the bureaucracy. The result was an inflexible approach toward foreign policy on the part of the Carter White House, rather than its reputation for indecision, that often hurt the political interests of the president. As a manager, Carter never provided the strength of character to control the Vance-Brzezinski dispute, which often resulted in him getting told what he wanted to hear rather than what he needed to know. In essence, the incompetence of the Carter Administration saved it from itself. It is no accident that most alumni of this White House make no mention of the boycott in their memoirs.

What of "soft power" and the Olympics in world affairs?

Carter and many of his subordinates never seriously respected the Olympic ideology. Going hand in hand with this lack of respect was the fact that they never fully appreciated that their opposites – the IOC and the various national Olympic committees – were nonstate actors and developed diplomatic approaches that were less than effective. Carter and his subordinates had a distorted idea of what the soft power of the international Olympic movement could do in world affairs. Soft power is hardly benign, but it is best understood to be something like water. It nourishes and its absence can be deadly. Hard power can cut though it easily, but when massed under pressure, soft power can be a powerful force that alters the landscape. The Olympic movement is hardly free of politics, but the IOC always preferred to channel such sentiment into athletic contests. Inclusion rather than exclusion has always been its main aim. Those that attempt to challenge this inclusive nature directly are almost always driving into a force similar to a wall of water. Only a social phenomenon like the two world wars could directly challenge its viability.

In 1980, the Carter administration was trying to do just that. With a weak argument and failure to respect the views of the Olympians, administration officials were unable to make arguments that convinced foreigners of the danger. They even lacked basic knowledge about the structure of international sports. The Americans assumed that the IOC had a political structure that was similar to that of the United Nations. That ignorance worked against their efforts and often allowed boycott opponents to ignore the substance of the administration's argument.

President Carter liked to think of himself as a "trustee president." Drawing upon the ideas of Edmund Burke, the eighteenth-century British politician and political philosopher, Carter believed that he owed his constituency his judgment on the various ideas that he would encounter rather than a willingness to blindly follow public sentiment, which was often ignorant of the details of various policy debates. Ignoring the fact that Burke was voted out of office for ignoring the views of his electoral borough, Carter proved himself quite ineffective in office. He was a technocrat and made it a habit to invest himself in the details of various policy matters. While it is useful for any executive to know what they are doing, Carter went too far in these efforts. He consistently had difficulty in determining priorities and making decisions between competing interests. The Olympic boycott was no different. His inability to pursue consistent foreign policies created an intense rivalry between Vance and Brzezinski. The contest between these two produced an atmosphere of court politics in the Carter White House, which made many administration officials reluctant to tell the truth to power. These two tendencies resulted in efforts that were counterproductive to Carter's own interests.

His involvement in the details of the boycott forced American officials to pursue certain options because the President was personally invested. Many people at the time claimed that the boycott was more about the President's reelection effort than about foreign policy. This view is simplistic but it contains a small element of truth. There is no evidence showing that the administration officials were pursuing the boycott campaign because they thought it was gaining votes for the president, but a number of White House documents show that administration officials believed that Carter's personal credibility was on the line and this fact ended discussion on the matter. These attitudes stripped U.S. diplomats of a good deal of flexibility in pursuing their objectives. In a strange combination of arrogance and naïveté, Carter and his lieutenants believed that the morality of their position was obvious and that their allies should do as they were told. The idea of alliance management, of consultations was foreign in this White House. This view came directly from the Oval Office itself and permeated the entire administration. The cold hard fact is that Carter has failed in his preferred role as a trustee. His judgment was quite poor, and if the American people used that as a criteria in making their electoral decision in 1980, then they were quite right in voting him out of office.

The boycott also failed because of the efforts of Lord Killanin. Many observers saw the Irishman as a weak leader compared to the authoritarian Avery Brundage who came before him and the dynamic Marquis Juan Antonio de Samaranch who succeeded him. It is true that Killanin was slow to appreciate the determination of the Americans to destroy the Olympics, but after Carter made his decision in mid-January, the battle lines were drawn. Carter's need to take what the American people saw as some sort of strong action in response to Afghanistan was intense, and his willingness to reconsider his position was nonexistent. After that point, nothing Killanin did or could have done would have mattered to Carter. Should Killanin have made an effort to meet with Carter and other officials before they reached this decision? One would think that the answer to this question would be "yes," but the administration was making no effort to consult with anyone involved in the Olympics, including Americans on the IOC or leaders of the USOC. There is no reason to believe that Killanin could have made contact with influential individuals within the White House or that they would have listened to him.

Another factor that shaped Lord Killanin's response is that the organization he led was exceptionally weak at this point in time. The IOC was particularly vulnerable to political pressure. The weakness was primarily the work of Brundage's idealistic but dated policies, and Killanin did much to rebuild the committee's strength, which Samaranch used to achieve even greater success. Killanin's approach of staying the course proved to be the wisest option he had available. A more stringent stand against boycott proponents might have easily splintered the international Olympic movement. When the

USOC decided to boycott the Moscow Games, it was grossly in violation of the Olympic charter, but retaliating against the Americans would only have damaged the movement given the fact that they would host the next summer Olympiad.

The fact that the boycott essentially became a civil war for control of the Olympic movement was another consideration that Lord Killanin had to keep in mind. That the movement was decentralized worked to his advantage. There were a number of turning points in the boycott campaign that ultimate determined its effectiveness, or ineffectiveness. The U.S. government lost most of these battles. There was no chance that the International Olympic Committee was going to strip Moscow of the hosting honors. Only three other Olympiads had been altered – actually cancelled – and these actions had been due to global war. The Soviet presence in Afghanistan, no matter how objectionable, failed to meet these criteria. The one important victory that the administration secured – the vote of the U. S. Olympic Committee – showed the weakness of the boycott. Had the USOC stood fast against and voted to attend the festival, the U.S. government had few tools left short of authoritarian, police-state measures to block the team from visiting the Soviet Union. Kane, Miller, and other leaders of the Committee worried instead about fundraising rather than the interests of their athletes and bent to the intense political pressure that the White House had directed against them. Although President Carter might have been willing to used authoritarian methods regardless of the political costs they entailed, his failure to convince his own national Olympic committee to support the boycott would have had a ripple effect throughout the international Olympic movement against the campaign. As it was, the vote of the USOC only set the stage for a series of battles that the Carter administration lost. The Americans invested a huge amount of time and energy in this effort, which produced only modest returns. Put in terms of poker, Killanin had a weak hand but he played it as well as one could.

What of the Cold War?

Although the boycott was an important issue in the history of the modern Olympics, how significant was it in the story of the American-Soviet confrontation? The boycott had no impact on the Soviet intervention in Afghanistan. Of that there can be no doubt. White House documents show, though, that no one ever thought keeping athletes from competing in Moscow stood a serious chance of forcing a withdrawal. Jimmy Carter had to take some stand against the Soviet Union, and the boycott was sufficient. The problem, though, was that an Olympic boycott was too weak to change Soviet actions but too strong for them to ignore. Soviet diplomats and political officials were stunned at the intensity of the American boycott effort. Afghanistan came during an election year for the United States, but so did the Soviet Union's intervention in Hungary in 1956 and in Czechoslovakia in 1968. Although Afghanistan was in Southwest Asia instead of Eastern Europe, all three countries were already Soviet satellites. Soviet actions did not really alter the balance of power in any of these areas. Punishing a wayward satellite is significantly different from launching an attack on another power. Dwight Eisenhower and Lyndon Johnson understood this distinction and responded accordingly in 1956 and 1968.

The intensity of Carter's reaction, on the other hand, was overkill. The President grossly exaggerated the threat and significance of the Soviet invasion of Afghanistan. Soviet actions in this country were cynical and brutal, but Americans had shown little interest in this region prior to 1979 and had little care or concern for helping rebuild Afghanistan once the Soviets were gone. It might be a harsh statement, but there was good reason for caring little about the fate of this land. Afghanistan is not a particular important region when it comes to international affairs. Carter's standing in foreign affairs, however, was far from secure in 1980, and the boycott played well politically. The soundness of this policy was another thing altogether.

Just as Carter and his subordinates refused to take the Olympics seriously, so too did the Soviet leadership disregard Jimmy Carter's moral objections to their actions in Afghanistan. It was also difficult for them to believe that the abrupt shifts in U.S. foreign policy under this President were anything other than intentional. The President's public remarks might have struck his countrymen as naïve, but the Soviets saw it as ideologically charged rhetoric that attacked the very legitimacy of the Soviet state. Carter, in their view, was looking for a return to the most frigid days of the Cold War, and the Olympics were the tool to that end. Observers were right in noting that the Soviets had invested a good deal of money and effort in the Olympiad, and the boycott was a stinging public slap in the face that could neither be forgiven nor forgotten. Afghanistan need not have killed détente, nor did the American reaction need to have restarted the Cold War; there were options available to American diplomats and statesmen that they could have taken without provoking and humiliating their opposites. Such calm and reasoned voices, though, had little influence in 1980, and the result was the return to a harsh confrontation between Moscow and Washington.

What about the nature of U.S. foreign policy?

On this issue, the boycott is most instructive. There are many who argue that this topic is narrow and involves only a small, select group of individuals, hardly representative or relative to the lives of most Americans or others. It is difficult to take this argument seriously. The foreign policy of the United States was and is a "national issue" in the truest sense of that phrase. The

Olympic boycott makes that point abundantly clear. World affairs in 1980 were discussed at the highest levels of government among a small elite that worked and lived in the Washington, D.C. area. That point is certainly true. But the foreign policy of the United States was also the subject of interest to people in California, Texas, and Georgia as well. All states, in fact. In 1980, the American people were still vigilant, determined to fight the good fight that was the Cold War. This ongoing commitment to oppose the evil of the Soviet Union was discussed, as was the boycott, on the editorial pages of *The Washington Post* and *The New York Times*, but also other papers like the *San Francisco Chronicle*, the *Austin American-Statesman*, and *The Augusta Chronicle*. The boycott – like foreign policy in general – affected the lives and careers of small businessmen, athletes, television producers, and bartenders, to name just a few. In short, foreign policy is a subject that engages and affects the entire populace. It is everywhere; it matters to everyone; it is national.

Epilogue

Jimmy Carter

After leaving office on a high note with the return of the hostages that Iranians had held captive in the U.S. embassy in Tehran, he returned to Plains, Georgia, profoundly depressed. He found relief in the physical labor of repairing his house, which had seen little upkeep during his political career. In his retirement, he became a prolific author, writing over twenty books that included several memoirs, a collection of poetry, a historical novel about the American Revolution, an illustrated children's story, a self-help book about aging, a work of theology, and a travelogue on fly fishing. In addition to establishing the Carter Presidential Library, he founded the Carter Center that would focus on promoting democracy and public health issues. The organization gave him a platform with which to address diplomatic and public policy issues. He had to wait until Reagan left office, though, before he was asked to perform diplomatic missions. "It was like opening a new door for me." The same intellectual arrogance that lead him to believe he could master all sorts of policy matters lead Carter to act on his own, independent of the Bush and Clinton administrations. This behavior so infuriated President Bill Clinton that the two had a yelling match in the Oval Office. Despite offending a number of administrations, Carter received the Nobel Peace Prize in 2002. In his acceptance speech, he said, "War may sometimes be a necessary evil. But no matter how necessary, it is always evil, never good. We will not live together in Peace by killing each other's children." When asked if the Nobel vindicated his presidency – a question based on the premise that his time at the White House was a failure – he replied, "I don't know of any decision I made in the White House that were basically erroneous."[1]

Lord Killanin

After stepping down as IOC president, Killanin put his name back in the Dublin phone book. The Soviet Union offered him the Order of Friendship of Peoples, which he declined. The IOC awarded him the Olympic Order and the title of Honorary Life President, both of which he accepted. He died on April 25, 1999 in his Dublin home where he had met Cutler twenty-nine years before. "Lord Killanin always represented Ireland at home and abroad with style, distinction and integrity," Irish Prime Minister Bertie Ahern observed. "He was a charismatic and dynamic individual who was passionate about every task he took on." Upon Killanin's death, his son Redmond became the fourth Baron Killanin of Galway, County Galway.[2]

Lloyd Cutler

Following Carter's defeat in 1980, Cutler returned to Wilmer, Cutler and Pickering, the law firm that he helped establish in 1962. In 2004, the firm merged with another and became Wilmer Cutler Pickering Hale and Dorr. He remained an influential figure in Washington and a powerful lawyer. In 1982, he argued before the U.S. Supreme Court in the case on behalf of the National Association for Advancement of Colored Persons and won. He maintained a reputation for bipartisanship. In 1987, he supported the nomination of Judge Robert Bork to the U.S. Supreme Court. He returned to the White House in 1994, serving again as White House Counsel to President Bill Clinton during the Whitewater scandal. In 2004, President George W. Bush appointed him to serve on the Commission on the Intelligence Capabilities of the United States Regarding Weapons of Mass Destruction, which investigated analyses from the U.S. spy agencies prior to the second Iraq war. Cutler died in 2005 at the age of 87. "He was a devoted public servant who had a profound influence on the legal profession," President Bush noted. In the many obituaries that followed, there was often no mention of his role in the Olympic boycott, and people knowing little of his actions in 1980 praised him for knowing when to not do what the client demanded.[3]

Joe Onek

After Carter left the White House, Onek established a small law firm in Washington, Onek, Klein & Farr, that quickly developed a reputation for being strong in appellate work and appearances before the U.S. Supreme Court. Half of the lawyers in the firm had been clerks for Supreme Court justices. Onek described the firm as "a place that had very interesting work, an enjoyable place, and that would always take precedence over financial considerations, so you don't end up doing things that you don't want to do or not doing things that you do want to do." When the firm dissolved in 1991, he became a partner in Crowell & Moring and then returned to public service in the Clinton administration, serving as Principal Deputy Associate Attorney General and State Department Rule of Law Coordinator. After working for a number of nonprofit organizations, he became Counsel to the Speaker of the U.S. House of Representatives in 2007.[4]

Walter Mondale

In 1984, Mondale ran for President of the United States. He secured the nomination of the Democratic Party before suffering a massive defeat at the hands of Ronald Reagan in the general election. In the Electoral College, he won only Minnesota, his home state, and the District of Columbia. In the immediate aftermath of that defeat, he would wake up in cold sweat, replaying his disappointing performance in his last televised debate with Reagan. "One of the virtues of getting whomped like I did is that there is less second-guessing," he observed twenty years later. When asked how long it took him to get over the defeat, he replied, "I'll call you when it happens." In 1987, he became a partner in Dorsey & Whitney law firm headquartered in Minneapolis, Minnesota. He left the legal practice from 1993 to 1996 to serve as U.S. Ambassador to Japan. In 2002, he briefly returned to politics, following the death of Senator Paul Wellstone just before Election Day. Mondale agreed to take Wellstone's place on the ballot. "I don't apologize for my experience," he said. "It's an asset." His return to politics ended poorly. He lost, making it the first time he had failed to carry the state. "I love Minnesota," he said conceding defeat. "And in what is obviously my last campaign, you always treated me decently … You always listened to me. I am so proud of this state and its people."[5]

Cyrus Vance

After he resigned as Secretary of State, Vance returned to his New York law firm, Simpson, Thacher & Bartlett. He carried out a number of diplomatic missions in the 1980s and served as chairman of the Federal Reserve Bank of New York at the end of the decade. The only comment he made on his feud with Brzezinski was to *The New York Times* reporter that interviewed him years in advance for his obituary: "I had some reservations about him," he said, "but I knew the president wanted him badly. I now realize my instinctive feeling on that was right." He died in 2002 after suffering from Alzheimer's disease. He was 84. "A champion for peace and human rights, he was a superb statesman who served me and other presidents well," Carter said in a statement he released on behalf of himself and his wife. "We will miss his friendship, and the world will miss his humanitarian work and goodness." When asked how he wanted to be remembered, he said, "I hope for being a reasonably decent, honest person who tried to do some things for the country that might have lasting effect and create a better life for a number of people."[6]

Zbigniew Brzezinski

The National Security Advisor returned to Columbia University when the Carter administration left office. His classes were immensely popular, drawing enrollments of over 300 students. He continued living in the Washington,

D.C. area and for a time he regularly ate lunch with Muskie and former Secretary of Defense Harold Brown. He also held a weekly reunion of his NSC staff at his office on K Street in Washington, which quickly became known in the nation's capital as the "Z.B. Brown Bag Lunch." Despite his ties to Jimmy Carter, he took a position with George Bush presidential campaign in 1988. The end of the Cold War vindicated to many his hardline positions toward the Soviet Union. He left Columbia for a position at Johns Hopkins University's Nitze School of Advanced International Studies. He published regularly, writing over a dozen books after leaving office, several of which became bestsellers, and numerous opinion pieces for newspapers, magazines, and scholarly journals that were quite critical of both Bush administrations and that of Bill Clinton.[7]

Warren Christopher

Before leaving office, Jimmy Carter awarded Christopher the Medal of Freedom, the highest civilian decoration the U.S. government can award. Christopher was absent from the ceremony when the President presented the medals, because he was in Algeria successfully negotiating the end of the Iranian hostage crisis. In his memoirs, Carter called him "the best public servant I ever knew." He returned to Los Angeles and resumed work with his law firm, O'Melvey & Myers. "He's a lawyer's lawyer," political commentator Daniel Pipes remarked. "He's Cyrus Vance without the charisma." He returned to Washington as Secretary of State under Bill Clinton from 1993 to 1997. Highlights of his tenure as the head of the State Department included overseeing the expansion of NATO, helping Israel and Jordan negotiate a peace treaty, establishing diplomatic relations with Vietnam, and negotiating an end to the war in Bosnia.[8]

F. Don Miller

He had a certain amount of contempt for the Carter administration after his experiences in 1980: "We concluded that the reason they were doing this was due to a complete lack of foreign policy. If there was a foreign policy, why of all things, would you choose the Olympic movement, which stood for good throughout the world, which built international amity and good will?" In 1984, he received the Olympic Order from the IOC and remained as executive director of the USOC until 1985. He resigned to become president of the new United States Olympic Foundation, which received 40 percent of the $215 million surplus that the Los Angeles Olympics produced. He died on January 17, 1996. "He was a visionary and he was also a doer," William E. Simon remarked. "You don't get that combination very often. His integrity was legend. He loved the Olympics like he loved his family. He understood sports."[9]

Robert J. Kane

He stepped down as president of the USOC in 1981 and was inducted into the United States Olympic Hall of Fame in 1986. Kane always believed that the Committee had acted properly in 1980. "I am persuaded it had to be our only course of action. To have defied the President of the United States, the Congress, and the will of the People would have been unpatriotic and perhaps suicidal for USOC. It would have been a hard setback for the Olympic athletes of the future for defiance could conceivably have led to governmental take-over of Olympic affairs. And after all we do represent the United States of America." He died on May 31, 1992.[10]

1980 U.S. Olympic Hockey Team

At the end of the year, the editors of *Sports Illustrated* named the entire team "Sportsmen of the Year." Other honors large and small would come in the years that followed. In 2002, they lit the Olympic flame at the Salt Lake City Winter Olympics and a year later, the entire team was inducted into the United States Hockey Hall of Fame. The team was also the subject of a made-for-television movie *Miracle on Ice* (1981) and a theatrical production *Miracle* (2004). Thirteen of the twenty players ended up playing in the NHL. Herb Brooks followed them into the professional ranks. He coached the New York Rangers, the Minnesota North Stars, the New Jersey Devils, and the Pittsburgh Penguins. Despite reaching 100 wins faster than any other coach in Rangers history, he had a rather mediocre NHL record of 219–222–66. He coached the French Olympic team at the 1998 Nagano Games and returned to lead the U.S. team a second time four years later at Salt Lake City. Coaching professionals instead of college players, Brooks led the team to the silver medal. It was the first medal in hockey for the United States since 1980. He died in an automobile accident in 2003.[11]

1980 U.S. Summer Olympic Team

Many of the athletes that were honored on the west steps of the U.S. Capitol building never competed in any Olympic festival. At the time, some knew such would be their destiny. Sue Walsh's fate was fairly typical. Walsh made the 1980 swim team in the 100-meter backstroke and was a serious candidate to win gold in Moscow. In 1984, she was the American-record holder in the event but swam with a sinus infection and finished third in the Olympic trials, failing to qualify for the U.S. team. In fact, for nearly half of the team, 1980 was the only time they qualified for the Olympics. Many moved on with their lives and careers but still retain a small amount of bitterness. Bill Wall, executive director of the Amateur Basketball Federation of the United States of America, remarked, "I will never forget or forgive."[12]

Margaret Thatcher

Most of Thatcher's career at 10 Downing Street still lay ahead of when the Moscow Olympics ended. When British athletes returned home, she refused to award them the honors and knighthoods that the crown had bestowed on Olympians in the past. Her time in office was important for initiating a number of economic reforms that included rewriting corporate tax codes, financial deregulation, strict money controls, privatization of state-owned industries, and union legislation. Together these actions initiated a period of strong economic growth not seen in the United Kingdom since the end of World War II, brought about a dramatic rise in home ownership, and halted the decline in Britain's share of world trade. The highlight of her time in office was the 1982 Falkland Islands War with Argentina that reversed the fading power of the British military. Despite strong support within the broad reaches of her party, she lost a fight for the leadership when most of her cabinet turned on her. In announcing her resignation, despite her popularity and accomplishments, she observed, "It's a funny old world." In 1992, she became a member of the House of Lords when she became Baroness Thatcher of Kesteven in the County of Lincolnshire.[13]

Helmut Schmidt

Schmidt won reelection in 1980. He stayed in office until 1982, losing support within his party to Helmut Kohl after a vote of no confidence in the *Bundestag* over arms control issues. In retirement from active politics, his life took a literary turn. He has written nine books and served as publisher of the weekly *Die Zeit*. On its pages, he has opposed the expansion of NATO and admission of Turkey into the European Union. In 2008 to celebrate his ninetieth birthday, he released a compact disc of him playing Bach on the piano.[14]

Pierre Trudeau

Trudeau's major achievements as Prime Minister still lay ahead of him. In 1982, he successfully got the British Parliament to surrender its role in the Canadian constitutional process, severing its last vestiges of legal authority over British North America. He also oversaw the process that made Canada officially bilingual in 1984. He divorced his wife, Margaret, and retired from politics that same year. He lived a private life afterward, dying in 2000.[15]

Joe Clark

Clark lost control of his party's leadership in 1983. He accepted this defeat, and when the Progressive Conservative party regained control of the government in 1984, he served as Foreign Minister and then Constitutional Affairs

Minister in the cabinet of Prime Minster Brian Mulroney. He retired from Canadian politics in 1993 but regained leadership of the party in 1998 after it had suffered enormous electoral defeats. He refused to stay in the party when it merged with another party to become the Conservative Party. When he retired from politics a second time, *Toronto Star* columnist James Travers observed, "Clark slips into history tonight as the most unfortunate of political creatures: A failure who was not quite magnificent." Since leaving politics, he has taught at American University in Washington, D.C., and McGill University in Montreal.[16]

Muhammad Ali

In October 1980, he fought his former sparring partner, Larry Holmes, and lost decisively. His last fight came against Trevor Berbick on December 11, 1981. He lost in the tenth round. "Time had finally caught up with me," he admitted. "The truth is if I won my last fight I would have kept going." He was already suffering from Parkinson's disease. Despite his illness, he returned to the Olympics in 1996 when Atlanta hosted the summer games. He carried the Olympic torch during the opening ceremonies. "It brought back a lot of memories of my early boxing days, and I count it among the most memorable moments of my life," he explained. "I showed the world that Parkinson's disease hadn't defeated me. I showed them that I was still the Greatest of All Time." On the subject of his legacy, he wished, "I would like to be remembered as a man who won the heavyweight title three times, who was humorous, and who treated everyone right. As a man who never looked down on those who looked up to him, and who helped as many people as he could. As a man who stood up for his beliefs no matter what. As a man who tried to unite all humankind through faith and love. And if all that's too much, then I'd settle for being remembered only as a great boxer who became a leader and a champion of his people. And I wouldn't even mind if folks forgot how pretty I was." President George W. Bush did many of these things in 2005 when he awarded Ali the Presidential Medal of Freedom. After reciting Ali's accomplishments, the President said, "The real mystery, I guess, is how he stayed so pretty. It probably had to do with his beautiful soul."[17]

Anita DeFrantz

She never competed in another Olympics. After the 1984 Olympics, she became president of the Amateur Athletic Foundation of Los Angeles, a nonprofit organization that uses the profits of these games to develop sports in the southern California region. In 1986, she became a member of the IOC. When asked about the 1980 boycott, she said, "I was right then and I'm right now."[18]

Peter Ueberroth

In October 1984, Ueberroth took another sports management position, becoming commissioner of Major League Baseball. "I've always hunted for challenges," he told a reporter for *Time* when the magazine named him "Man of the Year" three months later. He was commissioner of baseball for four and a half years, resigning before the start of the 1989 season. Active on the boards of a number of corporations, he ran for governor of California in the 2003 recall election as a Republican but never seriously challenged actor Arnold Schwarzenegger. In 2004, he returned to the Olympic movement, accepting the new position of chairman of the USOC after a series of corruption scandals forced another administrative reform of the committee.[19]

William E. Simon

Simon maintained an active business career. In the 1980s, he helped establish three corporations: the Wesray Corporation, WSGP International, and William E. Simon & Sons. In addition, he served on the boards of thirty companies. Simon maintained active involvement in the Olympic movement. He was one of the founders of the U.S. Olympic Foundation. In recognition of his service, the USOC awarded him the Olympic Torch, the highest award of that organization. The IOC gave him its highest honor, the Olympic Order. In 1991, he was inducted into the U.S. Olympic Hall of Fame. In 1998, he donated one million dollars and created the William E. Simon Olympic Trust to give grants that would underwrite training expenses. He was also one of the leaders of the effort to bring the World Cup to the United States. In his memoirs, Simon finally offered an apology in public for his speech to the House of Delegates: "I can think of only one major issue on which I supported President Carter – the boycott of the 1980 Olympics – and I regret it to this day."

He also became quite active as a philanthropist, giving away a good deal of his money. He endowed centers that bore his name at the U.S. Military Academy, the U.S. Air Force Academy, and Lafayette College, his alma matter. He also endowed chairs at Lafayette, the Air Force Academy, Georgetown University, and the Center for Strategic and International Studies. In 1986, the University of Rochester named its business school the William E. Simon Graduate School of Business Administration. He also created the William E. Simon Foundation with the mission "to strengthen the free enterprise system and the spiritual values on which it rests: individual freedom, initiative, thrift, self-discipline and faith in God." He died in 2000. He was 72.[20]

Juan Antonio Samaranch

Despite the boycott of 1984, Samaranch had a largely successful tenure as IOC president. During his tenure, women joined the Committee as members and the Olympic movement expanded to include another fifty nations. The Committee also expanded eligibility rules, allowing more athletes to compete in the Olympics, and developed new sources of finance, including sponsorship revenue and better television contracts. King Juan Carlos of Spain made him a Marquis. A corruption scandal, though, engulfed the IOC just before he left office, when a number of members took bribes in return for their votes on which city would get to host the games. "I used to be happy to open the door of my office. Now I am happy if I close it behind me," he said of that crisis. The IOC instituted a number of reforms including age limits that ended the lifetime membership, increase in the size of the committee, creating positions for athletes and representatives of the federations, and a ban on visiting candidate cities.[21]

Richard Pound

Pound remained active in the Olympic movement. Serving twice as IOC vice-president, he was Samaranch's main lieutenant. He was the main negotiator for the IOC's new television contracts and developed marketing ideas that Samaranch implemented. In 1999, he led the investigation into IOC corruption that led to the departure of ten members and a series of reforms. That effort probably cost him the chance to succeed Samaranch in 2001. Pound came in third in the balloting. Between 1999 and 2007, he has served as chairman of the World Anti-Doping Agency, which the IOC created to combat drug cheating among athletes. "We deal with Interpol, and they tell us they believe the illegal sport drug market exceeds the market for marijuana, cocaine and heroin combined," he remarked. "Everybody out there is somebody's kid." He used his writing to challenge drug usage in non-Olympic sports. When Tour de France winner Floyd Landis tested positive for artificially high levels of testosterone, Pound remarked, "I mean it was 11 to 1! You'd think he'd be violating every virgin within 100 miles. How does he even get on his bicycle?" He offered no apologies for his controversial style. "There are a significant number of people who think I might be a complete asshole – and they could be right. But I really don't care if I piss people off." As a partner in the Montreal law firm of Stikeman Elliot, he wrote two major works of Canadian legal history in addition to two books on the Olympics. He also served as Chancellor of McGill University.[22]

Malcolm Fraser

The Australian Prime Minister won reelection in 1980. At the time, he refused to view the boycott as a political defeat: "People didn't like the policy, but I think by and large more people would have respected the government for sticking with it."[23] In 1983, his conservative coalition government lost power to the Labour Party. He retired from politics. He has been active in charities in the years since, and has had his photography displayed in an artistic exhibition in the Collins Street district of Melbourne. In retirement, his political views have moved to the left, although he disputes this analysis. "Discrimination, or worse, racism has always appalled me. Claims I have moved to the left should be seen against a world environment in which policy differences between socialists and conservatives has changed, where the whole political spectrum has moved leagues to the right." In 2008, he admitted the boycott had been a mistake. "I never thought it was good policy because policy, to be successful, needs to be sustainable," he said. "Not only was it divisive between different sports, but also within sports."[24]

Notes

Introduction: Miracle on ice

1. John Powers and Arthur C. Kaminsky, *One Goal: A Chronicle of the 1980 U.S. Olympic Hockey Team* (New York: Harper & Row, 1984), 232; Dave Ogrean, "Ice Hockey," *The Olympian* (April 1980), 12; Wayne Coffey, *The Boys of Winter: The Untold Story of a Coach, a Dream, and the 1980 U.S. Olympic Hockey Team* (New York: Crown Publishers, 2005), 17, 247; *Do You Believe in Miracles? The Story of the 1980 U.S. Hockey Team* (New York: Home Box Office Home Video, 2001).

2. Powers and Kaminsky, *One Goal*, 232; Ogrean, "Ice Hockey," 12; Coffey, *The Boys of Winter*, 17, 247; *Do You Believe in Miracles? The Story of the 1980 U.S. Hockey Team* (New York: Home Box Office Home Video, 2001).

3. Powers and Kaminsky, *One Goal*, 232; Ogrean, "Ice Hockey," 12; Coffey, *The Boys of Winter*, 17, 247; *Do You Believe in Miracles? The Story of the 1980 U.S. Hockey Team* (New York: Home Box Office Home Video, 2001).

4. Powers and Kaminsky, *One Goal*, 232; Dave Ogrean, "Ice Hockey," *The Olympian* (April 1980), 12; Coffey, *The Boys of Winter*, 17, 247; *Do You Believe in Miracles? The Story of the 1980 U.S. Hockey Team* (New York: Home Box Office Home Video, 2001)

5. Powers and Kaminsky, *One Goal*, 19; Tim Wendel, *Going for the Gold: How the U.S. Won at Lake Placid* (Westport, CT: Lawrence Hill & Company, 1980), 11.

6. Powers and Kaminsky, *One Goal*, 29, 134; Wendel, *Going for the Gold*, 9; Coffey, *The Boys of Winter*, 8.

7. Powers and Kaminsky, *One Goal*, 27–9, 64, 78–9, 90–1, 94, 101–2, 108–10, 134, 146–7; Coffey, *The Boys of Winter*, 8, 84–5, 102, 228; Wendel, *Going for the Gold*, 9, 82.

8. Powers and Kaminsky, *One Goal*, 27–9, 64, 78–9, 90–1, 94, 101–2, 108–10, 134, 146–7; Coffey, *The Boys of Winter*, 8, 84–5, 102, 228; Wendel, *Going for the Gold*, 9, 82.

9. Powers and Kaminsky, *One Goal*, 27–9, 64, 78–9, 90–1, 94, 101–2, 108–10, 134, 146–7; Coffey, *The Boys of Winter*, 8, 84–5, 102, 228; Wendel, *Going for the Gold*, 9, 82.

10. Powers and Kaminsky, *One Goal*, 24, 34, 40, 57, 107, 132; Wendel, *Going for the Gold*, 5, 15.

11. Powers and Kaminsky, *One Goal*, 22, 62–3.

12. Powers and Kaminsky, *One Goal*, 80–1, 143, 148, 156.

13. Powers and Kaminsky, *One Goal*, 13, 71–2, 128–9, 254; Coffey, *The Boys of Winter*, 13; E. M. Swift, "The Boys of Winter," *Sports Illustrated*, January 25, 1980, p. 26; *Do You Believe in Miracles? The Story of the 1980 U.S. Hockey Team* (New York: Home Box Office Home Video, 2001).

14. Powers and Kaminsky, *One Goal*, 13, 71–2, 128–9, 254; Coffey, *The Boys of Winter*, 13; Swift, "The Boys of Winter," p. 26; *Do You Believe in Miracles?*.

15. Powers and Kaminsky, *One Goal*, 2–3, 166.

16. Powers and Kaminsky, *One Goal*, 167–8; Wendel, *Going for the Gold*, 84–5.

17. Wendel, *Going for the Gold*, 22, 29; Powers and Kaminsky, *One Goal*, 169–76; Coffey, *The Boys of Winter*, 116.

18. Wendel, *Going for the Gold*, 22, 29; Powers and Kaminsky, *One Goal*, 169–76; Coffey, *The Boys of Winter*, 116.

19. *Do You Believe in Miracles?*; Wendel, *Going for the Gold*, 30; Powers and Kaminsky, *One Goal*, 178–84; *Flint Journal*, February 21, 1980.

20. Powers and Kaminsky, *One Goal*, 186–8; *The Washington Post*, February 17, 1980.

21. Powers and Kaminsky, *One Goal*, 190–2.

22. Powers and Kaminsky, *One Goal*, 193–6; Wendel, *Going for the Gold*, 32; *The Washington Post*, February 21, 1980

23. Powers and Kaminsky, *One Goal*, 198–203.

24. *Do You Believe in Miracles?*; Powers and Kaminsky, *One Goal*, 200–1; Coffey, *The Boys of Winter*, 28.

25. *Do You Believe in Miracles?*; Powers and Kaminsky, *One Goal*, 203–7.

26. *Do You Believe in Miracles?*; Powers and Kaminsky, *One Goal*, 203–7.

27. *Do You Believe in Miracles?*; Powers and Kaminsky, *One Goal*, 203–7.

28. Coffey, *The Boys of Winter*, 90–1; Powers and Kaminsky, *One Goal*, 209; Wendel, *Going for the Gold*, 38.

29. Coffey, *The Boys of Winter*, 90–1; Powers and Kaminsky, *One Goal*, 209; Wendel, *Going for the Gold*, 38.

30. *Do You Believe in Miracles?*; *The Washington Post*, February 23, 1980; Powers and Kaminsky, *One Goal*, 210–13.

31. *Do You Believe in Miracles?*; Coffey, *The Boys of Winter*, 90–1, 234; Powers and Kaminsky, *One Goal*, 213, 215; *The Washington Post*, February 23, 1980.

32. *Do You Believe in Miracles?*; Coffey, *The Boys of Winter*, 90–1, 234; Powers and Kaminsky, *One Goal*, 213, 215; *The Washington Post*, February 23, 1980.

33. *Do You Believe in Miracles?*; *The Washington Post*, February 23, 1980; Powers and Kaminsky, *One Goal*, 216; Coffey, *The Boys of Winter*, 242.

34. Coffey, *The Boys of Winter*, 90–91, 243–4, 259; Powers and Kaminsky, *One Goal*, 216.

35. Coffey, *The Boys of Winter*, 90–91, 242–4, 259; Powers and Kaminsky, *One Goal*, 216; *The Washington Post*, February 23, 1980.

36. Coffey, *The Boys of Winter*, 90–1, 242–4, 259; Powers and Kaminsky, *One Goal*, 216; *The Washington Post*, February 23, 1980.

37. *Do You Believe in Miracles?*; Coffey, *The Boys of Winter*, 254.

38. *Do You Believe in Miracles?*; Powers and Kaminsky, *One Goal*, 224–7; E. M. Swift, "The Golden Goal," *Sports Illustrated*, March 3, 1980, 20.

39. Wendel, *Going for the Gold*, 17.

40. Jimmy Carter, *Keeping Faith: Memoirs of a President* (New York: Bantam Books, 1982). 489; Jack W. Germond and Jules Witcover, *Blue Smoke and Mirrors: How Reagan Won and Why Carter Lost the Election of 1980* (New York: Viking Press, 1981), 149–50; Powers and Kaminsky, *One Goal*, 228; Wendel, *Going for the Gold*, 44.

41. Jimmy Carter, *Keeping Faith: Memoirs of a President* (New York: Bantam Books, 1982). 489; Jack W. Germond and Jules Witcover, *Blue Smoke and Mirrors: How Reagan Won and Why Carter Lost the Election of 1980* (New York: Viking Press, 1981), 149–50; Powers and Kaminsky, *One Goal*, 228; Wendel, *Going for the Gold*, 44.

42. Lord Killanin, *My Olympic Years* (London: Secker and Warburg, 1983), 189. There are significant differences in pagination between the British and American publication of Killanin's memoirs. Unless otherwise noted, citations are to the version printed in London, not New York.

43. Killanin, *My Olympic Years*, 221–2.

44. The Olympics have been the subject of a good deal of historical inquiry, which has reflected the general historiographical trends of sport history, stressing social issues. Politics has been present in Olympic history as well. As an international sporting event, diplomatic and political issues are inherent in its nature. Most political histories have focused on the politics of participation. Much of the political inquiry has focused on the XXII Olympiad. The official Olympic history explains why: "In the entire history of the modern Olympic Games, it was on the occasion of the Moscow Olympic Games that the most widespread use was made of sport as a means of applying diplomatic pressure." Fernand Landy and Magdeleine Yerlès, *International Olympic Committee – One Hundred Years: The Idea – The Presidents – The Achievements, vol. 3, the Presidencies of Lord Killanin (1972–1980) and of Juan Antonio Samaranch (1980–)* (Lausanne, Switzerland: International Olympic Committee, 1994), 111. David B. Kanin

advances a similar argument in his book on Olympic politics. He argues that the boycott was a "qualified success" because it "robbed from Moscow the sense of international legitimacy that the Games normally provide the Olympic host." David B. Kanin, *A Political History of the Olympic Games* (Boulder, CO: Westview Press, 1981), 108, 145. Martin Barry Vinokur makes a similar argument about the boycott being important as a mechanism for public relations. Martin Barry Vinokur, *More Than A Game: Sports and Politics* (New York: Greenwood Press, 1988), 116. Derick L. Hulme, Jr. was the first scholar to focus on the boycott itself and bases his study on a contemporary American press accounts, public documents, and the memoirs of key individuals in the campaign. Although more critical of the Carter administration than Kanin, Hulme ultimately comes to a similar assessment, calling the boycott "only partially successful." He believes that the boycott was a safe form of protests against the invasion of Afghanistan that posed little risk to the United States. Derick L. Hulme, Jr., *The Political Olympics: Moscow, Afghanistan, and the 1980 U.S. Boycott* (New York: Praeger, 1990), x, 9, 17–18, 128. Tom Caraccioli and Jerry Caraccioli's *Boycott: Stolen Dreams of the 1980 Moscow Olympic Games* (Washington, DC: New Chapter Press, 2008) is a collection of oral histories of American Olympic athletes and the impact – usually negative – that the boycott had on their careers. Stephanie Wilson McConnell in a Ph.D. dissertation offers a historical account, and is the first scholar to utilize documents from the Carter White House. Athough basically following in Hulme's wake, she does claim that the boycott started the collapse of the Soviet Union. Stephanie Wilson McConnell, "Jimmy Carter, Afghanistan, and the Olympic Boycott: The Last Crisis of the Cold War?" (Ph.D. Dissertation, Bowling Green State University, 2001), 190–1, 210. This argument sounds convincing at first glance, but when one looks beyond the perspective that records in the Carter White House afford, it becomes less convincing. There have also been specialized studies on this boycott. Laurence Barton, Leon Chorbajian, and Vincent Mosco examined the coverage of the boycott in the U.S. media. Laurence Barton, "The American Olympic Boycott of 1980: The Amalgam of Diplomacy and Propaganda in Influencing Public Opinion," (Ph.D. Dissertation, Boston University, 1983); Leon Chorbajian and Vincent Mosco, "1976 and 1980 Olympic Boycott Media Coverage: All the News that Fits," *Arena Review* vol. 5 (1981), 3–28. John Deane and Michael Young have conducted similar studies on the Australian media. John Deane, "The Melbourne Press and the Moscow Olympics," *Sporting Traditions* vol. 1, no. 2 (May 1985), 27–42; and Michael Young, "The Melbourne Press and the 1980 Moscow Olympic Boycott Controversy," *Sporting Traditions* vol. 4, no. 2 (May 1988), 184–200. All of them find that the media was heavily biased in favor of the boycott, and this study borrows heavily from these studies at appropriate points. Baruch Hazan uses the boycott as a case study to examine Soviet propaganda techniques in Baruch Hazan, *Olympic Sports and Propaganda Games: Moscow 1980* (New Brunswick, NJ: Transaction Books, 1982). Stephen R. Wenn and Jeffrey P. Wenn examine an attention-getting episode when the Carter administration enlisted the aid of Muhammad Ali. Wenn and Wenn believe Ali's mission was far more successful than is commonly thought – the claim that is rejected in this account. Stephen R. Wenn and Jeffrey P. Wenn, "Muhammad Ali and the Convergence of Olympic Sport and U.S. Diplomacy in 1980: A Reassessment from Behind the Scenes at the U.S. State Department," *Olympika: The International Journal of Olympic Studies* vol. 2 (1993), 45–66. Sandra L. Kereliuk offered a preliminary account of the Canadian debate on the Olympics in Sandra L. Kereliuk, "The Canadian Boycott of the 1980 Moscow Olympic Games," Gerald Redmond, ed., *Sport and Politics* (Champaign, IL: Human Kinetics Publishers, 1986). For a more extensive study, see the fifth chapter of Donald Macintosh and Michael Hawes, with contributions from Donna Greenhorn and David Black, *Sport and Canadian Diplomacy* (Montreal: McGill-Queen's University Press, 1994), 90–107. Jane Crossman and Ron Lappage have also examined the impact the boycott had on the lives and careers of Canadian athletes in Jane Crossman and Ron Lappage, "Canadian Athletes' Perceptions of the 1980 Olympic Boycott," *Sociology of Sport Journal* vol. 9 (1992), 354–71. The account in this book is different in that it puts U.S. foreign policy in an international context and considers the Olympic point of view, looking at the politics of the Olympics, the political ideology of the international Olympic movement, and the process for selecting host cities. It also looks at the events in the arenas of Moscow and Los Angels and how the boycott affected the competitions themselves, which clearly shows that the boycott was nothing other than a failure.

45. Like most other presidents, the climate of the day has shaped Carter's historical reputation. Defeated in his reelection bid, he left office with his reputation in tatters. For a contemporary example, see Haynes Johnson, *In the Absence of Power: Governing America* (New York: Viking Press, 1980). For matters focusing on foreign policy, Gaddis Smith advanced a critical assessment, faulting Carter for naivette; see Gaddis Smith, *Morality and Reason: American Diplomacy in the Carter Years* (New York: Hill and Wang, 1986). For a historiography that examines the second half of the Cold War, see Robert D. Schulzinger, "Complaints, Self-justifications, and Analysis: The Historiography of American Foreign Relations since 1969," *Diplomatic History* vol. 15, no. 2 (Spring 1991), 245–64. Smith's assessment would be particularly popular among conservative commentators who offered early assessments of Carter's foreign policy, like Jeane Kirkpatrick and Joshua Muravchik; see Joshua Muravchik, *The Uncertain Crusade: Jimmy Carter and the Dilemmas of Human Rights Policy* (Lanham, MD: Hamilton Press, 1986). Kirkpatrick wrote the forward to Muravchik's book. In the 1980s, there were a number of scholar/ participants who produced hybrid memoirs/monographs that were the product of both original research and memory. Most of these works focused on specific episodes such as Nicaragua, the Camp David peace agreements, and Iran, and often provided ammunition for critics of the Carter administration. For examples, see the following: Robert A. Pastor, *Condemned to Repetition: The United States and Nicaragua* (Princeton, NJ: Princeton University Press, 1987); David Newsom, *The Soviet Brigade in Cuba: A Study in Political Diplomacy* (Bloomington, IN: Indiana University Press, 1987); Anthony Lake, *Somoza Falling: The Nicaraguan Dilemma* (Boston: Houghton Mifflin, 1989); William Quandt, *Camp David: Peacemaking and Politics* (Washington, DC: Brookings Institution, 1986); Gary Sick, *All Fall Down: America's Tragic Encounter with Iran* (New York: Random House, 1985). In the late 1980s, a number of political scientists began to advance a revisionist view of Carter. Noting that he liked to think of himself as a "trustee" of the public welfare along the lines that Edmund Burke recommended in eighteenth-century England, these scholars contend Carter pursued the best policy despite its political ramifications. See Charles O. Jones, *The Trusteeship Presidency: Jimmy Carter and the United States Congress* (Baton Rouge, LA: Louisiana State University, 1988); Erwin C. Hargrove, *Jimmy Carter as President: Leadership and the Politics of the Public Good* (Baton Rouge, LA: Louisiana State University, 1988); Richard V. Pierard and Robert D. Linder, *Civil Religion and the Presidency* (Grand Rapids, MI: Academie Books, 1988); Aaron Wildavsky, *The Beleaguered Presidency* (New Brunswick, NJ: Transatlantic Publishers, 1991); Mark J. Rozell, *The Press and the Carter Presidency* (Boulder, CO: Westview Press, 1989); Charles O. Jones, "Carter and Congress: From the Outside In," *British Journal of Political Science* vol. 15 (July 1985). Other scholars have also advocated a similar, positive reassessment of Carter's presidency. A number of historians have argued that Carter was a sound leader and that his emphasis on human rights was a strong, rational response rather than a naïve or simplistic one to the world affairs of his day. See Robert A. Strong, *Working in the World: Jimmy Carter and the Making of American Foreign Policy* (Baton Rouge, LA: Louisiana State University Press, 2000); David F. Schmitz and Vanessa Walker, "Jimmy Carter and the Foreign Policy of Human Rights: The Development

of a Post-Cold War Foreign Policy," *Diplomatic History* vol. 28, no. 1 (January 2004), 113–43; and Douglas Brinkley, "The Rising Stock of Jimmy Carter: The 'Hands on' Legacy of our Thirty-Ninth President," *Diplomatic History* vol. 20, no. 4 (Fall 1996), 505–29. Were that it were so. Historian Kenton Clymer shows that the Carter administration had not moved beyond the Cold War and was willing to ignore human rights concerns when geopolitical issues of power were involved; see Kenton Clymer, "Jimmy Carter, Human Rights, and Cambodia," *Diplomatic History* vol. 27, no. 2 (April 2003), 245–78. Burton I. Kaufman has rejected the trustee view in a broad study of the Carter's four years in the White House: "I am persuaded … that the earlier critics of his administration were justified in giving the president mediocre marks – and largely for the reasons they cited." Kaufman also rejected the arguments of the trustee revisionists. "I find that the people who have called for a fresh look at the Carter presidency have too easily passed over the elemental fact that, for better or worse, there is a political process in any system of representative government, which no leader can simply ignore on the basis of being above the fray, especially one who, like Carter, lacks a political mandate from the voters." Kaufman, though, saves his strongest comments for the actual achievements of this President and his White House staff: "The events of his four years in office projected an image to the American people of a hapless administration in disarray and of a presidency that was increasingly divided, lacking in leadership, ineffective in dealing with Congress, incapable of defending America's honor abroad, and uncertain about its purpose, priorities, and sense of direction." Burton I. Kaufman, *The Presidency of James Earl Carter, Jr.* (Lawrence, KS: University Press of Kansas, 1993), 3. At a conference on the Carter presidency that eventually produced an edited book, William Stueck came to similar conclusions on Carter's handling of foreign policy. See William Stueck, "Placing Jimmy Carter's Foreign Policy," Gary M. Fink and Hugh Davis Graham, eds., *The Carter Presidency: Policy Choices in the Post-New Deal Era* (Lawrence,

KS: University Press of Kansas, 1998), 247. Scott Kaufman argues that Carter's managerial style made his problems in world affairs even worse than they needed be. Scott Kaufman, *Plans Unraveled: The Foreign Policy of the Carter Administration* (DeKalb, IL: Northern Illinois University Press, 2008). It is difficult to disagree with these assessments. This study will show that in the Olympic boycott, Carter failed as a trustee, that his judgment was poor, and that his leadership was ineffective. His "hands on" approach toward leadership was often counterproductive.

46. The end of the Cold War has already generated a good deal of historiographical and political debate about who and what was responsible for ending this confrontation. The candidates for who include Ronald Reagan, Margaret Thatcher, and Mikhail Gorbachev. Geoffrey Smith gives a large amount of credit to the team of Reagan and Thatcher in Geoffrey Smith, *Reagan and Thatcher* (New York: Norton, 1991). Tony Smith believes it was Reagan alone, drawing on American political traditions: Tony Smith, *America's Mission: The United States and the Struggle for Democracy in the Twentieth Century* (Princeton, NJ: Princeton University Press, 1994). Beth A. Fisher agrees, arguing that it was Reagan himself who initiated his policies, but contends that the president changed his foreign policy positions while in office, and that these new views were responsible for ending the Cold War: Beth A. Fisher, *The Reagan Reversal: Foreign Policy and the End of the Cold War* (Columbia, MO: University of Missouri Press, 1997). Peter Schweizer disagrees. He believes Reagan was solely responsible, arguing that "Reagan embraced a vision for dealing with the Soviet Union and ending the Cold War that was remarkably consistent and proved to be decisive" in Peter Schweizer, *Reagan's War: The Epic Story of His Forty-year Struggle and Final Triumph Over Communism* (New York: Anchor Books, 2002), 3. Jack F. Matlock, Jr., a Foreign Service Officer who served on the staff of Reagan's National Security Council and then was the U.S. Ambassador in the Soviet Union, disagrees. "It really was not so simple." It was a combination of Reagan putting

pressure on the Soviet Union and Mikhail Gorbachev pursuing reform that ended the Cold War before Regan left office. Jack F. Matlock, Jr., *Reagan and Gorbachev: How the Cold War Ended* (New York: Random House, 2005). While Raymond L. Garthoff believes that the United States was primarily responsible for the death of détente, an argument similar to the one this study on the boycott advances, he does not believe the "hanging tough" policies of Reagan and Thatcher helped end this confrontation. He contends instead that it was due mostly to internal Soviet politics. He makes this argument in Raymond L. Garthoff, *Détente and Confrontation: American-Soviet Relations from Nixon to Reagan*, revised edition (Washington, DC: Brookings Institution, 1994); Raymond L. Garthoff, *The Great Transformation: American-Soviet Relations and the End of the Cold War* (Washington, DC: Brookings Institution, 1994). Don Oberdorfer provides a narrative of this era, stressing the importance of personalities in Don Oberdorfer, *The Turn: From the Cold War to a New Era* (New York: Poseidon Press, 1991); and Don Oberdorfer, *From the Cold War to a New Era: The United States and the Soviet Union, 1983–1991* (Baltimore, MD: Johns Hopkins University Press, 1998). John Lewis Gaddis offers a truly international perspective, giving Reagan, Thatcher, and Pope John Paul II credit for addressing ideas as well as policies. He has also argued that the death of détente was necessary to bring about the end of the Cold War in John Lewis Gaddis, *The Cold War: A New History* (New York: Penguin, 2005); but also see John Lewis Gaddis, *The United States and the End of the Cold War: Implications, Reconsiderations, Provocations* (New York: Oxford University Press, 1994). Scholars using Russian-language documents have confirmed some of these interpretations but have also given more agency – for better or worse – to Soviet officials. Vladislav M. Zubok argues that personality and ideology in both Washington and Moscow played significant roles in shaping the course of the Cold War, incuding its end. During the 1970s, when Soviet power began to fade, bureaucratic interia and factional politics had their say in Moscow as well. Vladislav M. Zubok, *A Failed Empire: The*

Soviet Union in the Cold War from Stalin to Gorbachev (Chapel Hill, NC: University of North Carolina Press, 2007). Norman Friedman examines the strategy of the Cold War, treating the U.S.-Soviet contrtation as World War III that ebbed and flowed. He argues that détente made certain parts of Europe vulnerable during a period of U.S. retrenchment, but ultimately American technology and Ronald Reagan intervened at a time when Soviet power was fading. Norman Friedman, *The Fifty Year War: Conflict and Strategy in the Cold War* (Annapolis, MD: Naval Institute Press, 2000). Melvyn P. Leffler comes to similar conclusions in his study. He believes there were five key moments when the Cold War turned. One of these was the late 1970s, when détente ended. He argues that forces such as bureaucracies and uncooperative allies often worked against the policies that statesmen wanted to pursue, or forced them into decisions they did not want to make. One of these was Brezhnev's authorization of the invasion of Afghanistan, which, he argues, killed détente, a policy that was close to the Soviet leader's heart. This assessment, though, ignores Carter's culpability in bringing about the same result, which he also wanted to avoid. Melvyn P. Leffler, *For the Soul of Mankind: The United States, the Soviet Union, and the Cold War* (New York: Hill and Wang, 2007). In a book on interventions in the Third World during the Cold War, Odd Arne Westad argues that the Soviet invasion reflected ideologies inherent in the politics of the Soviet Union. In Afghanistan, the Soviets were compelled to prove the universality of their ideology when it came into conflict with political Islam. He also makes the same claim of the United States in other places and places more responsibility on Americans for the death of détente that most other writers do. Odd Arne Westad, *The Global Cold War: Third World Interventions and the Making of Our Times* (New York: Cambridge University Press, 2005).

1. Lord Killanin and the Politics of the Olympics

1. Killanin, *My Olympic Years*, 4–5, 9; Alfred Erich Senn, *Power, Politics, and the Olympic*

Games (Champaign, IL: Human Kinetics, 1999), 21.

2. Killanin, *My Olympic Years*, 4–5, 9; Senn, *Power, Politics, and the Olympic Games*, 21.

3. Senn, *Power, Politics, and the Olympic Games*, 8; Christopher R. Hill, *Olympic Politics* (Manchester, England: Manchester University Press, 1992), 36; Hulme, *Political Olympics*, 2.

4. Richard W. Pound, *Inside the Olympics: A Behind-the-Scenes Look at the Politics, the Scandals, and the Glory of the Games* (Etobicoke, Ontario: J. Wiley & Sons Canada, 2004), 42.

5. Senn, *Power, Politics, and the Olympic Games*, 8–11.

6. Allen Guttmann, *The Olympics: A History of the Modern Games* 2nd edition (Urbana: University of Illinois Press, 2002), 8, 10, 11, 16; Senn, *Power, Politics, and the Olympic Games*, 33.

7. Senn, *Power, Politics, and the Olympic Games*, 28; Hill, *Olympic Politics*, 71.

8. Senn, *Power, Politics, and the Olympic Games*, 28–30; Hill, *Olympic Politics*, 52; Geoffrey Miller, *Behind the Olympic Rings* (Lynn, MA: H.O. Zimman, 1979), 82.

9. Senn, *Power, Politics, and the Olympic Games*, 22, 30; Guttmann, *The Olympics*, 19–20.

10. Senn, *Power, Politics, and the Olympic Games*, 45; Guttmann, *The Olympics*, 37–8.

11. Guttmann, *The Olympics*, 39

12. Senn, *Power, Politics, and the Olympic Games*, 37–45.

13. Guttmann, *The Olympics*, 60–9.

14. Guttmann, *The Olympics*, 60–9; *The Washington Post*, January 22, 1980.

15. Guttmann, *The Olympics*, 60–9.

16. *The Washington Post*, January 22, 1980; *Congressional Record*, January 22 and 24, 1980, vol. 126, part 1, 59 and 578; U.S. House of Representatives. Committee on Foreign Relations, *U.S. Participation in the 1980 Summer Olympic Games: Hearings and Markup Before the Committee on Foreign Relations* January 23 and February 4, 1980, 96th Congress, Second Session. (Washington, D.C.: Government Printing Office, 1980), 12.

17. *The Washington Post*, January 22, 1980; *Congressional Record*, January 22 and 24, 1980, vol. 126, part 1, 59 and 578; U.S. House of Representatives. Committee on Foreign Relations, *U.S. Participation in the 1980 Summer Olympic Games*, 12.

18. Guttmann, *The Olympics*, 73–5.

19. Guttmann, *The Olympics*, 76–8; Senn, *Power, Politics, and the Olympic Games*, 99.

20. Barbara J. Keys, *Globalizing Sport: National Rivalry and International Community in the 1930s* (Cambridge: Harvard University Press, 2006), 159.

21. Guttmann, *The Olympics*, 85–7.

22. Guttmann, *The Olympics*, 78, 88–9; Senn, *Power, Politics, and the Olympic Games*, 94–5.

23. Guttmann, *The Olympics*, 97; Senn, *Power, Politics, and the Olympic Games*, 90, 103.

24. Allen Guttmann, *The Games Must Go On: Avery Brundage and the Olympic Movement* (New York: Columbia University Press, 1984), 151–5; Senn, *Power, Politics, and the Olympic Games*, 105, 119.

25. Senn, *Power, Politics, and the Olympic Games*, 127; Guttmann, *The Olympics*, 95, 96.

26. Guttmann, *The Games Must Go On*, 142–50; Guttmann, *The Olympics*, 90–3.

27. Guttmann, *The Games Must Go On*, 142–50; Guttmann, *The Olympics*, 90–3.

28. Guttmann, *The Olympics*, 93–4.

29. Senn, *Power, Politics, and the Olympic Games*, 128–33.

30. Richard Espy, *The Politics of the Olympic Games* (Berkeley: University of California Press, 1979), 147–55.

31. Clive Gammon, "Lord of the Games," *Sports Illustrated*, February 9, 1976, 67; Vincent Browne and John Rodda, "Killanin in the Eye of the Storm," *Magill*, February, 1980, 44.

32. Gammon, "Lord of the Games," 67; Browne and Rodda, "Killanin in the Eye of the Storm," 44; Transcript of "Lord Killanin Being Interview by John Greenslade of BBC Overseas on Thursday 10th April [1980], Folder Identification 8047, Folder 0070948, Interview Files, Papers of Lord Killanin, Samarch Olympic Studies Centre, Olympic Museum, Lausanne, Switzerland.

33. Killanin, *My Olympic Years*, 174; Gammon, "Lord of the Games," 67; Transcript of "Lord Killanin Being Interview by John Greenslade of BBC Overseas on Thursday 10th April [1980], Folder Identification 8047, Folder 0070948, Interview Files, Papers of Lord Killanin, Samarach Olympic Studies Centre, Olympic Museum, Lausanne, Switzerland. [Spelling, punctuation, and capitalization errors in the transcript

corrected by the author without any indication in the text.]

34. Gammon, "Lord of the Games," 67; Transcript of "Lord Killanin Being Interview by John Greenslade of BBC Overseas on Thursday 10th April [1980], Folder Identification 8047, Folder 0070948, Interview Files, Papers of Lord Killanin, Samarach Olympic Studies Centre, Olympic Museum, Lausanne, Switzerland. [Spelling, punctuation, and capitalization errors in the transcript corrected by the author without any indication in the text.]

35. Browne and Rodda, "Killanin in the Eye of the Storm," 44; Transcript of "Lord Killanin Being Interview by John Greenslade of BBC Overseas on Thursday 10th April [1980], Folder Identification 8047, Folder 0070948, Interview Files, Papers of Lord Killanin, Samarach Olympic Studies Centre, Olympic Museum, Lausanne, Switzerland.

36. Gammon, "Lord of the Games," 69.

37. "Speech Give as Honorary Life President of the IOC at the XIth Olympic Congress in Baden-Baden," September 24, 1981, Lord Killanin, Lord Killanin's Speeches From 1972 to 1981 (Lausanne, Switzerland: Comité International Olympique, 1985), 120; Browne and Rodda, "Killanin in the Eye of the Storm," 44.

38. "Lord Killanin…Five Years of presidency and China," Olympic Review, September 1977, page 537; "Speech Given as Honorary Life President of the IOC at the XIth Olympic Congress in Baden-Baden," September 24, 1981, Lord Killanin's Speeches From 1972 to 1981, 121.

39. Guttmann, The Olympics, 142; Gammon, "Lord of the Games," 70.

40. "Speech Given as Honorary Life President of the IOC at the XIth Olympic Congress in Baden-Baden," September 24, 1981, Lord Killanin's Speeches From 1972 to 1981, 123; "Lord Killanin…Five Years of presidency and China," Olympic Review, September 1977, 537; Killanin, My Olympic Years, 223–4.

41. David Miller, Olympic Revolution: The Biography of Juan Antonio Samaranch (London: Pavilion, 1992), 33; Pound, Inside the Olympics, 230.

42. Gammon, "Lord of the Games," 67; Miller, Behind the Olympic Rings, 183.

43. Miller, Olympic Revolution, 11–12, 43–4; Guttmann, The Olympics, 156; Pound, Inside the Olympics, 233; Peter Ueberroth with Richard Levin and Amy Quinn, Made in America: His Own Story New York: William Morrow, 1985), 61.

44. James Worrall, My Olympic Journey: Sixty Years with Canadian Sport and the Olympic Games (Toronto: Canadian Olympic Association, 2000), 142; Browne and Rodda, "Killanin in the Eye of the Storm," 45; John Rodda, "Lord Killanin," Olympic Review, June-July, 1999, 82–3; Guttmann, The Olympics, 143–4; Artur Takač, Šezdeset Olimpijskih Godina [Sixty Olympic Years] (Novi Sad, Serbia: Prometej, 1999), 276.

45. Miller, Behind the Olympic Rings, 84–8, 169; Espy, Politics of the Olympic Games, 151–5; Takač, Olimpijskih Godina [Sixty Olympic Years], 283–4.

46. Guttmann, The Olympics, 133–6, 145–6; Miller, Behind the Olympic Rings, 89–93; Espy, Politics of the Olympic Games, 157–8.

47. Miller, Behind the Olympic Rings, 94–5, 187–8.

48. Miller, Behind the Olympic Rings, 188; "Lord Killanin…Five Years of presidency and China," Olympic Review, September 1977, 538.

49. "Speech Made at the Opening of the Meeting of the Intergovernmental Committee for Physical Education and Sport at UNESCO House, Paris, France," June 5, 1979, Lord Killanin's Speeches From 1972 to 1981, 99; Senn, Power, Politics, and the Olympic Games, 174.

2. Los Angeles versus Moscow

1. "Status of Los Angeles' Bid for 1976 Olympic Games," no date, enclosure to Rood to Haldeman, January 13, 1970, Folder 1976 Olympic Games, Box 170, Alpha Subject Files, Papers of H.R. Haldeman, Staff Member and Office Files, White House Special Files, NPP, NACP; Nixon to John B. Kilroy, June 20, 1969 and Reagan Statement in Los Angles '76 Bid Book, Call Number: MA 6901 721 Los, Library, Samarach Olympic Studies Centre, Olympic Museum, Lausanne, Switzerland.

2. Kilroy to Dent, January 9, 1970, Folder [EX] RE 14 Olympic Games, Box 8,

Recreation-Sports Files, Subject Files, White House Central Files; Rood to Haldeman, January 13, 1970 and enclosure "Status of Los Angeles' Bid for 1976 Olympic Games," no date, Folder 1976 Olympic Games, Box 170, Alpha Subject Files, Papers of H.R. Haldeman, Staff Member and Office Files, White House Special Files, NPP, NACP.

3. Kilroy to Dent, January 9, 1970, Folder [EX] RE 14 Olympic Games, Box 8, Recreation-Sports Files, Subject Files, White House Central Files; Rood to Haldeman, February 6, 1970; Kilroy to Sonnenfeldt, February 4, 1970, Folder 1976 Olympic Games, Box 170, Alpha Subject Files, Papers of H.R. Haldeman, Staff Member and Office Files, White House Special Files, NPP, NACP.

4. Wilkinson to Ehrlichman, February 3, 1970, Folder [EX] RE 14 Olympic Games, Box 8, Recreation-Sports Files, Subject Files, White House Central Files, NPP, NACP.

5. Rood to Haldeman, January 13, 1970 and enclosure "Status of Los Angeles' Bid for 1976 Olympic Games," no date, Folder 1976 Olympic Games, Box 170, Alpha Subject Files, Papers of H.R. Haldeman, Staff Member and Office Files, White House Special Files, NPP, NACP.

6. Emphasis in the original. Sonnenfeldt to Higby, February 13, 1970; Higby to Haldeman, February 27, 1970; Haldeman to Stuart, March 2, 1970, Folder 1976 Olympic Games, Box 170, Alpha Subject Files, Papers of H.R. Haldeman, Staff Member and Office Files, White House Special Files, NPP, NACP.

7. Emphasis in the original. Sonnenfeldt to Higby, February 13, 1970; Higby to Haldeman, February 27, 1970; Haldeman to Stuart, March 2, 1970, Folder 1976 Olympic Games, Box 170, Alpha Subject Files, Papers of H.R. Haldeman, Staff Member and Office Files, White House Special Files, NPP, NACP.

8. Emphasis in the original. Haldeman to Kissinger, March 4, 1970, Folder 1976 Olympic Games, Box 170, Alpha Subject Files, Papers of H.R. Haldeman, Staff Member and Office Files, White House Special Files, NPP, NACP.

9. Nixon to IOC members, no date, Folder: Games of the XXI Olympiad 1976 Bid Los Angeles, Calif. (1970–1971), Box 194, Papers of Avery Brundage, University of Illinois at Urbana-Champaign.

10. Stuart Memorandum for File, March 20, 1970; Haig to Eliot, March 25, 1970; Haldeman to Stuart, March 17, 1970; Stuart to Haldeman, April 29, 1970, Folder 1976 Olympic Games, Box 170, Alpha Subject Files, Papers of H.R. Haldeman, Staff Member and Office Files, White House Special Files, NPP, NACP.

11. Killanin, *My Olympic Years*, 4–5, 9.

12. Stuart to Haldeman, April 29, 1970; Stuart to Haldeman, March 18, 1970; Trent to Higby, March 3, 1970, Folder 1976 Olympic Games, Box 170, Alpha Subject Files, Papers of H.R. Haldeman, Staff Member and Office Files, White House Special Files; Ehrlichman to Kissinger, February 6, 1970; Haig to Kissinger, February 16, 1970; Kissinger to Ehrlichman, February 22, 1970, Folder [EX] RE 14 Olympic Games, Box 8, Recreation-Sports Files, Subject Files, White House Central Files, NPP, NACP.

13. Stuart to Haldeman, April 29, 1970; Stuart to Haldeman, March 18, 1970; Trent to Higby, March 3, 1970, Folder 1976 Olympic Games, Box 170, Alpha Subject Files, Papers of H.R. Haldeman, Staff Member and Office Files, White House Special Files; Ehrlichman to Kissinger, February 6, 1970; Haig to Kissinger, February 16, 1970; Kissinger to Ehrlichman, February 22, 1970, Folder [EX] RE 14 Olympic Games, Box 8, Recreation-Sports Files, Subject Files, White House Central Files, NPP, NACP.

14. Stuart to Haldeman, March 18, 1970; Stuart to Haldeman, April 29, 1970, Folder 1976 Olympic Games, Box 170, Alpha Subject Files, Papers of H.R. Haldeman, Staff Member and Office Files, White House Special Files; Eliot to Kissinger, May 14, 1970, Folder [EX] RE 14 Olympic Games, Box 8, Recreation-Sports Files, Subject Files, White House Central Files, NPP, NACP.

15. Stuart to Haldeman, April 29, 1970, Folder 1976 Olympic Games, Box 170, Alpha Subject Files, Papers of H.R. Haldeman, Staff Member and Office Files, White House Special Files, NPP, NACP.

16. Guttmann, *The Games Must Go On*.

17. On the views of the Los Angeles group and the relationship of Brundage with their bid, see Kilroy to Brundage, December 10, 1969; Brundage to Kilroy, December 17, 1969; "Status and Needs of the Los

Angeles 1976 Olympic Committee versus the Bid of Moscow for the XXIst Summer Olympiad, no date, Folder: Games of the XXI Olympiad 1976 Bid Los Angeles, Calif. (1968–1969); Kilroy to Brundage, January 2, 1970; Brundage to Kilroy, July 10, 1970; W. H. Nicholas to Brundage, June 30, 1970; Brundage to Nicholas, July 3, 1970, Folder: Games of the XXI Olympiad 1976 Bid Los Angeles, Calif. (1970–1971), Box 194, Papers of Avery Brundage, University of Illinois at Urbana-Champaign.

18. Kilroy to Brundage, December 10, 1969; Brundage to Kilroy, December 17, 1969; "Status and Needs of the Los Angeles 1976 Olympic Committee versus the Bid of Moscow for the XXIst Summer Olympiad, no date, Folder: Games of the XXI Olympiad 1976 Bid Los Angeles, Calif. (1968–1969); Kilroy to Brundage, January 2, 1970; Brundage to Kilroy, July 10, 1970; W. H. Nicholas to Brundage, June 30, 1970; Brundage to Nicholas, July 3, 1970, Folder: Games of the XXI Olympiad 1976 Bid Los Angeles, Calif. (1970–1971), Box 194, Papers of Avery Brundage, University of Illinois at Urbana-Champaign

19. Stuart to Haldeman, April 29, 1970, Folder 1976 Olympic Games, Box 170, Alpha Subject Files, Papers of H.R. Haldeman, Staff Member and Office Files, White House Special Files, NPP, NACP. There is only one letter from Nixon in the head of state file and a letter from the President to all IOC members in the file on Los Angeles: Nixon to Brundage, January 31, 1970, Folder: Heads of State – U.S.A., Box 332, Important Letters: Heads of State, 1931–1970 File; Nixon to IOC members, no date, Folder: Games of the XXI Olympiad 1976 Bid Los Angeles, Calif. (1970–1971), Box 194, Papers of Avery Brundage, University of Illinois at Urbana-Champaign. Guttmann, *The Games Must Go On.*

20. Kilroy to Sonnenfeldt, February 4, 1970; Stuart to Haldeman, April 29, 1970, Folder 1976 Olympic Games, Box 170, Alpha Subject Files, Papers of H.R. Haldeman, Staff Member and Office Files, White House Special Files, NPP, NACP.

21. Kilroy to Sonnenfeldt, February 4, 1970; Stuart to Haldeman, April 29, 1970, Folder 1976 Olympic Games, Box 170, Alpha Subject Files, Papers of H.R. Haldeman,

Staff Member and Office Files, White House Special Files, NPP, NACP.

22. *The New York Times*, May 13, 1970; Minutes of the 69th Session of the International Olympic Committee, May 12–16, 1970, pages 12–14, IOC Historical Archives, Samaranch Olympic Studies Centre, Olympic Museum, Lausanne, Switzerland.

23. Stuart to Haldeman, March 18, 1970; Stuart to Haldeman, April 29, 1970, Folder 1976 Olympic Games, Box 170, Alpha Subject Files, Papers of H.R. Haldeman, Staff Member and Office Files, White House Special Files; Eliot to Kissinger, May 14, 1970, Folder [EX] RE 14 Olympic Games, Box 8, Recreation-Sports Files, Subject Files, White House Central Files, NPP, NACP; *The New York Times*, May 13, 1970.

24. Fernand Landry and Magdeleine Yerlès, *International Olympic Committee – One Hundred Years: The Idea – The Presidents – The Achievements*, vol. 3, *the Presidencies of Lord Killanin (1972–1980) and of Juan Antonio Samaranch (1980-)* (Lausanne, Switzerland: International Olympic Committee, 1994), 80–4; Killanin, *My Olympic Years*, 4–5, 9; Minutes of the 69th Session of the International Olympic Committee, May 12–16, 1970, pages 12–14, IOC Historical Archives, Samaranch Olympic Studies Centre, Olympic Museum, Lausanne, Switzerland.

25. Landry and Yerlès, *International Olympic Committee – One Hundred Years*, 80–4; Killanin, *My Olympic Years*, 4–5, 9; Minutes of the 69th Session of the International Olympic Committee, May 12–16, 1970, pages 12–14, IOC Historical Archives, Samaranch Olympic Studies Centre, Olympic Museum, Lausanne, Switzerland.

26. Worrall, *My Olympic Journey*, 115.

27. *The New York Times*, May 13, 1970.

28. *The New York Times*, May 13, 1970; Worrall, *My Olympic Journey*, 115–16; Minutes of the 69th Session of the International Olympic Committee, May 12–16, 1970, pages 14–16, IOC Historical Archives, Samaranch Olympic Studies Centre, Olympic Museum, Lausanne, Switzerland.

29. Fell to Nixon, December 4, 1973; Harrigan to Cole, January 22, 1974; Nixon to Killanin, February 13, 1974, Folder [EX] RE 14 Olympic Games 1/1/73, Box 8, Recreation-Sports

Files, Subject Files, White House Central Files, NPP, NACP.

30. Minutes of the 75th Session of the International Olympic Committee, October 21–24, 1974, 7–11, IOC Historical Archives, Samaranch Olympic Studies Centre, Olympic Museum, Lausanne, Switzerland.

31. Minutes of the 75th Session of the International Olympic Committee, October 21–24, 1974, 7–11, IOC Historical Archives, Samaranch Olympic Studies Centre, Olympic Museum, Lausanne, Switzerland.

32. Killanin, *My Olympic Years*, 173, 4. There are significant differences between the American and British versions of Killanin's book. The introduction in the U.S. edition is shorter, with many bitter paragraphs about the Moscow Olympics and the boycott missing. The information in this section of this article comes from both versions, and from the Minutes of the 75th Session of the International Olympic Committee, October 21–24, 1974, pages 7–11, IOC Historical Archives, Samaranch Olympic Studies Centre, Olympic Museum, Lausanne, Switzerland.

33. "Lord Killanin … Five Years of presidency and China," *Olympic Review*, September 1977, 538.

34. *The New York Times*, July 21, 1976; "A U.S. Boycott of the Moscow Olympics," *U.S. News and World Report*, August 28, 1978, 33; *Congressional Record*, January 24, 1980, vol. 126, part 1, 575.

35. Resolution in Follows to Thatcher, March 7, 1980, Moscow Olympic Files, British Olympic Association Archives, London, England.

36. Stephen R. Wenn, "A Turning Point for IOC Television Policy: U.S. Television Rights Negotiations and the 1980 Lake Placid and Moscow Olympic Festivals," *Journal of Sport History* vol. 25, no. 1 (Spring 1998), 87–117.

37. "The Moscow Game Plan," *National Review*, August 12, 1977, 113.

38. Landry and Yerlès, *International Olympic Committee- One Hundred Years*, 80–4; Killanin, *My Olympic Years*, 224–5; Richard Perelman, editor, *Official Report of the Games of the XXIIIrd Olympiad Los Angeles, 1984*, vol. 1, *Organization and Planning* (Los Angeles: Los Angeles Olympic Organizing Committee, 1985), 8–12.

39. Perelman, *Official Report*, 12.

3. Jimmy Carter and U.S.-Soviet Relations

1. Jimmy Carter, *An Hour Before Daylight: Memories of a Rural Boyhood* (New York: Simon & Schuster, 2001), 15, 17; Kenneth E. Morris, *Jimmy Carter: American Moralist* (Athens: University of Georgia Press, 1996), 52.

2. Carter, *An Hour Before Midnight*, 255–6; Morris, *American Moralist*, 94.

3. Morris, *American Moralist*, 95, 100–1.

4. Morris, *American Moralist*, 95, 106–13.

5. Morris, *American Moralist*, 95, 106–13.

6. Morris, *American Moralist*, 95, 115–17; Jimmy Carter, *Turning Point: A Candidate, a State, and a Nation Come of Age* (New York: Times Books, 1992), 21–3.

7. Carter, *Turning Point*, xxiii, 72, 165, 179, 182–3; Morris, *American Moralist*, 133–40.

8. Morris, *American Moralist*, 141–2.

9. Morris, *American Moralist*, 141.

10. Peter G. Bourne, *Jimmy Carter: A Comprehensive Biography from Plains to Post-Presidency* (New York: Scribner, 1997), 179; Morris, *American Moralist*, 142–3.

11. Bourne, *Jimmy Carter*, 164–5; Morris, *American Moralist*, 144–5.

12. Morris, *American Moralist*, 183–4.

13. Morris, *American Moralist*, 138, 188–9.

14. Morris, *American Moralist*, 182–4, 187.

15. Morris, *American Moralist*, 188.

16. Morris, *American Moralist*, 198.

17. Morris, *American Moralist*, 197.

18. Jules Witcover, *Marathon: The Pursuit of the Presidency, 1972–1976* (New York: Viking Press, 1977), 168, 176–7, 255–64, 297, 313–16, 643; Morris, *American Moralist*, 201, 223–9.

19. Witcover, *Marathon*, 644–5.

20. Cyrus Vance, *Hard Choices: Critical Years in America's Foreign Policy* (New York: Simon and Schuster, 1983), 31.

21. John Lewis Gaddis, *Russia, the Soviet Union and the United States: An Interpretive History* second edition (New York: McGraw Hill, 1990), 296.

22. "Lord Killanin … Five Years of presidency and China," *Olympic Review*, September 1977, 538.

23. Anatoliy Dobrynin, *In Confidence: Moscow's Ambassador to America's Six Cold War Presidents (1962–1986)* (New York: Random House, 1995), 470–1; Andrei Gromyko, *Memories* Translated by Harold Shukman (New York: Doubleday, 1989), 292.

24. Leffler, *For the Soul of Mankind*, 267–8, 270.

25. Helmut Schmidt, *Menschen und Mächte* [Men and Powers] (Berlin: Wolf Jobst Siedler Verlag GmbH, 1987), 222, 224.
26. Zubok, *Failed Empire*, 230–2, 234, 241–2, 247.
27. Nicholas Cull, *The Cold War and the United States Information Agency: American Propaganda and Public Diplomacy, 1945–1989* (New York: Cambridge University Press, 2008), 360–98.
28. Gaddis, *Russia, the Soviet Union, and the United States*, 298–9; Zbigniew Brzezinski, *Power and Principle: Memoirs of the National Security Advisor, 1977–1981* (New York: Farrar, Straus, Giroux, 1983), 43.
29. Gaddis, *Russia, the Soviet Union, and the United States*, 298–99; Brzezinski, *Power and Principle*, 43.
30. Gromyko, *Memoirs*, 294; Vance, *Hard Choices*, 36–44.
31. Brzezinski, *Power and Principle*, 42; Vance, *Hard Choices*, 36–44.
32. Gaddis, *Russia, the Soviet Union, and the United States*, 301; Gromyko, *Memoirs*, 289.
33. Valéry Giscard d'Estaing, *Le Pouvoir et la Vie: Choisir* [Capacity and Life: To Choose] (Paris: Compagnie 12: 2006), 132
34. Brzezinski, *Power and Principle*, 145.
35. Gromyko, *Memoirs*, 288.
36. *The Washington Post*, June 8, 1978; Vance, *Hard Choices*, 102; Brzezinski, *Power and Principle*, 320–1.
37. Giscard d'Estaing, *Le Pouvoir et la Vie*, 133
38. Gaddis, *Russia, the Soviet Union, and the United States*, 295–305
39. Gaddis, *Russia, the Soviet Union, and the United States*, 295–305
40. Gaddis, *Russia, the Soviet Union, and the United States*, 295–305; Leffler, *For the Soul of Mankind*, 317.
41. Gaddis, *Russia, the Soviet Union, and the United States*, 308; Vance, *Hard Choices*, 358–64; Brzezinski, *Power and Principle*, 346–52; Jean A. Garrison, *Games Advisors Play: Foreign Policy in the Nixon and Carter Administrations* (College Station: Texas A&M University Press, 1999), 114–17.
42. Dobrynin, *In Confidence*, 476.

4. The Soviet Invasion of Afghanistan

1. Georgi Arbatov, *The System: An Insider's Life in Soviet Politics* (New York: Random House, 1992), 197.
2. Zubok, *Failed Empire*, 246; Arbatov, *The System*, 193–4; Concerning the Situation in "A," December 12, 1979, in "Documentation," *Cold War International History Project Bulletin* Issue 4 (Fall 1994), 76.
3. Dobrynin, *In Confidence*, 436–40.
4. Odd Arne Westad, *The Global Cold War: Third World Interventions and the Making of Our Times* (New York: Cambridge University Press, 2005), 314; Personal Memorandum, Andropov to Brezhnev, no date, in "U.S.-Soviet Relations and the Turn Towards Confrontation, 1977–1980 – New Russian & East German Documents," *Cold War International History Project Bulletin* Issues 8–9 (Winter 1996/1997), 159.
5. Westad, *The Global Cold War*, 316; William Maley, *The Afghanistan Wars* (New York: Palgrave Macmillan, 2002), 35–6; Andropov-Gromyko-Ustinov-Ponomarev Report on Events in Afghanistan on 27–28 December, 31 December 1979, in "U.S.-Soviet Relations and the Turn Towards Confrontation, 1977–1980 – New Russian & East German Documents," *Cold War International History Project Bulletin* Issues 8–9 (Winter 1996/1997), 160–1.
6. Zubok, *Failed Empire*, 262–3; Meeting of the Politburo of the Central Committee of the Communist Party of the Soviet Union, March 17, 1979 in Odd Arne Westad, editor, *The Fall of Détente: Soviet-American Relations during the Carter Years* (Boston: Scandinavian University Press, 1997), 287–310.
7. Zubok, *Failed Empire*, 227.
8. Aleksandr Antonovich Lyakhovskiy, *Inside the Invasion of Afghanistan and the Seizure of Kabul, December 1979*, Gary Goldberg and Artemy Kalinovsky translators Cold War International History Project Working Paper 51 (January 2007), 37; Maley, *Afghanistan Wars*, 35–36; Andropov-Gromyko-Ustinov-Ponomarev Report on Events in Afghanistan on 27–28 December, 31 December 1979, in "U.S.-Soviet Relations and the Turn Towards Confrontation," 160–1.
9. M. Hassan Kakar, *Afghanistan: The Soviet Invasion and the Afghan Response, 1979–1982* (Berkeley and Los Angeles: University of California Press, 1995), 45.
10. The Russian General Staff, *The Soviet-Afghan War: How a Superpower Fought and Lost* Translated and edited by Lester W. Grau and Michael A. Gress (Lawrence: University

Press of Kansas, 2002), 11, 15, 17; Maley, *Afghanistan Wars*, 43.

11. Anna Heinämaa, Maija Leppänen, and Yuri Yurchenko, *The Soldiers' Story: Soviet Veterans Remember the Afghan War* Translated by A.D. Haun. (Berkeley: International and Area Studies, University of California at Berkeley, 1994), 1; *Soviet-Afghan War*, 18; Lyakhovskiy, *Inside the Invasion of Afghanistan*, 39–40.

12. Lester W. Grau, "The Takedown of Kabul: An Effective Coup de Main," in William G. Robertson and Lawrence A. Yates, editors, *Block by Block: The Challenge of Urban Operations* (Fort Leavenworth, Kansas: U.S. Army Command and General Staff College Press, 2003), 302; Lyakhovskiy, *Inside the Invasion of Afghanistan*, 36.

13. Heinämaa, Leppänen, and Yurchenko, *Soldiers' Story*, 2; *Soviet-Afghan War*, 18; Lyakhovskiy, *Inside the Invasion of Afghanistan*, 44, 46.

14. Grau, "The Takedown of Kabul," 296–9, 303–12; Lyakhovskiy, *Inside the Invasion of Afghanistan*, 44, 46.

15. Lyakhovskiy, *Inside the Invasion of Afghanistan*, 52; Grau, "The Takedown of Kabul," 298.

16. Lyakhovskiy, *Inside the Invasion of Afghanistan*, 53–5.

17. Grau, "The Takedown of Kabul," 306–7.

18. Lyakhovskiy, *Inside the Invasion of Afghanistan*, 45.

19. Lyakhovskiy, *Inside the Invasion of Afghanistan*, 56.

20. Lyakhovskiy, *Inside the Invasion of Afghanistan*, 58–9.

21. Lyakhovskiy, *Inside the Invasion of Afghanistan*, 60–1.

22. Lyakhovskiy, *Inside the Invasion of Afghanistan*, 60.

23. Lyakhovskiy, *Inside the Invasion of Afghanistan*, 60.

24. Lyakhovskiy, *Inside the Invasion of Afghanistan*, 61.

25. Lyakhovskiy, *Inside the Invasion of Afghanistan*, 61.

26. Lyakhovskiy, *Inside the Invasion of Afghanistan*, 61.

27. Lyakhovskiy, *Inside the Invasion of Afghanistan*, 52, 62; Grau, "The Takedown of Kabul," 309.

28. Grau, "The Takedown of Kabul," 310–12.

29. Grau, "The Takedown of Kabul," 310–12.

30. *Soviet-Afghan War*, 16–18; Lyakhovskiy, *Inside the Invasion of Afghanistan*, 45.

31. *Soviet-Afghan War*, 18, 23–24; Lyakhovskiy, *Inside the Invasion of Afghanistan*, 39.

32. *Soviet-Afghan War*, 12–13.

33. Kakar, *Afghanistan*, 126; Scott R. McMichael, *Stumbling Bear: Soviet Military Performance in Afghanistan* (London: Brassey's, 1991), 10; *Soviet-Afghan War*, 18, 20, 23, 26.

34. McMichael, *Stumbling Bear*, 10; *Soviet-Afghan War*, 18, 20, 23, 26.

35. Robert F. Baumann, *Russian-Soviet Unconventional Wars in the Caucasus, Central Asia, and Afghanistan* (Combat Studies Institute, U.S. Army Command and General Staff College: Ft. Leavenworth, Kansas, 1993), 136; Mark Galeotti, *Afghanistan: The Soviet Union's Last War* (London: Frank Cass, 1995), 39.

36. *Soviet-Afghan War*, 20–21, 310.

37. *Soviet-Afghan War*, 29–30, 311–12; Haji Sayed Mohammed Hanif, "Defending Surkhab Base Camp," Ali Ahmad Jalali and Lester W. Grau, *The Other Side of the Mountain: Mujahideen Tactics in the Soviet-Afghan War* (Quantico: United States Marine Corps Studies and Analysis Division, 1995), 275.

38. *Soviet-Afghan War*, 29–30, 311–12; Edward Girardet, *Afghanistan: The Soviet War* (New York: St. Martin's Press, 1985), 46.

39. *Soviet-Afghan War*, 29–30, 311–12; Girardet, *Afghanistan*, 46.

40. Maley, *Afghanistan Wars*, 61.

41. *Soviet-Afghan War*, 35, 308–9; Gennady Bocharov, *Russian Roulette: Afghanistan Through Russian Eyes* Translated by Alyona Kojevnikov (New York: HarperCollins, 1990), 9.

42. *Soviet-Afghan War*, 19; Girardet, *Afghanistan*, 16; Maley, *Afghanistan Wars*, 46–7.

43. Lester W. Grau, translator and editor, *The Bear Went Over the Mountain: Soviet Combat Tactics in Afghanistan* (Washington, D.C.: National Defense University Press, 1996), 4–8, 11–13; *Soviet-Afghan War*, 312; Girardet, *Afghanistan*, 42–3; McMichael, *Stumbling Bear*, 16; Baumann, *Russian-Soviet Unconventional Wars*, 153.

44. Baumann, *Russian-Soviet Unconventional Wars*, 141–2, 153.

45. Baumann, *Russian-Soviet Unconventional Wars*, 165.

46. Galeotti, *Afghanistan*, 38; Baumann, *Russian-Soviet Unconventional Wars*, 156.

47. Girardet, *Afghanistan*, 45–47; Heinämaa, Leppänen, and Yurchenko, *Soldiers' Story*, 16.

48. McMichael, *Stumbling Bear*, 8.

49. Kakar, *Afghanistan*, 135–136.

50. Heinämaa, Leppänen, and Yurchenko, *Soldiers' Story*, 2; *Soviet-Afghan War*, 29.

51. Nawaz Khan, Abdul Qudus Alkozai, and Haji M. Siddiqullah, "Taking Alingar District Capital," and Haji Badshah Khan, "Carving Up Regiments on the Approach to Wazi," Jalali and Grau, *The Other Side of the Mountain*, 119–21, 149–51.

52. McMichael, *Stumbling Bear*, 14.

53. *Soviet-Afghan War*, 60–62, 72; McMichael, *Stumbling Bear*, 10.

54. Maley, *Afghanistan Wars*, 42; Gromyko-Andropov-Ustinov-Zagladin Report, April 7, 1980, in "U.S.-Soviet Relations and the Turn Towards Confrontation, 1977–1980 – New Russian & East German Documents," *Cold War International History Project Bulletin* Issues 8–9 (Winter 1996/1997), 170–2.

55. Bocharov, *Russian Roulette*, 15; Heinämaa, Leppänen and Yurchenko, *Soldiers' Story*, 15.

56. Maley, *Afghanistan Wars*, 60–61; Kakar, *Afghanistan*, 126–8.

57. Girardet, *Afghanistan*, 68; *Soviet-Afghan War*, 20.

58. Girardet, *Afghanistan*, 68; Heinämaa, Leppänen and Yurchenko, *Soldiers' Story*, 11.

59. Girardet, *Afghanistan*, 66.

60. Baumann, *Russian-Soviet Unconventional Wars*, 142.

61. Galeotti, *Afghanistan*, 44; Arbatov, *The System*, 209.

5. The American Response

1. Emphasis in the original. Brzezinski to the President, January 3, 1980, Folder: Southwest Asia/Persian Gulf – Afghanistan [1/5/80–10/1/80], Box 17, Geographic File, Papers of Zbigniew Brzezinski, Donated Historical Collections, Jimmy Carter Presidential Library, Atlanta, Georgia.

2. Brzezinski to the President, January 3, 1980, Folder: Southwest Asia/Persian Gulf – Afghanistan [1/5/80–10/1/80], Box 17, Geographic File, Papers of Zbigniew Brzezinski, Donated Historical Collections, Jimmy Carter Presidential Library, Atlanta, Georgia.

3. Jack W. Germond and Jules Witcover, *Blue Smoke and Mirrors: How Reagan Won and Why Carter Lost the Election of 1980* (New York: The Viking Press, 1981), 49, 55; David Farber, *Taken Hostage: The Iran Hostage Crisis and America's First Encounter with Radical Islam* (Princeton: Princeton University Press, 2005), 163–5.

4. Brzezinski to the President, January 3, 1980, Folder: Southwest Asia/Persian Gulf – Afghanistan [1/5/80–10/1/80], Box 17, Geographic File, Papers of Zbigniew Brzezinski, Donated Historical Collections, Jimmy Carter Presidential Library, Atlanta, Georgia.

5. Dobrynin, *In Confidence*, 441–2; Norman Friedman, *The Fifty Year War: Conflict and Strategy in the Cold War* (Annapolis, MD, Naval Institute Press, 2000), 436–7;Zubok, *Failed Empire*, 228.

6. "Afghanistan: Steps in the Framework of US-Soviet Relations attached to Tarnoff to Brzezinski, December 31, 1979, Folder: Southwest Asia/Persian Gulf – Afghanistan [1/5/80–10/1/80], Box 17, Geographic File, Papers of Zbigniew Brzezinski, Donated Historical Collections, Jimmy Carter Presidential Library, Atlanta, Georgia.

7. Carter notation on "Afghanistan: Steps in the Framework of US-Soviet Relations attached to Tarnoff to Brzezinski, December 31, 1979, Folder: Southwest Asia/Persian Gulf – Afghanistan [1/5/80–10/1/80], Box 17, Geographic File, Papers of Zbigniew Brzezinski, Donated Historical Collections, Jimmy Carter Presidential Library, Atlanta, Georgia.

8. Brezhnev to Carter, December 29, 1979, Cold War International History Project located at http://www.wilsoncenter.org/index.cfm?fuseaction=topics.home&topic_id=1409

9. Emphasis in the original. Carter notations on Vance, Memorandum, February 25, 1980, Folder: Southwest Asia/Persian Gulf – Afghanistan [1/5/80–10/1/80], Box 17, Geographic File, Papers of Zbigniew Brzezinski, Donated Historical Collections, Jimmy Carter Presidential Library, Atlanta, Georgia.

10. Schmidt, *Menschen und Mächte* [Men and Powers], 263, 300.

11. Carter, *Keeping Faith*, 481.

12. Ueberroth, *Made in America*, 79; Hulme, *Political Olympics*, 96.

13. Kane and Miller to Carter, January 3, 1980, Folder:Olympics–Memos/Correspondence to President 1–2/80, Box 103, Lloyd Cutler Files, Counsel's Office Files, Staff Office Files, Jimmy Carter Presidential Materials, Jimmy Carter Presidential Library.

14. Carter wrote in abbreviation and these condensed writings have been converted into full words in the text for clarity's sake. His actual handwritten comments are: "Leave min; no > 10 UK, Can – no recog It, FRG, Amb out Fr – no polit contact." Carter's handwritten comments are on Brzezinski to the President, January 3, 1980, Folder: Southwest Asia/Persian Gulf-Afghanistan [12/26/79–1/4/80], Box 17, Geographic File, Papers of Zbigniew Brzezinski, Donated Historical Collections, Jimmy Carter Presidential Library, Atlanta, Georgia.

15. National Security Council Meeting, January 2, 1980 in Odd Arne Westad, *The Fall of Détente: Soviet American Relations during the Carter Years* (Boston: Scandinavian University Press, 1997), 341–2; *The New York Times*, January 2, 1980.

16. National Security Council Meeting, January 2, 1980 in Westad, *The Fall of Détente*, 342–3.

17. Caraccioli and Caraccioli, *Boycott*, 62–3; Carter, *Keeping Faith*, 474.

18. Memorandum for the Vice President, the Secretary of State, the Secretary of Defense, January 2, 1980, Folder: Southwest Asia/Persian Gulf – Afghanistan [12/26/79–1/4/80], Box 17, Geographic File, Papers of Zbigniew Brzezinski, Donated Historical Collections, Jimmy Carter Presidential Library, Atlanta, Georgia.

19. Schmidt, *Menschen und Mächte* [Men and Powers], 244–5. Takač, *Olimpijskih Godina* [Sixty Olympic Years], 304.

20. "Soviet Invasion of Afghanstan," January 4, 1980, *Public Papers of the President: Jimmy Carter, 1980* (Washington, D.C.: U.S. Government Printing Office, 1981) [Hereafter abbreviated as *PPP*], 23–4.

21. Carter, *Keeping Faith*, 475–6.

22. *Newsweek*, January 14, 1980, 24.

23. Emphasis in the original. Carter to Key Advisors, January 9, 1980, Folder: Afghanistan, 1/9–31/80, Box 1, Country File, National Security Advisor Files, Staff Office Files, Jimmy Carter Presidential Materials, Jimmy Carter Presidential Library, Atlanta, Georgia.

24. Dobrynin, *In Confidence*, 434; Robert A.D. Ford, *Our Man in Moscow: A Diplomat's Reflections on the Soviet Union* (Toronto: University of Toronto Press, 1989), 320; Thomas J. Watson, Jr. and Peter Petre, *Father, Son & Co.: My Life at IBM and Beyond* (New York: Bantam Books, 1990), 429; Brement to Brzezinski, February 6, 1980, Folder: Meetings-Vance/Brown/Brzezinski: 1/80–2/80, Box 34, National Security Advisor Files, Staff Office Files, Jimmy Carter Presidential Materials, Jimmy Carter Presidential Library, Atlanta, Georgia.

25. Dobrynin, *In Confidence*, 434; Watson, Jr. and Petre, *Father, Son & Co.*, 429; Brement to Brzezinski, February 6, 1980, Folder: Meetings-Vance/Brown/Brzezinski: 1/80–2/80, Box 34, National Security Advisor Files, Staff Office Files, Jimmy Carter Presidential Materials, Jimmy Carter Presidential Library, Atlanta, Georgia.

26. Watson and Petre, *Father, Son & Co.*, 432–3; Brzezinski, *Power and Principle*, 433; Kaufman, *The Presidency of James Earl Carter, Jr.*, 165; Carter, *Keeping Faith*, 476; Daily Dairy, January 4, 1980, Folder: 1/4/80, Box PD-70, President's Daily Diary, Staff Office Files, Jimmy Carter Presidential Materials Jimmy Carter Presidential Library.

27. Watson and Petre, *Father, Son & Co.*, 432–3.

28. Mikahail Gorbachev, *Memoirs* (New York: Doubleday 1996), 116.

29. Brzezinski to the President, no date, Folder: Olympics 6/79–2/80, Box 48, Subject Files, National Security Advisor Files, Staff Office Files, Jimmy Carter Presidential Materials, Jimmy Carter Presidential Library, Atlanta, Georgia.

30. Lloyd Cutler Exit Interview, March 2, 1981; Brzezinski to the President, no date, Folder: Olympics 6/79–2/80, Box 48, Subject Files, National Security Advisor Files, Staff Office Files, Jimmy Carter Presidential

Materials, Jimmy Carter Presidential Library, Atlanta, Georgia.

31. *The Washington Post*, January 6, 1980; *The New York Times*, January 4, 16, 1980; Ira Berkow, *Red: A Biography of Red Smith* (New York: Times Books, 1986), 252–5; Chorbajian and Mosco, "1976 and 1980 Olympic Boycott Media Coverage: All the News that Fits," 3–28.

32. Turner to the President, January 9, 1980, Folder: Olympics 6/79–2/80, Box 48, Subject Files, National Security Advisor Files, Staff Office Files, Jimmy Carter Presidential Materials, Jimmy Carter Presidential Library, Atlanta, Georgia.

33. Underlining in the original. Brzezinski to the President, no date, Folder: Olympics 6/79–2/80, Box 48, Subject Files, National Security Advisor Files, Staff Office Files, Jimmy Carter Presidential Materials, Jimmy Carter Presidential Library, Atlanta, Georgia.

34. *Los Angeles Times*, January 11, 1980; Brzezinski, *Power and Principle*, 433.

35. *The New York Times*, January 16, 1980; "Moscow '80: An Olympics Under Siege," *Sports Illustrated*, January 21, 1980, 7; Ian Wooldridge, *Sport in the 80's: A Personal View* (London: Centurion Books, 1989), 10–11; Transcript of "BBC World at One," January 14, 1980, Folder Identification 8047, Folder 0070948, Interview Files, Papers of Lord Killanin, Samarach Olympic Studies Centre, Olympic Museum, Lausanne, Switzerland.

36. House Floor Resolution Number 80–120 January 18, 1980 attached to Tilly to Killanin, January 22, 1980, Folder Identification 8366, Folder 0072285, Telex Files, Papers of Lord Killanin, Samarach Olympic Studies Centre, Olympic Museum, Lausanne, Switzerland.

37. *The Washington Star*, January 20, 1980; *Boston Herald American*, January 21, 1980; *The Union Leader* January 18, 1980; *Chicago Tribune*, January 22, 1980; *San Francisco Chronicle*, January 8 and 10, 1980.

38. ABC-News Harris Survey, January 22, 1980, Folder: Olympics – Publications and Pamphlets, 1–4/80, Box 104, Lloyd Cutler Files, Counsel's Office Files, Staff Office Files, Jimmy Carter Presidential Materials; Hodding Carter to The Secretary, January 29, 1980, Folder: RE 15 1/1/80–3/31/80,

Box: RE2, Sports-Recreation Files, Subject Files, White House Central Files, Jimmy Carter Presidential Library.

39. Chorbajian and Mosco, "1976 and 1980 Olympic Boycott Media Coverage: All the News that Fits," 9, 13; *Akron Beacon Journal*, January 3, 1980; *Daily News*, January 20, 1980.

40. *The Washington Star*, January 4 and 18, 1980; *Rocky Mountain News*, January 11, 1980.

41. *The Philadelphia Inquirer*, January 17, 1980.

42. *Arkansas Democrat*, January 16, 1980; *The Wall Street Journal*, January 25, 1980.

43. *The Washington Post*, January 6, 1980.

44. *The Washington Post*, January 15 and 21, 1980; Allan J Mayer with Gloria Borger, Thomas M. DeFrank, Eleanor Clift, William E. Schmidt, Martin Kasindorf and Susan Agrest, "An Olympic Boycott?" *Newsweek*, January 28, 1980, 20.

45. *Cleveland Press*, January 18, 1980.

46. *The Washington Post*, January 17, 1980.

47. *The Boston Globe*, January 11, 1980; *Dallas Times-Herald*, January 15, 1980; *Milwaukee Sentinel*, January 7, 1980; *The Atlanta Journal*, January 4, 1980.

48. *The Washington Post*, January 11 and 24, 1980; Barton, "The American Olympic Boycott of 1980," 90–1, 93, 95, 100.

49. *The Washington Post*, January 11 and 24, 1980; Barton, "The American Olympic Boycott of 1980," 90–1, 93, 95, 100.

50. Margaret Thatcher, *The Downing Street Years* (New York: HarperCollins, 1993), 88; Thatcher to Follows, January 22, 1980, Moscow Olympic Files, British Olympic Association Archives, London, England; Prime Minister telephone conversation with Chancellor Schmidt, January 15, 1980 located in British Cabinet Office Freedom of Information Reading Room Website, Subject Sport and Recreation, Moscow Olympics-11 http://www.cabinetoffice.gov.uk/foi/reading_room/topic/sports.aspx

51. *The Economist*, January 19, 1980, 11; Carrington to British UN Embassy, January 10, 1980; Heseltine to Carrington, January 16, 1980 located in British Cabinet Office Freedom of Information Reading Room Website, Subject Sport and Recreation, Moscow Olympics-11 http://www.cabinetoffice.gov.uk/foi/reading_room/topic/sports.aspx

52. Thatcher to Follows, January 22, 1980, Moscow Olympic Files, British Olympic Association Archives, London, England.

53. Philip Ayers, *Malcolm Fraser: A Biography* (Richmond, Victoria, Australia: Willian Hienemann Australia, 1987), 395; Patrick Weller, *Malcolm Fraser PM: A Study in Prime Ministerial Power* (Ringwood, Victoria, Australia: Penguin, 1989), 344–5; Fraser to Grange, January 22, 1980, Annex 10 to Minutes of the Meeting of the Executive Board, February 8, 9, 12, and 15, 1980, pages 7–9, IOC Historical Archives, Samaranch Olympic Studies Centre, Olympic Museum, Lausanne, Switzerland.

54. Harry Gordon, *Australia and the Olympic Games* (St. Lucia, Australia: University of Queensland Press, 1994), 323.

55. Willi Knecht, *Der Boykott* [The Boycott] (Cologne: Verlag Wissenschaft und Politik, 1980), 39, 44–5, 55, 59–60.

56. Knecht, *Der Boykott*, 60–1, 70, 74.

57. Knecht, *Der Boykott*, 76.

58. Knecht, *Der Boykott*, 79–84.

59. McDonald to Cutler, January 16, 1980, Folder: Olympics – Memos, 1–2/80, Box 102, Lloyd Cutler Files, Counsel's Office Files, Staff Office Files; Notes, January 16, 1980, Folder: #21, Box 12, Steno Pad Chronology File, Papers of Alonzo L. McDonald, Donated Historical Collections; Daily Dairy, January 16, 1980, Folder: 1/16/80, Box PD-70, President's Daily Diary, Staff Office Files, Jimmy Carter Presidential Materials, Jimmy Carter Presidential Library.

60. Carter to Powell, January 17, 1980, Folder: Olympics–Memos/Correspondence to President 1–2/80, Box 103, Lloyd Cutler Files, Counsel's Office Files, Staff Office Files, Jimmy Carter Presidential Materials, Jimmy Carter Presidential Library.

61. Joe Onek Oral History by the Author, June 22, 2007.

62. Cutler and Onek to the President, January 17, 1980, Folder: Olympics – Memos/Correspondence to President 1–2/80, Box 103, Lloyd Cutler Files, Counsel's Office Files, Staff Office Files, Jimmy Carter Presidential Materials, Jimmy Carter Presidential Library.

63. Hamilton Jordan, *Crisis: The Last Year of the Carter Presidency* (New York: G.P. Putnam's Sons, 1982), 112–13.

64. *San Francisco Chronicle*, February 28, 1980; "Not in Mosocw," *Business Week*, February 4, 1980, 124; Pete Axthelm, "Boycott the Olympics," *Newsweek*, January 21, 1980, 63; Howard Cosell with Peter Bonventre, *I Never Played the Game* (New York: William Morrow and Company, 1985), 372–3.

6. Easy Victories

1. "Interview of the President on Meet the Press," January 20, 1980, Folder: Olympics 6/79–2/80, Box 80, Subject Files, National Security Advisor Files, Staff Office Files, Jimmy Carter Presidential Materials, Jimmy Carter Presidential Library, Atlanta, Georgia.

2. "The Olympic Ultimatum," *Sports Illustrated*, January 28, 1980, 7–8; *The Union Leader*, January 24, 1980; other editorials critical of the delay appeared in the *San Francisco Examiner*, January 24, 1980; *The Atlanta Constitution*, January 25, 1980; and *The Boston Globe*, January 25, 1980; Gromyko, *Memoirs*, 291–2; Derick Hulme in his study on the boycott is quite critical of this decision, calling it "premature and inflexible." Hulme, *Political Olympics*, 112–15.

3. "Interview of the President on Meet the Press," January 20, 1980, Folder: Olympics 6/79–2/80, Box 80, Subject Files National Security Advisor Files, Staff Office Files, Jimmy Carter Presidential Materials, Jimmy Carter Presidential Library, Atlanta, Georgia.

4. "Interview of the President on Meet the Press," January 20, 1980, Folder: Olympics 6/79–2/80, Box 80, Subject Files, National Security Advisor Files, Staff Office Files, Jimmy Carter Presidential Materials, Jimmy Carter Presidential Library, Atlanta, Georgia.

5. "Interview of the President on Meet the Press," January 20, 1980, Folder: Olympics 6/79–2/80, Box 80, Subject Files, National Security Advisor Files, Staff Office Files, Jimmy Carter Presidential Materials, Jimmy Carter Presidential Library, Atlanta, Georgia.

6. "Press Briefing with Lloyd Cutler, Counsel to the President and Jody Powell, Press Secretary," January 20, 1980, Folder: Olympics – Press, 5/79–1/80, Box 103, Lloyd Cutler Files, Counsel's Office Files, Staff Office Files, Jimmy Carter

Presidential Materials, Jimmy Carter Presidential Library, Atlanta, Georgia.

7. "Press Briefing with Lloyd Cutler, Counsel to the President and Jody Powell, Press Secretary," January 20, 1980, Folder: Olympics – Press, 5/79–1/80, Box 103, Lloyd Cutler Files, Counsel's Office Files, Staff Office Files, Jimmy Carter Presidential Materials, Jimmy Carter Presidential Library, Atlanta, Georgia.

8. "Press Briefing with Lloyd Cutler, Counsel to the President and Jody Powell, Press Secretary," January 20, 1980, Folder: Olympics – Press, 5/79–1/80, Box 103, Lloyd Cutler Files, Counsel's Office Files, Staff Office Files, Jimmy Carter Presidential Materials, Jimmy Carter Presidential Library, Atlanta, Georgia.

9. "Press Briefing with Lloyd Cutler, Counsel to the President and Jody Powell, Press Secretary," January 20, 1980, Folder: Olympics – Press, 5/79–1/80, Box 103; "Meet the Press Olympics Qs and As, no date, Folder: Olympics – Talking Points and Qs and As, 2–5/80, Box 105, Lloyd Cutler Files, Counsel's Office Files, Staff Office Files, Jimmy Carter Presidential Materials; *NBC Nightly News*, January 20, 1980 in The White House News Summary, January 21, 1980, Jimmy Carter Presidential Library, Atlanta, Georgia; *The Christian Science Monitor*, February 8, 1980.

10. *The New York Times*, January 21, 1980; Carter notation on Special Translation, February 1, 1980, Folder: 2/12/80 [2], Box 170, Staff Offices, Office of Staff Secretary, Handwriting File, Jimmy Carter Presidential Materials, Jimmy Carter Presidential Library, Atlanta, Georgia.

11. *St. Paul Pioneer Press*, January 23, 1980; *Akron Beacon Journal*, January 22, 1980; *Richmond Times-Dispatch*, January 22, 1980.

12. *Newsday*, January 24, 1980; *Dallas Times Herald*, January 23, 1980; *Oakland Tribune*, January 21, 1980.

13. English Translation of Joerg Wigan, "The Games Will Take Place in Moscow or Not at All," *Bild am Sonntag*, January 20, 1980 in Pueschel to MacManaway, January 22, 1980, attached to MacManaway to Killanin, January 28, 1980, Folder Identification 8047, Folder 0070948, Interview Files, Papers of Lord Killanin, Samarach Olympic Studies Centre, Olympic Museum, Lausanne, Switzerland.

14. Pound, *Inside the Olympics*, 230, 231, 233.

15. Pound to Killanin attached to Pound to Miller, January 16, 1980. Miller introduced these letters when he testified before Congress. U.S. Congress. House of Representatives. Committee on Foreign Relations, *U.S. Participation in the 1980 Summer Olympic Games: Hearings and Markup before the Committee on Foreign Relations* January 23 and February 4, 1980, 96th Congress, Second Session. (Washington, DC: Government Printing Office, 1980), 6–7.

16. Ueberroth with Levin and Quinn, *Made in America*, 77–9; *Detroit Free Press*, January 21, 1980; Ueberroth to Killanin, January 25, 1980, Folder Identification 8365, Folder 0072284, Telex Files, Papers of Lord Killanin, Samarach Olympic Studies Centre, Olympic Museum, Lausanne, Switzerland.

17. Cutler to the President, January 22, 1980, Folder: Olympics – Memos/Correspondence to the President 1–2/80, Box 103, Civiletti to the President, January 21, 1980; Civiletti to Cutler, January 29, 1980; Garland to the Attorney General, no date, Folder: Olympics – [working file] 3/18–1/80, Box 105, Lloyd Cutler Files, Counsel's Office Files, Staff Office Files, Jimmy Carter Presidential Materials, Jimmy Carter Presidential Library, Atlanta, Georgia.

18. *Congressional Record*, 216, 225–6; House of Representatives, Committee on Foreign Relations, *U.S. Participation in the 1980 Summer Olympic Games*, 1.

19. *Congressional Record*, 216, 225–6; House of Representatives, Committee on Foreign Relations, *U.S. Participation in the 1980 Summer Olympic Games*, 5, 8, 12, 14, 17–18.

20. House of Representatives, Committee on Foreign Relations, *U.S. Participation in the 1980 Summer Olympic Games*, 5, 8, 12, 13–18.

21. House of Representatives, Committee on Foreign Relations, *U.S. Participation in the 1980 Summer Olympic Games*, 3–4, 16, 26, 36, 39.

22. House of Representatives, Committee on Foreign Relations, *U.S. Participation in the 1980 Summer Olympic Games*, 41.

23. House of Representatives, Committee on Foreign Relations, *U.S. Participation in the 1980 Summer Olympic Games*, 43–4.

24. House of Representatives, Committee on Foreign Relations, *U.S. Participation in the 1980 Summer Olympic Games*, 46, 47, 63.

25. House of Representatives, Committee on Foreign Relations, *U.S. Participation in the 1980 Summer Olympic Games*, 42–3, 52, 57, 65.

26. House of Representatives, Committee on Foreign Relations, *U.S. Participation in the 1980 Summer Olympic Games*, 51, 65, 67, 69.

27. *The New York Times*, January, 24, 1980; Kane's observation is in speech notes he made for some public remarks he later delivered. Kane made a number of notes and speeches about the boycott. Internal evidence indicates that he wrote his comments at various times throughout the early to mid-1980s. There are no dates on any of the documents and most are on envelopes and other pieces of paper that offer no method of distinguishing from one another. Kane notes, Folder, 148, Box 9, Papers of Robert Kane, U.S. Olympic Committee Library and Archives, U.S. Olympic Committee Training Center, Colorado Springs, Colorado.

28. *The Atlanta Constitution*, January 25, 1980; *The Boston Globe*, January 25, 1980; *St. Louis Post-Dispatch*, January 24, 1980.

29. *Congressional Record*, 568–70, 576–80.

30. Gromyko, *Memoirs*, 291–2; Dobrynin, *In Confidence*, 444; Hazan, *Olympic Sports and Propaganda Games*, 127.

31. Dobrynin, *In Confidence*, 445, 452; "Transcript of a Meeting of the Central Committee of the Communist Party of the Soviet Union Politburo," January 17, 1980, in "U.S.-Soviet Relations and the Turn Towards Confrontation, 1977–1980 – New Russian & East German Documents," *Cold War International History Project Bulletin* Issues 8–9 (Winter 1996/1997), 162–3.

32. Dobrynin, *In Confidence*, 452–3.

33. Secretary of the Central Committee to Soviet Ambassador to West Germany, February 1, 1980, "U.S.-Soviet Relations and the Turn Towards Confrontation, 1977–1980 – New Russian & East German Documents," *Cold War International History Project Bulletin* Issues 8–9 (Winter 1996/1997), 125–7.

34. Hazan, *Propaganda Games*, 129, 131–2; Kanin, *Political History*, 122.

35. Hazan, *Propaganda Games*, 130–2.

36. Hazan, *Propaganda Games*, 134.

37. Dobrynin, *In Confidence*, 443, 446, 448.

38. *The Denver Post*, February 24, 1980; "A Joint Athletes Statement Concerning the Proposed Olympic Boycott," January 25, 1980; "Statement by U.S. Women's Team Handball Squad," no date; "Statement of Ms. Anita DeFrantz," all in U.S. Congress. Senate. Committee on Foreign Relations, *1980 Summer Olympics Boycott: Hearing before the Committee on Foreign Relations* January 28, 1980, 96th Congress, second session (Washington DC: U.S. Government Printing Office, 1980), 57–62; emphasis in the original of the Edwin Moses quote in Kenny More, "The 'Pawns' Make a Move," *Sports Illustrated*, February 4, 1980, 22.

39. *The Denver Post*, February 24, 1980; "A Joint Athletes Statement Concerning the Proposed Olympic Boycott," January 25, 1980; "Statement by U.S. Women's Team Handball Squad," no date; "Statement of Ms. Anita DeFrantz," all in U.S. Congress. Senate. Committee on Foreign Relations, *1980 Summer Olympics Boycott: Hearing before the Committee on Foreign Relations* January 28, 1980, 96th Congress, second session (Washington DC: U.S. Government Printing Office, 1980), 57–62; emphasis in the original of the Edwin Moses quote in More, "The 'Pawns' Make a Move," 22.

40. Onek to Cutler, January 16, 1980, Folder: Olympics Memos, 1–2/80, Box 102; Cutler Memorandum for the President, January 19, 1980, Folder: Olympics – Memos/Correspondence to the President, 1–2/80, Box 103, Lloyd Cutler Files, Counsel's Office Files, Staff Office Files, Jimmy Carter Presidential Materials, Jimmy Carter Presidential Library, Atlanta, Georgia; Kane notes, Folder, 148, Box 9, Papers of Robert Kane, U.S. Olympic Committee Library and Archives, U.S. Olympic Committee Training Center, Colorado Springs, Colorado.

41. Kane made a number of notes and speeches about the boycott. Internal evidence indicates that he wrote his comments at various times throughout the early to mid-1980s. There are no dates on any of the documents and most are on envelopes and other pieces of paper that offer no method of distinguishing one from the other. Kane notes, Folder, 148, Box 9, Papers of Robert Kane, U.S.

Olympic Committee Library and Archives, U.S. Olympic Committee Training Center, Colorado Springs, Colorado.

42. Carter notation on Cutler and Onek to the President, January 30, 1980, Folder: Olympics – Memos/Correspondence to the President, 1–2/80, Box 103, Lloyd Cutler Files, Counsel's Office Files, Staff Office Files, Jimmy Carter Presidential Materials, Jimmy Carter Presidential Library, Atlanta, Georgia.

43. Carter to Kane, January 20, 1980, *PPP*, 106–107; Vance to all diplomatic posts, January 20, 1980, Folder: Olympics, 6/79–2/80, Box 48, Subject Files, National Security Advisor Files, Staff Office Files, Jimmy Carter Presidential Materials, Jimmy Carter Presidential Library, Atlanta, Georgia.

44. Ron Fimrite, "Facing Bear Facts," *Sports Illustrated*, February 4, 1980, 20; "USOC Faces Critical Issues in a Tense World Situation/1980," *The Olympian*, March 1980, 6.

45. Fimrite, "Facing Bear Facts," 20; resolution in "USOC Faces Critical Issues in a Tense World Situation/1980," *The Olympian*, March 1980, 6.

46. Fimrite, "Facing Bear Facts," 20.

47. "Meeting of the Administrative Committee of the United States Olympic Committee Transcript," March 15, 1980, 23, U.S. Olympic Committee Library and Archives, U.S. Olympic Committee Training Center, Colorado Springs, Colorado.

48. *Los Angeles Times*, January 27, 1980; there is a different construction of Cutler's quote in Fimrite, "Facing Bear Facts," 20.

49. *Colorado Springs Sun*, January 26, 1980; *The Washington Post*, January 27, 1980.

50. "National Conference on Physical Fitness and Sports for All," February 1, 1980, *PPP*, 259–60.

51. Senate, Committee on Foreign Relations, *1980 Summer Olympics Boycott*, 2.

52. Senate, Committee on Foreign Relations, *1980 Summer Olympics Boycott*, 2–6.

53. Senate, Committee on Foreign Relations, *1980 Summer Olympics Boycott*, 31–3, 38.

54. Senate, Committee on Foreign Relations, *1980 Summer Olympics Boycott*, 40, 52; Senate Foreign Relations Committee Staff, "The Politics of the Olympics," in *Congressional Record*, 832.

55. Senate, Committee on Foreign Relations, *1980 Summer Olympics Boycott*, 46, 49–50.

56. Senate, Committee on Foreign Relations, *1980 Summer Olympics Boycott*, 54–7, 62–6.

57. Senate, Committee on Foreign Relations, *1980 Summer Olympics Boycott*, 77–86.

58. *Congressional Record*, 830, 835–7, 1052, 1056, 1059, 1122; Hulme, *Political Olympics*, 95.

59. *The Weekend Australian*, February 2–3, 1980; *The Age*, February 2, 1980; Philip Ayers, *Malcolm Fraser: A Biography* (Richmond, Victoria, Australia: Willian Hienemann Australia, 1987), 395; Patrick Weller, *Malcolm Fraser PM: A Study in Prime Ministerial Power* (Ringwood, Victoria, Australia: Penguin, 1989), 344–5; Gordon, *Australia and the Olympic Games*, 324; Fraser to Grange, January 22, 1980, Annex 10 to Minutes of the Meeting of the Executive Board, February 8, 9, 12, and 15, 1980, 7–9, IOC Historical Archives, Samaranch Olympic Studies Centre, Olympic Museum, Lausanne, Switzerland.

60. Kevan Gosper, with Glenda Korporaal, *An Olympic Life: Melbourne 1956 to Sydney 2000* (St. Leonards, Australia: Allen & Unwin, 2000), 134; Gordon, *Australia and the Olympic Games*, 324; Lisa Forrest, *Boycott: Australia's Controversial Road to the 1980 Moscow Olympics* (Sydney, Australia: ABC Books, 2008), 29.

61. Ayers, *Malcolm Fraser: A Biography*, 395; Patrick Weller, *Malcolm Fraser PM*, 344–5; Malcolm Fraser Oral History, April 14, 1994, Australian Biography, Special Broadcasting Service Television available at: http://www.australianbiography.gov.au/fraser/interview8.html.

62. *The Weekend Australian*, February 2–3, 1980; *The Age*, February 2, 1980; Ayers, *Malcolm Fraser*, 395; Weller, *Malcolm Fraser PM*, 344–5.

63. Visit of Mr. Fraser: Olympic Games, February 4, 1980, located in British Cabinet Office Freedom of Information Reading Room Website, Subject Sport and Recreation, Moscow Olympics-07 http://www.cabinetoffice.gov.uk/foi/reading_room/topic/sports.aspx

64. Gordon, *Australia and the Olympic Games*, 325.

7. Painful Losses

1. Killanin, *My Olympic Years*, 176.

2. Killanin, *My Olympic Years*, 177–8; "The Olympic System: A Political Primer,"

January 24, 1980, Folder: Olympics – Publications and Pamphlets 1–4/80, Box 104, Lloyd Cutler Files, Counsel's Office Files, Staff Office Files, Jimmy Carter Presidential Materials, Jimmy Carter Presidential Library, Atlanta, Georgia.

3. Killanin, *My Olympic Years*, 178.

4. Wenn and Wenn, "Muhammad Ali and the Convergence of Olympic Sport and U.S. Diplomacy in 1980," 49; Thomas Hauser, *Muhammad Ali: His Life and Times* (New York: Simon and Schuster, 1991), 396.

5. Wenn and Wenn, "Muhammad Ali and the Convergence of Olympic Sport and U.S. Diplomacy," 50–2.

6. Wenn and Wenn, "Muhammad Ali and the Convergence of Olympic Sport and U.S. Diplomacy," 50–2; Martin to the President, February 11, 1980, Folder: Olympics 6/79–2/80, Box 48, Subject Files, National Security Advisor Files, Staff Office Files, Jimmy Carter Presidential Materials, Carter Presidential Library, Atlanta, Georgia.

7. Wenn and Wenn, "Muhammad Ali and the Convergence of Olympic Sport and U.S. Diplomacy," 50–2; Martin to the President, February 11, 1980, Folder: Olympics 6/79–2/80, Box 48, Subject Files, National Security Advisor Files, Staff Office Files, Jimmy Carter Presidential Materials, Carter Presidential Library, Atlanta, Georgia.

8. *Des Moines Register*, February 6, 1980; *News & Courier*, February 6, 1980; *The Times-Picayune*, February 5, 1980; *New York Post*, February 6, 1980; *Los Angeles Times*, February 6, 1980; *The Washington Post*, February 5, 1980.

9. Wenn and Wenn, "Muhammad Ali and the Convergence of Olympic Sport and U.S. Diplomacy," 53–4; Martin to the President, February 11, 1980, Folder: Olympics 6/79–2/80, Box 48, Subject Files, National Security Advisor Files, Staff Office Files, Jimmy Carter Presidential Materials, Carter Presidential Library, Atlanta, Georgia.

10. Wenn and Wenn, "Muhammad Ali and the Convergence of Olympic Sport and U.S. Diplomacy," 54–5.

11. *The Washington Post*, February 5 and 18, 1980; "The Greatest, Not the Smartest," *The Economist*, February 8, 1980, p. 34.

12. Funk to Brzezinski, February 11, 1980; Martin to the President, February 11, 1980; "Muhammad Ali Presidential Mission: Summary of My Findings," no

date, Folder: Olympics 6/79–2/80, Box 48, Subject Files, National Security Advisor Files, Staff Office Files, Jimmy Carter Presidential Materials; Ali's hug is documented in the photos taken of that meeting: Contact Sheet C15530, Photo Book 156, White House Staff Photographer Photos, Jimmy Carter Presidential Library, Atlanta, Georgia.

13. Wenn and Wenn, "Muhammad Ali and the Convergence of Olympic Sport and U.S. Diplomacy," 57–9.

14. Carter, *Keeping Faith*, 482.

15. Schmidt, *Menschen und Mächte* [Men and Powers], 158.

16. Schmidt, *Menschen und Mächte* [Men and Powers], 244–5; Carrington to British Embassy in Rome, February 19, 1980 located in British Cabinet Office Freedom of Information Reading Room Website, Subject Sport and Recreation, Moscow Olympics-05 http://www.cabinetoffice.gov.uk/foi/reading_room/topic/sports.aspx

17. Schmidt, *Menschen und Mächte* [Men and Powers], 244–5.

18. *The Globe and Mail*, January 28, 1980; Kereliuk, "The Canadian Boycott of the 1980 Moscow Olympic Games," 156–7; Worrall, *My Olympic Journey*, 181.

19. *The Globe and Mail*, January 28, February 28, 1980; Macintosh and Hawes with Greenhorn and Black, *Sport and Canadian Diplomacy*, 94–7.

20. Macintosh, Hawes, Greenhorn and Black, *Sport and Canadian Diplomacy*, 97.

21. Ivan Head and Pierre Trudeau, *The Canadian Way: Shaping Canada's Foreign Policy, 1968–1984* (Toronto: McClelland and Stewart, 1995), 209–10; Kereliuk, "The Canadian Boycott," 157.

22. Schmidt, *Menschen und Mächte* [Men and Powers], 222, 229.

23. Kanin, *Political History of the Olympic Games*, 125; Knecht, *Der Boycott*, 85.

24. Schmidt, *Menschen und Mächte* [Men and Powers], 228–9, 249; Vance, Memorandum, February 25, 1980, Folder: Southwest Asia/Persian Gulf – Afghanistan [1/5/80–10/1/80], Box 17, Geographic File, Papers of Zbigniew Brzezinski, Donated Historical Collections, Jimmy Carter Presidential Library, Atlanta, Georgia.

25. Forrest, *Boycott*, 148.

26. Vance, Memorandum, February 25, 1980, Folder: Southwest Asia/Persian

Gulf – Afghanistan [1/5/80–10/1/80], Box 17, Geographic File, Papers of Zbigniew Brzezinski, Donated Historical Collections, Jimmy Carter Presidential Library, Atlanta, Georgia.

27. Killanin, *My Olympic Years*, 175; Brement to Cutler, February 13, 1980, Folder: Olympics, 6/79–2/80, Box 48, Subject Files, National Security Advisor Files, Staff Office Files, Jimmy Carter Presidential Materials, Culter and Onek to the Special Coordination Committee, February 25, 1980, Folder: Olympics – Memos/ Correspondence to President 1–2/80, Box 103, Lloyd Cutler Files, Counsel's Office Files, Staff Office Files, Jimmy Carter Presidential Materials, Jimmy Carter Presidential Library, Atlanta, Georgia.

28. Kane's views are evident in a number of speeches he made about the boycott. Internal evidence indicates that he wrote his comments at various times between 1980 and 1984, but there are no dates on any of the documents and most are on envelopes and other pieces of paper that offer no method of distinguishing one from the other. Kane notes, Folder, 148, Box 9, Papers of Robert Kane, U.S. Olympic Committee Library and Archives, U.S. Olympic Committee Training Center, Colorado Springs, Colorado; "Statement Made by Robert J. Kane, President of the United States Olympic Committee Concerning the Games of the XXIInd Olympiad in Moscow," Annex 9 to Minutes of the Meeting of the Executive Board, February 8, 9, 12, and 15, 1980, 7–9, 48–49, IOC Historical Archives, Samaranch Olympic Studies Centre, Olympic Museum, Lausanne, Switzerland; Proceedings of the Meeting of the Administrative Committee of the United States Olympic Committee, March 15, 1980, page 5, U.S. Olympic Committee Library and Archives, U.S. Olympic Committee Training Center, Colorado Springs, Colorado.

29. Weller, *Malcolm Fraser PM*, 344–5; Ayers, *Malcolm Fraser: A Biography*, 367; Fraser to Grange, January 22, 1980; Press Release Issued by the Australian Olympic Federation, January 24, 1980, Annex 10 and 11 to Minutes of the Meeting of the Executive Board, February 8, 9, 12, and 15, 1980, 7–9, 49–50, IOC Historical Archives,

Samaranch Olympic Studies Centre, Olympic Museum, Lausanne, Switzerland.

30. Killanin, *My Olympic Years*, 181–2.

31. Lord Killanin, "Opening of the 82nd Session of the International Olympic Committee in Lake Placid, United States of America," February 9, 1980, *Lord Killanin's Speeches From 1972 to 1981*, 101–3.

32. "Remarks by Mr. Cyrus Vance, Secretary [of] State of the United States," *Olympic Review*, 109–10.

33. Pound, *Five Rings Over Korea*, 16; Killanin, *My Olympic Years*, 184; Worrall, *My Olympic Journey*, 182–3; Takač, *Olimpijskih Godina* [Sixty Olympic Years], 304.

34. "Report by Mr. Ignati T. Novikov, President of the Organising Committee for the Games of the XXIInd Olympiad in Moscow," Annex 5 to Minutes of the 84th Session of the International Olympic Committee, Baden-Baden, Germany, 29 September to 2 October, 1981, 64, IOC Historical Archives, Samaranch Olympic Studies Centre, Olympic Museum, Lausanne, Switzerland.

35. Pound, *Five Rings Over Korea*, 16; Killanin, *My Olympic Years*, 184; Worrall, *My Olympic Journey*, 182–3; "Report by Mr. Ignait T. Novikov, President of the Organising Committee for the Games of the XXIInd Olympiad in Moscow," Annex 5 to Minutes of the 84th Session of the International Olympic Committee, Baden-Baden, Germany, 29 September to 2 October, 1981, 64, IOC Historical Archives, Samaranch Olympic Studies Centre, Olympic Museum, Lausanne, Switzerland.

36. Miller, *Olympic Revolution*, 86; Takač, *Olimpijskih Godina* [Sixty Olympic Years], 304.

37. Minutes of the 82nd IOC Session, Lake Placid, New York, USA, February 10–13, 1980, 6–19, IOC Historical Archives, Samaranch Olympic Studies Centre, Olympic Museum, Lausanne, Switzerland; Proceedings of the Meeting of the Administrative Committee of the United States Olympic Committee, March 15, 1980, 6, U.S. Olympic Committee Library and Archives, U.S. Olympic Committee Training Center, Colorado Springs, Colorado.

38. Minutes of the 82nd IOC Session, Lake Placid, New York, USA, February 10–13, 1980, 6–19, IOC Historical Archives, Samaranch Olympic Studies Centre, Olympic Museum,

Lausanne, Switzerland; Proceedings of the Meeting of the Administrative Committee of the United States Olympic Committee, March 15, 1980, 6, U.S. Olympic Committee Library and Archives, U.S. Olympic Committee Training Center, Colorado Springs, Colorado.

39. Minutes of the 82nd IOC Session, Lake Placid, New York, USA, February 10–13, 1980, 6–19, IOC Historical Archives, Samaranch Olympic Studies Centre, Olympic Museum, Lausanne, Switzerland.

40. *The New York Times*, February 13, 1980; Killanin, *My Olympic Years*, 186–8; Statement by Lord Killanin, President of the International Olympic Committee, Concerning the Games of the XXIInd Olympiad in Moscow, February 12, 1980, Annex 10 to Minutes of the 82nd IOC Session, Lake Placid, New York, USA, February 10–13, 1980, 6–19, 46–7, IOC Historical Archives and Transcript of Interview with Lord Killanin on *BBC Sportsnight*, June 4, 1980, Folder Identification 8047, Folder 0070948, Interview Files, Papers of Lord Killanin, Samarach Olympic Studies Centre, Olympic Museum, Lausanne, Switzerland. Samaranch Olympic Studies Centre, Olympic Museum, Lausanne, Switzerland.

41. Killanin, *My Olympic Years*, 191; Killanin to Kane, March 5, 1980 and Pound to Kane, March 4, 1980, Folder: Boycott Correspondence, Internal (USOC & IOC), Box 9, Papers of Robert Kane, U.S. Olympic Committee Library and Archives, U.S. Olympic Committee Training Center, Colorado Springs, Colorado.

42. "1980 Summer Olympics," February 12, 1980, *PPP*, 305–6; Aaron Beacom, "A Changing Discourse? British Diplomacy and the Olympic Movement," Roger Levermore and Adrian Budd, *Sport and International Relations: An Emerging Relationship* (London: Routledge, 2004), 102.

43. Forrest, *Boycott*, 38.

44. *The New York Times*, February 15, 1980.

45. Carter to Kane, February 15, 1980 and Carter to Kane, February 15, 1980, Folder: Boycott Correspondence, Carter, Jimmy, Box 9, Papers of Robert Kane, U.S. Olympic Committee Library and Archives, U.S. Olympic Committee Training Center, Colorado Springs, Colorado.

46. Joe Onek Oral History by the Author, June 22, 2007; Onek to Cutler, no date, Folder: Olympics – Statements & Transcripts, 1–2/80, Box 104, Lloyd Cutler Files, Counsel's Office Files, Staff Office Files, Jimmy Carter Presidential Materials, Jimmy Carter Presidential Library, Atlanta, Georgia; Kane notes, Folder, 148, Box 9, Papers of Robert Kane, U.S. Olympic Committee Library and Archives, U.S. Olympic Committee Training Center, Colorado Springs, Colorado.

47. *The Washington Post*, February 12, 1980.

48. *The Washington Post*, February 12, 1980.

49. Joe [Onek] to Lloyd [Cutler], January 31, 1980, Folder: Olympics – Memos, 1–2/80, Box 102; Lloyd Cutler, Memorandum for the Attorney General, February 13, 1980, Folder: Olympics – [Working File] 2–3/80, Box 105, Lloyd Cutler Files, Counsel's Office Files, Staff Office Files, Jimmy Carter Presidential Materials, Jimmy Carter Presidential Library, Atlanta, Georgia.

50. Lloyd Cutler, Memorandum for the Attorney General, February 13, 1980, Folder: Olympics – [Working File] 2–3/80, Box 105, Lloyd Cutler Files, Counsel's Office Files, Staff Office Files, Jimmy Carter Presidential Materials, Jimmy Carter Presidential Library, Atlanta, Georgia.

51. Civiletti to Cutler, February 15, 1980 and John M. Harmon, Memorandum for the Attorney General Re: Proposed Olympic Boycott Statute, February 15, 1980, Folder: Olympics – [Working File] 2–3/80, Box 105, Lloyd Cutler Files, Counsel's Office Files, Staff Office Files, Jimmy Carter Presidential Materials, Jimmy Carter Presidential Library, Atlanta, Georgia.

52. Civiletti to Cutler, February 21, Folder: Olympics – [Working File] 2–3/80, Box 105; Stanford Litvack, Memorandum for the Attorney General, February 15, 1980; Civiletti to Cutler, February 25, 1980, Folder: Olympics – Agreements, 2–4/80, Box 101, Lloyd Cutler Files, Counsel's Office Files, Staff Office Files, Jimmy Carter Presidential Materials, Jimmy Carter Presidential Library, Atlanta, Georgia.

53. Civiletti to Cutler, February 21, Folder: Olympics – [Working File] 2–3/80, Box 105; Stanford Litvack, Memorandum for the Attorney General, February 15, 1980; Civiletti to Cutler, February 25, 1980,

Folder: Olympics – Agreements, 2–4/80, Box 101, Lloyd Cutler Files, Counsel's Office Files, Staff Office Files, Jimmy Carter Presidential Materials, Jimmy Carter Presidential Library, Atlanta, Georgia.

54. Lloyd Cutler, Memorandum for the Attorney General, March 3, 1980, Folder: Olympics – [Working File] 2–3/80, Box 105, Lloyd Cutler Files, Counsel's Office Files, Staff Office Files, Jimmy Carter Presidential Materials, Jimmy Carter Presidential Library, Atlanta, Georgia.

55. McDonald to Cutler, February 15, 1980, Folder: Afghanistan and [Olympic Games], Box 8, Papers of Alonzo L. McDonald, Donated Historical Collections, Jimmy Carter Presidential Library, Atlanta, Georgia.

56. Cutler to McDonald, February 15, 1980, Folder: Afghanistan and [Olympic Games], Box 8, Papers of Alonzo L. McDonald, Donated Historical Collections, Jimmy Carter Presidential Library, Atlanta, Georgia.

8. The White House Games

1. *The Washington Post*, February 14, 1980.

2. "American Legion: Remarks at the Legion's Annual Conference, February 19, 1980, *PPP*, 346; *The Washington Post*, February 20, 1980; Cutler Memorandum for the SCC, February 20, 1980 and Brzesinski to Secretary of Defense, February 22, 1980, Folder: Olympics, 6/79–2/80, Box 48, Subject Files, National Security Advisor Files, Staff Office Files, Jimmy Carter Presidential Materials, Jimmy Carter Presidential Library, Atlanta, Georgia.

3. The White House News Summary, February 21, 1980, Jimmy Carter Presidential Library, Atlanta, Georgia; "1980 Summer Olympics: White House Statement on U.S. Withdrawal From the Games to be Held in Moscow," February 20, 1980, *PPP*, 356–7.

4. *Philadelphia Inquirer*, February 20, 1980; *The Atlanta Constitution*, February 21, 1980; *The Commercial Appeal*, February 22, 1980.

5. *New York Daily News*, February 21, 1980; *The Bergin County Record*, February 24, 1980; *The Des Moines Register*, February 22, 1980; *The Salt Lake Tribune*, February 22, 1980.

6. Memorandum for Zbigniew Brzezinski, February 19, 1980, Folder: Olympics, 6/79–2/80, Box 48, Subject Files, National Security Advisor Files, Staff Office Files, Jimmy Carter Presidential Materials, Jimmy Carter Presidential Library, Atlanta, Georgia.

7. *The New York Times*, March 2, 1980; Brement to Brzezinski, February 25, 1980, Folder: Olympics, 6/79–2/80, Box 48, Subject Files, National Security Advisor Files, Staff Office Files, Jimmy Carter Presidential Materials, Jimmy Carter Presidential Library, Atlanta, Georgia.

8. Zbigniew Brzezinski, *Power and Principle: Memoirs of the National Security Advisor, 1977–1981* (New York: Farrar, Straus, Giroux, 1983), 434.

9. Dyess to Deputy Secretary, March 21, 1980 attached to Cutler to Carter, March 24, 1980, Folder: Olympics – Memos/Correspondence to President, 3/80, Box 103, Lloyd Cutler Files, Counsel's Office Files, Staff Office Files, Jimmy Carter Presidential Materials, Jimmy Carter Presidential Library, Atlanta, Georgia.

10. "Report on the Meeting of the Foreign Secretaries of the Closely Cooperating Socialist Countries om Moscow on 26 February 1980," February 29, 1980, Csaba Békés, "Why was There No 'Second Cold War in Europe? Hungary and the Soviet Invasion of Afghanistan in 1979: Documents from the Hungarian Archives," *Cold War International History Project Bulletin Issue* 14/15 (Winter 2003–Spring 2004), 213.

11. "Interview with the President," February 25, 1980, *PPP*, 388.

12. Germond and Witcover, *Blue Smoke and Mirrors*, 149–50; "United States Olympic Team: Remarks at the Welcoming Ceremony for Participants in the 1980 Winter Games," February 25, 1980, *PPP*, 379–81.

13. "United Jewish Appeal: Remarks at the Organization's National Young Leadership Conference," February 25, 1980, *PPP*, 377.

14. Dave Ogrean, "Ice Hockey," *The Olympian*, April 1980, 15.

15. *The Washington Post*, February 26, 1980; "United States Olympic Team: Remarks at the Welcoming Ceremony for Participants in the 1980 Winter Games," February 25, 1980, *PPP*, 379–81.

16. *The Washington Post*, February 26, 1980; *Time*, February 11, 1980; The White House News Summary, February 26, 1980, Jimmy Carter Presidential Library, Atlanta, Georgia.

17. Jody Powell Exit Interview, page 7, Jimmy Carter Presidential Library, Atlanta, Georgia.

18. Wendel, *Going for the Gold*, 45.

19. Jordon, *Crisis*, 182.

20. *World News Tonight*, February 25, 1980, ABC News Transcripts, Lexis-Nexis Database, http://www.lexis-nexis.com; The White House News Summary, February 26, 1980, Jimmy Carter Presidential Library, Atlanta, Georgia.

21. *The Washington Post*, February 26, 1980; The White House News Summary, February 26, 1980, Jimmy Carter Presidential Library, Atlanta, Georgia.

22. *The Washington Post*, February 26, 1980; 1980 Winter Olympic Team to Carter, February 24, Folder: 3/18/80. Box 176, Handwriting File, Office of Staff Secretary, Jimmy Carter Presidential Materials, Jimmy Carter Presidential Library, Atlanta, Georgia.

23. Berenson and Jenkins to Cutler, February 27, 1980, Folder: Olympics – Memos, 1–2/80, Box 102, Lloyd Cutler Files, Counsel's Office Files, Staff Office Files, Jimmy Carter Presidential Materials, Jimmy Carter Presidential Library, Atlanta, Georgia.

24. Cutler and Onek to Special Coordination Committee, February 25, 1980, Folder: Olympics – Memos/Correspondence to President 1–2/80, Box 103, Lloyd Cutler Files, Counsel's Office Files, Staff Office Files, Jimmy Carter Presidential Materials, Jimmy Carter Presidential Library, Atlanta, Georgia.

25. Joe Onek Oral History with the Author, June 22, 2007.

26. *The Washington Post*, March 8, 1980; "Interview with the President," February 25, 1980, *Public Papers of the President: Jimmy Carter, 1980*, 388; Cutler to the President, February 18, 1980, Folder: Olympics – Memos/Correspondence to President 1–2/80, Box 103, Lloyd Cutler Files, Counsel's Office Files, Staff Office Files, Jimmy Carter Presidential Materials, Jimmy Carter Presidential Library, Atlanta, Georgia.

27. British Embassy in Bonn to Foreign and Commonwealth Office, January 17, 1980; British Embassy in Mexico City to Foreign and Commonwealth Office, January 17, 1980; British Embassy in Tokyo to Foreign and Commonwealth Office, January 17, 1980; "Olympic Games" Annex, no date, located in British Cabinet Office Freedom of Information Reading Room Website, Subject Sport and Recreation, Moscow Olympics-11 http://www.cabinetoffice.gov.uk/foi/reading_room/topic/sports.aspx; Lever to Alexander, February 11, 1980; Telegram 691, British Embassy in Washington to Foreign and Commonwealth Office, February 12, 1980; Record of a Meeting Held at the State Department, February 12, 1980 located in British Cabinet Office Freedom of Information Reading Room Website, Subject Sport and Recreation, Moscow Olympics-06 http://www.cabinetoffice.gov.uk/foi/reading_room/topic/sports.aspx; Thatcher to Carter, January 22, 1980 located in British Cabinet Office Freedom of Information Reading Room Website, Subject Sport and Recreation, Moscow Olympics-10 http://www.cabinetoffice.gov.uk/foi/reading_room/topic/sports.aspx

28. Lever to Alexander, February 11, 1980; Telegram 691, British Embassy in Washington to Foreign and Commonwealth Office, February 12, 1980; Record of a Meeting Held at the State Department, February 12, 1980 located in British Cabinet Office Freedom of Information Reading Room Website, Subject Sport and Recreation, Moscow Olympics-06 http://www.cabinetoffice.gov.uk/foi/reading_room/topic/sports.aspx

29. Record of a Meeting Held at the State Department, February 12, 1980 located in British Cabinet Office Freedom of Information Reading Room Website, Subject Sport and Recreation, Moscow Olympics-06 http://www.cabinetoffice.gov.uk/foi/reading_room/topic/sports.aspx

30. *The Washington Post*, March 8, 1980; "Interview with the President," February 25, 1980, *PPP*, 388; Cutler to the President, February 18, 1980, Folder: Olympics – Memos/Correspondence to President 1–2/80, Box 103, Lloyd Cutler Files, Counsel's Office Files, Staff Office Files, Jimmy Carter Presidential Materials,

Jimmy Carter Presidential Library, Atlanta, Georgia.

31. Record of Meeting (Extract) of Prime Minister and Secretary of State Vance 10 Downing St., February 21, 1980 located in British Cabinet Office Freedom of Information Reading Room Website, Subject Sport and Recreation, Moscow Olympics-05 http://www.cabinetoffice.gov.uk/foi/reading_room/topic/sports.aspx

32. Forrest, *Boycott*, 66.

33. Record of a Meeting Held at the State Department, February 12, 1980 located in British Cabinet Office Freedom of Information Reading Room Website, Subject Sport and Recreation, Moscow Olympics-06 http://www.cabinetoffice.gov.uk/foi/reading_room/topic/sports.aspx

34. *The Washington Post*, February 26, 1980; "Order of the American Hellenic Educational Progressive Association Remarks at the Annual Dinner of the Supreme Lodge," February 25, 1980, *Public Papers of the President: Jimmy Carter, 1980*, 381–3.

35. Lloyd Cutler Exit Interview, March 2, 1981, 8; Cutler to McIntyre, Folder: Olympics – Alternative Games 1–7/80, Box 101; McDonald to Cutler, March 21, 1980, Folder: Olympic – Memos, 3–4/80, Box 103, Lloyd Cutler Files, Counsel's Office Files, Staff Office Files, Jimmy Carter Presidential Materials; Special Coordination Committee Meeting, March 20, 1980, Folder: Meetings – SCC 291 3/20/80, Box 32, Brzezinski Donated Material, Jimmy Carter Presidential Library, Atlanta, Georgia.

36. Lloyd Cutler Exit Interview, March 2, 1981, 8; Cutler to McIntyre, Folder: Olympics – Alternative Games 1–7/80, Box 101; McDonald to Cutler, March 21, 1980, Folder: Olympic – Memos, 3–4/80, Box 103, Lloyd Cutler Files, Counsel's Office Files, Staff Office Files, Jimmy Carter Presidential Materials; Special Coordination Committee Meeting, March 20, 1980, Folder: Meetings – SCC 291 3/20/80, Box 32, Brzezinski Donated Material, Jimmy Carter Presidential Library, Atlanta, Georgia.

37. Carter, *Keeping Faith*, 500, 536–7.

38. Schmidt, *Menschen und Mächte* [Men and Powers], 253–63, 300; Carter, *Keeping Faith*, 500, 536–7; Special Coordination Committee, March 6, 1980, Folder: Meetings

SCC 284 3/6/80, Box 32, Papers of Zbigniew Brzezinski, Donated Historical Collections, Jimmy Carter Presidential Library, Atlanta, Georgia.

39. In his memoirs, Ueberroth says it was April, but internal evidence shows that it was actually March. He and his ghostwriters made a number of small factual errors of this type. Ueberroth, with Levin and Quinn, *Made in America*, 79–80; Hulme, *Political Olympics*, 108.

40. *The Christian Science Monitor*, February 21, 1980.

41. Brement to Cutler, February 13, 1980, Folder: Olympics, 6/79–2/80, Box 48, Subject Files, National Security Advisor Files, Staff Office Files, Jimmy Carter Presidential Materials, Jimmy Carter Presidential Library, Atlanta, Georgia.

42. Ledsky to Secretary of State, March 8, attached to Brement to Brzezinski and Aaron, March 10, 1980, Folder: Olympics, 3/80, Box 49, Subject Files, National Security Advisor Files, Staff Office Files, Jimmy Carter Presidential Materials, Jimmy Carter Presidential Library, Atlanta, Georgia.

43. Scott to Onek, February 13, 1980 and Berenson and Onek to Cutler, February 15, 1980, Folder: Olympics – Alternative Games 1–7/80, Box 101, Lloyd Cutler Files, Counsel's Office Files, Staff Office Files, Jimmy Carter Presidential Materials, Jimmy Carter Presidential Library, Atlanta, Georgia.

44. Memorandum of Conversation, February 26, 1980, Folder: Olympics – Memos, 1–2/80, Box 102, Lloyd Cutler Files, Counsel's Office Files, Staff Office Files, Jimmy Carter Presidential Materials, Jimmy Carter Presidential Library, Atlanta, Georgia.

45. Memorandum of Conversation, February 26, 1980, Folder: Olympics – Memos, 1–2/80, Box 102, Lloyd Cutler Files, Counsel's Office Files, Staff Office Files, Jimmy Carter Presidential Materials, Jimmy Carter Presidential Library, Atlanta, Georgia.

46. Cutler and Onek to Special Coordination Committee, February 25, 1980, Folder: Olympics – Memos/Correspondence to President 1–2/80, Box 103, Lloyd Cutler Files, Counsel's Office Files, Staff Office Files, Jimmy Carter Presidential Materials, Jimmy Carter Presidential Library, Atlanta, Georgia.

47. Cutler to the President, February 18, 1980, Folder:Olympics–Memos/Correspondence to President, 1–2/80, Box 103, Lloyd Cutler Files, Counsel's Office Files, Staff Office Files, Jimmy Carter Presidential Materials; emphasis in the in the original notation on Special Coordination Committee, March 6, 1980, Folder: Meetings SCC 284 3/6/80, Box 32, Papers of Zbigniew Brzezinski, Donated Historical Collections, Jimmy Carter Presidential Library, Atlanta, Georgia.

48. Memorandum from Cutler, March 20, 1980, Folder: Olympics, 3/80, Box 49, S Subject Files, National Security Advisor Files, Staff Office Files, Jimmy Carter Presidential Materials, Jimmy Carter Presidential Library, Atlanta, Georgia.

49. Killanin, *My Olympic Years*, 192.

50. *Cleveland Press*, January 18, 1980.

51. *The Washington Post*, March 9, 1980; *Los Angeles Times*, March 9, 1980.

52. Vance to Carter, March 10, 1980, Folder: State Department Evening Reports, 2/80, Box 40, Plains File, Jimmy Carter Presidential Materials, Jimmy Carter Presidential Library, Atlanta, Georgia.

53. Record of a Conversation between the Prime Minister and the Australian Prime Minister, Mr. Malcolm Fraser, March 4, 1980; Foreign and Commonwealth Office to High Commissioner in Canberra, no date; Alexander to Lever, March 4, 1980; Fraser to Thatcher, March 5, 1980 located in British Cabinet Office Freedom of Information Reading Room Website, Subject Sport and Recreation, Moscow Olympics-03 http://www.cabinetoffice.gov.uk/foi/reading_room/topic/sports.aspx

54. Ueberroth with Levin and Quinn, *Made in America*, 80; Onek, Memorandum for the File, March 12, 1980, Folder: Olympics – Alternative Games 1–7/80, Box 101; Cutler and Onek to Special Coordination Committee, February 25, 1980, Folder: Olympics – Memos/Correspondence to President 1–2/80, Box 103, Lloyd Cutler Files, Counsel's Office Files, Staff Office Files, Jimmy Carter Presidential Materials, Jimmy Carter Presidential Library, Atlanta, Georgia.

55. Killanin to Kane, March 5, 1980 and Kane to Killanin, March 20, 1980, Folder 824, Box 52a, Papers of Robert Kane, U.S. Olympic Committee Library and Archives, U.S. Olympic Committee Training Center, Colorado Springs, Colorado.

56. Ueberroth with Levin and Quinn, *Made in America*, 81–2; *Los Angels Times*, March 19, 1980.

57. Killanin, *My Olympic Years*, 192; *Tribune de Geneve*, March 18, 1980; *La Suisse*, March 18, 1980; *The Guardian*, March 19, 1980; *The Times*, March 19, 1980; *The New York Times*, March 19, 1980; Hurd and Cutler Press Conference Transcript in U.S. Mission Geneva to the Secretary of State, March 18, 1980, Folder: Olympics, 3/80, Box 49, Subject Files, National Security Advisor Files, Staff Office Files, Jimmy Carter Presidential Materials, Jimmy Carter Presidential Library, Atlanta, Georgia; British Mission in Geneva to Foreign and Commonwealth Office, March 17, 1980 located in British Cabinet Office Freedom of Information Reading Room Website, Subject Sport and Recreation, Moscow Olympics-16 http://www.cabinetoffice.gov.uk/foi/reading_room/topic/sports.aspx.

58. Hazan, *Olympic Sports and Propaganda Games*, 149.

59. Beacom, "A Changing Discourse?," 102; Denis Howell, *Made in Birmingham: The Memoirs of Denis Howell* (London: Queen Anne Press, 1990), 292, 296–7; Follows to Thatcher, February 1, 1980 located in British Cabinet Office Freedom of Information Reading Room Website, Subject Sport and Recreation, Moscow Olympics-08 http://www.cabinetoffice.gov.uk/foi/reading_room/topic/sports.aspx

60. Howell, *Made in Birmingham*, 296–7.

61. House of Lords, *The Parliamentary Debates (Hansard)* Fifth Series – Volume 404 (London: Her Majesty's Stationery Office, 1980), 981.

62. Memorandum for the Prime Minister, January 23, 1980 located in British Cabinet Office Freedom of Information Reading Room Website, Subject Sport and Recreation, Moscow Olympics-09 http://www.cabinetoffice.gov.uk/foi/reading_room/topic/sports.aspx

63. *The Daily Telegraph*, February 1, 1980.

64. *The Times*, February 6 and 7, 1980.

65. *The Daily Telegraph*, February 20, 1980.

66. Follows to Thatcher, March 7, 1980, Moscow Olympic Files, British Olympic Association Archives, London, England.

67. House of Commons, Minutes of Evidence taken Before the Foreign Affairs Committee, March 5, 1980, 5–6, located in British Cabinet Office Freedom of Information Reading Room Website, Subject Sport and Recreation, Moscow Olympics-02 http://www.cabinetoffice.gov.uk/foi/reading_room/topic/sports.aspx

68. House of Commons, Minutes of Evidence taken Before the Foreign Affairs Committee, March 5, 1980, 11–12, located in British Cabinet Office Freedom of Information Reading Room Website, Subject Sport and Recreation, Moscow Olympics-02 http://www.cabinetoffice.gov.uk/foi/reading_room/topic/sports.aspx

69. House of Commons, Minutes of Evidence taken Before the Foreign Affairs Committee, March 5, 1980, 7–8, 13, located in British Cabinet Office Freedom of Information Reading Room Website, Subject Sport and Recreation, Moscow Olympics-02 http://www.cabinetoffice.gov.uk/foi/reading_room/topic/sports.aspx

70. House of Commons, *Parliamentary Debates (Hansard)* Fifth Series – Volume 981(London: Her Majesty's Stationery Office, 1980) 31–168.

71. A Statement from the British Olympic Association to Members of Parliament, March 14, 1980 located in British Cabinet Office Freedom of Information Reading Room Website, Subject Sport and Recreation, Moscow Olympics-18 http://www.cabinetoffice.gov.uk/foi/reading_room/topic/sports.aspx

72. House of Commons, *Parliamentary Debates (Hansard)* Fifth Series – Volume 981(London: Her Majesty's Stationery Office, 1980) 31–168.

73. *Parliamentary Debates (Hansard)* Fifth Series – Volume 981, 31–168.

74. *Parliamentary Debates (Hansard)* Fifth Series – Volume 981, 31–168.

75. *Parliamentary Debates (Hansard)* Fifth Series – Volume 981, 31–168.

76. *Parliamentary Debates (Hansard)* Fifth Series – Volume 981, 31–168.

77. *The Daily Telegraph*, March 19, 1980.

78. The Howell-Cutler meeting has grown more dramatic and more confrontational with its retelling. The source for this rendering is Howell's fairly reserved account: Howell, *Made in Birmingham*, 303–4; Neil

79. Macfarlane with Michael Herd, *Sport and Politics: A World Divided* (London: Willow Books, 1986), 225–6.

79. Howell, *Made in Birmingham*, 303–4; Macfarlane with Herd, *Sport and Politics*, 225–6.

80. Memorandum from Cutler, March 20, 1980, Folder: Olympics, 3/80, Box 49, Subject Files, National Security Advisor Files, Staff Office Files, Jimmy Carter Presidential Materials, Jimmy Carter Presidential Library, Atlanta, Georgia.

81. *Los Angeles Times*, March 21, 1980.

82. Hulme, *Political Olympics*, 30; Berenson to Cutler and Ledsky, March 27, 1980, Folder: Olympics [Working File] 2–3/80, Box 105, Lloyd Cutler Files, Counsel's Office Files, Staff Office Files, Jimmy Carter Presidential Materials, Jimmy Carter Presidential Library, Atlanta, Georgia.

83. Hulme, *Political Olympics*, 30; Kenny Moore, "The Parisian Whirl," *Sports Illustrated*, March 24, 1980, 34; Berenson to Cutler and Ledsky, March 27, 1980, Folder: Olympics [Working File] 2–3/80, Box 105, Lloyd Cutler Files, Counsel's Office Files, Staff Office Files, Jimmy Carter Presidential Materials, Jimmy Carter Presidential Library, Atlanta, Georgia.

84. Hulme, *Political Olympics*, 30; Moore, "The Parisian Whirl," 34; Berenson to Cutler and Ledsky, March 27, 1980, Folder: Olympics [Working File] 2–3/80, Box 105, Lloyd Cutler Files, Counsel's Office Files, Staff Office Files, Jimmy Carter Presidential Materials, Jimmy Carter Presidential Library, Atlanta, Georgia.

9. Coca-Cola, NBC, and the Defeat of the Iron Lady

1. *The Wall Street Journal*, January 14, 1980; Dobrynin, *In Confidence*, 451.

2. Firmite, "Facing Bear Facts," 22; "Olympics: To Go or Not to Go," *Time*, January 28, 1980, 15–16; "What a Boycott Would Cost Moscow," *Business Week*, February 4, 1980, 30; *The Washington Post*, January 22, 1980; William R. Doerner, "Auditing the Capitalist Games," *Time*, May. 21, 1984, 30.

3. *The Atlanta Constitution*, March 24, 1980.

4. Allen to Carter, March 18, 1980, Folder RE 15 1/20/77–1/20/81, Box RE 2, Sports-Recreation File, Subject File, White House

Central Files, Jimmy Carter Presidential Library, Atlanta, Georgia.

5. Jaqua to Cutler, March 27, 1980, Folder: Olympics – Letters 3–4/80, Box 102, Lloyd Cutler Files, Counsel's Office Files, Staff Office Files, Jimmy Carter Presidential Materials, Jimmy Carter Presidential Library, Atlanta, Georgia.

6. *The New York Times*, March 5, 1980.

7. Frank Shorter with Marc Bloom, *Olympic Gold: A Runner's Life and Times* (Boston: Houghton Mifflin, 1984), 134; *The Washington Post*, June 6, 1980.

8. *The Washington Post*, June 6, 1980.

9. Onek and Cutler to the President, January 5, 1981; Cutler to the President, March 27, 1980, Folder: Olympics – Memos/Correspondence to President, 3/80; Lloyd N. Cutler, Memorandum: "Olympics – Broadcast Revenues," February 14, 1980; Cutler and Onek to the SCC, March 10, 1980, Folder: Olympics – National Broadcasting Company, 2/80–1/81, Box 103, Lloyd Cutler Files, Counsel's Office Files, Staff Office Files, Jimmy Carter Presidential Materials, Jimmy Carter Presidential Library, Atlanta, Georgia.

10. Emphasis in the original. Cutler and Onek to the SCC, March 10, 1980, Folder: Olympics – National Broadcasting Company, 2/80–1/81, Box 103, Lloyd Cutler Files, Counsel's Office Files, Staff Office Files, Jimmy Carter Presidential Materials, Jimmy Carter Presidential Library, Atlanta, Georgia.

11. Cutler to Aaron, Christopher, Carswell, Shenefield, Owen, and Mudheim, February 28, 1980, Folder: Olympics – Memos/Correspondence to President, 1–2/80, Box 103, Lloyd Cutler Files, Counsel's Office Files, Staff Office Files; Brzezinski to the Secretary of State, Secretary of Defense, Attorney General, Secretary of Agriculture, Secretary of Commerce, Chairman of the Council of Economic Advisers, Special Trade Representative, Director of Central Intelligence, February 22, 1980, Folder: Olympics, 3/80, Box 49, Subject Files, National Security Advisor Files, Staff Office Files, Jimmy Carter Presidential Materials, Jimmy Carter Presidential Library, Atlanta, Georgia.

12. Special Coordination Committee Meeting, March 20, 1980, Folder: Meetings – SCC

291 3/20/80, Box 32, Papers of Zbigniew Brzezinski, Donated Historical Collections, Jimmy Carter Presidential Library, Atlanta, Georgia.

13. Special Coordination Committee Meeting, March 20, 1980, Folder: Meetings – SCC 291 3/20/80, Box 32, Papers of Zbigniew Brzezinski, Donated Historical Collections, Jimmy Carter Presidential Library, Atlanta, Georgia.

14. Special Coordination Committee Meeting, March 20, 1980, Folder: Meetings – SCC 291 3/20/80, Box 32, Papers of Zbigniew Brzezinski, Donated Historical Collections, Jimmy Carter Presidential Library, Atlanta, Georgia.

15. Special Coordination Committee Meeting, March 20, 1980, Folder: Meetings – SCC 291 3/20/80, Box 32, Papers of Zbigniew Brzezinski, Donated Historical Collections, Jimmy Carter Presidential Library, Atlanta, Georgia.

16. Special Coordination Committee Meeting, March 20, 1980, Folder: Meetings – SCC 291 3/20/80, Box 32, Papers of Zbigniew Brzezinski, Donated Historical Collections, Jimmy Carter Presidential Library, Atlanta, Georgia.

17. Cutler to Carter, March 20, 1980, Folder: Olympics – Memos/Correspondence to President, 3/80, Box 103, Lloyd Cutler Files, Counsel's Office Files, Staff Office Files, Jimmy Carter Presidential Materials, Jimmy Carter Presidential Library, Atlanta, Georgia.

18. Memorandum for Dr. Zbigniew Brzezinski, Subject: NBC Payments to USSR, March 20, 1980, Folder: Olympics – National Broadcasting Company, 2/80–1/81, Box 103, Lloyd Cutler Files, Counsel's Office Files, Staff Office Files, Jimmy Carter Presidential Materials, Jimmy Carter Presidential Library, Atlanta, Georgia.

19. Turner, Memorandum for Deputy Assistant to the President for National Security Affairs," March 20, 1980, Folder: Olympics, 3/80, Box 49, Subject Files, National Security Advisor Files, Staff Office Files, Jimmy Carter Presidential Materials, Jimmy Carter Presidential Library, Atlanta, Georgia.

20. Civiletti, Memorandum for the President, March 27, 1980, Folder: Olympics – Agreement 2–4/80, Box 101, Lloyd Cutler

Files, Counsel's Office Files, Staff Office Files, Jimmy Carter Presidential Materials, Jimmy Carter Presidential Library, Atlanta, Georgia.

21. Mabry to Moyer, March 20, 1980; Moyer to Bergsten, March 21, 1980, Folder: Olympics [Working File], 2–3/80, Box 105; Joe [Onek] to Lloyd [Cutler], March 21, 1980, Folder: Olympics – National Broadcasting Company, 2/80–1/81, Box 103; Jaqua to Cutler, March 27, 1980, Folder: Olympics – Letters 3–4/80, Box 102, Lloyd Cutler Files, Counsel's Office Files, Staff Office Files, Jimmy Carter Presidential Materials, Jimmy Carter Presidential Library, Atlanta, Georgia.

22. Hulme, *Political Olympics*, 26; Berenson to Cutler, February 22, 1980, Folder: Olympics – Memos, 1–2/80, Box 102, Lloyd Cutler Files, Counsel's Office Files, Staff Office Files, Jimmy Carter Presidential Materials; Onek and Berenson to the Vice President, April 10, 1980, Folder: Olympics – Talking Points and Qs and As, 2–5/80, Box 105, Papers of Lloyd Cutler; Brement and Larrabee to Cutler, March 19, 1980, Folder: Olympics, 3/80, Box 49, Subject Files, National Security Advisor Files, Staff Office Files, Jimmy Carter Presidential Materials, Jimmy Carter Presidential Library, Atlanta, Georgia.

23. Kenny Moore, "Stating 'Iron Realities," *Sports Illustrated*, March 31, 1980, 16–17.

24. Moore, "Stating 'Iron Realities," 16–17.

25. Moore, "Stating 'Iron Realities," 16–17.

26. *The Washington Post*, March 22, 1980; Moore, "Stating 'Iron Realities," 16–17; "President Carter Speaks to Olympic Athletes," *World News Tonight*, March 21, 1980, ABC News Transcripts, http://www.lexis-nexsis.com

27. *The New York Times*, March 22, 1980; *The Washington Post*, March 22, 1980; Moore, "Stating 'Iron Realities," 16–17; "White House Briefing on the 1980 Summer Olympics, March 21, 1980, *PPP*, 517–20.

28. *The Washington Post*, March 22, 1980; Moore, "Stating 'Iron Realities," 16–17.

29. Moore, "Stating 'Iron Realities," 16–17; Anita DeFrantz Oral History with the Author, June 20, 1997.

30. *The Kansas City Times*, March 28, 1980; *The Virginian-Pilot*, March 30, 1980; *The Houston Post*, March 31, 1980; *Chicago Tribune*, April 1, 1980.

31. Thatcher to Follows, March 19, 1980, Moscow Olympic Files, British Olympic Association Archives, London, England.

32. Follows to Thatcher, March 19, 1980, Moscow Olympic Files, British Olympic Association Archives, London, England.

33. Record of Meeting Between the Hon. Douglas Hurd CBE MP, Minister of State, and Lt Col J Innes, Honorary Treasurer of the British Olympic Association, May 7, 1980 located in British Cabinet Office Freedom of Information Reading Room Website, Subject Sport and Recreation, Moscow Olympics-24 http://www.cabinetoffice.gov.uk/foi/reading_room/topic/sports.aspx

34. British Olympic Association Press Statement, March 25, 1980, Moscow Olympic Files, British Olympic Association Archives, London, England.

35. J. Riordan, "Great Britain and the 1980 Olympics: A Victory for Olympism," in Maaret Ilmarinen, editor, *Sport and International Understanding* (New York: Springer-Verlag, 1984), 142.

36. *The Washington Post*, March 29, 1980.

37. *Daily Mail*, April 16, 1980; *The Guardian*, April 16, 1980.

38. Thatcher to Tuke, March 26, 1980 located in British Cabinet Office Freedom of Information Reading Room Website, Subject Sport and Recreation, Moscow Olympics-14 http://www.cabinetoffice.gov.uk/foi/reading_room/topic/sports.aspx; Tuke to Thatcher, April 10, 1980 located in British Cabinet Office Freedom of Information Reading Room Website, Subject Sport and Recreation, Moscow Olympics-14 http://www.cabinetoffice.gov.uk/foi/reading_room/topic/sports.aspx

39. *Daily Mail*, April 16, 1980.

40. Memorandum from Cutler, March 20, 1980, Folder: Olympics, 3/80, Box 49, Subject Files, National Security Advisor Files, Staff Office Files, Jimmy Carter Presidential Materials, Jimmy Carter Presidential Library, Atlanta, Georgia.

41. *Chicago Tribune*, March 26, 1980.

42. Knecht, *Der Boykott*, 90.

43. *Financial Times*, March 19, 1980; Kanin, *Political History of the Olympic Games*, 136. The representatives of fifteen national committees had met in Brussels on March 22 and declared that they would all vote to

send teams to Moscow. Press Release by Western European NOCs, March 22, 1980, Annex 10 to Minutes of the Meeting of the IOC Executive Board, April 21, 22, 23, 1980, 52–3, IOC Historical Archives, Samaranch Olympic Studies Centre, Olympic Museum, Lausanne, Switzerland.

44. Barton, "The American Olympic Boycott of 1980," 90–1, 93, 95, 100; *Rocky Mountain News*, March 28, 1980; *Seattle Post-Intelligencer*, April 4, 1980; *Chicago Tribune*, March 21, 1980.

45. Barton, "The American Olympic Boycott of 1980," 90–1, 93, 95, 100; *Rocky Mountain News*, March 28, 1980; *Seattle Post-Intelligencer*, April 4, 1980; *Chicago Tribune*, March 21, 1980.

46. There is no time stamp to indicate when personal notations have been made on Special Coordination Committee Meeting, March 20, 1980, Folder: Meetings – SCC 291 3/20/80, Box 32, Papers of Zbigniew Brzezinski, Donated Historical Collections; Carter notations on Cutler to Carter, March 20, 1980, Folder: Olympics – Memos/ Correspondence to President, 3/80, Box 103, Lloyd Cutler Files, Counsel's Office Files, Staff Office Files, Jimmy Carter Presidential Materials, Jimmy Carter Presidential Library, Atlanta, Georgia, but a memo that Brzezinski sent to Cutler on March 21 reports on all these comments and establishes that the President made these comments quickly. Brzezinski to Cutler, March 21, Folder: Olympics, 3/80, Box 49, Subject Files, National Security Advisor Files, Staff Office Files, Jimmy Carter Presidential Materials, Jimmy Carter Presidential Library, Atlanta, Georgia.

47. The abbreviations in Carter's handwriting are "AG" for Attorney General, "nat" for national, "PR" for public relations and "Com" for Commerce. "Jody" is a reference to White House Press Secretary Jody Powell. Carter notations on Special Coordination Committee Meeting, March 20, 1980, Folder: Meetings – SCC 291 3/20/80, Box 32, Papers of Zbigniew Brzezinski, Donated Historical Collections; Carter notations on Cutler to Carter, March 20, 1980, Folder: Olympics – Memos/ Correspondence to President, 3/80, Box 103, Lloyd Cutler Files, Counsel's Office Files, Staff Office Files, Jimmy Carter

Presidential Materials, Jimmy Carter Presidential Library, Atlanta, Georgia.

48. Onek and Cutler to the President, January 5, 1981, Folder: Olympics – National Broadcasting Company, 2/80–1/81, Box 103; Cutler to the President, March 27, 1980, Folder:Olympics–Memos/Correspondence to President, 3/80, Box 103, Lloyd Cutler Files, Counsel's Office Files, Staff Office Files, Jimmy Carter Presidential Materials, Jimmy Carter Presidential Library, Atlanta, Georgia.

49. Memorandum on Prohibition of U.S. Transactions With Respect to the Olympic Games, March 28, 19; White House Statement on Prohibition of U.S. Transactions With Respect to the Olympic Games, March 28, 1980, *PPP*, 559–61.

10. The Vote in Colorado

1. "White House Briefing for Civic and Community Leaders," April 30, 1980, *PPP*, 804; McDonald to Speechwriters, April 2, 1980, Folder: Olympics 1/1/90–8/31/80, Box 18, Speechwriters Files, Staff Office Files, Jimmy Carter Presidential Materials, Jimmy Carter Presidential Library, Atlanta, Georgia.

2. Ueberroth to Berlioux, March 25, 1980, Notice 0071937, Memo 16 Février-30 Avril 1980, Papers of Lord Killanin, Samarach Olympic Studies Centre, Olympic Museum, Lausanne, Switzerland.

3. *Los Angeles Times*, March 26–27, 1980; *The Washington Post*, April 4, 1980.

4. *The San Diego Union*, February 29, 1980.

5. *The Washington Post*, April 4, 1980; *The Washington Star*, March 29, 1980.

6. *The Washington Post*, April 1, 1980; *Los Angeles Times*, April 3, 1980; *The Atlanta Constitution*, March 31, 1980; Mark Bowden, *Guests of the Ayatollah: The Iran Hostage Crisis: The First Battle in America's War with Militant Islam* (New York: Grove Press, 2006), 400–3, 408; Farber, *Taken Hostage*, 147–55; Germond and Witcover, *Blue Smoke and Mirrors*, 141–2, 148–9; Kaufman, *Plans Unraveled*, 210.

7. *The Washington Post*, April 1, 1980; *Los Angeles Times*, April 3, 1980; *The Atlanta Constitution*, March 31, 1980.

8. *Los Angeles Times*, April 3, 1980; "Pro Forma Letter Regarding Olympic Boycott,"

April 2, 1980 attached to Cutler to the President, April 2, 1980, Folder: Olympics – Memos/Correspondence to the President, 4/80, Box 103, Lloyd Cutler Files, Counsel's Office Files, Staff Office Files, Jimmy Carter Presidential Materials, Jimmy Carter Presidential Library, Atlanta, Georgia.

9. *Los Angeles Times*, April 3, 1980; *The New York Times*, April 6, 1980.

10. *Los Angeles Times*, April 9, 1980.

11. *Los Angeles Times*, April 9, 1980; *New York Daily News*, April 10, 1980; *Chicago Tribune*, April 6, 1980.

12. *The Washington Post*, April 10, 1980.

13. O'Neill, Wright, Brademas, Rhodes, Zablocki and Broomfield to USOC Officers and Members, April 1, 1980, Folder: Boycott: Correspondence: Politicos; Kane notes, Folder, 148, Box 9, Papers of Robert Kane, U.S. Olympic Committee Library and Archives, U.S. Olympic Committee Training Center, Colorado Springs, Colorado; Byrd, Inouye, Stennis, Cannon, Muskie, Cranston, Javits, Packwood, and Church to Kane, April 2, 1980 in *Congressional Record*, 7756.

14. William E. Simon with John M. Caher, *A Time for Reflection: An Autobiography* (Washington, D.C.: Regnery, 2004), 189; *Los Angeles Times*, April 5, 1980; *The Washington Post*, April 9, 1980; Lloyd Cutler Exit Interview, March 2, 1981, 8, Jimmy Carter Presidential Library, Atlanta, Georgia; Minutes of the United States Olympic Committee, volume 1, Minutes of the Administrative Committee, April 10, 1980, 10, 16, 25, U.S. Olympic Committee Library and Archives, U.S. Olympic Committee Training Center, Colorado Springs, Colorado.

15. Onek and Berenson to the Vice-President, April 10, 1980, Folder: Olympics – Talking Points and Qs and As, 2–5/80, Box 105, Papers of Lloyd Cutler, Jimmy Carter Presidential Library, Atlanta, Georgia.

16. The author has reconfigured the punctuation from the original in the oral history believing it more accurately and clearly reflects Cutler's intended meaning. Lloyd Cutler Exit Interview, March 2, 1981, 8, Jimmy Carter Presidential Library, Atlanta, Georgia; British Embassy in Washington to Foreign and Commonwealth Office, April 9, 1980 Thatcher to Tuke, March 26, 1980 located in British Cabinet Office Freedom of Information Reading Room Website, Subject Sport and Recreation, Moscow Olympics-13 http://www.cabinetoffice.gov.uk/foi/reading_room/topic/sports.aspx.

17. Caraccioli and Caraccioli, *Boycott*, 88.

18. *Los Angeles Times*, April 1, 1980; "Jesse Owens, Sports Legend and Humanist," *Olympic Review*, April 1980, 196.

19. *Los Angeles Times*, April 5, 1980; *The Washington Post*, April 9, 1980; *Colorado Springs Sun*, April 5, 1980; Simon, *A Time for Reflection*, 189–90.

20. Minutes of the United States Olympic Committee, volume 1, House of Delegates Session, April 12, 1980, 2, U.S. Olympic Committee Library and Archives, U.S. Olympic Committee Training Center, Colorado Springs, Colorado; Cutler to the President, April 7, 1980, Folder: Olympics – Memos/Correspondence to the President, 4/80, Box 103, Lloyd Cutler Files, Counsel's Office Files, Staff Office Files, Jimmy Carter Presidential Materials, Jimmy Carter Presidential Library, Atlanta, Georgia.

21. Simon, *A Time for Reflection*, 190–1; Notes of Phone Conversation with Colonel F. Don Miller, April 5, [1980], Folder 4/7/80 [1], Box 179, Handwriting File, Office of Staff Secretary, Jimmy Carter Presidential Materials, Jimmy Carter Presidential Library, Atlanta, Georgia.

22. Carter to Cutler, April 6, 1980, Folder: Boycott Correspondence: Carter, Jimmy, Box 9, Papers of Robert Kane, U.S. Olympic Committee Library and Archives, U.S. Olympic Committee Training Center, Colorado Springs, Colorado.

23. *Rocky Mountain News*, April 10, 1980; "American Society of Newspaper Editors," April 10, 1980, *PPP*, 631–6.

24. *The Des Moines Register*, April 7, 1980; *The Atlanta Journal*, April 10, 1980; *The Washington Post*, April 15, 1980; *The Philadelphia Inquirer*, April 7, 1980.

25. *Los Angeles Times*, April 20, 1980.

26. *Colorado Springs Sun*, April 8, 1980; Wayne Drehs, "DeFrantz Would Do it All Over Again," EPSN.com located at http://espn.go.com/oly/summeroo/s/boycott/defrantz.html; undated notes of phone conversation between Miller and Cutler, Folder: Olympics, Cutler, Lloyd N. Notes, 5/80, Box 101, Lloyd Cutler Files, Counsel's

Office Files, Staff Office Files, Jimmy Carter Presidential Materials, Jimmy Carter Presidential Library, Atlanta, Georgia.

27. The White House News Summary, April 4, 1980, Jimmy Carter Presidential Library, Atlanta, Georgia.

28. Anita DeFrantz Oral History with the Author, June 20, 2007; "Resolutions Adopted by the Administrative Committee of the United States Olympic Committee" in Minutes of the United States Olympic Committee, volume 1, Minutes of the Administrative Committee, April 10, 1980, 17, 88, 100, U.S. Olympic Committee Library and Archives, U.S. Olympic Committee Training Center, Colorado Springs, Colorado; Wayne Drehs, "DeFrantz Would Do it All Over Again," EPSN.com located at http://espn.go.com/oly/summeroo/s/boycott/defrantz.html

29. The White House News Summary, April 4, 1980, Jimmy Carter Presidential Library, Atlanta, Georgia; The Atlanta Journal, April 9, 1980; Colorado Springs Gazette Telegraph, April 11, 1980.

30. Undated notes of phone conversation between Miller and Cutler, Folder: Olympics, Cutler, Lloyd N. Notes, 5/80, Box 101, Lloyd Cutler Files, Counsel's Office Files, Staff Office Files, Jimmy Carter Presidential Materials, Jimmy Carter Presidential Library, Atlanta, Georgia.

31. Rocky Mountain News, April 26, 1980; Cutler to the President, April 7, 1980 and Carter notations on Cutler to the President, April 7, 1980, Folder: Olympics – Memos/Correspondence to the President, 4/80, Box 103, Lloyd Cutler Files, Counsel's Office Files, Staff Office Files, Jimmy Carter Presidential Materials, Jimmy Carter Presidential Library, Atlanta, Georgia; Minutes of the United States Olympic Committee, volume 1, Minutes of the Administrative Committee, April 10, 1980, 15–20, 35, 100, U.S. Olympic Committee Library and Archives, U.S. Olympic Committee Training Center, Colorado Springs, Colorado.

32. Rieckehoff to Killanin, April 10, Notice 0071937, Memo 16 Février–30 Avril 1980, Papers of Lord Killanin, Samarach Olympic Studies Centre, Olympic Museum, Lausanne, Switzerland; Cutler to the President, April 21, 1980, Folder:

Olympics – Memos/Correspondence to the President, 4/80; Carter to Iles, May 20, 1980, Folder: Olympics – Memos/Correspondence to the President, 5/80, Box 103, Lloyd Cutler Files, Counsel's Office Files, Staff Office Files, Jimmy Carter Presidential Materials, Jimmy Carter Presidential Library, Atlanta, Georgia.

33. The Wall Street Journal, April 10, 1980; The Christian Science Monitor, April 10, 1980; Los Angeles Times, April 9, 1980; Chicago Tribune, April 10, 1980.

34. Kenny Moore, "The Decision: No Go on Moscow," Sports Illustrated, April 21, 1980, 32.

35. Minutes of the United States Olympic Committee, volume 1, Minutes of the Administrative Committee, April 10, 1980, 35, 146–7, U.S. Olympic Committee Library and Archives, U.S. Olympic Committee Training Center, Colorado Springs, Colorado.

36. Minutes of the United States Olympic Committee, volume 1, Minutes of the Administrative Committee, April 10, 1980, 35, 146–147, U.S. Olympic Committee Library and Archives, U.S. Olympic Committee Training Center, Colorado Springs, Colorado.

37. Minutes of the United States Olympic Committee, volume 1, Minutes of the Administrative Committee, April 10, 1980, 149–50, U.S. Olympic Committee Library and Archives, U.S. Olympic Committee Training Center, Colorado Springs, Colorado.

38. Colorado Springs Gazette Telegraph, April 11, 1980.

39. Moore, "The Decision: No Go on Moscow," 31; Pound, Five Rings Over Korea, 33.

40. The Vice-President, "U.S. Call for an Olympic Boycott," April 12, 1980, State Department Bulletin, vol. 80, no. 2038 (May 1980), 14–15.

41. The Vice-President, "U.S. Call for an Olympic Boycott," April 12, 1980, State Department Bulletin, vol. 80, no. 2038 (May 1980), 14–15.

42. The Vice-President, "U.S. Call for an Olympic Boycott," 14–15.

43. "Digest of the Proceedings of the United States Olympic Committee's House of Delegates," April 12–13, 1980, Minutes of the United States Olympic Committee, volume

1, U.S. Olympic Committee Library and Archives, U.S. Olympic Committee Training Center, Colorado Springs, Colorado.

44. Simon, *A Time for Reflection*, 196–8; Minutes of the United States Olympic Committee, volume 1, House of Delegates Session, April 12, 1980, 364–71, U.S. Olympic Committee Library and Archives, U.S. Olympic Committee Training Center, Colorado Springs, Colorado.

45. Minutes of the United States Olympic Committee, volume 1, House of Delegates Session, April 12, 1980, 364–71, U.S. Olympic Committee Library and Archives, U.S. Olympic Committee Training Center, Colorado Springs, Colorado.

46. Minutes of the United States Olympic Committee, volume 1, House of Delegates Session, April 12, 1980, 364–71, U.S. Olympic Committee Library and Archives, U.S. Olympic Committee Training Center, Colorado Springs, Colorado.

47. Minutes of the United States Olympic Committee, volume 1, House of Delegates Session, April 12, 1980, 364–71, U.S. Olympic Committee Library and Archives, U.S. Olympic Committee Training Center, Colorado Springs, Colorado.

48. *The Washington Post*, April 14, 1980; Simon, *A Time for Reflection*, 198; Ueberroth with Levin and Quinn, *Made in America*, 83–4.

49. Minutes of the United States Olympic Committee, volume 1, House of Delegates Session, April 12, 1980, 373–80, U.S. Olympic Committee Library and Archives, U.S. Olympic Committee Training Center, Colorado Springs, Colorado.

50. *The Washington Post*, April 15, 1980; Simon, *A Time for Reflection*, 198; *The Christian Science Monitor*, April 14, 1980; C. Robert Paul, Jr., "Historic Decision at Colorado Springs Means USA will not Participate at Moscow," *The Olympian*, May/June, 1980, 4–7. This construction of Kane's comment is from *The Washington Post*. There are significantly different constructions in the other publications cited in this note.

51. *The Washington Post*, April 20, 1980.

52. "1980 Summer Olympics in Moscow," April 12, 1980, *PPP*, 668.

53. McDonald to Cutler, April 14, 1980, Folder: Afghanistan and [Olympic Games], Box 8, Papers of Alonzo L. McDonald, Donated Historical Collections, White House Material, Jimmy Carter Presidential Library, Atlanta, Georgia.

54. *Los Angeles Times*, April 20, 1980.

55. *Congressional Record*, 1980, 7764.

56. *The Christian Science Monitor*, April 14, 1980; Kane notes, Folder, 148, Box 9, Papers of Robert Kane, U.S. Olympic Committee Library and Archives, U.S. Olympic Committee Training Center, Colorado Springs, Colorado.

57. Macfarlane with Herd, *Sport and Politics*, 221.

58. Killanin, *My Olympic Years*, 194–5.

59. Emphasis in the original. Moore, "The Decision: No Go on Moscow," 32; *The Christian Science Monitor*, April 14, 1980.

60. For other editorials, see the following: *Pittsburgh Post-Gazette*, April 15, 1980; *Dallas Times-Herald*, April 15, 1980; *Chicago Sun-Times*, April 15, 1980; *Detroit Free-Press*, April 15, 1980; *Richmond News Leader*, April 15, 1980; *New York Daily News*, April 16, 1989; *St. Paul Pioneer Press*, April 15, 1980; *Baltimore Sun*, April 15, 1980; *The Boston Globe*, April 15, 1980; *Chicago Tribune*, April 16, 1980; *The Atlanta Constitution*, April 15, 1980; *The Philadelphia Inquirer*, April 15, 1980; *Los Angeles Times*, April 15, 1980; *Akron Beacon Journal*, April 14, 1980; *Detroit News*, April 16, 1980.

61. *The Washington Star*, April 15, 1980.

62. *The Washington Post*, April 13, 1980; Berenson to Cutler and Ledsky, March 27, 1980, Folder: Olympics [Working File] 2–3/80, Box 105, Lloyd Cutler Files, Counsel's Office Files, Staff Office Files, Jimmy Carter Presidential Materials, Jimmy Carter Presidential Library, Atlanta, Georgia.

63. Bowden, *Guests of the Ayatollah*, 550.

11. Civil Wars

1. Head and Trudeau, *The Canadian Way*, 209–10; Eric S. Morse, *Sport and Canadian Foreign Policy Behind the Headlines Series*. David Stafford, editor (Toronto: Canadian Institute of International Affairs, 1987), 12–13; Pound, *Inside the Olympics*, 101.

2. Macintosh, Hawes, Greenhorn, and Black, *Sport and Canadian Diplomacy*, 98; Pound, *Inside the Olympics*, 98; Worrall, *My Olympic Journey*, 186.

3. Macintosh, Hawes, Greenhorn, and Black, *Sport and Canadian Diplomacy*, 98–9; Pound, *Inside the Olympics*, 99.

4. Head and Trudeau, *The Canadian Way*, 210; Macintosh, Hawes, Greenhorn, and Black, *Sport and Canadian Diplomacy*, 99; Mark MacGuigan, *An Inside Look at External Affairs during the Trudeau Years* edited by P. Whitney Lackenbauer (Calgary: University of Calgary Press, 2002), 36–7.

5. Worrall, *My Olympic Journey*, 187; *The Globe and Mail*, April 23, 1980; Pound, *Inside the Olympics*, 98–9.

6. Pound, *Inside the Olympics*, 100.

7. *The Globe and Mail*, April 28, 1980.

8. Pound, *Inside the Olympics*, 98, 101.

9. "TV Interview for Granada TV Reports Politics," April 14, 1980, Christopher Collins, editor. *Complete Public Statements of Margaret Thatcher, 1945–1990* (New York: Oxford University Press, 1999).

10. *Sunday Express*, June 16, 1980.

11. Thatcher to Allhusen, April 30, 1980 located in British Cabinet Office Freedom of Information Reading Room Website, Subject Sport and Recreation, Moscow Olympics-12 http://www.cabinetoffice.gov.uk/foi/reading_room/topic/sports.aspx

12. Thatcher to Allhusen, April 30, 1980; Foreign and Commonwealth Office Memorandum: Why Britain Should not be Represented at the Olympics, March 27, 1980 located in British Cabinet Office Freedom of Information Reading Room Website, Subject Sport and Recreation, Moscow Olympics-12 http://www.cabinetoffice.gov.uk/foi/reading_room/topic/sports.aspx; Thatcher to Fraser, March 10, 1980, located in British Cabinet Office Freedom of Information Reading Room Website, Subject Sport and Recreation, Moscow Olympics-19 http://www.cabinetoffice.gov.uk/foi/reading_room/topic/sports.aspx

13. *The Guardian*, February 24, 2006.

14. *Le Figaro*, May 14, 1980.

15. *Le Figaro*, May 21, 1980.

16. Hulme, *Political Olympics*, 59–61; *Rocky Mountain News*, May 12, 1980; Robert Schneider, "Le front de la politique étrangère," *L'Express*, May 17–23, 19 Folder:Olympics–Memos/Correspondence to President 1–2/80, Box 103, Lloyd Cutler Files, Counsel's Office Files, Staff Office Files, Jimmy Carter Presidential Materials, Jimmy Carter Presidential Library.80, 111.

17. "The President's News Conference." February 13th, 1980, *PPP*, 307–15; Schmidt,

18. *Le Figaro*, May 14, 1980; *Le Monde*, May 15, 1980.

19. *Le Figaro*, May 14, 1980; *Le Monde*, May 15, 1980.

20. Kanin, *Political History*, 124–5, 127–8; Hulme, *Political Olympics*, 57–9; Helmut Schmidt, *Men and Powers: A Political Retrospective* translated by Ruth Hein (New York: Random House, 1989), 208–9; Special Coordination Committee, March 6, 1980, Folder: Meetings SCC 284 3/6/80, Box 32, Papers of Zbigniew Brzezinski, Donated Historical Collections, Jimmy Carter Presidential Library, Atlanta, Georgia.

21. Knecht, *Der Boykott*, 153–6, 162; *Le Figaro*, May 14, 1980; Goodall to Foreign and Commonwealth Office, April 24, 1980 located in British Cabinet Office Freedom of Information Reading Room Website, Subject Sport and Recreation, Moscow Olympics-11 http://www.cabinetoffice.gov.uk/foi/reading_room/topic/sports.aspx.

22. *Frankfurter Allgemeine Zeitung*, May 9 and 16, 1980.

23. *Frankfurter Allgemeine Zeitung*, May 16, 1980.

24. Muskie to the President, May 19, 1980, Folder: State Department Evening Reports, 5/80, Box 40, Plains File, Jimmy Carter Presidential Materials, Jimmy Carter Presidential Library, Atlanta, Georgia.

25. Richard N. Gardner, *Mission Italy: On the Front Lines of the Cold War* (New York: Rowman & Littlefield Publishers, 2005), 6–7, 254, 259.

26. Gardner, *Mission Italy*, 268.

27. Lichtenstein Press Bulletin Number 49, May 1, 1980 in *Congressional Record*, June 3, 1980, 13166.

28. Nordli to Mondale, April 24, 1980, Folder: RE 15 1/20/77–1/20/81, Box RE 2, Sports-Recreation File, Subject File, White House Central Files, Jimmy Carter Presidential Library, Atlanta, Georgia; Kanin, *Political History of the Olympic Games*, 132–6.

29. Dáil Éireann, *Parliamentary Debates*, vol. 318 (Dublin: The Stationary Office, 1980), 339–42.

30. *Irish Independent*, March 1, 1980; *The Irish Times*, March 3, 1980; Killanin to Kane, March 11, 1980, Folder 822, Box 52a, Papers

of Robert Kane, U.S. Olympic Committee Library and Archives, U.S. Olympic Committee Training Center, Colorado Springs, Colorado.

31. Seanad Éireann, *Parliamentary Debates* vol. 93 (Dublin: The Stationary Office of Seanad Éireann, 1980), 1434–93.

32. Text of Statement issued May 16,1980 in Dublin by Government of Ireland Information Services," Folder: Olympics – Statements and Transcripts, 3–5/80, Box 104, Lloyd Cutler Files, Counsel's Office Files, Staff Office Files, Jimmy Carter Presidential Materials, Jimmy Carter Presidential Library, Atlanta, Georgia.

33. *El Pais*, May 24, 1980; *ABC*, May 24, 1980.

34. *La Nacion*, May 10, 1980.

35. *La Nacion*, June 6,1980. This newspaper has the same title as one published in Argentina that is cited in notes that proceed and follow this one. Carter to Carazo, May 19, 1980; Carazo to Carter, May 23, 1980,

36. *El Imparcial*, May 29, 1980; *El Universal*, May 28, 1980.

37. *La Nacion*, May 10, 1980; *El Diario*, May 15, 1980; Méndez to Carter, February 13, 1980 and Carter notation on Brzezinski to the President, February 27, 1980, Folder: RE 15 1/20/77–1/20/81, Box RE 2, Sports-Recreation Files, Subject File, White House Central Files, Jimmy Carter Presidential Library, Atlanta, Georgia.

38. Hua to Carter, February 1, 1980; Demirel to Carter, May 23, 1980, Folder: RE 15 1/20/77–1/20/81, Box RE 2, Sports-Recreation Files, Subject File, White House Central Files, Jimmy Carter Presidential Library, Atlanta, Georgia

39. Allen Guttmann and Lee Thompson, *Japanese Sports: A History* (Honolulu: University of Hawaii Press, 2001), 202–3; Kiyokawa Masaji, *Supōtsu to Seiji* [Sports and Politics] (Tokyo: Baseball Magazine, 1987), 84–6; Sato Seizaburo, Koyama Kenichi and Kumon Shunpei, *Ohira Masayoshi: Hito to Shisō* [Ohira Masayoshi: Man and Ideas] (Tokyo: Ohira Masayoshi Kinen Zaidan, 1990), 546; Ono Akira, *Gendai Supōtsu Hihan* [A Critique of Modern Sports] (Tokyo: Taishūkan shoten, 1996), 139.

40. Guttmann and Thompson, *Japanese Sports*, 202–3; Sato, Koyama and Kumon, *Ohira Masayoshi*, 548–9.

41. Guttmann and Thompson, *Japanese Sports*, 202–3; Sato, Koyama and Kumon, *Ohira Masayoshi*, 548–9, 550; *The Washington Post*, April 16, 1980; Kiyokawa Masaji, *Supōtsu to seiji* [Sports and Politics], 125–32, 134.

42. *The Statesman*, March 29 and June 7, 1980.

43. Forrest, *Boycott*, 60–1, 70,73–5, 99–100, 113–16, 118–21.

44. Weller, *Malcolm Fraser PM*, 346–7; Alan Renouf, *Malcom Fraser and Australian Foreign Policy* (Sydney: Australian Professional Publications, 1986), 100–3; *The Australian*, February 7, 1980; *The Age*, February 14, 1980; Deane, "The Melbourne Press and the 1980 Moscow Olympics," 27–42; Gordon, *Australia and the Olympic Games*, 325.

45. Ayers, *Malcolm Fraser*, 367–8; Weller, *Malcolm Fraser PM*, 349; Forrest, *Boycott*, 71.

46. Gordon, *Australia and the Olympic Games*, 325; Forrest, *Boycott*, 110–11.

47. Gosper, *An Olympic Life*, 141–2; Miller, *Olympic Revolution*, 87; Young, "The Melbourne Press and the 1980 Moscow Olympic Boycott Controversy," 185, 196–7.

48. Forrest, *Boycott*, 125–7, 133, 192–3, 215.

49. Young, "The Melbourne Press and the 1980 Moscow Olympic Boycott Controversy," 184–200; Deane, "The Melbourne Press and the 1980 Moscow Olympics," 27–42; *The Age*, April 21, 1980; Forrest, *Boycott*, 60–1.

50. Forrest, *Boycott*, 128–30, 197–9.

51. Weller, *Malcolm Fraser PM*, 349; Ayers, *Malcolm Fraser*, 369; Gosper, *An Olympic Life*, 143.

52. *The Age*, May 24, 1980; Gosper, *An Olympic Life*, 143; Gordon, *Australia and the Olympic Games*, 326; Forrest, *Boycott*, 153, 155. The Luxton quote comes from Gordon. Forrest has a slightly different construction.

53. *The Age*, May 24, 1980; Gosper, *An Olympic Life*, 143; Gordon, *Australia and the Olympic Games*, 327–8.

54. *The Age*, May 24, 1980; Gosper, *An Olympic Life*, 143.

55. Emphasis in the original. *The Age*, May 24, 1980.

56. *The Herald*, May 28, 1980; *The Age*, May 24, 1980; Weller, *Malcolm Fraser PM*, 350; Ayers, *Malcolm Fraser*, 368–9; Gordon, *Australia and the Olympic Games*, 329.

57. Forrest, *Boycott*, 70, 159, 165–72; Fraser to Thatcher, May 28, 1980 located in British Cabinet Office Freedom of Information

Reading Room Website, Subject Sport and Recreation, Moscow Olympics-23 http://www.cabinetoffice.gov.uk/foi/reading_room/topic/sports.aspx

58. *The Herald*, May 28, 1980; *The Age*, May 24, 1980; Weller, *Malcolm Fraser PM*, 350; Ayers, *Malcolm Fraser*, 368–9; Gordon, *Australia and the Olympic Games*, 329; Forrest, *Boycott*, 196.

59. *The Evening Post*, January 23, 1980; *The New Zealand Herald*, January 21, 23, 1980.

60. *The Press*, May 9, 10, 1980; *The Evening Post*, January 23, 1980; Killanin, *My Olympic Years*, 222–3.

61. *The Press*, May 9, 10, 1980; *The Evening Post*, January 23, 1980; Killanin, *My Olympic Years*, 222–3.

62. *The Press*, May 9, 10, 1980; *The Evening Post*, January 23, 1980; Killanin, *My Olympic Years*, 222–3.

63. *The Evening Post*, May 10, 21, 27, 28, 29, 30, 1980; Kanin, *Political History of the Olympic Games*, 138; Forrest, *Boycott*, 146.

64. Kanin, *Political History of the Olympic Games*, 142; *Sunday Sketch*, June 8, 1980; Lamine Ba, "Wholehearted Support for the 1980 Olympic Games in Moscow," *Olympic Review* (April 1980), 161.

12. Carter versus Killanin

1. Killanin, *Olympic Years*, 191; Killanin to Kane, March 5, 1980, Folder 822, Box 52a, Papers of Robert Kane, U.S. Olympic Committee Library and Archives, U.S. Olympic Committee Training Center, Colorado Springs, Colorado.

2. Killanin, *Olympic Years*, 195–6; Ueberroth with Levin and Quinn, *Made in America*, 81–2; *Los Angels Times*, March 19, 1980.

3. Killanin, *Olympic Years*, 197; Minutes of the Meeting of the Executive Board, April 21, 22, and 23, 1980, 1, IOC Historical Archives, Samaranch Olympic Studies Centre, Olympic Museum, Lausanne, Switzerland.

4. Minutes of the Meeting of the Executive Board, April 21, 22, and 23, 1980, 6–8, IOC Historical Archives, Samaranch Olympic Studies Centre, Olympic Museum, Lausanne, Switzerland.

5. Minutes of the Meeting of the Executive Board, April 21, 22, and 23, 1980, 8–10, IOC Historical Archives, Samaranch Olympic

Studies Centre, Olympic Museum, Lausanne, Switzerland.

6. Minutes of the Meeting of the Executive Board, April 21, 22, and 23, 1980, 11–14, IOC Historical Archives, Samaranch Olympic Studies Centre, Olympic Museum, Lausanne, Switzerland.

7. Minutes of the Meeting of the Executive Board, April 21, 22, and 23, 1980, 14, IOC Historical Archives, Samaranch Olympic Studies Centre, Olympic Museum, Lausanne, Switzerland; Brement to Brzezinski, March 21, 1980, Folder: Olympics, 6/79–2/80, Box 48, Subject Files, National Security Advisor Files, Staff Office Files, Jimmy Carter Presidential Materials, Jimmy Carter Presidential Library, Atlanta, Georgia.

8. Carter to Killanin, April 22, 1980, Annex 17 to Minutes of the Meeting of the Executive Board, April 21, 22, and 23, 1980, 59, IOC Historical Archives, Samaranch Olympic Studies Centre, Olympic Museum, Lausanne, Switzerland.

9. Minutes of the Meeting of the Executive Board, April 21, 22, and 23, 1980, 25, IOC Historical Archives, Samaranch Olympic Studies Centre, Olympic Museum, Lausanne, Switzerland.

10. Minutes of the Meeting of the Executive Board, April 21, 22, and 23, 1980, 25–6, IOC Historical Archives; Berlioux to Novikov, January 26, 1980, Folder Identification 8365, Folder 0072284, Telex Files, Papers of Lord Killanin, Samarach Olympic Studies Centre, Olympic Museum, Lausanne, Switzerland.

11. Minutes of the Meeting of the Executive Board, April 21, 22, and 23, 1980, 25–6, IOC Historical Archives, Samaranch Olympic Studies Centre, Olympic Museum, Lausanne, Switzerland.

12. Killanin, *Olympic Years*, 197–9. There is a different construction of Keller's quote in the *Daily Mail*, April 23, 1980.

13. Killanin, *Olympic Years*, 197–9; *Daily Mail*, April 23, 1980.

14. Minutes of the Meeting of the Executive Board, April 21, 22, and 23, 1980, pages 31, 34–8, IOC Historical Archives, Samaranch Olympic Studies Centre, Olympic Museum, Lausanne, Switzerland.

15. Minutes of the Meeting of the Executive Board, April 21, 22, and 23, 1980, pages 31,

34–8, IOC Historical Archives, Samaranch Olympic Studies Centre, Olympic Museum, Lausanne, Switzerland.

16. Minutes of the Meeting of the Executive Board, April 21, 22, and 23, 1980, pages 31, 34–8, IOC Historical Archives, Samaranch Olympic Studies Centre, Olympic Museum, Lausanne, Switzerland.

17. Minutes of the Meeting of the Executive Board, April 21, 22, and 23, 1980, 38, IOC Historical Archives, Samaranch Olympic Studies Centre, Olympic Museum, Lausanne, Switzerland.

18. IOC Executive Board Resolution, April 23, 1980, Annex 22 to the Minutes of the Meeting of the Executive Board, April 21, 22, and 23, 1980 and the Minutes of the Meeting of the Executive Board, April 21, 22, and 23, 1980, 39–40, 67, IOC Historical Archives, Samaranch Olympic Studies Centre, Olympic Museum, Lausanne, Switzerland.

19. Killanin, *Olympic Years*, 206–7.

20. Dobrynin, *In Confidence*, 452–3; Killanin, *Olympic Years*, 207; "Seven Questions One Hundred Days Before the Games of the XXIInd Olympiad," *Olympic Review*, April 1980, 154–8.

21. "Seven Questions One Hundred Days Before the Games of the XXIInd Olympiad," *Olympic Review*, April 1980, 154–8.

22. Senn, *Power, Politics and the Olympic Games*, 180.

23. Killanin, *Olympic Years*, 211–12.

24. Cutler to the President, May 12, 1980, Folder: Memos/Correspondence to the President, 5–7/80, Box 103, Lloyd Cutler Files, Counsel's Office Files, Staff Office Files, Jimmy Carter Presidential Materials, Jimmy Carter Presidential Library, Atlanta, Georgia.

25. Brzezinski to the President, January 24, 1980, Folder 9 1/22/80–1/31/80, Box 13, President's Daily Reading File, Papers of Zbigniew Brzezinski, Donated Historical Collections, Jimmy Carter Presidential Library, Atlanta, Georgia.

26. Killanin, *Olympic Years*, 212.

27. Killanin, *Olympic Years*, 212.

28. The following account is based on a reading of three different versions of this meeting: the one offered in Killanin's memoirs, and the memos that Berlioux and Onek wrote. There are differences on when certain topics were discussed in the conversation and the importance of the subjects that the participants covered. The account here is generally the product of when two of the three sources agree. Killanin, *Olympic Years*, 212–14; Memorandum for the File, May 21, 1980, Folder: Olympics – Letters, 5–8/80, Box 102, Lloyd Cutler Files, Counsel's Office Files, Staff Office Files, Jimmy Carter Presidential Materials, Jimmy Carter Presidential Library, Atlanta, Georgia; Berlioux to Killanin, May 19, 1980, Folder Identification 8365, Folder 0072285, Telex Files, Papers of Lord Killanin, Samarach Olympic Studies Centre, Olympic Museum, Lausanne, Switzerland.

29. Killanin, *Olympic Years*, 212–14; Memorandum for the File, May 21, 1980, Folder: Olympics – Letters, 5–8/80, Box 102, Lloyd Cutler Files, Counsel's Office Files, Staff Office Files, Jimmy Carter Presidential Materials, Jimmy Carter Presidential Library, Atlanta, Georgia; Berlioux to Killanin, May 19, 1980, Folder Identification 8365, Folder 0072285, Telex Files, Papers of Lord Killanin, Samarach Olympic Studies Centre, Olympic Museum, Lausanne, Switzerland.

30. Killanin, *Olympic Years*, 212–14; Memorandum for the File, May 21, 1980, Folder: Olympics – Letters, 5–8/80, Box 102, Lloyd Cutler Files, Counsel's Office Files, Staff Office Files, Jimmy Carter Presidential Materials, Jimmy Carter Presidential Library, Atlanta, Georgia; Berlioux to Killanin, May 19, 1980, Folder Identification 8365, Folder 0072285, Telex Files, Papers of Lord Killanin, Samarach Olympic Studies Centre, Olympic Museum, Lausanne, Switzerland.

31. Killanin, *Olympic Years*, 212–14; Memorandum for the File, May 21, 1980, Folder: Olympics – Letters, 5–8/80, Box 102, Lloyd Cutler Files, Counsel's Office Files, Staff Office Files, Jimmy Carter Presidential Materials, Jimmy Carter Presidential Library, Atlanta, Georgia; Berlioux to Killanin, May 19, 1980, Folder Identification 8365, Folder 0072285, Telex Files, Papers of Lord Killanin, Samarach Olympic Studies Centre, Olympic Museum, Lausanne, Switzerland.

32. Killanin, *Olympic Years*, 212–14; Memorandum for the File, May 21, 1980,

Folder: Olympics – Letters, 5–8/80, Box 102, Lloyd Cutler Files, Counsel's Office Files, Staff Office Files, Jimmy Carter Presidential Materials, Jimmy Carter Presidential Library, Atlanta, Georgia; Berlioux to Killanin, May 19, 1980, Folder Identification 8365, Folder 0072285, Telex Files, Papers of Lord Killanin, Samarach Olympic Studies Centre, Olympic Museum, Lausanne, Switzerland.

33. Killanin, *Olympic Years*, 212–14; Memorandum for the File, May 21, 1980, Folder: Olympics – Letters, 5–8/80, Box 102, Lloyd Cutler Files, Counsel's Office Files, Staff Office Files, Jimmy Carter Presidential Materials, Jimmy Carter Presidential Library, Atlanta, Georgia; Berlioux to Killanin, May 19, 1980, Folder Identification 8365, Folder 0072285, Telex Files, Papers of Lord Killanin, Samarach Olympic Studies Centre, Olympic Museum, Lausanne, Switzerland.

34. Killanin, *Olympic Years*, 212–14; Memorandum for the File, May 21, 1980, Folder: Olympics – Letters, 5–8/80, Box 102, Lloyd Cutler Files, Counsel's Office Files, Staff Office Files, Jimmy Carter Presidential Materials, Jimmy Carter Presidential Library, Atlanta, Georgia; Berlioux to Killanin, May 19, 1980, Folder Identification 8365, Folder 0072285, Telex Files, Papers of Lord Killanin, Samarach Olympic Studies Centre, Olympic Museum, Lausanne, Switzerland.

35. Killanin, *Olympic Years*, 215.

36. Gosper, *An Olympic Life*, 149.

37. "Memorandum on Information Given by Comrade Pyotr A. Abrassimov to Comrade Erich Honecker about a Conversation between USSR Foreign Minister Comrade Adrei Gromyko with US Secretary of State Edmund S. Muskie," May 27, 1980, "More East-Bloc Sources on Afghanistan," *Cold War International History Project Bulletin Issue* 14/15 (Winter 2003-Spring 2004), 244.

13. Moscow: The Olympics Are the Olympics

1. "Guess Who's Coming to Moscow," *Time*, June 9, 1980, 66.

2. Killanin, *My Olympic Years*, 221.

3. Brzezinski to the President, June 6, 1980, Folder: Weekly Reports [to the President], 136–50, Box 42, Papers of Zbigniew Brzezinski, Donated Historical Collections, Jimmy Carter Presidential Library.

4. All information on Olympic medal statistics comes from the IOC's website, which includes a searchable database of all medal winners located at http://www.olympic.org

5. Draft letter From Prime Minister to Sir Denis Follows, no date; Thatcher to Follows, May 20, 1980 located in British Cabinet Office Freedom of Information Reading Room Website, Subject Sport and Recreation, Moscow Olympics-24 http://www.cabinetoffice.gov.uk/foi/reading_room/topic/sports.aspx

6. Carter, *Keeping Faith*, 526.

7. Joe Onek Oral History by the Author, June 22, 2007.

8. *The Christian Science Monitor*, May 27, 1980; "Medal Count," *Sports Illustrated*, May 26, 1980, 16.

9. *Berliner Morgenpost*, July 15, 1980; *Le Monde*, July 21, 1980.

10. Emphasis in the original. Miller, *Olympic Revolution*, 94.

11. Ueberroth, with Levin and Quinn, *Made in America*, 84; Kane notes, Folder, 148, Box 9, Papers of Robert Kane, U.S. Olympic Committee Library and Archives, U.S. Olympic Committee Training Center, Colorado Springs, Colorado.

12. *The Washington Post*, July 19, 1980.

13. *The Wall Street Journal*, July 22, 1980; *The New York Times*, July 21, 1980.

14. *The New York Times*, May 28, 1980; *Chicago Tribune*, May 10, 1980.

15. Plenum of Central Committee of the Communist Party of the Soviet Union, June 23, 1980, in "U.S.-Soviet Relations and the Turn Towards Confrontation, 1977–1980 – New Russian & East German Documents," *Cold War International History Project Bulletin* Issues 8–9 (Winter 1996/1997), 175.

16. Plenum of Central Committee of the Communist Party of the Soviet Union, June 23, 1980, in "U.S.-Soviet Relations and the Turn Towards Confrontation, 1977–1980 – New Russian & East German Documents," *Cold War International History Project Bulletin* Issues 8–9 (Winter 1996/1997), 176.

17. A. Kolodnyi, *"Igry" Vokrug Igr* ["The Games" Surrounding the Games] (Moscow: Sovetskaia Rossiia, 1981), 5.

18. Moore, "The 'Pawns' Make a Move," 22.

19. Joe Marshall, "High, Wide and Handsome," *Sports Illustrated*, March 10, 1980, 50–1.

20. Kenny Moore and E.M. Swift, "Detour on the High Road," *Sports Illustrated*, July 21, 1980, 26–43.

21. Emphasis in the original. Kenny Moore, "Trying Hard to Go Nowhere," *Sports Illustrated*, July 7, 1980, 12–17.

22. Kenny Moore, "The Agony and Ecstasy of the Trials," *Sports Illustrated*, June 30, 1980, 24; Moore, "Trying Hard to Go Nowhere," 12–17.

23. Moore and Swift, "Detour on the High Road," 26–43.

24. *Detroit Free Press*, May 28, 1980.

25. Fimrite, "Only the Bears Were Bullish," 10–17; Christopher Booker, *The Games War: A Moscow Journal* (London: Faber and Faber, 1981), 76–80.

26. Fimrite, "Only the Bears Were Bullish," 10–17; Booker, *The Games War*, 76–8.

27. *The New York Times*, July 23, 1980.

28. "The Undetered Yanks," *Sports Illustrated*, June 9, 1980, 9; Swift, "Detour on the High Road," 43; *The Washington Post*, August 1, 1980; Paul Zimmerman, "Voices from the Village," *Sports Illustrated*, July 28, 1980, 15.

29. "The Undetered Yanks," 9; Swift, "Detour on the High Road," 43; *The Washington Post*, August 1, 1980; Zimmerman, "Voices from the Village," 15.

30. Zimmerman, "Voices from the Village," 15.

31. A. Kolodnyi, *"Igry" Vokrug Igr* ["The Games" Surrounding the Games], 155.

32. *The Washington Post*, July 25, 1980; *The Christian Science Monitor*, July 31, 1980; Ron Fimrite, "One Slip and All Was Upside Down," *Sports Illustrated*, August 4, 1980, 16–19.

33. *The Washington Post*, July 25, 1980; *The Christian Science Monitor*, July 31, 1980; Fimrite, "One Slip and All Was Upside Down," 16–19.

34. Anita Verschoth, "Russia Gets in the Swim," *Sports Illustrated*, August 4, 1980, 18–19; C. Robert Paul, Jr. "East German Women Sweep as Soviet Men Take Down Top Swimming Honors" *The Olympian*, September 1980, 22–24.

35. Weller, *Malcolm Fraser, PM*, 351.

36. Kenny Moore, "Their Finest Hours," *Sports Illustrated*, August 4, 1980, 14.

37. Moore, "Their Finest Hours," 14–15; C. Robert Paul, Jr. "Was It the Best Ever Track and Field Olympics?" *The Olympian*, September 1980, 20.

38. Moore, "Their Finest Hours," 15–16; *The Christian Science Monitor*, July 28, 1980.

39. *The Washington Post*, July 25, 1980; C. Robert Paul, Jr. "Was It the Best Ever Track and Field Olympics?" *The Olympian*, September 1980, 19–20.

40. Kenny Moore, "How's This, Mrs. Mullory?" *Sports Illustrated*, August 11, 1980, 17–24.

41. *The Washington Post*, July 28, 1980; C. Robert Paul, Jr. "Was It the Best Ever Track and Field Olympics?" *The Olympian*, September 1980, 21; Moore, "How's This, Mrs. Mullory?" 17–24.

42. Moore, "How's This, Mrs. Mullory?" 17–24.

43. Moore, "How's This, Mrs. Mullory?" 17–24; *The Washington Post*, July 31, 1980.

44. *The New York Times*, July 25 and August 4, 1980.

45. *The Washington Post*, August 3, 1980; Booker, *Games War*, 195.

46. *The Christian Science Monitor*, July 31, 1980; "Soviet Union Medals in All Ten Team Sports on Program at Moscow," *The Olympian*, September 1980, 28.

47. Ueberroth with Levin and Quinn, *Made in America*, 87; I. T. Novikov, editor in chief, *Official Report of the Organising Committee of the Games of the XXII Olympiad*, volume 2, *Organisation* (Moscow: Progress Publishers, 1981), 299–306.

48. Ueberroth with Levin and Quinn, *Made in America*, 87; I. T. Novikov, editor in chief, *Official Report of the Organising Committee of the Games of the XXII Olympiad*, 299–306.

49. Killanin, *Olympic Years*, 217; Pound, *Inside the Olympics*, 102; Kiyokawa, *Supōtsu to seiji* [Sports and Politics], 136–41.

50. *The Boston Globe*, August 10, 1980.

51. *The Christian Science Monitor*, August 5, 1980; all information on participation figures comes from the IOC's website located at http://www.olympic.org

52. Report by Mr. Ignati T. Novikov, President of the Organising Committee for the Games of the XXIInd Olympiad in Moscow, Annex 5 to Minutes of the Meeting of the International Olympic Committee, September 29–October 2, 1981, 64–71, IOC Historical Archives, Samaranch Olympic Studies Centre, Olympic Museum, Lausanne, Switzerland.

53. *Le Quotidien de Paris*, July 22, 1980; *The Boston Globe*, August 10, 1980.

54. Booker, *Games War*, 196–9, 202–3; Fimrite, "Only the Bears Were Bullish," 17.

55. Booker, *Games War*, 196–9, 202–3; *The New York Times*, July 27, 1980; *The Wall Street Journal*, July 22, 1980; Fimrite, "Only the Bears Were Bullish," 17; *The Boston Globe*, August 10, 1980.

56. Report by Mr. Ignati T. Novikov, President of the Organising Committee for the Games of the XXIInd Olympiad in Moscow, Annex 5 to Minutes of the Meeting of the International Olympic Committee, September 29–October 2, 1981, 64–71, IOC Historical Archives, Samaranch Olympic Studies Centre, Olympic Museum, Lausanne, Switzerland.

57. Craig Neff, "… and Meanwhile in Philadelphia," *Sports Illustrated*, July 28, 1980, 18–19; *The Washington Post*, July 18, 1980.

58. "Consolation Prizes," *Sports Illustrated*, July 21, 1980, 12; *The Washington Post*, July 11 and 30, 1980; Bob Jaugstetter, "Party at the Nation's Capital," *The Olympian*, September 1980, 13; H.R. 7482, *Congressional Record*, volume 126, part 14, 17734; Carter notation on Cutler Memorandum for the President, June 3, 1980, Folder: Memos/Correspondence to President, Box 103, Lloyd Cutler Files, Counsel's Office Files, Staff Office Files, Jimmy Carter Presidential Materials, Jimmy Carter Presidential Library, Atlanta, Georgia.

59. "United States Summer Olympic Team: Remarks at the Medal Presentation Ceremony," July 30, 1980, *PPP*, 1440–1.

60. *The Washington Post*, July 31, 1980.

61. "Joy and Tears as U.S. Olympians are Honored by USOC in Washington," *The Olympian*, September 1980, 4–12; "Address by Senator Gary Hart to Olympic Athletes," *Congressional Record*, vol. 126. no. 16, 20433.

62. *The Washington Post*, July 31, 1980.

63. Joe Marshall, "All That Glitter Was Not Gold," *Sports Illustrated*, August 11, 1980, 32–5; *The New York Times*, August 4, 1980; "United States Olympic Swim Team: Remarks at a Medal Presentation Ceremony," August 5, 1980, *PPP*, 1492–3.

64. Diane K. Shah, "The Lost Class of '80," *Newsweek*, July 14, 1980, 47.

65. Anita DeFrantz Oral History by the Author, June 20, 2007.

14. Los Angeles: The Olympics Are the Olympics

1. Germond and Witcover, *Blue Smoke and Mirrors*, 148–51, 310–14.

2. Carter, *Keeping Faith*, 542.

3. Carter, *Keeping Faith*, 543.

4. "Venice Economic Summit: Exchange with Reporters Following the First Two Sessions," June 22, 1980; "Remarks Accepting the Presidential Nomination at the 1980 Democratic National Convention," August 14, 1980, and "Remarks and a Question-and-Answer Session at a Townhall Meeting," September 15, 1980, *PPP*, 1173, 1530–1, 1535, and 1728. Historian Douglas Brinkley, in a sympathetic account of Carter's life since leaving the White House, claims that Reagan used the boycott against Carter, ignoring the President's efforts to use the issue against the challenger. Brinkley, *The Unfinished Presidency*, 14.

5. Kaufman, *Presidency of Jimmy Carter*, 198–201.

6. Kaufman, *Presidency of Jimmy Carter*, 204–5; Carter, *Keeping Faith*, 543; Germond and Witcover, *Blue Smoke and Mirrors*, 312.

7. Dobrynin, *In Confidence*, 467, 469.

8. Pound, *Five Rings*, 33, 40; Pound, *Inside the Olympics*, 235–7.

9. Miller, *Olympic Revolution*, 100–1; Anita DeFrantz Oral History by the Author, June 20, 2007.

10. Ueberroth with Levin and Quinn, *Made in America*, 223, 228–9; Pavlov to Samaranch, August 10, 1982, Annex 22 to Meeting of the IOC Executive Board, October 10–13, 1982, Samaranch Olympic Studies Centre, Olympic Museum, Lausanne, Switzerland.

11. George P. Schultz, *Turmoil and Triumph: My Years as Secretary of State* (New York: Charles Scribner's Sons, 1993), 474–5.

12. Gramov to Samaranch, April 11, 1984, Annex 3 to Minutes of the Extraordinary Meeting of the IOC Executive Board, May 18–19, 1984, Samaranch Olympic Studies Centre, Olympic Museum, Lausanne, Switzerland.

13. Ueberroth, with Levin and Quinn, *Made in America*, 229; Juan-Antonio Samaranch, "1984 and Non-Participation: Declaration

14. Miller, *Olympic Revolution*, 88.
15. Ueberroth, with Levin and Quinn, *Made in America*, 235.
16. Ueberroth, with Levin and Quinn, *Made in America*, 235–40.
17. Ueberroth, with Levin and Quinn, *Made in America*, 239–40.
18. Ueberroth, with Levin and Quinn, *Made in America*, 240.
19. Miller, *Olympic Revolution*, 91.
20. Ueberroth, with Levin and Quinn, *Made in America*, 267; Reagan to Samaranch, May 8, 1984, Annex 5 to Minutes of the Extraordinary Meeting of the IOC Executive Board, May 18–19, 1984, Samaranch Olympic Studies Centre, Olympic Museum, Lausanne, Switzerland.
21. Ueberroth, with Levin and Quinn, *Made in America*, 267.
22. Ueberroth, with Levin and Quinn, *Made in America*, 267; Miller, *Olympic Revolution*, 90; Ronald Reagan, *The Reagan Diaries* edited by Douglas Brinkley (New York: HarperCollins Publishers, 2007), 220–1, 239.
23. "Statement of the USSR National Olympic Committee" attached to Gramov to Samaranch, May 9, 1984, Annex 2 to Minutes of the Extraordinary Meeting of the IOC Executive Board, May 18–19, 1984, Samarach Olympic Studies Centre, Olympic Museum, Lausanne, Switzerland.
24. Dobrynin, *In Confidence*, 553.
25. Miller, *Olympic Revolution*, 89.
26. Pound, *Five Rings*, 36; Simon, *A Time for Reflection*, 214; Minutes of the Extraordinary Meeting of the IOC Executive Board, May 18–19, 1984, Samarach Olympic Studies Centre, Olympic Museum, Lausanne, Switzerland.
27. Minutes of the Extraordinary Meeting of the IOC Executive Board, May 18–19, 1984, Samaranch Olympic Studies Centre, Olympic Museum, Lausanne, Switzerland.
28. Minutes of the Extraordinary Meeting of the IOC Executive Board, May 18–19, 1984, Samaranch Olympic Studies Centre, Olympic Museum, Lausanne, Switzerland.
29. "Presentation by the President of the United States Olympic Committee, Mr. William E. Simon" Annex 10 to Minutes of the Extraordinary Meeting of the IOC Executive Board, May 18–19, 1984, Samaranch Olympic Studies Centre, Olympic Museum, Lausanne, Switzerland.
30. "Presentation by the President of the United States Olympic Committee, Mr. William E. Simon" Annex 10 to Minutes of the Extraordinary Meeting of the IOC Executive Board, May 18–19, 1984, Samaranch Olympic Studies Centre, Olympic Museum, Lausanne, Switzerland.
31. "Presentation by the President of the United States Olympic Committee, Mr. William E. Simon" Annex 10 to Minutes of the Extraordinary Meeting of the IOC Executive Board, May 18–19, 1984, Samaranch Olympic Studies Centre, Olympic Museum, Lausanne, Switzerland.
32. Minutes of the Extraordinary Meeting of the IOC Executive Board, May 18–19, 1984, Samaranch Olympic Studies Centre, Olympic Museum, Lausanne, Switzerland.
33. William E. Simon, "Olympics for Olympians," *The New York Times*, July 29, 1984.
34. Miller, *Olympic Revolution*, 90; Pound, *Inside the Olympics*, 104; Minutes of the Extraordinary Meeting of the IOC Executive Board, May 18–19, 1984, Samaranch Olympic Studies Centre, Olympic Museum, Lausanne, Switzerland.
35. Kenneth Reich, "Doleful Days for the Games," and William Taaffe, "Shrewd Planning Should Keep ABC in the Money," *Sports Illustrated*, May 21, 1984, 19, 21, 22; Ueberroth, with Levin and Quinn, *Made in America*, 293–4.
36. Kenny More, "Oh, For the Days of a County Fair," *Sports Illustrated*, May 21, 1984, 31.
37. William Oscar Johnson, "Is There Life after Los Angeles," *Sports Illustrated*, May 21, 1984, 36.
38. *The Christian Science Monitor*, May 9, 1984; Johnson, "Is There Life after Los Angeles," 33.
39. Speech by Juan-Antonio Samaranch in Richard Perelman, editor, *Official Report of the Games of the XXIIIrd Olympiad Los Angeles 1984*, vol. 1, *Organization and Planning* (Los Angeles: Los Angeles Olympic Organizing Committee, 1985), 421–2.
40. Ueberroth, with Levin and Quinn, *Made in America*, 293–4; Kenny Moore, "Hey,

Russia, It's a Heck of a Party," *Sports Illustrated*, August 6, 1984, 26.

41. *USA Today*, April 13, 2005; *The Detroit News*, August 2, 2005; Caraccioli and Caraccioli, *Boycott*, 160.

42. Moore, "Hey, Russia, It's a Heck of a Party," 24–34.

43. Moore, "Hey, Russia, It's a Heck of a Party," 24–34.

44. Moore, "Hey, Russia, It's a Heck of a Party," 24–34.

45. Moore, "Hey, Russia, It's a Heck of a Party," 24–34.

46. Craig Neff, "It's a Bird, It's a Plane, It's Supergreg," *Sports Illustrated*, August 20, 80–4.

47. Craig Neff, "The U.S. Is Back … and How!" *Sports Illustrated*, August 13, 1984, 18–27.

48. Neff, "The U.S. Is Back … and How!" 18–27; Philip Whitten, "Still Kicking," *Swimming World Magazine* (April 2005), 19; *USA Today*, August 26, 2004.

49. Wayne Drehs, "Woodhead Was Devastated by Boycott," ESPN.com: http://espn.go.com/oly/summer00/s/boycott/woodhead.html

50. Bob Ottum, "A Vault Without Fault," *Sports Illustrated*, August 13, 1980, 42–58.

51. Kenny Moore, "They Got Off on the Right Track," *Sports Illustrated*, August 13, 1984, 60–81.

52. Moore, "They Got Off on the Right Track," 60–81; Kenny Moore, "Triumph and Tragedy in Los Angeles," *Sports Illustrated*, August 20, 1984, 20–55.

53. Moore, "Triumph and Tragedy in Los Angeles," 20–55.

54. Moore, "Triumph and Tragedy in Los Angeles," 20–55.

55. Pat Putnam, "Mining a Rich Vein of Gold … and Rancor," *Sports Illustrated*, August 20, 1984, 56–69.

56. Putnam, "Mining a Rich Vein of Gold … and Rancor," 56–69.

57. Moore, "Triumph and Tragedy in Los Angeles," 20–55.

58. Moore, "Triumph and Tragedy in Los Angeles," 20–55.

59. Moore, "Triumph and Tragedy in Los Angeles," 20–55; Robert Sullivan, "The Legacy of these Games," *Sports Illustrated*, August 20, 1984, 99; Moore, "They Got Off on the Right Track," 60–81.

60. Ron Fimrite, "A Gold Medal for Mettle," *Sports Illustrated*, August 20, 1984, 85–6.

61. Curry Kirkpatrick, "Oh, What Men! Ah, What Women!," *Sports Illustrated*, August 20, 1984, 72–78

62. Kirkpatrick, "Oh, What Men! Ah, What Women!," 72–78

63. Kirkpatrick, "Oh, What Men! Ah, What Women!," 72–78.

64. Frank Deford, "Cheer, Cheer, Cheer For the Home Team," *Sports Illustrated*, August 13, 1984, 38–41; William Taaffe, "Bold Strokes on a Big Canvas," *Sports Illustrated*, August 20, 1984, 79; Moore, "Triumph and Tragedy in Los Angeles," 20–55.

65. Landry and Yerlès, *The International Olympic Committee*, 80–4.

66. Landry and Yerlès, *The International Olympic Committee*, 120.

Epilogue

1. Mark K. Updegrove, *Second Acts: Presidential Lives and Legacies After the White House* (Guilford, CT: Lyons Press, 2006), 151, 160–1, 163, 167–9, 172–6.

2. Killanin, *My Olympic Years*, 224; *The Irish Times*, April 26, 1999; *The New York Times*, April 26, 1999; *The Independent*, April 28, 1999; *The Times*, April 26, 1999.

3. *The Washington Post*, May 9, 2005.

4. *The Washington Post*, April 22, 1986; July 1, 1991; December 3, 1997; April 4, 2006; Press Release: "Pelosi Names New Senior Staff to Speaker's Office," February 8, 2007, Speaker of the U.S. House of Representatives Web Site located at http://speaker.house.gov/newsroom/pressreleases?id=0069

5. Michael Leahy, "What Might Have Been," *The Washington Post Magazine*, February 20, 2005, 39; "On the Road Again," *The Lawyer*, September 20, 1999, 20–1; *The Scotsman*, November 1, 2002; *The Washington Post*, November 7, 2002.

6. *The Washington Post*, January 13, 2002; *The New York Times*, January 14, 2002.

7. *The New York Times*, April 2, 1981; *Newsweek*, July 6, 1981, 14; *The Washington Post*, March 14, 1982; *The New York Times*, January 23, 1985; *The Boston Globe*, September 13, 1988.

8. *The Washington Times*, December 23, 1992; *USA Today*, December 23, 1992; *The New York Times*, January 17, 1981; Carter, *Keeping Faith*, 521.

9. Simon, *A Time for Reflection*, 189–90; *The New York Times*, January 19, 1996.

10. *The New York Times*, June 1, 1992; Kane notes, Folder, 148, Box 9, Papers of Robert Kane, U.S. Olympic Committee Library and Archives, U.S. Olympic Committee Training Center, Colorado Springs, Colorado.

11. Powers and Kaminsky, *One Goal*, 236; Coffey, *Boys of Winter*, 58; *Sports Illustrated*, December 22, 1980; *USA Today*, August 12, 2003.

12. *The Virginian-Pilot*, August 18, 1994; *USA Today*, April 13, 2005; *The Detroit News*, August 2, 2005; Diane K. Shah, "The Lost Class of '80," *Newsweek*, July 14, 1980, 47; Caraccioli and Caraccioli, *Boycott*, 78.

13. *The Independent*, November 23, 25, 1990; *The Sunday Times*, November 25, 1990; *The Independent*, June 6, 1992; J. Riordan, "Great Britain and the 1980 Olympics: A Victory for Olympism," in Maaret Ilmarinen, editor, *Sport and International Understanding* (New York: Springer-Verlag, 1984), 142.

14. *The Irish Times*, December 22, 2008; *The Guardian*, November 4, 2008.

15. *The New York Times*, September 29, 2000.

16. *The Toronto Star*, May 29, 2003; *The Gazette*, October 3, 2006.

17. Muhammad Ali with Hana Yasmeen Ali, *The Soul of a Butterfly: Reflections on a Life's Journey* (New York: Simon and Schuster, 2004), 131, 181, 183, 205; "President Honors Recipients of the Presidential Medal of Freedom," November 9, 2005, White House Web Site located at http://www.whitehouse.gov/news/releases/2005/11/print/20051109-2.html

18. Takač, *Olimpijskih Godina* [Sixty Olympic Years], 262; Wayne Drehs, "DeFrantz would do it all over again," EPSN.com located at http://espn.go.com/oly/summeroo/s/boycott/defrantz.html

19. *The New York Times*, June 15, 2004; Robert Ajemian, "Master of the Games," *Time*, January 7, 1985, 32–9.

20. Simon, *A Time for Reflection*, 187; *The New York Times*, June 5, 2000; William E. Simon biography on U.S. Treasury Web Site located at: http://www.treas.gov/education/history/secretaries/wesimon.shtml; History and General Purpose of the William E. Simon Foundation on the William E. Simon Foundation Web Site located at: http://www.wesimonfoundation.org/found.nsf/history.htm?OpenPage&charset=iso-8859-1

21. *The Age*, July 10, 2001; *The Boston Globe*, July 15, 2001.

22. *The Globe and Mail*, November 17, 2007; *The New York Times*, January 7, 2007.

23. Weller, *Malcolm Fraser, PM*, 352.

24. *The Advertiser*, August 28, 2004; *The Age*, November 21, 2007, March 19, 2008.

Bibliography

Archives

Switzerland

Olympic Museum   Lausanne, Switzerland
   Samarach Olympic Studies Centre
      International Olympic Committee Historical Archives
         Minutes of the Executive Board
         Minutes of the International Olympic Committee
      Papers of Lord Killanin

United Kingdom

British Olympic Association   London, England
   Olympic Library
      Moscow Olympic Files

United States

Jimmy Carter Presidential Library   Atlanta, Georgia
   Jimmy Carter Presidential Materials
      Plains File
      Office of Staff Secretary
         Handwriting File
      White House Central Files
         White House Subject Files
           Recreation-Sport Files
      Staff Office Files
      Daily Diary
      National Security Advisor Files
      Counsel's Office Files
         Lloyd Cutler Files
      Presidential Speechwriters Files
   The White House News Summary
   White House Staff Photographer Photos
  Donated Historical Collections
   Papers of Zbigniew Brzezinski
   Papers of Alonzo L. McDonald

U.S. National Archives   College Park, Maryland
Nixon Presidential Project
  White House Central Files
    White House Subject Files
      Recreation-Sport Files
    White House Special Files
      Staff Member and Office Files
      Papers of H.R. Haldeman
U.S. Olympic Training Center   Colorado Springs, Colorado
  U.S. Olympic Committee Library and Archives
    Minutes of the Administrative Committee
    Minutes of the House of Delegates
    Papers of Robert Kane
University of Illinois   Urbana-Champaign, Illinois
  University Archives
    Papers of Avery Brundage

Government Publications

Ireland

Dáil Éireann, *Parliamentary Debates*, vol. 318 (Dublin: The Stationary Office, 1980).
Seanad Éireann, *Parliamentary Debates* vol. 93 (Dublin: The Stationary Office of Seanad Éireann, 1980).

United Kingdom

House of Commons, *Parliamentary Debates (Hansard)* Fifth Series – Volume 981 (London: Her Majesty's Stationery Office, 1980).
House of Lords, *The Parliamentary Debates (Hansard)* Fifth Series – Volume 404 (London: Her Majesty's Stationery Office, 1980).

United States

Public Papers of the President: Jimmy Carter, 1980 (Washington, D.C.: U.S. Government Printing Office, 1981).
U.S. Congress. *Congressional Record.*
U.S. Department of State. *State Department Bulletin* vol. 80, no. 2038 (May 1980).
U.S. House of Representatives. Committee on Foreign Relations, *U.S. Participation in the 1980 Summer Olympic Games: Hearings and Markup before the Committee on Foreign Relations* January 23 and February 4, 1980, 96th Congress, Second Session. (Washington, D.C.: Government Printing Office, 1980).
U.S. Senate. Committee on Foreign Relations, *1980 Summer Olympics Boycott: Hearing before the Committee on Foreign Relations* January 28, 1980, 96th Congress, second session (Washington D.C.: U.S. Government Printing Office, 1980).

Documents

Békés, Csaba. "Why Was There No 'Second Cold War' in Europe? Hungary and the Soviet Invasion of Afghanistan in 1979: Documents from the Hungarian Archives," *Cold War International History Project Bulletin Issue* 14/15 (Winter 2003–Spring 2004), 204–129.

Killanin, Lord. *Lord Killanin's Speeches From 1972 to 1981* (Lausanne, Switzerland: Comité International Olympique, 1985).

"More East-Bloc Sources on Afghanistan," *Cold War International History Project Bulletin Issue* 14/15 (Winter 2003–Spring 2004), 232–272.

Novikov, I.T. editor in chief. *Official Report of the Organising Committee of the Games of the XXII Olympiad*, volume 2, *Organisation* (Moscow: Progress Publishers, 1981).

Perelman, Richard, editor. *Official Report of the Games of the XXIIIrd Olympiad Los Angeles, 1984*, volume 1, *Organization and Planning* (Los Angeles: Los Angeles Olympic Organizing Committee, 1985).

The Russian General Staff. *The Soviet-Afghan War: How a Superpower Fought and Lost* Translated and edited by Lester W. Grau and Michael A. Gress (Lawrence, Kansas: University Press of Kansas, 2002).

"Documentation," *Cold War International History Project Bulletin* Issue 4 (Fall 1994).

"U.S.-Soviet Relations and the Turn Towards Confrontation, 1977–1980 – New Russian & East German Documents," *Cold War International History Project Bulletin* Issues 8–9 (Winter 1996/1997).

Websites

British Cabinet Office Freedom of Information Reading Room
http://www.cabinetoffice.gov.uk/foi/reading_room/topic/sports.aspx
Cold War International History Project
http://www.wilsoncenter.org/index.cfm?fuseaction=topics.home&topic_id=1409
ESPN.com
http://www.espn.com
International Olympic Committee
http://www.olympic.org
Lexis-Nexis
http://www.lexis-nexis.com
ABC News Transcripts
Speaker of the U.S. House of Representatives
http://speaker.house.gov
U.S. Department of the Treasury
http://www.treas.gov
White House
http://www.whitehouse.gov
William E. Simon Foundation
http://www.wesimonfoundation.org/

Videos

Do You Believe in Miracles? The Story of the 1980 U.S. Hockey Team (New York: Home Box Office Home Video, 2001).

Compact Disc/Read Only Material (CD/ROM)

Collins, Christopher, editor. *Complete Public Statements of Margaret Thatcher, 1945–1990* (New York: Oxford University Press, 1999).

Oral Histories

Oral History by Australian Biography, Special Broadcasting Service Television
Malcolm Fraser

Oral Histories by the Author
Anita DeFrantz
Joe Onek
Oral Histories by the Jimmy Carter Presidential Library
Lloyd Cutler
Jody Powell

Unpublished Items

Barton, Laurence. "The American Olympic Boycott of 1980: The Amalgam of Diplomacy and Propaganda in Influencing Public Opinion," (Ph.D. Dissertation, Boston University, 1983).
Los Angeles '76 Bid Book
McConnell, Stephanie Wilson. "Jimmy Carter, Afghanistan, and the Olympic Boycott: The Last Crisis of the Cold War?" (Ph.D. Dissertation, Bowling Green State University, 2001).

Newspapers and Magazines

Argentina

La Nacion

Australia

The Advertiser   *The Herald*
The Age   *The Weekend Australian*
The Australian

Bolivia

El Diario

Canada

The Gazette (Montreal)   *The Toronto Star*
The Globe and Mail (Toronto)

Costa Rica

La Nacion

France

L'Express   *Le Monde*
Le Figaro   *Le Quotidien de Paris*

Germany

Berliner Morgenpost   *Frankfurter Allgemeine Zeitung*

Bibliography 325

Guatemala

El Imparcial

India

The Statesman

Ireland

Irish Independent   *Magill*
The Irish Times

New Zealand

The Evening Post   *The Press*
The New Zealand Herald

Nigeria

Sunday Sketch

Spain

ABC   *El Pais*

Switzerland

La Suisse   *Tribune de Geneve*
Olympic Review

United Kingdom

Daily Mail   *The Lawyer*
The Daily Telegraph   *The Scotsman*
The Economist   *Sunday Express*
Financial Times   *The Sunday Times*
The Guardian   *The Times*
The Independent

United States

Akron Beacon Journal   *News & Courier* (Charleston)
Arkansas Democrat   *Newsday*
The Atlanta Constitution   *Newsweek*
The Atlanta Journal   *Oakland Tribune*
The Bergen County Record   *The Olympian*
The Boston Globe   *The Philadelphia Inquirer*
Boston Herald American   *Pittsburgh Post-Gazette*

Business Week
Chicago Sun-Times
Chicago Tribune
The Christian Science Monitor
  Cleveland Press
Colorado Springs Gazette Telegraph
Colorado Springs Sun
The Commercial Appeal (Memphis)
Daily News (New York)
Dallas Times-Herald
The Denver Post
Des Moines Register
Detroit Free-Press
Detroit News
Flint Journal
The Houston Post
The Kansas City Times
Los Angeles Times
Milwaukee Sentinel
National Review
New York Daily News
New York Post
The New York Times

Richmond News Leader
Richmond Times-Dispatch
Rocky Mountain News
Time
The Times-Picayune (New Orleans)
St. Louis Post-Dispatch
St. Paul Pioneer Press
The Salt Lake Tribune
The San Diego Union
San Francisco Chronicle
San Francisco Examiner
Seattle Post-Intelligencer
Sports Illustrated
The Sun (Baltimore)
Swimming World Magazine
U.S. News and World Report
USA Today
The Union Leader (Manchester)
The Virginian-Pilot (Norfolk)
The Wall Street Journal
The Washington Post
The Washington Post Magazine
The Washington Star

Venezuela

El Universal

Memoirs and Diaries

Ali, Muhammad, with Hana Yasmeen Ali. *The Soul of a Butterfly: Reflections on a Life's Journey* (New York: Simon and Schuster, 2004).
Arbatov, Georgi. *The System: An Insider's Life in Soviet Politics* (New York: Random House, 1992).
Brzezinski, Zbigniew. *Power and Principle: Memoirs of the National Security Advisor, 1977–1981* (New York: Farrar, Straus, Giroux, 1983).
Booker, Christopher. *The Games War: A Moscow Journal* (London: Faber and Faber, 1981).
Carter, Jimmy. *Keeping Faith: Memoirs of a President* (New York: Bantam Books, 1982).
  Turning Point: A Candidate, a State, and a Nation Come of Age (New York: Times Books, 1992).
  An Hour Before Daylight: Memories of a Rural Boyhood (New York: Simon & Schuster, 2001).
Cosell, Howard, with Peter Bonventre. *I Never Played the Game* (New York: William Morrow and Company, 1985).
Dobrynin, Anatoliy. *In Confidence: Moscow's Ambassador to America's Six Cold War Presidents (1962–1986)* (New York: Random House, 1995).
Ford, Robert A.D. *Our Man in Moscow: A Diplomat's Reflections on the Soviet Union* (Toronto: University of Toronto Press, 1989).
Gardner, Richard N. *Mission Italy: On the Front Lines of the Cold War* (New York: Rowman & Littlefield Publishers, 2005).
Giscard d'Estaing, Valéry. *Le Pouvoir et la Vie: Choisir* [Capacity and Life: To Choose] (Paris: Compagnie 12: 2006).
Gorbachev, Mikahail. *Memoirs* (New York: Doubleday 1996).
Gosper, Kevan with Glenda Korporaal. *An Olympic Life: Melbourne 1956 to Sydney 2000* (St. Leonards, Australia: Allen & Unwin, 2000).

Gromyko, Andrei. *Memories* Translated by Harold Shukman (New York: Doubleday, 1989).

Forrest, Lisa. *Boycott: Australia's Controversial Road to the 1980 Moscow Olympics* (Sydney, Australia: ABC Books, 2008).

Jordon, Hamilton. *Crisis: The Last Year of the Carter Presidency* (New York: G.P. Putnam's Sons, 1982).

Head, Ivan, and Pierre Trudeau. *The Canadian Way: Shaping Canada's Foreign Policy, 1968–1984* (Toronto: McClelland and Stewart, 1995).

Howell, Denis. *Made in Birmingham: The Memoirs of Denis Howell* (London: Queen Anne Press, 1990).

Killanin, Lord. *My Olympic Years* (London: Secker and Warburg, 1983).

My Olympic Years (New York: William Morrow and Company, 1983).

Kiyokawa, Masaji. *Supōtsu to Seiji* [Sports and Politics] (Tokyo: Baseball Magazine, 1987).

MacGuigan, Mark. *An Inside Look at External Affairs during the Trudeau Years* edited by P. Whitney Lackenbauer (Calgary: University of Calgary Press, 2002).

Macfarlane, Neil, with Michael Herd. *Sport and Politics: A World Divided* (London: Willow Books, 1986).

Matlock, Jr., Jack F. *Reagan and Gorbachev: How the Cold War Ended* (New York: Random House, 2005).

Morse, Eric S. *Sport and Canadian Foreign Policy* Behind the Headlines Series. David Stafford, editor (Toronto: Canadian Institute of International Affairs, 1987).

Pound, Richard W. *Five Rings over Korea: The Secret Negotiations Behind the 1988 Olympic Games in Seoul* (Boston: Little, Brown, 1994).

Inside the Olympics: A Behind-the-Scenes Look at the Politics, the Scandals, and the Glory of the Games (Etobicoke, Ontario: J. Wiley & Sons Canada, 2004).

Reagan, Ronald. *The Reagan Diaries* edited by Douglas Brinkley (New York: HarperCollins Publishers, 2007).

Schmidt, Helmut. *Menschen und Mächte* [Men and Powers] (Berlin: Wolf Jobst Siedler Verlag GmbH, 1987).

Men and Powers: A Political Retrospective translated by Ruth Hein (New York: Random House, 1989).

Schultz, George P. *Turmoil and Triumph: My Years as Secretary of State* (New York: Charles Scribner's Sons, 1993).

Shorter, Frank, with Marc Bloom. *Olympic Gold: A Runner's Life and Times* (Boston: Houghton Mifflin, 1984).

Simon, William E., with John M. Caher. *A Time for Reflection: An Autobiography* (Washington, D.C.: Regnery, 2004).

Takač, Artur. *Šezdeset Olimpijskih Godina* [Sixty Olympic Years] (Novi Sad, Serbia: Prometej, 1999).

Thatcher, Margaret. *The Downing Street Years* (New York: HarperCollins, 1993).

Ueberroth, Peter, with Richard Levin and Amy Quinn. *Made in America: His Own Story* New York: William Morrow, 1985).

Vance, Cyrus. *Hard Choices: Critical Years in America's Foreign Policy* (New York: Simon and Schuster, 1983).

Watson, Jr., Thomas J., and Peter Petre. *Father, Son & Co.: My Life at IBM and Beyond* (New York: Bantam Books, 1990).

Worrall, James. *My Olympic Journey: Sixty Years with Canadian Sport and the Olympic Games* (Toronto: Canadian Olympic Association, 2000).

Books

Ayers, Philip. *Malcolm Fraser: A Biography* (Richmond, Victoria, Australia: William Hienemann Australia, 1987).

Baumann, Robert F. *Russian-Soviet Unconventional Wars in the Caucasus, Central Asia, and Afghanistan* (Combat Studies Institute, U.S. Army Command and General Staff College: Ft. Leavenworth, Kansas, 1993).

Berkow, Ira. *Red: A Biography of Red Smith* (New York: Times Books, 1986).

Bocharov, Gennady. *Russian Roulette: Afghanistan Through Russian Eyes* Translated by Alyona Kojevnikov (New York: HarperCollins, 1990).

Bourne, Peter G. *Jimmy Carter: A Comprehensive Biography from Plains to Post-Presidency* (New York: Scribner, 1997).

Bowden, Mark. *Guests of the Ayatollah: The Iran Hostage Crisis: The First Battle in America's War with Militant Islam* (New York: Grove Press, 2006).

Brinkley, Douglas. *The Unfinished Presidency: Jimmy Carter's Journey Beyond the White House* (New York: Viking, 1998).

Caraccioli, Tom and Jerry Caraccioli. *Boycott: Stolen Dreams of the 1980 Moscow Olympic Games* (Washington, D.C.: New Chapter Press, 2008).

Coffey, Wayne. *The Boys of Winter: The Untold Story of a Coach, a Dream, and the 1980 U.S. Olympic Hockey Team* (New York: Crown Publishers, 2005).

Espy, Richard. *The Politics of the Olympic Games* (Berkeley, California: University of California Press, 1979).

Farber, David. *Taken Hostage: The Iran Hostage Crisis and America's First Encounter with Radical Islam* (Princeton, New Jersey: Princeton University Press, 2005).

Gaddis, John Lewis. *Russia, the Soviet Union and the United States: An Interpretive History* second edition (New York: McGraw Hill, 1990).

The United States and the End of the Cold War: Implications, Reconsiderations, Provocations (New York: Oxford University Press, 1994).

The Cold War: A New History (New York: Penguin, 2005).

Galeotti, Mark. *Afghanistan: The Soviet Union's Last War* (London: Frank Cass, 1995).

Garrison, Jean A. *Games Advisors Play: Foreign Policy in the Nixon and Carter Administrations* (College Station, Texas: Texas A&M University Press, 1999).

Garthoff, Raymond L. *Détente and Confrontation: American-Soviet Relations From Nixon to Reagan* revised edition (Washington, D.C.: Brookings Institution, 1994).

The Great Transformation: American-Soviet Relations and the End of the Cold War (Washington, D.C.: Brookings Institution, 1994).

Germond, Jack W. and Jules Witcover. *Blue Smoke and Mirrors: How Reagan Won and Why Carter Lost the Election of 1980* (New York: Viking Press, 1981).

Girardet, Edward. *Afghanistan: The Soviet War* (New York: St. Martin's Press, 1985).

Gordon, Harry. *Australia and the Olympic Games* (St. Lucia, Australia: University of Queensland Press, 1994).

Grau, Lester W. translator and editor. *The Bear Went Over the Mountain: Soviet Combat Tactics in Afghanistan* (Washington, D.C.: National Defense University Press, 1996).

Guttmann, Allen. *The Games Must Go On: Avery Brundage and the Olympic Movement* (New York: Columbia University Press, 1984).

The Olympics: A History of the Modern Games second edition (Urbana, Illinois: University of Illinois Press, 2002).

Guttmann, Allen, and Lee Thompson. *Japanese Sports: A History* (Honolulu, Hawaii: University of Hawaii Press, 2001).

Fisher, Beth A. *The Reagan Reversal: Foreign Policy and the End of the Cold War* (Columbia, Missouri: University of Missouri Press, 1997).

Friedman, Norman. *The Fifty Year War: Conflict and Strategy in the Cold War* (Annapolis, Maryland: Naval Institute Press, 2000).

Heinämaa, Anna, Maija Leppänen and Yuri Yurchenko. *The Soldiers' Story: Soviet Veterans Remember the Afghan War* Translated by A.D. Haun. (Berkeley, California: International and Area Studies, University of California at Berkeley, 1994).

Hargrove, Erwin C. *Jimmy Carter as President: Leadership and the Politics of the Public Good* (Baton Rouge, Louisiana: Louisiana State University, 1988).

Hauser, Thomas. *Muhammad Ali: His Life and Times* (New York: Simon and Schuster, 1991).

Hazan, Baruch. *Olympic Sports and Propaganda Games: Moscow 1980* (New Brunswick, New Jersey: Transaction Books, 1982).

Hill, Christopher R. *Olympic Politics* (Manchester, England: Manchester University Press, 1992).

Hulme, Jr., Derick L. *The Political Olympics: Moscow, Afghanistan, and the 1980 U.S. Boycott* (New York: Praeger, 1990).

Jalali, Ali Ahmad, and Lester W. Grau. *The Other Side of the Mountain: Mujahideen Tactics in the Soviet-Afghan War* (Quantico, Virginia: United States Marine Corps Studies and Analysis Division, 1995).

Johnson, Haynes. *In the Absence of Power: Governing America* (New York: Viking Press, 1980).

Jones, Charles O. *The Trusteeship Presidency: Jimmy Carter and the United States Congress* (Baton Rouge, Louisiana: Louisiana State University, 1988).

Kakar, M. Hassan. *Afghanistan: The Soviet Invasion and the Afghan Response, 1979–1982* (Berkeley and Los Angeles: University of California Press, 1995).

Kanin, David B. *A Political History of the Olympic Games* (Boulder, Colorado: Westview Press, 1981).

Kaufman, Burton I. *The Presidency of James Earl Carter, Jr.* (Lawrence, Kansas: University Press of Kansas, 1993).

Kaufman, Scott. *Plans Unraveled: The Foreign Policy of the Carter Administration* (DeKalb, Illinois: Northern Illinois University Press, 2008).

Keys, Barbara J. *Globalizing Sport: National Rivalry and International Community in the 1930s* (Cambridge, Massachusetts: Harvard University Press, 2006).

Knecht, Willi. *Der Boykott* [The Boycott] (Cologne: Verlag Wissenschaft und Politik, 1980).

Kolodnyi, A. *"Igry" Vokrug Igr* ["The Games" Surrounding the Games] (Moscow: Sovetskaia Rossiia, 1981).

Lake, Anthony. *Somoza Falling: The Nicaraguan Dilemma* (Boston: Houghton Mifflin, 1989).

Landry, Fernand and Magdeleine Yerlès. *International Olympic Committee – One Hundred Years: The Idea – The Presidents – The Achievements*, vol. 3, the Presidencies of Lord Killanin (1972–1980) and of Juan Antonio Samaranch (1980–) (Lausanne, Switzerland: International Olympic Committee, 1994).

Leffler, Melvyn P. *For the Soul of Mankind: The United States, the Soviet Union, and the Cold War* (New York: Hill and Wang, 2007).

Macintosh, Donald, and Michael Hawes with contributions from Donna Greenhorn and David Black. *Sport and Canadian Diplomacy* (Montreal: McGill-Queen's University Press, 1994).

Maley, William. *The Afghanistan Wars* (New York: Palgrave Macmillan, 2002).

McMichael, Scott R. *Stumbling Bear: Soviet Military Performance in Afghanistan* (London: Brassey's, 1991).

Miller, David. *Olympic Revolution: The Biography of Juan Antonio Samaranch* (London: Pavilion, 1992).

Miller, Geoffrey. *Behind the Olympic Rings* (Lynn, Massachusetts: H.O. Zimman, 1979).

Morris, Kenneth E. *Jimmy Carter: American Moralist* (Athens, Georgia: University of Georgia Press, 1996).

Muravchik, Joshua. *The Uncertain Crusade: Jimmy Carter and the Dilemmas of Human Rights Policy* (Lanham, Maryland: Hamilton Press, 1986).

Newsom, David. *The Soviet Brigade in Cuba: A Study in Political Diplomacy* (Bloomington, Indiana: Indiana University Press, 1987).

Oberdorfer, Don. *The Turn: From the Cold War to a New Era* (New York: Poseidon Press, 1991).

From the Cold War to a New Era: The United States and the Soviet Union, 1983–1991 (Baltimore: Johns Hopkins University Press, 1998).

Ono, Akira. *Gendai Supōtsu Hihan* [A Critique of Modern Sports] (Tokyo: Taishūkan shoten, 1996).

Pastor, Robert A. *Condemned to Repetition: The United States and Nicaragua* (Princeton, New Jersey: Princeton University Press, 1987).

Pierard, Richard V. and Robert D. Linder. *Civil Religion and the Presidency* (Grand Rapids, Michigan: Academie Books, 1988).

Powers, John and Arthur C. Kaminsky. *One Goal: A Chronicle of the 1980 U.S. Olympic Hockey Team* (New York: Harper & Row, 1984).

Quandt, William. *Camp David: Peacemaking and Politics* (Washington, D.C.: Brookings Institution, 1986).

Renouf, Alan. *Malcom Fraser and Australian Foreign Policy* (Sydney: Australian Professional Publications, 1986).

Rozell, Mark J. *The Press and the Carter Presidency* (Boulder, Colorado: Westview Press, 1989).

Sato, Seizaburo, Koyama Kenichi and Kumon Shunpei. *Ohira Masayoshi: Hito to Shisō* [Ohira Masayoshi: Man and Ideas] (Tokyo: Ohira Masayoshi Kinen Zaidan, 1990).

Schweizer, Peter. *Reagan's War: The Epic Story of His Forty-year Struggle and Final Triumph Over Communism* (New York: Anchor Books, 2002).

Sick, Gary. *All Fall Down: America's Tragic Encounter with Iran* (New York: Random House, 1985).

Senn, Alfred Erich. *Power, Politics, and the Olympic Games* (Champaign, Illinois: Human Kinetics, 1999).

Smith, Gaddis. *Morality and Reason: American Diplomacy in the Carter Years* (New York: Hill and Wang, 1986).

Smith, Geoffrey. *Reagan and Thatcher* (New York: Norton, 1991).

Smith, Tony. *America's Mission: The United States and the Struggle for Democracy in the Twentieth Century* (Princeton, New Jersey: Princeton University Press, 1994).

Strong, Robert A. *Working in the World: Jimmy Carter and the Making of American Foreign Policy* (Baton Rouge, Louisiana: Louisiana State University Press, 2000).

Updegrove, Mark K. *Second Acts: Presidential Lives and Legacies After the White House* (Guilford, Connecticut: Lyons Press, 2006).

Vinokur, Martin Barry. *More Than A Game: Sports and Politics* (New York: Greenwood Press, 1988).

Weller, Patrick. *Malcolm Fraser PM: A Study in Prime Ministerial Power* (Ringwood, Victoria, Australia: Penguin, 1989).

Wendel, Tim. *Going for the Gold: How the U.S. Won at Lake Placid* (Westport, Connecticut: Lawrence Hill & Company, 1980).

Westad, Odd Arne, editor. *The Fall of Détente: Soviet-American Relations during the Carter Years* (Boston: Scandinavian University Press, 1997).

The Global Cold War: Third World Interventions and the Making of Our Times (New York: Cambridge University Press, 2005).

Wildavsky, Aaron. *The Beleaguered Presidency* (New Brunswick, New Jersey: Transatlantic Publishers, 1991).

Witcover, Jules. *Marathon: The Pursuit of the Presidency, 1972–1976* (New York: Viking Press, 1977).

Wooldridge, Ian. *Sport in the 80's: A Personal View* (London: Centurion Books, 1989).

Zubok, Vladislav M. *A Failed Empire: The Soviet Union in the Cold War from Stalin to Gorbachev* (Chapel Hill, North Carolina: University of North Carolina Press, 2007).

Articles

Beacom, Aaron. "A Changing Discourse? British Diplomacy and the Olympic Movement," in Roger Levermore and Adrian Budd, eds., *Sport and International Relations: An Emerging Relationship* (London: Routledge, 2004).

Brinkley, Douglas. "The Rising Stock of Jimmy Carter: The 'Hands on' Legacy of our Thirty-Ninth President," Diplomatic History vol. 20, no. 4 (Fall 1996), 505–529.

Chorbajian, Leon and Vincent Mosco. "1976 and 1980 Olympic Boycott Media Coverage: All the News that Fits," Arena Review vol. 5 (1981), 3–28.

Clymer, Kenton. "Jimmy Carter, Human Rights, and Cambodia," Diplomatic History vol. 27, no. 2 (April 2003), 245–278.

Crossman, Jane and Ron Lappage. "Canadian Athletes' Perceptions of the 1980 Olympic Boycott," Sociology of Sport Journal vol. 9 (1992), 354–371.

Deane, John. "The Melbourne Press and the Moscow Olympics," Sporting Traditions vol. 1, no. 2 (May 1985), 27–42.

Grau, Lester W. "The Takedown of Kabul: An Effective Coup de Main," in William G. Robertson and Lawrence A. Yates, ed., *Block by Block: The Challenge of Urban Operations* (Fort Leavenworth, Kansas: U.S. Army Command and General Staff College Press, 2003).

Jones, Charles O. "Carter and Congress: From the Outside In," British Journal of Political Science vol. 15 (July 1985), 269–298.

Kereliuk, Sandra L. "The Canadian Boycott of the 1980 Moscow Olympic Games," in Gerald Redmond, ed., Sport and Politics (Champaign, Illinois: Human Kinetics Publishers, 1986).

Lyakhovskiy, Aleksandr Antonovich. *Inside the Invasion of Afghanistan and the Seizure of Kabul, December 1979* Gary Goldberg and Artemy Kalinovsky translators, Cold War International History Project Working Paper 51 (January 2007).

Riordan, J. "Great Britain and the 1980 Olympics: A Victory for Olympism," in Maaret Ilmarinen, ed., *Sport and International Understanding* (New York: Springer-Verlag, 1984).

Schmitz, David F. and Vanessa Walker. "Jimmy Carter and the Foreign Policy of Human Rights: The Development of a Post-Cold War Foreign Policy," Diplomatic History vol. 28, no. 1 (January 2004), 113–143.

Schulzinger, Robert D. "Complaints, Self-justifications, and Analysis: The Historiography of American Foreign Relations since 1969," Diplomatic History vol. 15, no. 2 (Spring 1991), 245–264.

Stueck, William. "Placing Jimmy Carter's Foreign Policy," Gary M. Fink and Hugh Davis Graham, *The Carter Presidency: Policy Choices in the Post-New Deal Era* (Lawrence, Kansas: University Press of Kansas, 1998).

Wenn, Stephen R. and Jeffrey P. Wenn. "Muhammad Ali and the Convergence of Olympic Sport and U.S. Diplomacy in 1980: A Reassessment from Behind the Scenes at the U.S. State Department," Olympika: The International Journal of Olympic Studies vol. 2 (1993), 45–66.

Wenn, Stephen R. "A Turning Point for IOC Television Policy: U.S. Television Rights Negotiations and the 1980 Lake Placid and Moscow Olympic Festivals," Journal of Sport History vol. 25, no. 1 (Spring 1998), 87–117.

Young, Michael. "The Melbourne Press and the 1980 Moscow Olympic Boycott Controversy," Sporting Traditions vol. 4, no. 2 (May 1988), 184–200.

Index

IN HER SHOES

WOMEN OF THE EIGHTH

During what was often a fraught and bitter campaign, some forgot the very real people behind the need for reproductive healthcare in Ireland. In Her Shoes helped put those people – and their vastly different backgrounds and stories – front and centre again. We will never know how many untold stories the Eighth Amendment left behind. In telling some of them, this book honours them all.
Tara Flynn, actress, writer and comedian

By changing the conversation, In Her Shoes helped the Repeal movement change Ireland, giving voice to experiences that had been silenced for far too long. This book is testimony to the power of those stories and a moving reflection on a history we should never forget.
Dr Mary McGill, researcher and journalist

It would be hard to overestimate the contribution of In Her Shoes to repealing the Eighth Amendment. I salute the honesty and bravery of the women who told their stories and Erin's strength and determination in bringing them into the open. This is a precious and valuable record of a remarkable project.
Ailbhe Smyth, Co-Director of Together For Yes and Convenor of the Coalition to Repeal the Eighth Amendment

IN HER SHOES

WOMEN OF THE EIGHTH

Collected, illustrated & introduced by

ERIN DARCY

NEW ISLAND

IN HER SHOES
First published in 2020 by
New Island Books
Glenshesk House
10 Richview Office Park
Clonskeagh
Dublin 14, D14 V8C4
Republic of Ireland
www.newisland.ie

Hardback ISBN: 978-1-84840-784-8
Paperback ISBN: 978-1-84840-762-6
eBook ISBN: 978-1-84840-785-5

British Library Cataloguing in Publication Data. A CIP catalogue record for this book is
available from the British Library.

Designed by Catherine Gaffney, caegaffney.com
Edited by Djinn von Noorden
Printed by L&C Printing Group, Poland

New Island Books is a member of Publishing Ireland

For my mother, Martha Jane, and the daughters of Ireland.

Born in the United States, **Erin Darcy** is a mother and a self-taught artist living in Galway, Ireland, since 2006. She has been a contributor to *The Rainbow Way: Cultivating Creativity in the Midst of Mothering* and *Creatrix: She Who Makes* by Lucy H. Pearce and *Rise Up & Repeal: A Poetic Archive of the 8th Amendment* edited by Sarah Brazil and Sarah Bernstein. *In Her Shoes: Women of the Eighth* is Erin's first book.

CONTENTS

AUTHOR'S NOTE

The Facebook page In Her Shoes – Women of the Eighth originated in early 2018 as an art project with the intention of changing
undecided voters' minds in the upcoming referendum on the
Eighth Amendment to the Constitution. The grassroots project
posted anonymous stories of the negative impacts of the Eighth
Amendment alongside a simple photo of a pair of shoes.

In the five months from its creation to the referendum vote
on 25 May 2018, the page grew to a following of over 115,000
with an organic reader reach of over four million per week. As
an artist, immigrant and mother of three living in rural Ireland,
creating and holding the space for these experiences became my
contribution to the movement to repeal the Eighth Amendment,
a referendum in which I could not vote.

Of the thousand stories sent to the In Her Shoes page, I
selected thirty-two for this book, as a representation of the
entire island of Ireland. I wanted to give these lived truths a
communal space that could be recognised the world over. The
anonymous stories are reproduced here with their authors'
consent and remain in their original words, with only minor
edits for accuracy and ease of reading. The stories published on
the Facebook page have been deposited by the Irish Qualitative

Data Archive in the Digital Repository of Ireland (DRI), accessible to the public and protected for future generations. By preserving these stories within the archives and in this book, we enshrine women's experiences in history where they are often written out.

In Her Shoes: Women of the Eighth, the book you now hold in your hands, describes a changing social landscape, an uprising within myself and within Ireland.

PROLOGUE

It's bitterly cold and windy but the sun is shining as I stand on the streets in my small conservative town in rural Catholic Ireland. This town is my home, but not my home place and so my American accent softens to match the gentler way of speaking. I'm asking strangers to support abortion rights in a place where it is illegal. The date is 13 January 2018.

Being a 'blow-in' is a privilege in many ways. It's far easier for me to campaign for choice than it is for the friends who have grown up here. In these small towns, where everyone knows everyone's business, being openly pro-choice can have both professional and personal implications. Abortion is a word said in a hushed tone, not something for which you broadcast support.

'Would you like to sign to support women's rights?'

I look for a way to encourage curiosity, to avoid the recoil the word 'abortion' can produce. The man passing by shakes his head automatically and moves on before pausing and doubling back. He's poised like a gundog.

'What did you say?' Furrowed brow, hands shoved deep into the pockets of his tan jacket, jaw clenched.

'I asked if you'd like to sign our sheet to support women's rights. We're looking for signatures of support for repealing the Eighth Amendment.'

'I have daughters!' he barks. 'Did you not hear about the woman who died after the abortion in England?'[1]

We've been told to move people like this on, but my adrenaline pulses, my heart races.

'Don't you think she should have been looked after better? Had she been able to get that help here, she wouldn't have been rushing out of a clinic to get her flight home. She would have been able to recover and take her time, under supervision of her own doctor.'

'I just don't think they should be using it as a form of birth control.'

I try not to feel exasperated and promise him that no one uses abortion as birth control. 'Do you think anyone *wants* to have an abortion?' I tell him how even the morning-after pill impacts our cycle and it's not a pleasant experience.

'Well there should be a cap – there's people that have three, four, five abortions. They need to take responsibility for their actions. They made that mess.'

The women standing at the stall with me continue talking to other people passing by. Trying to keep my voice steady, I ask him: 'Should she have those babies instead? Is that who you want raising a child, someone who doesn't want to be a mother?' I share with him that I have three kids. No one seems to expect a mother to advocate for abortion. 'Being pregnant shouldn't be a punishment. Children aren't a punishment. All children should be wanted, not raised by someone who didn't want to do this.'

I can see that he understands. 'I do think that women should be able to get an abortion in certain circumstances,' he concedes.

'Well, it sounds to me like you're pro-choice then,' I add quickly. 'The only way a person can get the abortion under any of the "certain circumstances" is if we vote to remove the Eighth Amendment. If you just put yourself in her shoes ...'

It doesn't come to me as a revelation. It's a turn of a phrase: don't judge someone until you've walked a mile in their shoes.

His entire disposition changes. 'I'm not sure I agree with abortion, but you've made me think. I need to read some things first.'

Heart racing, I hand him a few of our brochures before he moves on.

Oh my god, Erin, you're doing it. You've got this.

ERIN'S STORY

SELKIES

It was the selkies that brought me here. Selkies, I learned from *The Secret of Roan Inish*,[2] are mysterious mythological creatures, half-seal half-woman, that come to shore and shed their pelts to sunbathe in human skin. If someone takes a pelt home, the woman will stay but forever long for home, for the sea, for belonging. I longed for the sea.

*

When I was seven years old we moved from the Puget Sound of Washington to the purple Rocky Mountains of Colorado. High in the sky, as far from sea level as you can get, I would stand barefoot on boulders, surrounded by pines and aspen trees, making wishes into the wind to go to Ireland, to the ocean with selkies, to the land where my ancestors once lived. I roamed the mountains on horseback. In a small ghost town – population 49 – we lived an honest and simple life. I spent my time digging in the soil for remnants from Gold Rush days. I explored abandoned houses and created stories about pilgrims arriving by boat from far away. The days were endless and vast.

Adolescence smacked me in the face with a move back to my birthplace of Oklahoma. It was nowhere near the ocean and far from the mountains. We settled in a typical American neighbourhood of fenced-in back gardens and a paved road out front. The culture shock of school was immense: groups of jocks and geeks, skaters and preps, goths and band nerds. I craved the naivety and sweet simplicity of vast, wild spaces, although it didn't take long to find my tribe: the misfits, the shy, the artsy, the awkward, the rebels.

At home we were our own little unit, just the five of us: two older brothers, Cody and Trevor, Mom and Dad. My mother was my best friend. We had little money but lived like royalty. Mom and Dad took us on thrilling road trips: we'd sleep in motel rooms with a picnic spread of crackers and canned meats with cheese in a spray can – the height of luxury, I tell you. Living just above the poverty line in America meant brown paper bags from churches with cans of donated food, and yet we were never without.

I grew up with a passion to follow my dreams, like Mom and Dad. The ocean never stopped pulling me to her and I entertained fantasies of returning to Washington, of living in a houseboat near seals and whales and ocean mist, of becoming a marine biologist – a 'real job' with a side hobby of art. I considered the Atlantic and fantasised about Rhode Island School of Design, but art school was an impossible financial ask.

Around that time I began to search for a pen pal in Ireland, with the idea of becoming more familiar with the place and the stories I had grown to love. Dial-up internet churned into life, bringing me to the Irish chat rooms. Here were the poets and musicians, the older women looking for love, the perverts and the *craic*. Here was my escape from Oklahoma. I found a group of Irish people to chat with – and then I met him: a boy, sixteen and 'sound'. Here I was, talking to a *boy* from *Ireland*.

It wasn't long until I was in love, rushing home from school to see if Steven was online. Night after night he would stay awake into the early hours of the morning while I skipped homework to scheme out our future together, running up phone bills and a hefty collection of phone cards in the process. I drank in his Galway accent as I sat on the floor in my closet, beaming until my cheeks hurt, making him repeat words over and over again.

For two years we talked every day, sending letters and packages until, in the autumn of 2004, he asked his mom for a Christmas gift of a plane ticket that would bring me to Ireland and to him. I was seventeen. How would I even ask my parents for permission to go to Ireland during Christmas break to meet my internet boyfriend? I prepared the speech in my head. I would sit them down and tell them how important this was to me while guarding my heart for the inevitable no. To my surprise they said yes almost immediately. It was the experience of a lifetime, they conceded.

Mom and Dad's unwavering trust and faith in me led me to believe I could do anything, that I could be anyone. Yet rumours swirled around in school. I became the focus of our psychology class, the teacher dissecting my long-distance relationship, students joining in with jokes about a fat old sexual predator luring me to my death. I had always wanted to shake things up, so going against the grain of what was expected felt all the more thrilling. I would never be the one to stay in town, go to the local state college, have the two kids and a white picket fence. I wanted more. I wanted to travel to Ireland and meet the boy I was in love with. I counted down the days. I cashed in my fifty-dollar savings and applied for a passport.

The day after Christmas my parents hugged me at the departure gate. I navigated the Chicago layover on my own. On the 4,000-mile plane journey I was too nervous to find the toilets. I wasn't even sure where they were. I sat for six hours, thumbing through magazines and alarming the Irish man next to me with an account of my endeavour.

We landed in Dublin. My stomach all aflutter, I wheeled my giant bag through the exit doors to be met by a sea of faces looking for loved ones. I scanned the line until I found him: tall, dark hair, bright red cheeks and a giant grin. I was engulfed in his embrace, breathing him in, his shyness, excitement and familiarity. The world blurred around us. We were each other's first kiss in Dublin airport.

The countryside whirled by in a green fuzz. We held hands in the back seat of his uncle's car, giggly, delirious and lovesick. We arrived at the house, were welcomed in, and I met the entire family. I settled at the table with a cup of tea and stared at a plate piled high with rashers and sausages, eggs and beans, toast and black and white pudding. Aunts and uncles asked all of the questions. It was overwhelming.

During that magical fortnight we'd stay up until the early fog met the morning sun. It was bliss. I was in love with everything. In love with the damp cold air burning ice into our lungs. In love with the upturned umbrellas shoved angrily into bins. In love with the boy who held my hand and kissed me in public. How would I ever leave? Yet our idyll was fast coming to an end. We clung together, crying until our eyes were raw, not knowing when we would see each other again.

By saving money and travelling back and forth across the Atlantic, Steven got to experience my family and life in America while I continued going to school. And then, in 2006, I graduated high school and booked a one-way ticket to Ireland. Steven and I married within the year with just two witnesses. It was a simple affair, without a dress or a cake.

I was eager to begin our family but my body refused to cooperate and I was diagnosed with polycystic ovaries. The doctor dismissed me. 'You're young. You have time.' Depressed by my perceived infertility, I wrote blogs and took photos, explored art and photography. I found communities of women online where we shared our creative selves. We became fast friends, these women who took up space without apology; who wrote poetry, took photographs and spoke freely. I began to heal my relationship with my body. It shifted a dynamic within myself and clarified what I wanted to achieve.

The big freeze of 2009 brought snow, ice, and morning sickness. Forty-two weeks later I was induced – fortunate to be *allowed* to go past my due date – and became a mom for the first time. Like a selkie shedding her pelt and leaving her watery world, just minutes before midnight, with dark hair and searching eyes, my daughter was born.

The maternity and labour wards were a shock to the system, understaffed with overworked nurses and midwives doing their best to meet the needs of new mothers and their babies – it is between the lines that we are all failed. *Your baby made it out of your body alive. You are alive. Be grateful. What more do you want?*

Mom flew over for those delicate post-partum days, to mother and teach me how to nourish my babe at the breast, to coax my intuition into confidence and to make the stew that would always taste like home. After a month-long babymoon, I clung to her as she put her bags into the car for the airport. I took my daughter to the bed that Mom had been sleeping in and curled up in the scent of her.

Building my life in Ireland had been my dream. Now, as a new mother, I was desperate to belong in my new home place. While my online circles of women sustained me, I craved Irish women to befriend. Facebook groups opened up the world as I sat on my couch, baby at my breast, talking to other mothers around the country. Virtual breastfeeding support groups, baby-wearing groups and pregnancy groups – I learned about the politics of breastfeeding and the history of formula in Ireland and was initiated into the revelation of feminism. I learned how deep-seated misogyny seeped through our societies; how it had an impact on my choices as a woman, as a pregnant woman, as a birthing woman, as a mother. I was so angry.

Fuelled by my new-found hunger for change, I took a bus to the city to join a Galway birth gathering. We talked about the lack of choice to give birth how and where we wanted and discussed the rising intervention statistics: inductions, caesarean sections, instrumental deliveries, episiotomies. Around a kitchen table with children crawling underfoot and babies asleep in slings, we proposed ways in which we might improve local maternity services. I wanted to know everything.

I became pregnant for the second time, securing a home birth community midwife with the intention to stay away from the traditional maternity system.

Article 40.3.3 of the Eighth Amendment to the Constitution states:

> The State acknowledges the right to life of the unborn and, with due regard to the *equal* [my italics] right to life of the mother, guarantees in its laws to respect, and, as far as practicable, by its laws to defend and vindicate that right.

> Section 7.7.1: Because of the Constitutional provisions on the right to life of the unborn [Article 40.3.3] there is significant legal uncertainty regarding a pregnant woman's right to [consent].

Savita Halappanavar and I were both seventeen weeks pregnant when she died in University Hospital Galway on 28 October 2012 at the age of 31 from septic shock following what was diagnosed as an 'inevitable miscarriage'. Savita attended the hospital because of back pain, where she was advised physiotherapy and sent home. She returned to the hospital hours later with more pain. A foetal heartbeat was detected and blood tests later showed key signals of the risks of sepsis infection. However, the blood test results were not followed up at the time.

In the night her waters broke and she was told about the risk of infection. A scan showed the presence of a foetal heartbeat. Savita asked if there was any way to save the baby and was told it was not possible. 'Inevitable miscarriage' is recorded on her medical notes. Aware that her baby would not survive, Savita asked her obstetrician for a termination. She was told that in Ireland it was not legal to terminate a pregnancy on the grounds of poor prognosis for the foetus, and as her life was not currently at risk it was not legally possible to carry out a termination. Savita was given antibiotics to guard against infection. Communication broke down between all medical staff; information on Savita's health was not passed on. It was noted that she had failed to be monitored as often as hospital policy states. The obstetrician decided to carry out a termination, as it was now clear that Savita's life was at risk. Her condition deteriorated in theatre after the spontaneous birth of her dead baby, and she was moved to the high-dependency unit, where lifesaving measures continued and ultimately failed.

The baby that could never survive outside of the womb took precedence over Savita's own health. Savita Halappanavar died because the Constitution denied her rights to make healthcare decisions in pregnancy under the Eighth Amendment. Combined with an overcrowded and understaffed health service, Savita was failed on multiple levels, resulting in her tragic death.

*

I stood in the cold dark November rain at the first vigil in Galway city, staring at Savita's photo. My own baby tumbled within me as I cried, knowing how easily this could be me or any one of us. Candles flickered. There was a moment of silence. How can this have happened?

The awareness of my own mortality in pregnancy and the superstitions of trading one life for another had become an obsession. In February 2013, when I was 37 weeks pregnant, my 52-year-old dad suffered a heart attack, which required invasive open-heart surgery. As my due date approached and passed, I became certain that Dad would die when I gave birth to this baby. My anxiety only eased when Dad – released from hospital and signed off for travel – and Mom boarded a flight to Ireland. It was as if everything within me was waiting until Dad was safe and well before I could allow myself to give birth. The night of their arrival a babe came spiralling through my pelvis, velveteen head in the caul at my fingertips. My Pisces boy was born in my living room. Dad did not die. The spell was broken.

I updated my bio: *Artist and mother of two*. My online community became all the more important. Baby in sling, toddler in hand, I took buses across the country to sit at kitchen tables and solve the world's problems with other women. I ignored the heavier feelings that left me drained. I took herbal remedies and supplements and went to yoga. I had a supportive husband, an empowering birth and I loved being a mom. *Post-partum depression can't happen to me.* Yet I couldn't write or paint my way out of it. I was so tired. *Situational depression*, I told myself. *Motherhood is inherently lonely*, I decided. And then Mom lost her job, they lost their home, and Dad was diagnosed with early-onset dementia.

*

I sit on the stairs, pregnancy test in one hand, phone in the other, calling a community midwife while staring at the two solid lines in the little plastic window. *What the fuck are you doing? You already have two kids.* I don't know why I'm shocked. We hadn't used birth control: how ironic, given our infertility years, that I could become pregnant by accident. When Steven gets home we talk about how we'll figure out a way to make this work. Abortion never crosses my mind. I consider how I might miscarry, a thought that fills me with guilt. Days later I start bleeding.

The early pregnancy unit confirms a strong healthy heartbeat despite the blood telling me otherwise. The relief surprises me. I look at the screen. *I want that little blob.* Each bleed brings me back to the hospital for another scan and the reassurance of a growing babe. We celebrate Christmas and ring in the New Year. I'm out of the 'danger zone', society's magical twelve-week milestone after which the gestation can be revealed to the rest of the world. Excitement replaces fear at the thirteen-week scan to see that the blob and its heartbeat has grown legs and is bouncing around.

Two days later I toss and turn in my sleep, woken by my own whimpers, my body convulsing with cramps. I google 'pregnancy symptoms at the end of the first trimester'. Could it be round ligament pain? I stay in bed with a migraine, shivering with cold. I can't warm up. When the thermometer climbs to 39.4°C, I know something isn't right. I wrap up in a robe, put a bucket in front of me and close my eyes. Steven and the kids squeeze into the back of my mother-in-law's car and she drives us all in the dark to the hospital.

In triage I'm brought back to an isolation room to rule out meningitis. 'Why are you still breastfeeding your two-year-old?' 'How much longer are you planning on doing that for?' 'He doesn't need it. He's old enough.' I beg for pain relief, writhing in the bed, vomiting into cardboard kidney dishes until there's nothing left. I will be admitted to the ward for the night as a precaution. In the car park, the kids are asleep in the car. I send Steven home to get some rest.

'Sorry,' I call to the nurse, 'I think I wet myself – I just felt a gush down my legs.' We pull back the makeshift blanket of my dressing gown to discover the blood pouring from between my thighs.

'Not to worry!' the nurse trills. 'Let's just get you to sit on this pot so we can measure how much blood you're losing.'

As she helps me to stand, I can't stop the river. 'I'm so sorry! Oh god, I'm so sorry!' I apologise over and over again, trying to hold it in, trying not to make a mess. The floor, her shoes, her hands; I can't contain it. Clots escape, thick and black. More people come in to help move me back to the bed and to pull the soaked pyjamas off my legs.

'How long ago did you last eat or drink?' a doctor yells at me. Everything is moving fast forward but in slow motion. A primal bellow escapes from my throat, I recognise it as labour. I'm losing my baby. *I've made it happen.*

'Is your husband here? You need to call him – he has to come back.' Thick needles pierce my veins as I'm prepped for theatre as fast as possible. So many hands touching and pulling at me, asking questions, giving orders, moving quickly. A nurse presses my phone into my hand. I call Steven and leave a message, telling him that I'm going in for surgery. 'I love you,' I tell him. *What if I die?* I think.

As the bed is pushed through double doors and down the hallway, I watch the ceiling tiles and lights above my head and I pray. I pray that they won't do a scan and find a heartbeat. I think about Savita as they push the bed into the elevator. *Please stop bleeding. Please stop bleeding. Please stop bleeding.* They can take my uterus; I have two healthy kids at home. *Please stop bleeding.*

I wake to a warm hand holding mine.

'Erin?'

I'm in a hospital bed, in a gown, wearing mesh underwear packed with thick pads as Rebecca, my midwife, tells me that the baby I've lost was a boy. It's over, and I am relieved. And there is grief. Two nights of IV antibiotics. The chaplain brings me a little white box. Inside it, a tiny foetus I had seen bouncing on a screen just days before. *I've made it happen.*

Steven digs a hole in the garden as the January rain falls. Snowdrops dot the ground. I kneel and bury my hands in the soil, placing the babe I've wrapped in flower petals and silk into the tiny grave, baptising him with my tears and offering the earth around him seeds to nourish into life. I am a wild and wounded animal. From inside the house, a small voice calls for toast. I weep and we move on. This is women's work.

The notes I have requested from the hospital arrive, written evidence of the infection that had not been looked for nor diagnosed on previous hospital visits. I think about Savita. Had she received the healthcare she needed, she would still be alive. The baby I'd held in my palm was no more valuable than my own life. Of course he would have been loved, and I mourn for him, but he was not equal to me, nor equal to my other children. My children need their mother. My husband needs his wife. I need my life.

Spring arrives and seasonal hayfever sends me to the doctor. The moment she asks me how I am doing, I break down in tears. It all comes tumbling out: the undiagnosed post-partum depression, the surprise pregnancy, the anxiety about my parents, the miscarriage, the mothering being lonely as hell. She looks at me with gentle concern. I accept the prescription, feeling that my shame about taking antidepressants probably means I need them more than I think. I write about my miscarriage, about the duality of grief and relief, of not being ready to be a mother again and of the intrinsic sadness of losing a baby.

Miscarriage. A word that garners visible pity. And then the reasoning: the *higher plan*, the *at least you have kids*, the *you can try again*. My mom had an abortion and when I miscarried she blamed herself, as if the act of self-survival would one day punish her future daughter. Karma: trading one woman's abortion for another's miscarriage. My loss – a statistic, the one in four pregnancies that ends in miscarriage – became a personal responsibility and deal of fate. Yet loss gave me understanding and empathy and the taboo of miscarriage connected me to women around the world. It felt like a rite of passage in the experience of being a human, of being a fertile woman. I was safe, others were not. *I have to do something.*

*

While I was training as a doula – to become more involved in birth activism and to root myself into the community – the virtual circles remained a treasured resource. Monthly gatherings left me inspired and determined that we could change the world together. Later, the antidepressants help pull me out of the fog. I stop taking them. A few months later, I call Rebecca. Another baby will be joining our family. This time we are ready, but the familiar anxiety comes back to haunt me. *What if my dad dies during this pregnancy?*

Thirteen weeks pregnant, I travel to the States on my own, visiting my family for Thanksgiving. Though Dad's dementia is upsetting, there is much to be positive about. My parents are getting back on their feet financially. Things are looking up. Yet I can't shake off the birth/death paradox that had consumed my second pregnancy. When Dad stands up to greet family arriving through the door, the entire six foot three inches of him comes crashing down, leaving a dent from his head in the wooden coffee table. Mom's scream pierces the air. My pregnancy becomes an omen.

Dad doesn't die. We continue on with the festivities, carving the turkey and eating pumpkin pie. When he falls again the night before I'm due to fly back to Ireland, I realise I have no idea how the fuck I'm supposed to manage with the way things are going. Dementia or medication or both take him to a weird land of far away. *I miss him.* I say goodbye to Dad in the hospital before catching my flight and squeeze him tight. *Please don't die.*

Twenty-eight weeks later, a tidal wave crashes within me. Hot salty womb water pours down my shaking thighs. My voice trembles before finding the satisfying hum, the low moan, the vibration of shapeshift. My hands reach under the water, guiding a slip of a babe from one world into the next. I take her to my breast, her dark eyes gazing back at me. She is mysterious and wise, her black hair slicked to a velveteen head. My daughter, my seal pup.

*

Four months after giving birth I venture again to the States, this time with a newborn and two kids. It will be the first meeting of the youngest grandchild. Mom is exhausted. Coming home from work every evening she'd collapse straight into bed before getting up again to play with her grandchildren. It is so unlike her. She books routine blood tests with the family doctor who diagnoses elevated white blood cells – most likely a deficiency. Under the safety of a sleeping house I look up what the numbers are spelling out. I feel sick.

A second opinion sends her to a haematologist. I entertain the kids in the hospital waiting room with stickers and empty water cups. 'Are these the Irish grandkids?' The nurse calls us back. Despite having just endured a bone-marrow biopsy, Mom never missed an opportunity to show off and tell the stories of her children to anyone who asked, or didn't.

Under orders to enjoy the holidays, I curl her hair while she applies makeup.

'What if I lose my hair?' In that moment, looking at her face in the mirror, it feels like we both know.

'You won't. We don't know anything yet. Besides, there are so many different types of treatment these days. If you lose your hair, I'll shave mine off too.'

I won't allow myself to believe any of the potentials the doctors are looking to rule out. It won't be talked about today, not with extended family, not just yet. Loading up the truck with kids, we drive two hours south to Granny's, where we're joined by my brothers and their families for Thanksgiving. Pies and casserole dishes, stuffing and sweet potatoes.

The TV blares while the little cousins run around after each other. Dad's dementia is the main focus of conversation – what doctor's appointments are coming up, what medication is helping. I watch him zoning in and out. I watch Mom trying to make it through the day without falling asleep. I text Steven all of the gossip. *I wish you were here. It's taking everything within me to not say something. I wonder if he really voted for Trump?!* I eat pie and explain to Granny again how we don't have Thanks-giving in Ireland.

The holiday weekend is over with a bang. A family row and everyone goes home. And then we get the phone call.

'Get the kids ready. The hospital called. They want your mom up there right away.'

Dad rushes around the house in a panic. Mom is running errands, so while we wait for her to come home, everything speeds into overdrive. I gather the kids, dress them and pack a bag of toys and snacks. My heart is racing while I try to remain upbeat. Mom arrives back with the poinsettias she's picked out from the garden centre. They're her favourite. Her fifty-sixth birthday is approaching, just before Christmas, and our child-hood home was always filled with a pot of these lush flowers at this time of year. We drive the ten minutes to the hospital talking about flowers.

Elevator doors open and all I see is the word ONCOLOGY. The waiting room is full of people wearing colourful headscarves, offsetting their pale skin and the grey walls. My kids sit, eating snacks, swinging their feet from chairs in the waiting room. It feels important to pay attention to every detail. Mom and Dad disappear behind a set of doors. Minutes go by and then I'm called in with the kids.

'Acute myeloid leukaemia,' the doctor says firmly. 'Yes, you will lose your hair. I'm sorry.' She holds Mom's hand. 'You can go home and get your bag; you'll be admitted right now and need to begin treatment immediately.'

The air has been sucked out of the room. Oblivious, the toddler asks to go to the toilet. I am somewhere between having to be a mother and needing to be with my mother. I can't breathe. Back in the room, Mom meets my eyes. 'Can I come in tomorrow? Erin's leaving in the morning.'

The oncologist agrees as long as she returns first thing in the morning.

Blood-red poinsettias sit on the kitchen counter as we talk about DNR arrangements. Nothing feels real. A flurry of phone calls are made – insurance, work, sick leave. More calls to family and friends. I begin compiling a list of things to pack that might ease discomfort from the likely reactions of chemotherapy.

Mom and I drive to the mall. We walk around Gap, holding up fleece pyjamas and shirts with easy access for IV lines. We seek out the softest things we can find, carrying our secret like a bomb: the C word. Cancer. As we pack Mom's hospital bag, I pack my own, gathering bits to entertain three children on the long-haul flight. Leaving has always been hard, but this time it's unbearable. In the early morning darkness, we drive in silence to the airport. The only way I can part with Mom and Dad is knowing I'll be returning just as soon as I've brought my kids back home. It isn't goodbye, it's see you soon.

Back in Ireland I sink into a blessed rhythm, the packing of lunches, the walking to school. The prospect of Christmas leaves me numb, but I make myself be present for the kids. I want it to be magical for them. Santa arrives and leaves gold-covered chocolate coins dotted around the sitting room. I can only be certain of that because he does this every year. I'm tethered to my phone, to my mom thousands of miles across the ocean, checking the hospital app every day for blood counts, learning a new language to understand what that day's treatment entails. Each night brings no more than three hours of anxiety-ridden sleep.

Ringing in the New Year with the kids banging pots and pans and howling into the night sky like we did as children, I stir in an incantation and eat the traditional New Year black-eyed peas as if my life depended on this southern superstition: Every day I light

candles. I create rituals, I draw a talisman on my skin. I feel it in my gut. It's imperative I do these things to heal her.

I take my youngest on the flight back to Oklahoma. The road between hospital and house becomes a well-worn map in my mind. Mom's room is decorated with get-well-soon cards. Aromatherapy oils waft around and fairy lights twinkle, their gentle ambiance a refreshing contrast to the hospital's stark overhead lights and sharp chemical and antiseptic pungency. A six-month-old with fat pudding legs and round rosy cheeks strapped to my chest brings a grateful reprieve, baby babble and giggles each day, a reminder of light and life. We practise tying headscarves in different ways, but Mom's bald head is too stunning to cover. She carries it with confidence.

Hospital day 53 welcomes the sweetest word uttered from the oncologist. Remission.

'Go home and celebrate, book your holiday to Ireland.'

Promising to wait a couple of weeks before the celebratory margarita, we pack up the blankets and cards, balloons and socks. I drive the truck to the hospital door and bring my goddess home.

I return to Ireland, leaving Mom to recover at home while we plan out the future together over the phone. But my incantations, superstitions and spells have failed me. Concoctions of drugs and poisons and the latest medical science have failed her. The first clinical trial has failed. The leukaemia has returned and mutated. A new hospital, a more aggressive clinical trial, and a bone-marrow transplant will be necessary. New poisons, and a new dedication of hope.

'There's nothing more we can do for you here,' she is told after a month in a different hospital. Resources in Oklahoma have been exhausted and there are no more options in the state. Four hours south we find the place that will become her new and temporary home: a hospital in Dallas has offered a clinical trial that's covered by insurance. Mom travels the 216 miles by ambulance.

I fly to Texas with my baby, now a one-year-old, in a sling. As soon as I arrive, we run potential donor tests on me. It's unlikely, but worth a shot. 'Acute' sounds so innocuous. It doesn't imply how grave and ugly, how perilous a disease can be. In my mind it conjured a small and insignificant acute angle. How can something that sounds so small be so devastating?

My mother is like a frail, featherless bird in a giant bed. I'm unable to touch her without it hurting, so I don't. She sleeps for nearly twenty-four hours a day, Dad on a couch next to her bed. I sit in the chair for days, listening to her breathe, staring out of the high-rise window that looks out onto other wings of the hospital.

She cries out, delirious from medication, desperation in her voice, searching for her momma as if she were just beyond the doorway. I look for the ghost of her mother while I hold her leg in my arm, keeping her as still as possible while the doctor drills deep into the marrow of her hip. With my baby on my back, I sing soothing lullabies in her ear as if she were my baby too. I stroke her head as she falls asleep, her face never completely relaxing, whimpering through dreams. I walk the hallways to cry alone.

Despite everything, Dad and I successfully encourage Mom to eat. Slowly she gains strength and energy. She walks short shuffle steps in the hospital corridors, following behind the trying-to-learn-how-to-walk toddler. After three weeks I'm able to hug her for the first time. She still smells like her, still smells like home.

The Great American Eclipse of 2017 creates ripples of excitement on every news station. Mom is awake more often. She's regaining her old sense of humour. She is coming back to herself, and to us. Dad and I stand outside in the humid Texas air, our faces to the sky. We're a community of strangers, all sharing special filtered glasses, all connected by this one moment. It's a sign. I hold the amulet I wear around my neck, the one that matches hers. I smooth it between my fingers, repeating the mantra I call on daily: 'This is the spell that I intone / flesh to flesh, bone to bone / sinew to sinew, vein to vein / each shall be whole again.'

My suitcase is packed. We sit, side by side on the hospital bed, as Mom sings 'Itsy Bitsy Spider' and plays games with my babe. We wait anxiously for the results of the last biopsy. Just minutes before I have to leave for the airport, the oncologist arrives, bringing with him the provisional date for a bone-marrow transplant. This is the miracle we've been waiting for.

NINE MONTHS: 2017–2018

SEPTEMBER I continue to live astride two worlds; one where children grow like weeds, the other where parents are poised on the threshold of the unknown. There is much to celebrate: my youngest toddles across the floor in her first unaided steps to sibling cheers. The tooth fairy kisses the cheeks of my eldest as she sleeps and wakes to gold and remnants of magic. My middle child begins playschool, walking to school hand in hand with his sister, his backpack as big as himself.

I immerse myself back into birth activism, which has transitioned into the fight for abortion rights. 'Rebel Girl Repeal,'[3] a poem about the kind of girl my mama raised, is read in Galway city as part of Culture Night. Meanwhile, a date is set for the transplant – 4 October 2017 – when a hero stranger will give their bone marrow to save my mom's life. Could I possibly be there? It will be a year since the diagnosis. It would be the most perfect way to surprise her. I dream of the way it would feel to see her face. I'm moved to heaving sobs at the videos of Irish mammies being surprised by their children coming home from afar.

We settle into the new school routine, counting down the days for the transplant. I prepare my outfit for marching for

Repeal at the Sixth Annual March for Choice and look forward to my first abortion rights rally.

*

I'm on the night bus to Dublin in my Repeal jumper, my youngest curled into my lap. The annual march is tomorrow, 30 September. I'm heading to Dublin with a new purpose. I'm also travelling towards the worst moment of my life.

Just two days ago I texted with Mom. In the years since I'd left home, the past two months have been the only time we haven't talked every day. She's simply been too unwell. As I walk the kids to school, she texts that it hurts to breathe. I take it to be anxiety related and guide her through breathing techniques, breathing with her as I type out the words: *Inhale golden light down, down, down, swirling down through your body. Exhale a ribbon of light from your lips. Fill the room with the ribbon, slowly, let it dance around the room. Inhale golden healing light, let it soothe its way into every ache.* As the moon hangs in the early morning sky I let her know *I see the moon, we're under her together right now, it's just you and me.*

The fifteen-minute walk back home is interrupted by the ding of a text message. She is being moved to the intensive care unit. I video-call her and see her face now covered completely by an oxygen mask. Reluctant to waste any of her reserves, we speak in sign language – 'I love you' – and end the call so she can rest.

At noon, standing in the kitchen with a toddler on hip, my phone rings. It's Dad.

'You need to get home now. We have to put her on life support. The doctor says there's no time.' I can't breathe. The room is spinning, blood rushes in my ears. This can't be right. It's playschool collection and I have to go get my son. I tell him I'll find a way.

I call Steven at work. 'Come home, right now.' My mind races, calculating flight prices. I will have to go alone with my baby. I text

23

the women in my online circle. Behind the scenes, within hours and without my knowledge, they'd already begun gathering the money to get me home. The flights are booked. Nothing makes sense. My body carries me through the motions to get to the airport. Kissing my family in desperation, I climb into the bus for Dublin airport. *This cannot be real.*

'What are your reasons for travelling to the US?'

I can barely meet the immigration officer's face, the words thick in my throat, I choke them out. 'My mom ... I have to take her off life support.'

He asks no more questions. I get on the plane.

A layover somewhere. Chicago? Newark? Atlanta? I text to let her know I'm nearly there, as I do every time. I text into the void, to the phone by her bedside. She won't see it. One more flight. I pace the terminal, the weight of my daughter's body keeping me grounded. *Wait for me, wait for me, wait for me. I'm on my way. I'm here. Wait for me.*

The luggage carousal can't spit out my bag fast enough. Every minute that passes is a minute too long, a minute more that I've lost with her. I need to run. I need to run to her. *Come on, come on, come on.* I make strained small talk with my brother Cody during this fucked-up reunion and smile at my niece, adding some useless comment about how tall she's got. The humidity hits my lungs like a brick wall. Everything slows in the oppressive southern heat. Rush-hour traffic clogs the city's veins. I drink in the sticky molasses air as I pray to Mom over and over again, *Please wait for me, please wait for me, please wait.* Cody guides me through the hospital maze. I am feral, wild, my pulse is racing. *Where is she, where is she, where is she?* I hunt for her like an animal, searching through every partially open curtain and door.

Behind sliding glass doors, in the darkness, she lies still, tiny, consumed by tubes and wires. My beautiful, strong, fierce mama.

My first love. She waited for me. They waited for me. It isn't long before the doctors arrive to remove the machines that keep her body alive. *I'm here now, it's time.* I see her face again without the interference of tubes and tape. I moisten her lips with a wet sponge. My hand hovers over her chest, desperate to touch her, afraid to hurt her.

Twelve hours after my arrival she takes her last breath of earthly air. Just like that. Forever. The hum of machines still. The blush of her cheeks fades. Dad crumples over her bed. I sway with the weight of the child on my back. An envelope is pressed into my palm, containing a printout of the last recorded heartbeat of the woman who gave me life.

OCTOBER Oklahoma skies stretch blue and wide, sliced here and there by migrating geese. The crunch of dead grass underfoot. Autumn arrives, along with decisions to be made about the funeral. I write the obituary with my brother Trevor, both of us stretched across our parents' bed.

The tasks ahead are both profound and mundane. Shop for a funeral dress. Make sure Dad eats. Change the baby's nappy. Take the dog for a walk. Put one foot in front of the other.

Breathe.

At night, I share the bed with my dad and daughter so none of us sleeps alone. I spend days listening to him making phone calls, uttering 'My wife passed away' to bankers, insurance companies, lawyers.

I stare at her toothbrush in the bathroom, at the pillbox with its days of the week, some compartments empty, the rest forever waiting, at the nightgown crumpled in a pile on the floor. I want to create a museum, a shrine of her artefacts. Each vignette a poem. Everything is familiar and, at the same time, a precious new discovery. I build little altars everywhere. Everything she touched becomes a treasure. Smoothing on the lipstick that held the impression of her lips, I dress in a way that I can see her staring back at me from the mirror.

I never shaved my hair when I said I would.

People show up to the church, laughing, chatting, catching up with each other. They take selfies and group photos. Strangers who've known me my whole life, who've known my mother longer than I have, tell me I look just like her. I haven't dreamt of her again and I'm afraid the feeling of her will slip away too. I want to rip my skin off.

I stand at the front of the church reading the words that will never be enough. A funeral is for the people who come, I realise, not for the family. When the priest places the heavy box of ashes into my hands as we leave the church, it becomes my weight to carry. I am the matriarch.

There's no time to let anything settle. Dad's dementia worsens. It was only a matter of time with the trauma, stress and change of routine. The house they rent has to be packed up and cleaned out. Dad and I begin to sort through the treasures and memories; sell, donate and keep. We go out for dinner on my thirtieth birthday and I watch his eyes fading. I am losing him too. I feel so alone.

At night, as the house is stripped of her artefacts, the remnants of my parents' lives sealed in boxes, I find myself writing poetry and spilling inks and paint across a page. These become my last paintings for a year.

NOVEMBER

Back in Ireland I convince myself that Mom is still in hospital. *We haven't spoken in a while because she's resting, recovering from the transplant. When I fly home to surprise her, she'll be so excited ... I can't wait to see the look on her face.* I wake up, having bitten my tongue so hard that it bleeds. *Tomato soup,* she told me in my dream, *Tomato soup. The tubes ... my throat hurts.* I tell Dad about the soup. It turns out that that's all she was asking for in the days leading up to her death.

DECEMBER Days blur into each other. In the hour before dawn, she consumes my thoughts. *Just curl up. One more minute. One more hour. One more day. One more year.* I have to hold everything together. As we walk to school my mind flashes with all the ways that we might be killed by oncoming traffic. Images embed themselves into my vision: one wrong step, one trip, a driver not paying attention. My head splattered across the road, crushed beneath the wheels of a car. The entire scenario plays in a repeating reel. I nod as my son babbles away about hibernating animals. I listen, but I'm not really here. I'm there, splattered across the road. At school, I kiss them goodbye. I walk home, pushing the stroller faster and faster. I can't remember how to breathe. I'm late collecting my daughter – only by a few minutes, but to her they feel like a lifetime. I kneel down and look into her eyes full of tears and promise, 'I'll never leave you.' Yet as the words leave my mouth, I know this isn't true. Mothers will leave you one day, no matter how much they want to stay.

*

'Would you like to support women's rights?'

It's Saturday morning. Christmas lights line the streets. People are busy buying gifts and running errands. I find the three women I'd planned to meet, Aine, Rebecca and Marion, behind a trestle table, wearing Repeal jumpers and warm smiles. With no date yet set for a referendum to legalise abortion, I join them in the task to drum up support to sign an email list for Abortion Rights Campaign (ARC) in order to lobby our local conservative politicians. I need to find a way to focus my energy on something beyond this grief, I need a task.

We stand for a while in the cold as people pass by, ignoring us. *What would Mom do?* I step forward, call out to strangers and ask if anyone wants to sign to support women's rights.

'No.'

'Thanks anyway, have a great day!'

Undeterred, I continue to ask everyone and eventually their curiosity is piqued and people stop to talk. I silently promise that I will not only fight for my autonomy, but for theirs as well. I think about Savita. I think about my miscarriage. I think about my mother. I think about my daughters. I think about my new friends. The sense of belonging I had been searching for? The activists, those willing to push the boundaries, to fight against the system, to stand up for themselves and others? I found them. Wise women making ripples, who know how to play the game, who understand that change happens slowly, painfully slowly. The Repealers. I still want to burn shit down.

In 2006, the year I moved to Ireland, the word 'abortion' would garner a sharp inhale of air. Two years later a radical anti-abortion group, now called Youth Defence, rallied together to oppose the Lisbon Treaty because of its potential to include abortion. It worked. Fear, panic, disbelief. Abortion? *Not here. Not the babies.* 'Getting the boat' – that Irish euphemism – is met with quiet tuts and head-shaking. Pro-choice groups have been repeatedly prevented from holding public meetings on local premises. Abortion can happen, just not in Ireland.

I've spent years learning about the maternity system in Ireland and listening to the voices of others through the Association to Improve Maternity Services (AIMS Ireland) and Galway Birth Gatherings. I continue to dig: the historical physical and sexual abuse by the Catholic Church in Ireland and around the world that continues to this day and remains unprosecuted; the maternity wards run by religious orders; the mother and baby homes for unwed pregnant women – legal slavery hidden in plain sight. Contraception was only legalised in Ireland in 1980 and with strong restrictions, reflecting the Catholic teachings on sexual morality. Marital rape was not considered a criminal act until 1990, but it wouldn't be until 2002 that a man was prosecuted for it. The year 1995 brought the divorce referendum, making it legal (by a margin of 1 per cent) for couples to separate, yet the first divorce under the new amendment didn't take place until 1997. The last mother and baby home closed in 1996.

Oppressed by the church and government, denied the right of information and banned from travelling for abortion, women and girls in Ireland truly lived as second-class citizens under a tapestry of secrets. A blanket of shame. A rug under which to sweep the truth. Wash it away with holy water, bury it in an unmarked grave. History. Their history. They're history. There is a fire in my belly, a righteous anger for those who suffered before me, who are suffering now. I vow to join in the fight for reproductive equality and justice. The one thing I know to be true of Irish people is their rebellious nature, their compassion for others, their ways of taking care of community in need.

Galway East for Choice is a steering group of society misfits. A group of smart, witty, determined women. They welcome me among them. With information trickling down from the ARC

Headquarters in Dublin, we fall into our roles with ease: the time-keeper, the organiser, the creator, the feeder, the researcher and so on. When the 1983 referendum first introduced the Eighth Amendment into the constitution, the west was effectively forgotten. Because we lived beyond the pale, we would be doing this our own way. Galway East was determined that, this time, the west would not be left behind.

JANUARY On this winter's day, as a cold wind bites our faces, we stand in our small corner of conservative East Galway. People come and ask questions at the table I have dressed with the hand-sewn banner. We're learning as we go how to handle interactions. We find ways to answer questions to which we don't know the answer; we learn how to approach, how to engage, how to connect, how to move someone along. We make no assumptions; we talk to everyone. The triumphant joy when old men in their farm wellies press notes into our hands, telling us to use the money for someone who needs it. Young boys and girls preparing to vote for the very first time are happy to collect badges to pin to their school jumpers. We're learning, as some pass by with a nod of approval, that people might support abortion rights, but cannot be seen to do so. The stigma is heavy.

If you just walk in her shoes …

Who wears the shoes of someone who's had an abortion? I think about the families, the women passing by our stall. How many of them have had abortions? What if I wrote out the experiences of women who had had to travel abroad to have abortions and attached them to a pair of shoes, leaving them by the ATM, at the bus stop? Who owns these shoes? They could belong to anyone, not just 'that kind' of girl. That girl is every woman. That girl wears the shoes of a doctor, of a teacher, of a mother. That girl is someone we know and love. These shoes belong to anyone who has the potential to become pregnant. I know what I have to do. An art installation of sorts, but one that's bigger than something I can physically accomplish.

I'm not sure I agree with abortion, but you've made me think. His words stay with me, I'm determined to open his mind to the real circumstances of who needs an abortion. There are more like him, and I know that if they just hear something of the reality, they will change their minds. I finish at the stall and walk home to take photos of my shoes, like those you might see in a women's magazine: *What's In Her Bag? Travel (for an abortion) edition!*

Everything has been leading to this moment. The photography, blogs, poetry, groups, gatherings. I always knew that one day I'd turn that passion into something bigger than myself. I want to invite people to take a walk in her shoes. By sharing my project idea on my Facebook group and by offering the opportunity for anyone with a story to share anonymously, In Her Shoes – Women of the Eighth begins with the first line of one story: 'I was trying not to get sick on the way over, and trying not to bleed all over the seats on the way home ...' and continues with another: 'His [the doctor's] judgemental, intimidating attitude reminded me that my home country considered me a shameful criminal for daring to make decisions about my own body and my own life ...'

I upload the stories with pictures of my own shoes. My mother's words become my oath to the women of Ireland: *I trust you. I trust you to always make the best decision for yourself. And if you need help, I know you'll figure it out, and I will be here.*

Stories and photographs of shoes begin to trickle in. Each new post gains traction and attracts more, and then more, a tidal wave of experiences. People are desperate to tell what they have endured. Some are fearful of family, friends, or co-workers recognising their particular shoes. I'm trying to navigate an ethical way of holding these human experiences that are, after all, illegal in Ireland. I'm reluctant to advertise. I aim to build on trust. My gut guides me. When a story comes in, I reply, trying to meet the storyteller where she is in her vulnerability, in her bravery. I share it without changing the words, merely editing for pace and punctuation. What I have created is not a campaign: it is a gathering, and I am the facilitator.

Cáit, from our Facebook mothering group, messages me, asking if I need any help: *I suppose it could be an emotional toll taking on these stories – have you an outlet to debrief? I know even in breastfeeding counselling an emotional one can get me and I need an outlet for that. In fact, we're encouraged to have it. Anonymously of course. Just can be hard to shake a tough story, and they are nothing to the stories you're getting. x*

The project keeps me busy and offers a distraction, but it's hard going. I'm simply swapping out my own grief for that of others. Cáit has been sharing responses on Twitter about In Her Shoes and suggests I start a Twitter page. She offers to manage it for me. @InHerIrishShoes is born, bringing the platform deeper into a political atmosphere.

My phone is filled with photos of shoes. An article of clothing can say so much about a person. There is a creative freedom in being able to choose a pair of shoes that repaints the idea of *that* kind of girl. I'm constantly thinking how to best match up a story with a pair of shoes. What combination would afford a reader the best chance of seeing this person, who has had an abortion, as a human being, deserving of their compassion? The honour of holding this space comes with the duality of a larger responsibility. There are real people behind these stories.

Being available becomes a full-time job. I have to be there in an instant for anyone who needs me: *Is she in a crisis at this moment? Does she need resources near her? Does she need the phone number for the Rape Crisis Centre? Does she just need a listening ear?* I'm not trained for any of this, I'm just a woman listening. It's overwhelming, but taking it one story at a time and giving her my attention feels right. I put my own needs on the back burner. Steven has been stepping up to all the household and parenting duties while grief has pulled me far away. He's a constant champion for how important this is. It gives me purpose and keeps me above the surface.

I hadn't anticipated reading about so much sexual violence. Although I had created a space for abortion stories, others were coming forward with their experiences of rape and domestic abuse. No two stories are the same, yet they are all linked by common threads: being let down, being scared, alone, desperate. The stories leave me sobbing. I have to step away from the computer, put the phone down, talk it through with Steven. Yet the stories give me all the more reason to push through and past my own heavy heart. They have to be heard. Steven gives me strength and confidence to persevere. I find the Irish project 'Everyday Stories', a storytelling and illustration installation highlighting the Eighth Amendment, co-founded by Caoimhe Anglin and Mary McDermott in August 2017, which travels around the country with exhibitions for an immersive experience. People aren't just listening; they are actively seeking out these lived truths.

FEBRUARY In Her Shoes gains more and more momentum. Within a month we have over 6,000 followers. It's mind-boggling. By February we have 20,000 more followers and my butterflies are turning into full-blown palpitations. Grief consumes me, complex and layered. It competes with oxygen, filling my lungs with sediments of thick, heavy, sticky black missing, a desperate longing for my mother. I can't sleep. It sneaks up on me. There is no break from these women's tales. There is no break from monitoring the comments. I need help, and I don't know how to ask for it. I don't know what to do. There's so much to fight for.

An item of clothing falls out of my wardrobe and suddenly Mom's scent fills the air. I cup the fabric around my face and inhale deeply, willing it never to fade. It's been nearly five months since I last heard her voice. My final text to her remains forever marked unread.

MARCH Flights are grounded and there's a red weather warning in place. Storm Emma is making landfall. Anyone trying to get a flight in or out of Shannon and Dublin for an abortion is stranded.

News headlines focus on the sales of Brennans bread. Kids take delight in school closures and the post has halted all deliveries. Those not travelling for an abortion who have sourced illegal pills online are in limbo. Days tick away. Gestation waits for no one. My heart aches for those in Irish airports trying to get there, and those stuck in England trying to get home in order not to raise suspicions, to return to their children, to their bed where they can bleed with dignity. While the kids build snowmen in the garden, I try to bring awareness online to the distress the

Emma

In her shoes
The buses ran late.
After midnight,
Standing in the dark, the snow falling, the storm arrived.
The one that everyone has been chatting about with excitement
*   and cynicism.*

Bread and milk – and she can only think of the Panadol in her bag,
*   and if she has enough pads.*

Checking flight status in Dublin
Taking the chance that it might
*   still go*
A silent bus journey from
*   Limerick, Donegal, Cobh.*

Double-check passport is still in date
Anxious belly, it'll all have to wait …

Nine women
Taking ferry, plane and bus.

Medical tourist
Ireland's refugees
Silent, shameful, keeping reality
*   unseen.*

storm causes to a pregnancy that has to end. *I'm losing my way as a mother. My compass is broken. I don't know if I'm doing anything right. I'm distracted and distant, snappy and impatient. I want to dream about her. I want to curl up in bed next to her. I want so desperately to be crying out of homesickness, to know that I'll get to see her again.*

It's International Women's Day and the Galway East group will be speaking at a pro-choice rally in the city. I've opted to stay at home instead, sewing a *Blueberry Girl* costume for World Book Week. My revolution will take place behind the sewing machine, in the costume my daughter wears to school, in the books we read to our kids at night. *What would Mom do?* She would sew that dress, then stand in front of the large crowd to speak without a tremble in her voice. Instead, I'm having Susan read my letter about the women with no vote, women like me. I hope to inspire action in men to know that their vote on 'women's issues' is important; I hope to inspire someone who doesn't plan on voting to realise how their one vote is a voice for someone else:

> The women of Ireland are comprised of Irish citizens, permanent residents, temporary residents and people in direct provision. The only people with a voice in this referendum are Irish citizens. The only people fully able to leave the country to obtain a safe abortion are Irish citizens, EU passport-holders and certain temporary and permanent residents with enough money.
>
> Women who have made this country their home, who have given birth to their children here, who have settled into their communities here – they don't get a vote. They don't get a voice for themselves, or for the future of their Irish children. All women do not have freedom of movement across borders. Immigration restrictions mean many women are

unable to leave the country at short notice or unable to enter another EU country without a long process and expensive visa. Freedom to travel does not apply equally to all.

Women in direct provision cannot leave. These are women and girls who become pregnant through rape or incest; who find out they are pregnant with a baby that will never survive outside of the womb; who find out they are pregnant and are fighting addiction; who find out they are pregnant and are in an abusive relationship; who find out they are pregnant and are battling mental illness; who find out they are pregnant and are not ready; who find out they are pregnant and cannot afford to feed another mouth, nor heat their house. These are forgotten women.

These women and girls have no voice in this referendum, because they cannot vote. They are the ones left without choice, because they cannot travel. These women and girls who have made Ireland their home. These are our friends, these are our colleagues, our students, our artists, our athletes, our community. We are *mná na hÉireann*.

The following day Minister for Children Katherine Zappone and numerous politicians read In Her Shoes stories in Dáil Éireann. I feel as if I'm having an out-of-body experience. Our history is being cemented into the foundations of government. Politicians appeal for a date to be set for a referendum.

I wake multiple times during the night to breastfeed my daughter. Scrolling through my phone to check every comment and replying to desperate messages in the inbox is taking its toll. I wake early, panicking, double-checking that what I write in a half-sleep state makes sense. Did I actually send it or did I dream it all?

Mary notices the page taking on a momentum of its own and messages me, offering assistance. It's such a relief to say yes. I'm reluctant to accept help and bring somebody else into the heaviness of this work. I've known Mary since the first breastfeeding days and although we have yet to meet up in person, she feels like home.

Now it's just myself and Mary on the page. She moderates the comments; I do everything else. We swap out: *I'm gonna be off my phone for the next 15 minutes to get the kids, are you on?* Cáit sets up a firewall to stop the bots and trolls on Twitter. We work around the clock – pushing a stroller to school and typing out the drafts to share on the page into phone notes, stopping to take a picture of shoes along the way – but we need more help. I put the call out. Jenni, my good friend and our Galway Parents for Choice representative, suggests Jac, another member of Parents for Choice and a woman I have known from Gentle Parenting and feminist Facebook groups. I message her. So gracious and kind, she jumps on board to help in any way. The three of us are working well together. We have a WhatsApp group and find our rhythms for the tasks that suit in between taking care of children. Replying to each story with thought, care and love in a timely manner requires enormous emotional reserves. Our task is huge.

Cara, a fellow American from Cork, calls with questions about In Her Shoes. Although she's already home-educating three kids, Cara offers to help with reading, replying, organising, anything at all. It's weird how I left America and didn't want to *be* American, yet find myself befriending Americans in Ireland, grateful for our shared cultural understanding. None of us has a vote in this referendum; each one of us has been pregnant in Ireland under the Eighth Amendment. We're all mothers, finding the tiny pockets of time between the baths to be run, the toenails to be clipped, the lunches to be packed. We chat throughout the day, ask questions about the page, but it's mostly a reprieve from the intensity of the stories themselves and the often abusive comments. We are a united front in the face of what feels like an endless battle.

It's through Repeal that I learn more about the activists in Northern Ireland who smuggle illegal pills to those who need them. These activists are denied healthcare at home and are under threat to have their houses raided by the PSNI (Police Service of Northern Ireland). On 8 March 2017, International Women's Day, women's rights activist Helen Crickard had her office raided for abortion pills, with a warrant to seize all electronic devices with internet capability. Another raid happened at the home of a male pro-choice campaigner, and around twenty women who had packages seized were 'invited' for interviews at the police station. When they denied any knowledge of the packages, the police would show up at their doorsteps. Yet activists in Northern Ireland still remain determined to help anyone across any border to get the medication. Even though Northern Ireland is part of the United Kingdom (where abortion is legal), having an abortion in Northern Ireland is a prosecutable offence, risking a life prison sentence.[4]

I begin looking for a trusted voice to represent the unique climate, fight and struggles of Northern Ireland. Emer offers her time. She reads and replies with her whole heart, giving so much of herself to others. I rely on her experience, learning more about the gravity and tenderness of Northern Ireland's history. It informs so many of the cultural similarities and differences that I will never fully understand and I'm determined to maintain a united force of abortion activism across borders.

But even with a team of people picking up the pieces, my mental health is slipping. I worry about how the work will impact the well-being of these volunteers. I brought this work on them. More and more people offer to help but I don't know how to direct them to ways they can. Afraid to make decisions that will leave someone out, that will hurt someone's feelings, I do nothing instead.

It's like living in two separate worlds: the one in my hand with the constantly buzzing phone and the one around me with the kids, the housework, the dinners. A husband? Oh right, my husband. Two ships passing in the night. I listen to him laughing with the kids at bedtime. They are all doing fine without me and I'm grateful.

My son turns five. Milestones soaked in missing, dripping in yearning. I bury golden coins in a box, draw a treasure map, make the elaborate cake. If I can evoke the magic-making mama, the creator of memories, I can prove to myself that I am here.

The Government has confirmed that the referendum on the Eighth Amendment of the Constitution of Ireland will be held on Friday 25 May. It comes after the bill to hold a referendum passed all stages of the Seanad. – RTÉ, 28 March 2018

Hope

And so we pull back the covers.
We lift the veils that disguised and protected these secrets.
And when the sunlight shines all the dirt revealed that it was not
*   the women and girls who are dirty.*
It never was.
It is not their secrets to hold in shame. It is those who hold the
*   keys, the locks, the documents, the cross.*

It is those who wear the suits, the habit and the collar. It is the
*   laundries and the hospitals, the schools and the churches and*
*   there is no going back.*
No more rug to sweep it under.
*   The fire in the belly is lit and it will never be extinguished.*
*   Pandora's box is open.*
All the monsters come flooding out and there, hidden at the
*   bottom,*
there all along, is something called hope.

Emboldened by thousands of ancestors, we march forward. Two months to make history. Things will get dirty. This is battle. With a toddler asleep in my lap, I make my to-do lists. Mothers work a revolution with chicken nuggets and toast for dinners, drinking cups of tea gone cold.

APRIL The Facebook page receives at least ten stories per day. Nat, a mother, artist and Facebook friend, makes contact, offering to design our twelve-page booklet. I'm inspired by *The Healthy Birth Directory for the West*,[5] and decide to put together something for the undecided voter, for those voters who are not on social media and for rural Ireland. Information that can be read at the hairdresser's or in the doctor's waiting room; something tangible with which to start the conversation. It will have quotes and stories and a link to the Facebook page and will have to stay underground to avoid the attention of anti-choice groups. We'd have to fundraise on the quiet.

After nights spent pulling stories and quotes that would fit, Nat creates something really special and beautiful. We attribute funding to *mná na hÉireann* (women of Ireland). Abortion Rights Campaign call to ask what they can do to help. They share their resources of information for printing at cost. I email the PDF to every regional Together for Yes and pro-choice group I can find, giving them the freedom to print what their funds allow. Overnight we raise €1,056 in donations, ranging from €5 to €50, to cover printing costs.

Meanwhile, the Facebook page remains fully at grassroots level, allowing us to maintain the voice and intimacy I have worked so hard to create. While Together for Yes works alongside political parties and must tread carefully to maintain a message the entire coalition can agree upon, In Her Shoes can speak freely, unapologetically and apolitically, advocating for free, safe, legal abortion. It ends up being a cohesive approach to fill the gaps and appeal to everyone. Together for Yes, with an umbrella of seventy groups, was never part of In Her Shoes. For those of us in rural Ireland, the Coalition to Repeal the Eighth Amendment feels distant and Dublin-centric. Television debates are all about the politics. In Her Shoes focuses on the people, not the politicians. The stories are essential in bringing humanity into law reform.

A giant truck arrives from Dublin and lifts a pallet of booklets into my driveway. I laugh wildly. An idea come to fruition and here they are, printed and real. I create a logistics group, nominating one person in each county to receive a box of booklets along with distribution guidelines: *Please don't give them without consent, like the anti-choice literature in our letterboxes. Leave them in a place to be discovered, a place that allows someone to sit and read, to reflect.*

I envision people going home for Sunday roasts, leaving a booklet on Mam's table next to the newspaper and crosswords. Something that will pique curiosity and start conversation, that can be read in public without the 'a' word emblazoned across the front. I don't know how many we can give away in time. Each booklet on the pallet is precious and we plan on being conservative in their distribution.

On the In Her Shoes Facebook page, I emphasise how Catholicism doesn't automatically strike off the hardships and realities of life. One can maintain personal faith and still vote for others to have the freedom to choose their own healthcare.

My friend and neighbour stops by the house. Knowing that her Catholicism is important to her, I tentatively ask how she is feeling about the referendum. I am so anxious. I don't want our views to sour the friendship we have. 'It's not easy, I've been reading all of the stories on Facebook.' She lowers her voice. 'It's just awful ...'

She talks about the friends with diagnoses of babies who would not survive outside of the womb, who had no option but to continue with the pregnancy and face the devastation of a baby born sleeping. She takes a booklet. Later she sends me a text: *Simply heartbreaking, Erin. It's a tough read but I couldn't put it down. I had my decision made, but this just reassured me that it's the right one.* I read her text over and over and cry. I know that these booklets will make the difference.

In April our following is 66,000. I'm not sleeping, riddled with anxiety and the pressure of responsibility towards all these women sharing their most intimate experiences. I envision impossible things. I bargain with grief, and consider the possibility that if I do this really well, then perhaps the reality of Mom's death will change. If I succeed – if we win – I'll get to talk to Mom. I'll get to see her again.

The trolls arrive. Anti-choice, evangelical groups in America, coordinated by anti-choice groups in Ireland, launch an offensive to bring down the In Her Shoes Facebook page. They organise Facebook groups to flood our page with negative reviews; they report every post and exploit the time difference between the US and Ireland to drown the page while admin sleeps. But I'm not sleeping, and we are prepared.

The anti-choice lobbyists post their graphic foetus pictures in the comments. They aim to silence, shame, stun, vilify and hurt women. *Murderer. Slut. Bitch. Whore. Feminazi. Cold. Heartless. Cruel. Murderer. You're a murderer. You deserve to be raped. You deserve to die. I wish you would have been aborted. You're going to go to hell. I feel sorry for your children!*

The people of Ireland pull into formation to protect and claim their page. Over 5,000 positive reviews counteract the planned attack by anti-choice groups to bring the page down by reporting it as a scam. Without warning, Facebook places a 24-hour hold on the accounts while they investigate. Sky News, *The Journal*, *Irish Central* – even the satirical Waterford Whispers News report the failed cyberattack.

With a month until voting day, every hour is vital. We prepare for the responses we might get when canvassing door to door. Canvassing for marriage equality in 2015 meant advocating the freedom to love and marry. Canvassing for reproductive rights, for some people, means advocating for killing babies. We must be careful and deliberate. We must smile and stay *on message*, be *good girls*, remain polite in the face of someone who views us as criminals, as monsters.

American evangelical groups descend on Dublin and are bussed around the country. I'm enraged that these bigots with their baseball caps, backpacks and big white smiles are spreading misinformation and propaganda about our laws. They upload pictures to their social media about 'saving' Ireland. Because of them, I'm self-conscious of my American accent. Maybe canvassing with this accent is counterproductive to our cause. The first night we take to the streets, my hands tremble. I knock, hearing my pulse in my ears, and soften my voice on introduction. Inevitably, my background arises, my story pours out.

'Oklahoma, right above Texas. The musical ... Ah yes, married to a Portumna man. Three kids. Ah sure, you get used to the weather now.'

The grand stretch in the evening offers the usual back and forth before we talk about why I'm at the door. The reality is that I'm asking a stranger for rights to my own body because I'm not allowed to vote for myself.

As daunting as it first is to knock on a door and not know what to expect behind it, I have some beautiful and meaningful conversations with strangers. Once we move past the small chat and into the raw grit of their concerns, canvassing quickly feels like real progress is being made. Even if we aren't on the same page, I leave them with things to ponder.

One of my first doors leaves me in tears. An older man asks, 'Can you tell me why I should vote for this in five words?'

I hesitate for a moment and then reply, 'Autonomy in pregnancy and childbirth.'

He smiles. 'Ah you've got me there, that was a good answer.'

He asks about my story and as I begin to talk about Ireland being my home, about birthing my babies here, about not having a vote, I well up. I apologise and laugh through tears – I hadn't meant to get so emotional.

He talks about his daughter and her kids – *god I hope she's pro-choice* – and I assure him, 'This is about her healthcare, about her kids. About continued pregnancies and births as well.'

We chat for twenty minutes. He says I have his vote, shakes my hand and wishes us good luck. Every small interaction like that feels like a personal victory.

But it isn't always inspired. There are the moments when my blood runs cold and my body shakes with adrenaline as both men and women spew about sluts, hiss at me that I should be ashamed of myself and slam the door in my face. We canvass in pairs for safety, but to cover more ground we approach doors alone. After interactions that leave one of us shaken, we debrief quickly, offer a hug and pair up again. I'm approached for a leaflet and it is ripped from my hand and torn up. I'm told how disgusting I am. A man runs after us with a hurley, following us from house to house. I later learn that he is a former priest.

We wear badges on our clothes. Everywhere we go is an invitation to talk to someone about reproductive rights. It's also a target. An older woman with a kind face comes up to me and my toddler, leans down to look at my child and in a sing-song voice says, 'Aren't you glad your mam didn't kill you? That's what she wants to do to other babies.' I stand shocked, speechless at what was just said in the sweetest of tones, as she walks away.

Every evening we kiss our partners goodbye, put on hi-vis vests and grab our clipboards. Every evening we knock on doors. At weekends we hold information stalls. We organise steering group

meetings, write to newspapers, send letters to elected officials, organise fundraising events, look for volunteers. I run the Facebook page around the clock. It's taking its toll. We're mentally, emotionally and physically drained, but there's no time to stop. We exist on cake and beer, venting righteous anger in privacy. We force smiles. I can only imagine how much harder it is for those canvassing with us who have needed an abortion.

On 11 April I'm invited to interview with the founding members of Speaking of IMELDA,[6] Helena Walsh and Anne Rossiter. I have no idea who these people are, or what this is about, and so I look them up. *Look for Imelda, she'll be wearing red.* Legends. Badass activists. Rebels. Wise. Fearless. Artists. Putting aside my imposter syndrome, I agree to meet them at NUI Galway.

Members of IWASG[7] wore a red skirt at the train stations, ferry docks and airport terminals so as to be easily identifiable to women travelling for an abortion. As a nod to their predecessors, Speaking of IMELDA carries on the tradition of wearing red, and so I dress in red jeans, red boots and a red coat. I walk around NUIG campus searching for anyone else in red. I look like a walking blood clot. I find them, other women wandering around looking lost. 'Are you also here for IMELDA?' None of them resemble bloody billboards. They look smart, cool, casual. We introduce ourselves, fill in some background on why we were asked to be here, and eventually find the camera crew. We stand around while the couch is being inflated on the grass outside Áras na Mac Léinn, talking about our nerves and what we'll say on camera.

Helena and Anne – who are, of course, both dressed in red – immediately put me at my ease with their energy, playfulness, resilience and drive. I sink into the red couch and chat away, not knowing if I should look at them or at the camera and forgetting most of what I'd intended to say. But I did it! I watch for a while on the other side of the camera as several activists speak with poise and ease. I'm in awe of these smart, articulate and determined women.

*

I'm getting ready to head to Louisiana to see my dad. I couldn't be leaving the country at a more awkward time. Every single day matters, yet here I am, checking out for nine of them. Although I'm loath to leave at such a crucial time in the campaign, I know that the enforced break will do me good. I hand over to our eminently capable team, hoping to make my absence as smooth as possible. Steven sees me off at Shannon. I kiss him and the older children goodbye and get on a plane with the youngest.

I hadn't prepared for how I'd feel, flying into Dallas just over six months after my last arrival into the city. I forget how to breathe and as I exit the plane, the thick, heavy air compresses in my lungs. *Mom was here. I left her here.* I make it to baggage claim where Dad is waiting. He looks tired but is happy to see me. It's so strange to meet him at arrivals like this without Mom. We stand in silence, the tiles beneath our feet holding the history that clings to the spaces between my ribs.

As we sit in the Dallas rush-hour I'm taken back to being in the car with Cody when, in that same traffic, I prayed she would wait for me. Every cell in my body is on high alert. *Your mom is dead. You'll never see her again.* We drive through the night to get to deepest Louisiana and eventually turn off a small road and onto a long dirt driveway to the place Dad now calls home and the first place in all of my life where he's lived without his other half.

Swampy night air, a chorus of frogs and crickets, familiar and new all at the same time. I sleep on the bed under quilts that Mom made. This little RV camper of home, something that would have been an adventure dream for the two of them, is now just his, with her presence sprinkled throughout the soft furnishings. The only internet I can pick up is to be found around the tall grass near the chicken coop. I check in with home, catching up on emails and media requests. I pick ticks from my legs, sit under the stars at night talking to my brother and drink the margaritas my mom promised herself she'd have once she was out of hospital and celebrating remission. They taste bitter and sweet at the same time and leave me wonderfully numb. The days move slowly, and as anxious as I am to get back to work, I'm also grateful to have the control wrested from my hands. I dig through the boxes of Mom's belongings I packed months before, unravelling her scent all over again, choosing things I could fit in my bag to bring home.

Almost as soon as I arrive, I'm packing up again. Dad is coming home with me for the summer. Driving through the early morning darkness, the full moon following us, we reach Dallas to get on a plane to take us home to Ireland. Mom and I had planned this trip together. Now I travel with her ashes.

MAY Dad plays with his grandchildren, kicking a football in the garden, one hand on his cane, the other holding a glass of wine. The kids run around screaming with joy, savouring the late evenings of BBQs out the back. I waste no time getting back into Repeal mode – there are more booklets to be distributed across the country and stories are piling up. Emer and Cara try to catch up with the unread messages. We all feel guilty for not getting to them in a timely manner. We all feel overwhelmed.

Two weeks after his arrival, Dad spends three nights on a trolley in the hallways of A&E. I know it must be serious when that stubborn man agrees to see a doctor. The ambulance brings him from my local GP into Galway. I get a lift with a friend to the city, following the ambulance, and meet him in the most distressing, depressing place I have ever been in. Trolleys line both sides of the crowded hallway. Elderly people lie without privacy or dignity. This is where Savita died.

It's become so normalised to see trolleys in hospital hallways that it's no longer a shock, but it certainly doesn't feel like a first-world country that is part of the European Union. I'm ashamed that this is what the HSE offers to people in need and that healthcare professionals have to work in these conditions. It isn't just Galway hospitals – every public hospital in the country faces the same crisis.

Each morning I take the bus into Galway to keep Dad company. I relay information between hearing aids and accents. He spends three nights sleeping in a hallway before he's given a bed on the cardiac floor, and three more days on the ward before an angiogram can be scheduled. I pace the hallways, call Cody in Colorado to get the medical records sent over before surgery. I feel so alone. The weight of responsibility is heavy. This is my country now, and my dad is here in *my* hospital, with *my* health-care, and it feels like too much to hold. What if something bad happens? I need Mom. I don't know how to handle any of this.

Meanwhile, international journalists are constantly in touch. I agree to meet them selectively if I think their platform might help Ireland and Northern Ireland's cause. In between doctor rounds I meet a journalist in the car park of the hospital, drop a trail of In Her Shoes booklets on my way, and make it back to Dad's bed before he wakes up. In the coming days, as he recovers from his operation to insert a new stent, I sit by his bedside and organise stories to post. My body buzzes with stress, exhaustion and anxiety. Dad returns home with me after a week in hospital to continue his recovery.

As soon as he's back, I meet up with the volunteers again. Knowing that there is an end date in sight for the referendum is the only thing that pushes us on. Anti-choice campaigners arrive at our doors, and we run into them on the streets as we try to counteract the blatant lies being told while canvassing. People become visibly agitated at having these conversations at the door as the debate takes over social media, TV and radio. Signs are posted to every lamp post around the country. It is a conversation that cannot be escaped. It digs up trauma and wounds and leaves us on raw-edge nerves – we're never sure which way the conversation will go.

I'm invited to my first public speaking engagement in Tuam as the creator of In Her Shoes, a week before the referendum vote. Before now, the only people who know who I am are in the private Facebook groups. Remaining anonymous has been useful in creating a space that belongs to us all, a space where the stories speak for themselves. It doesn't matter who's behind it, it only matters that it's there.

When Facebook announced that it was blocking all foreign referendum advertising (most of which came from the US), anti-choice campaigners kicked up a fuss. They began digging to find out from where these women's stories originated, claiming they had been fabricated and orchestrated by the American pro-choice lobby. Yet In Her Shoes had never taken out an advertisement and relied solely on people to read and share at their discretion. As rumours and misinformation about the page began to elicit more questions, people on both sides demanded answers. I'd remained anonymous – but that was about to change.

*

The Bon Secours Mother and Baby Home in Tuam, County Galway, which operated between 1925 and 1961, housed unmarried mothers and their children.[8] Driving into the town, I can't help but feel a heaviness. What a place to talk of stories untold, of abortion, of choice for women. Dad sits in the audience, beaming with pride, taking a video with his phone. I try to stay calm so that the paper in my hands will stop trembling. My knees shake. I am not a public speaker.

> This space is not simply mine; it belongs to all of us. I feel that I am the guardian of it, and those that have shared with me have a special place in my heart. I feel protective of every

single one of you, and determined more than ever to hear and hold women's stories.

Currently we have a following of 100,000 people, with a reader reach of four million people per week. Without ads. Without sponsorship. Without anything but the reality of what we all face in Ireland, every single day. To date I have shared over 400 stories, and I have 643 currently waiting to be shared, with over 150 waiting to be read and replied to.

I never envisioned this project growing to this capacity, but of course it has. When women are joined together in support, when we share our honest lived truth, incredible things happen. Women's stories are power-filled. Not only are we freed from burdens we carry, we find ourselves being carried and cared for in the community. We all need our community, and In Her Shoes is carving out the support for which women have been hungry.

What started as my hope of achieving just one vote for me – because I don't have one – has become a healing space where women can finally find their voice, be heard, be cared for and mobilise change. I don't have a vote for myself, as a 30-year-old mother of three. And I don't have a vote for my daughters' futures. Despite having no voice in this referendum, I knew I had to do something.

I knew that if people just listened, they'd find the compassion to vote for a better country for women and girls and all of Ireland's people. I am proud to live here. I am proud to raise my children here. I will one day be proud to be an Irish citizen. I am proud to be part of the movement for improving this country.

Every day for the past five months I've received stories from women abandoned by their doctor, their community, their country. Stories of surviving abuse, surviving heartbreak, of

burying a much-wanted baby. Stories of desperation, depression, isolation. Stories of hopeful futures, of gratitude, of empowerment, from all ages and walks of life. There is not one face to represent the kind of person who needs an abortion, who deserves compassionate care.

Just the other night I received this message that I want to share. She writes: 'I don't have a story, but I would like to say that three months ago I was a strong No vote; I didn't even consider ever voting Yes. Your page has touched me in ways I can't explain. I've never felt so much pain in my heart and empathy for these women of the stories that you have shared. All of these women are so brave that I think I owe it to them, as an Irishwoman, to listen. This page has changed my mind and I'm so happy and proud to say I will be voting Yes because of it.'

We are currently rewriting history with her story. Women rising rooted, with big shoes to fill. And we will not stop. This referendum is just the beginning for our equality and liberation. Thank you for being on this journey with me and for holding the stories that the women of Ireland have been so gracious to share in strength, vulnerability and power. We are all her. We are *mná na hÉireann.*

After the final speaker finishes and we get up to move around, a woman comes up to me. 'I sent my story to you,' she says, tears in her eyes as she hugs me.

The room is decorated with shoes and candles. Stories printed on placards hang on the walls, the stories of women like her. The gravity of this meeting leaves me stunned. I hug her and cry with her. I remind her, 'It's because of you that people are coming out to support this. It's because of you that people are waking up to realise that this isn't good enough, that this has to stop, and that we have the ability to change it.' I thank her for trusting me.

I arrive home still wired. I feel electric, inspired and completely overcome with emotion. I call my friends to tell them about this encounter. I need to reach out to those who sent a story, and those who have not yet had a reply. It feels only right to be vulnerable in return for their trust.

I set up my camera on a tripod to record a video introducing myself to the world. For twelve minutes I sit on the beanbag in front of the bookcase, my daughter climbing in and out of my lap. The usual distractions of phone and background noise aside, here I am: vulnerable, a woman, a mother, a person without a vote. I upload the video in its raw, unedited state for over one hundred thousand people to witness. I am no longer anonymous.

REPEAL THE EIGHTH

It has all come down to this moment. The weight of lives in the ink of a pen, an X marked in a box. Will we move forward with compassion? Or will we close the lid on this box for another 35 years? If we win, we'll symbolically unbind the corsets of secrets, shame and indignity. A sigh of relief, a cry of overwhelming acceptance, an apology from society. *She is worthy.*

And if we don't win? We have made some of the greatest strides in healing a nation. Every person who set their story free will live with one less burden and the people who have read them will have been forever changed. It will not end here.

As in 2015, during the referendum for marriage equality when the hashtag campaign #HomeToVote encouraged thousands of people to travel across oceans to get home to vote Yes, Repeal has become the next pilgrimage, the opportunity for a generation to yet again change the status quo. We're witnessing the diaspora packing their bags, donning their black sweatshirts and creating an international conversation. People around the world are watching as we prove to them that we are better, that we can be a predominantly Catholic country and still be progressive as fuck.

People who can't travel home have been donating money so that others can get here. Through tears I watch as Twitter is taken over by strangers in comradery and generosity. The news

is full of footage of Dublin airport arrivals, which is flooded with welcome signs and resonates with cheers, hugs, tears, the orchestrated effort of a community coming together for democracy, for change, for human rights. For a generation that has been mocked and called 'snowflakes' for their compassion and willingness to talk about issues affecting them, #HomeToVote is an inspiration.

My stomach is like a pool of lead. My throat is like a cage full of wings. I'm too scared to feel excited, too hopeful to feel dread. We make our own pilgrimage to my daughters' school, the one with the convent attached, walls decorated with paintings of nuns and of the Virgin Mary, relics, artefacts, a gruesome execution, perfectly reasonable decor for children. I digress. This is the neutral space for Catholics to vote on matters of divorce, marriage equality and now abortion.

Steven takes our 8-year-old into the classroom to get a ballot paper: the irony of needing a man to vote for me when we have been talking to our children about this referendum, and what women did a hundred years ago to achieve their right to vote. They know that Daddy will vote for us. My eyes burn with tears of pride as I watch them disappear into the booth I'm not allowed to enter. My daughter hops, skips and jumps out of the door with a grin on her face.

'Dad marked the box for Yes, Yes for girls!'

The last flights arrive, the last lifts are given to zoom someone across the countryside to get them home to vote before the boxes are sealed. The news broadcasts the initial impressions of how the vote will go.

The crowd behind #HomeToVote once again leave me speechless. They've paid for all the final flights that can make it here in time; the leftover funds will go to activists in the community. Knowing I don't have one, they ask to pay the thousand euro towards giving me citizenship and a future vote. I feel as if I'm being handed my selkie pelt, returning and belonging, yet know I can't possibly accept it: the offer feels too grandiose and I ask them to donate it to Abortion Support Network instead. They assure me that they've donated money already to fund abortions for those who need them, then impress upon me how important it is to give to the community in this way as well, and that they have funded the citizenship application costs to a few others. I weep and squeal and text my friends, asking them what to do.

'Thank them and take it!'

*

26 May 2018. What will this day bring? The little crew of Galway East have become family to me. We barely know the names of each other's partners, or what anyone does for a living, and it doesn't matter.

The TV buzzes in the background, recounting the exit-poll results announced the night before. 'Landslide!' they keep saying. The exit-poll results, they report, have a margin error of 1.6 per cent. That means absolutely nothing to me. I will not allow myself to feel any semblance of hope of a win, not until the very final box is counted. Not until the real numbers are in. We cannot celebrate; not yet, not with what we're up against.

The count centre, a gymnasium set up with temporary barriers, is overwhelming. People mill around in bright yellow Together For Yes and neon pink Love Both high-vis vests. There are photographers and reporters, people in business suits and people in tracksuits. I push my way through the crowd to be as close to the barrier gates as possible. The walls can't contain the echoing sounds of people calling out numbers and names, running around, shuffling papers. The vibrations of the floor holding all of the pacing feet echo the anxiety vibrating in my core.

RTÉ request an interview. I stand at the high-rise section where all the reporters and number-runners will return to tables with tally sheets. It's an unofficial first count before the official ones can be logged. From up here, I try to make sense of the chaos and the excitement. *It's too good to be true, don't push your luck.* My Galway East sisters arrive. We hug, wish good luck to everyone else around us. Whatever happens, we have given it our all. We stand in a circle and sing.

Others from the count centre join in as we sing joyously over and over. No matter the results, we're in this together. The speaker takes to the podium. A hush falls across the room. We squeeze each other's hands, craning our necks to hear better. I can't silence my brain. I can't process what's happening. The speaker continues talking and I'm trying to hold on to every word coming out of her mouth. It's as if she's speaking another language I'm trying to piece together.

An eruption of cheers. Heaving sobs to the ceiling. Ecstasy. We made history. We did it.

In Her Shoes founder greets Yes landslide as Galway islands see 72 per cent Yes vote

Founder of the In Her Shoes Facebook campaign Erin Darcy, speaking at the Galway West count centre, said:

'Last night, I was trying to get my kids to bed – we were all up really, really late ... Then all the messages started rolling in. Women were just sending in their thanks for being able to tell their stories ... It just felt really good for them to see the exit polls last night. It's amazing to see everybody coming together. It's clear that we're ready for change.

'We've been talking to people of all generations – and they all have a story. Women have lived through so many things in Ireland. I've been desperate to tell the stories being sent to me. Some [of the stories] have been held onto for years. It's such a big, multi-generational shift.'[9]

In the chaos of cheers I search the crowd for mom. It hits me like a truck, as the joy is tempered with a stabbing reality. *Where are you?* I escape through a side door, gulping in the salty air. *I did good, Mama. I did really good. We did it. They want me here. They're taking care of me. I can do these big things. I did it. We did it. You would be so proud, Mom.*

We leave the count centre to await the official national results. Pubs have been reserved for watching the announcement. I walk with Jenni to the one that Parents for Choice have organised. The beer garden buzzes with children running around, and I hug the women and men I've met through birth gatherings and on the canvassing trail for Repeal.

It's the Champions League Final, Real Madrid versus Liverpool. We're packed into the smaller section of the pub, bodies pressing into bodies, giant TV screens blasting above us. On our tiny TV screen, the live scenes from Dublin Castle are relayed. We're fighting for bodily autonomy while across the room we're being shushed by men on the edge of their seats about football. We push in closer, calling people from the beer garden to hurry and crowd in with us. The results are about to be called!

The referendum to repeal the Eighth Amendment has been passed by a margin of more than 700,000 votes: 66.4 per cent. Donegal is the only constituency in the country to vote No.

The place erupts with more cheers. Drinks are spilled. We're drunk with love. We venture into the city centre to meet up with the rest of the Repealers. Tribeton Bar is hosting the after-party, with live music and cocktails with flames. We embrace strangers and we celebrate. Dancing, drinking, singing until our voices are raw, until the music has stopped and the lights come up.

*

Summer of 2018 comes crashing down around me. Up until then I had been living in survival mode. The momentous amount of work and the incredible feat of repealing the Eighth Amendment felt a million miles away. Having direction and a purpose bigger than me allowed for a disassociation. There was an imperative to do something that would make my mom proud. Bargaining with death made me feel that I might be able to rewrite the reality of her loss: if I did it all well enough, somehow she would be here again.

Dad flies back to the States on his own. I worry how he'll navigate the layover on his own. I wonder when I'll see him again. Everything has changed: I feel like I've lost more than just Mom, I feel like I've lost my entire family. My brothers and

Dad are so far away. The distance expands as we all grieve in our own ways.

Lost. Lost at sea. I spiral quickly. I walk for miles until I no longer feel like needing to crawl out of my skin, which is alive with electric anxiety. The cracks become chasms. I live through a veil, witnessing life happening around me. The rescuers come: alcohol, a joint, binge-eating or starvation. The rescuers become traitors. *I don't want to be here anymore.*

I reach out to Mara Clarke, an American in England running Abortion Support Network. I can't remember what I said to her in the email but it was desperate. Mara calls me, talking me off the ledge. 'I'm in the dead mother club too.' She shares the ups and downs of activism burnout, of doing this work in a country that is home but not our home, of mean girls and misunderstandings, of trying to do our best and still failing. Mara hands me back the pieces, giving me permission to trust myself. She gives me permission to know that I don't have to do anything at all.

I drift from my family, from my life. I tell Steven that I am the strongest I've ever been. I tell myself this too. It looks like I am enjoying myself. Marching, speaking publicly, organising, going out with friends. We dance. We laugh. We drink. I drink a lot. When we finally talk about where I'm really at, I'm scared to say the words out loud. Thoughts consume me, making me unrecognisable to myself: thoughts that make me scared to be alone with myself or with others, afraid of how I might sound, were I to speak them aloud. *I just want to go away.* Steven and friends gently encourage me to make that phone call. I sob into the phone to the receptionist and ask for an appointment.

I am suicidal.

The relief of a diagnosis washes over me. The anti-depressants begin to work despite my shame and the stigma around the need for them. The counsellor helps to process the previous three years of PTSD and grief.

I find myself searching for the ghost of my mother to guide me on how to be the person I need to be. I'm learning to be softer with myself, with grace and forgiveness. It isn't easy. I step away from social media for a while, I step away from the page. I remove myself from the loud noise and buzz of the incessant needs of activism. I try to learn how to set boundaries: how to say no, how to be involved without burning out. I practise, fail, try again.

I ask my mom what to do and her voice becomes my compass, my companion. I set goals and challenges for myself that would make her proud. I begin to paint again. I learn to drive. I check in with this inner knowing in order to navigate back to myself. I live for her so that I can begin to live for me. I'm not alone, I have a whole community of friends, a community I've had a part in shaping. For *her*, I did it for her.

It is through the immense love of my mother that I must continue. It is through the immense grief that I live with that I must push forward to do something in the world around me. It is the job of an artist to bring light to the darkness. I am only becoming aware of how this path of loss has been guiding me, connecting me to people around the world. A rite of passage; an opportunity to bury spring bulbs in the dark winter earth in hope and trust for the light of spring's return.

What do you want to do? she asks. *Do that*, she whispers. *Follow your intuition. Listen to it.* We don't always know what we're doing, or how we're going to do it, but we know we must do something.

*

It's the end of September. Jenny knocks at my door, phone in hand. She presses play on a recording of Aoife giving me instructions: 'Don't ask questions, bring your swimsuit, get in the car, I love you.' I do as I'm told. I hate surprises. I want to stay in bed and be sad. As we drive through the countryside, I can taste the salt in the air. I know we're getting closer.

I search around for familiar cars, for someone I recognise, and then I see it: a pink bell tent is waiting. A carpet of ferns has been laid across the sand, creating a soft forest-bed to the entrance. Candles and sunflowers line the path. I walk up to the gap in the canvas and dip my head within as my eyes slowly adjust to the darkness and the dark-pink glow. A circle of women wait for me.

It's been two years since I left my mother in Dallas. Among the pumpkins and flowers are pictures of Mom laughing, pictures of her pregnant with me, pictures of her in Ireland. Outside the thin veil of the tent, the ocean tide gently swells, inhales and exhales. One by one, these women, these Irish women who didn't know

me before the grief settled into my bones like a chill, read out letters and poetry to my mother. This is a funeral. This is a wake. This is a celebration. This is ceremony and ritual and my heart is bursting and also breaking into a thousand pieces.

Afterwards, with tears and laughter and chocolate warming our bellies, I strip off my clothes and wade past the giant mounds of seaweed into the welcoming cold Atlantic. I swim out into the setting sun, like a selkie returning to the sea, the pink sunset sky lapping at the horizon's edge, and in that moment it feels like my mom has returned me to the land of my namesake, to the island I call home, to the women, to belonging.

I am home.

THIRTY-TWO STORIES OF IRELAND

WOMEN gather naturally. Feasts are carried from cars into a waiting house. Floors are swept and kids run underfoot. We come together to nourish each other with food lovingly prepared in our kitchens. We share recipes passed down by our mothers, the tastes of home and history.

It becomes a natural rhythm. Women congregate in the kitchen, finding the plates, cutlery, boiling the water for tea. We all find our place. We eat without apology. There's always enough. We tend to each other's children as if they were our own.

Birth, blood, loss. We sit with the taboo. Silent nods all around. We let others weep while our own eyes spill over with tears. Candles burn down their wick and babies on breast fall asleep, rocked in their mother's arms. This is where the healing begins.

Long ago, it was forbidden for us to gather in these ways. Our history has been shunned and silenced, banned and burnt at the stake, drowned and beaten out of us. We have become disconnected from our roots, our mother tongue cut from our mouths. Yet we still navigate our way back together.

We will always find ways to mend the wound, to rekindle the fire and breathe life back into the world around us. When our history isn't important enough for men to write it down in ink, we take to needle and thread, sewing ourselves into the quilts for our daughters and sons, telling stories in embroidery. When our histories are not safe to voice aloud, we ensure they are folded in the hems of skirts, sharp daggers tucked in hats. We will not go silently. We write our own history into legislation, into the Dáil, in poems and books, in music and art. Our stories keep us alive.

We wait. For centuries, we wait.

I

I was working as a nurse in the UK, way back in 1993. I got married because I was pregnant, and then I miscarried. I was kind of like, Hmm it probably wasn't the right time. I was upset, obviously, but not devastated. A year later I got pregnant again and miscarried. I kind of did the whole, Ah sure it'll happen when it happens. We didn't use any contraception for a long time, but we weren't too worried about it.

We moved back to Ireland, where I continued working as a nurse. I went to see a doctor about IVF and he said, 'Oh you're too over-weight, I couldn't possibly start IVF, you'll have to come back after you've lost five or six stone.' I was really pissed off about that.

So I went to another fertility doctor. He monitored my cycle and got me to a stage where my hormones were good. I was so excited and nervous. Two blue lines. I was pregnant for the third time. Since I was being monitored by a specialist I thought, Oh brilliant, third time lucky.

I went to a very early scan, hopeful for a flickering heartbeat, holding my husband's hand. I was reassuring him that seeing the heartbeat wouldn't be a definite since we were so early. The doctor stopped and took the probe out, and then said to the nurse that we needed to chat. My heart sank, but being ever the optimist I thought it could be something mad like twins.

We sat in the office for what seemed like an hour, me reassuring my husband that the bloods were good so it would all be fine. The doctor came back in with the nurse and told us that there was a problem. He told me it was ectopic.[10] I couldn't breathe. I was devastated. As a nurse, I knew what that meant. I'd met a few patients who'd had one. I didn't understand exactly what it would mean for me though.

Questions wouldn't come out but I knew there were loads inside me. The doctor told me that I should go home because it was still early days and anything could happen. They gave me the idea that it would possibly sort itself out. They said, 'We don't know what will happen, come back if you get any pain in the area.'

I remember getting home and thinking that maybe I'll be lucky. I googled *chances of an ectopic pregnancy actually making it into the womb* and there were some stories that suggested it did – so I had a bit of hope for this baby we longed for.

Three days later I woke up in pain, so my husband and I decided to go to the hospital. We thought we'd beat the queues in the middle of the night. The pain got so much worse as I was waiting but the nurse told my husband that the theatre wasn't ready. I had no idea what she meant, I was crying with the pain by this stage. I knew the girls, I'd been working there at the time – yet I still didn't know what was really happening. The hospital seemed to spin around and everything was flying past me. I just remember being pushed into theatre.

I remember waking in agony. I had a pump for pain but no ability to press it, and no memory of why I should be so sore. My husband was sitting beside me and I looked at him, and he shook his head and told me that I had lost my tube. I also had a scar across my stomach as if I had had a caesarean section from the surgery. I'd needed a blood transfusion – the ectopic pregnancy had ruptured my fallopian tube. I was just thinking, *Oh my god, they saved my life!*

I was so sore from the surgery, I was sad about losing that pregnancy, I was grateful to be alive. I was out of work for four months to recover. I knew that ectopic pregnancies were an emergency, but it never dawned on me that they would send me home if it was such an emergency.

About two years later I got pregnant again. I had a procedure that pushes dye through to see everything and it cleared out the other tube; because of that I became pregnant. Each week that progressed, we got further and further: this was the longest pregnancy I had had and all things were going so well. We were so looking forward to finally having our family.

I was 22 weeks when she died. I didn't know she had died. I went to the hospital for a reassurance scan and they said that there was no movement, no heartbeat. It was devastating, she was our daughter. I was induced and gave birth to our little girl sleeping. It was a Sunday morning. I hated Sunday mornings for years after that. The hospital staff were all so lovely – they knew me well as we worked together, so they took good care of me and our family.

After that I had a *lot* of IVF. I knew no one else was going to help me. I went to the Sims Clinic, I went to Barcelona, I went to the Czech Republic. I had donor eggs, donor embryos, you name it. I injected myself with cocktails of medications. I was doing everything possible to conceive and carry a pregnancy to term. I miscarried every time.

When I went away on holidays in 2010, I randomly managed to get pregnant. It just happened on our own, after we had given up on all of the fertility treatment. When I went to the EPAU[11] there was a heartbeat, but two weeks later there was nothing. I decided to let things just happen naturally. That was the last time I was pregnant.

In 2011 we had started looking into adopting, but were told that we'd be waiting eight to nine years. We had already been foster parents in England just after we got married, so we decided to start fostering in Ireland because we just wanted kids around us, in our home – we wanted our family.

We've had such great kids with us. Some have kept in contact after growing up and moving on in the world. We've had really great experiences with fostering, but there are obviously a lot of difficulties. Only other foster parents can understand it, and we have a good community of support in each other. As foster parents, we know that the children might be placed back with the family – that's always the hope for them, to be reunited with their family. In some situations that will never happen, and at eighteen the child is then out of the system and on their own in the world.

With some of the families, you think of the biological mother and know that her life would have been better if she could have had a choice. Domestic violence, mental health issues, substance abuse, poverty, rape, incest ... How these children deserved to be wanted and cared for properly, and how she deserved to become a mother only if and when ready. Even the kids that come to us themselves, they too deserve autonomy. We've taken in teenagers that had babies in the UK: they had choice, and they turned into great kids. There are so many kids in the system, and so many who fall through the cracks. When the anti-choice side suggest adoption as the alternative to abortion, it's like they haven't even considered what situations people go through for their children to be put into the system for adoption or fostering. More resources need to be in place for those children already within the system, and the families that care for them.

I was always going to fight for repealing the Eighth Amendment – it's something I'm passionate about. It wasn't until I read something about In Her Shoes, I was talking to someone at the door canvassing and then it suddenly dawned on me: I was impacted by the Eighth Amendment. It just hit me as I was talking to this person, I had to stand over by the wall for a second in shock, processing that this had happened to *me*. I was sent home with an ectopic pregnancy, which is a medical emergency. They sent me home because they weren't going to do anything for that ectopic pregnancy when there was a heartbeat, and they should have done. I lost my tube because of it, and I could have lost my life. I'd spent all this time feeling grateful that they saved my life, when they really endangered my life – only to then save me.

When I was a nurse, I was never really aware of the impact of the Eighth Amendment. I know that mothers would come out into recovery after having caesarean sections and the babies would be gone, which to me was wrong, because they shouldn't be separated from their babies. Obviously they were prioritising the babies but it would have been easy to have them in with them. Even when they came down to theatre, when the baby was in a distressed state, they would open somebody up even before they were asleep: obviously they were trying to get them to sleep, but the baby was the priority. I know that we all want a good outcome for the baby, but in hindsight some of those mothers were terrorised. They weren't prioritising the mums at all – just 'get that baby out'. We all wanted those babies out alive, but we didn't even think of the mother. It was like, 'Did she have an epidural? Great, we can get the baby out.' I see it now.

I was there looking at this woman being cut open as they were trying to put her under and all I kept thinking was, *This woman is gonna remember this.* Even the ones that had been pushing for four days were refused caesareans, over and over, only until the baby's heart was showing distress and *then* they would move her to theatre. It didn't matter about what she had been through in those days, it only mattered that now the baby was done doing it.

There are so many more stories of those women impacted by the Eighth than the ones who've had to travel. They're the ones who couldn't travel, who never knew there was even an option to travel, the ones like myself who wanted babies and our lives put in danger in a medical emergency, the ones who were giving birth and couldn't make decisions for themselves; couldn't make an informed decision to have a caesarean. They never mattered. Only their babies did.

I'm so angry. And despite not having children of my own, I want everyone to repeal the Eighth Amendment – because it could have killed me. It's already been responsible for the deaths of too many.

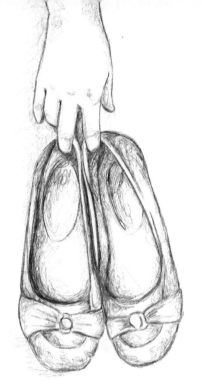

II

I was raised in a Catholic household and went to both a Holy Faith primary and secondary school. I am the youngest of five children. I grew up in the 1980s when you had the Kerry babies case[12], the Ann Lovett case[13] and where 'unmarried mothers' were stigmatised. We were in the middle of the AIDS epidemic. Where AIDS was concerned, homosexuality was never discussed, it was all down to drug use and shared needles.

In secondary school we had a nun who told us that tampons were the invention of the devil and took away your virginity. 'Nice' girls did not use tampons. Sex education did not include information on contraception as that, believe it or not, was illegal in Ireland at that time. I started my period at the age of nine. My mother handed me a brown paper bag, which contained huge sanitary towels and a book called *My Dear Daughter*, a Catholic publication that told me it was alright to touch my private parts to wash and to change pads but to say three Hail Marys afterwards.

I started caring for my mother at the age of fourteen. I was seventeen in May 1986. I had a best friend who had a boyfriend and he also had a best mate. I was groomed by them. It took me an extremely long time to internally accept this and to verbalise this. It was not in any way, shape or form, *my* fault. To cut a very long and complicated story short, I was raped and sexually assaulted by her boyfriend and his friend over two days. I was a virgin before that. I existed in a prolonged state of profound shock for a month. In the course of an argument with a sibling I blurted out that I had been raped. I think it was the first time I had acknowledged this fully to myself. I did what they say is the right thing to do and informed the Gardaí and went through examinations that were nearly as horrific, traumatic and intrusive as the crime itself.

I was told there was not enough evidence by the DPP [Director of Public Prosecutions] so there would be no court case. I was lucky in the sense that there was no pregnancy as I would have been sui-cidal if there had been. I would have had to carry that baby to term and most likely have the baby adopted as I could not raise that child. Which one of my rapists would have been the father? There was no paternity testing in 1986 as far as I know. I did attend the Rape Crisis Centre for a very short time. I think it was still too raw to gain any positive results from counselling. The one extremely important statement they made to me that set me on the path to healing was: *We believe you and we believe it did happen.*

I turned 18 that July. In October of the same year I met someone I thought would be gentle and understanding of my fragile mental and emotional state. He was not and I ended up becoming preg-nant, not forced, but certainly unplanned. I decided to have the baby and keep my child. I was eighteen and healthy. This was the 1980s and the stigma of lone parenthood was still within society. I had a normal and uneventful pregnancy but the birth was highly complex and eventually I had to undergo an emergency caesarean section. I remember after my son was born going to collect my first payment in the post office. I was handed this payment book with *Unmarried Mothers Allowance* printed in big black letters on the front. Over the years I discovered my child had various special needs so I became a carer for my child too.

I became celibate because of my past and found out that because of medical and personal reasons I could not use hormone-based contraception. I had no time for relationships. I was a carer and studying to gain some qualifications. I also worked part-time when I could.

My mother died in 2002 and my father became very ill so I started caring for him too. My son was now in his teens and life was becoming much better. I met someone and began a relationship. We were very careful. He had to go abroad for a year to complete his medical training. There was no contact or communication with him, the relationship was over. I discovered I was pregnant. I was frantic with worry. I was not in a position financially, emotionally, mentally, physically or had the energy to raise another child. I had no money to travel to England and had no idea where to obtain abortion pills. I eventually miscarried alone, scared and in great pain. I had and still have mixed emotions of deep relief and sadness but never one of regret.

I asked about sterilisation but was informed that because I was not married, only had one child – plus I was overweight – the answer was a firm no. They wanted me to accept a hormone-infused coil. I refused and left. I eventually went through an early menopause.

I am fully pro-choice. This includes full access to contraception including sterilisation and full access to safe legal abortion within the Republic of Ireland. For women giving birth to have full bodily autonomy with regard to birth plans and medical, surgical proce-dures during birth. To have the legal right to say no to anything they are uncomfortable with. I am fully pro-choice where adoption is concerned. I want to see legal open adoption in this country where at eighteen all adoptees have full unrestricted access to their files and biological families. I am fully pro-choice where I want to see financial, housing and support frameworks put in place so all parents can raise their children in comfort and with peace of mind. This includes parents of special-needs children and adults. I want to see comprehensive sexual and consent programmes implemented into all schools and colleges.

I also want to see fully legal and enforced exclusion zones at hospitals, doctor's surgeries, women's health centres and pharmacies so that all individuals with a womb can be safe and comfortable going about their lawful and private business. I want to see severe penalties if these exclusion zones are not adhered to.

I fully accept that the rape was not my fault, was never my fault. I accepted this a long time ago. It was not what I was wearing, It was not what I said or the manner in which I said it. I am a survivor. No means just that. NO.

Through the Freedom of Information Act I obtained a copy of my files from the Rotunda Hospital SATU.[14] To my utter astonishment, horror and fury, I discovered they had admitted they were guilty of some of the sexual acts they had forced on me. Nobody ever told me this. I would have felt so differently about this whole disgusting situation if they had. I am still processing the whole range of emotions this has made me feel. I am now going to write to the DPP to obtain a copy of my statement and any other relevant documents. To all individuals who have suffered sexual crimes I say to you: I BELIEVE YOU.

III

I wasn't raped. It just wasn't the right time.

IV

In February 2006, at the age of nineteen, I gave birth to my first child. About four months later I found out that I was pregnant again. I was petrified, but myself and my boyfriend focused on the positives and started to get excited at the thoughts of having 'Irish twins' as I was due two weeks before our first child's first birthday.

When I was nineteen weeks pregnant, we attended Holles Street for a foetal anomaly scan, and from the moment I saw the image I knew there was something wrong. The midwife said she would get one of her colleagues to come and have a look, which just confirmed my fears. After what felt like forever, we were told that while our baby's heart was beating perfectly, his chest cavity was open, leaving some of his vital organs exposed. We were devastated. I remember crying and being led to a private room where I rang my mam who was minding our firstborn and I explained that there was a problem with the baby and asked her to come and collect us. I just wanted to go home.

We left the hospital but got a phone call to say they were looking for us and could we come in the next day to be seen by a consultant. The next day the consultant scanned me again and we were told that our baby appeared to have a condition called amniotic band syndrome, which is when some of the membranes of the amniotic sac tear and wrap around the baby as they grow in the womb. Mine had wrapped around our baby and as he grew they had cut through his chest, leaving it open.

We were told that his chance of survival outside of the womb was zero. We were told that we had two options; travel to England for a termination (but that they wouldn't be able to assist us in that option) or we could continue with the pregnancy until I went into labour, which they expected would be premature. We had a six-month-old baby to care for so travelling was not an option.

We chose to continue on as normally as we could. The consultant was unsure of what exactly the outcome would be. Our baby could die in the womb or while I was in labour or he could live for minutes or hours after birth but inevitably he would die. We were told to prepare for everything. When I look back on it now I don't know how we carried on.

Knowing our baby was going to die but still having to encounter strangers on a daily basis who would congratulate us or ask when we were due and having to explain everything to our friends and family – it was all very awkward.

We were told by many that, 'Oh you can always try again' and, 'Oh these things happen for a reason.' It only added to our pain. We were trying to continue with a routine for the sake of our firstborn and my partner was trying to focus in work every day.

The stress was unreal. We were only nineteen and twenty years old. Even though I knew the most likely outcome, I didn't give up hope. I wouldn't even take a paracetamol for a headache in case it harmed our baby's slightest chance of survival.

Then, eight long weeks later, in the early hours of 14 November 2006, I woke with pains in my stomach. I rang Holles Street as I was told to do and then I just waited. My partner went to work as normal while I cared for our son who by then was eight months old. The pains got stronger and more regular so I rang my partner to come home. I went for a nap but when I woke and got out of the bed, my waters broke and I was bleeding. I went next door to my parents' house and my mother rang an ambulance.

I was 27 weeks pregnant and I was so scared. My mam tried to explain as best she could to the paramedics about our baby's condition as it was so rare. We arrived at the hospital and were quickly taken to the delivery room. I chose to have as natural a birth as possible, just as I had for my firstborn in the same hospital only eight months earlier. The labour is a blur but I remember that, as I was pushing, my partner was told to try and shield my face so as to stop me becoming distressed by our baby's abnormalities. I was very foggy from the gas and air and had no idea what the time was when our baby was born and whisked away. The midwife quickly returned with our son wrapped in a blanket with a tiny little hat on his head.

We were told his heart had beat for one minute, but he was gone. He weighed only 500g and we named him Christopher after his daddy.

The staff in the hospital were amazing. We have photos of our son to remember him by and we have his grave that we can visit but it is an experience that has affected us deeply. It is not something that I would like my sisters or daughters or anyone for that matter to go through. In Ireland the loss of a baby through miscarriage, stillbirth etc. is still very much a taboo subject, eleven years on, and I still feel like some people dismiss our baby's death as 'insignificant'. In this country you're damned if you do and damned if you don't. While we chose not to travel to England for a termination, who am I to judge or criticise what another woman feels is best for her? #RepealTheEighth #GiveWomenaChoice

V

It was a bright summer's day when we attended the EPAU at the hospital. I had some bleeding but as I'd had this during my pregnancy with my daughter, we weren't overly concerned. I was a day shy of twelve weeks pregnant, which is when we had planned on going public with this much-wanted pregnancy.

At the hospital we sat in a corridor outside the scanning room with other women and worried-looking couples. Some apprehensive smiles were exchanged before deep breaths were heard as the next name was called to enter the room. We seemed to be waiting forever, all the while seeing the mix of relieved and not-so-relieved faces of expectant parents trickle through as they left the room.

It was our turn and we were greeted by a lovely lady who was very engaging and chatty and explained what would happen. She began to scan and take measurements, all the while still chatting away about trivial things like the weather and holidays. It didn't take long before the eye contact lessened and the chatter stopped. Her expression changed enough that I knew something was wrong so I asked if this was the case. She said she was having difficulty seeing the lower limbs and wanted a second opinion. Her false smile of reassurance was totally lost on me as she left the room and returned with another doctor. Between the two of them they muttered to each other, scanning and measuring, and after what seemed like an eternity the doctor turned to me and said, 'I'm sorry but there is something very wrong with your baby.' Those dreaded words hung there in the air in front of me, in a jumble, making no sense, and I just looked at my husband and cried.

The baby was measuring very small for my dates and was not correctly formed. They could only find a partial leg and no other lower limbs. The nuchal translucency[15] was measuring high, suggesting a possible chromosomal defect. I felt ill and dizzy and confused and like I was outside myself looking down on this like it was a bad movie. This kind of thing doesn't happen in real life – does it?

We were told to come back the following day where a specialist would rescan and go through our options. We left the hospital in a haze and tried to reclaim some normality by picking our daughter up from crèche and carrying on with her as if there was nothing wrong but there was and we were terrified of what the following day had in store.

It took so much courage to even get dressed that morning and go back to the hospital, as if ignoring the appointment might make it all seem like a bad dream and everything was OK. But we attended nonetheless.

The doctor rescanned and confirmed the previous day's findings. It wasn't looking good. There was very little fluid around the baby and the growth was approximately two to three weeks behind what it should be. He started spouting off words that meant nothing to me – Edwards, Patau's, Turner syndrome. He also said, 'Don't google anything, whatever you do, you'll only freak yourself out.' It all whirled around my head like a storm.

An amniocentesis was scheduled for just under seven weeks' time when our baby would hopefully reach a gestational size of fifteen to sixteen weeks. He warned us of potential miscarriage in the meantime and to come straight back to the hospital should any further bleeding occur. He gave us a leaflet on amniocentesis and another on miscarriage and we were sent on our way.

The weeks that followed were a blur. Only for my then four-year-old daughter, I saw no reason to get up or dressed or even to eat. My husband's birthday came and went without fanfare or celebration – we were too devastated, not thinking things could get any worse. How wrong we were.

A week after that awful news, I began to haemorrhage. We felt this was it, I was losing the baby. I went to hospital and was admitted, terrified by the amount of blood leaving my body and for what was to come. They put me in a room opposite the labour ward where all the mothers and families of the healthy babies about to be born were celebrating. The chairs outside my room were taken up by happy family members chatting about their new arrivals as I listened from my bed, my hope and will passing out of me in scary clumps.

The next morning the master of the hospital arrived in my room with a group of student doctors and spoke of my case to them as if I were a case study in a book. Some sympathy was offered: 'I'm sorry you have to go through this. Miscarriage is a terrible thing. Would you like us to call the bereavement midwife?' So, I was definitely having a miscarriage? This was it then, the end of my pregnancy, nature taking its course. My bleeding had subsided, to my great relief – but what of the baby? A mobile ultrasound machine was brought into my room and there it was, beating away, that tiny heartbeat. Relief and worry merged in a confused ball inside me. What was happening? Was I still going to lose the baby? They saw the heart beating, saw the bleeding subside, explained how the miscarriage was likely to happen and I was sent home with the same miscarriage leaflet I had received a week earlier. It was a wait-and-see game.

This dance went on three more times over the course of the next few weeks. For each admission I was back in a room in the labour ward: bleeding would subside, there's the heartbeat, they sent me home. At each scan there was less and less fluid around the baby, which they said was needed to support and protect the baby from the pressure of my body. The baby wasn't growing and all signs were proving the baby was in severe trouble and this wasn't going to end well.

Every day was utterly terrifying. I was afraid to sleep in case I would bleed out in the night, leaving my husband and child without a wife and mother. I lived far from the hospital so I had to stay with my mother nearby, away from my husband and daughter. I couldn't be left on my own in case I haemorrhaged again and I was already weak and depressed. I cried uncontrollably. It encompassed my every moment. I worried about the lack of fluid around my baby and him being crushed. It was like a terrible nightmare that I just wanted to wake up from. I felt invalidated, uncared for by my country, unimportant – merely a vessel. It was all about the baby, who was slowly dying. I felt I was too. By the third haemorrhage I was desperate for them to do something but they couldn't. It was like death by a thousand cuts for both of us.

The day of the amniocentesis came and the specialist began to scan but it didn't take long for him to validate what I already suspected. The baby had died, and it wasn't recent. He indicated the broken skull on the screen and that there was no more fluid around my baby. I tried to hold it together but I couldn't. I cried like I never cried before. A sound came out of me that I didn't recognise but I now know that whatever that sound was, it was a mix of pain and relief. I felt so guilty for feeling that way. I loved and wanted my baby but I didn't want all this pain and suffering. It should never have gone this way.

A couple of days later I was taken in and they induced labour. I felt every contraction, every urge to push as if I were about to deliver a healthy baby – except I wasn't and by early evening, my baby was born still. I asked the midwife if it looked like a baby. She shook her head and said it looked 'very deformed' so I chose to keep the memory of what I had seen on the ultrasound screen so many times before in my head as the image of my baby instead. She took the baby away.

The following day I was discharged from the hospital. I had laboured the day before having gone through the same contractions as other women leaving with their babies. As I descended the stairs, a happy new father brushed past me in the corridor with a car seat and his new baby daughter asleep inside and the brightness of possibility in his eyes and I realised then the emptiness I felt at leaving with nothing but the trauma and pain I had endured in the preceding six-and-a-half weeks.

We found out she was a girl. We named her. She deserved a name. She mattered! Later we were told she had an incredibly rare neural tubal defect called Sirenomelia, or mermaid syndrome. Her lower body never fully formed and never would. What would have been legs were fused and formed what looked like a mermaid's tail. She had no kidneys, no bladder, no genitals or openings of any kind in her lower body, which is why she was unable to process or produce amniotic fluid. She had no hope. She was buried in the hospital plot and we visit from time to time but she is with me every single moment of every day.

It was known from that first scan that this was a very troubled pregnancy, doomed not to continue to the end, and yet all the while the medical professionals could do nothing for me or my baby. The Eighth Amendment prolonged our suffering to the point that she was crushed without the support of the necessary fluid needed to protect her. She was never going to survive! Where was the Eighth Amendment's so-called protection of the unborn then? How was that a dignified end? It wasn't! That is why the Eighth needs to go. Yes, she mattered. Yes, she left an indelible mark on our lives. Yes, I will never get over this and the extended and unnecessary trauma of this, the most horrific time in my life, all at the hands of the Eighth Amendment.

We need to stop treating women so badly in this country. We need to trust women to know what is best for them with the support of their family and healthcare professionals. This does not belong in our constitution and as long as it does, women like me will continue to suffer needlessly.

VI

I am terrified to share my story. I think I have typed and deleted it twenty times so far. I am just so scared to share it because the shame eats away at me and has done every day for the last two years.

I was not a teenager. I was not a victim of rape. There were no foetal fatality illnesses. I was just a girl in my mid- to late twenties. I had just returned from travelling. I managed to bag myself my dream job and started to date a nice guy. Then a week or two later I discovered I was pregnant. I was shocked, as I was being careful, but I was mainly distraught.

This wasn't the right time for me. I had no money after my travels. I was living at home with my sick mother. I hadn't known my partner for very long. And I had just started a new job. I wasn't ready for a baby. And mainly I couldn't give it the life it deserved. I had grown up in a poor, broken and abusive home and I did not want that for my child. I wanted something better for them. Stability and love. A mam and a dad together. Someone who was strong and could provide for them. I didn't have that at the time. I was devastated. I knew what I had to do.

I spent the following two days putting on a fake smile while inside I was dying. I couldn't talk to anyone about this. Everyone would hate me. They would think I was a bad person. I kept it to myself. The morning I flew to England I felt like a scared child. I was so frightened. The feelings of fear and shame were overbearing. I will never ever forget it.

After I took my second pill, I got a taxi back to the airport. The toughest journey of my life. I felt as if my insides were being ripped apart, I wasn't sure if this was supposed to happen but I just sat in the seat crying silently, hugging myself and praying it was normal. I sat in the airport waiting on my flight, seething in pain. I had four sanitary towels in my underwear. Each time I stood up I felt a river of blood flow down me. I was terrified. I just wanted someone to tell me I would be OK. But I was alone.

The blood and cramps lasted for weeks. It was embarrassing, many clothes and chairs were stained from the blood. I hated life.

I was never the same after this. I remember months later my mother telling me I had changed. 'Something in you isn't right,' she said, 'it's broken.' Little did she know how right she was.

Yes, it was my decision. I chose to have this happen. But I wish I'd had someone to tell. Someone to talk to. Someone to be there for me at a time I needed them the most. But I couldn't tell anyone. I never have. I'm too ashamed. I think about it every day. I think I'll never have a baby because I don't deserve one now. It's killing me. My country has played a massive part in this.

I know it was the best decision for me at the time. But it was the hardest decision for me too. This is NOT by any means an easy option. It is NOT a form of contraception. How little credit we give the women of Ireland if we think so. Irish women are some of the greatest in the world. We can trust them to do what is best for them. It will never be a decision taken lightly. In fact it is the toughest option for us. And all I know is I do not want anyone in this country to have to feel how I did and still do. So ashamed. So alone. Don't let us down anymore.

VII

I was fifteen when I discovered I was pregnant. I wish I could say it was by my first love and despite my young age I was blissfully happy. But the reality, albeit with hindsight, was a different story. As a carefree fifteen-year-old at the local youth club I should have been safe, protected. It started slowly, with a man, a youth officer ten years my senior, paying me more attention than he should have. And to begin with I could see that this was inappropriate but I brushed it off and went about enjoying the games with my peers.

But slowly slowly catchy monkey, he started to make me feel very special, buy me presents, and about six months down the line I thought I was in love; it would be another few months before it became sexual. The first time I said no but he didn't stop. However, for the next month or so he made me think I was the most beautiful, special person in the world, even if I didn't particularly like the sex. But It was only when he had taken my virginity and had his playtime, and I was no longer shiny and new (after about a month) that his interest in me began to wane. I then caught him with another girl, the same age as me, and discovered that he had got another girl (aged thirteen) pregnant the year before. There was a pattern here. Yes, I was groomed, but this was 1981 and the word 'groomed' didn't exist in the context it does today.

Anyway, it didn't occur to me to have an abortion (as it wasn't available). Furthermore, my schools had all been run by nuns. I wore those miniature feet on my blazer. I was indoctrinated. I was unimportant, I would live through the shame and the slurs on my character. I was a *wee slut*, as someone nicely told me by private Messenger just this Christmas. No, they didn't do it under their real name. Coward. I now know that I am, and always was, important.

So as my belly swelled over the next few months, and my childish body quickly stretched into that of a woman's, some of the midwives in the hospital looked down their noses at me and made me feel dirty and ashamed. No one, especially a child, should ever be made feel like that.

I had my baby, a boy, but almost died in the process, an emergency section and nine units of blood later (sixteen-year-olds are not meant to have babies). I carried my shame as bravely as I could, but my son was here, and he deserved the best I could give him. Times were very hard. While I had some family support, we moved into our own home when I was seventeen. Much too young, but hey, I coped. This is not the life I would have chosen for either him or me, but it was my reality.

While I know that I could never have handed him over for adoption, I don't judge those who do: maybe they are right, and he could have had a better life. But I did my best. If this happened to me now, would I make the same decision? Truthfully, I'm not sure that I would. Either way, sixteen-year olds should not be forced to have babies. Or be judged because they have been abused. I BELIEVE IN WOMEN. I don't believe anyone makes these decisions lightly, as this page has already shown.

My son is 36 this year: it hasn't always been easy, growing up without a father can mess with a young man's head. But he's out the other end of it now. Don't make children have children. Don't make those who are abused suffer more abuse. I believe in choice. #RepealTheEighth

VIII

In 2005 I suspected I was pregnant and bought a test in a chemist, which confirmed it. I had no access to the internet at home, and my phone was a Nokia 3310. If I needed to go online, I would use internet cafés. There was no way I was looking up abortion services in an internet café, so I went to the phone book and found a few advertisements for crisis pregnancy agencies. I rang Marie Stopes (Dublin) first, and was told that an appointment was €90. I rang another one on Dorset Street that offered a free appointment for testing and scan. They would also arrange the abortion in the UK for you.

When I attended the appointment a few days later, a woman greeted me and brought me to a room for a 'holistic consultation'. They took a lot of personal data from me, including 'name of [baby's] father'.

I was quite young at the time, eighteen years old, and had very little experience of any kind of medical clinic. I assumed I was giving my information to a nurse, because she carried out a urine test to confirm my pregnancy. She sent me to a bathroom down the hall and told me to urinate into a white plastic cup she had left in there; then I was to come back to the room and she would go in and test it. The cup was the plastic disposable type you use at children's birthday parties – that really should have been a big clue that I was not in a legitimate medical clinic, but I don't think I had ever given a urine sample up until that point. I had no experience, so no expectations.

After she had tested it, she came back and her demeanour had changed significantly. She said: 'You seem like a really nice girl – why would you want to cause harm to your baby?' I didn't answer. It felt like I was in trouble at school. She continued. 'You do realise your baby can feel pain?' and 'Do you think that's fair to do that to your baby?' Then she spoke about adoption, and told me they had a place in Donegal where I could go and have the baby in secret. I refused this option completely and she didn't push adoption any further.

She dated my pregnancy to somewhere between four and six weeks and told me abortions couldn't be performed until the gestation was at least eight weeks. So she sent me home to wait, and when I reached eight weeks they would make the arrangements for me.

Over the next few weeks I was contacted by them at least twice on my mobile when I was at home. They wanted to know if I had made a decision yet, and had I given any more thought to the Donegal option – I told them I still wanted to go to the UK for an abortion. She told me they would have to arrange a scan with a doctor in Cavan first. I never heard from them again.

My lowest point was probably when I finally realised they weren't coming back to help me. I had no idea where to go next and collapsed on the floor by my bedroom window, heaving and sobbing. After a while I calmed down and remembered the other advertisement for Marie Stopes around the corner from Dorset Street, and decided I'd have to figure out a way to get the €90 together for the appointment. Even now, in my early thirties, I would struggle to get a spare €90 together in a hurry. I lied to my parents about needing €20 here and there, and eventually pulled the money together.

I got the scan done in Dublin and was given all the information I needed to book the abortion in the UK, which I did from a phone box. They told me I could pay in euro when I arrived; they would convert the currency to save me having to get sterling before I got there. I didn't have a bank card at the time (I can't remember, but I don't think I even had a bank account) so I made my way to Dublin airport and booked the flight tickets at the Ryanair desk using cash.

By the time I got to the clinic in Essex I was fourteen weeks pregnant and it was recommended I had a general anaesthetic. The abortion was booked for 23 July, but I had to be there the day before for a scan, so I flew into Stansted airport on 22 July. On the 21st there had been a terror incident in London. It was two weeks after the 7 July bombs. I was petrified something would happen while I was there, but mainly I was worried if something happened that would delay or cancel flights. My parents thought I was staying in a friend's house down the country. *Nobody* knew I was overseas.

I stayed in a hotel down the road from the clinic. I felt mortified checking in at the hotel reception – it must have been so obvious what I was doing there. Irish teenager, female, one night, a three-minute walk from abortion clinic. The girl checking me in was engrossed in Sky News, so I felt like I got away with it. It was a weird atmosphere in the hotel, everybody was sitting around the lobby watching the news. I had to fast from that evening until after it was over.

My appointment was at 8 am. I woke from the anaesthetic around 9.15 am, wrapped up tightly in a blanket, the back of it wet with blood. This made me panic, but a nurse said it was normal for fourteen weeks. She brought me tea and a biscuit and told me to stay in bed for at least an hour or two, but I wanted to get going in case anything happened that would cancel flights or close the motorway. I just needed to get to the airport ASAP and know what was going on.

When I was dressed and ready to go, a doctor came in to see me. She checked me over and signed me out. She walked me down the stairs to reception (where I could see blue flashing lights) and gently explained that the police were outside due to a protest across the road. She never said what the protest was for. She told me that when I was ready to leave, a staff member would walk me to the gate and the police would ensure that the protesters didn't come past the gate, but once I was outside there was nothing they could do. 'They will approach you', she said, 'but just keep walking and don't interact.' She apologised profusely and said this was very common on Saturdays.

Intense nausea from the anaesthetic had kicked in. I smiled and said 'OK, no problem' and made a beeline to the bathroom in reception. I vomited tea everywhere. I made a half-arsed attempt to clean up and left. Two women on reception asked if I was ready to leave. I said yes and mumbled an apology for the mess in the bathroom.

They both walked me to the gate. On the other side of the road there was a group of about ten people, along with a few nuns and monks. The monks unnerved me the most: they stood separate from the group with their hoods up, holding large wooden posts. They weren't chanting or shouting; they were singing hymns. It was very eerie.

As I moved away from the police area, a girl broke off from the group and jogged after me. She tried to hand me a leaflet and I spat a very strong 'piss off' at her. I felt really guilty for this afterwards because of the look of deep concern on her face. When I got farther up the road, I realised that I still had a cotton-wool ball stuck on with a plaster in the crook of my arm, from where the anaesthetic had gone in. It was summer and I was wearing short sleeves. I walked on to my hotel, collected my stuff and waited in the pub next door for my taxi.

I felt utterly violated and exposed when leaving the clinic in Essex. As for my experience in Ireland, I don't have the language to describe how furious I am that a group of people could be allowed to set up and advertise a clinic in Ireland that gives out false information on a medical procedure.

The delay they caused me meant I was already about 9–10 weeks pregnant when I got to Marie Stopes in Dublin. The doctor I met there helped me work out when I would be able to afford to get to the UK. The price keeps rising with gestation, so by the time I would have enough money gathered it was going to be a fourteen-week abortion. A fourteen-week abortion is classified as a second trimester abortion, that upset me a lot.

I never felt any relief after the abortion. I felt shaky and numb, and I felt like that for some time afterwards.

IX

I was one of those people who was categorically against abortion. I was one of those women who couldn't understand why you would have an abortion. I AM one of those women who was left with NO CHOICE but to travel on the flight of shame to the UK.

I had three very-much-wanted children and in my plan I wanted four. I was going to have one more, but then I got sick – so sick I could hardly look after myself and my family. On looking at medication options I spoke with the consultant. With this medication I had to be finished having babies. At this point we had made the decision that we would have no more children.

I nodded at the consultant. 'Yes, we are having no more children.'

'Have you contraceptive arrangements in place?'

'Yes.'

'Good. It's important you don't conceive on this medication as it will cause severe abnormalities even if you stop the medication and you decide to have more children.'

I told him we were definitely having no more children. We were blessed with the three we had, which in fact we were told we may never have.

Fast forward.

I woke up violently sick. I thought it was a bug. The 'bug' continued and I found out I was pregnant. I had never in my life got 'caught'. Why the hell did I get caught now? I remember myself and my husband crying so hard. Abortion was never in our mindset, ever. Out of desperation I paid a lot of money to several online American doctors telling them my story and the name of the medication I was on. All had the same answers: severe abnormalities and termination suggestion. I didn't even know where to start with arranging one. Google became my friend.

I rang the UK. As I was just over five weeks pregnant, I had the option of a day procedure. I booked in. My husband was home from work to look after the other children so that no one would question where I was going. I was getting sicker with each day that passed.

I searched for flights and operators that accepted a driver's licence instead of passport. My passport was out of date. I booked a female taxi firm on the advice of forums, and I travelled alone. I felt it was written all over my face what I was doing as I sat surrounded by people going to a match. I spotted a local on the plane. I shrank with fright, hoping they wouldn't see me.

The flight is a blur. I remember waiting for my taxi. She was so nice. I felt I had to tell her all and justify myself. 'I'm a mother, you know, I just wouldn't do this, only I have no choice.' She really put my mind at ease. She told me such sad stories about women she'd picked up from Ireland and thought it was barbaric that each Irish person felt such shame and guilt. She said she'd never met a person who wanted an abortion for an easier life. As we approached the clinic, she warned me of pro-life campaigners and told me to keep pushing through past them.

I nearly died. My god, I was one of those pro-life people. I felt like screaming *You have no idea how little choice I have*. As I walked through the doors the words 'Don't do it, come back' echoed from the protesters.

I was met by lovely receptionists who seemed to really take extra care of the Irish. I entered the waiting room. Half the waiting room

was Irish women. I knew this as I heard their accents. Each woman like myself – ALONE.

The Irish always tend to seek each other out abroad and talk. Not in this case. Each woman looked pastier than the next, and hung her head, embarrassed, trying to hide her nationality. I was called for a scan and counselling session. It confirmed I was just six weeks pregnant and that there were two babies. They highlighted the higher risk of abnormalities given the medication I was on. During my counselling session it became clearer and clearer I was doing the right thing for me and my family. I went out to the waiting room once more, waiting to be called for the procedure.

My procedure was delayed for hours as a woman was rushed in with severe complications that had her life in risk. I was sick with anxiety as I waited, afraid I would miss my flight home, wondering was this the universe telling me change my mind? As time pushed on, I spoke to the receptionist and advised her I needed to be at the airport in two hours. She totally empathised and got me and another Irish woman in the same situation into the theatre. I opted for the suction procedure as I was so early on. I must have nearly broken the nurse's hand. They were so kind. I sat in the post-op room. Again, staff would hear Irish accents and look at us with such pity and they definitely gave us extra care, dignity and support. I got a taxi back to the airport.

My legs were jelly. I was on my own. I prayed to god I wouldn't fall down or get sick. I prayed I would make it home. Again, the airport is a blank. As I attempted to drive home I took a wrong turn. I ended up in the dark in a totally unfamiliar place. Again, I pleaded with god to get me home.

When I finally arrived home the relief was immense. It totally came over me and my husband that we had done the right thing but the whole travelling alone was horrendous for both of us. I am lucky and glad to say I have absolutely no regrets or guilt. I have no doubt I did the right thing.

As a previous pro-life, anti-abortion person I quickly learned that not all situations are black and white and there are so many justified reasons for abortion. Nobody knows the day or hour they may have no option. I was one of those women. Vote Yes. Women deserve more than this. Their partners and husbands deserve more than this. None of us knows when we will have no choice.

X

In late 2008, when I was eighteen, we buried our baby girl. She was five months old and died in her sleep from SIDS.[16] This is something that we will never recover from. We were only just old enough to be considered adults and we had lost a piece of ourselves.

In 2016 I fell pregnant again and was just terrified. I could never face that again. I could not survive that again. We had just got our lives back and had both gone to college. I was a month away from my final-year exams. Who was going to hire a pregnant woman? We spoke and my partner wanted a termination. With my fears and his requests, I felt that I had to terminate the pregnancy.

On this day two years ago, we travelled to Manchester. There were five women on the plane who were also in the clinic – we shared awkward glances, but rarely looked up from our paperwork. You could tell the Irish women from the English. The degree of shame was palpable in the Irish women.

It was painful. It was physically and psychologically draining. It led to some quite severe mental-health issues. Something that I attribute to the lack of aftercare for women when they return home – the shame associated and the fact that it is such a private situation, where nobody can know what you did.

Yes, I am ashamed. Yes, this is all my fault. Men walk away from their living, breathing children. But as women, we feel like monsters for removing a group of cells from our bodies that have the potential to become a human being.

My point here is this: as women, we are held to a different standard to men, we are told that we should be nurturing and are built for this process. Sometimes that is not the case. When something like this happens, we have to leave our homes in the early hours of the morning, fighting pregnancy symptoms to get on a plane at 5 am to put our bodies through unspeakable things and pay thousands for the 'privilege'.

Women are smart human beings, who should be trusted to do as they wish with their own bodies. No woman wants an abortion. No woman will stop using birth control if the Eighth Amendment is removed. The Eighth Amendment is harming women.

If I told my friends and family, would what I did be judged? If he told his friends and family, would he be judged? We would probably both be judged but I would be the villain in the story because I am the 'cold' woman who had an abortion.

XI

I was twelve years old. We were visiting my grandmother and my mother was bringing her to the hairdressers after they'd finished their cup of tea. My baby brother was finally seated and happy at the kitchen table. My uncle walked in and said he needed a hand to get stuff out from the dormer attic. My mum said, 'You go, you can crawl in.' I really didn't want to. I started to pull and play at my brother but my mum said, 'Leave him alone, off you go and help out.'

I walked up the stairs with my uncle behind. This was a familiar feeling and scenario for me; he always managed to get me alone. He had pinned me to his bed the previous Sunday and forced himself inside me. This he had done for some time now; it hurt my small body so much. His heavy body always smelling of stale sweat and unwashed grubby hands groping me and forcing me down. On this particular day I was bleeding and when he reached into my pants I was embarrassed: I was wearing the maxi pad my mother had given me the previous day. We'd had that awkward conversation about the birds and the bees and she'd handed me a book on teenage puberty, and pads that you probably wear after you've had a baby. My first period!

The way I remember the days is that my granny would get her hair set every second Tuesday and my mum would bring her, and it was also the day I found myself alone with my uncle. And the compulsory visit after mass on Sunday of course. So that particular Tuesday, as I was feeling embarrassed for bleeding, he put his hand inside me, withdrew it with haste, looked at his blood-stained hand, grabbed my face holding my chin and pulled my face up. I thought he was going to take the head off my shoulders, such was the disgust in his eyes. I felt so dirty and ashamed, more than ever on this particular day. He let go of my now blood-stained face and turned. I thought he was walking away and to my surprise he spun round and with all his strength and power fuelled with his disgust he punched me in the stomach. The force of it sent me flying backwards, bringing a bedside lamp with me as I fell up against the wall behind me, tangled up in a lamp flex. I threw up and passed out. I did not have an abortion. He kicked and punched me enough to prevent a foetus surviving the violation he'd subjected my body to.

All the talk of the Eighth Amendment of late has made me think – what if I'd been pregnant at twelve years old?

I know for certain that my parents would not know how to support me. We lived in a society of 'please be quiet' and 'don't make a fuss' and 'just be a good girl', and this was over twenty years ago, 1994 to be exact. It's an embarrassing and disturbing history we have here in Ireland. And it is the victims who are left to deal with the shame and stigma. We need to stop doing this to women, to girls. We have come so far, so please repel the Eighth so we can cross the threshold into love and understanding. No one should be subjected to the guilt, shame and isolation felt by so many women, even today in 2018. In an ideal world, no woman would need to seek an abortion. Partners would not be abusive, rapists would not exist, incest would not exist, contraception would not fail and all pregnancies would be timed perfectly and result in healthy babies. Had the rape resulted in a pregnancy, I can safely say that it would have destroyed and killed me. I would have missed out on a life, and on the privilege of being a mother to two incredible human beings, and the most loving and supportive partner. I will forever endeavour to give a voice to the victims of sexual abuse and to be an advocate for women. For the sake of Irish women's dignity. Every story is different, but every choice is personal. And we should be allowed to make the decisions that affect our bodies and our futures. Repeal the Eighth.

XII

I was in my mid-twenties, with a beautiful daughter, but the black cloud of an incredibly toxic relationship with a man I should have never have been with hung over our little family. He wasn't my daughter's father, thankfully, but the impact he had during the time we were together was huge and I'm grateful she is the thriving, intelligent and, more so, happy child that she is today.

I could have never envisioned being in an abusive relationship. I thought of myself as strong, but I wasn't. I was stuck: if I threatened to leave, I was harassed with messages of love, hate, threats of rape.

After he'd riled me by calling my daughter names, or with comments crafted with the intent of destroying the psyche of another, he'd record my retort and then jokingly play those segments of the arguments to his pals. Passports were hidden on holidays. I was hit and punched a few times, nothing compared to the more insidious things he'd do that would slowly but surely derail you. Anyway, he'd tamper with condoms too, an example being not putting them on properly so they would fall off during sex, or he'd slide them off. I fell pregnant, as was his plan. He was elated, I was terrified.

I never considered having an abortion; it wasn't for me, although I was always a believer in women doing whatever was right for themselves, their bodies, their lives. Pregnancy is damn hard. It shouldn't be enforced. I couldn't imagine another unsupported pregnancy, this time controlled by a man who spoke of me like trash while laying claim to what was forming inside of me. He wanted an abortion one moment, and in the next breath would call me every name under the sun for 'murdering his child'.

I had to have a termination. I knew it was the only right thing to do for my life, and for my daughter's life.

I researched. I didn't know what to do, where to go, who to turn to when I desperately needed someone to help me.

As a mature student, I wasn't exactly rolling in money to travel to London and pay for the procedure. I booked an appointment at seven weeks, but he, a very wealthy man at the time, wouldn't help. I cancelled the appointment, panicking all the more, like a bomb was about to go off inside of me. I needed help. I booked another appointment, at nine weeks. He decided he would pay half and come with me.

On the flight I couldn't hold back the tears. I felt like everyone knew I was en route to have an abortion. A mother travelling to have an abortion. I felt guilt. I felt relieved that I could afford to travel. The trauma of needing to leave your country to avail of the procedure added such an unexplainable dimension to something already so hard. I think you need to go through that, one of the exiled many, to comprehend the otherwise incomprehensible feeling of betrayal.

I cried, cried more, and a bit more. I just wanted to be free. On the tube I felt as if people were noticing my Irish accent, my sadness, and knew why I was travelling. I felt so anxious, on top of everything else, that I might have to walk through a mob of 'pro-life' protesters that I had read plagued that particular clinic. Obviously they were tormenting women in unenviable positions at another place that day. I was thankful their hate wasn't on display.

I cried a bit more, I cried when faced with such compassion from complete strangers in a country that was affording me a chance at saving my life, my daughter's. I cried entering the theatre. Is guilt etched into our DNA because we've grown up in a society that's in the shadow of the cross? I think so. Meanwhile, he was in a café, with not a care in the world.

I had a surgical abortion[17] under general anaesthetic. When I awoke and was moved to the general recovery area, I was sat next to a young medical student from Ireland who had made the exact same journey. Two Irish women side by side in a clinic in some strange part of London. I was in pain. I thought it was normal, but everyone else in the recovery area seemed fine as the nurse handed us tea and biscuits. I hadn't eaten since before the surgery.

Back at the hotel I lay in bed crying while he told me to stop – it was actually more along the lines of 'shut the fuck up'. I put in earphones and listened to music so I couldn't hear the abuse. I felt so alone. Even thinking about it brings burning tears to my eyes. I'm not the only one who has been through it. Some Irish woman has been through it today. It's a scandal.

That day London was celebrating the birth of Princess Charlotte: it was like the universe was mocking me. It was the right thing to do, I knew it once the relief washed over me upon waking, but I was shrouded in a crushing guilt too. Free, but not quite.

Back home I was still in pain, passing black blood. I was ignorant: back in a land that never provided me with information relating to abortion, I thought it was normal. I tried to resume normal life.

The abortion was incomplete. I was actually in a dangerous situation. Naturally, I'd be one of the statistical few where things didn't go to plan. Surgical abortion, like any surgery, carries small risks. That's why I despair when I see comments saying women will be accessing it as a form of contraception – so clueless, ill-informed and downright insulting. It's not an easy way out but a hard decision made for the right reasons. I had a D&C[18] in my home town.

The staff, who knew my story, displayed such humanity. I felt safe. I was safe. Everything was fine. I went home afterwards. No plane rides, no guilt, humiliation. It took a further year to be free of the relationship. I regret so much, but one thing I do not regret is the abortion. I had a right to life. I do not want this story repeated endlessly, for other Irish women to find themselves in the shoes of the women who have shared their stories with you. I hope our country finally acknowledges the need for this basic medical procedure to be available to women who desperately seek it. FYI, today I'm the happiest I've ever been, and feel no shame thanks to strong women speaking out, challenging the stigma and fighting the good fight.

XIII

I had just started seeing this boy & we were crazy about each other. We became inseparable, spending every minute we could together. I was on the pill at the time but somehow I fell pregnant. I told him first and we were so excited and scared but mainly excited. He told his parents first and his mam flipped the lid and said I was going on the first flight out to have an abortion. Then came my mam who had the same reaction as my boyfriend's mam. We were young & felt like we had no options so I went home to start making calls to clinics in Manchester & I found a clinic that could fit me in two weeks, which was the cheapest. My boyfriend wasn't allowed to come for fear we wouldn't go ahead. So me and mam were booked to go.

We flew out on a 6 am flight & a 7 pm home because we couldn't afford to stay the night as we had to borrow the money from my grandparents. I arrived at the clinic and was in and out in an hour and half. I'll spare you the horror of the details but the place wasn't the best clinic I could have chosen. Arriving back to the airport, we were told the flight had been delayed to 11 pm. I had to now face the long wait on the flight home. After two hours I began to feel extremely sick. The pain in my stomach became so unbearable I eventually asked Mam to get some help from the airport staff as I couldn't even keep a drink of water down. Due to the pain I was experiencing they called an ambulance and I was rushed to hospital in Manchester. The ambulance journey felt like a lifetime.

On arrival at the A&E the nurse had to give me morphine due to the level of pain I was in & Mam had to relay the events of what had gone on that morning. The doctors were shocked at how quickly I'd been allowed leave the clinic. It turned out the procedure had not been carried out correctly and I had to have several tests and scans to see what was going on. All the while they told Mam she had to leave the hospital. We had 10 pounds with us and nowhere to go. I told them I was going to discharge myself if she couldn't stay & thankfully they set us up in a room where Mam could sleep on the chair. Two days pass and I'm still in hospital. Family sent money for Mam to go to Tesco and buy us some leggings & necessary items with the nurses providing us with meals and toiletries as we had nothing. I just wanted to go home.

Eventually by the fourth day I was allowed leave. It turned out they didn't remove everything correctly during the procedure and I again won't to go into detail of what I had to go through for this to be fixed. Finally, after having to borrow more money for the €2,000 flights, I made it home.

However, I felt different. I was angry at everyone including myself. I blamed everyone including myself and this went on for months. I pushed everyone away: family, friends, my boyfriend, and with everything falling apart I started to become depressed. I wanted to get help but I was so, so terrified that I would get into trouble for what I had done. I had severe anxiety every time I heard an ambulance. I was so afraid I would be unable to have kids again due to damage caused to me in that clinic. I cried every time I saw a pregnant woman on the telly, in a movie. When I eventually got help it was too late. I was already damaged and with counselling not helping I was put on antidepressants. My relationship ended and my life felt ruined.

Thankfully, I'm now on the mend and me & my boyfriend found our way back to each other. I will vote Yes on 25 May so no other young girl has to experience what I did. We as women should be able to access safe & legal abortion at home with the much-needed aftercare. Not risking our lives by booking the cheapest clinic in England we can find. #RepealTheEighth

XIV

My story isn't the same as the beautiful, strong, inspiring women who share theirs here using the voice of this amazing page. Mine doesn't end in tragedy or abortion, like so many of our women. I have not lived a sheltered life and yet my experience has left me scarred and full of anger. Mine is the story of having a baby while the Eighth Amendment is still in place. The 'normalcy' that women accept in this country even though it is absolutely not normal to be traumatised after the birth of your child.

In 2010 I was pregnant with my first child, a son. I was twenty-two. I had a good, well-paying job, a partner and a supportive family surrounding me. Although I was young and fearful that I had little to no life experience to offer a child, he was very much wanted and loved. My pregnancy progressed well besides the usual symptoms – being very sick morning, noon and night for a long time, and kidney infections. I was scanned once at fourteen weeks and not scanned again until almost 30 weeks due to my bump measuring 'small'. It's probably important to note that I am a tall lady with a long torso so my baby bump spread upwards instead of outwards. That day I was told he wasn't growing as he should, and to come back the following week for another scan. When I returned they said there had been no change; I was told then that I had to go on bed rest so that I wouldn't be using any energy and my baby could use it to gain weight. She told me to eat, eat, eat. Naturally enough I wanted to do anything I could for my baby and I did what I was told, as though it was all my fault. The worry, fear and blame was all placed on my shoulders. I barely slept; I didn't qualify for disability but they couldn't care less. I had to give up work and take to my bed for the remaining ten weeks of my pregnancy, without any second opinions, different scanning machine, nothing.

I was to return every two weeks for ultrasounds, all which showed no improvement. At one point we were told that his abdomen was disproportionately smaller than the rest of his body and his head was measuring three weeks ahead of his body as well. I felt sick.

At 39 weeks, a final scan concluded that my baby was still severely underweight even though I had done everything I was told to. I force-fed myself even when I wasn't hungry, barely moved from the bed or the couch and worried constantly. He was still measuring 4.5 lbs at full term so I was forced into an induction to 'get that baby out and feed him'. The consultant was cold, heartless and couldn't care less about me or my wishes. I never saw her again. Not during the labour, the birth, or after.

I started induction. The special care unit was arranged and ready for him when he was born, so they could put a feeding tube down his throat. It took a full 24 hours of excruciating pain as my body wasn't ready and neither was my baby. I had an epidural at 2 cm as the pain was so bad I was throwing up. The drip was started, my waters had broken, absolutely nothing was natural or normal. When the time came, after two hours of pushing he wouldn't come out so they performed an episiotomy without my knowledge or consent. I didn't know until after it was done. Again, I wanted anything possible for my baby to be born safely but can you imagine that? I wasn't even made aware it was happening.

After the entire ordeal, my baby boy was born over 8.5 lbs, abdomen and head perfectly proportioned and completely healthy. Admittedly the midwives in attendance were looking at me perplexed and one of them even said, 'There's no way you should have been induced.' She then proceeded to cancel the special care unit. There was nothing wrong with my baby. The consultant's registrar entered the room soon after and I was told 'it happens'. Was this supposed to be an apology for all they had put me through? It took over an hour for me to be stitched. At the time I had no idea that this entire experience was because of the laws we have in place. They didn't need to apologise to me because I didn't matter. I was insignificant.

It took me twelve weeks to heal from the birth. I had post-natal depression and anxiety. I catastrophised so badly that I wouldn't let anyone hold my baby for fear of anything happening to him.

It's been the bones of ten years since then. TEN years and we are still living with these laws. I have a daughter now, and I absolutely hate the thought of her having an experience like mine. When I went in for subsequent pregnancies, I had birth preferences – including avoiding an episiotomy – and I was laughed at. I had no choice.

It isn't JUST about abortion. It's about our women, our sisters, our daughters being treated inhumanely in many cases, their feelings, values or choice ignored. We have no say over our bodies in any sense of the word. It's about the women who are ill and in need of treatment. It's about actually being able to parent post birth, without trauma. My story is that of hundreds of women. #RepealTheEighth

XV

As I sit down to write about this, a wave of sadness comes over me and I feel the pain, raw and consuming, once more. Now, almost two years later, I have been through two rounds of counselling, many cathartic letters or bits written for this and that, some published, some still only handwritten on an A4 pad. This one, though, feels like the last desperate attempt to save someone the suffering I had to endure; to use my heartache to bring about change. Feeling lucky enough to have it in me to do it, yet dirty and wrong that it has to be this way. My private life, a time of utter despair, now a thing to be voted on. I really hope this is the last time.

It was a sunny and warm June day when I went for my twelve-week scan. I was literally full of the joys, and having already had a healthy baby boy four years earlier, the thought of any issues never crossed my mind. I couldn't wait to tell him he was going to be a big brother. I just needed that precious scan picture. The excitement and giddiness mounted as I waited to be called.

And there it was, a heartbeat, a hand, a foot. The little bundle I was creating, much loved and wanted. But I could tell within seconds that something wasn't right. The room too quiet, too many clicks of the machine, the too-hard pressing on my tummy. Most of all the shape of my little bean was not what you would expect. She turned to me and held my hand and said she was so, so sorry. No chance for my little one to make it outside of me.

My heart stopped and everything sounded strange, like I was under water. Anencephaly,[19] a word unknown by me, a word I was unable to pronounce or retain. And from this underwater place I move my feet to the consultant's room and wait. Big hot wet tears flowing down my face. Shock and hurt and pain, and yet an unwavering understanding that this pregnancy must come to an end. So I rally myself to ask the question: 'What do I do now?' Please, please don't tell me to go to England. Don't turf me out like I hear ye do. Mind me, help me, show me care and compassion. All I got were whispers and side looks, and a suggestion to google the condition. The shame of this country laid bare to me. These professionals, who I believe were wanting to help me, being made cruel by our constitution.

I found myself out on the street in my underwater bubble wondering what in the world was going on. Looking across at the hospital, feeling like a dumped piece of rubbish. Not even a leaflet with information to guide me. No contact numbers. No assistance whatsoever. All I had was that green folder with the usual pregnancy stuff and one single piece of paper with those words I couldn't even look at. Others walked past me, holding theirs proudly. I wanted to puke. I wanted to die. Autopilot set in so I could get myself home.

I will be honest here, I screamed the house down. I screamed for my mammy. I screamed in pain and loss and anger. Eventually though, I pulled myself together. I knew deep down this was going to need careful and timely attention. I rang my mum and sister, and after the tears we made a plan. In a harsh twist, they were both out of the country at the time.

I called my GP and then the consultant I had seen from the hospital. My GP was unable to comment on something he could not see. I had to leave a message with the hospital administrator who actually scoffed at me when I asked to speak with the consultant. I explained the situation as best I could, trying to get across the urgency of it.

Over the course of the next two days I tried several times to get in contact with that doctor. No one from the hospital ever called me back at any stage.

So then I googled it. I was afraid to look. And when I say afraid, I mean I had to force my head to turn to look at the screen. Force my eyes to open, force them to focus. My stomach dropping like a stone. Something invisible crushing against my chest. The info and images a harsh reality I needed to see. I cried and cried and held my stomach and told my little bundle that I was so, so sorry. When I could breathe again a resolve came over me. Push through, girl. Be strong and end this suffering.

Passport checks. One of them was out of date. Why is this relevant at a time like this? But it was. When you export healthcare, patients need the correct documents. Sorting this problem caused a major headache, even more phone calls and worse, more explaining. Too tired and confused to make up a story, you have to go over and over it again and again. I found myself on a train at 7 am the next morning, heading to Dublin. Once it turned 9 am I was back planning my funeral from the comfort of a semi-full carriage. More calls, more explaining. My heart becoming more of a rock with every insult this situation brought. This was the time when I should have been coming to terms with this tragedy, grieving for my loss.

A trip to Dublin Zoo while we waited for the passport process. A handy excuse for this ridiculous trip to my clever four-year old. While we're there I tell him, as happily as I can muster: 'And guess what? Tomorrow we're going on a plane to see your auntie and uncle!'

And somehow I make it home to Galway and somehow I pack a bag, make more phone calls, have a harrowing phone consultation with the clinic. Next morning up a 2 am with my son in tow and drive to Dublin (because €400 more to fly from Shannon was a luxury I could not afford). Forty-eight hours after getting the

diagnosis. Forty-eight hours of little to no sleep. Forty-eight hours of pure torture, but we made it the airport. I'm just about able to hold it together. To not scream, 'Will somebody help me?!' as we pass through security. As the plane takes off and everyone is safely tied to their seats, I allow a little bit out. I can feel that pain now, it is still here. I will never be the same. I will never have the same connection to my country. A place for which I always felt pride and love. You tossed me out in my greatest time of need and I will fight every day until you stop punishing tragedy. Until you treat pregnant women equally, and give us back our autonomy.

It was another week before I finally got home. And again, I was lucky at that. When I did get to the clinic, they wanted to send me away. I was so sick from the stress of the previous days, they said I was not fit. An understanding nurse and two doctors examined me later and finally agreed to do it, considering the circumstances.

Honestly, a part of me, despite this, still feels so lucky. Lucky that so many women have stood up before me so that I at least knew this was so wrong. Lucky to have had the financial support to pay for the termination and the flights. Lucky to have been brought up in a house where there is no shame or stigma, only love and compassion. A place where we were encouraged to use our voice. Vote Yes on the 25th of May and end this torture.

XVI

Two years ago, while I was still living in Ireland, I got pregnant. I had just started a new job and the guy I had been seeing had recently left my city and would return to his home country soon. I noticed changes in my body before I had even missed my period. Deep down I knew the result when I was taking the test, but that didn't stop it feeling dreamlike and surreal when I saw the result on the small digital screen: *Pregnant, 1–2 weeks.*

My first step was to google 'abortion pills Ireland'. I had spent my entire adult life being terrified of pregnancy, with many days of paranoia waiting for my period, and I had already done my research on the site that ships abortion medication to the various countries around the world where it's still illegal.

I emailed them, then got into bed and cried. I was living at home at the time and when my mother came to check on me, I told her. It was uncomfortable, but I knew I was extremely lucky to have such a supportive reaction from her. She was behind me no matter what I decided. I told her I definitely wanted an abortion and was going to order the pills. She was worried and desperately wanted me to take some days off work and fly to England, but I was vehement that I didn't want that.

There were a few reasons why. Partly it was because it would feel like a much bigger event in my life than if I stayed in my home

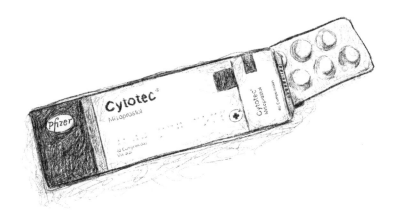

and took a pill. I didn't want it to be a big deal and I dreaded the unpleasantness of travel, a clinic and a strange hotel room. Partly it was because I would need her financial help to go, and although she could afford it, I wanted to sort it out on my own. I had got myself into this situation, I thought, and I would get myself out of it. The pills cost around a hundred euro, which I could manage.

And partly it was defiance. I wanted to give the abortion law the middle finger. I wanted to take control of my own body. When I had done my previous research into abortion, I had come across very old, home-remedy-style methods involving parsley and pennyroyal tea. This was how women dealt with unwanted pregnancies in the past, by themselves. The abortion pill felt closer to that and the idea of it somehow made me feel more powerful in the situation than the thought of a surgical abortion.

I had the pills shipped to a village in Northern Ireland. It was impossible to have them sent anywhere in the South. I was in anxious knots waiting to get an update on its arrival, each day crawling by slowly as I tried to pretend everything was normal. Then I found out that in my panic I had made a mistake when ordering them and the post office had rejected the package. It was being sent back to the other side of the world. This was a huge blow, and I sobbed out of frustration and fear. I just wanted it to be over.

I contacted the organisation who sent the pills and they told me that to prevent them being returned again, it would be ideal to have them sent to a residential address. The problem with this was that I didn't know anyone who lived in the North. In desperation, I went on Reddit and searched for a pro-choice group in Northern Ireland. Through this I found the profile of a woman who I could see had posted in that group previously. I took a chance and messaged her, telling her about my situation and basically begging her to help me.

I've never met this woman face to face, but she showed me so much kindness. She was understandably very nervous about letting me send the package to her house, with her full name on it. She was understandably suspicious that I could be an anti-choice activist who meant her harm. But she still helped me. Once the package arrived, she left it for me in a café in Belfast. My mother drove me up to get it on my day off, and then back home. An all-day trip.

That alone was such an anxious, miserable journey that I'm really not sure if I made the right choice in not going to England. When I got the pills in my hand, it all became more real. I won't pretend that I felt nothing for the embryo growing inside me. In all honesty, I did. Looking back, I think hormones played a big role in this. Your body wants to be pregnant, and wants you to protect the pregnancy. Before that I was pretty sure I never wanted children. But being pregnant woke maternal feelings in me, which I guess isn't surprising.

Mostly I was ready for the ordeal to be over and to get back to all the plans I had for my life that a child would totally disrupt. Mostly I knew that I was still unable to look after myself properly, never mind another person. Mostly I knew that if I was ready to have this child, I wouldn't have bought abortion pills. So I took them. I told the father what my decision was. While he had been very supportive of me and said he would be on board either way, I could hear relief in his voice when he heard I was going ahead with the abortion.

When I started to bleed, I cried. I grieved. The cramps were the worst pain I've ever been through. I had planned to go to work the following day but I was dizzy and weak and had to call in sick. I'm pretty sure my boss thought I had faked it to go to a festival for the weekend.

It was difficult not being able to tell her, or other people, what I had been through. I did tell a few people, and some of them tried their best to help me through it. But overall, it was a very lonely time. I also had trouble finding a place that provided aftercare for a medical abortion.[20] The sadness, guilt and shame took quite a while to go away. But it's gone now. These days I feel nothing but relief that I made the decision I did. And immense gratefulness towards the organisation that sent me the pills, the stranger who helped me get them and my mother who was supportive to me throughout the whole thing and long afterwards.

XVII

It was in March 2017 that I found out I was pregnant. I was happily in a relationship, planning our wedding and our life together.

Myself and my partner would often talk about the future life we wanted to build and children have never been part of our dream. So for the test to show up positive was a bit of shock to the system. I told him over the phone while he was in work and he said, 'It will all be OK,' which became our soothing mantra for the next few weeks. We discussed our options, but honestly, for me, having a child was never one of them. We made an appointment with the IFPA[21] and met with the counsellor. I was a bit nervous but she immediately put us at ease. She walked us through all of our options and we decided that the best option for us was for us to travel to the UK.

When we got home that day, we tried making an appointment. Unfortunately, the clinics were fully booked for three weeks. We discussed waiting but I felt physically ill and mentally unable to wait for that long so I researched getting the pills online. I found two organisations that were able to help us. I asked both organisations to send me the tablets, one to my home address and one to an address in Belfast just in case one of them got stopped and confiscated. I read all the information and I remember reading that if something went wrong there wasn't a test that could prove I had taken the tablets, which put me at ease somewhat.

One Friday I gave an excuse to my employers and drove up to Northern Ireland early to collect the tablets. The moment I had the tablets in hand I felt relief. I took the first tablet there and then and drove straight back to work. I planned to take the second tablet at home the following day when my partner was there. I had read about a few experiences online and was very nervous and scared; but for us, for me, it was the only option. I took the tablets on the Saturday and to my relief the experience wasn't a bad one: I had a little bleeding and cramping but overall I was just relieved it was all over. I went back to work on Monday with a weight lifted off my shoulders. Tuesday passed and my back was a little sore, there was just this pressure that got progressively worse until on Friday morning I woke up covered in blood. It was scary – none of the articles had prepared me for seeing that much blood, or the feeling of the blood and clots gushing out of you. I was also at a loss about what to do. We decided to go to my GP and showed up at their surgery at nine on the dot with my story rehearsed: 'I'm having a miscarriage.' At this stage I had already bled through my clothes and long coat – we had to put a plastic bag on the seat of the car. The nurse saw me but there was nothing she could do, so she referred me to Holles Street. We drove straight there, rehashing our story over and over again to ensure we wouldn't slip up.

I told the reception desk that I was having a miscarriage and a nurse brought me into a little office where she asked me to do a pregnancy test. I told her I was bleeding too much and showed her my clothes. She called for a doctor and they brought me into a different room for an examination. My partner hadn't come back yet and I just felt emotionally and physically overwhelmed. The doctor tried to reassure me and the nurse held my hand as I cried inconsolably while they manually scraped the clots out. They did this twice and then told me they were admitting me to the ward upstairs for monitoring. To monitor the bleeding and clots they gave me these cardboard bowls to use anytime I went to the bathroom. The bleeding and passing of the clots continued until around 5 pm at which point we were both just drained. I wanted to go home. The doctor came by around 7 pm and told me I could go home so I jumped at the opportunity. We got home around half past eight and went to sleep, just relieved it was now finally over.

The following morning. I woke up at around 6 am – again the bed and myself were covered in blood. I cleaned up and tried to go back to sleep but at this stage I was getting up to go to the bathroom every 10–15 minutes to pass clots and change my sanitary towel. It was around 10 am, when I was in the bathroom, that I felt really dizzy and faint. I screamed for my partner. He found me in the bathroom, pale, clammy and with my eyes rolling to the back of my head. He tidied me up best he could and carried me to the bed where I just wanted to sleep. I couldn't stay awake, so he decided to ring the emergency services and asked what he should do. I remember he kept trying to keep me awake by shaking me and tapping my cheek but I was just so incredibly tired. The person on the other end of the phone kept my partner calm and told him he was doing the right thing, that the ambulance was on its way, all he needed to do was open the door for them.

They came in and examined me, put my feet up so that the blood flow was stemmed slightly and after spending around half an hour stabilising me, brought me to the ambulance for transport back to Holles Street. We were back at the hospital in no time and I was brought straight into an examination room. No time was wasted and I received an internal examination and another manual clear-out. They were going to bring me back up to the ward and asked me to stand up and when I did, the blood just streamed out of me. I completely lost control of my emotions. I've never been so scared in my life. I looked at my partner and saw the fear in his face too. They wheeled me up to the ward where a nurse brought me to the bathroom – in there I lost consciousness and the poor nurse had to catch me and call for a doctor. They got me to the ward and I lost consciousness again and woke up on the floor. My partner stood next to the curtain, paralysed with fear. It turns out that because I had been steadily bleeding for two days I had lost too much blood. They gave me four blood transfusions and that night they scheduled me for a D&C, which went smoothly.

I was in hospital for three days. Then I was at home trying to get my blood levels back up to a level where I didn't feel faint all the time for two weeks. It took me another two months to get my strength back and it's taken me twelve months to come to terms with it all. I have not once, not even for a second, regretted making the decision to have an abortion. But this experience has mentally scarred me and my partner for life.

I'M ANGRY at this country for failing me, I'M ANGRY I had to lie, I'M ANGRY that I was made to feel shame for making the best decision for me, I'M ANGRY that I am not allowed to make a decision that not only affects MY body, but also my entire future and that of my partner. I'M ANGRY that I'm not trusted to decide what's best for me. #RepealtheEighth

XVIII

I've wavered about writing something for the campaign for ages now. The current wave of #MeToo allegations, the Belfast rape trial[22] and the debate surrounding the referendum have brought up some very difficult memories. But if I'm ever going to tell my story, it should be now.

I come from an abusive family. There was violence, both physical and sexual, as well as emotional abuse. There was hardly ever any peace or safety at home. At the age of twelve I went to my first ever school disco in my new secondary school. Some of my friends went outside to smoke. I went with them to try it. An older boy from 5th year started chatting to me. I was really flattered by his attention and his interest in me. I was very concerned with wanting to be one of the cool kids, and wanted to seem much more worldly than I was. My friends went back inside and I stayed outside talking to him.

Before I knew it he was kissing me. I didn't have much time to process what was happening, but I thought it was OK. I was delighted that this guy liked me, but I had no idea what was really happening. Next thing he's pushing me onto the ground with all his weight. I protested as I didn't want to lie down. I didn't want to get my cool disco clothes wrecked and dirty. He used his strength and raped me right there in the trees opposite the school hall. I asked him to stop. I was crying. It hurt a lot and seemed to go on forever. When he was finished, he got up off me and asked me if I wanted a cigarette.

I didn't, so we both pulled our clothes back on and returned to the disco. I went into the toilet to check my clothes. I wanted to leave, but my mam wasn't due to collect me for an hour. I wiped away my tear-stained make-up, fixed my hair and went back into the disco and danced with my friends until it was finished. He stayed for a while, but ignored me once we came back inside. I was dying with shame. I told nobody. They could never find out. It was all clearly my fault, I knew that, so I just pretended it hadn't happened.

I kept pretending for the next six weeks. Sometimes I saw my rapist on the bus to school. He never acknowledged me. I pretended none of this was happening. I totally dissociated from reality. Even when I started throwing up in the mornings. Even when I kept falling asleep every time I sat down. Even when my breasts started to really hurt. Even when I went off certain foods that suddenly started to turn my stomach. My mother worked out that I was pregnant. I denied it, but she knew. She blamed me, just as I knew she would. I couldn't face any of it. I came very close to taking my own life. There were horrified whispered conversations with my granny. My younger brother wanted to know what was going on, but nobody told him. A day after my thirteenth birthday my mother brought me to Liverpool by boat to have an abortion. We couldn't afford this trip, she told me several times. My overwhelming feeling during the trip was shame. There was absolutely no way I could bring a baby into the world. I was much too messed up and unstable. I knew I couldn't bring a child up, but especially in the abusive home I came from. I also knew I couldn't give birth and hand my child over to anybody else. I wouldn't survive it.

I was much younger than the other girls in the clinic. I wanted everyone to think I was older. I think even the staff in the clinic were shocked by my age. Nobody ever suggested contacting the author-ities, or pursuing an investigation. Those things simply weren't

considered. Everyone's attitude was to say as little as possible. Me included. I just felt shame and despair. The procedure itself was painful. I remember feeling relief that I wouldn't be bringing a life into the world to be hurt and abused. The trip home was endless. The sea was very rough, and I vomited for a lot of the journey. I kept throwing up my painkillers.

The following Monday I went back into school and carried on pretending none of it had happened. What a lonely journey.

These events remained buried for a very long time. In my forties I went to therapy and spoke about what happened for the first time. It's a long road of recovery for survivors of rape or abuse, but there is hope. Hope starts when we share our stories with someone who won't judge us or shame us.

My thoughts on the referendum: I'm sick and tired of women being ashamed. I'm sick and tired of the secrecy and hypocrisy. Having to travel to England plays a big part in this shame and secrecy. Ireland exports us, because this country has a hard time dealing with reality. Babies should be wanted, and mothers should be willing. Any girl or woman who does not feel able to be an adequate parent, for any reason, should be able to make a decision whether to continue her pregnancy or not. There is nothing evil about ending a pregnancy if the conditions for the baby are not ideal. This goes for the much-wanted pregnancies that will have catastrophic outcomes also. As one of the 'hard cases' I feel very strongly that all women should be given choices. No woman should be judged or shamed for making the best choice for herself and the potential life she is carrying. And, finally, suicidal children should not be forced to travel to another country to end a pregnancy. Child rape happens more than we like to acknowledge. Do we really want a society that would force a child to carry on an unwanted pregnancy?

XIX

I had an extreme premature baby in 2000. Born at 27 weeks' gestation, she weighed 2lbs 4oz. I talk freely about how small she was, how stressful it was for myself and my partner to go through caring for her and how wonderful it is that she grew up to be such a fine young woman that we are so, so proud of. It was easy to talk about the nice stuff, the milestones she reached, her amazing personality, the fact that she suffered no long-term disability.

What's harder to talk about is the effect her birth had on him and myself. What I don't speak about is the trauma we went through at the time of her birth, and how the Eighth Amendment put my life at risk.

We were delighted to be pregnant. The congratulations and preparations were the complete opposite to my previous pregnancy. Six years previously I was a lone parent on welfare and living in a shitty two-roomed flat. This time, I had the support of an amazing man. This pregnancy was full of hope of a future with a mum, a dad and two kids. Perfection.

At about 24 weeks I had a bleed. Panicked, I rang him and he came to collect me. We walked the short distance to the hospital but my doctor was away. Another doctor checked me out. Baby's heartbeat was strong. 'Go home, you'll probably miscarry.' We got a taxi home and didn't even speak. If we didn't say the words then maybe it wouldn't happen. My next appointment was the following week. No bleeding! I was hopeful. Everything was going to be OK.

At the next week's appointment, the doctor checked my files and was surprised to see I had been in with a bleed. 'We'll get you a scan.' The diagnosis was Grade 4 placenta praevia.[23] I had never heard of it. I was admitted straight away. Two weeks of lying on my back, missing my son terribly and desperately wanting to go home. I'd had no bleeding, no pain. Against the doctor's advice I packed my bags and went home.

Three days later, at 7.15 pm, I went to the bathroom. I will never forget the blood. Quickly, a friend ushered me into his car and we made the hospital in minutes. I had been warned that if this was to happen, I had fifteen minutes to get medical help, or else.

Arriving at the hospital was the start of the nightmare. Standing at reception my partner desperately tried to explain the situation to the receptionist. I was numb, I just stood there. A woman in the waiting room jumped up and ran over. She started to yell at the receptionist to get help. I didn't realise how much I was haemorrhaging. Still no pain, nothing.

The next thirteen hours were the worst of my life. I was admitted onto a ward and left to slowly bleed to death. But the baby's heartbeat was strong. I went into labour at 11.30 pm. I received some pain relief but they ignored my requests for a doctor. A nurse called Ann, the kindest person I have ever met, stayed with me all night. She held my hand and pleaded with the matron to get help. The matron lost the rag with her, threatened her with disciplinary action if she didn't leave me and get back to work. And told me to stop crying as I was upsetting the other women. Ann never left my side. She held my hand all night. I knew it was bad when I saw tears streaming down her face. At 8 am my doctor arrived. He sat at the edge of the bed. 'Unfortunately we have to take the baby out.'

As they wheeled me down to theatre, I felt my life ebbing away. I didn't think of the baby. Does that sound awful? All I could think about was my beautiful little boy at home and how he would cope without a mother. It was breaking my heart. He was my last thought before the anaesthetic knocked me out.

What I didn't know until years later, because we didn't talk about it, was what the doctor said to my partner outside the theatre that morning. 'We don't know if she'll make it: it's 20 per cent but the baby is 50/50.'

Although it all worked out in the end, being told that the woman you love only has a 20 per cent chance of survival has had devastating long-term effects. You don't just get over it. He had to be strong. He had to be the man who cares for his partner and children, keeps working, stays strong. The trauma I went through, feeling life leave me, being so close to death that I could taste it.

The Eighth Amendment meant that the doctor had to wait until my life was 'at serious risk' before he could intervene. My life was not as important to them as the life of a baby. I was a mother, a partner, a sister, a daughter and a friend. I had people in my life who loved me. What would their lives have been like if I had died? Who was there defending my right to life? Who was there defending the rights of my son to have a mother? Who was there defending the rights of my partner to have the woman he loved survive?

I was twelve in 1983 and did not have a vote in my future. My daughter will be three months away from her eighth birthday on 25 May. She does not have a vote in her future. We all need to take responsibility now for the pain and suffering the Eighth Amendment has had on thousands of women's lives over the last 35 years. We must never forget Mother B.,[24] the X Case,[25] Savita.

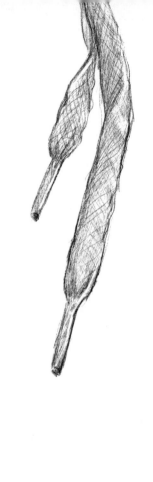

XX

Just before my 21st birthday I discovered I was pregnant. I was in the very early days of thinking I was in love with my boyfriend. We had been careful, but my pill didn't work. In the first couple of months I had three 'threatened' miscarriages. I ended up being admitted on the third occasion as it was feared that hostile circumstances at home were causing complications in my pregnancy and could risk me losing the baby. Placed in a ward with heavily pregnant women, all I could do was hope and plead that I wouldn't lose my baby while I could hear the cries of new lives around me.

Early one morning a midwife woke me. I remember she was older than most of the midwives there, it was barely 6 am and she woke me to chastise me for taking up a bed in the hospital. I didn't deserve to be there or cared for because, as she put it, it was my choice to make such a mess of my life getting pregnant so young and before I was prepared or ready for such a commitment. She made me feel worthless and an inconvenience. I had a horrific pregnancy, countless scares and hospital admissions, and my relationship became a misery. There followed months of being ridiculed and living with emotional and verbal abuse.

Thankfully the physical abuse didn't start until after I gave birth to a healthy baby. Then the manipulation and coercive control and torment escalated. I was terrified of becoming a single mother. I had been raised by one and saw my mother struggle, how the glass ceiling stifled her and society shunned her. Amidst the conflict of my fear to become a single mam and the torment of the abuse I lived with, it wasn't long before my contraception failed me AGAIN! I needed a miracle and thought maybe this would change things, it was naive but I tried. My boyfriend was livid. I thought he'd come around once the shock wore off but he didn't. My opinion didn't matter, he pulled all the strings in my life. He had control of every-thing, or so I believed at the time. As is typical in abusive relation-ships, I lived in fear of life with him and without him.

Before I knew it, we had an appointment in a family planning clinic. He was at the helm of every decision and one step in front of me the whole way. He was in the room in the clinic watching the screen as the doctor checked to confirm a heartbeat – they said they had to confirm it before they could make any arrangements, I couldn't look, I was sick. My heart was breaking. The clinic arranged the termination to be done in Holland: they told us the UK did too many every day so they wouldn't take as good care of me as they would in Holland. His mind was made up and I wasn't allowed a voice, I wasn't to discuss it or bring it up again. He told me I had to terminate the pregnancy or he'd walk away from me and our first child, that I'd have to explain why and cope with having two kids by myself. I was silenced in my fear. I was under his control and felt weak, worthless. But still I pleaded with him to reconsider. I held my stomach and I talked about the due date; he looked at me with a demonic stare and warned me to shut up. He arranged the flights and hotel and the money required. I was sworn to secrecy, not only by my boyfriend but by society. It wasn't something to be discussed or revealed.

He took our toddler to his parents under the pretence that he was taking me away for a weekend break. The night before we were due to travel, he was out drinking at a work party. I prayed he wouldn't come home so we'd miss the flight but I cried myself to sleep and he came home.

He booked the taxi and got us to the airport. It only took one look from him to send chills down my spine so I knew not to try anything. We landed in a country where people were speaking a foreign language, the signs were foreign, the place was foreign and the people were foreign. I was foreign, a stranger to them. I was terrified the closer it got but couldn't call for help then, I didn't know where I was and he had all the money. He repeatedly warned me that I couldn't back out. In the clinic I was in the medical chair in a gown and I couldn't stop crying. At the moment I begged them not to do it, with tears streaming down my face, they put me to sleep.

When I woke the nightmare wasn't over. I clutched my stomach and I wailed, I prayed that it would be one of the 'unsuccessful' procedures that I'd read about. I had pleaded with all of my might at that last moment for it all to stop but he was there by my side through the whole thing while the nurse shushed me and put me to sleep. I wasn't 'at home'. I didn't know these streets, the people, their language or their rules. I didn't know who I could call to save me from him or to take me somewhere safe. It was a foreign country; I had no money and couldn't run or ask for help. He was my only way home to the country that doesn't trust me, or trust women to walk in or out of a clinic on streets they know. It's taken me a very long time to stop blaming myself for not being stronger, for not standing up to him, for not being braver. Someday I hope to forgive myself for not finding a way out, to stop it from happening. I eventually did realise that I was stronger as a single mother, and I finally walked away from him for good.

Our country needs to trust women to make the right choice for their bodies, their lives. The Eighth Amendment helps abusers

to isolate their vulnerable girlfriends away from home, the Eighth silences women. A No vote won't stop abortions, it just stops people accessing safe abortions, legal services in the country they call home, where they have more chance of feeling safe and some hope of getting help and support when needed.

I deeply regret my abortion, I regret being coerced and manipulated, feeling forced into it and abandoned so many miles from home. I regret the shame in our country and being terrified to call out for help before reaching the airport, for fear of judgement or worse still, punishment. I regret the lack of support I had as a victim in an abusive relationship and the lack of support to parent alone. I regret so much of it because I didn't have a choice, which is wrong: we should absolutely have a choice and I implore people to please vote in favour of choice. The Love Both campaign claims to be pro-life but they're not, they're pro-birth and to hell with what happens after birth. We have a country where single parents still struggle and are stigmatised; our foster care services are under excessive pressure and adoption processes are far from ideal. So to take away a woman's right to essential healthcare on top of this broken system is completely unethical. Regretting my abortion does not mean I would vote No. Abortion wasn't the right option for me and I'm certain others who regret theirs would agree. It's the most difficult decision a woman should ever have to make, so it's imperative that it IS the woman's decision.

We need a Yes vote to keep women safe. We need our country to trust us, and to respect our choice whether to keep a pregnancy or not. We need to move forward; we need to repeal the Eighth.

XXI

I was sixteen, it was the mid-1990s. I don't think we even had divorce yet in Ireland. It was my first relationship, if you could even call it that at that age. He came from the new family who had moved into our small town and for some reason I was drawn to him. I was in 6th year at school, top of all my classes. Nice little weekend job at the local café and good circle of friends. This guy, Dave we'll call him. He told me that all the girls where he'd come from were having sex for years at my age. He called me a backwards culchie & said when I got to college that September that nobody would be into me cos they'd all know I was frigid. He said he'd met my father in the bar and even my father told him to 'break her in'.

I was such an idiot that I believed every word he said. I now know, after years of denial & eventual counselling, that he was technically grooming me and that what happened that night was rape. He told me he'd done me a favour and that I should be grateful. I eventually saw sense and realised that he was a bad guy and I got away from him.

Unfortunately, I was pregnant by then. I had to visit the hospital to get a test done in my school uniform as I was supposed to be at after-school study. They sent the results to my GP who I then had to attend the next week to find out the result – again in my school uniform. My GP told me it was positive and we worked out I was about ten weeks by then.

He told me there were some special homes I could go live in until the baby was born. He said there was one he knew in Dublin and they'd look after me. He told me that was probably the best thing as the whole town would be talking about me in no time. I'd be mortified and my family would be destroyed. He also told me I had 24 hours to tell my parents or else he would.

My parents didn't even know I had a boyfriend. They are lovely people but typically old-fashioned Irish, very religious and heavily involved in the community. Terrified doesn't come close to describing how I felt. I was sixteen, pregnant and alone. The confusion was insurmountable.

I confided in an older cousin that evening who told me to keep it a secret and get an abortion. She told me the rough details of how to go about arranging one. I was trying to figure out how to get off school, how to get the money together and how to get out of the country without anyone finding out. My cousin was a great support but she'd no money. I had about £120 in the post office but that wasn't near enough. Plus I had to get to a travel agent to book the boat, we'd no phone in the house and the internet hadn't been invented. I was trying to process all of this knowing I had less than a day before the GP told my parents.

I took the hard route. I had no other option other than to seek the support of my parents. I told my parents the next afternoon. My mother was shell-shocked, my father shouted & roared. Threw things around. Called my siblings into the room and told them, 'Look what she has done to all of us.' I was called awful names by them. It was an incredibly traumatic evening.

The next day I approached my still silent mother. I asked her to help me 'go on the boat'. Never before or since have I seen such repulsion & vehemence on her face. Now she found her voice and told me that it was bad enough her daughter was a hussy but she could never live with herself knowing her daughter was also a murderer! In my bedroom all that evening and night I planned my suicide. It was the only solution. There was simply nothing else to be done. The next morning my mother came to me and said that even though she didn't agree with it she would try and get the money together.

The next couple of days were a rollercoaster. I didn't want an abortion but I didn't want a baby either. I *was* a baby. Nobody spoke to me. I was kept home from school. No visitors allowed. Then I was sent to a cousin's house for a week or so. When I came home, Mum told me that there was no money. If I wanted to go on the boat, I would have to arrange it myself. By this stage I was twelve weeks pregnant. My leaving cert mock exams were looming.

Back in school that week, the rumours were rife. The career guidance counsellor called me into her office and asked me if they were true. I told her they were. When she heard I was over the twelve weeks she said it was too late to have an abortion. I said this to my mother that evening and she replied, 'Well you made your bed – you may lie in it now.'

I tried to find out how to cause a miscarriage but I couldn't bring myself to do it. I had one good friend, I told her everything and without her unwavering support I would have killed myself that night.

I spent the rest of the pregnancy knowing I was the talk of the town. I didn't stand up for myself when people slagged me off or crossed the street in disgust. My dying grandfather's last words to me were, 'You're a terrible daughter – you broke your mother's heart.' Not one single person ever asked how I'd got pregnant. It was just assumed I was a slut.

I swung between loving my baby to resenting it, many times a day. I missed hospital visits because I couldn't bear all the older women & couples looking at me in disgust as we shared the waiting room. I sat my leaving cert obviously pregnant. One examiner exclaimed loudly that they couldn't supervise the room I was in as they were so offended by my presence.

Eventually the baby was born. When I knew the day was drawing near, I got a little excited. I had decided I would do my best to look after this poor baby. Then I swung back into sheer panic. I was allowed live at home but I was told the baby was wholly my responsibility and to never ask for any help. I wished again & again that somehow I could have had an abortion.

I had a baby girl. She was a beautiful baby. She was also a very ill baby. She had to be resuscitated a couple times at birth, she had heart & lung problems. After a while in intensive care in Dublin they found out she had a disability. My family are carriers. We didn't know until we had tests. My sisters have decided to never have children because of it and I have a suspicion that one sister had an abortion because of it.

Since then my daughter has needed full-time care. She is now an adult. I have never had another relationship or any further children. My life is spent looking after my daughter's needs. I work during the few hours she is at day services. She is a happy, beautiful soul, trapped in a broken body. She is oblivious to her traumatic beginnings and I'm thankful that she will never experience it first-hand.

I will say this here for the purposes of this post only: I often wonder how different my life would have been had abortion been more accessible in Ireland. In times when I'm exhausted from looking after her, I wish I'd had an abortion. Or at least, I wish I'd had the choice. An available choice. I may have chosen to keep the pregnancy anyway.

Repeal the Eighth so that women, daughters, sisters & mothers can have at least the basic amount of sensible real-time support in the event of a pregnancy. Only then will Ireland's attitude change for the better and girls here will live their lives a little easier.

XXII

Eight years ago, myself & my husband were days away from the induction of our second son. I was almost 39 weeks pregnant. We had all the plans made, Babygros, baby hat, teddy bear, all ready for his arrival. However, these plans were not made for his life, they were made for his death.

At our 31-week scan, we discovered that all was not well with our much-wanted son. We had brought our first son to the scan with us so he could share in the excitement of his new sibling. The scan went on for what felt like an eternity, but we were oblivious until the doctor said that there was an issue with our son's heart and brain. There was no consultant there for us to talk to, so we were sent home and had to come back a few days later. After two further appointments and an amniocentesis, it was confirmed that our beloved son had Edwards' syndrome[26] and my son would not live after birth.

We immediately asked about having an early induction, but were told were not allowed at that time and we would have to wait until I was full term before an induction could be done. It was a 'process' that we had to go through. We received no other choices and we were sent on our way with instructions to come back every week for a scan.

The following weeks and scans were horrific. Going into the maternity hospital every week to see if our son was still alive was unbearable. I had two mental breakdowns: one happened on my birthday and I was hospitalised for four days. My mind had gone into shock and my body started to violently shake. I was not able to stop the shaking, the doctors thought I could be helped by thinking happy thoughts. It was decided that I needed to be medicated. I was unable to look after my son, so my mother had to move in with us.

My husband had to continue to work every day, pretending all was OK with the pregnancy. How he managed I'll never know. He was also planning our son's funeral and helping me through the many hysterical crying fits. We clung to the hope that our son would live through his birth so we could look into his eyes and he could feel our kiss before he died. However, knowing that we would have to watch him die in our arms just haunted us.

So, after eight weeks of hell, we arrived at our induction date. We were sent for our final scan & there was no heartbeat. We were too late. He had died approximately four days earlier. All that suffering was in vain. We would never get that kiss after all.

The following morning our son came silently into this world. He was so fragile and he was the first dead person I had ever touched. Our hearts were shattered. We had his funeral two days later, his teddy bear with him in his tiny white coffin. He was buried with my grandmother.

Eight years later I am still profoundly affected by our experience. Our choice was to have an early induction but the Eighth said we couldn't. We had no choice, nothing. I was forced to be life support for our dying son for eight weeks. Eight weeks! However, we consider ourselves lucky. We got to say goodbye to our son in our own country. We left the hospital with our son's tiny white coffin between us in the back of the funeral car. He had a lovely funeral. We were surrounded by our loving family at all times.

Was it worth waiting eight weeks? My answer is no. The mental and physical torture was too high a price to pay. It should never happen to anyone. The Eighth must be repealed. Please give us parents the choices we deserve. Not every pregnancy has a happy ending or is black and white. Please vote Yes on May 25th. I beg you. Thank you.

XXIII

I lost my firstborn two years ago at just six months old to a terminal genetic condition. We were told it was unlikely to happen again so we started trying for another little one. I'm now just over fourteen weeks pregnant and last week we received results from a CVS[27] test. It has happened again. Our desperately wanted and loved baby is also sick.

We were told this in a very kind and gentle way and then that was it. No help, no phone numbers, no direction in which to go. I spent the last week trying to contact hospitals in the UK to see if they could take us. Having to explain and ask if we could talk to someone about a termination several times made this awful, heartbreaking situation so much worse.

This has broken me. We were lost after losing our firstborn but it was a terrible situation that nobody had control over. This, however, is just cruel. Pure and simple. I hate this country and its old ways of just ignoring the problem until it goes away. Having to wait a couple of weeks, grieving the baby I still have growing in me, is a torture that no woman should have to go through. I'm so sad and so, so angry.

The procedure will be done on Wednesday in the UK, away from our supportive families in a country we don't know. We have been abandoned and it's so cold and cruel. I've never felt so alone.

XXIV

I entered into my first sexual relationship when I was eighteen and I, being a natural worrier and then having the fear of god if I ever got pregnant, was overly careful. I was on the pill and we used condoms and I thought everything was great.

Until it wasn't. I started to have terrible stomach pains one evening while I was at work. This had happened before as I had problems with cysts since starting my contraceptive the year before. I went home that evening after a nightshift. I woke that afternoon to a pain so excruciating I struggled to speak in coherent sentences. My boyfriend woke and jumped out of the bed and helped me up. We both realised quickly that the white sheets were covered in blood. I had soaked through my underwear onto the bed. It looked like a horror scene.

We rushed to the doctor's office, which was close to us. I knew her well. She was our family doctor and had prescribed me my contraception and had helped through all the health issues. She was achingly kind and horrified at how much pain I was in. She asked me if I'd done a pregnancy test. I told her straight out there was no way I could be pregnant. No way. She asked me when I was due my period. I realised I was a week late. She took a test and told me there was a chance I could be very early-stage pregnant – no more than a few weeks. She told me that most people don't even know they are pregnant at this stage but I could be having a massive bleed. I needed to go to hospital.

I begged for pain medication. From the second that test came out I was treated differently. She told me under Irish law I could not get pain medication as it could harm the baby. The baby we weren't even sure was there. I don't remember how I got to the hospital. The whole day seems like a blur. With hindsight I realise that's because I was drifting in and out of consciousness because of the pain. The pain. That I can remember. Vividly. Every single time I walk into a hospital and smell that clinical smell the pain comes back to me in waves, like being doused in a bucket of ice-cold water. By the time we got to the hospital it was late afternoon and the place was jammed. I waited for hours to see the triage nurse, she made me take a pregnancy test when she heard my symptoms and saw the referral letter. I was told to wait – still no pain relief of any kind. Another hour or so passed when I was called in again and told the test was still not conclusive. I was still in total agony at this stage and had bled through my clothes and the dressing gown I was wearing to cover the stains. I also bled onto the seats. My boyfriend had his shift starting – I told him to go to work and that I would be fine. I didn't tell my parents at this stage. I was so afraid they would be so angry that I had possibly got pregnant.

The day is so hazy. I remember begging for pain relief and being told that I couldn't have it in case it damaged the baby. After I collapsed going to the bathroom I was put into a bed in a corridor. They kept taking about getting a scan to see if I was miscarrying. They had no free technicians. I stopped listening and begged them for pain relief. I don't remember the details so well. I remember they kept talking to me about 'the baby'. I kept thinking about the pain. I wanted the pain to stop. At one point I wished I was dead. I was in and out on consciousness. I was woken eventually when someone came and gave me pain relief. They had done two more pregnancy tests within an hour of each other. Both apparently 'seemed normal'. I still don't know what that meant.

I was told by a nurse that a doctor would come and explain. Later, when the pain relief had started to kick in and the bleeding was stopping, I was now on fluids because of dehydration and they had also put me on meds for blood clots. I never had that scan. It was a young male doctor who had explained the final result. He was tired and had a cold demeanour. He only explained the medication he was giving. He told me he was discharging me. I asked him had I been pregnant. I will never forget what he said. 'We're not sure, it doesn't matter now anyway because the worst is over.' It doesn't matter anyway? It mattered hours before while I cried in agony. That's when I learned that my life did not matter as much as a possible foetus. As soon as I became sexually active I became nothing but a possible incubator. All the other times I had had a cyst burst I had been treated like a human because I had not been having sex. This time I was nothing more than a life-support machine. At one point they thought it was a baby. To this day, I still don't know if I was pregnant or not. But I grieved the loss of a baby and felt incredible shame that I had brought all this on myself.

I didn't tell my family the full extent of what happened for years after. There are parts of the aftermath of that incident and I can't and won't talk about. My relationship with that boyfriend fizzled out for many reasons but one of them was because I couldn't look at him without thinking of that day. The whisper of miscarriage went to both families but we didn't discuss it fully and we were both treated differently than we were before. It was hidden and we were made to feel like it was something not to be talked about.

I didn't talk about it again for three years until I told my current partner. He held me while I bawled because we'd been watching something on TV with the topic of miscarriage. After I told him, my shame came out in abundance. I had so much shame. I still do. I still feel like I am a drama queen to be so affected. I still feel like I am not worthy to be a mother. I still feel like even though I tried to be responsible, I was still a disgrace. He, because he is wonderful, loved me anyway.

The biggest impact? I had a scan recently and was told that I had scarring on the uterus wall, more than likely from a haemorrhage of a cyst. This could impact me having children in the future. It will more than likely mean I will miscarry at some point. I am terrified. I would love to be a mother one day. My partner of many years now is the kindest man I have ever encountered. He is decent and supportive and so very angry at what I have had to go through. He was made to be a dad. He will make the most wonderful father one day. I feel guilty that he may not be a dad because of me. I still have shame. This incident has meant we will start trying sooner than we planned to help our chances. This still terrifies me.

I was naive and didn't ask questions at eighteen. I get so very angry when I hear people saying 'love both'. That is a lie. Not ONE doctor or nurse had any concern for me. All they cared about was that 'baby'. I don't blame them though. They were busy and under-staffed and they have laws to follow. I am not angry at them. I am angry at a country that allows this and countless other things like it to happen to women like me.

No one mentioned the Eighth Amendment and I guarantee I would have heard it from the rooftops had I not miscarried and decided to get an abortion. Yet the Eighth Amendment is why I was treated the way I was. I was nothing but an inconvenience and they had to put that possible baby first. I was not equal. I was inferior. I continued to feel inferior for the next eight years. If anyone thinks the Eighth Amendment is about abortion then take it from me, it's not. It's about healthcare, medical consent and human rights. My story is not as heartbreaking as so many others I have read. I am one of the lucky ones. Yet I found writing this gut-wrenchingly difficult. I felt I needed to release some of that guilt and show that this referendum is not all about abortion.

It is the bravery of Irish women standing up and saying enough is enough. This page has given me a huge amount of courage to tell my small story and I will be holding my head up high while I walk hand in hand with my partner and we vote Yes in the referendum.

XXV

In November 1976 I turned 19. The memory I have of the weeks after my birthday is of checking time and time again to see if I'd finally started my period.

My first boyfriend had just broken up with me. I'd miscalculated my fertile dates. We'd been very much in love but were both a bit green about accessibility to condoms or the pill. All I knew was that I didn't want to be pregnant; I was far too young and not ready to be a parent. What I wanted was an abortion; what I didn't have was the knowledge of how to get one.

I had sympathetic bosses who arranged a job transfer from Dublin to a different city and I moved there when I was 15 weeks pregnant. This allowed me to have some privacy, which was especially important as it seemed at that point that I'd have no realistic option but to go down the adoption route. I did not tell my family that I was pregnant. I also did not want neighbours knowing my story.

My new colleagues were welcoming and supportive. They had found me a bedsit in a fairly rundown part of town, for which I was most grateful. But I soon discovered how uncomfortable it was living in a dingy, damp place. With hindsight, I see the judgement implicit in that choice of location. I cringe at my gratitude, my naivety at not seeing the underlying assumption that this was good enough for the kind of girl I was. After all, I was going to be an *unmarried mother*.

I just got on with it. My relationship was off and, although we spoke occasionally, I did not let go easily. I had good friends who supported me but I felt so deeply that this was my mistake, therefore my responsibility to sort it. The adoption 'solution' hung heavily over me. I only knew of two girls who had been in my situation: one had secretly given up her baby, the other had kept her child with support from her partner and family.

I saw a social worker from a Catholic adoption society, a young woman without warmth or sympathy. I was independent, not beholden to a mother and baby home and it was clearly not a situation she was used to. I told her that I didn't see how I could possibly make any decisions until my baby was born, although adoption was certainly something I would have to consider. I gave her an edited version of my background, that my father had died seven years ago. I mentioned the private schools and respectable family – anything I thought would put me and therefore my baby in the best light. I did not disclose that my mother was a manic depressive who spent three to four months every year in St Patrick's; that my home life was dysfunctional and that I was the 'responsible' one of three siblings, the one who tried to keep home life going.

As soon as my bump was visible, I was given notice to leave the bedsit. Luckily I found a sympathetic landlord who was willing to rent to me as long as I promised not to bring the baby back there. I agreed, glad to have a roof over my head. It was a nicer area and I felt safer there.

The due date of 5 August 1977 came and went. When I was overdue by ten days I was admitted to be induced. After a 24-hour labour I underwent an emergency Caesarean and gave birth to a healthy, beautiful baby boy. I called him Damian.

A nurse from the hospital informed the social worker that I'd given birth and she came to see me two days later. Back on the ward I was refused access to my son by hospital staff, the idea being that as he was possibly going to be adopted, I shouldn't bond with him. After numerous unsuccessful requests I caused ructions until I was put in a wheelchair and brought to him. Then I could finally hold him. I knew I could not let him go. I recall so vividly my tears dropping on his little blond head.

His dad, who'd travelled from Dublin, was also refused access to see him, even through a window. I saw him three times and fed him once. Then I was told that he'd be moved on to The Nursery in Bessborough, where he'd be taken care of, and I would have five weeks to make my decision. I asked to see him before he left the hospital and I was allowed to say goodbye. I was so sad, so empty. I couldn't stop crying, I was a mother, but had no baby.

Before I went back to Dublin, I asked the social worker to make arrangements to see Damian. His father and I saw him once in Bessborough. It was a horrendous experience as we had no privacy and were watched the whole time. On numerous occasions I tried to see my son at the agency instead, but was told each time that he either had or was recovering from a small infection. When he was two months old, I was told that Damian had been placed with wonderful adoptive parents and was now called Paul. I decided that I would sign the final papers sooner than legally required in order to take away the uncertainty that his new 'parents' must be feeling.

In November the social worker called to inform me that Damian had been found dead in his cot – probable cause being cot death aka SIDS (Sudden Infant Death Syndrome) – and that his adoptive parents were devastated. His funeral would take place in a matter of days. The same evening a priest, who was connected to the adoption agency, telephoned to confirm when and where the funeral would take place. I was told that I should not attend as the adoptive parents didn't want us there; the paperwork had yet to be signed and it was with reluctance and only because of their legal obligation that they were keeping me informed.

Damian's father and I attended the funeral; the adoptive parents did not attend. There was a short religious ceremony and then Damian was carried in a shoebox-like white coffin to be buried. I have thought of this couple so often over the years, imagining how devastating their experience must have been.

In late 2011, after I'd lived abroad and then come back to Ireland, I decided to delve more into the details of the adoption. I believed that I'd come to terms with the loss as well as the horrendous coldness and cruelty, the judgemental society that had caused me such gut-wrenching pain. I contacted the HSE who put me in touch with Tusla.

What I found profoundly shocked me. There were gaping errors in the original notes: details of Damian's burial, for example, were not entered into the cemetery records, his birthdate was recorded incorrectly and medical records showed that he was not thriving while he was in The Nursery. A medical examination at eight weeks indicates he was 'very thin', having only gained 2 lbs in their care. The doctor recommended for him to be moved to a foster home. It was at this foster home that he was cared for, gained weight and recovered from his time at The Nursery. The medical examination done the day before he died stated that he was well and fit for adoption.

Thirty-four years later I came to find out the truth. There were no devastated adoptive parents. He was not called Paul. He was not 'doing very well' as claimed in the letter from the social worker. His foster mother had been the one to find his lifeless little body and deal with the Garda and whatever else had to be done. She has since passed away, but her daughter told me that she was bullied and forbidden to attend the funeral by someone involved with the adoption agency. Her daughter remembered Damian well and she told me he had been splashing and laughing in his bath the night before he died. This picture in my mind means the world to me, as I know he experienced some love and affection for the short time he lived with the family. This was obviously not the case for his time in the nursery. Why all the lies?

Mine is a story of not having the choice to have the abortion I wanted. The sense of guilt, loss and sadness have altered somewhat, but they never leave me. Nor does the memory of Damian, holding my finger as babies do, my tears falling on his blond hair. I knew then and I know now that an abortion would have been the right decision for me. I would perhaps still have feelings of loss and sadness but I would have had the choice to make *my own decision*. Please, please vote to Repeal the Eighth, so girls and women have the choice to handle their lives as they want.

XXVI

I was born to first-time teenage parents in the early eighties. From as far back as I can remember, maybe from the age of four, I was sexually and physically abused by my father. This abuse continued frequently, sometimes daily, for about nine years until he finally left the family home. My story is not uncommon, sad but true. I endured abuse under threat to myself, my mother, and most effective of all, the threat that my sisters would be abused. I endured in silence, in fear, in anguish, in anger and in despair. I knew what was being done to me was wrong but I could see no way out without someone else suffering. As I got a little older, I became aware that what was being done to me might lead me to become pregnant. I knew I would kill myself if that happened. There was a pair of scissors in the house and I often visualised lodging them on the taps in the bath and plunging myself onto them and slipping into the warm water. I was eleven or twelve years old.

One vivid memory I have is of the X Case being on the news. I was alone in the living room with my father who was undergoing some sort of religious conversion. He took to repeatedly citing passages of the Bible to me as if I was the person who had committed some evil act. On this day, as I sat at the table in my uniform doing my homework, he asked me what I thought about the case. I said I believed the girl should be allowed an abortion. I couldn't articulate the words because she had been raped quite possibly by her own father, suffering the same fate that I had for years. Instead, when he pressed me, I said children shouldn't be having children. He said abortion was murder. Children were a gift from god and not having children was a punishment. He said that his own sister was a slut who had so many men that her womb rotted and she couldn't have children. The hypocrisy was startling yet I felt powerless by his words just as if he had me pinned to the bed. The law was being used to disempower victims of sexual violence. I understood that and knew it had to change.

I eventually found my voice some years later when I learned that he had raped another child. I had naively thought that in keeping the secret I was sparing other girls, my sisters, friends, cousins, the same fate. I sought justice for myself and achieved it in some measure though sacrificed my privacy to do so. I pursued a career in human rights law, advocating for the rights of children and woman affected by sexual violence, abuse and exploitation and continue to find a way to help the disempowered. I am lucky. I've met countless women who shared my history and were consumed by it, unable to overcome the societal barriers that victims face – some suffering, even dying by their own hand. I'm still haunted by my past but I have my voice and I will use it for myself and for those who feel unable to. I won't stand by and let our society disempower women and girls a second longer. The Eighth Amendment is a tool of female oppression. It's time for change.

XXVII

I never thought I would be writing to In Her Shoes again. Yesterday, when I was driving home from work, I heard that there was a GDPR[28] breach on a patient from Holles Street hospital. This woman had chosen to end her pregnancy in dignity and in privacy but instead she received a text message from a rogue crisis pregnancy agency in Dublin. The message described where the 'clinic' was and the lady soon got a call – from a male – giving her abuse for *her* choice. The lady who received this call bravely shared her story in social media to warn other pregnant people. This made me so angry as I was a victim of a rogue crisis pregnancy agency called Gianna Care.

I am writing again to share my experience with these people so that another person will not be hurt or manipulated like I was. I hope that this story will educate all people who can get pregnant and (hopefully) bring about a ban on these 'clinics'.

My loving, caring boyfriend was there by my side when the Clearblue test told us I was 1–2 weeks pregnant. It was March 2017. I had just turned 24 and had applied to college as a mature student. I was looking forward to studying and having a new career. My boyfriend had just started his new job in a career that he loved. Everything was great until that evening when I took that Clearblue test. We panicked at the thought of being parents; we had no money and we lived with our families. I was only getting a little above minimum wage in a full-time job and I could barely afford petrol to get to work most days. It was a crisis. We talked about the pros and cons if I was to continue with the pregnancy but there were more cons than pros – we looked into ending the pregnancy. With a heavy heart we knew it was the best thing. It was not easy.

While my boyfriend was in training with his new job he could not come to appointments although he tried to convince me that he would leave the job to be there, but I made sure he stayed. I could sort this on my own. So I thought. I researched around for information, I got hold of Reproductive Choices, a clinic on Berkeley Street run by Marie Stopes International. I could get my assessment done there and fly out to the UK to have the abortion. Simple. I made my way to Dublin to attend the appointment. I was nervous as you can imagine, I had my Google maps on my phone to make sure I was going to the right place. I was walking up towards Berkeley Street and I obviously looked lost. I thought that there would be a protester, something you'd see in *Juno* (LOL) but there were just two ladies having a chat on the street, nothing I would've thought to be suspicious. I looked up at the green-framed clinic and one of the ladies said to me, 'You going in there?'

I told her I was, thinking something had happened.

'Did you pay for your appointment? We do free scans in our clinic, you should try us out,' said the lady.

The other lady was much younger – I'd say in her thirties – and she handed me a leaflet, but the lady who'd first approached me distracted me from reading it and asked when my appointment was. I told her it wasn't for another 35 minutes. She got overexcited and the younger lady said, 'I'll bring you to our clinic; it's only around the corner [on Upper Dorset Street].'

I naively agreed to go with this one. The older lady told us she would meet us there as she needed to go to the shop.

What made me go with these ladies? What made me go to the clinic with some random person on the street? I was extremely isolated, I had to hide this all from family and it's much harder when you live with them. These women seemed liked they cared about my welfare and wanted to help me. That all changed once I entered the building of this fake clinic. There was a desk with a computer and a little kitchenette in the corner with teacups and a kettle. In the middle of the room they had black leather couches with a coffee table and a little plate of biscuits. On the walls were pictures of foetuses at weekly development along with prayers and certs of volunteers' counselling-skills courses.

I sat down and immediately felt uneasy. The younger lady put the kettle on and gave me a form to fill out. General questions: GP, number, email, date of last period and next of kin. As soon as I finished filling out the form the older lady came to the office and they both sat across from me. They started to ask If I was in a relationship, so I was telling them all about my boyfriend and then they asked about my family and parents & my job and they seemed like genuine getting-to-know-you questions and they acted like they had an interest in me.

Then the bomb dropped. The older lady asked me, 'Why were you going into Reproductive Choices?'

I explained my situation and the younger lady replied, 'You are aware that you are going to kill your unborn baby?'

It was then I knew I was trapped. I thought, *Fuck – what am I going to do?* So I just played nice and tried to agree with the reasons they were giving me not to have an abortion. The older lady said that if I was going to end my pregnancy, I'd get breast cancer and lose my reproductive organs. I remember saying that can't be true (I work in the medical sector). The younger lady said confidently that they have evidence from medical journals. They were telling

me stories of other women who they saved from 'post-abortion syndrome' (DOES NOT EXIST), that they refer women to a retreat called Rachel's Vineyard after their abortions. They told me my relationship with my boyfriend would be ruined. They said that I would ruin my life and regret my choice. They told me that my dad (who passed away in February 2016) would be disappointed in me and that a grandchild would heal my mother's grief of losing her husband and that if I abort it will be a selfish act.

I felt completely attacked by this point but I challenged them. I did not want to carry this pregnancy, I told them. Adoption was not an option and I could not afford to raise a child. They said that they could offer financial assistance. I asked them, 'What if my family won't support me?' They said that they could offer a 'companion' to attend appointments with me. I told them both that I wasn't ready. At this point they tried to break me and got frustrated and the younger lady said in a stern tone, 'Your baby is made out of love! Think of those who don't have that!'

I was taken back and the older lady had to intervene. They then persuaded me to have a scan. I said that I had ten minutes until my appointment. They were quick to say, 'Forget them – you're with us and we will take care of you here. They only care about your money and not you.' I went upstairs where they had a sonogram machine and boxes of donated clothes. The younger lady put the scan in front of me and said, 'You'll see your baby's heartbeat and realise it's yours.' I just smiled.

She couldn't find the pregnancy. She tried pressing harder into my pelvis but no luck, I was too early for an abdominal scan. I needed a vaginal scan. They said that they could bring me to the Beacon Hospital to see their doctor. I said, 'I've paid for my appointment so I'll go to Reproductive Choices.' The older lady said they could refund my money but I said I'd rather go to them as it's closer. They knew they had to let me go.

The younger lady said she'd phone me later and I just thanked them. They handed me a brown envelope with leaflets and pro-life foetal development cards and a pack of folic acid supplements. I ran over to Berkeley Street to the green-framed building.

Once at Reproductive Choices I explained to them what happened and why I was late. The midwife was so kind I started to cry and she made me a sweet tea and advised me to call the Gardaí as other women had been targeted by them when entering the clinic. She scanned me and said, 'It's just not your time yet,' and smiled empathically at me. She understood how I felt and took MY welfare into account. She showed me all her certs, that she was qualified to read and use sonograms, and her nursing qualifications.

The lady from Gianna Care who scanned me did not have any qualifications to use or read scans. I could've walked away from Gianna Care thinking there was nothing wrong because they are not medical professionals. The midwife told me that I was very early and I had to come back next week. I had to look out the peephole on the door before leaving the clinic to see if the same ladies from Gianna Care were waiting for me outside, which the older lady was. I opened the door and the older lady said, 'How did you get on?'

I told her to fuck off and walked away as fast as I could. I went to a bar on South William street and ordered two cocktails and started to cry, I was afraid that all the information they got out of me would be put on social media and that they would contact my family or my boyfriend's workplace.

Gianna Care rang me an hour later to apologise for waiting outside and asked me how I felt. I just said thank you and that I was keeping the pregnancy and would see them next week. As soon as I hung up, I blocked the number and thankfully never heard from them again. The following week I brought my friend to Reproductive Choices and we swapped coats and I had a scarf over my head and glasses on as we passed another two ladies outside the clinic. I thought I was going to be sick but thankfully I had my friend with me to tell them to go away. I travelled to Manchester a week later to get the abortion pill.

Five weeks after I travelled, I ended up in hospital due to an 'incomplete abortion'. I was given a D&C and strong antibiotics. I was told if I had left my symptoms any longer, I would've gone into septic shock. Due to the lack of aftercare given to women after they travel to have an abortion, I was too afraid to see IFPA or Reproductive Choices because I was so afraid of bumping into the ladies again. I had no trust in any organisation.

My family could've buried me at 24 years old because of Gianna Care. I was lucky I just went straight to the hospital but had I been a younger person it could have been fatal. I ask all who read this please contact your TDs and Simon Harris. Share your story if you were affected by these people, share my story if you have to. WE NEED TO SHUT THESE FAKE CLINICS DOWN NOW FOR THE SAFETY OF PREGNANT PEOPLE.

XXVIII

I was 29, I should have known better. It was a one-night stand. I really should have known better. I took the morning-after pill. Neither this nor the one-night stand were a habit of mine but I'd taken the steps to correct my irresponsible behaviour.

Four weeks later I felt off. I didn't notice I was late and didn't worry, sure that pill does funny things to your cycle. I couldn't smoke, the cigarettes I'd always loved were making me gag. Then I noticed that my breasts were sore, really sore. Moving my arms and brushing against them caused pain. The penny dropped. Where was my period? I bought a test. I was pregnant.

If I was ever going to have a baby now was a good time. I was in a decent job, I had no excuses. But I'd never wanted to be pregnant, I never got that urge. Also, I never felt mentally well enough to care for another person. I'd struggled with my mental health all my life and a pregnancy meant I'd have to come off my antidepressants. This wasn't an option for me. I knew what I needed to do. I went to the clinic and they helped me to arrange everything.

I took a day off work, drove to the airport and boarded my flight. I was quite cold in my mindset but I knew that this was what I needed to do. Maybe I deserved it for being an idiot, maybe this was karma.

On the day of my appointment I was nine weeks along. I waited for the guilt. I wondered why it didn't come. I was so sure what I was doing was wrong and selfish but I never felt the guilt. I even asked the doctor in the clinic to show me the ultrasound. This was my absolute test. Surely I'd feel guilt when I saw it. No, I saw something the size of a peanut that had caused me weeks of sleepless nights, that was going to cause me months and maybe years of mental health challenges. I was certain.

I woke up and felt relief. I shouldn't have done it only a few hours after an anaesthetic but I drove home from the airport. What was the alternative? I went back to my life and pretended nothing had happened, keeping my secret.

A few weeks later I was still spotting. Who could I ask? I certainly couldn't tell my GP, it'd be on my medical history that I'd had an abortion. I was sure it'd stop when it all settled down and my periods returned to normal.

Six weeks after my abortion I was rushed from work to the hospital with heavy and uncontrollable bleeding. I would later learn that I'd had a post-abortive infection. I was fast-tracked through A&E and admitted immediately.

I spent four days in hospital. This was now definitely going to be on my medical history yet what kept me up at night was, what excuse could I use to justify being hospitalised? The care I received was excellent, the staff were lovely, but while they tried to treat me for a severe infection in my uterus, my biggest concern was the fear of anyone knowing the truth. I'm not sorry. I did what was right for me. What happened to me was a direct result of the shame and stigma that prevented me seeking help earlier.

Looking back, I feel very lucky. I knew immediately what was right for me and I had the money to follow through. I never once regretted my decision or wondered what might have been but I'm furious that I was allowed to become sick enough to be rushed to hospital.

Today I fight with thousands of people to break down that stigma.

XXIX

My family and closest friends still don't know to this day that I was pregnant. I never want them to know because of the shame I would feel if they did.

My relationship with the father, while I cared about him deeply, was unstable to say the least. It was a non-exclusive arrangement, but he sometimes became possessive, hovering imposingly if I was talking to male friends. He showed aggression on occasion – he never became physical, but it shook me enough to intervene. He had issues with his family and despite horror stories of their treatment of each other, he still kept them close, the cycle of behaviour repeating again and again. He also had substance-abuse issues.

I had mental health issues myself. For the most part I was OK, but there were days when just being able to keep going was an exhausting struggle. I managed, but only just about.

When I realised I was pregnant, everything became clear: if things were unstable now when life was relatively uncomplicated and it was only me and him to think about, how would things be when a child completely reliant on us came into the picture? The fact that I hadn't told my family about his presence in my life and the fact that I couldn't trust him enough to tell him I was pregnant spoke volumes. Would he be there? Would I be largely on my own, scraping to provide? Would I be able to afford to move to accommodation suitable for a child when I could barely afford what I was renting at the time? If he was there, would he be able to keep his cool, stay sober and make sure the issues that were continuing in his home life did not spill over and affect this child? Maybe he could, but it would be a miracle I couldn't rely on.

Regarding my own stability, I'd heard that you'd find wells of strength you never knew you had when you became a mother: but what happened when the wells didn't provide and things were tough? Life isn't perfect, but if you don't have a stable foundation you can't build on it and the situation at the time was no foundation for a happy, healthy human life.

I was certain I wanted to terminate and began to research it. The cost of the abortion alone was something I could not afford, never mind the flights and accommodation. What would I say to people? Why was I suddenly going to England for no obvious reason? I couldn't even cry, the panic and fear were so overwhelming. I felt like I had nobody to turn to. I've never felt so alone and desperate in my entire life.

A few days later, still panicking, desperately trying to find a way out, the pains started. I had a miscarriage. It was a brutal, painful few days and I felt like I deserved every second of the pain inflicted on me. I was also relieved – relieved that this was my way out, that I was spared the journey, the excuses, the fear of being found out and forced into something I was not able to do, and my guilt increased tenfold. I carried this with me, going about my day-to-day life, which led to a breakdown months later. I began therapy and built myself up again but years later I'm still affected by it.

When I hear people talking about voting against Repeal or I see 'pro-life' marches on the television I'm taken back to those days sitting at my computer, frantically trying to find a way out while the clock ticked on, feeling completely desperate, trapped and abandoned. I think about if the referendum fails: how many other women and girls will feel as I did, how many have done so in the past and how many carry these feelings around with them every day? The thought of it is unbearable and I hope beyond hope that people genuinely take into consideration these stories before they condemn more women and girls to fear, silence and shame.

XXX

It was 1994, I was 26 years old, my partner and I were living together and had both just got jobs that we enjoyed. I didn't think much of my late period as I was never 'regular' so hardly registered the extra week. I decided to get a pregnancy test just to rule out the possibility. I'm polycystic[29] and was told it was unlikely I would get pregnant. My partner had gone to visit his mam and I was at home alone when I did the test. It was positive.

I remember feeling complete terror. I panicked, and the first person I told was my father. I would have preferred to speak to my mother, but she had died thirteen years earlier. She had been sick for a long time and when she was finally diagnosed with cancer and they decided what treatment she should have it was discovered she was pregnant. So, in this 'good' Catholic country where our hospitals are 'overseen' by these 'good' Catholic people, my mother had no choice but to continue with her pregnancy, all the while getting sicker and sicker. By the time the baby was born it was too late to treat her – she died eight months later.

So ... back to me. I went to my father and somewhat hysterically tried to explain my situation. I remember crying and shaking and waving this stick with the two blue lines in front of his face. He was great ... really great. He calmed me down and told me whatever I decided he would support 100 per cent. I've often thought since then about his words. He said to me, 'This is your decision, no one

else's. Whatever you decide to do, I'll be there,' and he was true to his word.

I was lucky I suppose – one of my best friends had 'got the boat', a horrible euphemism that was regularly used in those days, and she had all the information I needed. We talked and talked, my partner and I (by the by, 26 years later we're still together) and came to the decision that we were not in the position to become parents. There are a myriad of reasons we chose this route and none of them were trivial. I made the calls, booked the flights and we took the weekend off work (we both worked in the same company). Colleagues asked had we anything nice planned. We lied.

It was the first time my husband (then boyfriend) had ever flown. We got to our destination airport and from there took a taxi to a B&B that was used by the clinic. We didn't speak a word. The lady and man in the B&B were beyond compassionate, so welcoming and warm to us.

There was a couple staying there also, but it wasn't the woman who was having the procedure, it was her twelve-year-old daughter, I'll never forget that child's face. She was a young-looking twelve-year-old with red hair and freckles. Her story is horrifying, it's not mine to tell but I feel I should touch on it: her mother and father told me she was raped by a family 'friend' and that social services knew about it and would not let her travel to have a termination; they took her anyway and knew they would be in trouble when they returned. They did what was best for their daughter. And I applaud them for it. Another girl, Irish of course (we all were, in that B&B) had told her family and her partner she was staying with a friend for the weekend. She was completely alone. My heart broke for these girls – at least I had the support of my partner and family.

I went to the clinic for a consultation. Before we left, the lady of the house told me there may be some protesters outside the clinic and if so, to keep my head up and ignore them. Luckily there weren't any that day.

I waited hours to be called. I cried quietly and told this tiny embryo in my tummy that I was sorry (I was only eight weeks pregnant), so very sorry. When the nurse called me in I was so scared and disorientated that when she told me to get on the bed I sat the wrong way round. To this day I can still hear her chuckle, 'Ah don't go all Irish on me now, sit the other way.' When I awoke I cried bitter tears but I knew then and still do that this was the right decision.

When it was over they told me I could travel the next day. My partner came to get me and bring me back to the B&B: the young girl had already left, so had the other Irish girl. The lady of the house told me my partner had paced the garden for the whole time I was gone. My heart broke for him. He felt so helpless. The pain that followed was incredible, I'll never forget it. At one point I even felt I deserved it. How wrong is that?

I often think of that little girl. I hope she is happy in her life. I know how traumatising it was for me to have to leave my home, my family and my support network. So for all the women who for their own reasons cannot continue with a pregnancy, for women like my mother who had no choice and left four children motherless, please, please do the right thing. #RepealTheEighth

XXXI

In 1996 I was nineteen and ready to go to university when I found out I was pregnant. Terrified did not describe how frightened I was. I had a scan at my local hospital (in the North) and told the nurse I couldn't have a baby and she told me to 'go home, tell my mother and enjoy the pregnancy'. I walked away in tears. My boyfriend and I found a group that could help make an appointment in London for a termination. We didn't have the close to £1000 needed and this meant I was fourteen weeks pregnant by the time we gathered money and took a loan from the credit union. We told everyone we were going away for a few days and began the journey to Belfast before flying to London.

I have vivid memories of some of the trip: being afraid of the protesters, keeping my head down in the waiting room, the clothes I was wearing, waking up after the anaesthetic, the pain and loneliness. I didn't stay after the procedure and didn't have any follow-up medical care. The short flight home seemed to take hours and I have never felt sadness and emptiness like it. I struggled with feelings of deep shame and guilt and it's only now, all these years later, that I believe this was created by the culture of silence and stigma that made me feel like a fugitive, when the truth was I was a young woman in need of support and healthcare in my own town. The accounts on this page and the recent crowdfunding campaign have in themselves been healing for me and I no longer feel alone. Twenty-one years later I am angry that twelve women and girls still have to make the same journey every day. It needs to stop: Repeal the Eighth.

XXXII

I have a different story to many of the young, brave women here. I was 40 and trying for my second baby. It was harder to get pregnant than the first time and I was over the moon when it finally worked out. But at ten weeks I started to have a miscarriage. I went to Holles Street and a scan confirmed this. There was no foetal heartbeat. I asked them what I was supposed to do next and they gave me a brochure and told me to come back in a week when they could confirm the miscarriage.

I went home completely distraught and started to bleed very heavily, passing tissue, large clots and blood. I had to go back to the hospital the next day as it became so bad. As I lay there literally soaked down to the ankles with blood, they told me there was nothing they could do. I asked my mum and sister – both doctors – what I should do and they both advised a D&C to stop the bleeding and to prevent infection. I asked for one and was told that they don't do these in Ireland on demand and again, to come back in a week. I went to my mum's house and had the rest of the miscarriage there.

I will never forget the weekend that followed: having contractions in the middle of the night, bleeding everywhere; it was horrific. I wasn't alone – I had my husband, my baby son, my beautiful mum and sisters – I had the best support you can get. My story is nothing even approaching some of the harrowing ones I've read here but it was still a really traumatic and horrible experience where I was denied any basic healthcare options due to this abhorrent regulation. I was lucky enough not to get an infection or anything worse and went on to have another baby – a beautiful girl – but I will never forget the experience and how incapacitated we have made our health services.

I'm sharing this as I believe this vote is not just for young women: it's for all ages, all genders and anyone who believes in basic rights to healthcare. My sister is a GP and is heartbroken to see her patients forced to the UK with completely unviable pregnancies, including severe and fatal foetal abnormalities. This has to stop. Please have compassion, please use logic, please give women of all ages the right to choice, to privacy and dignity, and please vote Yes to repeal this amendment.

THE
KEEPERS'
STORIES

Cáit Ni Charthaigh, *County Cork*
In Her Shoes Twitter media manager
Activist, mother of three

After the marriage equality referendum, a colleague said during tea break, 'Look at us now, what a modern society we are!' To which I replied, 'Yeah, except for our archaic abortion laws.'

The silence was deafening. I tried to explain that we had some of the most draconian abortion laws in the world. We were extreme. We were an outlier. They were oblivious. I couldn't see how things would change. I hadn't heard of the Repeal movement. It seemed like quite the mountain to climb.

As In Her Shoes started to gain momentum I offered to run the Twitter account, and so became part of the team. It was frantic, particularly in the last few days. We had so many stories that desperately needed to be told. There were times I sat in my car, on the phone, outside my child's school, crying at a story, angry that our country was putting us through this. Letting the stories speak for themselves, we had one fundamental purpose – to share them. We kept our heads down and continued. Just keep sharing.

I often thought that these women shouldn't have to tell their stories. These are private stories. Why should they have to bare their souls in order to obtain basic human rights? It seems oxymoronic that one should have to completely expose oneself in order to be afforded one's dignity. But it was clear that it was cathartic for many of those who contributed. People felt validated. Those who had been made to feel shame and guilt through the illegality of abortion were taking their power back.

Since Repeal, I remain politically engaged. Being part of the Repeal movement sparked a fire that won't be extinguished. It has empowered me. I have faith that things can change. Power structures can be dismantled. Societal norms can be reshaped to be more compassionate, more inclusive. It has made me love and respect my country and its citizens all the more. We are a kind people at our core.

Mary Lalor, *American, living in County Wexford*
In Her Shoes admin and moderator
Activist, photographer, mother of four

I was raised pro-life. My family was conservative and Catholic. When you are raised in a religious home, it takes baby steps to untangle the years of indoctrination. When I had my own children, I began challenging nearly every ideology I was raised with. I left religion, changed how I look at everything. The last to change were my views on abortion. It took me so long – because of this, I felt like a fraud being involved in this campaign. I wanted this, but everyone I knew who was fighting for Repeal had been fighting for women's rights for their entire adult lives. It's in their blood, but I don't feel it's in my blood. I had to put my personal feelings of doubt in myself as an activist aside and focus on the end goal.

I felt honoured, absolutely privileged, to be given the enormous task of minding the stories on the page. I still feel that way today. Several evenings a week I would sit down and read through the stories. I was no stranger to the loss of a pregnancy: I lost two boys in separate pregnancies in my second trimester. Both times I lost my babies, they had died inside my body. I stopped feeling kicks, then went to the hospital for a scan where I was told that my babies had died. Because of that I was given the best care. Midwives treated me respectfully and acknowledged my grief – yet how strange to feel happy that my babies died *in the correct way* so that I could be spared the unfair treatment so many women received under the Eighth Amendment.

There was rarely a person I met at the doors who didn't have some compassion towards the women who had to travel. There were only a handful of people who had cold hearts, who blocked off their ability to allow themselves to feel what the women felt. The women of Ireland and their stories were the driving force in repealing the Eighth Amendment.

Jac Sinnott, *County Waterford*
In Her Shoes admin and moderator
Activist, mother of two

I was an accidental activist. Hearing Claire Cullen-Delsol tell of her heartbreak and suffering when her baby was diagnosed with a fatal foetal anomaly fuelled a rage that would spur me on to become involved in any way I could. When the country was striking for Repeal, I organised a group of Parents for Choice in Waterford. In just a few short months, parents were coming out to show their support.

We began canvassing with no proper leaflets, knocking on doors before Together for Yes had launched. Behind my very first door was a young man who told me that women should just close their legs and then they wouldn't have to be baby-killers. It was definitely not going to be an easy, yet every interaction with a stranger was an opportunity for a conversation. When I was asked to help admin In Her Shoes, I said yes, of course yes.

For months I felt as if I was barely engaging with my family, missing so much of normal life but never wanting to lose a second of time spent on the campaign. I read the stories locked behind my bathroom door so that little people wouldn't see me cry. I read them after bedtime so that I was fully able to digest what was being said, so that the woman who took the time to send this would get the reply she deserved.

I left my family most evenings and almost every weekend to go out and knock on doors. I hated that we had to beg people to imagine these women as their mother, sister, or daughter for them to realise that she is someone in her own right. Soon we had done everything we could to get Repeal over the line. There was nothing left. I was so exhausted on that Friday morning that I couldn't even get excited as the exit-poll results were announced as a landslide. In a sort of joyful stupor, everything happened in slow motion: we celebrated, we hugged each other hard.

I am forever changed for this experience, forever grateful to the Women of the Eighth for allowing us to share their stories, and forever relieved that the people of Ireland answered those stories by voting Yes to Repeal.

Cara Shank, *American, living in County Cork*
In Her Shoes admin and moderator
Activist, anthropologist, writer, mother of three

I was pressured into an unnecessary induction with my third baby, my first in Ireland. In Ireland, you comply. When I argued with my caregivers, I was met with anger. How dare I push back against 'the system' – a system that cared more about my foetus than me and my living children? The system violated me.

Being raised in the era of Planned Parenthood bombings and healthcare providers being shot at their clinics, I find the explicitly anti-choice activists frightening. Despite this, and because I didn't have a vote in the referendum, I went to a protest march at eight months pregnant. I thought it was important to show support when so visibly pregnant. Men took pictures of me, yelled at me, crowded me, called me disgusting. I had prepared myself for this, but I was shaken. I didn't know how I could get involved in this campaign. I didn't think I was strong enough.

I asked a friend what I could do from home for our Cork group. She told me to contact Erin. We'd been friends for years. I dropped everything and offered to help. I had been damaged by my birth experiences. I was scared to canvass, wear a pin, speak my mind, but I could read stories, and so I did. Night after night of heart-wrenching stories. I would cry at the coffee shop, cry into our WhatsApp group, cry at night, nursing my baby. And I healed. The people who wrote so beautifully breathed life into me. I'd been scared to go canvassing, but the stories helped me to knock on doors. I was still scared, but I also felt proud, and even though a man spat in my direction as I walked past, I didn't care. We didn't come at this from the same experiences, but those stories became the most important thing in the world. I am forever grateful that I could help amplify them, even in my small way.

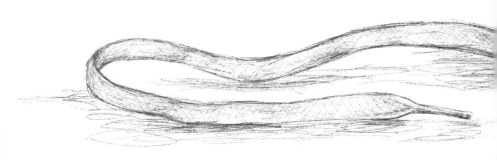

AFTERWORD

On 20 December 2018 President Michael D. Higgins signed into law the legislation passed for abortion in Ireland. The Health (Regulation of Termination of Pregnancy) Act 2018 provides the framework for the provision of abortion care from 1 January 2019. So long as a three-day waiting period has elapsed, abortion care is lawful on request for up to twelve weeks of pregnancy. Abortion is also lawful for reasons of risk to a woman's life and of serious harm to her health and in cases of fatal foetal anomaly. Abortion remains criminalised in all other cases. However, the criminal provisions do not apply to a woman in respect of her own pregnancy. Abortion is free to persons normally resident in Ireland. The legislation is not perfect, and it is also not protected to remain as is. The legislation in place is to be reviewed three years after it has been signed into law.

A three-day 'cooling-off' period prevents a woman from getting the pill prescribed and administered on the first appointment with a GP. She must return three days later to receive the medication she needs. Apart from infantilising women, this creates an additional strain on already limited resources and risks gestation progressing past the twelve-week cut-off. Legislation for termination beyond twelve weeks after the diagnosis of fatal foetal anomaly rests on projections of likelihood of the foetus' expectation to die either before or within twenty-eight days of birth. Neither of these restrictions is based on international best practice. While we have made great progress, it is not enough.

The establishment of safe-access zones surrounding GP practices and hospitals, designed to prevent harassment to patients from protesters, has yet to be implemented. As GPs must opt in to provide the medication, so-called 'conscientious objection', insufficient information and lack of support have prevented many from signing up to My Options, the HSE freephone line that provides information and counselling to people experiencing an unplanned pregnancy. The slow uptake by healthcare professionals in the community has left many outside of major cities without access to legal medication. Importing abortion pills from abroad and taking them without medical supervision continues to be a concern.

Managing the rights of asylum seekers and those living in direct provision centres adds restrictions to women needing access to a termination past twelve weeks' gestation. We await legislation for free contraception and the free morning-after pill.

Northern Ireland[30]

On 21 January 2019 we launched the In Her Shoes – Northern Ireland Facebook page, which tells the stories of those living in a province where abortion was a criminal offence – despite, paradoxically, that province being part of the United Kingdom, where abortion is legal. In February 2018 the United Nations found that the UK violates the rights of women in Northern Ireland by unduly restricting their access to abortion: 'The situation in Northern Ireland constitutes violence against women that may amount to torture or cruel, inhuman or degrading treatment,' said CEDAW Vice Chair Ruth Halperin-Kaddari.[31]

On 3 October 2019 Belfast's High Court ruled that Northern Ireland's abortion law breaches the UK's human rights commitments after Northern Irish woman Sarah Ewart challenged the law on being denied a termination in the province after the diagnosis of a fatal foetal anomaly in the pregnancy with her daughter in 2013, forcing her to travel to England for the procedure.

Abortion was decriminalised in Northern Ireland on 22 October 2019, repealing sections 58 and 59 of the Offences Against the Persons Act in Northern Ireland. MPs in Westminster had passed a bill in July 2019 for the British government to change the law in Northern Ireland for the decriminalisation of abortion as well as for granting marriage equality. As of April 2020, medical abortions are provided on two hospital sites in Northern Ireland. It is thought that just over a thousand terminations will take place. Northern Ireland will be the first jurisdiction to introduce buffer zones around hospital sites, preventing people from protesting in those areas. Pregnant people choosing an abortion will no longer face prosecution.

We are no longer criminals.

In solidarity with activists fighting for abortion rights where it is illegal, criminalised or heavily restricted

Afghanistan, Algeria, Andorra, Angola, Antigua, Argentina, Bahamas, Bangladesh, Barbuda, Benin, Bhutan, Bolivia, Botswana, Brazil, Brunei, Burkina Faso, Burundi, Cameroon, Central African Republic, Chad, Chile, Colombia, Comoros, Congo, Costa Rica, Djibouti, Dominica, Dominican Republic, Ecuador, Egypt, El Salvador, Equatorial Guinea, Eritrea, Ethiopia, Gabon, Gambia, Ghana, Guatemala, Guinea, Guinea-Bissau, Grenada, Haiti, Honduras, Indonesia, Iran, Iraq, Israel, Ivory Coast, Jamaica, Jordan, Kenya, Kiribati, Kuwait, Laos, Lebanon, Lesotho, Liberia, Libya, Liechtenstein, Madagascar, Malawi, Malaysia, Maldives, Mali, Malta, Myanmar, Marshall Islands, Mauritania, Mauritius, Mexico, Micronesia, Monaco, Morocco, Mozambique, Namibia, Nauru, New Zealand, Nicaragua, Niger, Nigeria, Oman, Panama, Papua New Guinea, Paraguay, Palau, Philippines, Pakistan, Peru, Poland, Qatar, Rwanda, Samoa, San Marino, São Tomé and Príncipe, Saudi Arabia, Senegal, Seychelles, Sierra Leone, Solomon Islands, Somalia, South Korea, South Sudan, Sri Lanka, St Kitts & Nevis, St Lucia, Sudan, Suriname, Swaziland, Syria, Tanzania, Thailand, Timor-Leste, Togo, Tonga, Trinidad and Tobago, Tuvalu, Uganda, United Arab Emirates, Venezuela, Vanuatu, West Bank & Gaza, Yemen, Zimbabwe.

ACKNOWLEDGEMENTS

To the thirty-two storytellers within this book, and every person who sent their story to the Facebook page: it has been my greatest honour and privilege to hold your experiences, to be entrusted with your lived truths and to give them a space to bring change, solidarity and healing to others.

Thank you to the In Her Shoes admin team: Mary Lalor, Cara Shank, Jac Sinnott, Emer Smith, Cáit Ní Charthaigh and all the volunteers along the way: I am forever in debt to you. Not only did you hold these stories with the utmost care and respect, you also held me through the most devastating grief of my life. You trusted and believed, and were a sounding board of guidance, graciousness and laughter. I have learned so much from you.

To Nat Kunachowicz, thank you for your time, talent and heart. You created the In Her Shoes booklet, a real work of art that influenced so many.

Galway East for Choice: Yvone Aherne, Niamh Bonner, Rebecca Clifford, Helena Conlon, Jenny Cooper, Ciara Coy, Sarah Daly, Ronnie Daly-Osemwegie, Gina Dooley, Louise Glavey, Susan McGrady, Jennie O'Connell, Moirin O'Donovan, Shona O'Flaherty, Aine O'Neill and Marion O'Neill. You have become the sisterhood I've been searching for, a home where I belong, and the biggest cheerleaders, champions and example of women supporting women.

To the underground network of mothers, others, dedicated Repealers. Those who donated to make the booklets and those who carried the stories into rural communities. Those who stood fiercely and bravely in the face of opposition and every person who travelled home to vote or helped someone to get here in time. The activists who have been on the ground for longer than I've been alive, and the younger generations of activists rising up the ranks. I am so inspired by you.

The dearest men in my life: my papa Tom Connelly and my husband Steven. Your constant support, love and protection are a reminder that I am capable and that I am doing important work.

My humble gratitude to Aoife K. Walsh and everyone at New Island Books for holding the first skeleton bones of this book and for envisioning it before I ever could. It is so beautiful to work with an Irish publisher that has grown from the sweetest grassroots beginnings.

To my editor Djinn von Noorden, midwife to the words: I don't think there could be anyone more perfect to help me bring this book to life. Thank you to Catherine Gaffney for her incredible design talent in weaving my illustrations and these words together.

Last but not least, my best friend, rebel riser, earth shifter and creative manager, Aoife Moore: I would be lost without you.

ADDITIONAL RESOURCES

The book *We've Come A Long Way: Reproductive Rights of Migrants and Ethnic Minorities in Ireland* (MERJ 2018) is an invaluable resource. Migrants and ethnic minorities were rarely represented on main stages in the campaign to repeal the Eighth Amendment. It is imperative to have the representation of minorities when implementing changes to our laws and society.

In writing about the events surrounding the death of Savita Halappanavar, I consulted with the investigation notes provided by the HSE's final report to ensure I had a factual timeline of events. In writing about the untimely death of Aisha Chithira, I relied on news articles from the BBC and RTÉ.

The Digital Repository of Ireland (DRI) is a national digital repository for Ireland's humanities, social sciences, and cultural heritage data: www.repository.dri.ie/.

Republic of Ireland

Abortion Access Campaign West (AAC West):
    www.aacwest.wordpress.com
Abortion Rights Campaign (ARC): www.abortionrightscampaign.ie
Abortion Support Network: www.asn.org.uk
Amach! LGBT: www.amachlgbt.com
Association to Improve Maternity Services Ireland (AIMSI):
    www.aimsireland.ie
HSE Unplanned pregnancy support services: www2.hse.ie/abortion

Inclusion Ireland: www.inclusionIreland.ie
Irish Family Planning (IFPA): 1850 49 50 51; www.ifpa.ie
London Irish ARC: www.londonirisharc.com
MERJ – Migrants and Ethnic Minorities for Reproductive Justice:
    www.merjireland.org
My Options: 00353 (0)1 687 7044
National Women's Council Ireland (NWCI): www.nwci.ie
Rape Crisis Network Ireland: www.rcni.ie; 1800 778 888
Suicide Ireland: www.suicideireland.com
Termination for Medical Reasons (TFMR): www.tfmrireland.com;
    www.lmcsupport.ie
Transgender Equality Network Ireland (TENI): www.teni.ie
Well Woman Centre: www.wellwomancentre.ie
Women's Aid: www.womensaid.ie; 1800 341 900
Women Help Women: www.consult.womenhelp.org/en/get-abortion-pills
Women on Web: www.womenonweb.org/en/i-need-an-abortion

Northern Ireland

Alliance for Choice: www.alliance4choice.com;
    alliancechoice4@gmail.com; 0044 (0)7894 063965
Alliance for Choice Derry: www.facebook.com/a4cderry
BPAS: www.bpas.org/abortion-care/considering-abortion/northern-ireland-
    funded-abortion-treatment; 0044 (0)333 2342184
In Her Shoes Northern Ireland: www.facebook.com/InHerShoesNI;
    ihsnorth@gmail.com
Informing Choices NI: www.informingchoicesni.org;
    0044 (0)28 9031 6100
Rally for Choice Ireland: www.facebook.com/rallyforchoice

NOTES

1   Aisha Chithira was a Malawian woman living in Ireland since 2009. When she became pregnant in 2011 and developed stomach pains, she and her husband decided that a termination was in the best interest of her health. Aisha needed a visa to travel to the UK, which took a month to obtain. At 20 weeks pregnant she travelled alone while her husband stayed behind to look after their toddler. Following the procedure, Aisha became ill and collapsed later that night. She died as a result of a significant intra-abdominal bleed.

2   *The Secret of Roan Inish* is a 1994 American-Irish film of Irish magical realism, written and directed by John Sayles.

3   From *Rise Up & Repeal – A Poetic Archive of the 8th Amendment*, edited by Sarah Brazil and Sarah Bernstein.

4   The intention, were we to be successful in repealing the Eighth, was always to switch the focus of the page towards maintaining awareness to the cause of Northern Ireland.

5   A booklet printed as a result of the work done by birth activists within AIMS (Association for Improvements in the Maternity Services) in Galway.

6   Ireland Making England the Legal Destination for Abortion. 'Speaking of IMELDA' was a direct-action feminist performance group focused on challenging the anti-choice laws in Northern Ireland and the Republic of Ireland. 'Imelda' was the code word for abortion. It enabled Irish women travelling to England for abortions to keep their plans secret and avoid stigma and criminalisation, as the right to travel for an abortion was illegal up until 1992.

7   Irish Women's Abortion Support Group (IWASG) provided support to women travelling from Ireland to England for abortions between 1980–2000.

8   The Bon Secours order is under investigation for the mass grave discovered in a septic tank in the grounds of the mother and baby home where, in 2014, local historian and activist Catherine Corless named and made public the remains of 796 children.

9   https://www.breakingnews.ie/ireland/8thref-results-referendum-passed-by-a-majority-of-706349-votes-845230.html.

10   An ectopic pregnancy is a medical emergency where a fertilised egg grows outside the uterus.

11   Early Pregnancy Assessment Unit.

12   A 1984 investigation in County Kerry into the killing of a newborn baby and the alleged killing of another. The mother who concealed the second baby, Joanne Hayes, was arrested and charged with the murder of the first baby, of which she was erroneously thought to be the mother.

13   Ann Lovett, a fifteen-year-old schoolgirl from Granard, County Longford, died giving birth beside a grotto on 31 January 1984. Her baby son died at the same time.

14   Sexual Assault Treatment Unit.

15   A prenatal scan taken to detect foetal chromosomal abnormalities.

16   Sudden Infant Death Syndrome, also known as cot death or crib death, is the sudden unexplained death of a child of less than one year of age.

17   A surgical abortion involves having surgery to end a pregnancy. All surgical abortions happen in a hospital, and are usually booked as a day case.

18   D&C (dilation and curettage) refers to the dilation of the cervix and surgical removal of part of the lining of the uterus and/or contents of the uterus. It is a therapeutic gynaecological procedure as well as the most often used method of first trimester miscarriage or abortion.

19   Anencephaly is the absence of a major portion of the brain, skull and scalp that occurs during embryonic development.

20   A medical abortion – also known as a medication abortion – occurs when pills are used to bring about an abortion. The recommended regimen consists of a combination of medications, starting with mifepristone and followed a day later by misoprostol.

21 Irish Family Planning Association.

22 The 2018 trial in which two professional rugby players were found not guilty of raping a young woman in a house in south Belfast in June 2016. Two other men were found not guilty of lesser charges.

23 A condition in which the placenta partially or wholly blocks the neck of the uterus, interfering with vaginal delivery of a baby.

24 The 2016 case in which a High Court judge refused to grant the HSE orders forcing a pregnant woman to have a caesarean section against her will so as to vindicate the right to life of her unborn child.

25 The 1992 landmark case which established the right to an abortion in Ireland if a pregnant woman's life was put at risk because of pregnancy, including the risk of suicide.

26 A genetic disorder, also known as trisomy 18, caused by the presence of a third copy of all or part of chromosome 18.

27 Chorionic villus sampling (CVS) is a prenatal diagnosis to determine chromosomal or genetic disorders in the foetus.

28 The General Data Protection Regulation (GDPR) is a legal framework that sets guidelines for the collection and processing of personal information from individuals who live in the European Union.

29 Polycystic ovary syndrome (PCOS) is a condition that affects a woman's hormone levels. Women with PCOS produce higher-than-normal amounts of testosterone, which causes missed periods and makes it harder to become pregnant.

30 See *Abortion Law in Northern Ireland: Eighth Report of Session 2017–19* (House of Commons, 2019).

31 www.ohchr.org, 23 February 2018.